PHILIP'S

GN00580043

First published 2001 by

Philip's, a division of
Octopus Publishing Group Ltd
2–4 Heron Quays
London E14 4JP

Second edition 2003
First impression 2003

ISBN 0 540 08466-2 (spiral-bound)
ISBN 0 540 08467-0 (perfect-bound)

© Philip's 2003

Ordnance Survey®

Printed and bound in Spain
by Cayfosa-Quebecor.

Contents

II Key to map pages

IV Administrative and Postcode boundaries

VI Key to map symbols

1 Street maps

77 Keys to enlarged map pages and symbols

78 Enlarged street maps

174 Index

267 List of numbered locations

280 London Underground

282 Central London theatres and cinemas

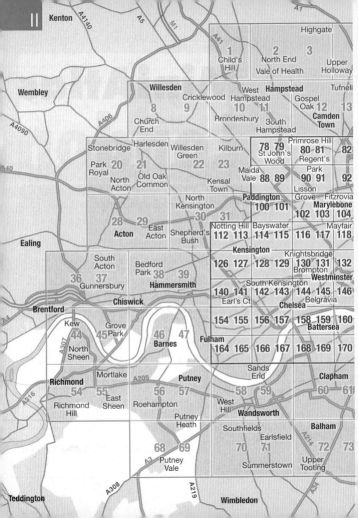

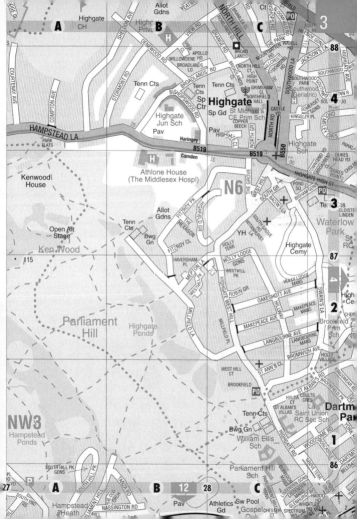

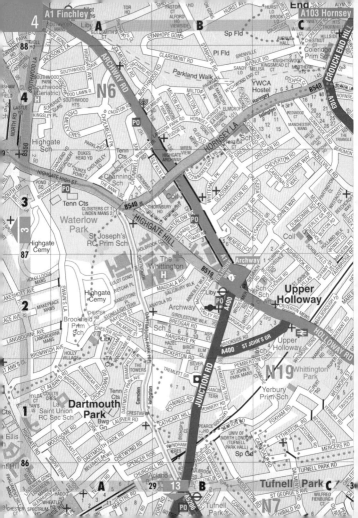

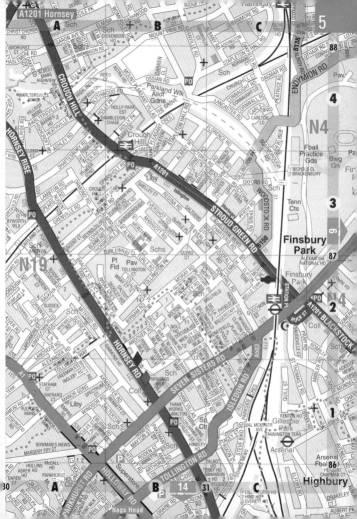

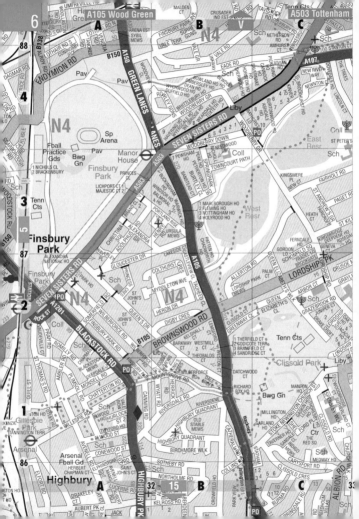

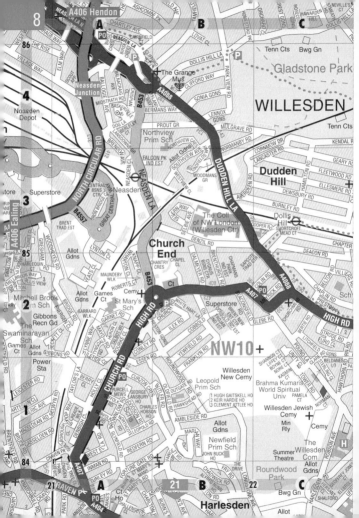

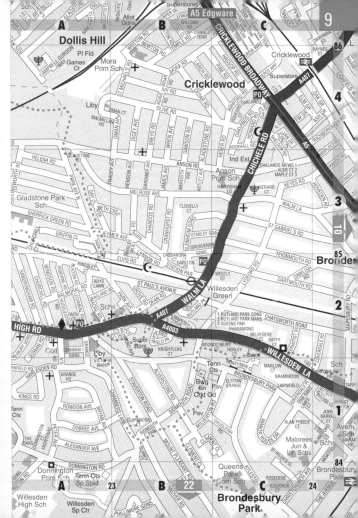

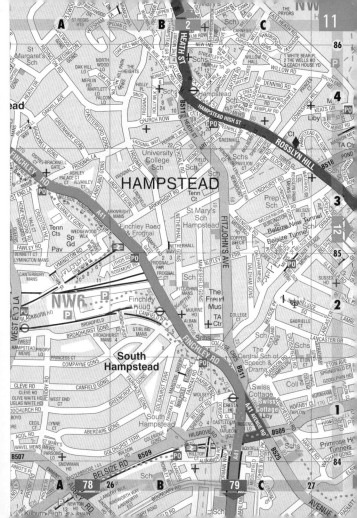

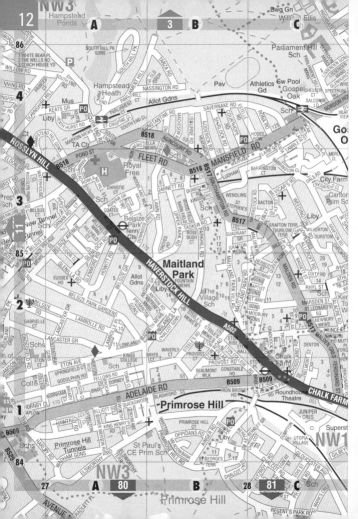

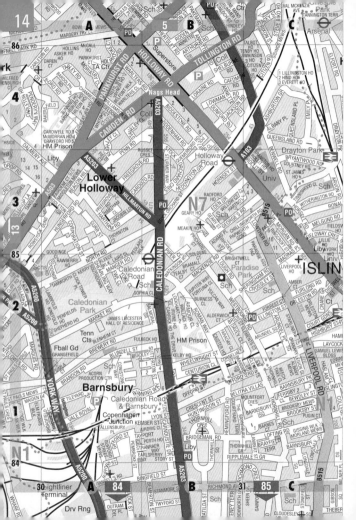

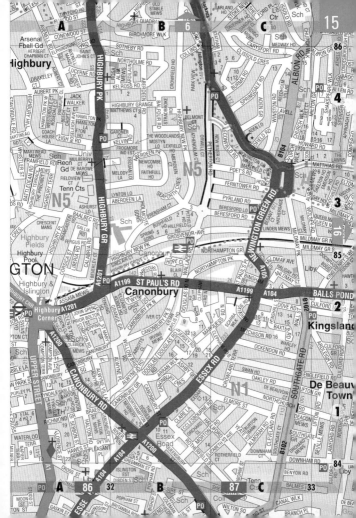

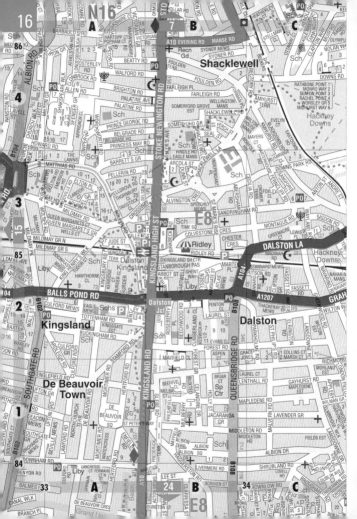

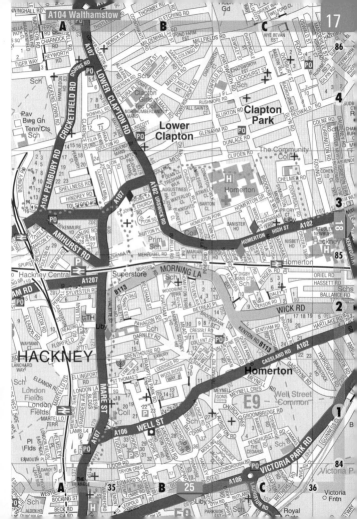

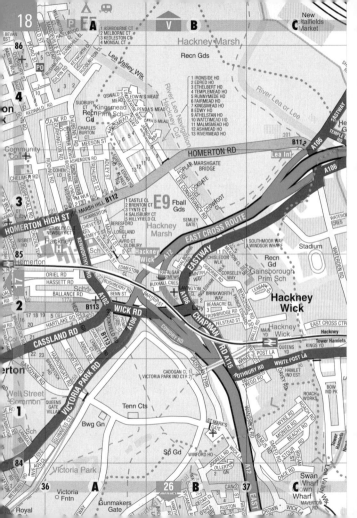

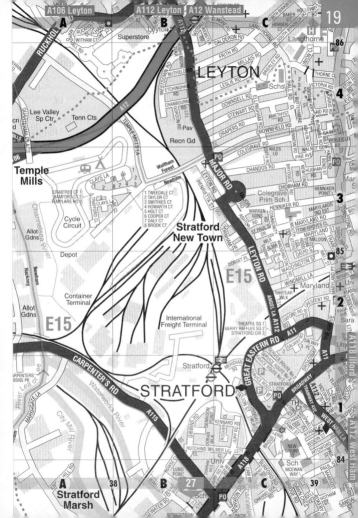

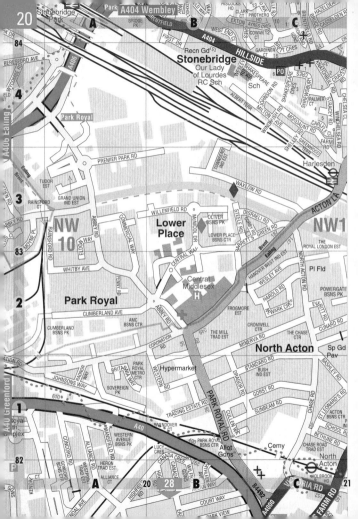

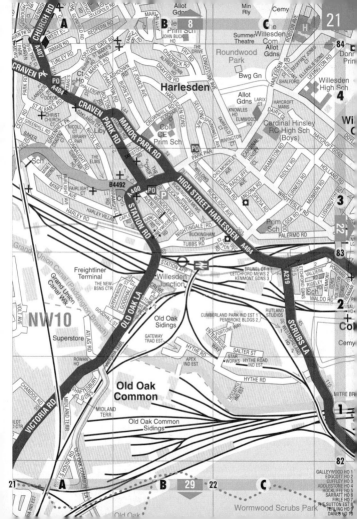

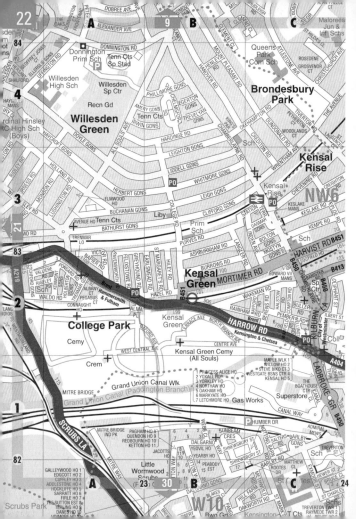

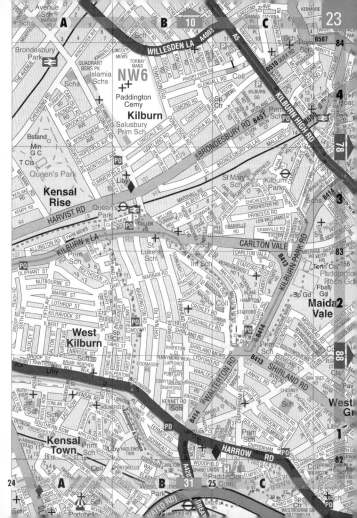

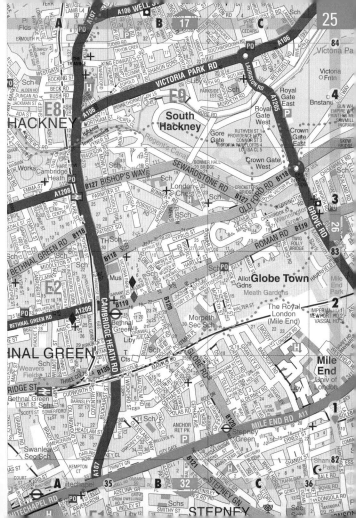

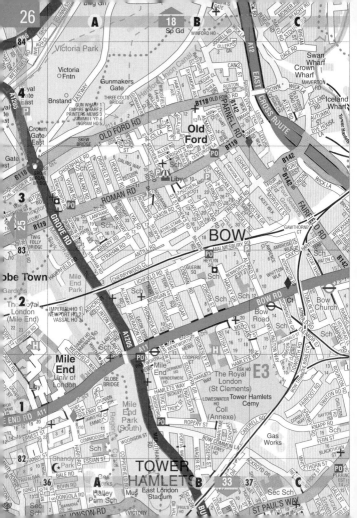

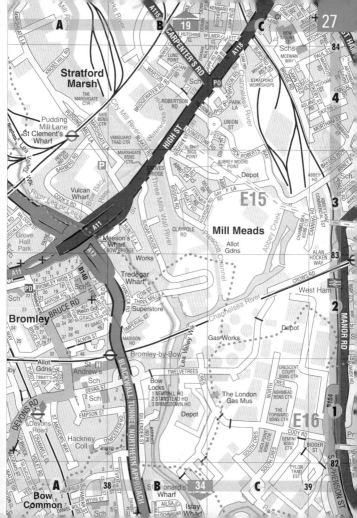

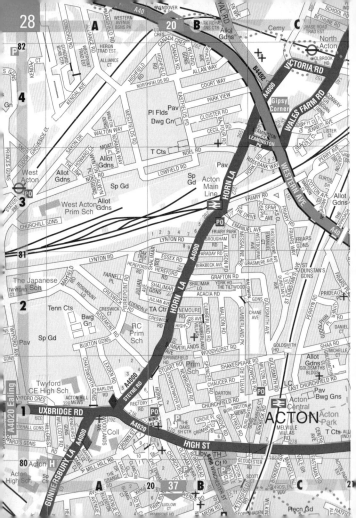

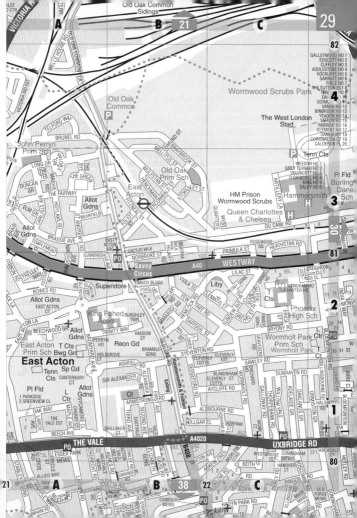

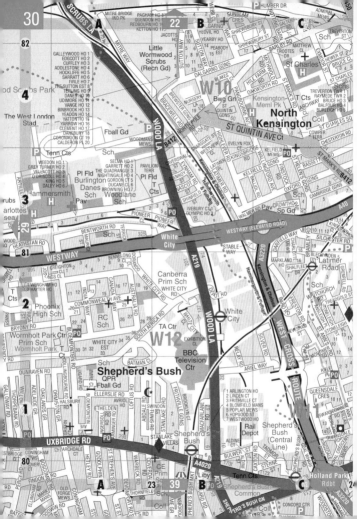

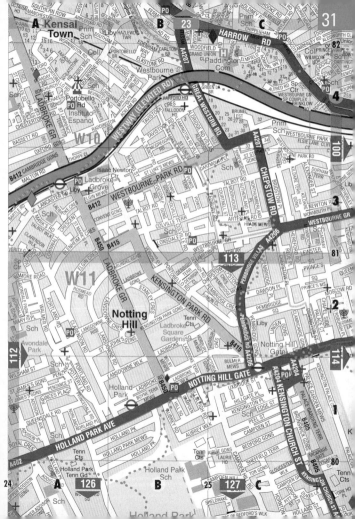

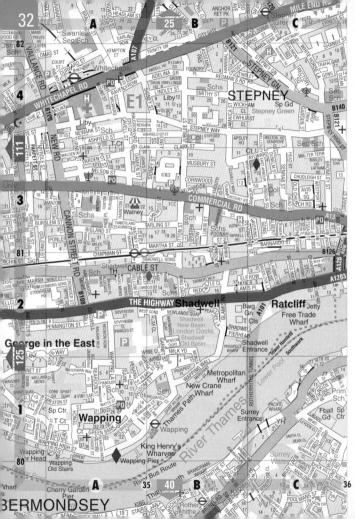

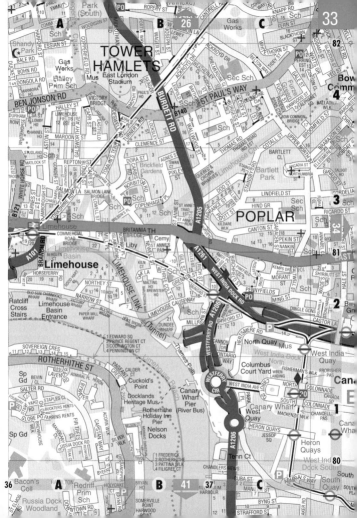

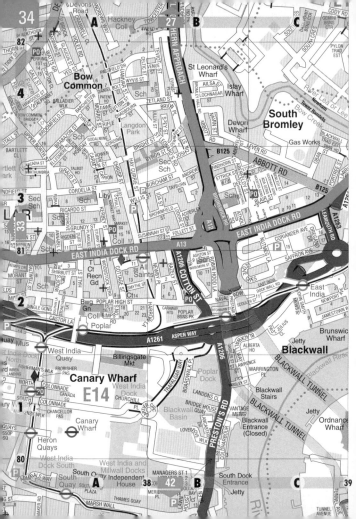

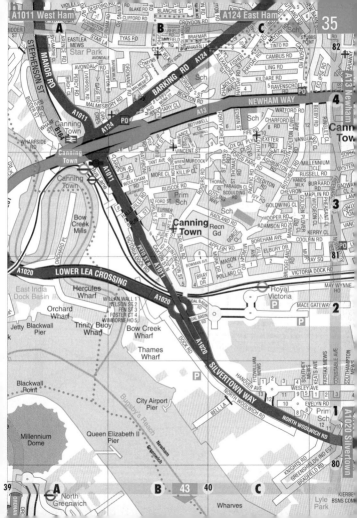

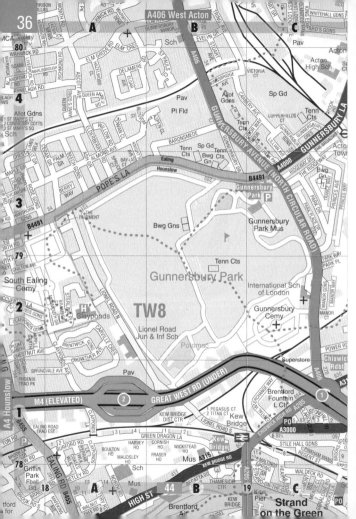

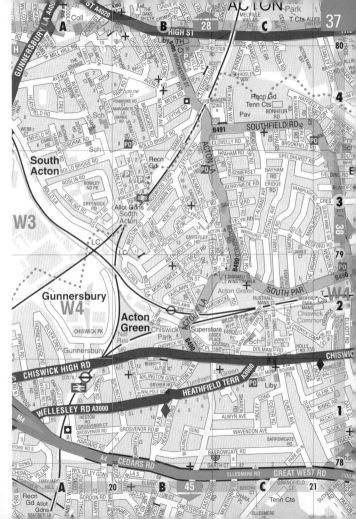

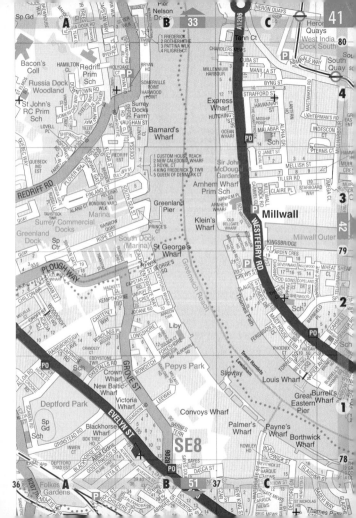

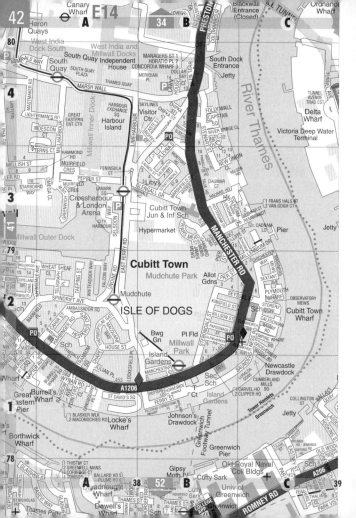

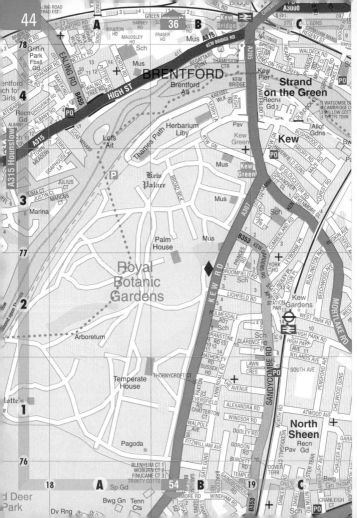

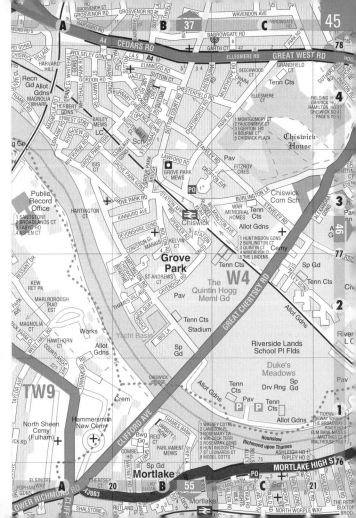

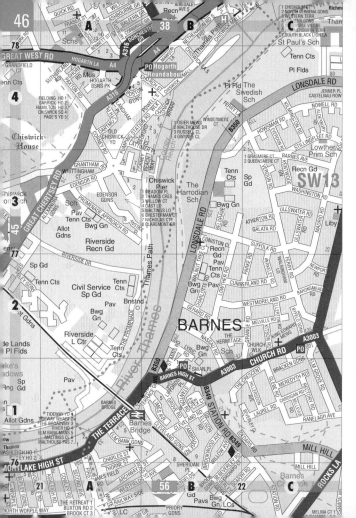

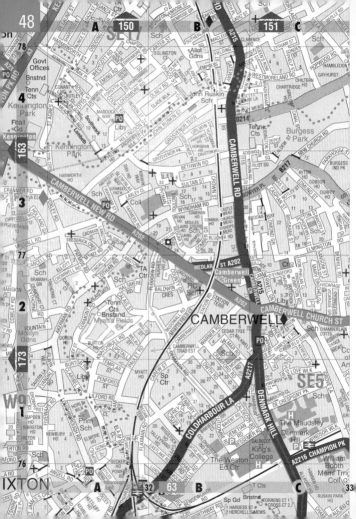

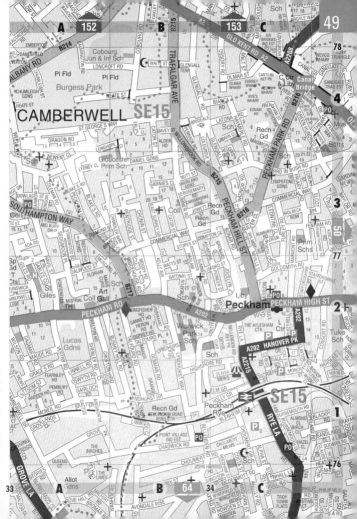

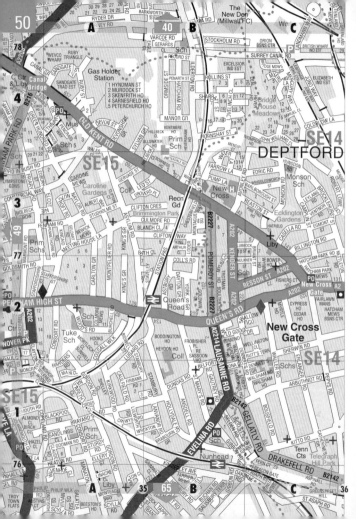

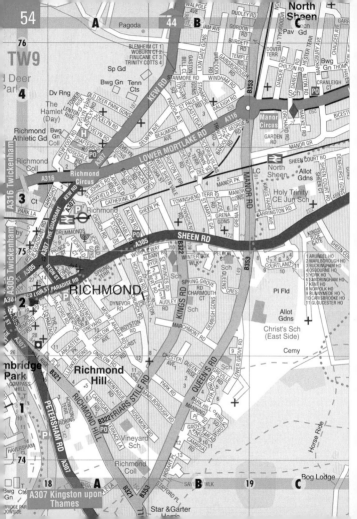

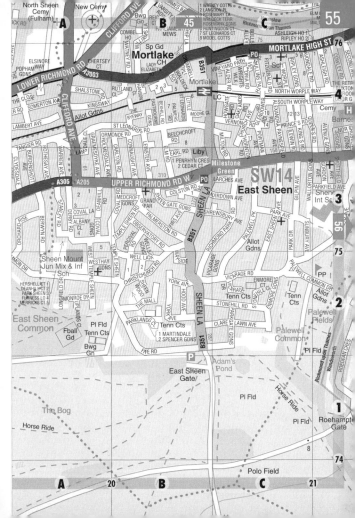

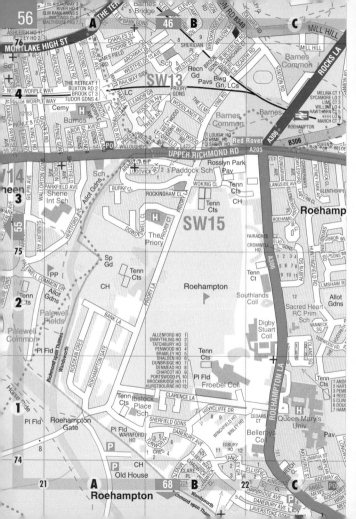

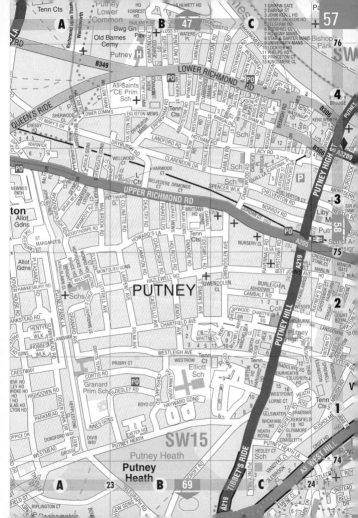

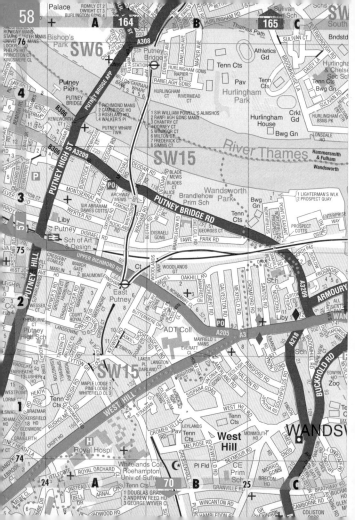

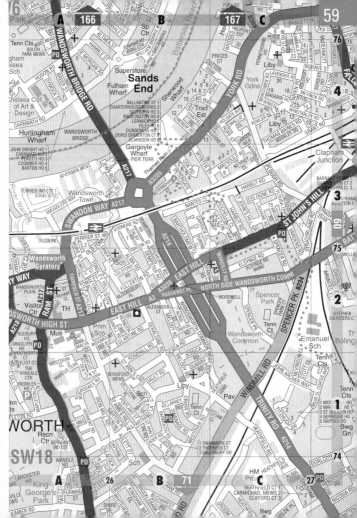

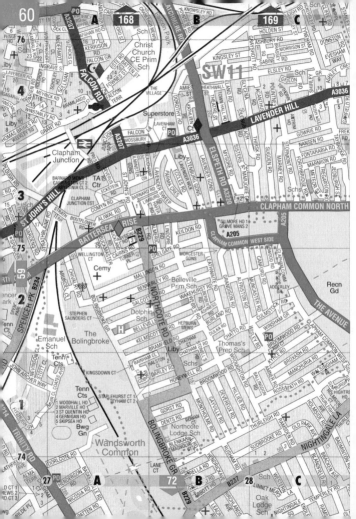

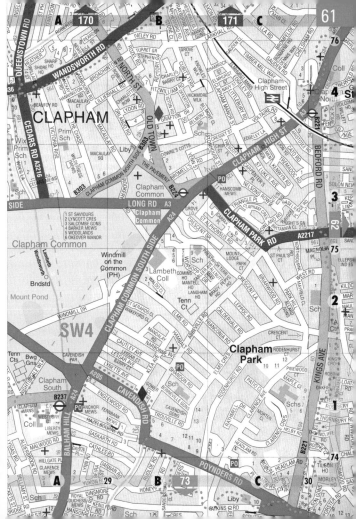

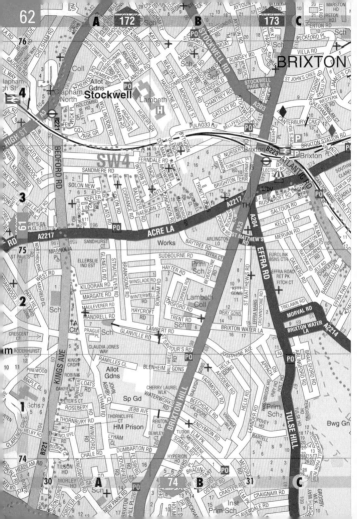

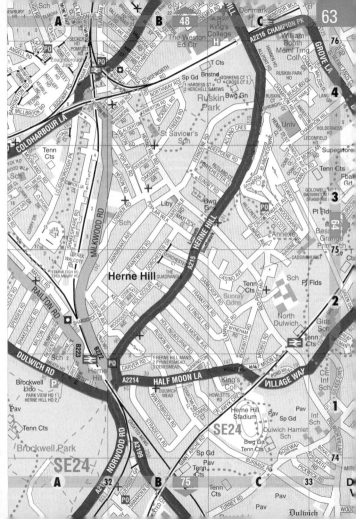

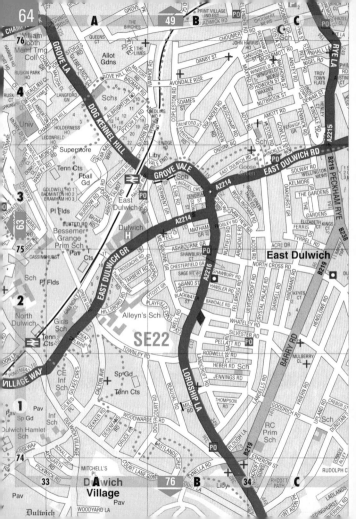

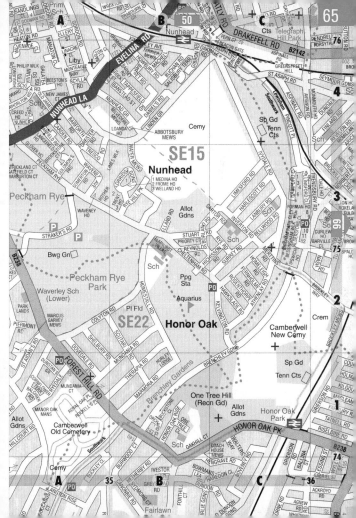

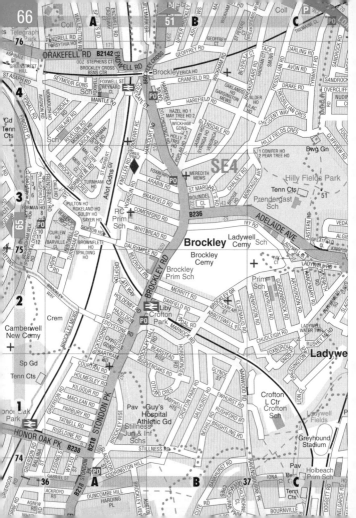

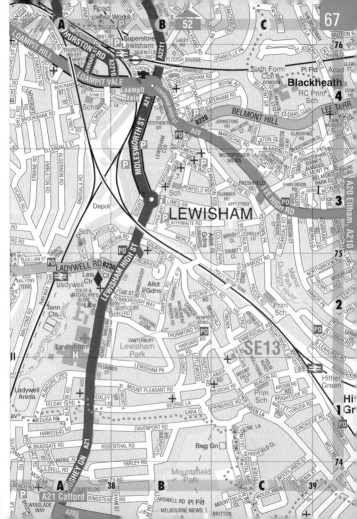

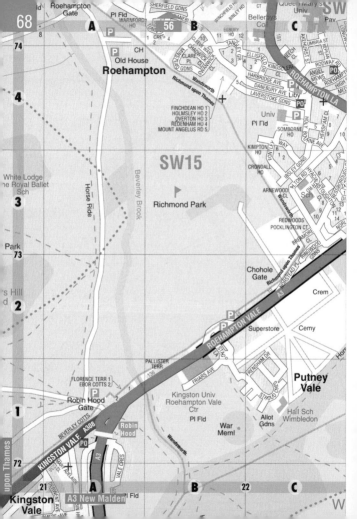

68

Roehampton Gate

PI Fld
WARNFORD HO

A

P

56

B

SHERFIELD GDNS

WINCHFIELD HO

BINLEY HO

EGBURY

Queen Mary's Univ

SW

Bellerbys Col

C

Pav

74

8

CH
P

Old House

Roehampton

Wandsworth

Richmond upon Thames

TANG GR

CRES

CHEWKWELL CT
CLARE PL
DANWICK CL

ELLISROAD CT

KINGSCLERE

CL

UMBRIA ST

NEPAUL RD

RODWAY RD

ROEHAMPTON LA

ANGEL
MEWS

ROEHAMPTON

HIGH

PO

MED

HARBRIDGE AVE

DANEBURY AVE

LAVERSTOKE GDNS

Liby

P

PO

4

FINCHDEAN HO 1
HOLMSLEY HO 2
OVERTON HO 3
REDENHAM HO 4
MOUNT ANGELUS RD 5

Univ
PI Fld

SOMBORNE HO

HERSHAM CL

P

KIMPTON HO

CONT LEY WAY

HOLY HOW

URM ONE AVE

White Lodge
The Royal Ballet Sch

Horse Ride

Beverley Brook

SW15

CRONDALL HO

INSLEY GDNS

UPTON RD

WAYLANDS

HAGGARD RD

School

MED

3

Richmond Park

ARNEWOOD

Wandsworth

Sch

REDWOODS
POCKLINGTON CT

Park
73

BREAMORE CL
RINGWOOD GDNS

s Hill
d

2

Chohole Gate

Richmond upon Thames

A3

Crem

Crem

ROEHAMPTON VALE

P

Superstore

Cemy

Putney Vale

1

PALLISTER TERR

FLORENCE TERR 1
EBOR COTTS 2

Robin Hood Gate

A436

FRIARS AVE

Kingston Univ
Roehampton Vale
Ctr
PI Fld

War Meml

FRENSHAM DR

STROUD CL

Allot Gdns

Hall Sch Wimbledon

Hom

BEVERLEY COTTS

Robin Hood

Wandsworth

72

KINGSTON VALE

A308

PO

A3

VALE CRES

ADELAIDE

upon Thames

21

A

22

C

Kingston Vale

A3 New Malden

B

l Fld

W

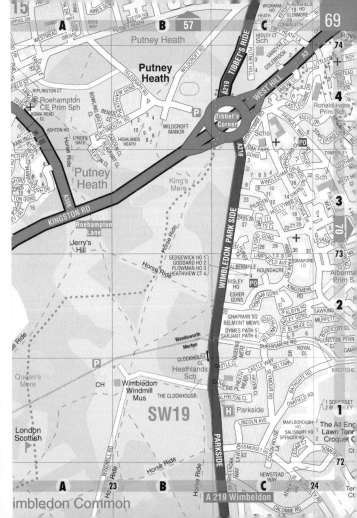

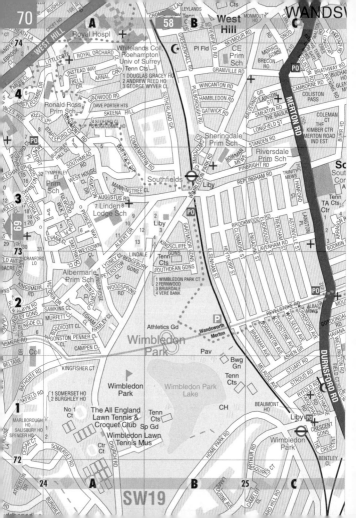

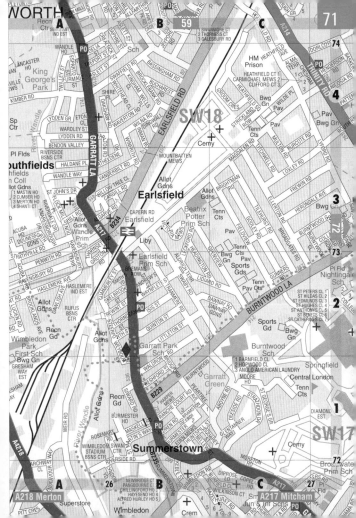

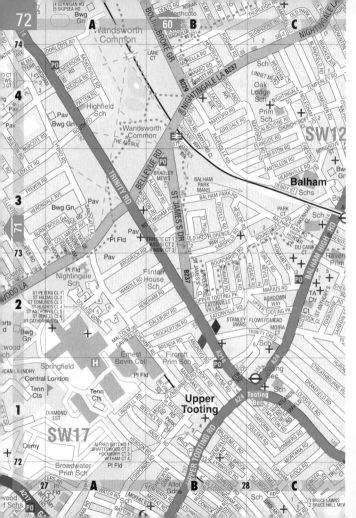

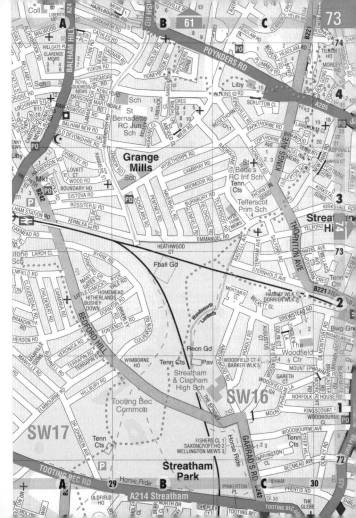

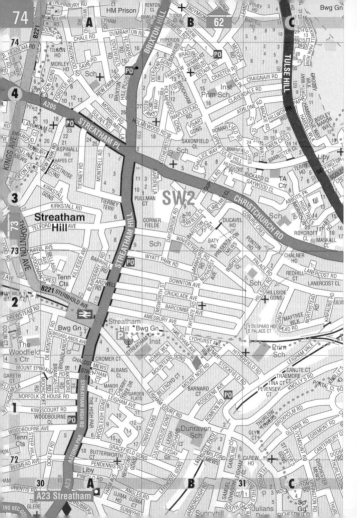

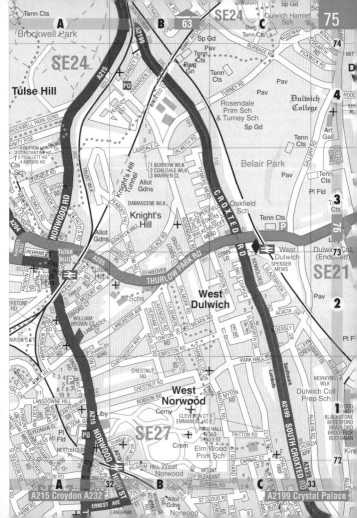

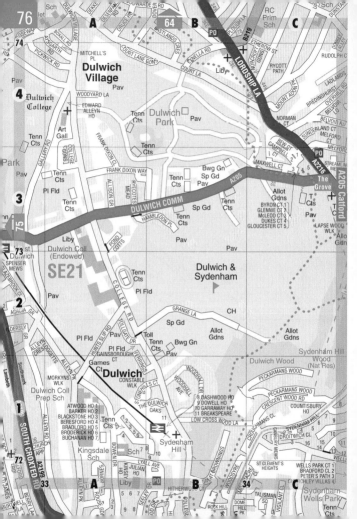

Key to enlarged map pages

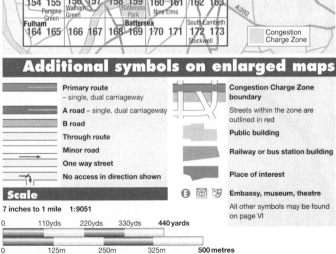

				Islington		A10
78 79 St John's Wood	Primrose Hill 80 81 Regent's	82 83 Somers Town	84 85 King's Cross	86 87		
Maida Vale 88 89 Westbourne Green	Park 90 91 Lisson Grove	92 93	St Pancras 94 95 Bloomsbury	Finsbury Shoreditch 96 97	98 99 Bethnal Green	
Paddington 100 101	Marylebone 102 103	Fitzrovia 104 105	Holborn 106 107 St Giles	108 109 City	110 111 Whitechapel	Spitalfields A11 A13
Notting Hill 112 113	Bayswater 114 115 Kensington	Mayfair 116 117 Hyde Park	Strand 118 119 St James	120 121 South Bank	122 123 Southwark	124 125 St George in the East
Kensington Holland Pk 126 127 West Kensington	Gardens 128 129 South Kensington	Knightsbridge 130 131 Brompton	Green Park 132 133	Waterloo 134 135	The Borough 136 137	138 139 Bermondsey
140 141 Earl's Ct	142 143	Westminster 144 145 Belgravia	146 147 Pimlico	Lambeth 148 149 Vauxhall	Newington 150 151 Kennington	152 153 Walworth
West Brompton Chelsea 154 155 Parsons Green	156 157 Walham Green	158 159 Battersea Park	160 161 Nine Elms	162 163		A2
Fulham 164 165	166 167	Battersea 168 169	170 171	South Lambeth 172 173 Stockwell		A202

A40 · A3220 · A4

Congestion Charge Zone

Additional symbols on enlarged maps

Primary route – single, dual carriageway	Congestion Charge Zone boundary
A road – single, dual carriageway	Streets within the zone are outlined in red
B road	Public building
Through route	Railway or bus station building
Minor road	
One way street	Place of interest
No access in direction shown	Embassy, museum, theatre

All other symbols may be found on page VI

Scale

7 inches to 1 mile 1:9051

0   110yds   220yds   330yds   **440 yards**

0   125m   250m   325m   **500 metres**

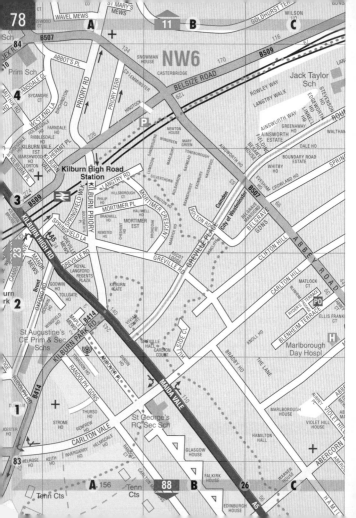

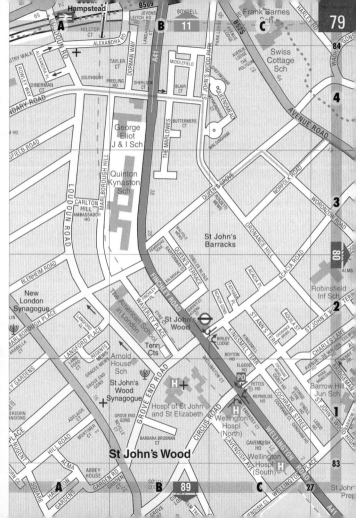

A
B
C

84
4
3
2
1
83
80

Frank Barnes Sch

HARLEY RD
BOYDELL
JEVONS
LEITCH HO
LANGHORNE
PARK LODGE
AVENUE LODGE THE POLYG
Swiss Cottage Sch

HILLTOP CT
ALEXANDRA RD
ALEXANDRA RD
DORMAN WAY
TAYLER CT
SOUTHBURY
FREELING HO
SHERLOCK CT
MIDDLEFIELD
ST JOHN'S WOOD PARK
BLAIR CT
SHEFFINGHAM

AVENUE ROAD

LOUDOUN RD
ROWLEY WAY
GANTRY WALK
DINERMAN
ALEXANDRA ROAD
BOUNDARY ROAD

WADHAM GDNS

THE MARLOWES
BUTTERMERE CT
WALSINGHAM
QUEENSMEAD

George Eliot J & I Sch

Quinton Kynaston Sch

MARLBOROUGH HILL
CARLTON HILL
AMBASSADOR HO

QUEEN'S GROVE
COSSHIN MEWS
NORFOLK ROAD
WORONZOW ROAD

ORDNANCE HILL

LOUDOUN ROAD

WALPOLE MEWS
PROBOROSE
BADMINTON
QUEEN'S TERRACE
JUBILEE BLDGS
BALMORAL

St John's Barracks

ACACIA RD
ACACIA PL
ACACIA GDNS
LATHAM PL

BLENHEIM ROAD

New London Synagogue

FINCHLEY ROAD
WAVERLEY PLACE
The American School in London

ST JOHN'S WD TERR
ST ANN'S TERR
AQUILA ST

Robinsfield Inf Sch

MARLBOROUGH PLACE
LANGFORD PLACE
LANGFORD CL
ARABELLA CT

EVRE CT

St John's Wood

BIRLEY LODGE
BOYTON CL
KINGSMILL TERR
KINGSMILL

CHARLES LANE
AVENUE DE WILDEN
ORDNANCE MEWS

GRACES MEWS
GROVE END GDNS
Tenn Cts

Arnold House Sch

St John's Wood Synagogue

WELLINGTON RD
WELLINGTON CT

ELGOOD HO
FETTES HO
REYNOLDS HO
COCHRANE ST
COCHRANE CT
O'NEILL
CAVE
GEORGE ELIOT

Barrow Hill Jun Sch

PERCORN MANSIONS
ABERCORN MANSIONS
ADELAIDE RD
MORTIMER CT
GROVE END RD
NEVILLE CT

Hospl of St John and St Elizabeth

H

CIRCUS ROAD
GROVE END ROAD

Wellington Hospl (North)

LORDS VIEW
BRIDGEMAN
PARK MANSIONS

HILL ROAD
ALMA
ABBEY HOUSE
GARDEN RD
SOUTH LODGE
BARBARA BROSNAN CT

CAVENDISH HO
CAVENDISH AVE

Wellington Hospl (South)
H

WELLINGTON PLACE
COCHRANE STREET

St John's Wood

GARDENS
NUGENT
PLACE
SQUARE

A
B
89
C
27
83
St John
Prep

CAVENDISH CL

GROVE

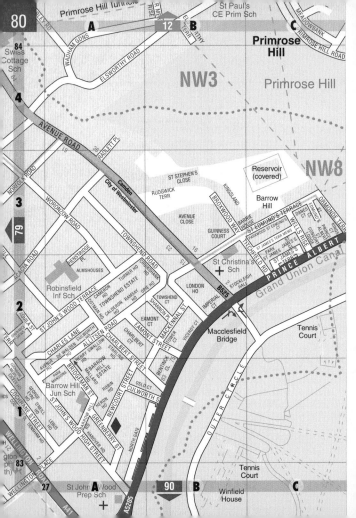

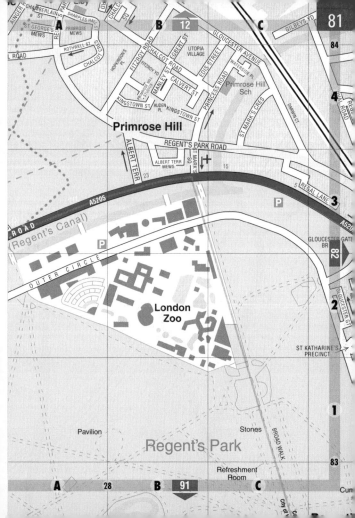

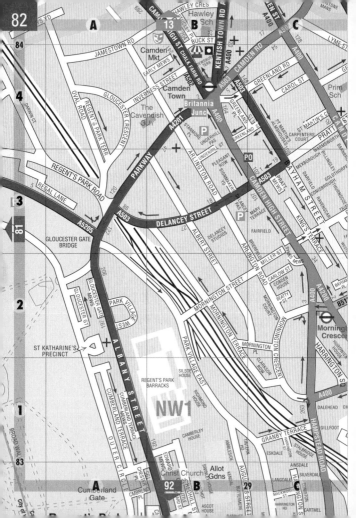

A   13   B   C

84

Hawley
Sch
Hawley Cres

HAWLEY YD
CAMDEN ST
HIGH ST
CHALK FARM RD
KENTISH TOWN RD
A400
ASH
LYME ST

BUCK ST

4

JAMESTOWN RD
Camden
Mkt
EARLY MEWS
INVERNESS STREET
Camden
Town
The
Cavendish
3.in
Britannia
Junc
CAMDEN RD
GREENLAND RD
CAROL ST
Prim
Sch
GREENLAND
ST MARTIN'S C
CARPENTERS
COURT
PRATT

OVAL ROAD
REGENT'S PARK TERR
GLOUCESTER CRESCENT
A5201
STRATFORD
PARKWAY
UNDERHILL PAS
UNDERHILL ST
PLEASANT
ROW
SHOEMAKERS
ARLINGTON ROAD
PO
PRATT
MEWS
CAMDEN HIGH STREET
A503
BAYHAM STREET

REGENT'S PARK ROAD
REGAL LANE
A5205
A503
GLOUCESTER GATE
BRIDGE
DELANCEY STREET
DELANCEY
STUDIOS
JAMES'S
PLACE
MARY
TERRACE
FAIRFIELD
KING'S TERRACE
P
ALBERT STREET
ARLINGTON ROAD
BREWERY
MILLER ST
CARLOW ST
COBDEN
HOUSE
BEATTY
ST

2

GLOUCESTER GT
GLOUCESTER MEWS
PARK VILLAGE WEST
ST KATHARINE'S
PRECINCT
MORNINGTON STREET
MORNINGTON TERRACE
PARK VILLAGE EAST
MORNINGTON
PL
MORNINGTON COURT
MORNINGTON CRESCENT
HARRINGTON SQ
Mornin
Cresc
A400
B51

REGENT'S PARK
BARRACKS
SILSOE
HOUSE
RICHMOND
HOUSE
CLARKSON
ROW
A400

1

NW1
ALBANY STREET
CUMBERLAND TERRACE
CUMBERLAND MEWS
OUTER CIRCLE
CAMBERLEY
HOUSE
HAMPSTEAD ROAD
DALEHEAD
GILLFOOT

83

EDWARD MEWS
GRANBY TERRACE
AMBLESIDE
ESKDALE
AINSIDE
LANGDALE
SILVERDALE
STARLING
HOUSE
MACKWORTH
HO
HARRINGTON HO
CARTMEL

A   92   B   29   C

Cumberland
Gate
Christ Church
Sch
Allot
Gdns
ASCOT
HOUSE

4   3   2   1
81

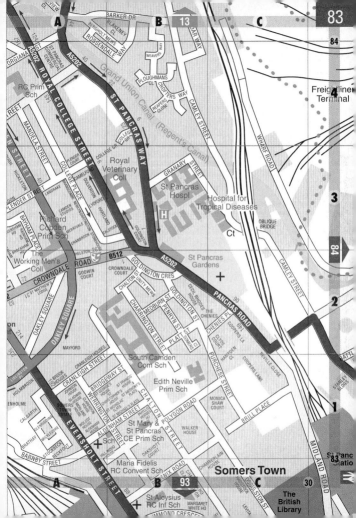

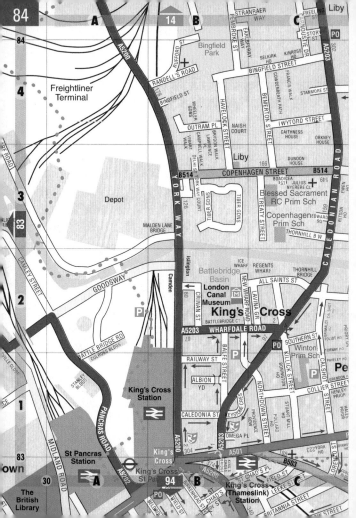

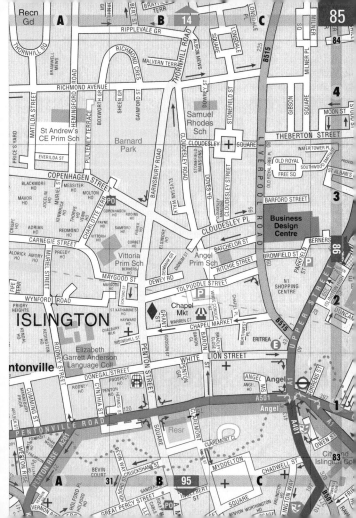

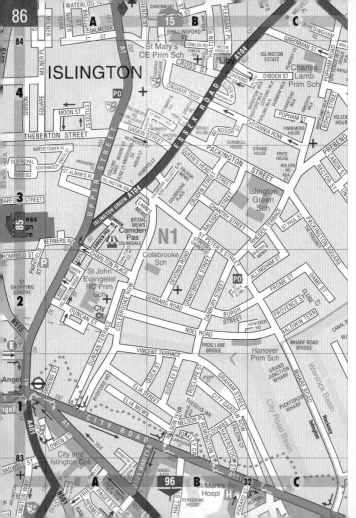

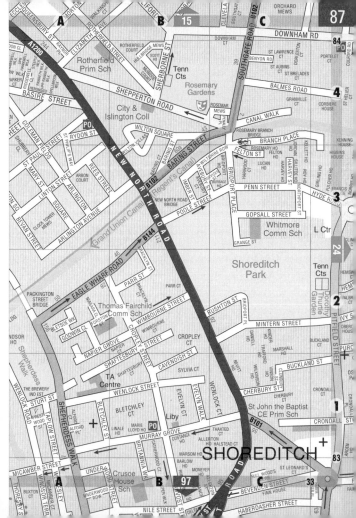

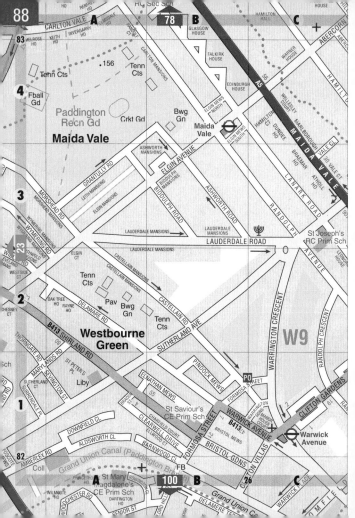

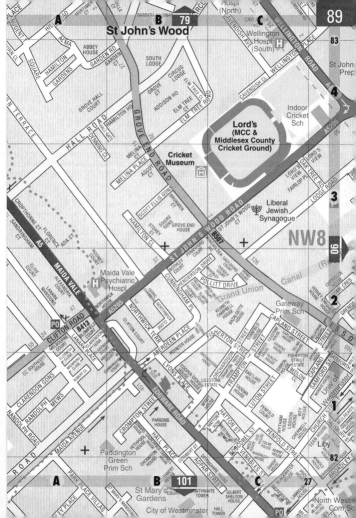

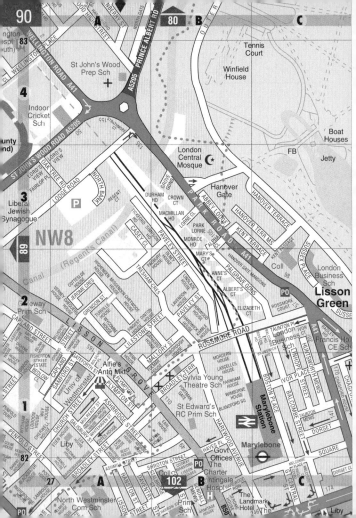

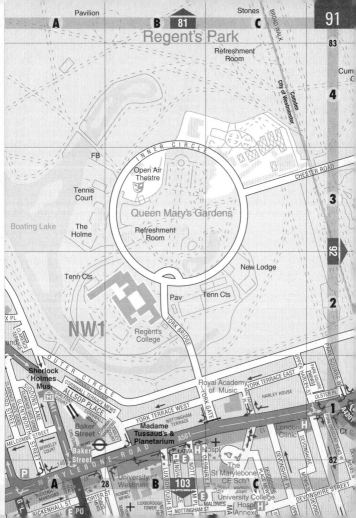

A   Pavilion   B   81   Stones   C   BROAD WALK

Regent's Park

83

Refreshment Room

Cum

City of Westminster Camden   4

INNER CIRCLE

FB

Open Air Theatre

CHESTER ROAD

Tennis Court

3

Queen Mary's Gardens

Boating Lake

The Holme

Refreshment Room

92

New Lodge

Tenn Cts

2

Pav   Tenn Cts

NW1

Regent's College

YORK BRIDGE

OUTER CIRCLE

Sherlock Holmes Mus

CORNWALL TERRACE MEWS

Royal Academy of Music

YORK TERRACE EAST

UPPER HARLEY ST

PARK SQUARE EAST

PARK SQUARE WEST

HARLEY HOUSE

ULSTER PL

A41

ALLSOP PLACE

CORNWALL TERRACE

YORK GATE

1

CLARENCE TERRACE

GLENTWORTH STREET

SIDDONS LANE

GLENTWORTH STREET

MELCOMBE STREET

BERKELEY COURT

CHILTERN COURT

Baker Street

Baker Street

YORK TERRACE WEST

NOTTINGHAM TERRACE

Madame Tussaud's & Planetarium

London Clinic

HARLEY ST

DEVONSHIRE PLACE MEWS

DEVONSHIRE PL

H

PX PL

CLARENCE GATE GDNS

ROMNEY MEWS

A501

MARYLEBONE ROAD

LATVIA

E

Hospl

+

St Marylebone CE Sch

H

82

P

BICKENHALL MANSIONS

A

BICKENHALL STREET

28

University Westmins

PORTER ST

B

LUXBOROUGH TOWER

LUXBOROUGH ST

103

NOTTINGHAM ST

MALDIVES

E

DBURY PL

University College Hospl Annexe

C

DEVONSHIRE STREET

GL

P

O

F

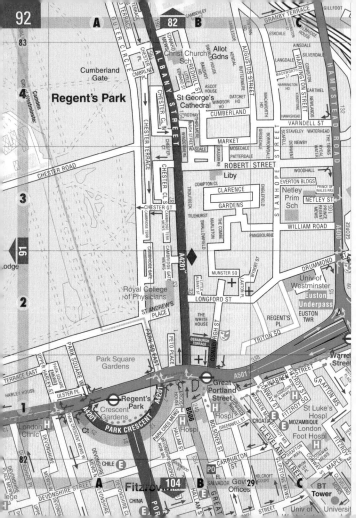

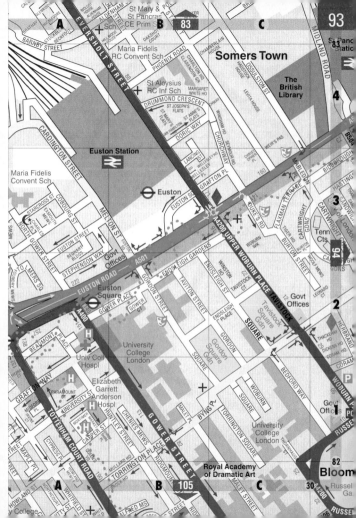

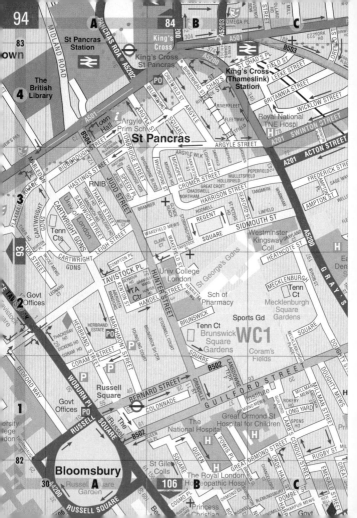

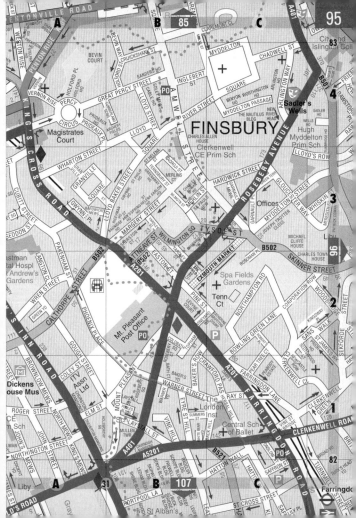

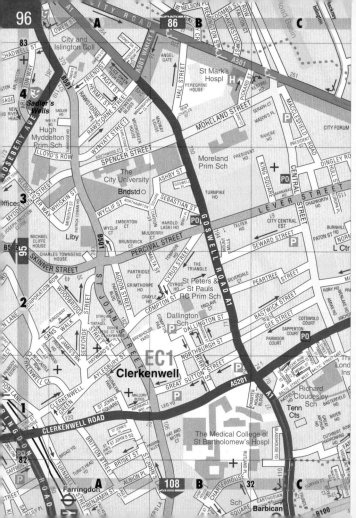

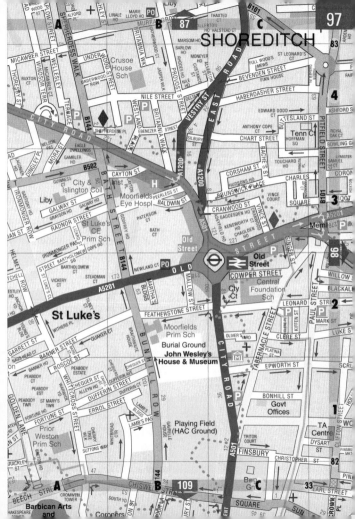

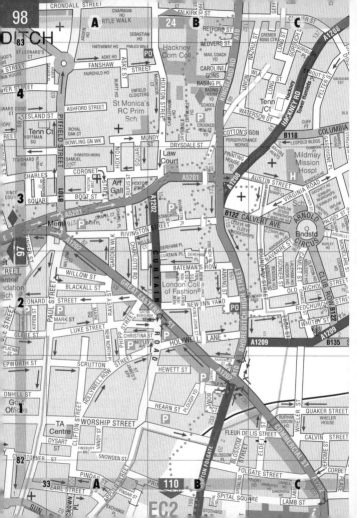

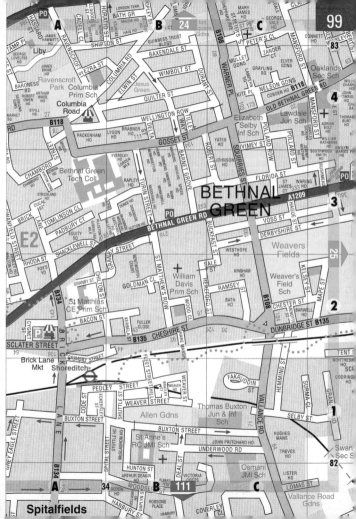

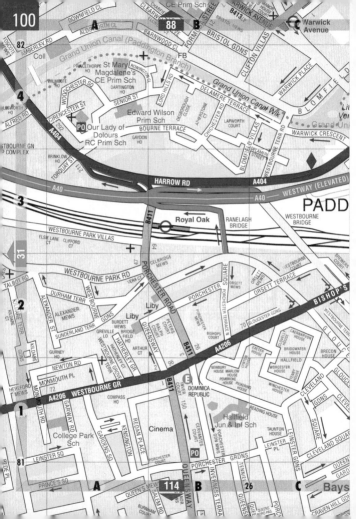

Grid references: A, B, C (columns); 1, 2, 3, 4 (rows)

Streets and Labels:

- MAIDA AVENUE
- CROMER
- PARSONS STREET
- PENFOLD STREET
- BROADLEY
- HARROW ROAD
- RANDOLPH ROAD
- PARK PLACE VILLAS
- HOWLEY PLACE
- Paddington Green Prim Sch
- St Mary's Gardens
- City of Westminster Coll
- St Mary's Ter
- St Mary's Sq
- ST MARY'S MANSIONS
- JOHN AIRD COURT
- PORTEUS RD
- INGHAM MEWS
- FLEMING COURT
- PHILIP COURT
- CHILTERN HOUSE
- CROMPTON HOUSE
- CUTHBERT STREET
- BRAITHWAITE TOWER
- GILBERT SHELDON HOUSE
- HALL TOWER
- WINDGROVE
- Canal
- HARROW ROAD (UNDER)
- (Paddington Branch)
- PADDINGTON
- W2
- BISHOPS ROAD BRIDGE
- BRIDGE ROAD
- A4206
- HERMES STREET
- DUDLEY STREET
- DUDLEY HOUSE
- NORTH WHARF ROAD
- North Westminster Com Sch
- SIDONS HOUSE
- HARBET ROAD
- Marylebone Flyover
- Paddington Basin
- EASTBOURNE TERRACE
- Paddington Station
- P
- WESTBOURNE TERRACE
- CLEVELAND TERRACE
- EASTBOURNE MEWS
- CHILWORTH STREET
- CHILWORTH MEWS
- DEVONSHIRE MEWS
- UPBROOK MEWS
- GLOUCESTER MEWS
- CRAVEN ROAD
- St James & St Michael's CE School
- CRAVEN HILL MS
- CRAVEN HILL
- Bayswater
- SOUTH WHARF ROAD
- St Mary's Hospital
- Medical School
- H
- WINSLAND STREET
- WINSLAND MEWS
- PRAED STREET
- BOUVERIE PL
- NORFOLK PLACE
- LONDON MEWS
- NORFOLK SQUARE
- PO
- Hilton London Paddington Hotel
- Paddington
- A4205
- CONDUIT STREET
- SPRING STREET
- TALBOT SQUARE
- B410
- CONDUIT MEWS
- A4209
- WESTBOURNE CRES
- SUSSEX GARDENS
- SUSSEX MEWS
- RADNOR MEWS
- RADNOR PLACE
- SUSSEX PLACE
- GLOUCESTER SQUARE
- BATHURST MEWS
- CLIFTON PL
- SUSSEX SQUARE
- STANHOPE TERRACE
- HYDE PARK GDNS MEWS
- HYDE PARK GARDENS
- SOMERS
- STAR STREET
- ST MICHAEL'S STREET
- MILES PLACE
- PENFOLD PLACE
- Lisson Grove
- Edgware Rd (Bakerloo)
- North Westmin Com Sch
- VENABLES ST
- SALE ST
- HERMITAGE ST
- WINDSOR
- KENNET HOUSE
- BLACKWATER
- JEROME CRES
- PO
- A5
- A40
- A404
- A4206
- A4205
- E SRI LANKA

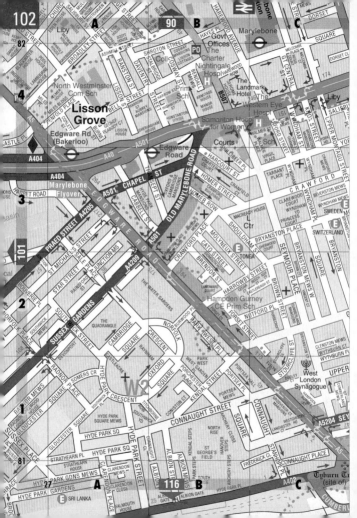

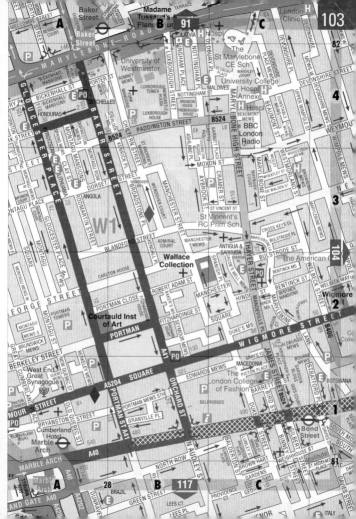

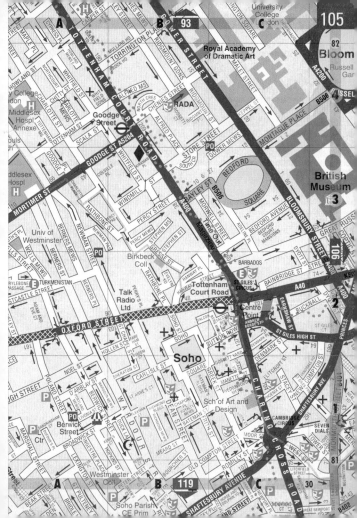

University
College
London

82
Bloom
Russell
Gar

Royal Academy
of Dramatic Art

A4200

B506

'SSEL

y College
don
Middlesex
Hospl
Annexe
uls
h'

RADA

MONTAGUE PLACE

**British
Museum**
ℹ︎3

Goodge
Street

STORE STREET
PO

GOODGE ROAD A5204

BEDFORD
SQUARE

BEDFORD AVENUE

BLOOMSBURY STREET

GREAT RUSS

106

Middlesex
Hospl

MORTIMER ST

WINDMILL ST

PERCY STREET

B506

BAYLEY ST

MORWELL STREET

Univ of
Westminster

Birkbeck
Coll

RATHBONE ST

BARBADOS

BAINBRIDGE ST

A40

KEY

Talk
Radio
Ltd

HANWAY PL

Tottenham
Court Road

St GILES
CIRCUS

Centre
Point

EARNSHAW ST

BUCKNALL

2

OXFORD STREET

SOHO

SUTTON ROW

DENMARK ST

ST GILES HIGH ST

ANDREW
BORDE

ST GILES
CT

PRINCES

Soho

SOHO
SQUARE

DENMARK STREET

FLITCROFT

STACEY'S

SHAFTESBURY AVE

A400

B402

Sch of Art and
Design

CAMBRIDGE
CIRCUS

SEVEN
DIALS

P

PO
Berwick
Street

OLD COMPTON STREET

CHARING CROSS RD

WEST ST

MONMOUTH

81

P

Ctr

BROADWICK ST

P

WARDOUR STREET

ROMILLY ST

LITCHFIELD
STREET

P

Westminster
Coll

SHAFTESBURY AVENUE

Soho Parish
CE Prim

P

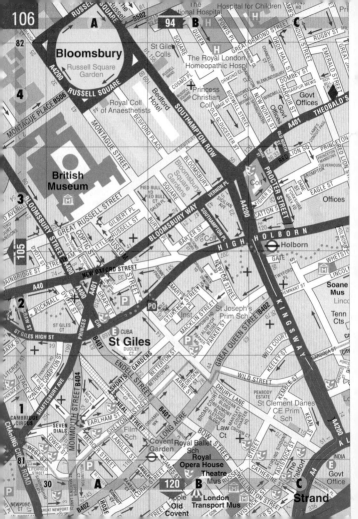

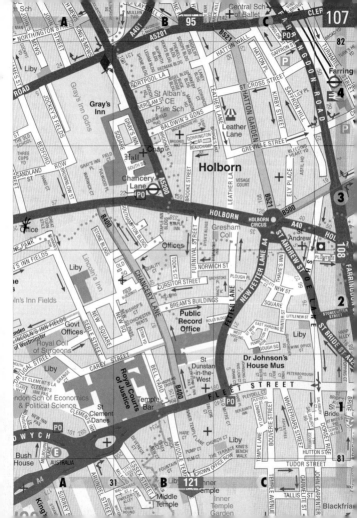

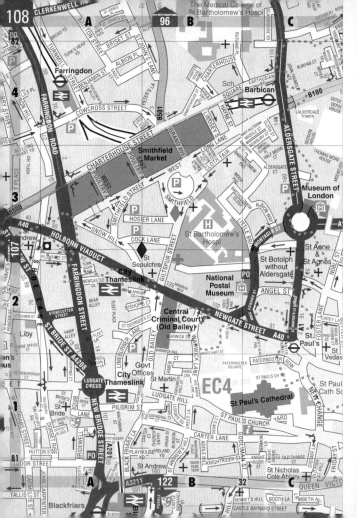

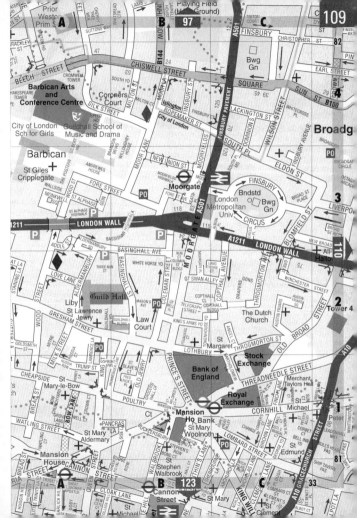

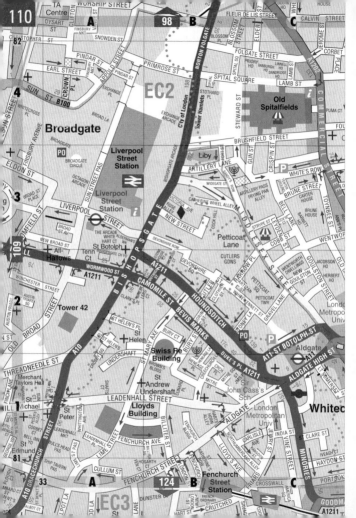

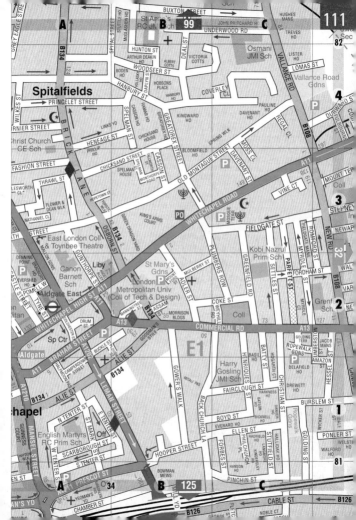

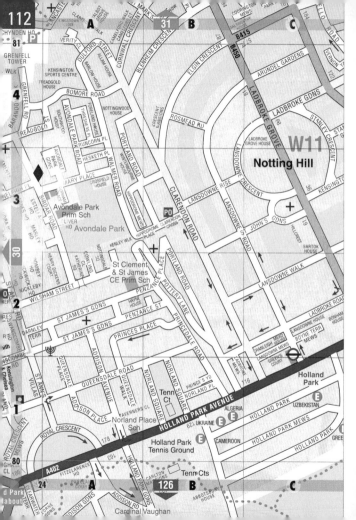

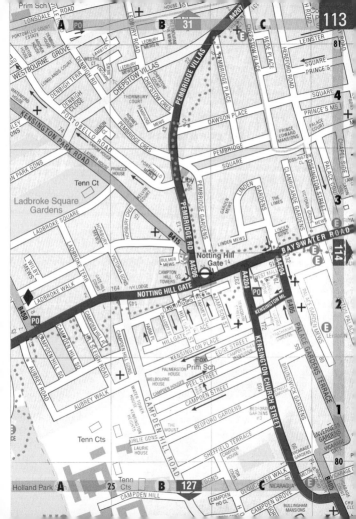

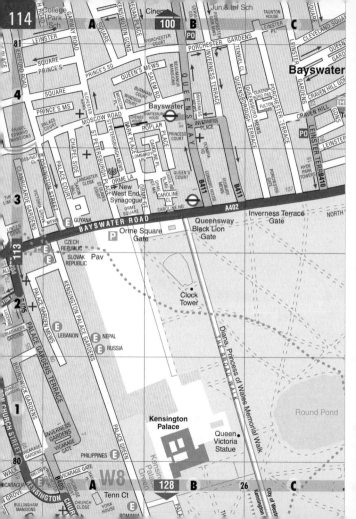

A
102 B
C

SQUARE MEWS
HYDE PARK SQ
HYDE PARK SQ
STRATHEARN PL
HYDE PARK SQUARE
STRATHEARN HOUSE
CLARENDON PLACE
CLARENDON MEWS
CLARENDON CLOSE
FALMOUTH HOUSE
HYDE PARK STREET
ALBION STREET
ALBION MEWS
ALBION CL
ALBION
25 ALBION GATE
ALBION GATE

CONN
NORTH RISE
ST GEORGE'S FIELD
PARK STEPS
SOUTH RISE
ARCHERY CLOSE
NORTH ROW
SQUARE
FREDERICK CL
CONNAUGHT PLACE

A520
A5

81
HYDE PARK GDNS MEWS
HYDE PARK GARDENS
E SRI LANKA

A402
Tyburn
(site of)
CUMBERL

4
Victoria Gate
BAYSWATER ROAD
NORTH CARRIAGE DRIVE
P
A402

NORTH RIDE

3

115
BUCK HILL WALK
WEST CARRIAGE DRIVE
NORTH RIDE

Nursery
New Lodge
Diana, Princess of Wales Memorial Walk
Resn (cov)

Bird Sanctuary

2
◆

◆
Ranger's Lodge
Ranger's Cottage
Hyde Park

P
Serpentine Lodge
SERPENTINE ROAD

ntine ge

1
Boat Houses
Pier
Resta

The Serpentine

P
80
The Lido
Diana, Princess of Wales Memo
k

27 A
130 B
C

ROTTEN ROW

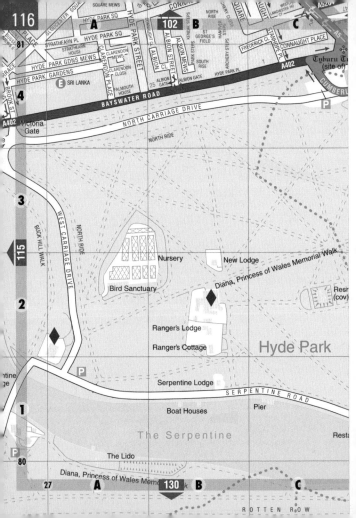

PO

Marble
Arch

A40

MARBLE ARCH

A40

A4202

A40

TYBURN WAY

Marble
Arch

AND GATE

A4202

Speakers'
Corner

DUNRAVEN ST

BRAZIL E

CYPRUS E

NORTH ROW

GREEN STREET

LEES CT

LEES PL

WOOD'S MEWS

UPPER BROOK

CULROSS STREET

NORTH AUDLEY STREET

RED PL

SHEPHERDS PL

BLACKBURNE'S MEWS

PARK

STREET

W1

Grosvenor
Ho

UPPER GROSVENOR ST

GROSVENOR ST

USA E

REEVES
HOUSE

REEVES MEWS

PROVIDENCE
CT

GEORGE YD

GROSVENOR

Roosevelt
Memorial
Grosvenor Sq
Gardens
Meml

SQUARE

INDONESIA E

ADAM'S ROW

Connaught

PO

CARLOS PL

BROWN HART
GARDENS
CHESHAM ST

DUKE ST

ST ANSELM'S
PLACE

DAVIES STREET

ARGENTINE

81

4

ITALY E

THREE KINGS
YD

CANADA E

PO

MOUNT R

MAURETANIA

3

MOUNT STREET

Liby
Mount St
Gardens
St Georges
Hanover Square
Sch

SOUTH AUDLEY STREET

BALFOUR

REX PL

ALDFORD ST

BALFOUR
PLACE

FOUNTAIN
HOUSE

SOUTH STREET

EGYPT E

The
Dorchester

DEANERY ST

DEANERY
MEWS

TILNEY ST

STANHOPE GATE

Fountain

Subway

PARK LANE

Horse Ride

LOVER'S WALK

Subway

BROAD WALK

Diana, Princess of Wales Memorial Walk

Bandstand

War
Meml

Statue
of Achilles

Weir

Holocaust
Memorial
Garden

The De...

aurant

FARM STREET

118

HILL ST

BURMA
(MYANMAR)

2

WATERLOO STREET

AUDLEY
SQUARE

RED LION
YD

QATAR E

CHESTERFIELD
GDNS

BAHAMAS E

CURZ

MARKET MEWS

MEXICO

CURZON

PITT'S HEAD MEWS

DERBY ST

The
Hilton

P

HERTFORD STREET

CURZON GATE

ACHILLES WAY

A4202

PARK

A4202

HAMILTON PLACE

Wellington
Museum
Apsley House

BRICK

SHEPHERD ST

1

80

HAMILTON
MEWS

M

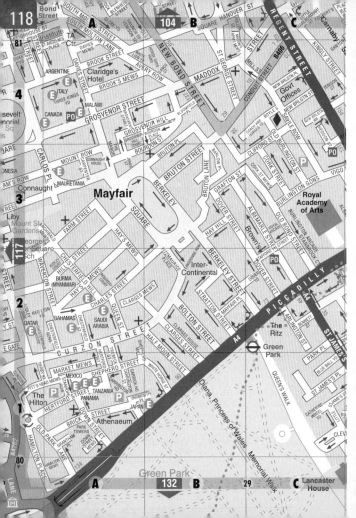

Bond Street

SOUTH MOLTON STREET

A

104

B

SQUARE HANOVER ST

C

Carnaby

REGENT STREET

KINGLY STREET

81

DUKE STREET

SOUTH MOLTON LANE

NEW BOND STREET

B406

MILL ST

Govt Offices

NEW BRIGHTN

ARGENTINE

Claridge's Hotel

BROOK STREET

AVERY ROW

MADDOX

ST GEORGE STREET

CONDUIT STREET (R)

SAVILE ROW

NEW BRIGHTN

4

ITALY

THREE KINGS YD

MALAWI

GROSVENOR STREET

BLOOMFIELD ST

NEW BRIGHTN

CANADA

PO

GROSVENOR HILL

GROSVENOR STREET

COACH AND HORSES YD

OLD BURLINGTON STREET

CLIFFORD STREET

BOYLE ST

PO

sevelt morial Sq

CARLOS PLACE

MOUNT ROW

THE MANOR

BOURDON PLACE

BOURDON STREET

BRUTON PL

BRUTON STREET

GRAFTON ST

CORK STREET

BURLINGTON GDNS

VIGO

AM'S ROW

MAURETANIA

Connaught

CONNAUGHT HOUSE

JONES

BRUTON LANE

BURLINGTON ARCADE

Royal Academy of Arts

3

Liby

Mount St Gardens

Fs

117

er Square Sch

Mayfair

FARM STREET

BERKELEY SQUARE

HAY HILL

DOVER STREET

ALBEMARLE STREET

OLD BOND STREET

Brown's

CHESTERFIELD HILL

HAY'S MEWS

FARMAURICE PLACE

Inter-Continental

BERKELEY STREET

STAFFORD

STRATTON STREET

DOVER STREET

PO

BURMA (MYANMAR)

HAY'S MEWS

CHARLES STREET

QUEEN STREET

PICCADILLY

A4

2

AUDLEY

RED LION

QATAR

BAHAMAS

SAUDI ARABIA

CLARGES MEWS

BOLTON STREET

CLARGES STREET

A4

The Ritz

ST JAMES'S

CURZON STREET

HALF MOON STREET

WHITE HORSE ST

Green Park

PARK PL

BLUE BALL YD

MARKET MEWS

SHEPHERD STREET

SHEPHERD MKT

YARMOUTH PL

Diana, Princess of Wales Memorial Walk

QUEEN'S WALK

ST JAMES'S

MEXICO

PITT'S HEAD MEWS

P

TANZANIA

P

CATHERINE WHEEL YD

CLEV

The Hilton

HERTFORD STREET

PANAMA

JAPAN

1

P

BRICK STREET

DOWN STREET

Athenaeum

PARK TOWERS

GRANTHAM PL

DOWN STREET MEWS

HAMILTON PLACE

A4202

80

HAMILTON

LANE

M

Green Park

A

132

B

29

C

Lancaster House

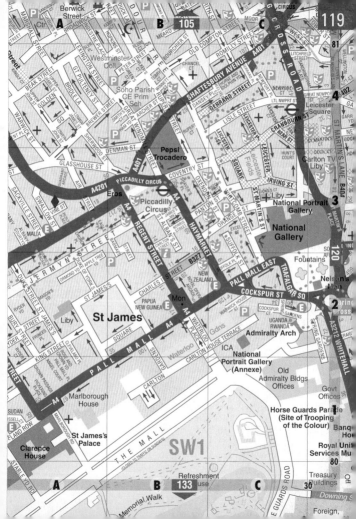

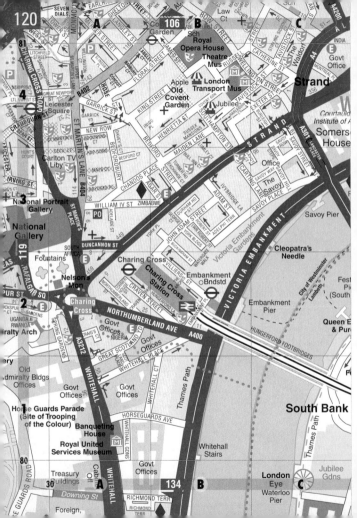

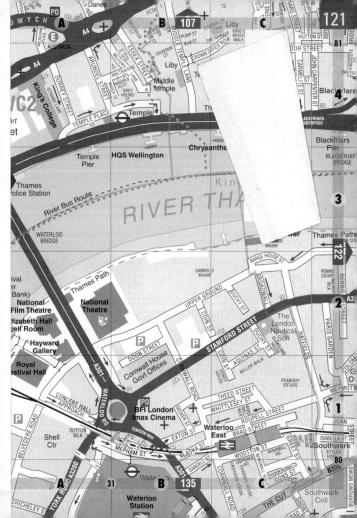

WYCH A4 P0 A
OWYCH 101 265
A4
AUSTRALIA E

B 107 Liby C
Church CT
PUMP CT
CROWN OFFICE ROW KING'S BENCH WALK
THE TERRACE
ESSEX STREET
FOUNTAIN CT Liby

ARUNDEL STREET
SURREY STREET
MALTRAVERS STREET Middle Temple

King's College
Art Street

TEMPLE PLACE
GREY HOUND CT

Temple

HUTTON ST
CARMELITE ST
TUDOR STREET
JOHN CARPENTER ST

Blackfriars 4
60

Temple Pier
HQS Wellington
Chrysanthe

BLACKFRIARS UNDERPASS

Blackfriars Pier
BLACKFRIARS BRIDGE

Thames Police Station
River Bus Route

Kin

RIVER THA

3

Thames Path

WATERLOO BRIDGE

Thames Path

BARGE HOUSE ST

Wharf
122

RENNIE COURT
WILLOW WLK
RENNIE STREET

GABRIEL'S WHARF

Festival (er Bank)
National Film Theatre
Elizabeth Hall cecil Room
Hayward Gallery
Royal estival Hall

National Theatre

UPPER GROUND
COIN ST
DUCHY ST
52
BROADWALL

2 A3
PARIS GARDEN

STAMFORD STREET
The London Nautical Sch
HATFIELDS

COIN ST 102

DOON STREET
P
P
Cornwall House Govt Offices
CORNWALL ROAD
51

AQUINAS ST
COIN ST
HENRY ST
MILLER WALK
PEABODY ESTATE

MEYMOTT

SOLOM CO

BELVEDERE ROAD A3200
P
CONCERT HALL APPROACH
WATERLOO RD A301
SUTTON WLK
Shell Ctr

P0
BFI London Imax Cinema

THEED STREET
WHITTLESEY ST
ROUPELL STREET

Waterloo East

BRAD STREET
ISABELLA ST
Southwark
STYLES HO
80

JOAN 1

TENISON WAY

EXTON ST
Alaska ST
SANDELL ST

WOOTTON ST
CORNWALL ROAD
CHARING HOUSE
CONS ST

GREET ST
B300

MEPHAM ST
A301
Waterlo

CHICHELEY ST
YORK ROAD A3200

A 31 B 135 Waterloo Station
C
Southwark Coll
THE CUT

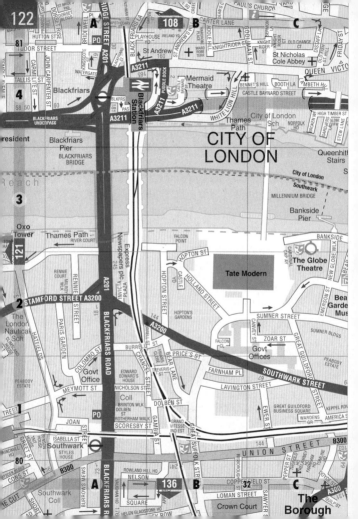

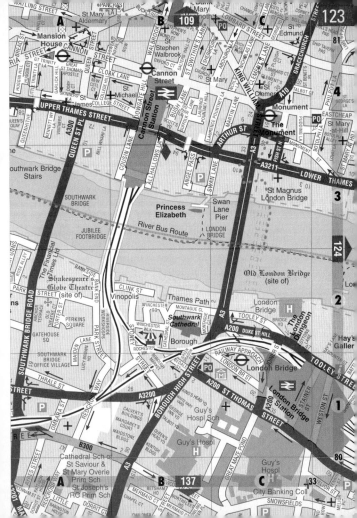

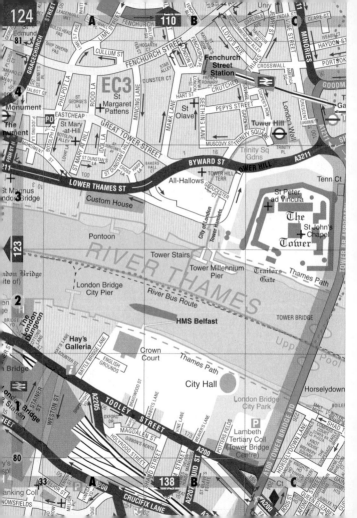

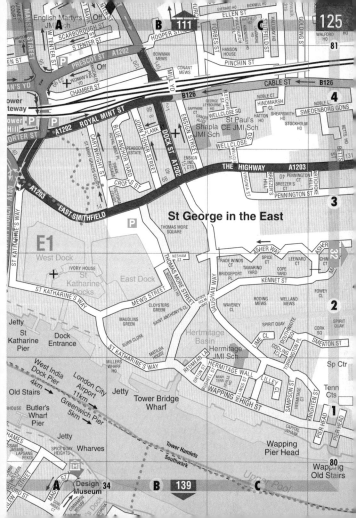

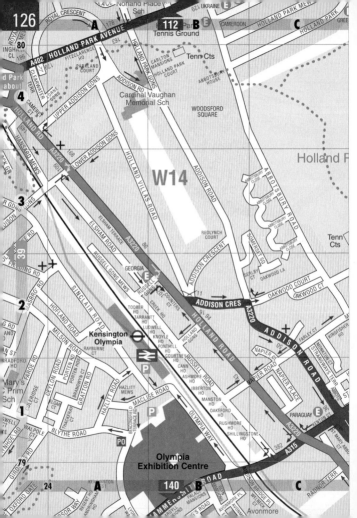

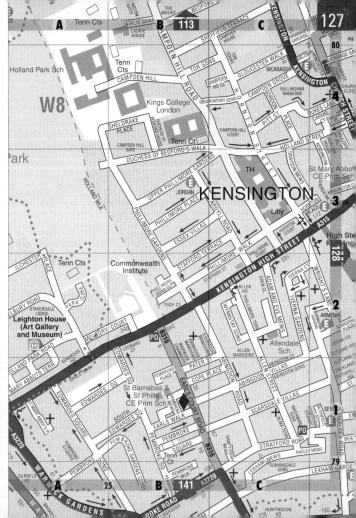

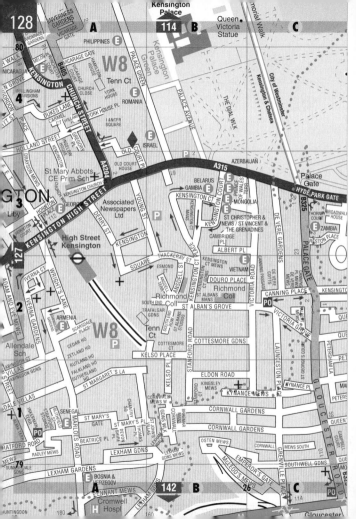

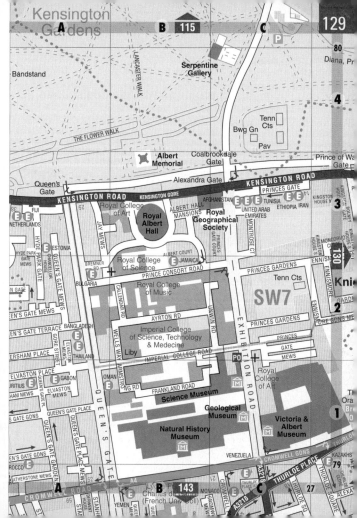

Kensington Gardens

A **B** 115 **C**

80

Diana, Pr

Bandstand

Serpentine Gallery

THE FLOWER WALK

LANCASTER WALK

P

4

Tenn Cts

Bwg Gn

Pav

Albert Memorial

Coalbrookdale Gate

Alexandra Gate

Prince of Wa Gate

Queen's Gate

KENSINGTON ROAD   KENSINGTON GORE

KENSINGTON ROAD

PRINCES GATE

3

E NETHERLANDS

E FIJI

Royal College of Art

Royal Albert Hall

ALBERT HALL MANSIONS

Royal Geographical Society

AFGHANISTAN **E** **E** TUNISIA

UNITED ARAB EMIRATES

ETHIOPIA IRAN

KINGSTON HOUSE

KINGSTON HOUSE N

KINGSTON GORE

JAY MEWS

BREMNER RD

E ESTONIA

CHANDLER HOUSE

HYDE PARK GATE MEWS

PRINCE'S GATE COURT

MONTROSE CT

Royal College of Science

ALBERT COURT

E JAMAICA

130

MONCORVO

KINGSTON HOUSE S

ENNISMORE GATE

Kni

BULGARIA

PRINCE CONSORT ROAD

PRINCES GARDENS

QUEEN'S GATE

Royal College of Music

Tenn Cts

EXHIBITION ROAD

ENNISMORE

SW7

2

N GATE

EN'S GATE MEWS

CALENDAR RD

AYRTON RD

PRINCES GARDENS

GARDI

ENNISMORE GDNS MI

PRINCES GATE MEWS

QUEEN'S GATE TERRACE

GORE STREET

E BANGLADESH

WELLS WA

ELVAS

UNWIN RD

ARMSTRO

Imperial College of Science, Technology & Medecine

ERSHAM PLACE

E **E** THAILAND

Liby

IMPERIAL COLLEGE ROAD

PO

+

Royal College of Art

T Ora Bre

ELVASTON PLACE

E GABON

E OMAN

VG RD

FRANKLAND ROAD

M

RITIUS

EN'S GATE ELVASTON MEWS

Science Museum

1

HAM MEWS

QUEEN'S GATE PLACE

Geological Museum

M

Victoria & Albert Museum

S GATE GDNS

QUEEN'S GATE PLACE MEWS

Natural History Museum

M

ROCCO

QUEEN'S GATE GDNS

VENEZUELA

CROMWELL GDNS

KAZAKHS

79

ATHERSTONE MEWS

A CROMWELL ROAD

A4

B 143

Charles de (French Univ oll)

MONACO

E PLACE

THURLOE PLACE

A3218

C THURLOE PLACE

27

THURLO

YEMEN

STANHO

QUEEN

QU

E

A3218

CROMWELL

THURLOE SQUARE

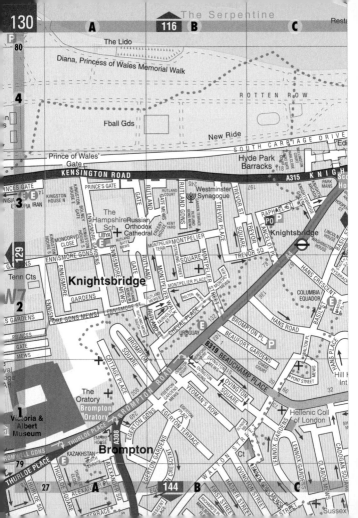

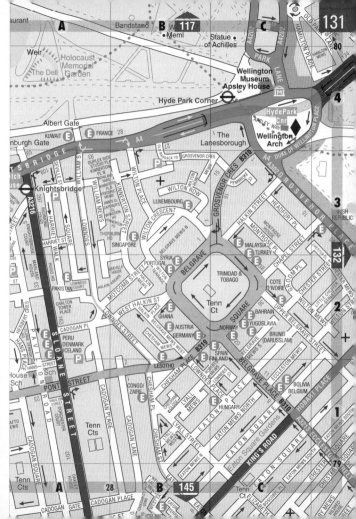

A   Bandstand   B   117   C

aurant
Meml
Statue
of Achilles

Weir
Holocaust
Memorial
Garden
The Dell

PARK
LANE
HAMILTON PLACE

HAMILTON MEWS

80

Wellington
Museum
Apsley House

4

Hyde Park Corner

HydePark
Cnr

Albert Gate
KUWAIT   FRANCE 28   A4
nburgh Gate

APSLEY WAY

Wellington
Arch

The
Lanesborough

DUKE OF WELLINGTON PLACE
GROSVENOR PLACE

A4 A3212

IRISH
REPUBLIC

KNIGHTSBRIDGE
A3216

P
Knightsbridge

SCOVILLE ST
WILLIAM S

DUPLEX RIDE
STUDIO PL
KINNERTON
PL N
BOWLAND
YD CAPENERS
CL
KINNERTON ST
CAPENER'S
CL
KINNERTON YD
THORBURN
HD

WILTON PLACE
GROSVENOR CRES

WILTON ROW
WILTON

GROSVENOR CRES   B310

PEMBROKE

HALKIN STREET

HEADFORT ST

MONTROSE
HOUSE

3

132

LUXEMBOURG

MONTROSE PL

MALAYSIA
TURKEY

CHAPEL STREET

CHESTER STREET

WILTON MEWS

LITTLE CHESTER STREET

inburgh Gate

RICHMOND
COURT

HARRIET ST
HARRIET
WALK
HUGO RD

SLOANE

LOWNDES

P
PAKISTAN

CARLTON
TOWER PL

CADOGAN PL

WILTON STREET
WILTON CRESCENT

WILTON PLACE

BELGRAVE MEWS N

SINGAPORE

PORTUGAL

MOTCOMB STREET
HALKIN STREET
GREVILLE
HOUSE

BELGRAVE MEWS N
WILTON
TERRACE

WEST HALKIN ST

HALKIN MEWS

BELGRAVE
SQUARE

BELGRAVE

SYRIA

TRINIDAD &
TOBAGO

Tenn
Ct

BAHRAIN

MALAYSIA
TURKEY

COTE
D'IVOIRE

NORWAY
YUGOSLAVIA

UPPER BELGRAVE STREET

2

House
Sch

HERBERT CRES

HANS PLACE

PAVILION RD

P

PERU
DENMARK
ICELAND

GHANA
AUSTRIA
GERMANY

CHESHAM MEWS WEST

LESOTHO

CHESHAM PLACE
B319
SPAIN
FINLAND

LOWNDES STREET

LYALL
MEWS

LOWNDES
PLACE

BELGRAVE
MEWS S

BRUNEI
(DARUSSLAM)

ECCLESTON MEWS

BELGRAVE PLACE

B310

BOLIVIA
BELGIUM

CHESTER MEWS

1

House
Sch

PONT STREET

CADOGAN PLACE

CADOGAN LANE

CONGO/
ZAIRE

CHESHAM PL
CHESHAM
MEWS W

LYALL
STREET
LYALL
MEWS W

EATON
MEWS
WEST

HUNGARY

EATON   SQUARE

EATON MEWS NORTH

EATON SQUARE

SQUARE

Eaton Square Gardens

LOWER BELGRAVE STREET

A217 EBURY STREET

EATON MEWS SOUTH
CHESTER SQUARE

79

Tenn
Cts

PAVILION
STREET
DRAYCOTT
PLACE

RAFTO
MEWS

Tenn
Cts

A   28   B   145   C

CADOGAN GATE
CADOGAN PLACE

CADOGAN SQUARE

KING'S ROAD

Tenn
Ct

ELIZABETH ST
ROSCOBIE PL

EATON

WILDING MEWS

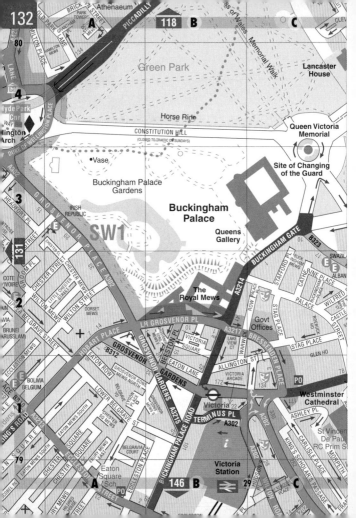

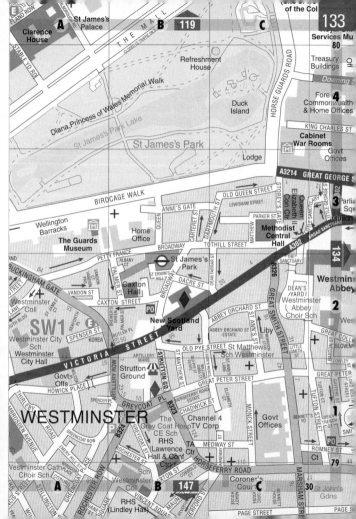

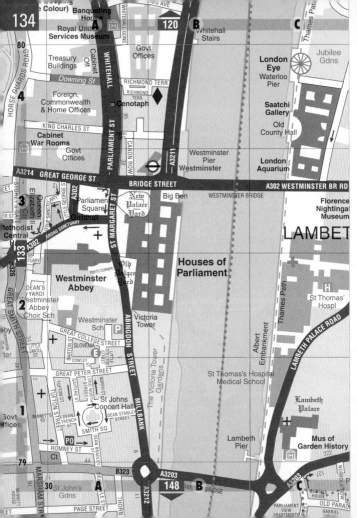

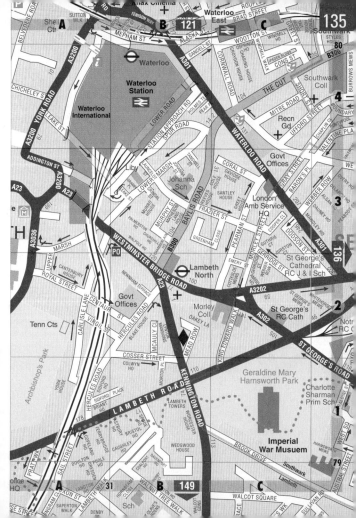

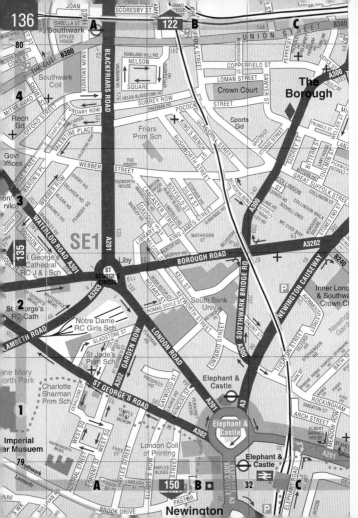

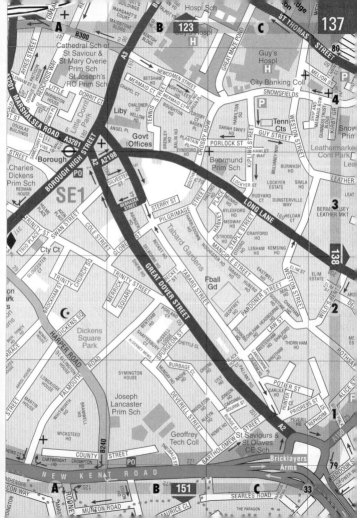

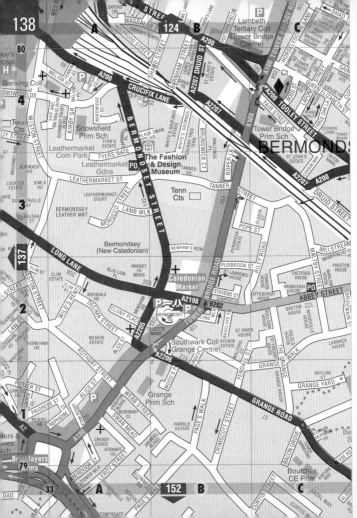

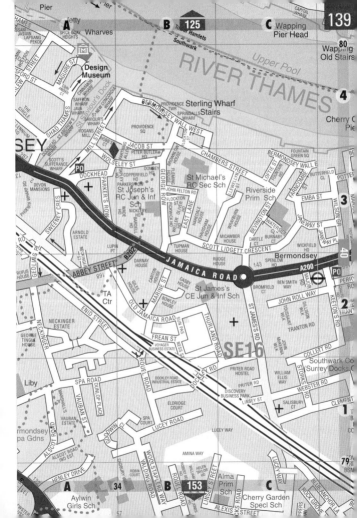

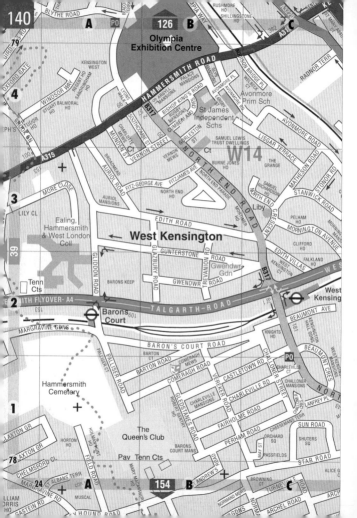

BLYTHE ROAD

A

PO

126 B

C

Olympia
Exhibition Centre

HAMMERSMITH ROAD

RUSHMORE HO
SHILLINGSTONE

BIRD ST

OXFORD GATE

79

WINDSOR WAY

KENSINGTON
WEST

REGENT HO
SANDRINGHAM

STUART BALMORAL
HO

CHARLOTTE
DESPARD AVE

SOUTHCOMBE

4

A315

MUNDEN ST

VERNON STREET

Ct

B317

BISHOP KING'S ROAD

RUGBY
MANSIONS

GIBBONS ARC

GORLESTON

PALACE
MANSIONS

AVONMORE PL

AVONMORE RD

WRECCLESHAM

Avonmore
Prim Sch

St James
Independent
Schs

RADNOR TERR

AVONMORE ROAD

LISGAR TERRACE

W14

SAMUEL LEWIS
TRUST DWELLINGS

THE
GRANGE

MORE CLOSE

AURIOL ROAD

FITZ-GEORGE AVE

FITZJAMES AVE

NORTH END PARADE

VERNON
MEWS

Ct

BURNE JONES

SAMUEL
RICHARDSON

STANWICK ROAD

MATHESON ROAD

STONOR RD

3

39

LILY CL

Ealing,
Hammersmith
& West London
Coll

AURIOL
MANSIONS

NORTH END
HO

EDITH ROAD

GLIDDON ROAD

GLAZBURY ROAD

GUNTERSTONE

BARONS KEEP

TREVANION ROAD

GWENDWR

NORTH END HO

NORTH END ROAD

West Kensington

MORNINGTON AVENUE

EDITH VILLAS

WEST
KENSINGTON

Gwendwr
Gdn

GWENDWR ROAD

PELHAM
HO

CLIFFORD
HO

FALKLAND
HO

MORNING

B317

Liby

NORTH END CRESCENT

MUNDER HO

WE

2

SMITH FLYOVER - A4

MARGRAVINE GDNS

163

Barons
Court

109

TALGARTH ROAD

BEAUMONT AVE

KENSINGTON
HALL GDNS

KNIGHTS
HO

West
Kensin

NORTH

BEAUMONT CRES

1

Hammersmith
Cemetery

PALLISER ROAD

BARTON
CT

BARON'S COURT ROAD

BARTON ROAD

COMERAGH
MEWS

COMERAGH ROAD

CASTLETOWN RD

CHARLEVILLE RD

CHALLONER STREET

PO

CHARLEVILLE
CT

CHALLONER
MANSIONS

LANFREY PL

NORTH

78

LAXTON GR

HORTON
HO

HOLMAINE HO

CHARLEVILLE
MANSIONS

GLEDSTANES ROAD

VEREKER ROAD

FAIRHOLME ROAD

PERHAM ROAD

CHEESEMANS TERR

ORCHARD
SQ

SUN ROAD

SHUTERS
SQ

LAXTON GR

The
Queen's Club

BEAUMONT

STAR ROAD

CHELMSFORD CL

ST ALBANS TERR

MUSCAL

FIELD RD

MARY MACARTHUR HO

BARONS
COURT MANS

Pav Tenn Cts

MAY ST

ANDREW'S

PASSFIELDS

BROWNING

TURNEY

ALICE RD

ARCH

LLIAM
ORRIS
HO

GASTEIN RD

24

A

154 B

C

ARCHEL ROAD

NORMAND

GDNS

HOUND ROAD

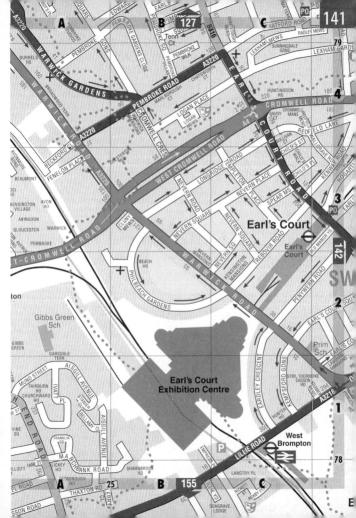

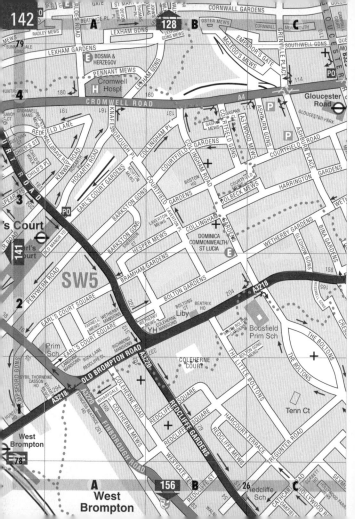

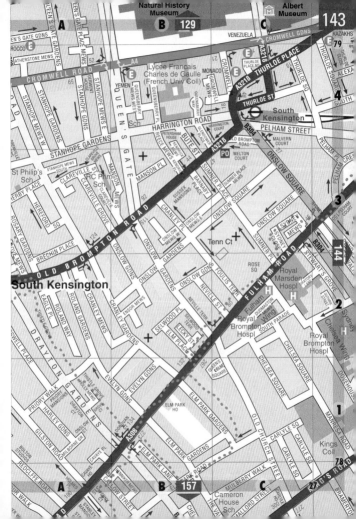

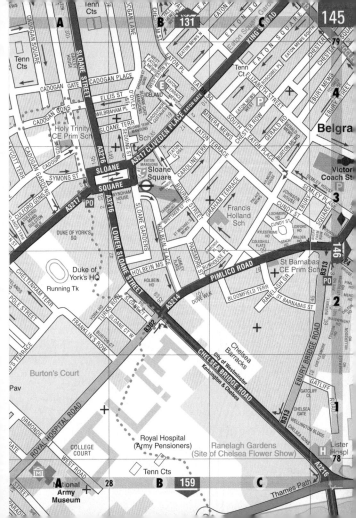

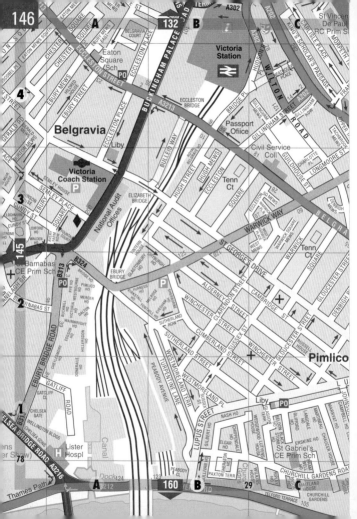

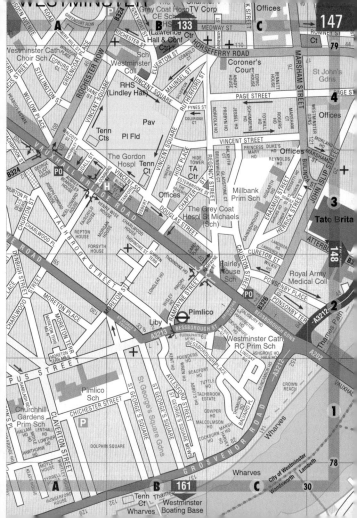

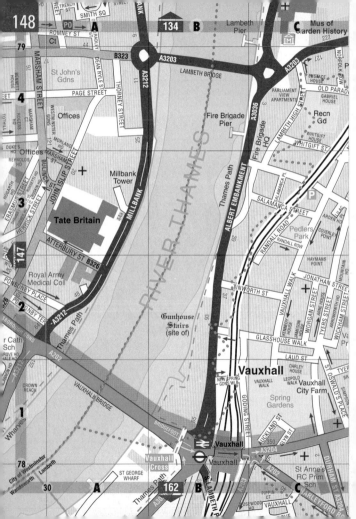

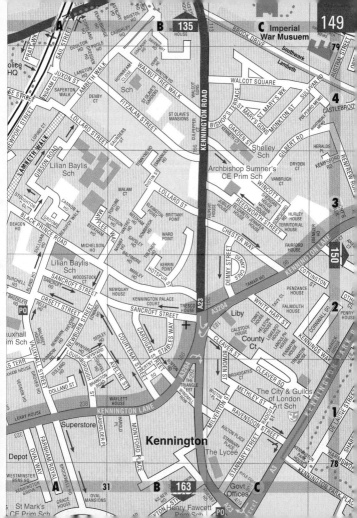

Grid references (top): **A** | **B** 135 | **C** | **4** | **3** | **2** | **1**

Grid references (bottom): **A** | 31 | **B** 163 | **C**

Key streets and locations:

- Imperial War Musuem
- BROOK DRIVE
- Southwark / Lambeth
- WALCOT SQUARE
- Police HQ
- PRATT WALK
- SAIL STREET
- BRISTOL
- CAUGHLEY
- HOUSE
- DOULTON ST
- POOLE
- DRESDEN
- REDCLIFFE
- ASHBY
- JUXON ST
- LANGTON
- WALNUT TREE WALK
- HORNBEAM CLOSE
- MINTON HO
- GILLPEPPER ST
- WALCOT GDNS
- CASTLEBROOK
- ST MARY'S TERRACE
- ST MARY'S GDNS
- OAKDEN ST
- MONKTON ST
- SULLIVAN RD
- LAMBETH WALK
- NORMAN ST
- SAPERTON WALK
- DEMBY CT
- FITZALAN STREET
- ST OLAVE'S GARDENS
- ST OLAVE'S MANSIONS
- BISHOP'S TERRACE
- KENNETH CT
- Shelley Sch
- GILBERT RD
- HERALDS PL
- KEMPSFORD
- RD
- RENFREW RD
- Sch
- LOLLARD STREET
- LUPINO CT
- GIBSON ROAD
- Lilian Baylis Sch
- SAUNDERS HO
- TONKIN HO
- DISTIN ST
- MALAM CT
- EMMANUEL
- KENNINGTON ROAD
- Archbishop Sumner's CE Prim Sch
- WINCOTT ST
- SHERIDAN
- VANBRUGH
- DRYDEN CT
- STOUGHTON CL
- CANNON HO
- BROOME
- WALNUT TREE WALK
- BEAUFOY WALK
- SCOTSON CT
- LOLLARD ST
- ELKINGTON POINT
- NEEDHAM
- BRITTANY POINT
- RUPERT HOUSE
- REEDWORTH STREET
- JUBILEE
- MATHAM
- JENNIFER
- HOUSE
- HURLEY HOUSE
- Territorial House
- EBENEZER HO
- BLACK PRINCE ROAD
- DEACON HO
- BURCHELL HO
- SULLIVAN HO
- MICHELSON HO
- WYVIL WAY
- BECKHAM HO
- GAYSLEY HO
- BALTIMORE
- TINDALE
- WARD POINT
- MANLEY HO
- HOTSPUR HO
- KERRIN POINT
- CHESTER WAY
- DENNY STREET
- FAIRFORD HOUSE
- CORKINGTON ST
- 150
- APIA CT
- Lilian Baylis Sch
- BLAND HO
- SANCROFT STREET
- WOODSTOCK HO
- NEWQUAY HOUSE
- DENNY CRES
- TAMAR HO
- PENZANCE HOUSE
- ORSETT STREET
- PELLA HO
- KENNINGTON PALACE COURT
- SANCROFT STREET
- TRESCO HOUSE
- A23
- A3204
- WHITE HART ST
- GRAY CT
- FALMOUTH HOUSE
- Liby
- PENRY HOUSE
- VAUXHALL
- Prim Sch
- MAULEY HOUSE
- NEWBURN STREET
- DUNRAVEN
- WYNYARD
- SEELEY ST
- BRANSTON
- COURTENAY STREET
- CARDIGAN STREET
- STABLES WAY
- CALSTOCK HOUSE
- TOWNEY
- HOLSTER
- WHEATLEY
- LISGARD HO
- LANGDON HO
- PRIMROSE HO
- County Ct
- CORNWALL ST
- KENNINGS WAY
- OTHE
- VERNON HO
- LOUGHBOROUGH
- DOMINION
- DOLLAND ST
- AVELINE ST
- WAYLETT HOUSE
- 238
- KENNINGTON LANE
- CLEAVER STREET
- BOWDEN ST
- BROADGATES CT
- CLEAVER SQ
- The City & Guilds of London Art Sch
- KENNINGTON FOR PARK?
- LEARY HOUSE
- FARNHAM ROYAL
- VAUXHALL GROVE
- GRAHAM HOUSE
- HAROLD CT
- RASHLEIGH PL
- METHLEY ST
- RAVENSDON STREET
- MILVERTON ST
- WILTON CT
- KENNEDY
- DELAVERNE ST
- 78
- Superstore
- MONTFORD PLACE
- Kennington
- AULTON PLACE
- RIFLE PL
- HARMSWORTH
- KENNINGTON PARK RD
- Depot
- OVAL WAY
- BROXHOLM
- THE TRIANGLE EST
- STANNARY STREET
- STANNARY PLACE
- The Lycée
- SHARP
- WESTMINSTER
- BSNS SQ
- KENNINGTON GROVE
- GRACE HOUSE
- OVAL MANSIONS
- KILNER
- Govt Offices
- 409
- St Mark's CE Prim Sch
- Henry Fawcett Prim Sch

Page references: 135, 163, 150, 149, 79

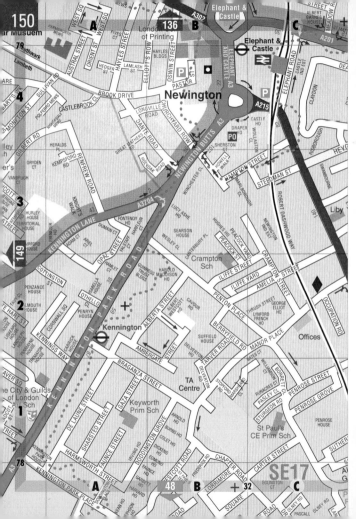

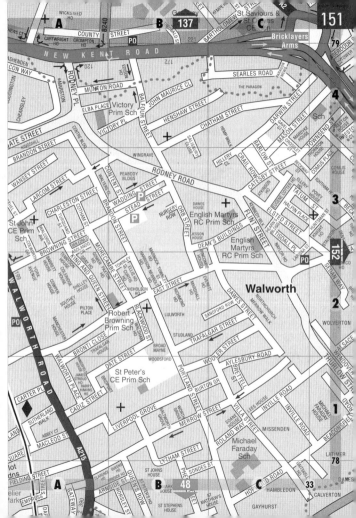

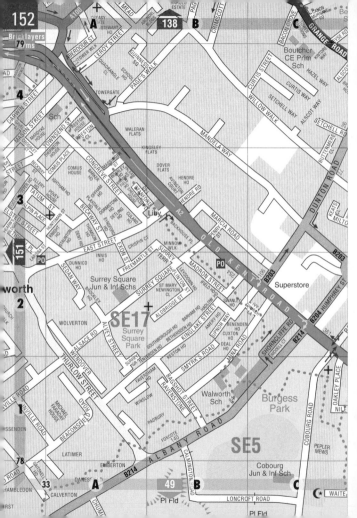

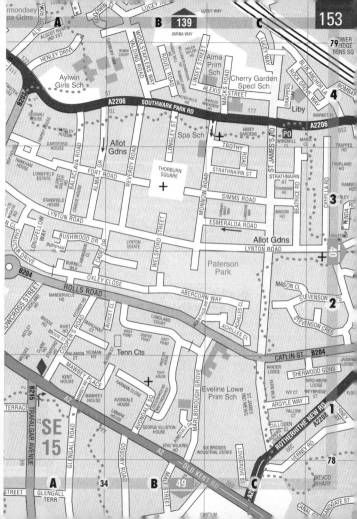

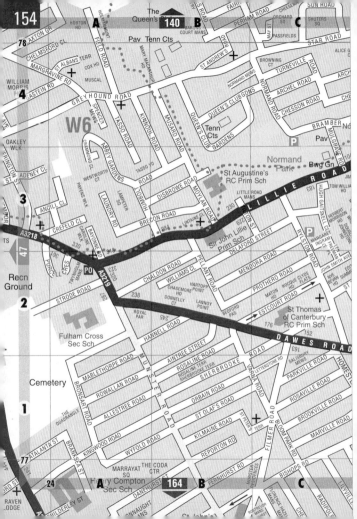

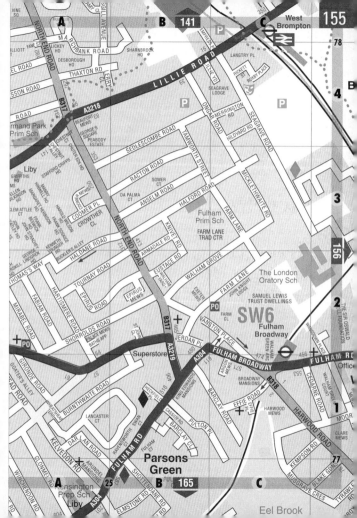

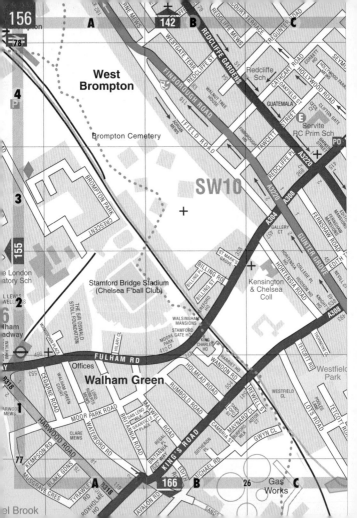

A

B

C

West Brompton

Brompton Cemetery

Redcliffe Sch

GUATEMALA

Servite RC Prim Sch

PO

E

SW10

Brompton Cemetery

155

The London Laboratory Sch

L LEWIS WELL

Stamford Bridge Stadium (Chelsea F'ball Club)

Kensington & Chelsea Coll

GALLERY CT

2

ham adway

THE SIR OSWALD STOLL FOUNDATION

WALSINGHAM MANSIONS

STAMFORD MOORE GATE HO

KING CHARLES HO

HARRIET HO

Westfield Park

WESTFIELD CL

Offices

Walham Green

FULHAM RD

HOLMEAD ROAD

WANDON RD

RUMBOLD ROAD

77

HARWOOD ROAD

KING'S ROAD

166

EDITH

26

Gas Works

C

A

B

el Brook

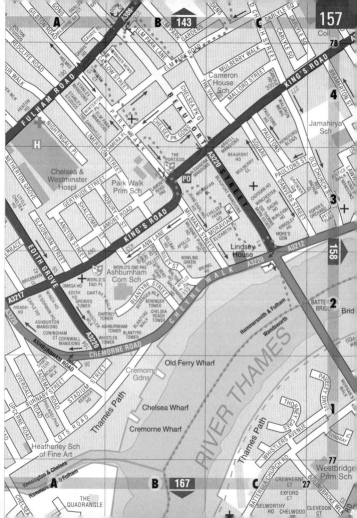

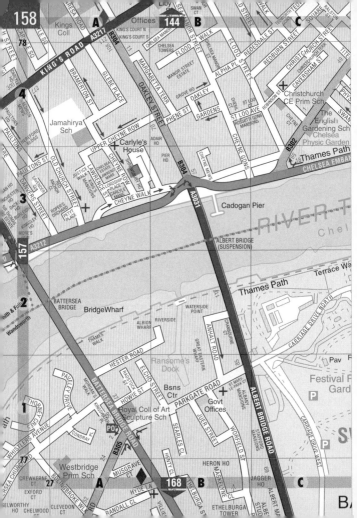

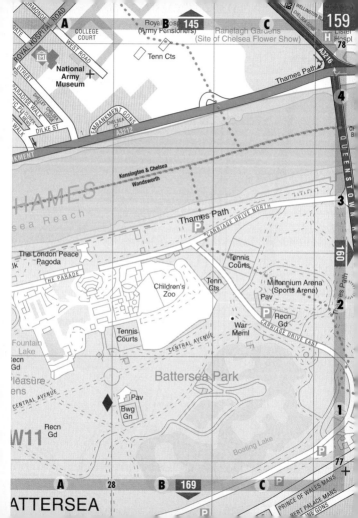

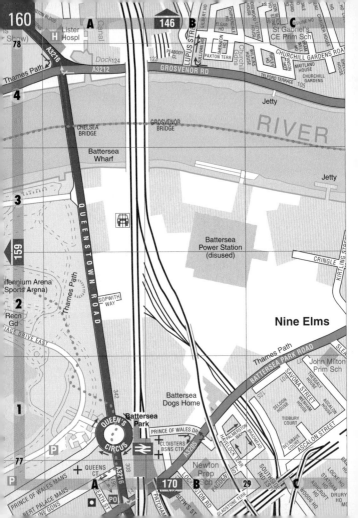

- **RIVER** (Thames)
- **Battersea Power Station (disused)**
- **Nine Elms**
- **Battersea Dogs Home**
- **Battersea Park**
- **QUEEN'S CIRCUS**
- **Chelsea Bridge**, **Grosvenor Bridge**
- **Battersea Wharf**
- **QUEENSTOWN ROAD**
- **Thames Path**
- **GROSVENOR RD** (A3212)
- **A3216**
- **LUPUS STREET**
- **St Gabriel's CE Prim Sch**
- **CHURCHILL GARDENS ROAD**
- **Churchill Gardens**
- **PAXTON TERR**
- **TELFORD TERRACE**
- **Lister Hospl**
- **Peabody Cl**
- **SOPWITH WAY**
- **Millennium Arena (Sports Arena)**
- **Recn Gd**
- **CARRIAGE DRIVE EAST**
- **BATTERSEA PARK ROAD**
- **John Milton Prim Sch**
- **SAVONA STREET**
- **ASCALON STREET**
- **PRINCE OF WALES DR**
- **CLOISTERS BSNS CTR**
- **Newton Prep Sch**
- **QUEENS CT**
- **PRINCE OF WALES MANS**
- **CRINGLE**
- **KIRTLING STREET**
- **Jetty**

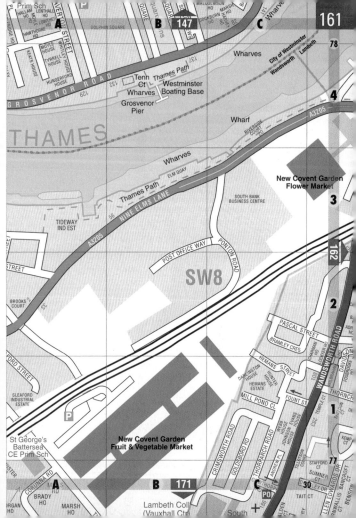

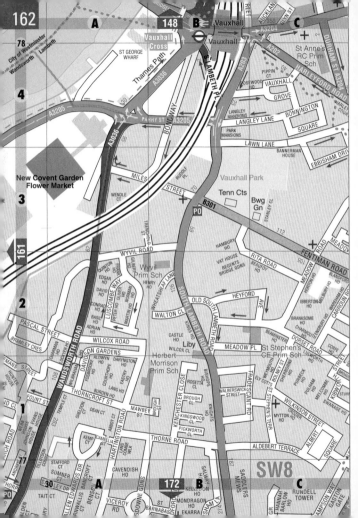

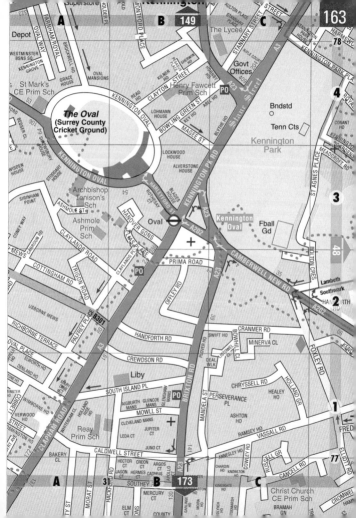

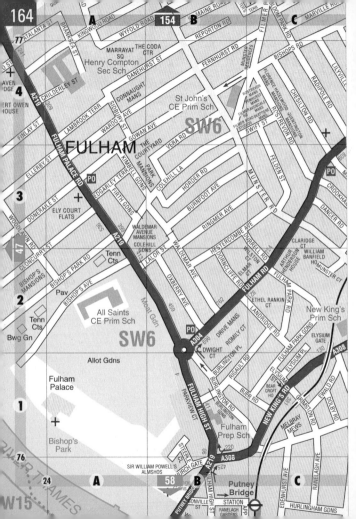

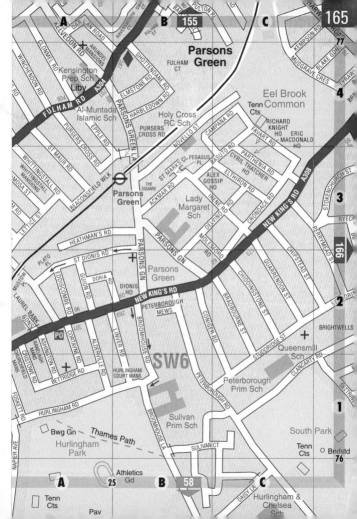

A B **155** C

Parsons Green

FULHAM CT

KELVEDON RD
DAR
AN ROAD
RAVENSCROFT SW CT
FULHAM RD
PULTON RD
BARCLAY RD

77
KEMPSON RD
BLAKE GDNS
MUSGRAVE CRES
TYRAW...
4
BP...

CLONMEL RD
WINCHENDON RD
Kensington Prep Sch Liby
ARUNDEL MANSIONS
SHOTTENDANE RD

Eel Brook Common
Tenn Cts

FULHAM RD A304

Al-Muntada Islamic Sch

ST MAUR RD
EPPLE RD
ELMSTONE RD
HARBLEDOWN RD
PARSONS GREEN LA
PURSERS CROSS RD
Holy Cross RC Sch
NOVELLO ST
CAMPANA RD

RICHARD KNIGHT HO
ERIC MACDONALD HO
TAVART RD
PARTHENIA RD
CYRIL THATCHER HO

WHITTINGSTALL RD
TIMOSA ST
BEACONSFIELD WLK
ST MARKS CL
PEGASUS PL
BASUTO RD
ALEX GOSSIP HO
ELTHIRON RD

⊖ **Parsons Green**

THE SQUARE
ACKMAR RD
IRENE RD
DEVINE RD
Lady Margaret Sch

CRONDACE RD
NEW KING'S RD A308
STOKENCHURCH RD
3
RYEC...

LETTICE ST

HEATHMAN'S RD
PLATO PL
ST DIONIS RD
PARSONS GN

MOLESFORD RD
QUARRENDON ST
CHIPSTEAD ST
PERRYMEAD ST

166

MUSTON RD
EDDISCOMBE RD
GUION RD
DORIA RD
Parsons Green
DIONIS HO
NEW KING'S RD
CONIGER RD
BRADBOURNE ST
CHIDDINGSTONE ST
2

LAUREL BANK GDNS
ASHINGTON RD
CORVANE RD
PETERBOROUGH MEWS
BRIGHTWELLS

PO
RANELAGH MANS
CRAISTONE RD
ALDERVILLE RD
LINVER RD
BROOMHOUSE RD
SW6
STUDDRIDGE ST
Queensmill Sch +
CLANCARTY RD

CHURCHFIELD MANS
BETTRIDGE RD
HURLINGHAM COURT MANS
PETERBOROUGH RD
Peterborough Prim Sch

FOSKETT RD
HURLINGHAM RD
SETTRI...
1

NAPIER AVE
☐ Bwg Gn
Thames Path
Hurlingham Park
BROOMHOUSE LA
Sulivan Prim Sch
SULIVAN CT
South Park
Tenn Cts
○ Bndstd
76

A ☐ Tenn Cts
Athletics Gd 25
B **58** C
DAISY LA
Hurlingham & Chelsea Sch
Pav

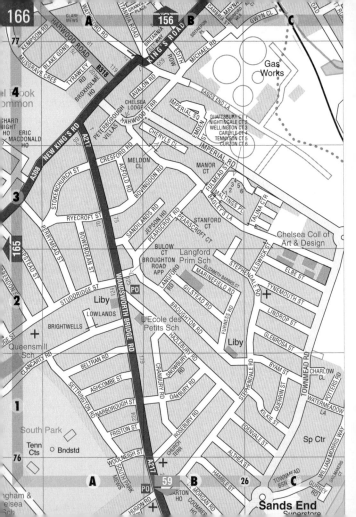

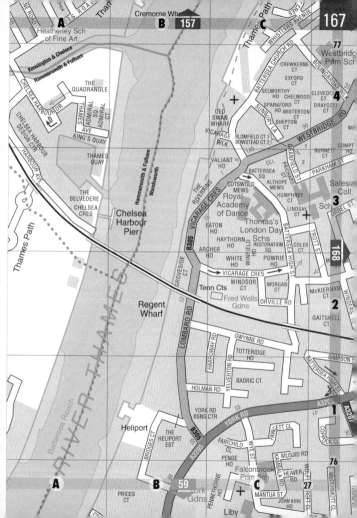

A B 157 C

Cremorne Whf

Thames Path

WHISTLERS AVENUE

77
Westbridge
Prim Sch

Heatherley Sch
of Fine Art

Kensington & Chelsea
Hammersmith & Fulham

THE
QUADRANGLE

CHELSEA HARBOUR

CHELSEA HARBOUR DESIGN CTR

HARBOUR AVE

THAMES
ADMIRAL
SQ
ADMIRAL
CT

KING'S QUAY

THAMES
QUAY

THE
BELVEDERE

CHELSEA
CRES

Hammersmith & Fulham
Wandsworth

THE
RIVERAINS

VICARAGE CRES

Chelsea
Harbour
Pier

Chelsea Harbour Pier

Thames Path

Battersea Reach

RIVER THAMES

Regent
Wharf

GROVESIDE CT

LOMBARD RD

B305

Heliport

BRIDGES CT

THE
HELIPORT
EST

B305

A3205

PRICES
CT

A

York
Gdns

B 59

BATTERSEA CHURCH RD

BOLINGBROKE RD

CREWKERNE
CT

EXFORD
CT

SELWORTHY
HO CHELWOOD
CT

SPARKFORD
HO MISTERTON
CT

SHEPTON
CT

CLEVEDON
CT

DRAYCOTT
CT

WESTBRIDGE RD

4

SUNBURY LA

OLD SWAN
WHARF

VICARAGE
VICARAGE
WLK

BLOMFIELD CT 1
BOWSTEAD CT 2

GRANFIELD ST

PRIORY

BURNETT
CT

COMPTON CT

PARKHAM ST

VALIANT
HO

BATTERSEA
SQ

COTSWOLD
MEWS

ALTHORPE
MEWS

Royal
Academy
of Dance

HUMPHREY
CT

Salesian
Coll

3

ORBEL ST

EATON
HO

LINDSAY
CT

BATTERSEA HIGH ST

HAYTHORN
HO

WINFIELD
HO

RESTORATION
SQ

COLES
CT

168

ARCHER
HO

WHITE
HO

POWRIE
HO

Thomas's
London Day
Schs

ROTT ST

VICARAGE CRES

Tenn Cts

Fred Wells
Gdns

WINDSOR
CT

MORGAN
CT

ORVILLE RD

McKIERNAN

2

WINDERS

GAITSKELL
CT

GWYNNE RD

HARROWAY RD

YELVERTON RD

TOTTERIDGE
HO

BADRIC CT

SIMPSON

BATTERSEA HIGH ST

HOLMAN RD

YORK RD
BSNS CTR

YORK RD

A3205

A320

1

FAIRCHILD
CL

FAWCETT CL

COPCOCK CL

PENGE
HO

WEST

MUSJID RD

KAMBALA
RD

WOFFINGTON

76

Falconbrook
Prim Sch

HEAVER
RD

McMERMOTT CL

27

PENNETHORNE

MANTUA ST

JOHN KIRK

C

Liby

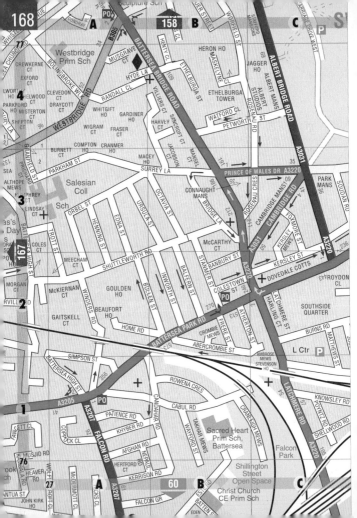

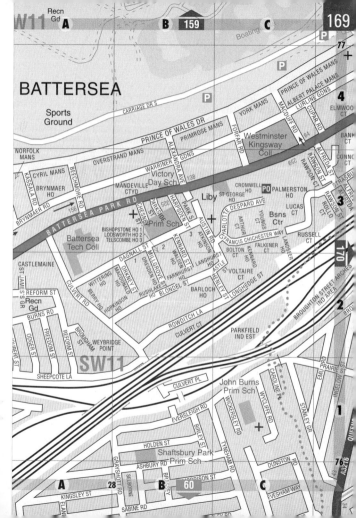

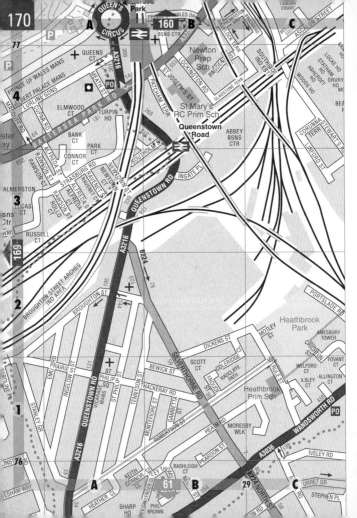

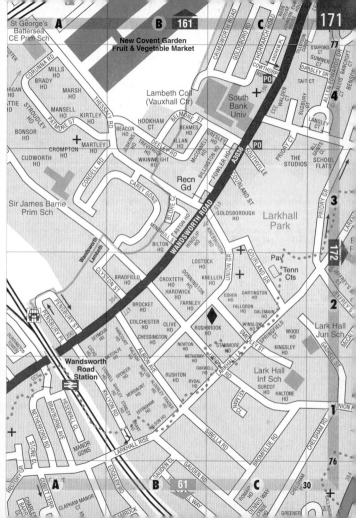

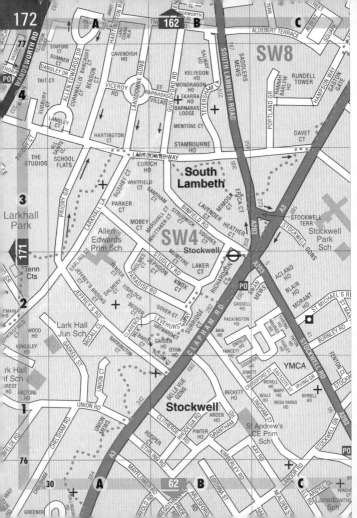

Index

Church Rd **6** Beckenham BR2..........**53** C6 **228** C6

Place name	Location number	Locality, town or village	Postcode district	Standard scale reference	Enlarged scale reference
May be abbreviated on the map	Present when a number indicates the place's position in a crowded area of mapping	Shown when more than one place (outside London postal districts) has the same name	District for the indexed place	Page number and grid reference for the standard mapping	Page number and grid reference for the central London enlarged mapping, underlined in red

Public and commercial buildings are highlighted in magenta
Places of interest are highlighted in blue with a star ★

Index of localities, towns and villages

A
Acton 28 C1
Acton Green 37 B2

B
Balham 72 C3
Barbican 109 A3
Barnes 46 B2
Barnsbury 14 A1
Battersea 169 A4
Bayswater 114 C4
Bedford Park 38 A3
Belgravia 146 A4
Belsize Park 12 A3
Bermondsey 40 A4
Bethnal Green 25 A2
Blackheath
Vale 53 B1
Blackwall 34 C2
Bloomsbury 106 A4
Borough The 136 C4
Bow 26 B3
Bow Common 34 A4
Brixton 62 C4
Broadgate 110 A4
Brockley 66 B3
Bromley
(Tower Hamlets) ...27 A2
Brompton 130 A1
Brondesbury 10 A2
Brondesbury
Park 22 C2
Brook Green 39 C2

C
Camberwell 48 B2
Camden Town 13 A1
Canary Wharf 34 A1
Canning Town 35 B3
Canonbury 15 B2
Chelsea 144 B1
Child's Hill 1 C6
Chiswick 38 B1
City of London 122 B4
Clapham 61 A4
Clapham
Common 61 A3
Clapham Junction 60 A3
Clapham Park 61 C2
Clapton Park 17 C4
Clerkenwell 96 A1
College Park 22 A2
Covent Garden 120 B4
Cricklewood 9 B4
Cubitt Town 42 B2

D
Dalston 16 C2
Dartmouth Park 4 A3
De Beauvoir Town ...16 A1
Deptford 50 C3
Dollis Hill 9 A4
Dudden Hill 8 C3
Dulwich 76 A2
Dulwich Village 76 A4

E
Earl's Court 141 C3
Earlsfield 71 B3
East Acton 29 A1
East Dulwich 64 C2
East Sheen 55 C3
Euston 93 A3

F
Finsbury 95 C4
Finsbury Park 5 C3
Fitzrovia 104 A4
Fulham 47 C1

G
Globe Town 25 C2
Gospel Oak 12 B2
Greenwich 53 A4
Grove Park
(Hounslow) 45 B2
Gunnersbury 37 A2

H
Hackney 17 A2
Hackney Wick 18 C2
Haggerston 24 B3
Hammersmith 39 B2
Hampstead 11 B3
Harlesden 21 B4
Herne Hill 63 B2
Highbury 15 A4
Highgate 3 C4
Holborn 107 C3

Homerton 17 C1
Honor Oak 65 B2
Hoxton 24 A3
Hyde Park 116 C2

I
Isle of Dogs 42 B2
Islington 14 C2

K
Kennington 149 B1
Kensal Green 22 B2
Kensal Rise 22 C3
Kensal Town 23 A1
Kensington 127 C3
Kentish Town 13 B2
Kew 44 C4
Kilburn 23 B4
King's Cross 84 C2
Kingsland 16 A2
Knightsbridge 130 A1

L
Ladywell 66 C1
Lambeth 134 C3
Lewisham 67 B3
Leyton 19 C4
Limehouse 33 A2
Lisson Green 90 B2
Lisson Grove 102 A4
Lower Clapton 17 B4
Lower Holloway 14 A3
Lower Place 20 B3

M
Maida Vale 88 A4
Maitland Park 12 C2
Marylebone 104 B2
Mayfair 118 A3
Mile End 26 A1
Mill Meads 27 C3
Millwall 41 C3
Mortlake 55 B4

N
New Cross 51 B2
New Cross Gate 50 C2
Newington 150 B4
Nine Elms 160 C2
North Acton 20 C2
North End 2 B2
North Kensington ...30 C4
North Sheen 44 C1
Notting Hill 112 C3
Nunhead 65 B3

O
Old Ford 26 B4
Old Oak Common 21 B1

P
Paddington 100 C3
Park Royal 20 A4
Parsons Green 165 B4
Peckham 49 A2
Pentonville 85 A1
Pimlico 146 C1
Poplar 33 C3

Primrose Hill	12 B1	Shoreditch	87 C1	St John's	51 C1	
Putney	57 B2	Soho	105 B1	St John's Wood	79 B1	
Putney Heath	57 B1	Somers Town	93 C4	St Luke's	97 A2	
Putney Vale	68 C1	South Acton	37 A3	St Pancras	94 B4	
		South Bank	120 C1	Stamford Hill	7 A3	
		South Bromley	34 C4	Stepney	32 C4	
R		South Hackney	25 B4	Stockwell	62 A4	
Ratcliff	32 C2	South Hampstead	11 B1	Stoke Newington	7 A2	
Regent's Park	92 A4	South		Stonebridge	20 B4	
Richmond	54 A2	Kensington	143 A3	Strand	120 C4	
Richmond Hill	54 A1	South Lambeth	172 B3	Strand on		
Roehampton	68 A4	Southfields	71 A3	the Green	44 C4	
Rotherhithe	40 C3	Southwark	40 B2	Stratford	19 B1	
		Spitalfields	110 A4	Stratford Marsh	27 A4	
S		St George in		Stratford New Town	19 B3	
Sands End	59 B4	the East	32 A2	Streatham Hill	74 A3	
Shacklewell	16 B4	St Giles	106 A2	Summerstown	71 B1	
Shadwell	32 B2	St James	119 B2			
Shepherd's Bush	30 A1					

T		Wapping	32 A2	
Temple Mills	19 A3	Waterloo	135 B4	
Tower Hamlets	33 B4	West Brompton	156 A4	
Tufnell Park	13 C4	West Dulwich	75 A2	
Tulse Hill	75 A4	West Hill	58 B1	
		West Hampstead	10 C4	
U		West Kensington	140 B3	
Upper Holloway	4 C2	West Kilburn	23 A2	
Upper Tooting	72 B1	West Norwood	75 B1	
		Westbourne Green	88 A2	
V		Westminster	133 A1	
Vale of Health	2 C1	Whitechapel	110 C1	
Vauxhall	148 B1	Willesden	8 C4	
		Willesden Green	22 A4	
W		Wimbledon Park	70 B3	
Walham Green	156 A1			
Walworth	151 C2			
Wandsworth	58 C1			

Abbreviations used in the index

Acad	Academy	Ent Ctr	Enterprise Centre	Mus	Museum
App	Approach	Ent Pk	Enterprise Park	Obsy	Observatory
Arc	Arcade	Est	Estate	Orch	Orchard
Art Gall	Art Gallery	Ex Ctr	Exhibition Centre	Par	Parade
Ave	Avenue	Ex Hall	Exhibition Hall	Pas	Passage
Bglws	Bungalows	Fst	First	Pav	Pavilion
Bldgs	Buildings	Gdn	Garden	Pk	Park
Bsns Ctr	Business Centre	Gdns	Gardens	Pl	Place
Bsns Pk	Business Park	Gn	Green	Prec	Precinct
Bvd	Boulevard	Gr	Grove	Prep	Preparatory
Cath	Cathedral, Catholic	Gram	Grammar	Prim	Primary
CE	Church of England	Her Ctr	Heritage Centre	Prom	Promenade
Cemy	Cemetery	Ho	House	RC	Roman Catholic
Cir	Circus	Hospl	Hospital	Rd	Road
Circ	Circle	Hts	Heights	Rdbt	Roundabout
Cl	Close	Ind Est	Industrial Estate	Ret Pk	Retail Park
Cnr	Corner	Inf	Infant	Sch	School
Coll	College	Inst	Institute	Sec	Secondary
Com	Community	Int	International	Sh Ctr	Shopping Centre
Comm	Common	Intc	Interchange	Sp	Sports
Comp	Comprehensive	Jun	Junior	Specl	Special
Con Ctr	Conference Centre	Junc	Junction	Sports Ctr	Sports Centre
Cotts	Cottages	La	Lane	Sq	Square
Cres	Crescent	L Ctr	Leisure Centre	St	Street, Saint
Cswy	Causeway	Liby	Library	Sta	Station
Ct	Court	Mans	Mansions	Stad	Stadium
Ctr	Centre	Mdw/s	Meadow/s	Tech	Technical/Technology
Crkt	Cricket	Meml	Memorial	Terr	Terrace
Ctry Pk	Country Park	Mid	Middle	Trad Est	Trading Estate
Cty	County	Mix	Mixed	Twr/s	Tower/s
Ctyd	Courtyard	Mkt	Market	Univ	University
Dr	Drive	Mon	Monument	Wlk	Walk

A

Abady Ho SW1 .... **147** C4
Abberley Mews **4**
SW8 .... **61** A4
Abbess Cl SW2 .... **75** A3
Abbeville Mews **3**
SW4 .... **61** C3
Abbeville Rd SW4 ...... **61** C3
Abbey Bsns Ctr
SW8 .... **170** B4
Abbey Cl SW8 .... **78** C2
SE17 .... **151** C1
6 London W12 .... **38** A3
Abbeyfield Rd SE16 .. **40** B2
Abbey Gdns NW8 ...... **79** A1
W6 .... **154** A3
Abbey Ho NW8 .... **89** A4
SE17 .... **151** A4
Abbey Lo E15 .... **27** C3
Abbey Lo NW8 .... **90** B3
Abbey Orchard St
SW1 .... **133** C2
Abbey Orchard Street
Est SW1 .... **133** C2
Abbey Rd NW8 .... **78** C2
Wembley NW10 .... **20** A3
Abbey St SE1 .... **138** C2
Abbey Tutorial Coll
W2 .... **31** C3 **113** A4
Abbot Cl SW8 .... **162** A1
Abbot Ho **6** E14 ...... **34** A2
Abbotsbury Cl E15 .... **27** B3
W14 .... **126** C3
Abbotsbury Ho
W14 .... **126** B4
Abbotsbury Mews
SE15 .... **65** B4
Abbotsbury Rd
W14 .... **126** C3
Abbotshade Rd **15**
SE16 .... **32** C1
W14 .... **126** C1
Abbots La SE1 .... **124** B1
Abbot's Pl NW6 .... **78** A4
Abbotstone Ho **4** E5 .. **7** C2
Abbotstone Rd
SW15 .... **57** B4
Abbotswell Rd SE4 .. **66** B2
Abbotswood Rd
London SE22 .... **64** A3
Streatham SW16 ...... **73** C1
Abbott Ho SW12 ...... **72** B4
Abbott Rd E14 .... **34** C3
Abbotts Cl N1 .... **15** B2
Abchurch La EC2,
EC4 .... **123** C4
Abchurch Yd EC4 .... **123** B4
Abdale Rd W12 .... **30** A1
Abel Ho SE11 .... **163** B4
Aberavon Rd E3 .... **26** A2
Abercorn Cl NW8 ...... **88** C4
Abercorn Ho SE10 .... **52** A3
Abercorn Mans
NW8 .... **79** A1
Abercorn Mews **15**
TW10 .... **54** B3
Abercorn Pl NW8 ...... **78** C2
Abercorn Way SE1 .. **153** B2
Abercrombie Ho **1**
W12 .... **30** A2

Abercrombie St
SW11 .... **168** B2
Aberdale Ct **22**
SE16 .... **40** C4
Aberdare Gdns
NW6 .... **11** A1
Aberdeen Ct W2 ...... **89** B1
Aberdeen La N5 .... **15** B3
Aberdeen Mans
WC1 .... **94** A2
Aberdeen Pk N5 ...... **15** B3
Aberdeen Pk N5 **8** .. **89** B2
Aberdeen Rd
London N5 .... **15** B4
London NW10 .... **8** B3
Aberdeen Terr SE3 .. **52** C1
Aberdour St SE1 ...... **152** A4
Aberfeldy Ho SE5 .. **48** A3
Aberfeldy St E14 ...... **34** B3
Abersham Rd E8 ...... **16** B3
Abingdon W14 .... **141** A3
Abingdon Cl NW1 .... **13** C2
Abingdon Cl **5**
London SE1 .... **153** A2
London NW1 .... **13** C2
Abingdon Ct W8 ...... **127** C1
Abingdon Gdns
W8 .... **127** C1
Abingdon Ho **2** .. **98** C2
Abingdon Mans
W8 .... **127** C1
Abingdon Rd W8 .... **127** C1
Abingdon St SW1 .... **134** A2
Abingdon Villas
W8 .... **127** C1
Abinger Ct **8** SE8 .. **51** B4
Abinger Gr SE8 .... **51** B4
Abinger Ho **11** SE5 .. **48** B3
Abinger Mews W9 .... **23** C1
Abinger Rd W4 .... **38** A3
Ablett St **16** SE16 .. **40** B1
Abney Gdns **5** N16 .. **7** B2
Abney Park Cemetery **7** ★
Abney Park Ct N16 .. **7** B2
Aborfield **8** NW5 .. **13** B3
Aboyne Rd SW17 .... **71** C1
Abyssinia Cl SW11 .. **60** A3
Abyssinia Rd SW11 .. **60** A3
Acacia Cl SE8 .... **41** A2
Acacia Gdns NW8 .... **79** C2
Acacia Gr SE21 .... **75** C2
Acacia Ho N16 .... **6** C2
Acacia Ho **8** NW3 .. **79** C2
London W3 .... **28** B2
Acacia Pl NW8 .... **79** C2
Acacia Rd **2** N8 .... **157** A1
Acacia Rd London W3 .. **28** B2
Academy Ct **2** E2 .. **25** B2
Academy The **2** N19 .. **4** B3
Acanthus Dr SE1 .... **153** B2
Acanthus Rd SW11 .. **60** C4
Accommodation Rd
NW11 .... **1** B3
Acer Ct **3** NW2 ...... **10** A3
Acfold Rd SW6 .... **166** B3
Achilles Cl SE1 .... **153** C2
Achilles Ho **16** E2 .. **25** A3
Achilles Rd NW6 ...... **10** C3
Achilles St SE14 ...... **51** A3
Achilles Way W1 .... **117** C1
Acklam Rd W10 ...... **31** B4
Ackmar Rd SW6 ...... **165** B3
Ackroyd Dr E3 .... **33** C4
Acland Burghley Sch
NW5 .... **13** A4
Acland Cres SE5 ...... **63** C4
Acland Ho SW9 ...... **172** C2
Acol Ct **3** NW6 ...... **10** C1
Acol Rd NW6 .... **11** A1

Acorn Gdns W3 .... **28** C4
Acorn Par **7** SE15 .. **50** A3
Acorn Production Ctr
N7 .... **14** A1
Acorns The **41**
SW19 .... **69** C3
Acorn Wharf SE1 .... **49** C4
Acorn Wlk SE16 ...... **33** A1
Acre Dr SE22 .... **64** C3
Acre La SW2 .... **62** B3
Acris St SW18 .... **59** B2
Acton Bsns Ctr
NW10 .... **20** C1
Acton Central Ind Est **4**
W3 .... **28** A1
Acton Central Sta
W3 .... **28** B1
Acton High Sch W3 .. **36** C4
Acton Hill Mews
W3 .... **28** A1
Acton Ho **10** E8 ...... **24** B4
5 London W3 .... **28** B3
Acton La London W4 .. **36** C4
Acton Main Line Sta
W3 .... **28** C3
Acton Mews E8 .... **24** B4
Acton Park Est W3 .. **37** C4
Acton Park Ind Est
W3 .... **37** C4
Acton St WC1 .... **94** C3
Acton Town Sta W3 .. **36** C4
Acton Vale Ind Pk
W3 .... **29** B1
Acuba Ho SW18 ...... **71** A3
Acuba Rd SW18 ...... **71** A2
Ada Ct N1 .... **86** C3
Ada Ct W9 .... **89** A3
Ada Gdns E14 .... **34** C3
Ada Ho **22** E2 .... **24** C4
Adair Ho SW3 .... **158** B4
Adair Rd W10 .... **23** A1
Adair Twr **7** W10 .. **23** A1
Ada Kennedy Ct **6**
SE10 .... **52** B3
Adam Ct SE11 .... **150** A3
Adam & Eve Ct
W1 .... **105** A2
Adam & Eve Mews
W8 .... **127** C2
Adamfields N15 ...... **13** A4
Adams Gardens Est **5**
SE16 .... **40** B4
Adamson Rd E16 .... **35** C3
London NW3 .... **11** C1
Adams Pl N7 .... **14** B3
Adam's Row W1 ...... **117** C3
Adam St WC2 .... **120** B3
Adam Wlk SW6 ...... **47** B3
Ada Pl E2 .... **24** C4
Ada St E8 .... **25** A4
Adare Wlk SW16,
SW2 .... **74** B1
Adderley Gr SW11 .. **60** C2
Adderley St E14 ...... **34** B3
Addey Ho SE8 .... **51** B3
Addey & Stanhope Sch
SE14 .... **51** C2
Addington Ct **7**
SW14 .... **55** C4
Addington Ho
SW9 .... **173** A1
Addington Rd E3 ...... **26** C2
Addington Sq SE5 .. **48** C3

Addington St SE1 .. **135** A3
Addison Ave
W11 .... **31** A1 **112** A1
Addison Bridge Pl
W14 .... **140** C4
Addison Cres W14 .. **126** B2
Addison Gdns W14 .. **39** C3
Addison Gr W4 .... **38** A3
Addison Ho NW8 ...... **89** B4
Addison Park Mans **17**
W14 .... **39** C4
Addison Pl
W11 .... **31** A1 **112** A1
Addison Prim Sch
W14 .... **39** C3
Addison Rd W14 .... **126** C2
Addle Hill EC4 .... **108** B1
Addle St EC2 .... **109** A3
Addlestone Ho W10 .. **30** B4
Addy Ho SE16 .... **40** B2
Adela Ho **8** W6 ...... **39** B1
Adelaide Ave SE4 .. **66** C3
Adelaide Ct NW8 ...... **79** C1
Adelaide Gr W12 ...... **29** C1
Adelaide Rd
London NW3 .... **12** A1
2 London SW18 .. **58** C2
Richmond TW9 .... **54** B3
Adelaide St WC2 .... **120** A3
Adela St W10 .... **23** A1
Adelina Gr E1 .... **32** B4
Adelina Mews
SW12 .... **73** C3
Adeline Pl WC1 ...... **105** C3
Adelphi Ct **22** SE16 .. **40** C4
Adelphi Terr WC2 .. **120** B3
Adeney Cl W6 .... **47** C4
Aden Gr N16 .... **15** C4
Aden Ho **8** E1 .... **32** C4
Aden Lo N16 .... **15** C4
Adeyfield Ho EC1 .... **97** C3
Adie Rd W6 .... **39** B3
Adisham Ho **4** E5 .. **17** A3
Adler St E1 .... **111** B2
Adley St E5 .... **18** A3
Admiral Ct SW10 .... **167** A4
12 London SW1 .. **124** C3
Admiral Hyson Ind Est
SE16 .... **40** A1
Admiral Mews W10 .. **22** C1
Admiral Pl SE16 ...... **33** A1
Admirals Ct SE1 .... **124** C1
82 Putney SW19 .. **69** C3
Admirals Gate SE10 .. **52** A2
Admiral Sq SW10 .. **167** A4
Admiral St SE8 .... **51** C2
Admirals Way E14 .. **41** C4
Admiralty Arch ★
SW1 .... **119** C2
Admiralty Cl **3** SE8 .. **51** C4
Admiral Wlk W9 ...... **31** C4
Adolphus Rd N4 ...... **6** A3
Adolphus St SE8 ...... **51** B3
Adpar St W2 .... **101** B4
Adrian Bolt Ho **2**
E2 .... **25** A2
Adrian Ho N1 .... **85** A3
London NW10 .... **21** A3
Adrian Mews
SW10 .... **156** B4
Adriatic Ho **18** E1 .. **25** C1
Adriatic Bldg **17**
E14 .... **33** A2
Adron Ho **6** SE16 .. **40** B2
Adstock Ho **5** N1 .. **15** A1
ADT Coll SW15 ...... **58** B2

Adventurers Ct **6**
E14 .... **34** C2
Adys Lawn NW2 ...... **9** A2
Adys Rd SE15 .... **64** B4
Affleck St N1 .... **85** A1
Afghan Rd SW11 .... **168** A1
Agamemnon Rd
NW6 .... **10** B3
Agar Gr NW1 .... **13** C1
Agar Pl NW1 .... **13** B1
Agar St WC2 .... **120** B3
Agate Rd W6 .... **39** B3
Agatha Cl E1 .... **32** B1
Agave Rd NW2 .... **9** B4
Agdon St EC1 .... **96** A2
Agincourt Rd NW3 .. **12** B4
Agnes Ct **11** SW18 .. **59** C3
Agnes Ho **9** W11 .. **30** C2
Agnes Rd W3 .... **38** B4
Agnes St E14 .... **33** B3
Aigburth Mans
SW9 .... **163** B1
Ailsa St E14 .... **34** B4
Ainger Rd NW3 ...... **12** B1
Ainsdale NW1 .... **92** C4
Ainsdale Dr SE1 .... **153** B1
Ainsley St E2 .... **25** A2
Ainsty St **14** SE16 .. **40** B4
Ainsworth Cl SE5 .. **49** A1
Ainsworth Est NW8 .. **78** B3
Ainsworth Ho NW8 .. **78** B3
Ainsworth Rd E9 .... **17** B1
Ainsworth Way
NW8 .... **78** C4
Aintree St SW6 ...... **154** B2
Aird Ho SE1 .... **136** C1
Airdrie Cl N1 .... **14** B1
Airedale Ave W4 ...... **38** B1
Airedale Ave S W4 .. **38** B1
Airedale Rd SW12 .. **72** B4
Airlie Gdns
W8 .... **31** C1 **113** B1
Air St W1 .... **119** A3
Aisgill Ave SW5 ...... **141** A1
Aiten Pl W6 .... **38** C2
Aithan Ho **9** E14 .. **33** B3
Aitken Cl E8 .... **24** C4
Ajax Ho **8** E2 .... **25** A3
Ajax Rd NW6 .... **10** C3
Akbar Ho **7** E14 .... **42** A2
Akehurst St SW15 .. **68** C4
Akenside **8**
NW3 .... **11** C3
Akenside Rd NW3 .. **11** C3
Akerman Rd SW9 .. **48** A2
Akintaro Ho **7** SE8 .. **51** B4
Alamaro Lo SE10 .... **43** B3
Aland Ct SE16 .... **41** A3
Alan Preece Ct NW6 .. **9** C1
Alaska St SE1 .... **121** B1
Albacore Cres SE13 .. **67** A1
Alba Mews SW18,
SW19 .... **70** C2
Alban Ho NW3 .... **11** B2
Albans Cl SW16 ...... **74** A1
Albany W1 .... **118** C3
Albany Cl SW14 ...... **55** A3
Albany Ct E10 .... **19** A4
NW10 .... **133** B2
Albany Ctyd W1 .... **119** A3
Albany Ho **6** TW8 .. **44** A4
Albany Mans SW11 .. **158** B1
Albany Mews SE5 .. **48** B4
London N1 .... **14** C1
Albany Par **4** TW8 .. **44** A4
Albany Pas **12** TW10 .. **54** A2
Albany Rd N7 .... **14** C1

Albany Rd SE5 ....49 A4
Richmond TW10 ....54 A2
Albany St NW1 ....92 B4
Albany Terr **6**
TW10 ....54 B2
Alba Pl W11 ....31 B3
Albemarle SW19 ....69 C2
Albemarle Ho SE8 ....41 B2
Albemarle Mans
NW3 ....11 A4
Albemarle Prim Sch
SW19 ....70 A2
Albemarle St W1 ....118 C3
Albemarle Way EC1 ....96 A1
Albermarle Ho **5**
SW9 ....62 C4
Alberta Ct **1** TW10 ....54 B2
Alberta Ho E14 ....34 B1
Alberta St SE17 ....150 B2
Albert Ave SW8 ....162 C1
Albert Barnes Ho
SE1 ....136 C1
Albert Bigg Point
E15 ....27 B4
Albert Bridge Rd
SW11 ....158 C1
Albert Cl **11** E9 ....25 A4
Albert Cotts E1 ....111 A4
Albert Ct SW7 ....129 B3
2 Putney SW19 ....70 A3
Albert Dr SW19 ....70 A3
Albert Emb SE1 ....148 B2
Albert Gate Ct
SW1 ....130 C3
Albert Gdns E1 ....32 C3
Albert Gray Ho
SW10 ....157 B2
Albert Hall Mans
SW7 ....129 B3
Albert Mans SW11 ....168 C4
London N8 ....5 A4
Albert Memorial*
SW7 ....129 B3
Albert Mews W8 ....128 C2
Albert Palace Mans
SW11 ....169 C4
Albert Pl W8 ....128 B3
Albert Rd NW6 ....23 B3
London N4 ....5 B4
Richmond TW10 ....54 B2
Albert's Ct NW1 ....90 B1
Albert Sq SW8 ....162 C1
Albert St NW1 ....82 B3
Albert Starr Ho **7**
SE8 ....40 C2
Albert Studios
SW11 ....168 C4
Albert Terr NW1 ....81 B3
London NW10 ....20 B4
Albert Terr Mews
NW1 ....81 B3
Albert Way SE15 ....50 A3
Albion Ave SW8 ....171 B1
Albion Cl **2** 116 B4
Albion Ct **7** W6 ....39 A2
Albion Dr E8 ....16 C1
Albion Est SE16 ....40 B4
Albion Gate W2 ....116 A4
Albion Gdns **1** W6 ....39 A2
Albion Ho **6** SE8 ....51 C3
W2 ....116 B4
6 London W6 ....39 A2
Albion Pl EC1 ....108 A4
EC2 ....109 C3

Albion Pl continued
London W6 ....39 A2
Albion Prim Sch
SE16 ....40 B3
Albion Rd N16 ....15 C4
Albion Sq E8 ....16 B1
Albion St SE16 ....40 B4
W2 ....116 B4
Albion Terr E8 ....16 B1
Albion Way EC1 ....108 C3
London SE13 ....67 B3
Albion Wharf
SW11 ....158 A2
Albion Yd N1 ....84 B1
Albon Ho
London SE14 ....51 B2
Wandsworth SW18 ....58 C1
Albrighton Rd SE5,
SE22 ....64 A4
Albury Bldgs SE1 ....136 B3
Albury Ct SE8 ....51 C4
Albury St SE8 ....51 C4
Albyn Rd SE8 ....51 C2
Alconbury Rd E5 ....7 C2
Aldbourne Rd W12 ....29 C1
Aldbridge St SE17 ....152 B2
Aldburgh Mews
W1 ....103 C2
Aldbury Ho SW3 ....144 A3
Aldebert Terr SW8 ....162 C1
Aldeburgh Pl SE10 ....43 C2
Aldeburgh St SE10 ....43 C1
Aldenham Ho NW1 ....83 B1
Aldenham St NW1 ....83 B1
Alden Ho E8 ....25 A4
Aldensley Rd W6 ....39 A3
Alderbrook Prim Sch
SW12 ....73 A4
Alderbrook Rd
SW12 ....61 A1
Alderbury Rd SW13 ....46 C4
Aldergrove Ho **3** E5 ....7 C2
Alder Ho SE15 ....49 B4
1 London NW3 ....12 B1
London SE4 ....66 C4
Alderley Ho SW8 ....171 B1
Alder Lo SW6 ....47 C2
Aldermanbury EC2 ....109 A2
Aldermanbury Sq
EC2 ....109 A3
Alderman's Wlk
EC2 ....110 A3
Alder Mews **1** N19 ....4 B2
Alderney Ho **10** N1 ....15 B2
Alderney Mews
SE1 ....137 B1
Alderney Rd E1 ....25 C1
Alderney St SW1 ....146 B2
Alder Rd SW14 ....55 C4
Aldersford Cl SE4 ....65 C3
Aldersgate Ct EC1 ....108 C3
Aldersgate St EC1 ....108 C3
Aldershot Rd NW6 ....23 B4
Alderson St W10 ....23 A1
Alderton Rd SE24 ....63 B4
Alderville Rd SW6 ....165 A1
Alderwick Ct N7 ....14 B2
Aldford St W1 ....117 C2
Aldgate EC3 ....110 B1
Aldgate East Sta
E1 ....111 A1
Aldgate High St

Aldred Rd NW6 ....10 C3
Aldren Rd SW17 ....71 B1
Aldrich Terr SW18 ....71 B2
Aldrick Ho N1 ....85 A2
Aldridge Ct W11 ....31 B4
Aldridge Road Villas
W11 ....31 B4
Aldsworth Cl W9 ....88 A1
Aldworth Gr SE13 ....67 B1
Aldwych WC2 ....107 A1
Aldwych Bldgs
WC2 ....106 B2
Aldwyn Ho SW8 ....162 A1
Alexander Ave NW10 ....9 A1
Alexander Cl SE8 ....59 B2
Alexander Ho **9**
E14 ....41 C3
Alexander Mews
W2 ....100 A2
Alexander Pl SW7 ....144 A4
Alexander Rd N19 ....5 A1
Alexander Sq SW3 ....144 A4
Alexander St W2 ....31 C3
Alexandra Ave
SW11 ....169 B3
Alexandra Cotts
SE14 ....51 B2
Alexandra Ct **4**
SW11 ....89 A2
6 London W9 ....88 C4
5 London W12 ....38 C4
Alexandra Gdns W4 ....46 A3
Alexandra Gr N4 ....6 A3
Alexandra Ho **8**
W6 ....39 B1
Alexandra Mans
SW3 ....157 B3
6 London NW6 ....10 C3
Alexandra National Ho
N4 ....6 A2
Alexandra Pl NW8 ....79 A4
Alexandra Rd
London NW8 ....11 C1
London W4 ....37 C4
Mortlake TW9 ....55 C4
Richmond TW9 ....54 B4
Alexandra St E16 ....35 C4
2 London SE14 ....51 A3
Alex Gossip Ho
SW6 ....165 B3
Alexis St SE16 ....153 C4
Alfearn Rd E5 ....17 B4
Alford Ct N1 ....87 A1
Alford Pl N1 ....87 A1
Alfreda Ct SW11 ....170 A3
Alfreda St SW11 ....170 A3
Alfred Butt Ho
SW17 ....72 B1
Alfred Cl W4 ....37 C2
Alfred Ho E9 ....18 A3
Alfred Mews W1,
WC1 ....105 B4
Alfred Nunn Ho
NW10 ....21 B4
Alfred Pl WC1 ....105 B4
Alfred Rd W2 ....31 C4
London W3 ....28 B1
Alfred Salter Ho
SE1 ....153 A3
Alfred Salter Prim Sch
SE16 ....40 C3
Alfred St E3 ....26 B2
Afferton Ct SW9 ....69 C1
Afriston Rd SW11 ....60 B2
Algar Ho SE1 ....136 A3
Algarve Rd SW18 ....71 A3
Algernon Rd NW6 ....23 C4

Algernon Rd continued
London SE13 ....67 A3
Algiers Rd SE13 ....66 C3
Alice Ct SW15 ....58 B3
Alice Gilliott Ct
W14 ....155 A4
Alice La E3 ....26 B4
Alice Owen Tech Ctr
EC1 ....96 A4
Alice Shepherd Ho **7**
E14 ....42 B4
Alice St SE1 ....138 A1
Alice Walker Cl **3**
SE24 ....63 A3
Alie St E1 ....111 A1
Aliwal Rd SW11 ....60 A3
Alkerden Rd W4 ....38 A1
Alkham Rd N16 ....7 B2
Allam Ho W11 ....112 A4
Allanbridge N16 ....7 A4
Allan Way W3 ....28 B4
Allard Gdns SW4 ....61 C2
Allardyce St SW4,
SW9 ....62 B3
Allbrook Ho **4**
SW15 ....68 C4
Allcroft Rd NW5 ....12 C2
Allendale Cl SE5 ....48 C2
Allendale Sch W8 ....127 C2
Allen Edwards Dr
SW8 ....172 A4
Allen Edwards Prim Sch
SW4 ....172 A3
Allenford Ho **1**
SW15 ....56 B1
Allen Ho W8 ....127 C2
Allen Mans W8 ....127 C2
Allen Rd E3 ....26 B3
London N16 ....16 A4
Allensbury Pl
London NW1 ....14 A1
1 London NW1 ....13 C1
Allen St W8 ....127 C1
Allenswood **12**
SW19 ....70 A3
Allerdale Ho **7** N4 ....6 C4
Allerton Ho N1 ....87 C1
Allerton Rd N16 ....6 B2
Allerton St N1 ....97 C4
Allerton Wlk **11** N7 ....5 B2
Allestree Rd SW6 ....154 A1
Alleyn Cres SE21 ....75 C2
Alleyn Ho EC1 ....97 A1
SE1 ....137 B1
Alleyn Pk SE21 ....76 A1
Alleyn Rd SE21 ....76 A1
Alleyn's Sch SE22 ....64 A2
Allfarthing La SW18 ....59 B1
Allfarthing Prim Sch
SW18 ....59 B1
Allgood St **10** E2 ....24 B3
Allhallows La EC4 ....123 B3
Alliance Ct W3 ....28 A4
Alliance Rd W3 ....20 A1
Allied Ind Est W3 ....29 A1
Allied Way W3 ....38 A4
Allingham Ct NW3 ....12 A3
Allingham St N1 ....86 C2
Allington Cl SW19 ....69 C1
Allington Ct SW8 ....170 C1
Allington Rd W10 ....23 A3
Allington St SW1 ....132 B1
Allison Cl SE10 ....52 B2

Allison Gr SE21 ....76 A3
Allison Rd W3 ....28 B2
Alliston Ho 22 ....99 A3
Allitsen Rd NW8 ....80 A2
Allnutt Way SW4 ....61 C2
Alloa Rd SE8 ....41 A1
Allom Ct **4** 172 B1
Allonby Ho E14 ....33 A4
Alloway Rd E3 ....26 A2
Allport Ho SE5 ....63 C4
Allport Mews **18** E1 ....25 B1
All Saints CE Prim Sch
SW15 ....57 B4
All Saints' CE Prim Sch
London NW2 ....1 B1
London SE3 ....53 A1
All Saints Ct **9** E1 ....32 B2
All Saints Dr SE3 ....53 B1
All Saints Ho **2** 31 B4
All Saints Pas SW18 ....58 C2
All Saints Rd W3 ....37 B3
All Saints Rd W11 ....31 B3
All Saints Rd N1 ....84 C2
All Saints Sta E14 ....34 A2
Allsop Pl NW1 ....91 A1
All Souls' Ave NW10 ....22 A4
All Souls Pl W1 ....104 C3
Alma Birk Ho **1**
NW6 ....10 B1
Almack Rd E5 ....17 B4
Alma Gr SE1 ....153 A3
Alma Ho **7** TW8 ....44 A4
Alma Pl NW10 ....22 A4
Alma Prim Sch
SE16 ....153 C4
Alma Rd SW18 ....59 B3
Alma Sq NW8 ....89 A4
Alma St London E15 ....19 C2
London NW5 ....13 A2
Alma Terr W8 ....127 C1
Wandsworth SW18 ....71 C4
Almeida St **10** N1 ....15 A1
Almeric Rd SW11 ....60 B3
Almington St N4 ....5 B3
Almond Ave W5 ....36 A3
Almond Cl SE15 ....49 C1
Almond Ho SE4 ....51 B1
Almond Rd SE16 ....40 A2
Al-muntada Islamic Sch
SW6 ....164 C2
Alperton St W10 ....23 B1
Alphabet Sq E3 ....33 C4
Alpha Cl NW8 ....90 B3
Alpha Gr E14 ....41 C4
Alpha Ho NW6 ....23 C3
NW8 ....90 B1
London SW4 ....62 B3
Alpha Pl NW6 ....23 C3
SW3 ....158 B4
Alpha Rd SE14 ....51 B2
Alpha St SE15 ....49 C1
Alpine Gr **19** E9 ....17 B1
Alpine Rd SE16 ....40 C1
Alroy Rd N4 ....5 C4
Alsace Rd SE17 ....152 A2
Al Sadiq & Al Zahra
Schs NW6 ....23 A4
Alscot Rd SE1 ....139 A1
SE1 ....139 A1
Alscot Way SE1 ....152 C4

Altenburg Gdns SW11 ...60 B3
Althea St SW6 ...59 A4
Althope Mews SW11 ...167 C3
Althorp Rd SW17 ...72 B3
Alton Ho 4 E3 ...27 A2
Alton Rd Richmond TW10,TW9 .54 A3
Roehampton SW15 ...68 C3
Alton St E14 ...34 A4
Alumni Ct SE1 ...139 A4
Alvaney Cl NW3 ...11 A3
Alvanley Gdns NW6 ...11 A3
Alvaney Ho NW9 ...173 B4
Alverstone Ave SW18,SW19 ...70 C2
Alverstone Ho SE11 ...163 B3
Alverton St SE8 ...51 B4
Alvey St SE17 ...152 A2
Alvington Cres E8 ...16 B3
Alwyn Ave W4 ...37 C1
Alwyne La N1 ...15 A1
Alwyne Pl N1 ...15 B1
Alwyne Rd N1 ...15 B1
Alwyne Sq N1 ...15 B2
Alwyne Villas N1 ...15 A1
Alwyn Gdns W3 ...28 A3
Alzette Ho 11 E2 ...25 C3
Amazon St E1 ...32 A3
Ambassador Ct 9 NW6 ...10 C3
Ambassador Ho NW8 ...79 A3
Ambassador Sq E14 ...42 A2
Amber Ct N7 ...14 C2
Ambergate St SE17 ...150 B2
Amberley Ct 2 SW9 ...63 A4
Amberley Rd W9 ...23 C1
Amber Wharf 22 E2 ...24 B4
Ambler Prim Sch N4 ...6 A2
Ambler Rd N4 ...6 A1
Ambleside NW1 ...82 C1
8 Putney SW15 ...70 A3
Ambleside Cl E9 ...17 B3
Ambleside Point 1 SE15 ...50 B3
Ambleside Rd NW10 ...8 B1
Ambrosden Ave SW1 ...133 A1
Ambrose Ho 9 E14 ...33 C4
Ambrose Mews SW11 ...168 C2
Ambrose St SE16 ...40 A2
Ambrose Wlk E3 ...26 C3
AMC Bsns Ctr W10 ...30 C4
Amelia Cl W3 ...37 A4
Amelia Ho 5 W6 ...39 B1
Amelia St SE17 ...150 C2
Amen Cnr EC4 ...108 B1
Amen Ct EC4 ...108 B1
American Coll The W1 ...103 C2
American Sch in London The NW8 ...79 B2
America Sq EC3 ...124 C4
America St SE1 ...122 C1
Amerland Rd SW18 ...58 B1
Amersham Gr SE14 ...51 B3
Amersham Rd SE14 ...51 B3

Amersham Vale SE14,SE8 ...51 B3
Amery Gdns NW10 ...22 A4
Amery Ho SE17 ...152 B2
Amesbury Ave SW2 ...74 B2
Amesbury Twr SW8 ...170 C2
Ames Cotts 14 E3 ...33 A4
Ames Ho 10 E2 ...25 C3
Amethyst Rd E15 ...19 C4
Amherst Prim Sch E8 ...16 C3
Amhurst Ct N4 ...6 C4
Amhurst Par N16 ...7 B4
Amhurst Pk N4,N16 ...7 B4
Amhurst Rd E8,N16 ...16 C4
Amhurst Terr E8 ...16 C4
Amias Ho EC1 ...96 C2
Amiel St 8 E1 ...25 B1
Amies St SW11 ...60 B4
Amigo Ho SE1 ...135 C2
Amina Way SE16 ...139 B1
Amner Rd SW11 ...60 C1
Amor Rd W6 ...39 B3
Amory Ho N1 ...85 A2
Amott Rd SE15 ...64 C4
Amoy Pl E14 ...33 C2
Ampton Pl WC1 ...94 C3
Ampton St WC1 ...94 C3
Amstel Ct 18 SE15 ...49 B3
Amsterdam Rd E14 ...42 B3
Amwell St EC1 ...95 B4
Amyruth Rd SE4 ...66 C2
Anatola Rd N19 ...4 B2
Anchorage Point E14 ...41 C4
Anchor Ho EC1 ...96 C2
Anchor Mews SW11 61 A1
Anchor Ret Pk E1 ...25 B1
Anchor St SE16 ...40 A2
Anchor Terr SE1 ...123 A2
Anchor Yd EC1 ...97 A2
Ancill Cl W6 ...154 A3
Ancona Rd NW10 ...21 C3
Andalus Rd SW9 ...62 A4
Andaman Ho 8 E1 ...33 A4
Anderson Cl W3 ...28 C3
Anderson Ho 10 E14 ...34 B2
Anderson Rd E9 ...17 C2
Andersons Sq N1 ...86 B4
Anderson St SW3 ...144 C2
Anderton Cl SE5 ...63 C4
Andover Ho 6 N7 ...5 B2
Andover Pl NW6 ...78 A1
Andover Rd N7 ...5 B2
Andoversford Ct 7 SE15 ...49 A4
Andre St E8 ...16 C3
Andrew Borde St WC2 ...105 C2
Andrew Ho 2 EC2 ...109 A3
Andrew Ho London SE4 ...51 B1
6 Putney SW15 ...56 C2
Andrew Marvell Ho 11 N16 ...16 A4
Andrew Pl SW8 ...171 C4
Andrew Reed Ho SW18 ...70 A4
Andrews Crosse WC2 ...107 B1
Andrew's Rd E8 ...25 A4
Andrews Wlk SE17 ...48 A4
Anfield Cl SW12 ...73 B4
Angel EC1 ...86 A1

Angela Davis Ind Est 21 SW9 ...63 A3
Angel Alley 1 E1 ...111 A2
Angel Ct EC2 ...109 C2
SW1 ...119 A1
Angel Gate EC1 ...96 B4
Angel Ho N1 ...85 C1
Angelina Ho 2 SE15 ...49 C2
Angel La E15 ...19 C2
Angell Park Gdns 5 SW9 ...62 C4
Angell Rd SW9 ...63 A4
Angel Mews N1 ...85 C1
Putney SW15 ...68 C4
Stepney E1 ...32 A2
Angel Pas EC4 ...123 B3
Angel Pl 1 SE1 ...137 B4
Angel Prim Sch N1 ...85 C2
Angel Sq EC1 ...86 A1
Angel Wlk W6 ...39 B2
Angerstein Bsns Pk SE10 ...43 C2
Angerstein La SE3 ...53 B2
Anglebury 5 W2 ...31 C3
Anglers La NW5 ...13 A2
Anglesey Ho 9 E14 ...33 C3
Anglia Ho 10 E14 ...33 A3
Anglo American Laundry SW17 ...71 B1
Anglo Rd 20 E3 ...26 B3
Angrave Ct 8 E8 ...24 B4
Angrave Pas 5 E8 ...24 B4
Angus Ho 12 SW12 ...73 C4
Angus St SE14 ...51 A3
Anhalt Rd SW11 ...158 B2
Anley Rd W14 ...39 C4
Annabel Cl E14 ...34 A3
Anna Cl E8 ...24 B4
Annandale Prim Sch SE10 ...43 B1
Annandale Rd SE10 ...43 B1
London W4 ...38 A1
Anne Goodman Ho 1 E1 ...32 B3
Anne Kerr Ct 13 SW15 ...57 C1
Anne's Ct NW8 ...90 B1
Annesley Ho SW9 ...173 B4
Annesley Wlk N19 ...4 B2
Annette Cres 1 N1 ...15 B1
Annette Ct N7 ...5 B2
Annie Besant Cl E3 ...26 B4
Anning St E2 ...98 B2
Annis Rd E9 ...18 A2
Ann La SW10 ...157 B3
Ann Moss Way SE16 ...40 B3
Ann's Cl SW1 ...131 A3
Ann's Pl E1 ...110 C3
Ansdell Rd SE15 ...50 B1
Ansdell St W8 ...128 B2
Ansdell Terr 4 W8 ...128 B2
Ansell Ho 1 E1 ...32 B4
Ansell Rd SW17 ...72 B1
Anselm Rd SW6 ...155 B3
Ansleigh Pl W11 ...30 C2
Anslie Wlk 6 SW12 ...73 A4
Anson Ho 6 E1 ...26 A1
Anson Prim Sch NW2 .9 C3
Anson Rd London N7 ...13 C4
London NW2 ...9 B3
Anstey Ct 6 W3 ...37 A4
Anstey Ho 8 E9 ...25 B4
Anstey Rd SE15 ...64 C4

Anstice Cl W4 ...46 A3
Antenor Ho 18 E2 ...25 A3
Anthony Cope Ct N1 ...97 C4
Anthony Ho NW8 ...90 A1
Anthony St E1 ...32 A3
Antilles Bay 7 E14 ...42 B4
Antill Rd E3 ...26 A2
Antill Terr 8 E1 ...32 C3
Antony Ho 4 SE14 ...50 C3
2 SE16 ...40 B2
Antrim Gr NW3 ...12 B2
Antrim Ho SW11 ...60 C4
Antrim Mans NW3 ...12 B2
Antrim Rd NW3 ...12 B2
Antrobus Rd W4 ...37 B3
Aoex Ind Est NW10 ...21 B1
Apollo Bldg 4 E14 ...41 C2
Apollo Ho 10 E2 ...25 A3
London N6 ...3 B4
Apollo Ind Bsns Ctr 27 SE8 ...50 C4
Apollo Pl SW10 ...157 B2
Apollo Studios 18 NW5 ...13 B3
Apothecary St EC4 ...108 A1
Appach Rd SW2 ...62 C1
Appleby Rd E16 ...35 C3
London E8 ...16 C1
Appleby St E2 ...24 B3
Appledore Cl SW12, SW17 ...72 B2
Appleford 8 NW5 ...13 B3
Appleford Ho 6 W10 ...23 A1
Appleford Rd W10 ...23 A1
Applegarth Ho SE1 136 B4
8 SE15 ...49 C3
Applegarth Rd W14 ...39 C3
Apple Mkt WC2 ...120 B4
Appleshaw Ho 4 SE5 ...64 A4
Appletree Ct SE7 ...43 C1
Apple Tree Yd SW1 ...119 A2
Appold St EC2 ...110 A4
Appollo Ct SW9 ...173 B4
Apprentice Way 5 E5 ...17 A4
Approach Cl N16 ...16 A4
Approach Rd E2 ...25 B3
The Approach W3 ...28 C3
April Ct 20 E2 ...24 C3
April St E8 ...16 B4
Apsley Ho E1 ...32 B4
Apsley Way W1 ...131 C4
Aquila St NW8 ...79 C2
Aquinas St SE1 ...121 C1
Arabella Ct NW8 ...79 A2
Arabella Dr SW15 ...56 A3
Arabian Ho 3 E1 ...26 A1
Arabin Rd SE4 ...66 B3
Aragon Twr SE8 ...41 B2
Arakan Ho 4 N16 ...15 C4
Aral Ho 4 E1 ...25 C1
Arapiles Ho 6 E14 ...34 C3
Arbery Rd E3 ...26 A3
Arbon Ct N1 ...87 A3
Arbor Ct N16 ...6 C2
Arborfield Ho 6 E14 ...33 C2
Arbourfield Cl SW2 ...74 B3
Arbour Ho 3 E1 ...32 C3
Arbour Sq E1 ...32 C3

Arbuthnot Rd SE14 ...50 C1
Arbutus St E8 ...24 B4
Arcade The 2
1 London N7 ...14 A4
Arcadia St E14 ...33 C3
Archangel St SE16 ...40 C4
Archbishop Michael Ramsey Tech Coll SE5 ...48 A3
Archbishop's 1 SW2 ...74 B4
Archbishop Sumner's CE Prim Sch SE11 ...149 C3
Archbishop Tenison's Sch SE11 ...163 A3
Archdale Ct W12 ...30 A1
Archdale Ho SE1 ...138 A2
Archdale Rd SE22 ...64 B3
Archel Rd W14 ...154 C4
Archer Ho 8 N1 ...24 A4
W11 ...113 A4
London SW11 ...167 C3
Archers Lo 6 SE1 ...153 C3
Archer Sq 1 SE14 ...51 A4
Archer St W1 ...119 B4
Archery Cl W2 ...102 B1
Archery Fields Ho WC1 ...95 B4
Archery Steps W2 ...116 B4
Arches The 4 WC2 ...120 B2
Archibald Mews W1 ...118 A3
Archibald Rd N7 ...13 C4
Archibald St E3 ...26 C2
Arch St SE1 ...136 C1
Archway N19 ...4 B2
Archway Bsns Ctr 5 N19 ...4 C1
Archway Cl W10 ...30 C4
London SW19 ...70 C1
Archway Hts 5 N19 ...4 B3
Archway Mews SW15 ...58 A3
Archway Rd N6 ...4 A4
Archway St SW13, SW14 ...56 A4
Archway Sta N19 ...4 B2
Arcola St E8 ...16 B3
Arctic St NW5 ...13 A3
Ardbeg Rd SE24 ...63 C2
Arden 26 SW19 ...69 C3
Arden Cres E14 ...41 C2
Arden Ho 21 N1 ...24 A3
SE11 ...148 C3
London SW9 ...172 B1
Ardent Ho 28 E3 ...26 A3
Ardilaun Rd N5 ...15 B4
Ardleigh Rd N1 ...16 A2
Ardlui Rd SE27 ...75 B2
Ardmere Rd SE13 ...67 C1
Ardshiel Cl SW15 ...57 C4
Ardwell Rd SW2 ...74 A2
Ardwick Rd NW2 ...10 C4
Ares Ct 3 E14 ...41 C2
Arethusa Ho 8 E14 ...42 A2
Argon Mews SW6 ...155 C1
Argos Ct SW9 ...173 B4
Argos Ho 8 E2 ...25 A3
Argosy Ho SE8 ...41 A2
W1 ...92 B1
Argyle Pl W6 ...39 A2
Argyle Prim Sch WC1 ...94 A4
Argyle Rd E1 ...25 C1
Argyle Sq WC1 ...94 B4
Argyle St WC1 ...94 B4
Argyle Way SE16 ...153 C4

Argyle Wlk WC1 . . . . .94 B3
Argyll Cl SW9 . . . . .62 B4
Argyll Ct 1 SW2 . . . . .74 A4
Argyll Mans SW3 . . . . .157 C2
   W14 . . . . .140 B4
Argyll Rd W8 . . . . .127 C3
Argyll St W1 . . . . .104 C1
Arica Ho SE16 . . . . .40 A3
Arica Rd SE4 . . . . .66 A4
Ariel Ct SE11 . . . . .150 A3
   London W12 . . . . .38 C3
Ariel Rd NW6 . . . . .10 C2
Ariel Way W12 . . . . .30 B1
Aristotle Rd SW4 . . . . . . .61 C4
Arklow Ho 7 SE17 . . . . . .48 C4
Arklow Rd SE14 . . . . .51 B4
Arklow Road Trad Est
   SE14 . . . . .51 B4
Arkwright Ho 23
   SW2 . . . . .74 A4
Arkwright Mans
   NW3 . . . . .11 B3
Arkwright Rd NW3 . . . . . .11 B3
Arlesey Cl SW15 . . . . . . .58 A2
Arlesford Rd SW9 . . . . . .62 A4
Arlingford Rd SW2 . . . . . .62 C1
Arlington Ave N1 . . . . . . .87 A3
Arlington Gdns W4 . . . . . .37 B1
Arlington Ho EC1 . . . . . . .95 C4
   3 SE8 . . . . .51 B4
   London W12 . . . . .30 A1
Arlington Lo SW2 . . . . . . .62 B3
Arlington Park Mans
   4 . . . . .37 B1
Arlington Pl 7
   SE10 . . . . .52 B3
Arlington Rd NW1 . . . . . . .82 B3
Arlington Sq N1 . . . . .87 A3
Arlington St SW1 . . . . . .118 C2
Arlington Way EC1 . . . . . .95 C4
Armada Ct 11 SE8 . . . . . .51 C4
Armadale Rd SW6 . . . . .155 B3
Armada St 10 SE8 . . . . . .51 C4
Armagh Rd E3 . . . . .26 B4
Arminger Rd W12 . . . . . . .30 A1
Armitage Ho NW1 . . . . .102 A4
Armitage Rd SE10 . . . . . .43 B1
   London NW11 . . . . .1 B3
Armour Cl N7 . . . . .14 B2
Armoury Ho SE8 . . . . . . .52 A1
Armoury Way SW18 . . . .58 C2
Armsby Ho 15 E1 . . . . . . .32 B4
Armstrong Ho 8
   SW15 . . . . .57 C1
Armstrong Rd
   SW7 . . . . .129 B1
   London W3 . . . . .29 B1
Arnal Cres SW18 . . . . . . .70 A4
Arncliffe NW6 . . . . .78 B3
Arne Ho SE11 . . . . .148 C2
Arne St WC2 . . . . .106 B1
Arneway St SW1 . . . . . .133 C1
Arnewood Cl SW15 . . . . .68 C3
Arnhem Pl E14 . . . . .41 C3
Arnhem Way 3
   SE22 . . . . .64 A2
Arnhem Wharf E14 . . . . . .41 C3
Arnhem Wharf Prim Sch
   E14 . . . . .41 C3
Arnold Cir E2 . . . . .98 C3
Arnold Est SE1 . . . . .139 A3
Arnold Ho SE17 . . . . . . .150 B1
   9 London N16 . . . . .7 A1
Arnold House Sch
   NW8 . . . . .79 C1
Arnold Rd E3 . . . . .26 C2

Arnot Ho 27 SE5 . . . . . . .48 B3
Arnott Cl W4 . . . . .37 C2
Arnould Ave SE5 . . . . . . .63 C3
Arnside Ho 2 SE17 . . . . .48 C4
Arnside St SE17 . . . . . . .48 B4
Arodene Rd SW2 . . . . . . .62 B1
Arragon Rd SW18 . . . . . .70 C3
Arran Ho N16 . . . . .7 C3
Arran Wlk N1 . . . . .15 B1
Arrol Ho SE1 . . . . .137 A1
Arrowe Ct 7 E5 . . . . .17 A4
Arrow Ho 24 N1 . . . . .24 A4
Arrow Rd E3 . . . . .27 A2
Arrowsmith Ho
   SE11 . . . . .148 C2
Arsenal Sta N5 . . . . .5 C1
Artemis Ct 6 E14 . . . . . . .41 C2
Artesian Rd W2 . . . . .31 C3
Arthur Ct 1 SW11 . . . . .169 C3
   10 London W2 . . . . .31 C4
   London W2 . . . . .100 A2
Arthur Deakin Ho
   E1 . . . . .111 B4
Arthurdon Rd SE4 . . . . . .66 C2
Arthur Henderson Ho
   Fulham SW6 . . . . .164 C2
   9 London N19 . . . . .4 C4
Arthur Newton Ho 9
   SW11 . . . . .59 C4
Arthur Rd N7 . . . . .14 B4
Arthur St EC4 . . . . .123 C4
Arthur Wade Ho E2 . . . . .99 A4
Artichoke Hill 9 E1 . . . . .32 A2
Artichoke Mews 5
   SE5 . . . . .48 C2
Artichoke Pl SE5 . . . . . . .48 C2
Artillery La E1 . . . . .110 B3
   London W12 . . . . .29 C3
Artillery Pass E1 . . . . . . .110 B3
Artillery Row SW1 . . . . .133 B1
Artizan St E1 . . . . .110 B2
Arton Wilson Ho 12
   SW15 . . . . .56 C2
Arts Educational Sch
   The W4 . . . . .38 A2
Arundel Bldgs SE1 . . . . .138 B1
Arundel Cl SW11 . . . . . . .60 A2
Arundel Ct 1 SW13 . . . .144 B2
   Barnes SW13 . . . . .47 A4
   Putney SW15 . . . . .57 C2
Arundel Gdns
   W11 . . . . .31 B2 112 C4
Arundel Gr N16 . . . . .16 A3
Arundel Ho N1 . . . . .86 B4
   3 London W3 . . . . .37 A4
Arundel Mans
   SW6 . . . . .165 A4
   Barnes SW13 . . . . .47 A4
Arundel Pl N1,N7 . . . . . . .14 C2
Arundel Sq N7 . . . . .14 C2
Arundel St WC2 . . . . . . .121 A4
Arundel Terr SW13 . . . . .47 A4
Arvon Rd N5 . . . . .14 C3
Asaph Ho SE14 . . . . .51 B2
Ascalon Ct 10 SW2 . . . . .74 B4
Ascalon Ho SE8 . . . . . . .160 C1
Ascalon St SW8 . . . . . . .160 C1
Ascham St NW5 . . . . .13 B3
Ascot Ct NW8 . . . . .89 B3
   8 London SW4 . . . . .62 A3
Ascot Ho NW1 . . . . .92 B4
   1 W9 . . . . .31 C4
   London W3 . . . . .37 B1
Ascot Lo NW6 . . . . .78 B2
Ascot Par 2 SW4 . . . . . . .62 A3
Ascott Ave W5 . . . . .36 A4
Asfil Ho EC1 . . . . .107 C3

Ashbourne Ct E5 . . . . . . .18 A4
Ashbourne Gr
   London SE22 . . . . .64 B3
   London W4 . . . . .38 A1
Ashbridge St NW8 . . . . . .90 A1
Ashbrook Rd N19 . . . . .4 C3
Ashburn Gdns
   SW7 . . . . .142 C4
Ashburnham Com Sch
   SW10 . . . . .157 B2
Ashburnham Gr
   SE10 . . . . .52 A3
Ashburnham Pl
   SE10 . . . . .52 A3
Ashburnham Rd
   SW10 . . . . .157 A1
   London NW10 . . . . .22 B3
Ashburnham Retreat 5
   SE10 . . . . .52 A3
Ashburnham Twr
   SW10 . . . . .157 B2
Ashburn Pl SW7 . . . . . . .142 C3
Ashburton Gr N7 . . . . . . .14 C4
Ashburton Mans
   SW10 . . . . .157 A2
Ashbury Rd SE16 . . . . . . .35 C3
Ashby Ct NW8 . . . . .89 C2
Ashby Ho 1 N1 . . . . .15 B1
   6 London SW9 . . . . .48 A1
Ashby Mews SE4 . . . . . . .51 B1
Ashby Rd SE4 . . . . .51 B1
Ashby St EC1 . . . . .96 B3
Ashchurch Ct W12 . . . . . .38 C3
Ashchurch Gr W12 . . . . . .38 C3
Ashchurch Park Villas
   W12 . . . . .38 C3
Ashchurch Terr
   W12 . . . . .38 C3
Ashcombe Ct 4
   SW15 . . . . .58 A2
Ashcombe Ho 39 E3 . . . .27 A2
Ashcombe St SW6 . . . . .166 A1
Ashcroft Ho SW8 . . . . . .170 C4
Ashcroft Rd E3 . . . . .26 A2
Ashcroft Sq 6 W6 . . . . . .39 B2
Ash Ct W1 . . . . .102 C2
   London N19 . . . . .4 B2
   London SW11 . . . . .60 C3
Ashdale Ho N4 . . . . .6 C4
Ashdene 6 SE15 . . . . . . .50 A3
Ashdown SW15 . . . . .57 C2
Ashdown Cres NW5 . . . . .12 C3
Ashdown Ho 6 E5 . . . . . . .7 C2
Ashdown Rd NW10 . . . . .21 A4
Ashdown Way
   SW17 . . . . .72 C2
Ashdown Wlk 15
   E14 . . . . .41 C2
Ashenden SE17 . . . . . . .151 A4
Ashenden Rd E5 . . . . . . .18 A3
Ashen Gr SW19 . . . . .70 C2
Ashentree Ct EC4 . . . . . .107 C1
Asher Way E1 . . . . .125 C3
Ashfield Ho 5 N5 . . . . . . .15 B3
Ashfield Rd W3 . . . . .29 B1
Ashfield St E1 . . . . .32 B4
Ashford Ct NW2 . . . . .9 C4
Ashford Ho 11 SE8 . . . . .51 B4
   14 London SW9 . . . . . . .63 A3
Ashford Rd NW2 . . . . .9 C4
Ashford St N1 . . . . .98 A4
Ash Gr E8 . . . . .25 A4
   London NW2 . . . . .10 A4
   London W5 . . . . .36 A3
Ashgrove Ct 2 W9 . . . . . .31 C4

Ashgrove Ho SW1 . . . . .147 C2
Ash Ho 3 E14 . . . . .42 B4
   SE1 . . . . .153 A3
Ashington 1 NW5 . . . . . .13 A2
Ashington Ho 10 E1 . . . . .25 A1
Ashington Rd SW6 . . . . .165 A1
Ashland Pl W1 . . . . .103 B4
Ashleigh Ho SW14 . . . . . .56 A4
Ashleigh Rd SW14 . . . . . .56 A4
Ashley Cres SW11 . . . . . .60 C4
Ashley Ct
   19 London N16 . . . . . . .16 A3
   London NW3 . . . . .11 A3
Ashley Pl SW1 . . . . .132 C1
Ashley Rd London N19 . . . .5 A4
Ashlin Rd E15 . . . . .19 C4
Ash Lo SW6 . . . . .47 C2
Ashlone Rd SW15 . . . . . .57 C4
Ashmead Bsns Ctr
   E16 . . . . .27 C1
Ashmead Ho E9 . . . . .18 A3
Ashmead Prim Sch
   SE8 . . . . .51 C1
Ashmead Rd SE8 . . . . . . .51 C1
Ashmere Gr 11 SW2 . . . . .
   SW2 . . . . .62 A3
Ashmere Ho 10
   SW2 . . . . .62 A3
Ashmill St NW8 . . . . . . .102 A4
Ashmole Prim Sch
   SW8 . . . . .163 A3
Ashmole St SW8 . . . . . . .163 A3
Ashmore NW1 . . . . .13 C1
Ashmore Cl SE15 . . . . . . .49 B3
Ashmore Ho W14 . . . . . .126 B1
Ashmore Rd W9 . . . . .23 B2
Ashmount Prim Sch
   N6 . . . . .4 A4
Ashmount Rd N19 . . . . .4 C4
Ashness Rd SW11 . . . . . .60 B2
Ashpark Ho 4 E14 . . . . . .33 B3
Ashtead Ct 18 SW19 . . . .69 C3
Ashtead Rd E5 . . . . .7 C4
Ashton Ho SW9 . . . . .163 C1
   Roehampton SW15 . . . .69 A4
Ashton Rd E15 . . . . .19 C3
Ashton St E14 . . . . .34 B2
Ashurst Lo N5 . . . . .15 A3
Ashwin St E8 . . . . .16 B2
Ashworth Cl SE5 . . . . . . .48 C1
Ashworth Mans W9 . . . . .88 B3
Ashworth Rd W9 . . . . .88 B3
Aske Ho N1 . . . . .98 A4
Asker Ho N7 . . . . .14 A4
Aske St N1 . . . . .98 A4
Askew Cres W12 . . . . .38 C4
Askew Mans 14
   W12 . . . . .38 C4
Askew Rd W12 . . . . .38 C4
Askham Ct W12 . . . . .29 C1
Askham Rd W12 . . . . .29 C1
Askill Dr SW15 . . . . .58 A2
Asland Rd E15 . . . . .27 C4
Aslett St SW18 . . . . .71 B4
Asmara Rd NW2 . . . . .10 A3
Asolando Dr SE17 . . . . . .151 A3
Aspen Cl
   London N19 . . . . .4 B2
   London W5 . . . . .36 B4
Aspen Ct 16 E8 . . . . .16 B2
   Richmond TW9 . . . . .44 C3
Aspen Gdns W6 . . . . .39 A1
Aspen Ho 5 SE15 . . . . . . .50 B4
   4 London NW3 . . . . .12 B2
Aspenlea Rd W6 . . . . .47 C4
Aspen Way E14 . . . . .34 B2

Aspern Gr NW3 . . . . .12 A3
Aspinall Ho SW12 . . . . . .74 A3
Aspinall Rd SE4 . . . . .65 C4
Aspinden Rd SE16 . . . . . .40 A2
Aspley Rd SW18 . . . . .59 A2
Assam SE1 . . . . .125 A1
Assam St E1 . . . . .111 B2
Assata Mews N1 . . . . .15 A2
Assembly Pas E1 . . . . . . .32 B4
Assisi Ct SW12 . . . . .72 B3
Astbury Ho SE11 . . . . . . .135 B1
Astbury Rd SE15 . . . . . . .50 B2
Astell St SW3 . . . . .144 B2
Aste St E14 . . . . .42 B4
Astey's Row 1 N1 . . . . . . .15 B1
Astle St SW11 . . . . .169 C2
Aston Ho SW8 . . . . .171 B3
   W11 . . . . .113 A4
Astonville St SW18 . . . . . .70 C3
Astor Ct SW6 . . . . .156 C1
Astoria Mans 18
   SW16 . . . . .74 A1
Astoria Par SW16 . . . . . . .74 A1
Astoria Wlk SW9 . . . . . . .62 C4
Astra Ho 4 E3 . . . . .26 B2
   London N4 . . . . .5 B4
Astrop Mews W6 . . . . . . .39 B3
Astrop Terr W6 . . . . .39 B4
Astwood Mews
   SW7 . . . . .142 C4
Asylum Rd SE15 . . . . .50 A3
Atalanta St SW6 . . . . . . .154 A1
Athelstan Gdns 6
   NW6 . . . . .10 A1
Athelstane Gr E3 . . . . . . .26 B3
Athelstane Mews N4 . . . . .5 C3
Athelstan Gdns 6
   NW6 . . . . .10 A1
Athelstan Ho
   London E9 . . . . .18 B3
   London N16 . . . . .16 A4
Athena Ct NW8 . . . . .79 B2
Athenia Ho 7 E14 . . . . . . .34 C3
Athenlay Rd SE15 . . . . . .65 C2
Athenoeum Ct N5 . . . . . .15 B4
Athens Gdns W9 . . . . .23 C1
Atherden Rd E5 . . . . .17 B4
Atherfield Ct SW18 . . . . .59 A1
Atherfold Rd SW9 . . . . . .62 A4
Atherstone Ct W2 . . . . . .100 B4
Atherstone Mews
   SW7 . . . . .143 A4
Atherton Rd SW13 . . . . . .46 C3
Atherton St SW11 . . . . . .168 B2
Athlone Cl E5 . . . . .17 A3
Athlone Ho 9 E1 . . . . . . .32 B3
   16 London N16 . . . . .7 A1
Athlone Rd SW4,SW12 . .73 C4
Athlone St NW5 . . . . .12 C2
Atkins Ct 8 E3 . . . . .26 B4
Atkinson Ho 13 E2 . . . . . .24 C3
   SE17 . . . . .151 C3
Atkins Rd SW4,SW12 . . . .73 C4
Atlantic Ct 6 E14 . . . . . . .34 C2
Atlantic Ho 4 E1 . . . . .33 A4

Atlantic Ho *continued*
4 Putney SW15 .....58 B2
Atlantic Rd SW2,
SW9,SE24 ....62 C3
Atlas Mews E8 ....16 B2
Atlas Rd NW10 ......21 A2
Atley Rd E3 ....26 C4
Atney Rd SW15 .....58 A3
Atterbury St SW1 ..148 A3
Attilburgh Ho SE1 .138 C2
Attneave St WC1 ...95 B3
Atwater Cl SW2 .....74 C3
Atwell Rd 4 SE15 ..49 C1
Atwood Ave TW9 ...44 C1
Atwood Ho SE21 ...76 A1
Atwood Rd W6 .....39 A2
Aubert Ct N5 ....15 A4
Aubert Pk N5 ....15 A4
Aubert Rd N5 ....15 A4
Aubrey Beardsley Ho
SW1 ....147 A3
Aubrey Mans NW1 .102 A4
Aubrey Moore Point
E15 ....27 B3
Aubrey Pl NW8 .....78 C1
Aubrey Rd
W14 ....31 B1 113 A1
Aubrey Wlk
W14 ....31 B1 113 A1
Auburn Cl SE14 .....51 A3
Aubyn Sq SW15 .....56 C2
Auckland Ho 11
W12 ....30 A2
Auckland Rd SW11 .60 A3
Auckland St SE11 ..148 C1
Auden Pl NW1 ......81 B4
Audley Ct W1 .....118 A2
Audley Rd TW10 ....54 B2
Audley Sq W1 .....117 C2
Audrey St E2 ....24 C3
Augustas Cl W12 ...39 A3
Augustine Rd W14 ..39 C3
Augustines Ct E9 ...17 B3
Augustus Ct
8 Putney SW19 .....70 A3
Streatham SW16 ....73 C2
Augustus Rd SW19 ..70 A3
Augustus St NW1 ...92 B4
Aulton Pl SE11 ....149 C1
Auriga Mews N1 ....15 C3
Auriol Mans W14 ..140 A3
Auriol Rd W14 ....140 A3
Austen Ho 2 NW6 ..23 C2
Austin Friars EC2 ..109 C2
Austin Friars Sq
EC2 ....109 C2
Austin Ho 1 SE14 ...51 B3
6 London SW2 .....62 B2
Austin Rd SW11 ...169 B3
Austins Ct SE15 .....64 C4
Austin St E2 ....98 C3
Australia Rd W12 ...30 A2
Austral St SE11 ...150 A4
Autumn St E3 ....26 C4
Avalon Rd SW6 ....166 A4
Avebury Ct N1 ......87 B3
Avebury St N1 ......87 B3
Aveline St SE11 ....149 B1
Ave Maria La EC4 ..108 B1
Avenell Mans N5 ...15 A4
Avenell Rd N5 ....6 A1
Avenfield Ho W1 ..117 A4
Avening Rd SW18 ...70 C4
Avening Terr SW18 ..70 C4
Avenue Cl NW8 .....80 B3
Avenue Cres W3 ....37 A4
Avenue Ct SW3 ....144 C3
London NW2 ....1 A1
Avenue Gdns
London W3 ....37 A4
Mortlake SW14 ......56 A4
Avenue Ho NW8 ....80 A1
London N16 ....7 C2
London NW10 ....22 A3
Avenue Lo 12 NW8 ..11 C1
Avenue Mans NW3 ..11 A3
Avenue Park Rd
SE21,SE27 ....75 A2
Avenue Rd NW8 ....80 A4
London N6 ....4 C4
London NW10 ....21 B3
London W3 ....37 A4
Avenue Sch The
NW6 ....10 A1
Avenue The NW6 ...23 A4
SE10 ....52 C3
London SW4 ....60 C2
London W4 ....38 A3
Richmond TW9 ......44 B1
Wandsworth SW18,
SW12 ....72 A4
Averill St W6 ....47 C4
Avery Farm Row
SW1 ....146 A3
Avery Hill Coll (Mile End
Annexe) E3 ....26 B1
Avery Row W1 .....118 B4
Aviary Cl E16 ....35 B2
Avigdor (Jewish) Prim
Sch N16 ....6 C2
Avignon Rd SE4 ....65 C4
Avington Ct SE1 ...152 B3
Avis Sq E1 ....32 C3
Avocet Cl SE1 .....153 B2
Avon Ct
1 London W3 ....28 B3
11 Putney SW15 ....58 A2
Avondale Ct E16 ....35 A4
Avondale Ho SE1 ..153 B1
6 Mortlake SW14 ...55 C4
Avondale Mans
SW6 ....164 C4
Avondale Park Gdns
W11 ....112 A3
Avondale Park Prim Sch
W11 ....31 A2 112 A3
Avondale Park Rd
W11 ....31 A2 112 A4
Avondale Rd E16 ...35 A4
Mortlake SW14 .....55 C4
Avondale Rise SE15 .64 B4
Avondale Sq SE1 ..153 B1
Avon Ho W14 .....141 A3
14 London N16 ......15 C4
Avonhurst Ho NW6 .10 A1
Avonley Rd SE14 ....50 B3
Avonmore Gdns
W14 ....141 A3
Avonmore Pl W14 .140 B4
Avonmore Prim Sch
W14 ....140 B4
Avonmore Rd W14 140 C4
Avonmouth St SE1 .136 C2
Avon Pl SE1 ....137 A3
Avon Rd SE4 ....66 C4
Avriol Ho W12 ......30 A1
Avro Ct E9 ....18 A3
Axford Ho SW2 .....75 A3
Axis Bsns Ctr E15 ...27 A4
Axminster Rd N7 .....5 B1
Aybrook St W1 ....103 B3
Aycliffe Rd W12 ....29 C1
Aylesbury Ho 13
SE15 ....49 C4
Aylesbury Rd SE17 .151 C1
Aylesbury St EC1 ...96 A1
Aylesford Ho SE1 ..137 C3
Aylesford St SW1 ..147 B1
Aylesham Ctr The
SE15 ....49 C2
Aylestone Ave NW6 .22 C4
Aylmer Ho SE10 ....42 C1
Aylmer Rd W12 .....38 B4
Aylton Est 22 SE16 ..40 B4
Aylward St E1 ......32 C3
Aylwin Est SE1 ....138 B2
Aylwin Girls Sch
SE1 ....153 A4
Aynhoe Mans W14 ..39 C2
Aynhoe Rd W14 ....39 C3
Ayres St SE1 ......137 A4
Ayrsome Rd N16 .....7 A1
Ayrton Gould Ho 9
E2 ....25 C2
Ayrton Rd SW7 ....129 B2
Aysgarth Rd SE21 ...76 A4
Ayston Ho 19 SE8 ...40 C2
Ayton Ho SE5 ....48 C3
Aytoun Ct SW9 ....173 A1
Aytoun Pl SW9 ....173 A1
Aytoun Rd SW9 ....173 A1
Azalea Ho SE14 .....51 B3
Azenby Rd SE15 ....49 B1
Azof St SE10 ....43 A2
Azov Ho 9 E1 ......26 A1

B

Baalbec Rd N5 ......15 A3
Babington Ct WC1 .106 B3
Babington Ho SE1 .137 A4
Babmaes St SW1 ..119 B3
Bacchus Wlk 12 N1 .24 A3
Bache's St N1 ......97 C3
Back Church La
E1 ....111 B1
Back Hill EC1 ....95 C1
Backhouse Pl SE1 .152 B3
Back La NW3 ....11 B4
Bacon Gr SE1 .....138 C1
Bacon's Coll SE16 ...41 A4
Bacon's La N6 ....3 C3
Bacon St E2 ..24 C1 99 A2
Bacton NW5 ....12 C3
Bacton St E2 ....25 B2
Baddeley Ho SE11 .149 A2
Baddow Wlk N1 ....86 C4
Baden Pl SE1 ......137 B4
Badminton Ct 9 N4 .6 B4
Badminton Ho SE22 .64 A3
Badminton Mews 10
E16 ....35 C1
Badminton Rd
SW12 ....60 C1
Badric Ct SW11 ....167 C1
Badsworth Rd 3
SE5 ....48 B2
Bagley's La SW6 ..166 B3
Bagnigge Ho WC1 ..95 B3
Bagshot Ho NW1 ...92 B4
Bagshot St SE17 ..152 B1
Baildon 28 E2 ......25 B3
Baildon St SE8 ......51 B3
Bailey Ct 9 W12 ...38 C4
Bailey Mews W4 ....45 A4
Bainbridge St
WC1 ....105 C2
Bain Ho SW9 ......172 B2
Baird Ho 29 W12 ...30 A2
Baird St EC1 ....97 A2
Baizdon Rd SE3 .....53 A1
Baker Ho 12 E3 .....27 A2
Baker Rd NW10 .....21 A4
Bakers Field N7 .....14 A4
Bakers Hall Ct EC3 .124 B3
Baker's Mews W1 .103 B2
Bakers Rents E2 ....98 C3
Baker's Row EC1 ....95 B1
Baker St W1 ......103 A4
Baker Street W1 ....91 A1
Baker Street Sta
NW1 ....91 A1
Baker's Yd EC1 ......95 B1
Bakery Cl SW9 .....162 C1
Balaclava Rd SE1 .153 A3
Balchier Rd SE22 ...65 A1
Balcombe Ho NW1 .90 C2
3 Streatham SW2 ...74 B3
Balcombe St NW1 ..90 C1
Balcorne St E9 .....17 B1
Balderton Flats
W1 ....103 C1
Balderton St W1 ..103 C1
Baldock Ho 32 SE5 ..48 B1
Baldock St E3 ......27 A3
Baldrey Ho 1 SE10 .43 B1
Baldwin Cres SE5 ...48 B2
Baldwin Ho 15 SW2 .74 C3
Baldwin's Gdns
EC1 ....107 B4
Baldwin St EC1 .....97 B3
Baldwin Terr N1 ....86 C2
Baldwyn Gdns W3 ..28 C2
Bale Rd E1 ....33 A4
Bales Coll W10 .....22 C2
Balfern Gr W4 ......38 A1
Balfern St SW11 ...168 B2
Balfe St N1 ....84 B1
Balfour Ho W10 ....30 C4
Balfour Mews W1 .117 C2
Balfour Pl W1 .....117 C3
Putney SW15 ....57 A3
Balfour Rd
London N5 ....15 B4
London W3 ....28 B4
Balfour St SE17 ....151 B4
Balfron Twr 2 E14 ..34 B3
Balham Gr SW12 ....72 C4
Balham High Rd
SW12,SW17 ....72 C3
Balham Hill SW12 ..61 A1
Balham New Rd
SW12 ....73 A4
Balham Park Mans
SW12 ....72 B3
Balham Park Rd
SW12,SW17 ....72 C3
Balham Sta SW12 ...73 A3
Balham Station Rd
SW12 ....73 A3
Balin Ho SE1 ......137 B4
Balkan Wlk E1 ......32 A2
Balladier Wlk E14 ...34 A4
Ballance Rd E9 ......18 A2
Ballantine St SW18 .59 B3
Ballantrae Ho NW2 .10 B4
Ballard Ho SE10 ....52 A4
Ballast Quay SE10 ...42 C1
Ballater Rd SW2,
SW4 ....62 A3
Ball Ct EC3 ....109 C1
Ballin Ct 9 E14 .....42 B4
Ballingdon Rd
SW11 ....60 C1
Ballinger Point 18
E3 ....27 A2
Balliol Ho 11 SW15 .57 C1
Balliol Rd W10 .....30 C3
Ballogie Ave NW10 ...8 A4
Ballow Cl 23 SE5 ....49 A3
Ball's Pond Pl 3
N1 ....15 C2
Ball's Pond Rd N1 ..16 A2
Balman Ho 3 SE16 .40 C2
Balmer Rd E3 ......26 B3
Balmes Rd N1 ......87 C4
Balmoral Cl 1
SW15 ....57 C1
Balmoral Ct NW8 ...79 B2
21 SE16 ....32 C1
Balmoral Gr N7 .....14 B2
Balmoral Ho W14 .140 A4
London N4 ....6 B3
Balmoral Mews
W12 ....38 B3
Balmoral Rd NW2 ....9 A2
Balmore St N19 ......4 A2
Balmuir Gdns SW15 .57 B3
Balnacraig Ave
NW10 ....8 A4
Balniel Gate SW1 ..147 C2
Balsam Ho 8 E14 ...34 A2
Baltic Ho 7 SE5 ....48 B1
Baltic St E EC1 .....96 C1
Baltic St W EC1 .....96 C1
Baltimore Ho SE11 149 B2
Balvaird Pl SW1 ...147 C1
Balvernie Gr SW18 ..70 C4
Bamborough Gdns 12
W12 ....39 B4
Bamford Ct E15 .....19 A3
Banbury Ct WC2 ...120 A4
Banbury Ho 5 E9 ...17 C1
Banbury Rd E9 ......17 C1
Banbury St SW11 ..168 B2
Bancroft Ct SW8 ..172 A4
Bancroft Ho 10 E1 ..25 B1
Bancroft Rd E1 .....25 C1
Banff Ho 1 NW3 ....12 A2
Banfield Rd SE15 ...65 A4
Bangabandhu Prim Sch
E2 ....25 B2
Bangalore St SW15 .57 C4
Banim St W6 ....39 A2
Banister Ho SW8 ..171 A4
London E9 ....17 C3
15 London W10 .....23 A2
Banister Rd W10 ...22 C2
Bank Ct SW11 .....170 A4
Bank End SE1 .....123 A2
Bank La SW15 ......56 A2
Bank of England★
EC2 ....109 B1
Banks Ho SE1 .....136 C1
Bankside SE1 .....122 C3
SE1 ....123 A2
Bankside Pier SE1 .122 C3
Bank Sta EC3 ......109 C1
Bank The N6 ....4 A3
Bankton Rd SW2 ...62 C3
Banner Ho EC1 .....97 A1
Bannerman Ho
SW8 ....162 C3
Banner St EC1 ......97 A2
Banning Ho 4
SW19 ....69 C3
Banning St SE10 ....43 A1
Bannister Cl SW2 ...74 C3
Bannister Ho 28
SE14 ....50 C4
Banqueting House★
SW1 ....120 A1
Banstead Ct N4 ......6 B3

Banstead St SE15 ....65 B4	

Banstead St SE15 ....65 B4
Bantock Ho 14 W10 ..23 A2
Bantry Ho 5 E1 ....25 C1
Bantry St SE5 ....48 C3
Banyan Ho 6 NW3 ....11 A2
Banyard Ho SE16 .....40 A3
Baptist Gdns NW5 ....12 C2
Barandon Wlk 6
  W11 ....30 C2
Barbanel Ho EC1 .....97 B4
Barbara Brosnan Ct
  NW8 ....79 B1
Barbauld Rd N16 .....7 A1
Barber Beaumont Ho 5
  E1 ....25 C2
Barbers Rd E15 ....27 A3
Barbican * EC2 ......109 B3
Barbican Arts & Con Ctr
  EC2 ....109 A4
Barbican Sta EC1 ....108 C4
Barb Mews W6 ....39 B3
Barbon Cl WC1 ....106 C4
Barbrook Ho E9 ......17 B2
Barchard St SW18 ....59 A2
Barchester St E14 ....34 A4
Barclay Cl SW6 ......155 B1
Barclay Ho 21 E9 ....17 B1
Barclay Rd SW6 .....155 C1
Barcombe Ave SW2 ..74 B2
Bardell Ho 51 SE1 ...139 B3
Bardolph Rd
  London N7 ....14 A4
  Richmond TW9 ....54 B4
Bard Rd W10 ....30 C2
Bardsey Pl 54 E1 ....25 B1
Bardsley Ho 5
  SE10 ....52 B4
Bardsley La SE10 ....52 B4
Barents Ho 10 E1 ....25 C1
Barfett St W10 ....23 B1
Barfleur Ho SE8 .....41 B2
Barford Ho 15 E3 ....26 B3
Barforth Rd SE15 ....65 A4
Barge House St
  SE1 ....121 C2
Barham Ho SE17 ....152 B2
Baring Ct N1 ....87 B3
Baring Ho 11 E14 ....33 C3
Baring St N1 ....87 B3
Barker Dr NW1 ......13 C1
Barker Ho SE17 .....152 A3
  Dulwich SE21 ....76 A1
Barker Mews SW4 ...61 A3
Barker St SW10 .....156 C4
Barker Wlk SW16 ....73 C1
Bark Pl W2 ....114 A4
Barkston Gdns
  SW5 ....142 A3
Barkway Ct N4 ....6 B2
Barkwith Ho 5
  SE14 ....50 C4
Barkworth Rd SE16 ..40 B1
Barlborough St
  SE14 ....50 C3
Barlby Gdns W10 ....22 C1
Barlby Prim Sch
  W10 ....22 C1
Barlby Rd W10 ......22 C1
Barleycorn Way E14 .33 B2
Barley Mow Pas
  EC1 ....108 B3
Barlow Ho 6 N1 .....24 A2 2
Barling 6 NW1 ....13 A1
Barling Ct SW4 .....172 A2
Barlings Ho 2 SE4 ..65 C3

Barloch Ho SW11 ...169 B2
Barlow Ho 57 W4 ...
Barlow Ho N1 ....97 B4
  14 SE16 ....40 A2
Barlow Pl W1 ....118 B3
Barlow Rd Acton W3 .28 A1
London NW6 ....10 B2
Barlow St SE17 .....151 C3
Barmouth Ho 6
  N7 ....5 B2
Barmouth Rd SW18 ..59 B1
Barnabas Ho EC1 ....96 C3
Barnabas Lo SW8 ...172 B4
Barnabas Rd E9 .....17 C3
Barnaby Pl SW7 ....143 B3
Barnard Ct SW16 ....74 B1
Barnard Ho 12 E2 ...25 A2
Barnard Lo 19 W9 ...31 C4
Barnard Mews
  SW11 ....60 A3
Barnard Gdns 6 E1 ..32 C2
  E1 ....32 C2
Barnardo Gdns 2
  E1 ....32 C2
Barnard Rd SW11 ...60 A3
Barnard's Inn EC4 ..107 C2
Barnbrough NW1 ....82 C3
Barnby St NW1 ......93 A4
Barn Cl 18 NW5 .....13 C3
Barnersbury Ho N7 ..14 A4
Barnes Ave SW13 ...46 C3
Barnes Bridge Sta
  SW13 ....46 A1
Barnes Common
  SW13 ....56 C4
Barnes Ct N1 ....14 C1
Barnes High St
  SW13 ....46 B1
Barnes Ho 14 E2 ....25 B3
  20 SE14 ....51 A4
London SW1 ....147 C3
Barnes Hospl SW14 .56 A4
Barnes St E14 ....33 A3
Barnes Terr SE8 .....41 B1
Barnet Gr E2 .....24 C2 99 B3
Barnett Ho E1 ....110 C3
Barnett St 15 E1 ....32 A3
Barn Field NW3 .....12 B3
Barnfield Cl
  London N4 ....5 A4
Wandsworth SW17 ..71 B1
Barnfield Pl E14 ....41 C2
Barnham St SE1 ....138 B4
Barnsbury Gr N7 ....14 B1
Barnsbury Pk N1 ....14 C1
Barnsbury Rd N1 ....85 B3
Barnsbury Sq N1 ....14 C1
Barnsbury St N1 .....14 C1
Barnsbury Terr N1 ...14 B1
Barnsdale Ave E14 ..41 C2
Barnsdale Rd W9 ....23 B1
Barnsley St E1 ......25 A1
Barn St N16 ....7 A2
Barnstaple La SE13 .67 B3
Barnston Wlk N1 ....86 C4
Barnwell Ho 5 SE5 ..49 A2
Barnwell Rd SW2 ....62 C2
Barnwood Cl W9 .....88 B1
Baron Cl N1 ....85 B2
Baroness Rd E2 .....24 B2 99 A4
Barons Court Mans
  W14 ....140 B1
Baron's Court Rd
  W14 ....140 B2

Barons Court Sta
  W14 ....140 A2
Barons Gate 13 W4 ..37 B3
Barons Keep W14 ...140 A2
Barons Lo 6 E14 ....42 B2
Baronsmead Rd
  SW13 ....46 C2
Baronsmede W5 .....36 B4
Baron's Pl SE1 .....135 C3
Baron St N1 ....85 B2
Baron Wlk E16 ......35 B4
Barque Mews SE8 ...51 C4
Barratt Ho 15 N1 ...15 A1
Barratt Ind Pk E3 ...27 B1
Barret Ho NW6 .....23 C4
Barrett's Gr N16 ....16 A3
Barrett's Green Rd
  NW10 ....20 C3
Barrett St W1 ....103 C1
Barrhill Rd SW2 .....74 A2
Barriedale SE14 .....51 A1
Barrie Ho NW8 ......80 B3
  W2 ....115 A3
  Acton W3 ....37 B4
Barrington Ct NW5 ..12 C3
London SW9 ....172 B1
Barrington Rd SW9 .63 A4
Barrowgate Ho W4 ..37 C1
Barrowgate Rd W4 ..37 C1
Barrow Hill Est
  NW8 ....80 A1
Barrow Hill Jun Sch
  NW8 ....80 A1
Barry Ho 4 SE16 ....40 A1
Barry Lo N4 ....5 B4
Barry Par SE22 .....64 C3
Barry Rd SE22 ......64 C2
Barset Rd SE15 .....65 B4
Barston Rd SE27 ....75 B1
Barstow Cres SW2 ..74 B3
Bartell Ho SW2 .....62 C1
Barter St WC1 ......106 B3
Bartholomew Cl
  EC1 ....108 C3
London SW18 ......59 B3
Bartholomew Ct
  E14 ....34 C2
  5 Poplar E14 ....34 C2
Bartholomew Ho 22
  SE5 ....48 B1
Bartholomew La
  EC2 ....109 C1
Bartholomew Pas
  EC1 ....108 B3
Bartholomew Pl
  EC1 ....108 C3
Bartholomew Rd
  NW5 ....13 B2
Bartholomew Sq 18
  E1 ....25 A1
Bartholomew St
  SE1 ....137 C1
Bartholomew Villas
  NW5 ....13 B2
Bartle Rd W11 ......31 A3
Bartlett Cl E14 ......33 C3
Bartlett Ct EC4 .....107 C2
Bartok Ho W11 .....112 C3
Bartolomew Sq EC1 97 A2
Barton Cl London E9 .17 B3
London SE15 ....65 A4
Barton Ct W14 .....140 B2

Barton Ct continued
  London SW4 ......172 A2
Barton Ho 8 E3 .....27 A2
  N1 ....15 A1
  London SW6 ......59 A4
Barton Rd W14 .....140 B1
Bartonway NW8 .....79 B2
Bartram SE4 ....66 A1
Bartrip St E9 ....18 B2
Barville Cl SE4 ......66 A3
Barwell Ho 2 ....99 B2
Barwick Ho 7 W3 ...37 B4
Bascome St 13 SW2 62 C1
Basevi Way SE8 ....52 A4
Bashley Rd NW10 ...20 C1
Basil Ho E1 ....111 C2
  SW8 ....162 A2
Basil Mans SW1 ....130 C3
Basil St SW3 ....130 C3
  SW1,SW3 ....130 C2
Basin App E14 .....33 A3
Basing Ct 12 SE15 ..49 B2
Basingdon Way SE5 63 C3
Basinghall Ave
  EC2 ....109 B2
Basinghall St EC2 ..109 B2
Basing Hill NW11 ....1 B3
Basing House Yd
  E2 ....98 B4
Basing Pl E2 ....98 B4
Basing St W11 ......31 B3
Basire St N1 ....87 A4
Baskerville Gdns
  NW10 ....8 A4
Baskerville Rd
  SW18 ....72 A4
Baslow Wlk E5 .....17 C4
Basnett Rd 8 SW11 .60 C4
Basque Ct 21 SE16 ..40 C4
Bassano St SE22 ....64 B2
Bassein Park Rd
  W12 ....38 B3
Bassett Rd W10 .....30 C3
Bassett St NW5 .....12 C2
Bassingbourn Ho 6
  N1 ....15 A1
Bassingham Rd
  SW18 ....71 B4
Bassishaw Highwalk
  EC2 ....109 B3
Basswood Cl SE15 ..65 A4
Basterfield Ho EC1 ..96 C1
Bastwick St EC1 .....96 C2
Basuto Rd SW6 ....165 C3
Batavia Ho 8 SE14 .51 A3
Batavia Mews 3
  SE14 ....51 A3
Batavia Rd SE14 ....51 A3
Batchelor St N1 .....85 C3
Bateman Ho 6
  SE17 ....48 A4
Bateman's Bldgs
  W1 ....105 B1
Bateman's Row
  EC2 ....24 A1 98 B2
Bateman St W1 ....105 B1
Bate St 10 E14 .....33 B2
Bath Cl SE15 ....50 A3
Bath Ct EC1 ....95 B1
  EC1 ....97 B3
  5 Forest Hill SE26 76 C1
Bathgate Ho 8
  SW9 ....48 A2
Bathgate Rd SW19 ..69 C1
Bath Gr E2 ....24 C3
Bath Ho E2 .....24 C1 99 C2

Bath Ho continued
  SE1 ....137 A2
Bath Pl EC2 ....98 A3
  16 London W6 ...39 B1
Bath Rd W4 ....38 A2
Baths App SW6 ....155 A2
Bath St EC1 ....97 B3
Bath Terr SE1 ......136 C2
Bathurst Gdns
  NW10 ....22 A3
Bathurst Ho 12 W12 30 A2
Bathurst Mews
  W2 ....115 C4
Bathurst St W2 .....115 C4
Batley Pl 5 N16 .....7 B1
Batley Rd N16 ......7 B1
Batman Cl W12 .....30 A1
Batoum Gdns W6 ...39 B3
Batson Ho 1 ....111 C1
Batson St W12 .....38 C4
Batten Ho
  1 London SW4 ...61 B2
  London W10 .....23 A2
Batten St SW11 .....60 A4
Battersea Bridge Rd
  SW11 ....158 A1
Battersea Church Rd
  SW11 ....167 C4
Battersea Dogs Home
  SW8 ....160 B1
Battersea Park * ...159 B1
Battersea Park Rd
  SW11,SW8 ....169 C3
Battersea Park Sta
  SW8 ....160 A1
Battersea Power
  Station(dis) SW8 .160 B1
Battersea Rise
  SW11 ....60 B3
Battersea Sq 1
  SW11 ....167 C3
Battersea Tech Coll
  SW11 ....169 A3
Battishill St 1 N1 ...15 A1
Battlebridge Ct
  NW1 ....84 B2
Battle Bridge Ctr
  NW1 ....84 B2
Battle Bridge La
  SE1 ....124 A1
Battle Bridge Rd
  NW1 ....84 B2
Battledean Rd N5 ...15 A3
Battle Ho 8 SE15 ...49 C4
Batty St E1 ....111 C2
Baty Ho SW2 ....74 B3
Baulk The SW18 ....70 C4
Bavaria Rd N19 .....5 A2
Bavent Rd SE5 .....48 B1
Bawdale Rd SE22 ...64 B2
Bawtree Rd SE14 ...51 A3
Baxendale St
  E2 ....24 C2 99 B4
Baxter Ho 11 E3 ....27 A2
Baxter Rd N1 ....15 C2
Baycliffe Ho 8 E9 ..17 C2
Bay Ct 7 E1 ....25 C1
  London W5 ......36 A3
Bayer Ho EC1 ......96 C1
Bayes Ct NW3 ......12 B1
Bayfield Ho 3 SE4 ..65 C3
Bayford Rd NW10 ..22 C2
Bayford St 5 E8 ....17 A1

Bayford St Ind Ctr **4**
E8 ....17 A1
Bayham Pl NW1 ....83 A3
Bayham Rd W4 ....37 C3
Bayham St NW1 ....82 C3
Bayhurst Lo N4 ....6 B4
Bayley St WC1 ....105 B3
Baylis Rd SE1 ....135 B3
Baynes Mews **2**
NW3 ....11 C2
Baynes St NW1 ....13 B1
Bayon Ho **7** N1 ....9 C4
Bayonne Rd W6 ....154 A3
Bayston Rd N16 ....7 B1
Bayswater Rd W2 ....115 B3
Bayswater Sta W2 ....114 B4
Baythorne St **5** E3 ....33 B4
Bayton Ct **2** E8 ....16 C1
Baytree Rd SW2 ....62 B3
Bazalgette Ho NW8 ....89 C2
Bazely St E14 ....34 B2
Bazely St E14 ....34 B2
BBC Television Ctr
W12 ....30 B1
Beach Ho SW5 ....141 B2
Beachy Rd E3 ....18 C1
Beaconfield Terrace Rd
W14 ....126 A1
Beacon Gate SE14 ....65 C4
Beacon Hill N7 ....14 A3
Beacon Ho **5** SE5 ....49 A3
Beacon Rd SE13 ....67 C1
Beaconsfield Cl SE3 ......53 C4
London W4 ....37 B1
Beaconsfield Rd
SE17 ....152 A1
Greenwich SE3 ....53 C3
London NW10 ....8 B2
London W4 ....37 C3
Beaconsfield Wlk
SW6 ....165 A3
Beadon Rd W6 ....39 B2
Beak St W1 ....119 A4
Beale Ho SW9 ....172 C1
Beale Pl E3 ....26 B3
Beale Rd E3 ....26 B4
Beames Ho SW8 ....171 B4
Beaminster Ho
SW8 ....162 C2
Beamish Ho **5**
SE16 ....40 B2
Beanacre Cl E9 ....18 B2
Bear Alley EC4 ....108 A2
Bear Croft Ho
SW6 ....164 C1
Beardsley Way W3 ....37 C4
Bear Gardens Mus
SE1 ....122 C2
Bear Gdns SE1 ....122 C2
Bear La SE1 ....122 B1
Bear St WC2 ....119 C4
Bearstead Rise SE4 ......66 B2
Beaton Cl SE15 ....49 B2
Beatrice Ho
1 London SW2 ....62 B2
4 London W6 ....39 B1
Beatrice Pl W8 ....128 A1
Beatrice Rd SE1 ....153 C3
London N4 ....5 C4
2 Richmond TW10 .....54 B2
Beatrice Tate Sch
E2 ....25 A2
Beatrice Webb Ho **3**
E3 ....26 A3

Beatrice Ho SW5 ....142 B2
Beatrix Potter Prim Sch
SW18 ....71 B3
Beattie Ho SW8 ....171 A4
Beatty Rd N16 ....16 A4
Beatty St NW1 ....82 C2
Beauchamp Cl **10**
W4 ....37 B3
Beauchamp Pl
SW3 ....130 B1
Beauchamp Rd
SW11 ....60 B3
Beauchamp St EC1 ......107 B3
Beauclerc Rd W6 ....39 A3
Beauclerk Ho **10**
SW16 ....74 A1
Beaufort Cl SW19 ....69 A4
Beaufort Gdns
SW3 ....130 B2
Beaufort Ho SW1 ....147 B1
SW3 ....157 C3
London SW1 ....168 A2
Beaufort Mans
SW3 ....157 C3
Beaufort Mews
SW6 ....155 A4
Beaufort St SW3 ....157 B4
3 West Norwood
SE27 ....75 A1
Beaufoy Rd **1** SW8 .....61 A4
Beaufoy Wlk SE11 ....149 A3
Beaulieu Cl SE5 ....63 C4
Beaulieu Pl W4 ....37 B3
Beaumanor Mans
W2 ....114 B4
Beaumaris Twr **2**
W3 ....37 A4
Beaumont W14 ....141 A3
Putney SW15 ....58 A2
Beaumont Ave
W14 ....140 C2
Richmond TW9 ....54 B4
Beaumont Bldgs
WC2 ....106 B1
Beaumont Cres
W14 ....140 C1
Beaumont Ct **10** W4 ..37 B1
Wimbledon SW19 ....70 C1
Beaumont Gdns NW3 ...1 C1
Beaumont Gr **1** E1 .....25 C1
Beaumont Ho
5 Streatham SW2 ....74 A3
4 Wimbledon SW19 ...70 C1
Beaumont Pl NW1,
WC1,W1 ....93 A2
Beaumont Rd
London W4 ....37 C3
Putney SW15,SW19 ....70 A4
Beaumont Rise N19 ....4 C3
Beaumont Sq E1 ....32 C4
Beaumont St W1 ....103 C4
Beaumont Wlk NW3 .....12 B1
Beauvale **6** NW1 ....12 C1
Beauval Rd SE22 ....64 B1
Beaux Ho N16 ....16 C4
Beavor La W6 ....38 C1
Beccles St E14 ....33 B2
Beck Cl SE13 ....52 A2
Beckers The N16 ....16 C4
Becket Ho SE1 ....137 B3
Becket St SE1 ....137 B2
Beckett Cl
London NW10 ....8 A2
Streatham SW16 ....73 C2
Beckett Ho **12** E1 ....32 B4

Beckett Ho continued
London SW9 ....172 B1
Beckford Ho **3** N16 .....16 A3
Beckford Cl W14 ....140 C4
Beckford Ho N16 ....16 A3
Beckford Prim Sch
NW6 ....10 B3
Beckham Ho SE11 ....149 A3
Beckley Ho **5** E3 ....26 B1
Beckton Ho **2** E5 ....17 A1
Becklow Rd W12 ....38 C4
Beck Rd E8 ....25 A4
Beckton Rd E16 ....35 B2
Beckway St SE17 ....152 A3
Beckwith Ho **2** E2 ......25 A3
Beckwith Rd SE24 ....63 C2
Bective Pl SW15 ....58 B3
Bective Rd SW15 ....58 B3
Bedale St SE1 ....123 B1
Bedefield WC1 ....94 B3
Bede Ho
London SE14 ....51 B2
London SW15 ....57 C1
Bedford Ave WC1 ....105 C3
Bedfordbury WC2 ....120 A3
Bedford Cl W4 ....46 B4
Bedford Cnr **3** W4 ....38 A2
Bedford Court Mans
WC1 ....105 C3
Bedford Ct WC2 ....120 A3
Bedford Gardens Ho
W8 ....113 C1
Bedford Gdns
W8 ....31 C1 113 C1
Bedford Hill SW12 ....73 A2
Bedford Ho
7 London SW4 ....62 A3
2 London W4 ....38 A2
Bedford Park Cnr **5**
W4 ....38 A2
Bedford Park Mans
W4 ....37 C2
Bedford Pas SW6 ....154 B2
Bedford Pl WC1 ....106 A4
Bedford Rd
London SW2,SW4 ....62 A3
London W4 ....38 A3
Bedford Row WC1 ....107 A3
Bedford Sq WC1 ....105 C3
Bedford St WC2 ....120 B3
Bedford Way WC1 ....93 C1
Bedgebury Gdns
SW19 ....70 A2
Bedlow Cl NW8 ....89 B1
Bedser Cl SE11 ....163 A4
Bedser Ct **2** SW4 ....172 A2
Beech Ave W3 ....29 A1
Beech Cl SE8 ....51 B4
Putney SW15 ....68 C4
Beechcroft Ave
NW11 ....1 B4
Beechcroft Cl **2**
SW16 ....74 B1
Beechcroft Ct **3**
NW11 ....1 B4
Beech Croft Ct N5 ....15 A4
Beechcroft Rd
Mortlake SW14 ....55 B4
Upper Tooting SW17 ......72 A2
Beech Ct W1 ....102 C2
London NW2 ....1 B2
Beech Gdns **12**
London N16 ....7 A1

Beechdene **4** SE15 .....50 A2
Beeches Rd SW17 ....72 B1
Beeches The **1** N19 .....5 A3
Beechey Ho **11** E1 ......32 A1
Beech Gdns W5 ....36 A3
Beech Ho SE16 ....40 B4
5 London N16 ....16 A4
Beechmore Rd
SW11 ....169 A3
Beechmount Rd
SE15 ....150 A4
Beech St EC2 ....109 A4
Beech Tree Cl N1 ....14 C1
Beechwood Ave
TW9 ....44 C1
Beechwood Ct
Chiswick W4 ....45 C4
London N16 ....7 A4
Beechwood Gr W3 ....29 A2
Beechwood Ho **22**
E2 ....24 C3
Beechwood Rd E8 ....16 B2
Beechworth Cl NW3 .....1 C2
Beecroft Rd SE4 ....66 A2
Beecroft Rd SE4 ....66 A2
Beehive Cl E8 ....16 B1
Beehive Pl SW9 ....62 C4
Beeston Cl **8** E8 ....16 C3
Beeston Pl SW1 ....132 B2
Beethoven St W10 ....23 A2
Begbie Ho SW9 ....173 A2
Begonia Wlk W12 ....29 B3
Beira St SW12 ....73 A4
Beis Rachel D'Satmar
Girls Sch N16 ....7 A4
Bekesbourne St **11**
E14 ....33 A3
Beldanes Lo NW10 ....8 C1
Belenoyd Ct SW16 ....74 B1
Belfont Wlk N7 ....14 A4
Belford Ho **7** E8 ....24 B4
Belfort Rd SE15 ....50 B1
Belfry Cl **5** SE16 ....40 A1
Belgrade Ho N16 ....16 A4
Belgrade Rd N16 ....16 A4
Belgrave Cl **1** W3 ....37 B4
Belgrave Ct **4** W4 ....37 B1
Belgrave Gdns NW8 .....78 C3
Belgrave Mans
NW8 ....78 C3
Belgrave Mews N
SW1 ....131 B3
Belgrave Mews S
SW1 ....131 C2
Belgrave Mews W
SW1 ....131 B2
Belgrave Pl SW1 ....131 C1
Belgrave Rd SW1 ....146 C3
Barnes SW13 ....46 B3
Belgrave Sq SW1 ....131 B2
Belgrave St E1 ....32 C3
Belgrave Yd SW1 ....132 A1
Belgravia Ct SW1 ....132 A1
Belgravia Ho **11**
SW4 ....61 C1
Belgrove St WC1 ....94 B4
Belham Wlk **13** SE5 ...48 C2
Belinda Rd **3** SW9 ......63 A4
Belitha Villas N1 ....14 C1
Bellamy Cl **7** E14 ....41 C4
SW5 ....141 A1
Bellamy's Ct **18**
SE16 ....32 C1
Bellamy St SW12 ....73 A4
Bellasis Ave SW2 ....74 A2
Bell Dr SW18 ....70 A4

Bellefields Rd SW9 ....62 B4
Bellenden Rd SE15 ....49 B1
Bellenden Rd Ret Pk
SE15 ....49 C2
Bellenden Sch SE15 .....49 C1
Bellendon Road Bsns
Ctr SE15 ....49 B1
Bellerbys Coll SW15 ....56 C1
Belleville Prim Sch
SW11 ....60 B2
Belleville Rd SW11 ....60 B2
Belle Vue Gdns
SW9 ....172 B1
Bellevue Pl E1 ....25 B1
Bellevue Rd
Barnes SW13 ....46 C1
Upper Tooting SW17 .....72 B3
Bellew St SW17 ....71 B1
Bellgate Mews NW5 .....4 A1
Bell Ho SE10 ....52 B4
12 Streatham SW2 .....74 A4
Bellina Mews NW5 ....13 B4
Bell Ind Est **8** W4 ......37 B2
Bell Inn Yd EC3 ....109 C1
Bell La E1 ....110 C3
E16 ....35 C1
Bellmaker Ct **10** E3 ....33 C4
Bell Moor NW3 ....2 B1
Bello Cl SE24,SW2 ....75 A3
Bellot Gdns **1** SE10 ...43 A1
Bellot St SE10 ....43 A1
Bell St NW1 ....102 A4
Bell Wharf La EC4 ....123 A4
Bellwood Rd SE15 ....65 C3
Bell Yd WC2 ....107 B1
Belmont Cl SW4 ....61 B4
Belmont Ct
6 London N16 ....7 B3
London N5 ....15 B4
Belmont Gr
London SE13 ....67 C4
London W4 ....37 C2
Belmont Hall Ct
SE13 ....67 C4
Belmont Hill SE13 ....67 C4
Belmont Mews
SW19 ....69 C2
Belmont Prim Sch
W4 ....37 C2
Belmont Rd
London SW4 ....61 B4
London W4 ....37 C2
Belmont Terr W4 ....37 C2
Belmore Ho N7 ....13 C3
Belmore St SW8 ....171 B4
Beloe Cl SW15 ....56 C3
Belsham St E9 ....17 B2
Belsize Ave NW3 ....12 A3
Belsize Court Garages
1 NW3 ....11 C3
Belsize Cres NW3 ....11 C3
Belsize Ct NW3 ....11 C3
Belsize Gr NW3 ....12 A2
Belsize La NW3 ....11 C3
Belsize Mews NW3 ....11 C2
Belsize Park Gdns
NW3 ....12 A3
Belsize Park Mews **1**
NW3 ....11 C2
Belsize Park Sta
NW3 ....12 A3
Belsize Pk NW3 ....12 A3
Belsize Pl NW3 ....11 C3
Belsize Rd NW6 ....78 B4
Belsize Sq NW3 ....11 C2
Belsize Terr NW3 ....11 C2

Beltane Dr SW19 .....69 C1
Belthorn Cres SW12 73 B4
Belton Rd NW2 ....9 C2
Belton Way E3 ....33 C4
Beltran Rd SW6 ....166 A1
Belvedere Bldgs
  SE1 ....136 B3
Belvedere Ct
  London NW2 ....9 C2
  7 London SW4 ......61 C1
  Putney SW15 ....57 B3
Belvedere Heights
  NW8 ....90 B1
Belvedere Mews
  SE15 ....65 B4
Belvedere Pl SE1 ..136 B3
  10 London SW2 ....62 B2
Belvedere Rd SE1 ..121 A1
Belvedere The
  SW10 ....167 A3
Belvoir Lo SE22 .....76 C4
Belvoir Rd SE22 ....76 C4
Bembridge Cl NW6 ..10 A1
Bembridge Ho
  8 SE8 ....41 B2
  Wandsworth SW18 ..59 A1
Bemerton St N1 .....84 C4
Bemish Rd SW15 ....57 C4
Benabo Ct 6 E8 .....16 C3
Benbow Ct W6 ......39 A3
Benbow Ho 12 SE8 ..51 C4
Benbow Rd W6 .....39 A3
Benbow St SE8 .....51 C4
Bence Ho 5 SE8 ....41 A2
Bendall Mews
  NW1 ....102 B4
Bendemeer Rd
  SW15 ....57 C4
Benden Ho SE13 ....67 B2
Bendon Valley
  SW18 ....71 A4
Benedict Rd SW9 ...62 B4
Benedon Ho SE17 .152 B2
Ben Ezra Ct E17 ...151 A3
Benfleet Ct 6 E8 ....24 B4
Bengal Ct EC3 .....109 C1
Bengal Ho E1 ......32 C4
Bengeworth Rd SE5 63 B4
Benham Cl 1 SW11 59 C4
Benham's Pl 5
  NW3 ....11 B4
Benhill Rd SE5 .....48 C2
Benjamin Cl E8 ....24 C4
Benjamin St EC1 ..108 A4
Ben Jonson Ct 8
  N1 ....24 A3
Ben Jonson Prim Sch
  E1 ....26 A1
Ben Jonson Rd E1 ..33 A4
Benledi St E14 .....34 C3
Bennelong Cl W12 ..30 A3
Bennerley Rd SW11 60 B2
Bennet's Hill EC4 ..122 B4
Bennet Ct London NW1 1
  12 London W3 .....37 B4
Bennett Gr SE13 ...52 A2
Bennett Ho SW1 ...147 C4
  2 Streatham SW4 ..73 C4
Bennett St London W4 38 A1
  SW1 ....118 C2
Bennett's Yd SW1 .133 C1
Benn Ho E1 ....18 A2
Benns Wlk 8 TW9 ..54 A3
Bensbury Cl SW15 ..69 B4
Ben Smith Way
  SE16 ....139 C2

Benson Ct SW8 .....172 A4
  1 London N19 .....13 B4
Benson Ho 2 ....98 C2
  SE1 ....121 C1
Benson Quay E1 ....32 B2
Benthal Ct N16 ......7 C1
Benthal Prim Sch
  N16 ....7 C1
Benthal Rd N16 .....7 C1
Bentham Ct 10 N1 ..15 B1
Bentham Ho SE1 ...137 B1
Bentham Rd E9 ....17 C2
Bentinck Cl NW8 ...80 B1
Bentinck Ho 7
  W12 ....30 A2
Bentinck Mans
  W1 ....104 A2
Bentinck Mews
  W1 ....103 C2
Bentinck St W1 ....103 C2
Bentley Cl SW19 ...70 C1
Bentley Ho
  8 Bow E3 ....26 C1
  5 Camberwell SE5 .49 A2
Bentworth Ct 2 .....99 B2
Bentworth Prim Sch
  W12 ....30 A3
Bentworth Rd W12 .30 A3
Benville Ho SW8 ...163 A1
Benwell Rd N7 .....14 C3
Benwick Cl SE16 ...40 A2
Benworth St E3 ....26 B2
Benyon Ho EC1 .....95 C4
Benyon Rd N1 ......87 C4
Beormund Prim Sch
  SE1 ....137 B3
Bequerel Ct SE10 ..43 B3
Berberis Ho 15 E14 33 C2
Berber Pl 13 E14 ...33 C2
Berber Rd SW11 ...60 B2
Berebinder Ho 17
  E3 ....26 B3
Berenger Twr
  SW10 ....157 B2
Berenger Wlk
  SW10 ....157 B2
Berens Rd NW10 ...22 C2
Beresford Ct E9 ...18 A3
Beresford Ho
  Dulwich SE21 ......76 A1
  14 London SW4 ....62 A3
Beresford Lo N4 ...15 C3
Beresford Rd N5 ...15 C3
Beresford Terr 3
  N5 ....15 B3
Bere St E1 ....32 C2
Berestede Rd 4
  W6 ....38 B1
Bergen Ho 1 SE5 ..48 B1
Bergen Sq SE16 ...41 A3
Berger Prim Sch E9 17 C2
Berger Rd E9 ......17 C2
Berghem Mews
  W14 ....39 C3
Bergholt Cres N16 ..7 A4
Bergholt Mews 4
  NW1 ....13 C1
Bering Sq E14 .....41 C1
Berisford Mews
  SW18 ....59 B1
Berkeley Ct
  1 London NW11 ....1 B4
  10 Streatham SW2 74 C3
Berkeley Gdns W8 113 C3
Berkeley Ho 17 E3 .26 C2

Berkeley Mews
  W1 ....103 A1
Berkeley Rd SW13 .46 C2
Berkeley Sq W1 ....118 B3
Berkeley St W1 ....118 B2
Berkeley The NW11 .2 A4
Berkeley Wlk 1 N7 ..5 B2
Berkley Gr NW1 ....12 C1
Berkley Rd NW1 ...12 C1
Berkshire Rd E9 ...18 B2
Bermans Way NW10 .8 B4
Bermondsey Leather
  Mkt SE1 ....138 A3
Bermondsey Mkt*
  SE1 ....138 B2
Bermondsey Sq
  SE1 ....138 B2
Bermondsey St
  SE1 ....138 A3
Bermondsey Sta
  SE16 ....40 B3
Bermondsey Trad Est
  SE16 ....40 B1
Bermondsey Wall E
  SE16 ....40 A4
Bermondsey Wall W
  SE1,SE16 ....139 B4
Bernard Angell Ho 4
  SE10 ....52 C4
Bernard Cassidy St 4
  E16 ....35 B2
Bernard Shaw Ct 3
  NW1 ....13 B1
Bernard Shaw Ho 2
  NW10 ....20 C4
Bernard St WC1 ....94 B1
Bernay's Gr SW9 ..62 B3
Berners Mews W1 .105 A3
Berners Pl W1 .....105 A2
Berners Rd N1 .....86 A3
Berners St W1 ....105 A2
Berner Terr E1 ....111 B2
Bernwood Ho 4 N4 .6 C4
Berridge Mews
  NW6 ....10 C3
Berriman Rd N7 ....5 B1
Berry Cl NW10 .....8 A1
Berryfield Rd SE17 150 B2
Berry Ho 25 E1 ....25 A1
  London SW11 ....169 A2
Berrymead Gdns
  W3 ....37 B4
Berrymede Jun Sch
  W3 ....37 B4
Berrymede Rd W4 ..37 C3
Berry Pl EC1 ....96 B3
Berry St EC1 ....96 B1
Berry Way W5 .....36 A3
Bertha Neubergh Ho 6
  SE5 ....48 B2
Berthon St SE8 ....51 C4
Bertie Rd NW10 ....8 C2
Bertram St N19 ....4 A2
Bertrand Ho 11
  SW16 ....74 A1
Bertrand St SE13 ..67 A4
Bertrum House Sch
  SW17 ....72 C2
Berwick St W1 ....105 A1
Berwyn Ho 3 N16 ..7 B3
Berwyn Rd
  Mortlake SW14,TW10 55 A3

Berwyn Rd continued
  Streatham SE24 ...75 A3
Beryl Rd W6 ....39 C1
Besant Cl NW2 .....1 A1
Besant Ct N1 ......15 C3
Besant Ho NW8 ....78 C3
Besant Rd NW2 ....10 A4
Besant Wlk N7 .....5 B2
Besford Ho 2 E2 ..24 C3
Bessant Dr TW9 ...45 A2
Bessborough Gdns
  SW1 ....147 C2
Bessborough Pl
  SW1 ....147 C2
Bessborough Rd
  SW15 ....68 C3
Bessborough St
  SW1 ....147 B2
Bessemer Ct 5
  NW1 ....13 B1
Bessemer Grange Prim
  Sch SE5 ....64 A3
Bessemer Park Ind Est
  3 SE24 ....63 A3
Bessemer Rd SE5 .48 B1
Bessingham Wlk
  SE4 ....65 C2
Besson St SE14 ...50 C2
Bessy St E2 ....25 B2
Bestwood St SE8 ..40 C2
Beswick Mews 1
  NW6 ....11 A2
Beta Pl 20 SW4 ...62 B3
Betchworth Ho 6
  N7 ....13 C3
Bethersden Ho
  SE17 ....152 B2
Bethlehem Ho 14
  E14 ....33 B2
Bethnal Green Mus of
  Childhood* E2 ....25 B2
Bethnal Green Rd
  E2 ....24 B1 99 B3
Bethnal Green Sta
  E1 ....25 A1
  E2 ....25 A2
Bethnal Green Tech Coll
  E2 ....99 A3
Bethune Rd
  London N16 ....7 A4
  London NW10 .....20 C1
Bethwin Rd SE5 ...48 B3
Betsham Ho SE1 ..137 B4
Betterton Ho 2 WC2 106 B2
Betterton St WC2 ..106 B1
Bettridge Rd SW6 165 A1
Betts Ho E1 ....32 A2
Betts St E1 ....32 A2
Betty Layward Prim Sch
  N16 ....6 C1
Betty May Gray Ho 1
  E14 ....42 B2
Bevan St N1 ....87 A3
Bev Callender Cl 1
  SW8 ....61 A4
Bevenden St N1 ...97 C4
Beveridge Rd 1
  NW6 ....10 B1
Beverley Cl
  Barnes SW13 .....46 C1
  5 London SW11 ...59 C3
Beverley Cotts
  SW15 ....68 A1
Beverley Ct
  London N5 ....15 A2
  London SE4 ......66 B4
  3 London W12 ....30 A3

Beverley Ct continued
  9 London W4 .....37 B1
Beverley Gdns
  Barnes SW13 .....56 B4
  London NW11 ......1 A4
Beverley Lo 6
  TW10 ....54 A2
Beverley Path 9
  SW13 ....56 B1
Beverley Rd
  Barnes SW13 .....56 B4
  London SW13 .....38 B1
Beversbrook Rd N19 4 C1
Beverstone Rd SW2 62 B2
Beverston Mews
  NW1 ....102 C3
Bevin Cl SE16 .....33 A1
Bevin Ct WC1 ......95 A4
Bevington Rd W10 .31 A4
Bevington Sch W10 31 A4
Bevington St SE16 .40 A4
Bevin Ho 2 E2 .....25 B2
  2 ....26 C2
Bevin Sq SW17 ....72 B1
Bevin Way WC1 ....95 B4
Bevis Marks EC3 ..110 B2
Bewdley Ho N4 ....6 B4
Bewdley St N1 ....14 C1
Bewick Mews SE15 50 A3
Bewley Ct SW2 ....62 B1
Bewley Ho 2 ....32 A2
Bewley St E1 ......32 A2
Bexhill Rd
  Mortlake SW14 ...55 B4
Bexley Ho SE4 ....66 A3
BFI London Imax
  Cinema SE1 ......121 B1
Bianca Rd SE1,SE15 49 C4
Bicester Rd TW9 ..55 A4
Bickenhall Mans
  W1 ....103 A4
Bickenhall St W1 ..103 A4
Bickerton Rd N19 ..4 B2
Bicknell Ho E1 ....111 C1
Bicknell Rd SE5 ...63 B4
Bicknor Ho 2 E5 ..17 A3
Bidborough St N1,
  WC1 ....94 A3
Biddenham Ho 13
  SE16 ....40 C2
Bidder St E16 .....35 A4
Biddesden Ho
  SW3 ....144 C3
Biddestone Rd N7 .14 B4
Biddulph Mans W9 88 B3
Biddulph Rd W9 ...88 B3
Bidwell St SE15 ...50 A2
Big Ben* SW1 ....134 B3
Biggerstaff Rd E15 27 B4
Biggerstaff St N4 ..5 C2
Biggs Row SW15 ..57 C4
Bigland Green Prim Sch
  E1 ....32 A3
Bigland St E1 .....32 A3
Bilberry Ho 13 E3 .33 C4
Billingford Cl SE4 .65 C3
Billing Ho 6 E1 ...32 C3
Billingley NW1 ....82 C3
Billing Pl SW10 ...156 B2
Billing Rd SW10 ..156 B2

Billingsgate Mkt
E14 .....115 C4
Billing St SW10 ...156 B2
Billington Ho SW8 ...171 C3
Billington Rd SE14 ...50 C3
Billiter Sq EC3 ...110 B1
Billiter St EC3 ...110 B1
Billson St E14 ...42 B2
Bilton Ho SW8 ...171 B3
Bilton Twrs W1 ...103 A1
Bina Gdns SW5 ...142 C3
Binbrook Ho W10 ...30 B4
Binden Rd W12 ...38 B3
Binfield Ct SE5 ...48 B1
Binfield Rd SW4 ...172 B3
Bingfield St N1 ...84 C4
Bingham Pl W1 ...103 B4
Bingham St N1 ...15 C2
Binley Ho SW15 ...56 B1
Binney St W1 ...103 C1
Binnie Ho SE1 ...136 C1
Binns Rd W4 ...38 A1
Binns Ter **3** W4 ...38 A1
Binstead Ho SW18 ...59 C3
Binyon Ho **8** N16 ...16 A4
Bircham Path SE4 ...65 C3
Birch Cl E16 ...35 A4
  London N19 .....4 B2
  London SE15 ...49 C1
Birchdown Ho **12**
  E3 ...27 A2
Birches The SE5 ...49 A1
Birchfield Ho **2**
  E14 ...33 C2
Birch Ho
  London SE14 ...51 B2
  8 London SW2 ...62 C1
Birchington Ct NW6 ...78 A4
Birchington Ho **1**
  E5 ...7 C3
Birchington Rd
  NW6 ...23 C4
Birchin La EC3 ...109 C1
Birchlands Ave
  SW12 ...72 B4
Birchmere Lo **18**
  SE16 ...40 A1
Birchmere Row SE3 ...53 B1
Birchmore Wlk N5 ...6 B1
Birch Vale Ct NW8 ...89 C2
Birchwood Dr NW3 ...2 A1
Birdcage Wlk SW1 ...133 B3
Birdhurst Rd SW18 ...59 B2
Bird In Bush Rd
  SE15 ...49 C3
Bird In Hand Yd **4**
  NW3 ...11 B4
Birdsall Ho **5** SE5 ...64 A4
Birdsfield La **1** E3 ...26 B4
Bird St W1 ...103 C2
Birkbeck Ave W3 ...28 B2
Birkbeck Coll W1 ...105 B2
Birkbeck Ct W3 ...28 C1
Birkbeck Gr W3 ...37 C4
Birkbeck Hill SE21 ...75 A3
Birkbeck Mews **5**
  E8 ...16 B3
Birkbeck Pl SE21 ...75 B2
Birkbeck Rd
  London E8 ...16 B3
  London W3 ...28 C1
  London E17 ...25 A2
Birkdale Cl **10** SE16 ...40 A1

Birkenhead Ho **1**
  N7 ...14 C3
Birkenhead St WC1 ...94 B4
Birkwood Cl SW12 ...73 C4
Birley Lo NW8 ...79 C2
Birley St SW11 ...169 B1
Birnam W4 N4 ...5 B2
Birrell Ho SW9 ...172 C1
Birse Cres NW10 ...8 A4
Birtwhistle Ho **5**
  E3 ...26 B4
Biscay Ho **11** E1 ...25 C1
Biscay Rd W6 ...39 C1
Biscott Ho **3** E3 ...27 A1
Bisham Gdns N6 ...3 C3
Bishop Challoner
  Collegiate Sch
  E1 ...32 B3
Bishop Ct **2** SW2 ...62 C1
Bishop Duppa's
  Almshouses **7**
  TW10 ...54 A2
Bishopgate **8**
  W14 ...140 B3
Bishop's Ave The SW6 ...164 A2
Bishop's Bridge Rd
  W2 ...100 C2
Bishops Cl N19 ...4 B1
Bishops Cl W4 ...37 B1
Bishop's Ct EC4 ...108 A2
  WC2 ...107 B2
Bishops Ct W2 ...100 B2
Bishopsgate Ho **8**
  NW6 ...23 C4
Bishopsgate EC2 ...110 A2
Bishopsgate Arcade
  E1 ...110 B3
Bishopsgate Church Yd
  EC2 ...110 A2
Bishops Ho SW8 ...162 B1
Bishop's Mans SW6 ...47 C1
Bishops Mead SE5 ...48 B3
Bishop's Park Rd
  SW6 ...47 C1
Bishops Rd SW11 ...164 B1
Bishop St N1 ...86 C4
Bishop's Terr SE11 ...149 C4
Bishopstone Ho
  SW6 ...166 B2
Bishop's Way E2 ...25 B3
Bishopswood Rd N6 ...3 B4
Bishop Wilfred Wood Cl
  SE15 ...49 C1
Bisley Ho SW19 ...69 C2
Bissextile Ho SE13 ...52 A1
Bisson Rd E15 ...27 B3
Bittern Ct **8** SE8 ...51 C4
Bittern Ho SE1 ...136 C3
Bittern St SE1 ...136 C3
Blackall St EC2 ...98 A2
Blackburne's Mews
  W1 ...117 B3
Blackburn Rd NW6 ...11 A2
Blackdown Ho E8 ...16 C4
Blackett St SW15 ...57 C4
Blackfriars Bridge
  EC4 ...122 A3
Blackfriars Ct EC4 ...122 A4
Black Friars La
  EC4 ...108 A1

Blackfriars Pas
  EC4 ...122 A4
Blackfriars Pier
  EC4 ...122 A4
Blackfriars Rd SE1 ...122 A2
Blackfriars Sta
  EC4 ...122 A4
Blackfriars Underpass
  EC4 ...121 C4
Blackheath Ave SE3 ...53 A3
Blackheath Bsns Est
  SE3 ...53 B2
Blackheath Gr SE3 ...53 B1
Blackheath High Sch
  SE3 ...53 B3
Blackheath High Sch
  (Girls) SE3 ...53 B1
Blackheath High Sch
  GPDST (Jun Dept)
  SE3 ...53 B1
Blackheath Hill
  SE10 ...52 B2
Blackheath Rd SE10 ...52 A2
Blackheath Rise
  SE13 ...52 B1
Blackheath Vale
  SE3 ...53 A1
Blackheath Village
  SE3 ...53 B1
Black Horse Ct
  SE1 ...137 C2
Blackhorse Rd SE8 ...51 A4
Blacklands Terr
  SW3 ...145 A3
Black Lion La **4** W6 ...38 C2
Black Lion Mews **4**
  W6 ...38 C2
Blackmore Ho N1 ...85 A3
  2 London SW18 ...59 A2
Blackmore Twr **1**
  W3 ...37 B3
Blackpool Rd SE15 ...50 A1
Black Prince Rd
  SE1,SE11 ...149 A3
Black Roof Ho **5**
  SE5 ...48 A2
Black's Rd **6** W6 ...39 B2
Blackstock Ho N5 ...6 A2
Blackstock Mews N4 ...6 A1
Blackstock Rd N4,N5 ...6 A2
Blackstone Ho
  SW1 ...146 C1
  Dulwich SE21 ...76 A1
Blackstone Rd NW2 ...9 B4
Black Swan Yd
  SE1 ...138 A4
Blackthorn Ct
  10 SE15 ...49 B3
  4 London E16 ...19 C4
Blackthorn St E3 ...26 C1
Blacktree Mews **12**
  SW9 ...62 C4
Blackwall Sta E14 ...34 B2
Blackwall Trad Est
  E14 ...34 C4
Blackwall Tunnel
  E14,SE10 ...43 C4
Blackwall Tunnel App
  SE10 ...43 C4
Blackwall Tunnel
  Northern Approach
  E14,E3 ...27 B1
Blackwall Way E14 ...34 B2
Blackwater Ho
  NW8 ...101 C4
Blackwater St SE22 ...64 B2

Blackwell Cl **10** E5 ...17 C4
Blackwell Ho **3**
  SW4 ...61 C1
Blackwood Ho **1**
  E1 ...25 A1
Blackwood St
  SE17 ...151 B2
Blade Ho SW15 ...58 B3
Bladen Ho **4** E1 ...32 C3
Blades Ct SW15 ...58 B3
Blades Ho SE11 ...163 B3
Blades Lo **3** SW2 ...62 C1
Blagdon Rd SE13 ...67 A1
Blagrove Rd **1** W10 ...31 B4
Blair Cl N1 ...15 B2
Blair Ct NW8 ...79 B4
Blairderry Rd SW2 ...74 A2
Blair Ho SW9 ...172 C2
Blair St E14 ...34 C3
Blake Ct **8** SE16 ...40 A1
  London NW6 ...23 C2
Blake Gdns SW6 ...166 A4
Blake Ho **4** SE1 ...135 B2
  2 SE8 ...51 C4
  London N16 ...16 A4
  1 London N19 ...13 C4
Blake Mews **14** TW9 ...44 C2
Blakemore Rd
  SW16 ...74 A1
Blakeney Cl **4**
  E8 ...16 C3
Blaker Rd E15 ...27 B4
Blakes Cl W10 ...30 B4
Blake's Rd SE15 ...49 A3
Blanca Ho **8** N1 ...24 A3
Blanchard Way E8 ...16 C2
Blanch Cl SE15 ...50 B3
Blanchedowne SE5 ...63 C3
Blanche Ho NW8 ...90 A1
Blandfield Rd SW12 ...72 C4
Blandford Ct
  London N1 ...16 A1
  2 London NW6 ...10 A1
Blandford Ho SW8 ...162 C2
Blandford Rd W4 ...38 A3
Blandford Sq NW1 ...90 B1
Blandford St W1 ...103 B3
Bland Ho SE11 ...149 A2
Blantyre St SW10 ...157 B2
Blantyre Twr
  SW10 ...157 B2
Blantyre Wlk
  SW10 ...157 B2
Blashford St SE13 ...67 C1
Blasker Wlk E14 ...42 A1
Blaxland Ho **12** W12 ...30 A2
Blechynden Ho **17**
  W10 ...30 C3
Blechynden St W10 ...30 C2
Bleeding Heart Yd
  EC1 ...107 C3
Blemundsbury
  WC1 ...106 C4
Blendworth Point **1**
  SW15 ...69 A3
Blenheim **20** SW19 ...69 C3
Blenheim Cres
  W11 ...31 A3 112 B4
Blenheim Ct
  17 SE16 ...32 C1
  London N19 ...5 A2
  London N7 ...14 A2
  Richmond TW9 ...54 B4
Blenheim Gdns
  London NW2 ...9 B3

Blenheim Gdns continued
  London SW2 ...62 B1
Blenheim Gr SE15 ...49 C1
Blenheim Pas NW8 ...78 C2
Blenheim Rd NW8 ...78 C2
  London W4 ...38 A3
Blenheim Rd NW8 ...104 A1
Blenheim Terr NW8 ...78 C2
Blenkarne Rd SW11 ...60 B1
Blessed John Roche RC
  Sch The E14 ...33 C3
Blessed Sacrament RC
  Prim Sch N1 ...84 C3
Blessington Cl SE13 ...67 C4
Blessington Rd
  SE13 ...67 C3
Bletchley Ct N1 ...87 B1
Bletchley St N1 ...87 A1
Bletsoe Wlk N1 ...87 A2
Blick Ho **1** SE16 ...40 B3
Blincoe Cl SW19 ...69 C2
Blissett St SE10 ...52 B2
Blisworth Ho **2** E2 ...24 C4
Blithfield St W8 ...128 A1
Bloemfontein Ave
  W12 ...30 A1
Bloemfontein Rd
  W12 ...30 A2
Blomfield Ct SW11 ...167 C4
  W9 ...89 A2
Blomfield Mans
  W12 ...30 B1
Blomfield Rd W9 ...100 C4
Blomfield St EC2 ...109 C3
Blomfield Villas
  W9 ...100 C4
Blondel St SW11 ...169 B2
Blondin St E3 ...26 C3
Bloomburg St
  SW1 ...147 A3
Bloomfield Ho E1 ...111 B3
Bloomfield Pl W1 ...118 B4
Bloomfield Terr
  SW1 ...145 C2
Bloom Gr SE27 ...75 A1
Bloom Park Rd
  SW6 ...154 C2
Bloomsbury Ct
  WC1 ...106 B3
Bloomsbury Ho **10**
  SW4 ...61 C1
Bloomsbury Pl
  WC1 ...106 B3
  London SW18 ...59 B2
Bloomsbury Sq
  WC1 ...106 B3
Bloomsbury St
  WC1 ...105 C3
Bloomsbury Way
  WC1 ...106 B3
Blore Cl SW8 ...171 B3
Blore Ct W1 ...119 B4
Blossom Cl W5 ...36 A4
Blossom Pas SW8 ...98 B1
Blossom St
  E1 ...24 A1 98 B1
Blount St E14 ...33 A3
Blucher Rd SE5 ...48 B3
Blue Anchor Alley **4**
  TW9 ...54 A3
Blue Anchor La
  SE16 ...40 A2
Blue Ball Yd SW1 ...118 C1
Bluebell Cl **10** E9 ...25 B4

Blue Gate Fields Jun & Inf Schs E1 ... 32 B2
Bluegate Mews E1 ... 32 A2
Blundell St N7 ... 14 A2
Blurton Rd E5 ... 17 C4
Blyth Cl E14 ... 42 C2
Blythe SE11 ... 163 C4
Blythe Mews **2** W14 ... 39 C3
Blythendale Ho **31** E9 ... 24 C3
Blythe Rd W14 ... 126 A1
Blythe St E2 ... 25 A2
Blyth's Wharf E14 ... 33 A2
Blythwood Rd N4 ... 5 A4
Boadicea St N1 ... 84 C3
Boadoak Ho NW6 ... 78 B3
Boardwalk Pl E14 ... 34 B1
Boarley Ho **2** SE17 ... 152 A3
Boathouse Ctr The W10 ... 22 C2
Boat Lifter Way **18** SE16 ... 41 A2
Bobbin Cl SW4 ... 61 B4
Bobington Ct WC1 ... 106 B4
Bob Marley Way **11** SE24 ... 62 C3
Bocking St E8 ... 25 A4
Boddicott Cl SW19 ... 70 A2
Boddington Ho SE14 ... 50 B2
Bodeney Ho **10** SE5 ... 49 A2
Boden Ho E1 ... 111 B4
Bodington Ct **7** W12 ... 39 C4
Bodley Manor Way SE24 ... 74 C4
Bodmin St SW18 ... 70 C3
Bodney Mans **14** E8 ... 17 A3
Bodney Rd E5,E8 ... 17 A3
Bohemia Pl **1** E8 ... 18 A2
Bohn Rd E1 ... 33 A4
Boileau Rd SW13 ... 47 A4
Boilerhouse SE1 ... 124 C1
Boisseau Ho **27** E1 ... 32 B4
Bolden St SE8 ... 52 A1
Boldero Pl NW8 ... 90 A1
Boleyn Rd N16 ... 16 A3
Bolina Rd SE16 ... 40 B1
Bolingbroke SW11 ... 60 B1
Bolingbroke Hospl The SW11 ... 60 A2
Bolingbroke Rd W14 ... 39 C3
Bolingbroke Wlk SW11 ... 168 A4
Bollo Bridge Rd W3 ... 37 A4
Bollo Ct **2** W3 ... 37 B3
Bollo La W3 ... 37 A3
Bolney Gate SW7 ... 130 A3
Bolney St SW8 ... 162 C1
Bolsover St W1 ... 92 B1
Bolt Ct EC4 ... 107 C1
Bolton Cres SE5 ... 48 A3
Bolton Ct SW11 ... 169 C3
Bolton Gdns NW10 ... 22 C3
 London NW10 ... 22 C3
Bolton Gdns Mews SW10 ... 142 B2
Bolton Ho **4** SE10 ... 43 A1
Bolton Rd NW8 ... 78 B3
 Chiswick W4 ... 45 B3
 London NW10 ... 21 A4
Bolton St SW1 ... 118 B2
Boltons The SW10 ... 142 C2

Bolton Studios SW10 ... 143 A1
Bolton Wlk N7 ... 5 B2
Bombay St SE16 ... 40 A2
Bomore Rd W11 ... 31 A2 112 A4
Bonar Rd SE15 ... 49 C3
Bonchurch Rd W10 ... 31 A4
Bond Ct EC4 ... 109 B1
Bond Ho **4** NW6 ... 23 B3
Bonding Yard Wlk SE16 ... 41 A3
Bond Street Sta W1 ... 103 C1
Bondway SW8 ... 162 B4
Bonfield Rd SE13 ... 67 B3
Bonham Ho W11 ... 112 C3
Bonham Rd SW2 ... 62 B2
Bonheur Rd W4 ... 37 C4
Bonhill St EC2 ... 97 C1
Bonington Ho N1 ... 84 C1
Bonita Mews SE15 ... 65 C4
Bonner Ho **3** SW15 ... 56 C2
Bonner Prim Sch E2 ... 25 B2
Bonner Rd E2 ... 25 B3
Bonner St E2 ... 25 B3
Bonneville Gdns SW4 ... 61 B1
Bonneville Prim Sch SW4 ... 61 B1
Bonnington Sq SW8 ... 162 C4
Bonny St NW1 ... 13 B1
Bonsor Ho SW8 ... 171 A4
Bonsor St SE5 ... 49 A3
Bonthron Ho SW15 ... 47 B1
Booker Cl **15** E3 ... 33 B4
Boord St SE10 ... 43 A3
Boothby Rd N19 ... 4 C2
Booth Cl **10** E9 ... 25 A4
Booth Ho **2** SW2 ... 74 C4
Booth La EC4 ... 122 C4
Booth's Pl W1 ... 105 A3
Boot St N1 ... 98 A3
Bordon Wlk **5** SW15 ... 68 C4
Boreas Wlk N1 ... 86 B1
Boreham Ave E16 ... 35 C3
Boreman Ho **10** SE10 ... 52 B4
Borland Rd SE15 ... 65 B3
Borneo St SW15 ... 57 B4
Borough High St SE1 ... 123 B1
Borough Mkt* SE1 ... 123 B1
Borough Rd SE1 ... 136 B2
Borough Sq SE1 ... 136 C3
Borough Sta SE1 ... 137 A3
Borrett Cl SE17 ... 150 C1
Borrodaile Rd SW18 ... 59 A1
Borrowdale NW1 ... 92 C3
Borthwick St SE8 ... 41 C1
Boscastle Rd NW5 ... 4 A1
Boscobel Ho **4** E8 ... 17 A2
Boscobel Pl SW1 ... 145 C4
Boscobel St NW8 ... 89 C1
Boscombe Cl E5 ... 18 A3
Boscombe Rd W12 ... 38 C4
Boss Ho SE1 ... 138 C4
Boss St SE1 ... 138 C4
Boston Gdns W4 ... 46 A4
Boston Ho NW1 ... 90 C2
 SW5 ... 142 B3
 2 London SE5 ... 48 B1
Boston Pl NW1 ... 90 C1

Bosun Cl **8** E14 ... 41 C4
Boswell Ct WC1 ... 106 B4
 3 London W14 ... 39 C3
Boswell Ho WC1 ... 106 B4
Boswell St WC1 ... 106 B4
Bosworth Ho **4** W10 ... 23 A1
Bosworth Rd W10 ... 23 A1
Botha Rd E13 ... 35 B4
Bothwell Cl E16 ... 35 B2
Bothwell St **4** W6 ... 47 C4
Botolph Alley EC3 ... 124 A4
Botolph La EC3 ... 124 A4
Bott's Mews W2 ... 31 C3
Boughton Ho SE1 ... 137 B4
Boulcott St E1 ... 32 C3
Boulevard The **4** SW17 ... 72 C2
Boulogne Ho SE1 ... 138 C2
Boulter Ho SE14 ... 50 B2
Boulton Ho **9** TW8 ... 36 A1
Boundaries Mans **3** SW12 ... 72 C3
Boundaries Rd SW12 ... 72 C3
 Balham SW12 ... 73 A4
Boundary La SE17 ... 48 B4
Boundary Pas E2 ... 98 C2
Boundary Rd NW8 ... 79 A4
Boundary Road Est NW8 ... 78 C3
Boundary Row SE1 ... 136 A4
Boundary St E2 ... 24 B1 98 C2
Bourchier St W1 ... 119 B4
Bourdon Pl W1 ... 118 B4
Bourdon St W1 ... 118 B3
Bourke Cl London NW4 ... 62 A1
 London NW10 ... 8 A2
Bourlet Cl W1 ... 104 C3
Bourne Ho **5** SW4 ... 61 B3
Bournemouth Cl SE15 ... 49 C1
Bournemouth Rd SE15 ... 49 C1
Bourne Pl W4 ... 37 C1
Bourne St SW1 ... 145 B3
Bourne Terr W2 ... 100 B4
Bousfield Prim Sch SW10 ... 142 C2
Boutcher CE Prim Sch SE1 ... 152 C4
Boutflower Rd SW11 ... 60 A3
Bouverie Mews N16 ... 7 A2
Bouverie Pl W2 ... 101 C2
Bouverie Rd N16 ... 7 A2
Bouverie St EC4 ... 107 C1
Bovingdon Cl **1** N19 ... 4 B2
Bovingdon Rd SW6 ... 166 B3
Bowater Cl SW2 ... 62 A1
Bowater Ho EC1 ... 97 B1
Bow Brook The **20** E2 ... 25 C3
Bow Churchyard EC2,EC4 ... 109 A1
Bow Common La E3 ... 33 C4
Bowden Ho **29** E3 ... 27 A2

Bowden St SE11 ... 149 C1
Bowditch SE8 ... 41 B1
Bowen Ct **2** N5 ... 15 A4
Bowen Dr SE21 ... 76 A1
Bowen St E14 ... 34 A3
Bower Ave SE3 ... 53 A3
Bowerdean St SW6 ... 166 A3
Bower Ho SE14 ... 50 C2
Bowerman Ave SE14 ... 51 A4
Bowerman Ct **1** N19 ... 4 C2
Bowes Rd W3 ... 29 A2
Bowfell Rd W6 ... 47 B4
Bowhill Cl SW9 ... 163 C2
Bowie Cl SW4 ... 73 C4
Bow Ind Pk E15 ... 18 C1
Bow La EC2,EC4 ... 109 A1
Bowland Ho N4 ... 6 B4
Bowland Rd SW4 ... 61 C3
Bowland Yd SW1 ... 131 A3
Bowl Ct EC2 ... 24 A1 98 B1
Bowles Rd **1** SE1 ... 49 C4
Bowley Ho SE16 ... 139 B2
Bowling Green Cl SW19 ... 69 A4
Bowling Green Ho SW10 ... 157 B2
Bowling Green La EC1 ... 95 C2
Bowling Green Pl SE1 ... 137 B4
Bowling Green St SE11 ... 163 B4
Bowling Green Wlk N1 ... 98 A4
Bowman Ave E16 ... 35 B2
Bowman Mews E1 ... 125 B4
 Wandsworth SW18 ... 70 B3
Bowman's Mews N7 ... 5 A1
Bowman's Pl N7 ... 5 A1
Bowmore Wlk NW1 ... 13 C1
Bowness Cl **6** E8 ... 16 B2
Bowness Ho SE15 ... 50 B3
Bowood Rd SW11 ... 60 C2
Bow Rd E3 ... 26 C2
Bow Road Sta E3 ... 26 C2
Bowry Ho **14** E14 ... 33 B4
Bowsprit Point **5** E14 ... 41 C3
Bow St WC2 ... 106 B1
Bowstead Ct SW11 ... 167 C3
Bow Triangle Bsns Ctr **2** E3 ... 26 C2
Bowyer Ho **22** N1 ... 24 A4
 Wandsworth SW18 ... 59 A1
Bowyer Pl SE5 ... 48 B3
Bowyer St **15** SE5 ... 48 B3
Boxall Rd SE21 ... 64 A4
Boxley Ho **5** E5 ... 17 A3
Boxmoor Ho **16** E2 ... 24 C4
 9 London W11 ... 30 C1
Box Tree Ho SE8 ... 41 A1
Boxworth Gr N1 ... 85 A4
Boyce Ho **1** W10 ... 23 B2
Boyce St SE1 ... 121 B1
Boyd Ct SW15 ... 57 B1
Boydell Ct NW8 ... 11 C1
Boyd St E1 ... 111 C1
Boyfield St SE1 ... 136 B3
Boyle St W1 ... 118 C4
Boyne Ct NW10 ... 8 C1
Boyne Rd SE13 ... 67 C4
Boyne Terr Mews W11 ... 31 B1 112 C2

Boyson Rd **10** SE17 ... 48 C4
Boyton Cl E1 ... 25 C1
Boyton Ho NW8 ... 79 C2
 SE11 ... 149 B1
Brabazon St E14 ... 34 A4
Brabner Ho **2** E2 ... 99 B4
Brabourn Gr SE15 ... 50 B1
Bracer Ho **1** N1 ... 24 A3
Bracewell Rd W10 ... 30 B4
Bracey St N4 ... 5 A2
Bracken Ave SW12 ... 72 C4
Brackenbury N4 ... 5 B3
Brackenbury Gdns W6 ... 39 A3
Brackenbury Prim Sch W6 ... 39 A2
Brackenbury Rd W6 ... 39 A3
Bracken Gdns SW13 ... 46 C1
Bracken Ho **14** E3 ... 33 C4
Brackley Ct NW8 ... 89 C2
Brackley Rd W4 ... 38 A1
Brackley St EC1 ... 109 A4
Brackley Terr **6** W4 ... 38 A1
Bracklyn Ct N1 ... 87 B2
Bracklyn St N1 ... 87 B2
Bracknell Gate NW3 ... 11 A3
Bracknell Gdns NW3 ... 11 A4
Bracknell Way NW3 ... 11 A4
Bradbeer Ho **27** E2 ... 25 B2
Bradbourne St SW6 ... 165 C2
Bradbury Ct **3** SE3 ... 53 C3
Bradbury Ho E1 ... 111 A2
Bradbury St **28** N16 ... 16 A3
Bradby Ho NW8 ... 78 B1
Braddon Rd TW9 ... 54 B4
Braddyll St SE10 ... 43 A1
Bradenham **13** SE17 ... 48 C4
Bradenham Cl SE17 ... 48 C4
Braden St W9 ... 88 A1
Bradfield Ct **14** NW1 ... 13 A1
Bradfield Rd E16 ... 35 C1
Bradgate Rd SE6 ... 67 A1
Brading Rd SW2 ... 74 B4
Brading Terr W12 ... 38 C3
Bradiston Rd W9 ... 23 B2
Bradley Cl N7 ... 14 B2
Bradley Ho **6** E3 ... 26 C2
 3 E3 ... 27 A2
 SE16 ... 40 A2
Bradley Mews SW12 ... 72 B3
Bradley's Cl N1 ... 85 C2
Bradlord Rd SE21 ... 76 A1
Bradmead SW8 ... 160 C1
Bradmore Park Rd W6 ... 39 A2
Brad St SE1 ... 121 C1
Bradstock Ho E9 ... 18 A1
Bradstock Rd E9 ... 17 C2
Bradwell Ho NW6 ... 78 A3
Brady Ho SW8 ... 171 A4
 London SW4 ... 61 C3
Brady St E1 ... 25 A1
Braefoot Ct SW15 ... 57 C2
Braemar Ave SW18,SW19 ... 70 C2

Braemar Ho W9 ......88 C3
Braemar Mans W8 **128** B1
Braemore Ho **21**
SE15 ......49 C3
Braganza St SE17 **150** A1
Braham St E1 ......**111** A2
Brahma Kumaris World
Spiritual Univ NW10 ..8 C2
Braid Ave W3 ......29 A3
Braid Ho SE2 ......52 B2
Braidwood St SE1 ..**124** A1
Brailsford Rd SW2 ..62 C1
Braintree Ho **5** E1 ..25 B1
Braintree St E2 ......25 B2
Braithwaite Ho EC1 ..97 B2
14 South Bromley
E14 ......34 C3
Braithwaite Twr
W2 ......**101** B4
Bramah Gn SW9 ..**173** C4
Bramall Ct N7 ......14 B2
Bramber WC1 ......94 A3
Bramber Ct TW8 ......36 A2
Bramber Rd W14 ..**154** C4
Brambledown **4** N4 ..5 A4
Bramcote Gr SE16 ..40 B1
Bramcote Rd SW15 ..57 A3
Bramerton NW6 ......9 C1
Bramerton St SW3 ..158 A4
Bramfield Ct N4 ......6 B2
Bramfield Rd SW11 ..60 B2
Bramford Rd SW18 ..59 B3
Bramham Gdns
SW5 ......**142** B2
Bramham Ho SE22 ..64 A3
Bramlands Cl SW11 ..60 A4
Bramley Cres SW8 ..**161** C2
Bramley Ho
10 London W10 ......30 C3
5 Roehampton
SW15 ......56 B1
Bramley Rd W10 ..30 C3
Bramshaw Rd E9 ..17 C2
Bramshill Gdns NW5 ..4 A1
Bramshill Rd NW10 ..21 B3
Bramshurst NW8 ..**78** B3
Bramston Rd
London NW10 ......21 C3
Wandsworth SW17 ..71 B1
Bramwell Ho SE1 ..**137** A1
SW1 ......**160** C4
Bramwell Mews N1 ..85 A4
Brancaster Ho
22 E1 ......25 C2
Brancaster Rd
SW16 ......74 A1
Branch Hill NW3 ......2 B1
Branch Pl N1 ......87 C4
Branch Rd E14 ......33 A2
Branch St SE15 ......49 A3
Brand Cl N4 ......6 A3
Brandlehow Rd
SW15 ......58 B3
Brandon Mews
EC2 ......**109** B4
Brandon Rd N7 ......14 A1
Brandon St SE17 ..**151** A3

Brandrams Wharf
SE16 ......40 B4
Brandreth Rd SW17 ..73 A2
Brandon St SE10 ......52 B3
Brangton Rd SE11 ..**149** A1
Brankway St SW6 ..**154** A1
Branksome Ho
SW8 ......**162** C2
Branksome Rd SW2 ..62 A2
Bransby Ct **4** N16 ..16 A4
Branscombe NW1 ..83 A3
Branscombe St
SE13 ......67 A4
Bransdale Cl NW6 ..23 C4
Branstone Ct **9**
TW9 ......44 B2
Branstone Rd TW9 ..44 B2
Branston Ho N7 ......14 C3
Brantwood Ho **5**
SE5 ......48 B3
Brantwood Rd SE24 ..63 B2
Brasenose Dr SW13 ..47 B4
Brassey Ho **1** E14 ..42 A2
Brassey Rd NW6 ......10 B2
Brassey Sq SW11 ..60 C4
Brassie Ave W3 ......29 A3
Brass Talley Alley **51**
SE16 ......40 C4
Brathay NW1 ......83 A1
Brathway Rd SW18 ..70 C4
Bratley St E1 ......99 B1
Bravington Pl W9 ..23 B1
Bravington Rd W9 ..23 B2
Brawne Ho **12** SE17 ..48 A4
Braxfield Rd SE4 ......66 B3
Bray NW3 ......12 A1
Brayard's Rd SE15 ..50 A1
Braybrook St W12 ..29 B3
Brayburne Ave
SW4 ......**171** A1
Bray Cres SE16 ..40 C4
Braydon Rd N16 ......7 C3
Bray Dr E16 ......35 B2
Brayfield Terr N1 ..14 C1
Brayford Sq **12** E14 ..32 B3
Bray Pl SW3 ......**144** C3
Bread St EC2,EC4 ..**109** A1
Breakspeare SE21 ..76 B1
Breakspears Mews
SE4 ......51 C1
Breakspears Rd SE4 ..66 C4
Breakwell Ct **16**
W10 ......23 A1
Breamore Cl SW15 ..68 C3
Bream's Bldgs EC4 ..**107** B2
Bream St E3 ......18 C1
Breasley Cl SW15 ..57 A3
Brechin Pl SW7 ..**143** A3
Brecknock Prim Sch
NW1 ......13 C2
Brecknock Rd N19 ..13 C3
Brecon Ho **2** N16 ..7 A3
London N19 ......7 B3
Wandsworth SW18 ..70 C4
Brecon Rd W6 ......**154** B3
Bredel Ho **1** E14 ..33 C4
Bredgar SE13 ......67 A2
Bredgar Rd N19 ......4 B2
Bredhurst Rd SW15 ..57 C4
Bredinghurst SE22 ..76 C4
Bredinghurst Sch
SE15 ......65 C3
Breer St SW6 ......59 A4
Breezer's Ct **1**
E1 ......**125** C3
Breezer's Hill **1**
E1 ......**125** C3
Bremans Row SW18 ..71 B2
Bremner Rd SW7 ..**129** A2

Brenchley Gdns
SE15,SE22,SE23 ......65 C1
Brenda Rd SW17 ......72 B2
Brendon Ave NW10 ..8 A4
Brendon Ho W1 ......**103** B4
Brendon St W1 ......**102** B2
Brenley Ho SE1 ..**137** B4
Brent Ct **5** W12 ......38 A3
Brentford Fountain
Leisure Centre W4 ..36 C1
Brenthouse Rd E9 ..17 B2
Brenthouse Rd E9 ..17 B2
Brenthurst Rd NW10 ..8 B2
Brent New Ent Ctr
NW10 ......8 B2
Brenton Ct E9 ......18 A3
Brenton St E14 ......33 A3
Brent Rd E16 ......35 C4
Brent Trad Est NW10 ..8 A3
Brentwick Gdns
TW8 ......36 A2
Brereton Ho **2**
SW2 ......74 C4
Bressenden Pl
SW1 ......**132** C2
Breton Ho EC2 ......97 A1
Breton St SW8 ......**138** C2
Bretton Cl N16 ......7 C4
Brett Cl N16 ......7 A3
Brett Cres NW10 ..20 C4
Brettell St SE17 ..**151** C1
Brett Ho **1** SW15 ..69 C4
Brett House Cl **2**
SW15 ......69 C4
Brettinghurst SE1 ..**153** B1
Brett Manor E8 ......17 A3
Brett Pas **28** E8 ......17 A3
Brett Rd E8 ......17 A3
Brewers Bldgs EC1 ..96 A4
Brewer's Gn SW1 ..**133** B2
Brewer St W1 ......**119** A4
Brewery Ind Est The
N1 ......86 C2
Brewery Rd EC2 ......**100** C2
Brewery Sq SE1 ..**124** C1
Brewhouse La E1 ..32 A1
Brewhouse La
Putney SW15 ......58 A4
Brewhouse St
SW15 ......58 A4
Brewhouse Wlk
SE16 ......33 A1
Brewhouse Yd EC1 ..96 A2
Brewster Gdns W10 ..30 B4
Brewster Ho E14 ..33 B2
SE1 ......**153** A4
Briant Ho SE1 ......**135** A1
Briant St SE14 ......50 C2
Briar Ct E8 ......16 B1
Briardale SW19 ......70 B3
Briardale Gdns NW3 ..1 C1
Briarbank Ho N16 ..7 A3
Briar Rd NW2 ......9 B4
Briar Wlk W10 ......23 A1
Putney SW15 ......57 A3
Briarwood Rd SW4 ..61 C2
Briarwood Rd E11 ..**82** C3
Briary Cl NW3 ......12 A1
Brickbarn Cl SW10 ..**157** A2
Brick Ct EC4 ......**107** B1
Brick Farm Cl TW9 ..45 A2
Bricklayers Arms
SE1 ......**137** C1
Brick St W1 ......**118** A1
Brickworth Ho **5**
SW2 ......**62** C2
Bridal Mews N1 ......85 B4
Brideale Cl SE15 ......49 B4

Bride Ct EC4 ......**108** A1
Bride La EC4 ......**108** A1
Bride St N7 ......14 B2
Bridewain St SE1 ..**138** C2
Bridewell Pl **20** E1 ..32 A1
EC4 ......**108** A1
Bridford Mews W1 ..**104** B4
Bridge App NW3 ......12 C1
Bridge Ave W6 ......39 B1
Bridge Avenue Mans **1**
W6 ......39 B1
Bridge Cl **1** W10 ..30 C3
Bridge Field Ho
W2 ......**100** A2
Bridgefoot SE1 ......**148** B1
Bridge Ho London SE7 ..12 A1
1 London NW1 ..12 C1
London SE4 ......66 B3
Bridge House Quay
E14 ......34 B1
Bridge La SW11 ..**168** B3
Bridgeland Rd E16 ..35 C2
Bridgeman Ho **19**
E9 ......17 B1
Bridgeman Rd N1 ..14 B1
Bridgeman St NW8 ..**80** A1
Bridge Meadows
SE14 ......50 C4
Bridgend Rd SW18 ..59 B3
Bridgen Ho **15** E1 ..32 A3
Bridge Pk **2** SW11 ..60 A4
Bridge Pl SW1 ......**146** B4
Bridgeport Pl **1** ..**125** C2
Bridge Rd E15 ......**27** C4
London NW10 ......8 A2
London SW1 ......**167** B1
Bridges Ct SW11 ..**167** B1
Bridges Ho SE5 ......48 C3
Bridge St SW1 ......**134** B3
London W4 ......37 C2
Bridge Terr E15 ......19 C1
Bridgeview **2** W6 ..39 B1
Bridgewater Rd E15 ..**27** B4
Bridgewater Sq
EC2 ......**108** C4
Bridgewater St
EC2 ......**108** C4
Bridgeway St NW1 ..83 A1
Bridge Wharf **17** E2 ..25 C3
Bridge Yd SE1 ......**123** C2
Bridgford St
SW18 ......71 B1
Bridgman Rd W4 ..37 B3
Bridgnorth Ho **10**
SE15 ......49 C4
Bridgwater Ho W2 ..**100** C2
Bridle La W1 ......**119** A4
Bridlington Ho
N1 ......89 B3
Bridport SE17 ......**151** A1
Bridport Ho N1 ......87 C3
Bridport Pl N1 ......87 C3
Bridstow Pl **2** W2 ..31 C3
Brief St SE5 ......48 A2
Brierfield NW1 ......82 C3
Brierley Rd
London E11 ......19 C4
Upper Tooting SW12 ..73 B2
Brierly Gdns E2 ......25 B3
Brigade St SE3 ......53 B1
Briggeford Cl **5** E5 ..7 C2
Briggs Ho **2** 99 A4
Brightfield Rd SE4 ..66 B1
Brightlingsea Pl **5**
E14 ......33 B2
Brightman Rd SW18 ..71 C3
Brighton Bldgs
SE1 ......**138** A1

Brighton Ct SW15 ..58 B1
Brighton Gr SE14 ..51 A2
Brighton Ho **7** SE5 ..48 C2
Brighton Rd N16 ......16 A4
Brighton Terr SW9 ..62 B3
Brightside Rd SE13 ..67 C1
Bright St E14 ......34 A4
Brightwells Rd N7 ..14 B3
Brightwells **5** **166** A2
Brig Mews SE8 ......51 C4
Brigstock Ho SE5 ..48 B1
Brill Pl NW1 ......83 C1
Brimsdown Ho E3 ..27 B1
Brindley Ho
7 London W2 ......31 C4
3 Streatham SW12 ..74 A4
Brindley St SE14 ......51 B2
Brinc Ho **10** E3 ......26 A3
Brinklow Ho W2 ......**100** A3
Brinkworth Way E9 ..18 B2
Brinsley Ho **3** E1 ..32 B3
Brinsley St E1 ......32 A3
Brinsley St **21** E1 ..32 A3
Brion Wlk SE1 ......**122** A1
Brion Pl E14 ......34 B4
Brisbane Ho **3**
W12 ......30 A2
Brisbane St SE5 ......48 C3
Briset Rd SE9 ......53 B4
Briset St EC1 ......96 A1
Briset Way N7 ......5 B2
Bristol Gdns W9 ......88 B1
Bristol Ho SE11 ......**135** B1
SE11 ......**135** B1
Britannia Cl SW4 ......61 C3
Britannia Gate **12**
E16 ......35 C1
Britannia Junc NW1 ..82 B4
Britannia Rd **11** E14 ..41 C2
SW6 ......**156** A1
Britannia Row N1 ..86 C4
Britannia St WC1 ..94 C4
Britannia Way
NW10 ......20 A1
Britannia Wlk N1 ..97 B4
British Gr W4 ......38 B1
British Grove Pas **2**
W4 ......38 B1
British Grove S **3**
W4 ......38 B1
British Library The *
WC1 ......93 C4
British Mus* WC1 ..**106** A3
British St E3 ......26 B2
British Wharf Ind Est
SE14 ......50 C4
Britley Ho **10** E14 ..33 B3
Brittany Ho SW15 ..57 B3
Brittany Point
SE11 ......**149** B3
Britten Cl NW11 ......2 A3
Britten Ho SW3 ..**144** B2
Britten St SW3 ......**144** B2
Britton St EC1 ......96 A1
Brixton Day Coll
SW9 ......**62** A4
Brixton Hill SW2 ..**62** A1
Brixton Hill Ct **5**
SW2 ......**62** B2
Brixton Hill Pl SW2 ..74 A4
Brixton Mkt SW9 ..**62** C3
Brixton Oval **7**
SW2 ......**62** C3
Brixton Rd SW9 ..**173** B2
Brixton Sta SW9 ..**62** C4
Brixton Station Rd
SW9 ......**62** C4
Brixton Water La
SW2 ......**62** B2

Broadbent Cl N6 ....4 A3
Broadbent St W1 ....118 A4
Broad Bridge Cl
SE3 ....53 C3
Broad Common Est
N16 ....7 C3
Broad Ct WC2 ....106 B1
Broadfield NW6 ....11 A3
Broadfield La NW1 ....14 A1
Broadfields Way
NW10 ....8 B3
Broadford Ho ⊞ E1 ..26 A2
Broadgate EC2 ....110 A4
Broadgate Circ
EC2 ....110 A3
Broadgates Ct
SE11 ....149 C1
Broadgates Rd
SW18 ....71 C3
Broadhinton Rd
SW4 ....61 B4
Broadhurst Cl
London NW6 ....11 B2
⑨ Richmond TW10 ..54 B2
Broadhurst Gdns
NW6 ....11 A2
Broadhurst Mans
NW6 ....11 A3
Broad La EC2 ....110 A4
Broadlands N6 ....3 C4
Broadlands Ave
SW16 ....74 A2
Broadlands Cl
London N6 ....3 C4
Streatham SW16 ......74 A2
Broadlands Ct TW9 ..44 C3
Broadlands Lo N6 .....3 B4
Broadlands Mans ⑫
SW16 ....74 A2
Broadlands Rd N6 .....3 B4
Broadley St NW8 ....102 A4
Broadley Terr NW1 ..90 B1
Broadmayne SE17 ...151 B2
Broadmead SE6 ....54 A1
Broadmead ⑭
SW9 ....62 C4
Broadoak Ho NW6 ...78 B3
Broad Sanctuary
SW1 ....134 A3
Broad St Ave EC2 ...110 A3
Broadstone Ho
SW8 ....162 C1
Broadstone Pl W1 ..103 B3
Broad St Pl EC2 ......109 C3
Broadwalk Ho
SW7 ....128 C3
Broadwalk La NW11 ..1 B4
Broadwall SE1 ....121 C2
Broadway SW1 ....133 B2
London E15 ....19 C1
Broadway Arc ⑧
W6 ....39 B2
Broadway Ho ⑳ E8 ..25 A4
Broadway Mans
SW6 ....155 C1
Broadway Market
E8 ....25 A4
Broadway Market Mews
㉑ E8 ....24 C4
Broadway Mews E5 ..7 B4
Broadway The
Barnes SW13 ....46 A1
London W3 ....36 C4
Broadwick St W1 ....105 A1
Broad Wlk NW1 ....81 C1
W1 ....117 B2
Richmond TW9 ....44 B3

Broad Wlk The W8 ..114 B1
Broadwood Terr
W14 ....141 A4
Broad Yd EC1 ....96 A1
Brocas Cl NW3 ....12 A1
Brockbridge Ho ⑪
SW15 ....56 B1
Brocket Ho SW8 .....171 B2
Brockham Dr SW2 ...74 B4
Brockham Ho NW1 ...83 A3
⑤ Streatham SW2 ...74 B4
Brockham St SE1 ....137 A2
Brock Ho WC1 ....105 B4
Brockhurst Ho N4 ......6 C4
Brockill Cres SE4 ......66 A3
Brocklebank Rd
SW18 ....71 B4
Brocklebank Road Ind
Est SE7 ....43 C2
Brocklehurst St
SE14 ....50 C3
Brockley Cross SE4 ..66 B4
Brockley Cross Bsns Ctr
SE4 ....66 A4
Brockley Gdns SE4 ..51 B1
Brockley Gr SE4 ....66 B2
Brockley Hall Rd
SE4 ....66 A2
Brockley Ho SE17 ...152 A2
Brockley Mews SE4 ..66 A2
Brockley Prim Sch
SE4 ....66 B2
Brockley Rd SE4 ......66 B2
Brockley Sta SE4 ......66 A4
Brockley Way SE4 ....66 A2
Brockmer Ho ⑤ E1 ..32 A2
Brock Pl E3 ....27 A1
Brock St SE15 ....65 B4
Brockweir ⑫ E2 ......25 B3
Brockwell Ct ②
SW2 ....62 C2
Brockwell Ho
SE11 ....163 A4
Brockwell Park
SE24 ....63 A1
Brockwell Park Gdns
SE24 ....75 A4
Broderick Ho SE21 ..76 A1
Brodia Rd N16 ....7 A1
Brodick Ho ⑪ E3 .....26 B3
Brodie Ho SE1 ....153 A2
Brodie St SE1 ....153 A2
Brodlove La E1 ....32 C2
Broken Wharf EC4 ..122 C4
Brokesley St E3 ....26 B2
Broke Wlk E8 ....24 B4
Bromar Rd SE5 ....64 A4
Bromehead St ⑧
E1 ....32 B3
Bromell's Rd SW4 ...61 B3
Bromfelde Rd
London E9 ....18 A2
London W4 ....37 C4
Bromfield Ct SE16 ..139 C2
Bromfield St N1 ....85 C2
Bromleigh Ho SE1 ..138 C2
Bromley-by-Bow Sta
E3 ....27 A2
Bromley Cl SE13 ......67 C2
Bromley Hall Rd
E14 ....27 B2
Bromley High St E3 ..27 A2
Bromley Lo ② W3 ...28 B3
Bromley Pl W1 ....104 C4
Bromley St E1 ....32 C3
Brompton WC1 ....106 C3

Brompton Arc
SW1 ....131 A3
Brompton Oratory
SW3 ....130 A1
Brompton Park Cres
SW6 ....156 A3
Brompton Pl SW3 ...130 B2
Brompton Rd SW3 ..130 A1
Brompton Sq SW3 ...130 A2
Bromstone Ho
SW9 ....173 B3
Bromwich Ave N6 .....3 C2
Bromwich Ho ⑧
TW10 ....54 A1
Bromyard Ave W3 ...29 A2
Bromyard Ho ⑧
SE15 ....50 A3
Bron Ct NW6 ....23 C4
Brondesbury Coll for
Boys NW6 ....10 A3
Brondesbury Mews ②
NW6 ....10 C1
Brondesbury Park Sta
NW6 ....23 A4
Brondesbury Pk NW2 9 C1
Brondesbury Rd
NW6 ....23 C3
Brondesbury Sta
NW6 ....10 B1
Brondesbury Villas
NW6 ....23 C3
Bronsart Rd SW6 ....154 A1
Bronte Ct ⑧ W14 .....39 C3
Bronte Ho
⑥ London N16 ....16 A3
London NW6 ....23 C2
Bronti Cl SE17 ....151 A2
Bronwen Ct NW8 .....89 B3
Bronze St SE8 ....51 C3
Brookbank Sd SE13 ..67 A4
Brook Cl SW17 ....72 C2
Brook Ct London E15 56 B4
Brookdale Rd SE6 ....67 A1
Brook Dr SE11 ....150 A4
Brooke Ho ⑤ SE14 ..51 A2
Brookes Ct EC1 ....107 B4
Brookes Mkt EC1 ....107 C4
Brooke's Mkt EC1 ...107 C4
Brooke St EC1 ....107 B3
Brookfield N6 ....3 C1
⑤ London N4 ....5 C2
Brookfield Ho NW5 ..4 A1
Brookfield Prim Sch
N19 ....4 A2
Brookfield Rd
London E9 ....18 A2
London W4 ....37 C4
Brook Gate W1 ....117 A3
Brookgate N16 ....6 C2
Brook Gdns SW13 ....56 B4
Brook Gn ⑨ W6 ....39 C2
Brook Green Flats ⑪
W14 ....39 C3
Brook Ho
⑬ London SW4 ....61 B2
④ London SW4 ....36 C1
④ London W3 ....28 B2
Brook Hos NW1 ....83 A1
Brooklands Ave
SW18 ....71 A2
Brooklands Court
Apartments ⑧
NW6 ....10 B1
Brooklands Ct ⑩
NW6 ....10 B1

Brooklyn Ct W12 ......30 B1
Brookmarsh Ind Est
SE10 ....52 A3
Brook Mews N ② W2 114 C4
Brookmill Rd SE8 .....51 C2
Brooksbank Ho ⑦
E9 ....17 B2
Brooksbank St ⑨
E9 ....17 B2
Brooksby St N1 ....14 C1
Brooksby's Wlk E9 ..17 C3
Brooks Ct SW8 ....161 A2
London SW4 ....172 A2
Brooks Ho ⑥ SW2 ...74 C3
Brookside Rd N19 .....4 B2
Brooks La W4 ....44 C4
Brooks Rd W4 ....36 C1
Brookstone Ct SE15 ..65 A3
Brooksville Ave
NW6 ....23 A4
Brookville Rd SW6 ..154 C1
Brookwood Ave
SW13 ....46 B1
Brookwood Ho
SE1 ....136 B3
Brookwood Rd
SW18 ....70 C3
Broome Ct ⑧ E3 ......26 C3
Broome Ho ⑦ E5 .....17 A3
Broome Way ⑧ SE5 ..48 C3
Broomfield ⑦ NW1 ..12 C1
Broomfield Ho
SE17 ....152 A3
Broomfield House Sch
TW9 ....44 B2
Broomfield Rd TW9 ..44 B2
Broomfield St E14 ....34 A4
Broomgrove Rd
SW9 ....173 A1
Broomhill Rd SW18 ..58 C2
Broomhouse La
SW6 ....58 C4
Broomhouse Rd
SW6 ....165 B1
Broomsleigh St
NW6 ....10 B3
Broomwood Hall Sch
SW12 ....72 C4
Broomwood Rd
SW11 ....60 C2
Brougham Rd E8 ....24 C4
Brougham St
SW11 ....169 A2
Brough Cl SW8 ....162 B1
Brough St SW8 ....162 B1
Broughton Dr ⑳
SW9 ....63 A3
Broughton Rd
SW6 ....166 B2
Broughton Road App
SW6 ....166 A2
Broughton St SW8 ..170 A2
Broughton Street
Arches Ind Area
SW11 ....170 A2
Brouncker Rd W3 .....37 B4
Browne Ho ⑱ SE8 ..51 C3
Brownfield St E14 .....34 B3
Brownflete Ho ⑧ SE4 66 A3
Brown Hart Gdns
W1 ....117 C4
Browning Cl W9 ....89 A1

Browning Ct W14 ....154 C4
Browning Ho
⑩ London N16 ....16 A4
London W12 ....30 B3
Browning Mews
W1 ....103 C3
Browning St SE17 ...151 A3
Brownlow Ho SE16 ..139 B3
Brownlow Mews
WC1 ....95 A1
Brownlow Rd E8 ......24 C4
London NW10 ....8 A1
Brownlow St WC1 ...107 A3
Brownlow St WC1 ...107 A3
Brownlow St WC1 ...102 C2
Browns Bldgs EC3 ..110 B1
Brownswood Rd N4 ..6 B2
Broxash Rd SW11 ....60 C1
Broxbourne Ho ⑪
E3 ....27 A1
Broxholme Ho
SW6 ....166 A4
Broxholm Rd SE27,
SW16 ....74 C1
Broxwood Way
NW8 ....80 B3
Bruce Cl W10 ....30 C4
Bruce Glasier Ho ⑬
N19 ....4 C4
Bruce Ho
④ London SW4 ....61 C1
④ London W10 ....30 C4
⑱ Putney SW15 ....57 A2
Bruce Rd E3 ....27 A2
Bruckner St W10 ......23 B2
Bruges Pl ⑰ NW1 ....13 B1
Brune Ho E1 ....110 C3
Brunei Ho NW10 ......21 C2
Brunel Est W2 ....31 C4
Brunel Ho E14 ....42 A1
SW10 ....157 C2
Brunel Rd SE16 ....32 B1
London W3 ....29 A4
Brunel St E16 ....35 B1
Brunel St E1 ....110 C3
Brunlees Ho ⑨
SE1 ....137 A1
Brunswick Ct EC1 ....96 A3
SE1 ....138 B4
SW1 ....147 C3
Brunswick Gdns
W8 ....31 C1 113 C1
Brunswick Ho ④ ② 24 B3
NW1 ....90 C2
Brunswick Mews
W1 ....103 A3
Brunswick Park Prim
Sch SE5 ....48 C3
Brunswick Pk SE5 ...49 A2
Brunswick Pl N1 ......97 C3
Brunswick Quay
SE16 ....40 C3
Brunswick Rd E14 ...34 B3
Brunswick Sh Ctr
WC1 ....94 B2
Brunswick Sq WC1 ..94 B2
Brunswick Villas ②
SE5 ....49 A2
Brunton Pl E14 ....33 A3
Brushfield St E1 ......110 C4
Brushwood Ho ④
E14 ....34 A4
Brussels Rd SW11 ...59 C3
Bruton La W1 ....118 B3
Bruton Pl W1 ....118 B3

Bruton St W1 ....**118** B3
Bryan Ave NW10 ....9 A1
Bryan Ct W1 ....**102** C2
Bryan Ho SE16 ....41 B4
Bryan Rd SE16 ....41 B4
Bryanston Ct W1 .....**102** C2
Bryanston Ho **11**
SE15 ....49 C3
Bryanston Mans
W1 ....**102** C4
Bryanston Mews E
W1 ....**102** C2
Bryanston Mews W
W1 ....**102** C2
Bryanston Pl W1 ....**102** C2
Bryanston Sq W1 ....**102** C2
Bryanston St W1 .....**103** A1
Bryant Ct E2 ....24 B3
Bryantwood Rd N5,
N7 ....14 C3
Bryce Ho **22** SE14 ....50 C4
Brydale Ho **9** SE16 ...40 C2
Brydges Pl WC2 .....**120** A3
Brydges Rd E15 ....19 C3
Brydon Wlk N1 ....84 C4
Bryer Ct EC2 ....**108** C4
Brydett Rd N7 ....37 B1
Bryher Ho W14 ....37 B1
Brymay Cl E3 ....26 C3
Brymon Ct W1 ......**103** A3
Brynmaer Ho
SW11 ....**169** A3
Brynmaer Rd
SW11 ....**169** A3
Bryony Rd W12 ....29 C2
BT Telecom Twr*
W1 ....**104** C4
Buccleuch Ho E5 ......7 C4
Buchanan Ct **10**
SE16 ....40 C2
Buchanan Gdns
NW10 ....22 A3
Buchanan Ho
Dulwich SE21 ......76 A1
Wandsworth SW18 ..70 C4
Buchan Ho W3 ....37 A4
Buchan Rd SE15 ......65 B4
Bucharest Rd SW18 .71 B4
Buckfast St
E2 ....24 C2 **99** C3
Buck Hill Wlk W2 ...**115** C3
Buckhold Rd SW18 ...58 C1
Buckhurst Ho **6** N7 .13 C3
Buckhurst St E1 ....25 A1
Buckingham Gate
SW1 ....**133** A2
Buckingham Ho
London N4 ....6 B3
Richmond TW10 ....54 C2
Buckingham Mans
NW6 ....11 A3
Buckingham Mews
SW1 ....**132** C2
7 London N1 ......16 A3
London NW10 ......21 B3
Buckingham Palace*
SW1 ....**132** C1
Buckingham Palace Rd
SW1 ....**146** B4
Buckingham Pl
SW1 ....**132** C2
Buckingham Rd
London N1 ....16 A2
London NW10 ......21 B3

Buckingham St
WC2 ....**120** B3
Buckingham Yd
NW10 ....21 B3
Buckland Cres NW3 12 C2
Buckland Ct **6** N1 ..24 A3
Buckland St N1 ....87 C1
Buckland Wlk **2**
W3 ....37 B4
Buckler's Alley
SW6 ....**155** A2
Bucklersbury EC2,
EC4 ....**109** B1
Buckle St E1 ....**111** A2
Buckley Ct **5** NW6 ..10 B1
Buckley St SE1 ......**121** A1
Buckmaster Cl
SE17 ....**150** C2
1 London SW9 ....62 C4
Buckmaster Ho **1**
N7 ....14 B4
Buckmaster Rd
SW11 ....60 A3
Bucknall St WC1 ....**106** A2
Bucknell Cl SW2 .....62 B3
Buckner Rd SW2 .....62 B3
Buckridge Bldg
EC1 ....**107** C3
Buckshead Ho **19**
W2 ....31 C4
Buck St NW1 ....13 A1
Buckstone Cl SE23 ..65 B1
Buckters Rents
SE16 ....33 A1
Buckthorne Rd SE4 ..66 A2
Budge Row EC4 ....**109** B1
Budge's Wlk W2 ....**115** A2
Budleigh Ho **19**
SE15 ....49 C3
Buer Rd SW6 ....**164** C1
Bugsbys Way SE10 ..43 A2
Buick Ho **8** E3 ......26 C1
Bulinca St SW1 .....**147** C3
Bullace Row SE5 .....48 C2
Bullards Pl **8** E2 ....25 C2
Bulleid Way SW1 ...**146** B3
Bullen Ho **13** E1 ....25 A1
Bullen St SW11 .....**168** B2
Buller Cl SE15 ....49 C4
Buller Rd NW10 .....22 C2
Bullfinch Ct **3** SE21 75 C2
Bullingham Mans
W8 ....**127** C4
Bull Inn Ct WC2 ....**120** B3
Bullivant St **8** E14 .34 B2
Bulls Alley SW14 ...**45** C1
Bull's Gdns SW3 ...**144** B4
Bull's Head Pas
EC3 ....**110** A1
Bull Yd SE15 ....49 C2
Bulmer Mews
W11 ....31 C1 **113** B2
Bulow Ct SW6 ......**166** B3
Bulstrode Pl W1 ....**103** C3
Bulstrode St W1 ....**103** C2
Bulwer St W12 ....30 B1
Bunbury Ho SE15 ...49 C3
Bunhill Row EC1 ....**97** B1
Bunhouse Pl SW1 ..**145** C2
Bunkers Hill NW11 ..2 B4
Bunning Ho **7** N7 ..14 A4
Bunning Way N7 ....14 B1
Bunsen Ho **1** E3 ....26 A3
Bunsen St **3** E3 ....26 A3
Bunyan Ct EC2 .....**108** C4

Buonaparte Mews
SW1 ....**147** B2
Burbage Cl SE1 ....**137** B1
Burbage Ho N1 .....**87** C3
16 SE14 ....50 C4
Burbage Rd SE21,
SE24 ....75 C4
Burbage Sch N1 .....24 A3
Burcham St E14 .....34 B3
Burchell Ho SE11 ..**149** A2
Burchell Rd SE15 ...50 A2
Burcote Rd SW18 ...71 C4
Burder Ho SW8 ....**162** A1
Burdenham Ave
TW10 ....**54** A3
Burder Cl N1 ....16 A2
Burder Rd N1 ....16 A2
Burdett Coutts &
Townshend CE Prim
Sch SW1 ....**147** C4
Burdett Mews **2**
W2 ....**100** A2
Burdett Rd E3 ....33 B4
Burdett St SE1 .....**135** C2
Burford Ho
3 Brentford TW8 ..36 A1
London SW9 ....**173** A1
Burford Rd E15 ......27 C4
Brentford TW8 .....36 A1
Burford Wlk SW6 ..**156** B1
Burgate Ct **5** SW9 .62 C4
Burgess Hill NW2 ...10 C4
Burgess Ho **5** SE5 .48 B3
Burgess Ind Pk SE5 .48 B3
Burgess Park Mans
NW6 ....10 C4
Burgess St E14 ......33 C4
Burge St SE1 ....**137** C1
Burgh St N1 ....86 B2
Burghley Hall Cl
SW19 ....70 A3
Burghley Ho SW19 .70 A3
Burghley Rd NW5 ...13 A4
Burghley Twr W3 ....29 B2
Burgh St N1 ....86 B2
Burgon St EC4 .....**108** B1
Burgos Gr SE10 .....52 A2
Burgoyne Rd SW9 ..62 B4
Burhan Uddin Ho
E1 ....**98** C1
Buriton Ho **9** SW15 58 A3
Burke Cl SW15 ....56 A3
Burke Ho **5** SW11 .59 C3
Burke St E16 ....35 B2
Burland Rd SW11 ...60 B2
Burleigh Ho SW3 ..**157** C3
London W10 ....30 C4
Burleigh Pl SW15 ...57 C2
Burleigh St WC2 ...**120** C4
Burley Ho E1 ....32 C3
Burlington Arc W1 .**118** C3
Burlington Ave TW9 44 C2
Burlington Cl W9 ...**23** C1
Burlington Ct W4 ....45 B3
Burlington Danes Sch
W12 ....30 A3
Burlington Gdns
W1 ....**118** C3
Fulham SW6 ....**164** B1
London W3 ....28 B1
London W4 ....45 B4
Burlington Ho NW3 .11 C4
Burlington La SW14 .45 C1
Burlington Mews
London W3 ....28 B1
1 Putney SW15 ....58 B2
Burlington Pl SW6 .**164** B1

Burlington Rd
Fulham SW6 ....**164** B1
London W4 ....37 B1
Burma Rd N16 ....15 C4
Burmarsh **6** NW5 ..12 C2
Burmester Ho SW17 71 B1
Burmester Rd SW17 71 B1
Burnaby Cres W4 ...45 A4
Burnaby Ct SE16 ..**139** C3
Burnaby Gdns W4 ..45 A4
Burnaby St SW10 ..**157** A1
Burnand Ho **8** W14 .**39** C3
Burnaston Ho **5** E5 ..7 C1
Burnbury Rd SW12 .73 B3
Burne Jones Ho
W14 ....**140** B3
Burnell Ho **10** SW2 .74 C3
Burnell Wlk SE1 ...**153** A2
Burness Cl N7 ....14 B2
Burne St NW1 ......**102** A4
Burnett Cl E9 ....17 B3
Burnett Ho **6** SE13 ..52 B1
Burnett Cl SW11 ...**168** A3
Burney St SE10 .....52 B3
Burnfoot Ave SW6 ..54 C1
Burnham NW3 ....12 A1
Burnham Cl SE1 ...**153** A3
Burnham Ct W2 ...**114** B4
Burnham Est **8** E2 .25 B2
Burnham St E2 ....25 B2
Burnhill Ho EC1 ....**96** C3
Burnley Rd
London NW10 ....8 C3
London SW9 ......**172** C2
Burnsall St SW3 ..**144** B2
Burns Ho **12** E2 ....25 B2
11 London N16 ....16 A4
London N7 ....14 B2
Burn's Ho NW10 ...21 A4
Burn's Rd NW10 ...21 B4
Burnthwaite Rd
SW6 ....**155** A1
Burntwood Cl SW18 72 A3
Burntwood Ct SW17 71 B1
Burntwood Grange Rd
SW18 ....72 A3
Burntwood La
SW17 ....71 C2
Burntwood Sch
SW17 ....71 C2
Buross St E1 ....32 A3
Burrage Ct **17** SE16 .40 C2
Burrard Ho **5** E2 ....25 B3
Burrard Rd NW6 ....10 C4
Burr Cl E1 ....**125** B2
Burrell St SE1 .....**122** A2
Burrell's Wharf Sq
E14 ....42 A1
Burrhill Ct SE16 .....40 C3
Burrow Ho SW9 ...**173** A1
Burrow Rd SE22 ....64 A3
Burrows Mews
SE1 ....**136** A4
Burrows Rd NW10 ..22 B2
Burrow Wlk SE21 ...75 B4
Burr Rd SW18 ....70 C4
Bursar St SE1 .....**124** A1
Burslem St E1 ......**111** B2
Burstock Rd SW15 .58 A3
Burston Rd SW15 ..57 C2
Burtley Cl N4 ....6 B3
Burton Bank **4**
N1 ....15 C1
Burton Ct SW3 ....**145** A2
Burton Gr SE17 ....**151** B1

Burton Ho **8** SE16 .40 A4
London SE5 ....48 A3
Burton Lo **5** SW15 .58 B2
Burton Mews SW1 .**145** C3
Burton Pl WC1 ....**93** C3
Burton Rd
London NW6 ....10 B1
London SE5 ....48 A1
London SW9 ....**173** B2
Burtons Ct E15 .....19 C1
Burton St WC1 ......**93** C2
Burtonwood Ho N4 ..6 C4
Burtt Ho N1 ....98 A4
Burwash Ho SE1 ...**137** C3
Burwell Cl **21** E1 ...32 A3
Burwell Rd E10 .....19 A4
Burwell Wlk **14** E3 ..26 C1
Burwood Ho **11**
SW9 ....63 A3
Burwood Pl W2 ....**102** B2
Bury Cl SE16 ....32 C1
Bury Ct EC3 ....**110** B2
Bury Pl WC1 ....**106** B3
Bury St EC3 ....**110** B2
London SW1 ....**119** A2
Bury Wlk SW3 ......**144** A2
Busbridge Ho **16**
E14 ....33 C4
Busby Pl NW5 ....13 C2
Bushaby Cl SE1 ....**138** A1
Bushberry Rd E9 ...18 A2
Bush Cotts **12** SW18 58 C2
Bush Ct **7** W12 ....39 C4
Bushell Cl SW2 ......74 B2
Bushell St E1 ....**125** C1
Bushey Down SW12 73 A2
Bushey Hill Rd SE5 .49 B2
Bushey Rd N15 .....49 B2
Bushey Hill Rd SE5 .49 B2
Bushfield Ho N5 ....15 B3
Bush Ind Est NW10 .20 C1
Bush La EC4 ....**123** B4
Bushnell Rd SW17 .73 A1
Bush Rd E8 ....25 A4
SE8 ....40 C2
Richmond TW9 .....44 B4
Bushwood Dr SE1 .**153** A3
Bushwood Rd TW9 .44 C4
Business Design Ctr*
N1 ....**85** C3
Buspace Studios **3**
W10 ....23 A1
Butcher Row E1 .....32 C3
Butchers Rd E16 ...35 C3
Bute Gdns W6 ....39 C2
Bute House Prep Sch
W6 ....39 C2
Bute St SW7 ....**143** B4
Butfield Ho **6** E9 ...17 B2
Butler Ho **13** E14 ..33 B3
2 E2 ....25 B2
5 London SW9 ...48 A3
Butler Pl SW1 ......**133** B2
Butler Rd NW10 .....8 B1
Butler St **13** E2 ....25 B2
Butler's Wharf W
SE1 ....**124** C1
Butley Ct **7** E3 .....26 A3
Butterfield Cl **1**
SE16 ....40 A4
Butterfly Wlk **2**
SE5 ....48 C2
Buttermere NW1 ....92 B4
Buttermere Cl SE1 .**152** C3
London E11 ....19 C4
Buttermere Ct NW8 79 B4
Buttermere Dr
SW15 ....58 A2

Buttermere Ho 11
E3 ....26 B2
Buttermere Wlk 9
E8 ....16 B2
Butterwick W6 ....39 B2
Butterworth Ct
SW16 ....74 A1
Buttesland St N1 ....97 C4
Buxhall Cres E9 ....18 B2
Buxted Rd London E8 ...16 B1
London SE22 ....64 A3
Buxton Ct N1 ....97 A4
Buxton Gdns W3 ....28 A2
Buxton Ho SW11 ....59 C3
Buxton Rd N19 ....4 C3
London NW2 ....9 A2
Mortlake SW14 ....56 A4
Buxton St E1 .....24 C1 99 B1
Byam Shaw Sch of Art
N19 ....4 C2
Byam St SW6 ....166 C1
Byards Ct SE16 ....40 C3
Byas Ho 8 E3 ....26 B2
Byfeld Ct SE16 ....40 B2
Byelands Cl 12 SE16 ....32 C1
Bye The W3 ....29 A3
Byeway The SW14 ....55 B4
Byfeld Gdns SW13 ....46 C2
Bygrove Prim Sch
E14 ....34 A3
Bygrove St E14 ....34 A3
Byng Pl WC1 ....93 B1
Byng St E14 ....41 C4
Byrne Ho 82 SW2 ....62 B2
Byrne Rd SW12 ....73 A2
Byron Cl E8 ....24 C4
Byron Ct SW3 ....144 B3
W9 ....23 C1
WC1 ....94 C2
Dulwich SE21 ....76 C3
3 London NW6 ....11 B1
Byron Mews NW3 ....12 A4
Byron St E14 ....34 B3
Bythorn St SW9 ....62 B3
Bywater Pl SE16 ....33 A1
Bywater St SW3 ....144 C2
Bywell Pl W1 ....104 C3
Byworth Wlk N19 ....5 A3

C

Cabbell St NW1 ....102 A3
Cabinet Off SW1 ....134 A4
Cabinet War Rooms ★
SW1 ....133 C4
Cable Ho WC1 ....95 B4
Cable Pl SE10 ....52 B2
Cable St E1 ....32 A2
Cabot Ct SE16 ....40 C3
Cabot Sq E14 ....33 C1
Cabul Rd SW11 ....168 B1
Cactus Cl SE5 ....49 A1
Cactus Wlk W12 ....29 B3
Cadbury Way 3 SE16 ...153 B4
Caddington Rd NW2 .....1 A1
Cadell Cl E2 ....24 B3
Cadell Ho 12 E2 ....24 B3
Cade Rd SE10 ....52 C2
Cader Rd SW18 ....59 B1
Cadet Dr SE1 ....153 A2
Cade Tyler Ho 10
SE10 ....52 B2
Cadiz St SE17 ....151 A1
Cadman Cl SW9 ....48 A3
Cadmore Ho 4 N1 ....15 A1
Cadmus Cl 5 SW4 ......61 C4

Cadmus Ct SW9 ....173 B4
Cadnam Lo E14 ....42 C3
Cadnam Point 15
SW15 ....69 A3
Cadogan Cl E9 ....18 B1
Cadogan Ct SW3 ....144 C3
Cadogan Ct Gdns
SW1 ....145 B4
Cadogan Gate
SW1 ....145 A4
Cadogan Gdns
SW3 ....145 A3
Cadogan Ho 3 SW3 .....157 C3
Cadogan La SW1 ....131 B1
Cadogan Pl SW1 ....131 A1
Cadogan Sq SW1 ....131 A1
Cadogan St SW3 ....144 C3
Cadogan Terr E9 ....18 B1
Caedmon Rd N7 ....14 B4
Caernarvon Ho
W2 ....100 C2
Caesar Ct 22 E2 ....25 C3
Cahill St EC1 ....97 A1
Cahir St E14 ....42 A2
Caine Ho 3 N7 ....14 A4
Caird St W10 ....23 B2
Cairns Ho 3 N7 ....14 B4
Cairns Rd SW11 ....60 A2
Caister Ho
10 Balham SW12 ....73 A4
London N7 ....14 B2
Caister Mews SW12 .....73 A4
Caistor Rd SW12 ....73 A4
Caithness Ho N1 ....84 C4
Caithness Rd W14 ....39 C3
Calabria Rd N5 ....15 A3
Calais Gate SE5 ....48 A2
Calais St SE5 ....48 A2
Calbourne Rd SW12 .....72 C4
Calcraft Ho 10 E2 ......25 B3
Caldecot Ct SE5 ....48 B1
Caldecot Rd SE5 ....48 B1
Calder Ct SE16 ....33 B1
Calderon Ho 8 NW8 .....80 A2
Calderon Pl W10 ....30 B4
Caldervale Rd SW4 .....61 C2
Caldew St SE5 ....48 C3
Caldwell St SW9 ....163 B1
Caldy Wlk 15 N1 ....15 B2
Caleb St SE1 ....137 A4
Caledonia Ho
E14 ....33 A3
Caledonia Market
SE1 ....138 B2
Caledonian Rd N1 ......84 C3
London N7 ....14 B2
**Caledonian Road &
Barnsbury Sta** N7 ......14 B1
Caledonian Road Sta
N7 ....14 B2
Caledonian Wharf Rd
E14 ....42 C2
Cale St SW3 ....144 A2
Caletock Way SE10 ......43 B1
Calgarth NW1 ....83 A1
Calgary Ct 24 SE16 ....40 B4
Caliban Twr 9 N1 ....24 A3
Calico Ho 4 SW11 ....59 B4
Calico Row 5 SW11 .....59 B4
Calidore Cl SW2 ....62 B1
Callaby Terr 1 N1 ......15 C2
Callahan Cotts 8
E1 ....32 B4
Callcott Ct NW6 ....10 B1
Callcott Rd NW6 ....10 B1
Callcott St W8 ....113 B2

Callendar Rd SW7 ......129 B2
Callingham Cl 17
E14 ....33 B4
Callingham Ho 4
SW4 ....62 A1
Callow St SW3 ....157 B4
Calmington Rd SE5 .....49 A4
Calshot Ho N1 ....84 C2
Calshot St N1 ....84 C1
Calstock NW1 ....83 B3
Calstock Ho SE11 ......149 C2
Calthorpe St WC1 ......95 A2
Calton Ave SE21 ....64 A1
Calver 6 NW5 ....13 A4
Calverley Gr N19 ....4 C3
Calvert Ave E2 ....98 C3
Calvert Ct
1 London N19 ....4 B3
5 Richmond TW9 ....54 B4
Calvert Ho 9 W12 ......30 A2
Calverton SE5 ....49 A4
Calvert Rd SE10 ....43 B1
Calvert's Bldgs
SE1 ....123 B1
Calvert St NW1 ....81 B4
Calvin St E1 ......24 B1 98 C1
Calypso Cres 5
SE15 ....49 B3
Calypso Way SE8,
SE16 ....41 B2
Cambalt Ho 5
SW15 ....57 C2
Cambalt Rd SW15 ....57 C2
Cambay Wlk N1 ....84 C4
Camber Ho 4 SE15 ......50 B4
Camberley Ho NW1 .....82 B1
Camberwell Church St
SE5 ....48 C2
Camberwell Coll of Arts
SE5 ....49 B3
London SE5 ....48 C2
Camberwell Glebe
SE5 ....49 A2
Camberwell Gn SE5 .....48 B2
Camberwell Gr SE5 .....49 A1
Camberwell Green
SE5 ....48 B2
Camberwell New Rd
SW9 ....48 A3
Camberwell Rd SE5 .....48 B3
Camberwell Station Rd
SE5 ....48 B2
Camberwell Trad Est
SE5 ....48 B2
Camborne Rd SW18 .....70 C4
Cambourne Mews 6
W11 ....31 A3
Cambray Rd SW12 ....73 B3
Cambria Ho 18 E14 .....33 A3
Cambria Rd TW10 ....54 B1
Cambria St SW6 ....156 B1
Cambridge Ave
NW6 ....23 C3
Cambridge Cir
WC2 ....105 C1
Cambridge Cotts
TW9 ....44 C4
Cambridge Cres 25
E2 ....25 A3
Cambridge Ct 23 E2 ....25 A3
2 NW6 ....23 C3
London N16 ....7 A4
Cambridge Gate
NW1 ....92 A2

Cambridge Gate Mews
NW1 ....92 B2
Cambridge Gdns
NW6 ....23 C3
W10 ....31 A3
Cambridge Gr W6 ....39 A2
Cambridge Heath Rd
E1,E2 ....25 A2
Cambridge Heath Sta
E2 ....25 A3
Cambridge Ho W6 ....58 A4
Cambridge Mans
SW11 ....168 C3
Cambridge Pas 3
E9 ....17 B1
Cambridge Pl W8 ......128 B3
Cambridge Rd NW6 .....23 C2
Barnes SW13 ....46 B1
London NW6 ....23 C3
London SW11 ....168 C3
Richmond TW9 ....44 C3
Cambridge Rd N
W4 ....37 A1
Cambridge Rd S 8
W4 ....37 A1
Cambridge Sch W6 .....39 A2
Cambridge Sq W2 ......102 A2
Cambridge St SW1 .....146 C2
Cambridge Terr
NW1 ....92 A3
Cambridge Terr Mews
NW1 ....92 B3
Cambus Rd E16 ....35 C4
Cam Ct 2 SE15 ....49 B4
Camden Gdns NW1 .....13 A1
Camden High St
NW1 ....82 C3
Camden Ho 6 SE8 ......41 B1
Camdenhurst St
E14 ....33 A3
Camden Lock Pl
NW1 ....13 A1
Camden Mews NW1 ....13 C2
Camden Mkt* NW1 ....82 B4
Camden Park Rd
NW1 ....13 C2
Camden Pas N1 ....86 A3
Camden Rd NW1 ....82 C4
Camden Road Sta
NW1 ....13 B1
Camden Row SE3 ....53 A1
Camden Sch for Girls
The NW5 ....13 B2
Camden Studios
NW1 ....83 A3
Camden Town Sta
NW1 ....82 C4
Camden Wlk N1 ....86 A3
Cameford Ct 20
SW2 ....74 A4
Camelford Ho SE1 .....148 B1
Camelford Ct 7
W11 ....31 A3
Camelford Wlk 8
W11 ....31 A3
Camellia Ho SE8 ....51 B3
Camellia St SW8 ....162 A1
Camelot Ho 6 NW1 .....13 C2
Camelot Prim Sch
SE15 ....50 A4
Camera Pl SW10 ....157 B4
Cameret Ct 6 W11 .....30 C1
Cameron Ct 3
SW19 ....70 A3
Cameron Ho NW8 ....80 A2

Cameron Ho continued
SE5 ....48 B3
Cameron House Sch
SW10 ....157 B3
Camerton Cl 8 E8 ......16 B2
Camilla Rd SE16 ....40 A2
Camlet St E2 ....98 C2
Camley St NW1 ....83 C2
Camomile St EC3 ......110 B2
Campaign Ct W9 ....23 B1
Campana Rd SW6 ......165 C4
Campbell Ct SW7 ......128 C1
Dulwich SE21 ....76 C3
Campbell Gordon Way
NW2 ....9 A4
Campbell Ho SW1 ......146 C1
W2 ....89 B1
30 London W12 ....30 A3
Campbell Rd E3 ....26 C2
Campdale Rd N7 ....4 C1
Campden Gr W8 ....127 C4
Campden Hill W8 ......127 B4
Campden Hill Ct
W8 ....127 C4
Campden Hill Gate
W8 ....127 B4
Campden Hill Gdns
W8 ....113 B2
Campden Hill Mans
W8 ....113 C2
Campden Hill Pl
W14 ....113 B2
Campden Hill Rd
W8 ....127 B4
Campden Hill Sq
W14 ....113 A1
Campden Ho 4
W8 ....113 C2
4 London NW6 ....11 C1
Campden House Cl
W8 ....113 C2
Campden Hos The
W8 ....127 C4
Campden St
W8 ....31 C1 113 B2
Campen Cl SW19 ....70 A2
Camperdown St
E1 ....111 A1
Campion Ho 19 N16 ....16 A3
Campion Rd SW15 ......57 B2
Camplin St SE14 ....50 C3
Campshill Pl SE13 .....67 B2
Campshill Rd SE13 .....67 B2
Campton Hill Twrs
W8 ....113 C2
Cam Rd E15 ....27 C4
Camsey Ho 3 SW2 .....62 B2
Canada Cres W3 ....20 B1
Canada Gdns SE13 .....67 B2
Canada Rd W3 ....28 B4
Canada Sq E14 ....34 A1
Canada St SE16 ....40 C4
Canada Way W12 ....30 A2
Canada App SE8 ....51 A4
Canal Bldg N1 ....86 C2
Canal Bridge SE15 .....49 C4
Canal Cl E1 ....26 A1
London W10 ....22 C1
Canal Gr SE15 ....50 A4
Canal Head Public Sq
SE15 ....49 C2
Canal Path 22 E2 ......24 B4
Canalside Studios 17
N1 ....24 A4
Canal St SE5 ....48 C4
Canal Way W10 ....22 C1
Canal Wlk N1 ....87 C4

Canary Wharf★ E14 . . 34 C4
Canary Wharf Pier
 (River Bus) E14 . . . . 33 B1
Canary Wharf Sta
 E14 . . . . 33 C1
Canberra Prim Sch
 W12 . . . . 30 A2
Canbury Mews
 SE26 . . . . 76 C1
Cancell Rd SW9 . . .173 C4
Candahar Rd 168 B1
Candida Ct ⑨ NW1 . . 13 A1
Candishe Rd 138 C4
Candover St W1 . . .104 C3
Candy St E3 . . . . 26 B4
Canfield Gdns NW6 . . 11 A1
Canfield Pl NW6 . . . . 11 B2
Canford Rd SW11 . . .60 C2
Canham Rd W3 . . . . . 38 A4
Cann Ho W14 . . . . . . 126 B2
Canning Cross SE5 . . 49 A1
Canning Ho ❷ W12 . . 30 A2
Canning Pas W8 . . . 128 C2
Canning Pl W8 . . . . 128 C2
Canning Pl Mews
 W8 . . . . 128 C2
Cannington ⑮ NW5 . 12 C2
Cannington Town E16 . 35 B3
Cannington Town Sta
 E16 . . . . 35 A4
Cannock Ho N4 . . . . . . 6 C4
Cannon Dr E14 . . . . . 33 C2
Cannon Hill NW6 . . . . 10 C3
Cannon Ho SE11 . . . 149 A3
Cannon La NW3 . . . . . 2 C1
Cannon Pl NW3 . . . . . 2 C1
Cannon Street Rd
 E1 . . . . 32 A3
Cannon Street Sta
 EC4 . . . . 123 B4
Cannon Wharf Bsns Ctr
 ⑫ SE8 . . . . 41 A2
Canon Barnett CE Prim
 Sch E1 . . . . .111 A2
Canon Beck Rd
 SE16 . . . . 40 B4
Canonbury Cres ⑮ . 15 B1
Canonbury Ct ⑤ N1 . 15 A1
Canonbury Gr N1 . . . 15 B1
Canonbury La N1 . . . . 15 A1
Canonbury Pk N N1 . . 15 B2
Canonbury Pk S N1 . . 15 B2
Canonbury Pl N1 . . . . 15 A2
Canonbury Prim Sch
 N1 . . . . 15 A2
Canonbury Rd N1 . . . 15 A1
Canonbury Sq N1 . . . 15 A1
Canonbury St N1 . . . . 15 B1
Canonbury Sta N1,
 N5 . . . . 15 B3
Canonbury Villas
 . . . . 15 A1
Canon Murnane Rd
 SE1 . . . . .138 C1
Canon Row SW1 . . .134 A3
Canons Cl N2 . . . . 2 C4
Canon St N1 . . . . . . 86 C3
Canrobert St E2 . . . . 25 A2
Cantelowes Rd
 NW1 . . . . 13 C2
Canterbury SE13 . . . .67 B2

Canterbury Cl ⑯
 SE5 . . . . 48 B1
Canterbury Cres
 SW9 . . . . .62 C3
Canterbury Ct NW6 . .23 C3
Canterbury Ind W3 . . .29 A1
Canterbury Gr SE27,
 SW16 . . . . 74 C1
Canterbury Ho
 ❻ E3 . . . . 27 A2
 SE1 . . . . 135 A2
Canterbury Ind Pk ⑮
 SE15 . . . . 50 B4
Canterbury Mans
 NW6 . . . . 11 A2
Canterbury Pl
 SE17 . . . . 150 B3
Canterbury Rd NW6 . 23 C3
Canterbury Terr
 . . . . 23 C3
Cantium Ret Pk SE1 . 49 C4
Canton St E14 . . . . . . 33 C3
Cantrell Rd E3 . . . . . . 26 C1
Canute Ct SW16 . . . . 74 C1
Canute Gdns SE16 . . . 40 C2
Cape Henry Ct ❼
 E14 . . . . 34 C2
Capel Ho ⑰ E9 . . . . .17 B1
Capel Lo
 ⓫ Richmond TW9 . . .44 B2
 ❷ Streatham SW2 . . .74 B4
Capener's Ct SW1 . . 131 B3
Capern Rd SW18 . . . . 71 B3
Capital Interchange Way
 TW8 . . . . 36 C1
Capital Wharf E1 . . . 125 C1
Capland Ho NW8 . . . 89 C2
Capland St NW8 . . . . 89 C2
Caple Ho SW10 . . . . 157 A2
Caple Rd NW10 . . . . . 21 B3
Capper St WC1 . . . . . 93 A1
Capstan Ho ❹ E14 . . 42 B2
Capstan Sq E14 . . . . . 42 B4
Capstan Way SE16 . . 33 A1
Capulet Mews ❶
 E16 . . . . 35 C1
Caradoc Cl W2 . . . . . 31 C3
Caradoc St SE10 . . . . 43 A1
Caranday Villas ❸
 W11 . . . . 30 C1
Caravel Cl E14 . . . . . . 41 C3
Caravel Mews ⑭
 SE8 . . . . 51 C4
Caraway Hts E14 . . . . 34 B2
Carbery Ave W3 . . . . 36 B4
Carbis Rd E14 . . . . . . 33 B3
Carbroke Ho ⑩ E9 . . 25 B4
Cardale St ❶ E14 . . . 42 B3
Cardale St SE15 . . . . 65 A4
Cardiff Ho ⑱ SE15 . . 49 C4
Cardigan Rd E3 . . . . . 26 B3
 Barnes SW13 . . . . . . 46 C1
 Richmond TW10 . . . . 54 A1
Cardigan St SE11 . . .149 B2
Cardigan Wlk ❷ N1 . 15 B1
Cardinal Bourne St
 SE1 . . . . .137 C1
Cardinal Cap Alley
 SE1 . . . . .122 C3
Cardinal Hinsey Cl
 NW10 . . . . 21 C3
Cardinal Hinsey RC
 High Sch (Boys)
 NW10 . . . . 21 C4

Cardinal Pl SW15 . . . .57 C3
Cardinal Pole RC Sch
 London E9 . . . . 18 A2
 London E9 . . . . 17 C1
Cardinals Way N19 . . . 4 C3
Cardinal Vaughan
 Memorial Sch
 W14 . . . . 126 A4
Cardine Mews SE15 . 50 A3
Cardington St NW1 . 93 A3
Cardozo Rd N7 . . . . . 14 A3
Cardwell Rd N7 . . . . . 14 A4
Career Ct ⑪ SE16 . . 40 C4
Carew Ct ❼ 5 B2
Carew Cl ⑮ SE14 . . .50 C3
Carew St SE5 . . . . . . 48 B1
Carew St SE5 . . . . . . 74 C1
Carey Ct ⑳ SE5 . . . . 48 B3
Carey Gdns SW8 . . 171 B3
Carey La EC2 . . . . . . 108 C2
Carey Pl SW1 . . . . . 147 B3
Carey St WC2 . . . . . 107 A1
Carfax Pl SW4 . . . . . 61 C3
Carfree Cl ❸ N1 . . . . . 14 C1
Cargill Rd SW18 . . . . 71 B3
Carinthia Ct ❺ SE8 . 41 A2
Carisbrook Ct ❶
 SW16 . . . . 74 B1
Carisbrooke Ct W3 . . 37 A4
Carisbrooke Gdns
 SE15 . . . . 49 B3
Carisbrooke Ho
 TW10 . . . . 54 C2
Carleton Gdns N19 . . 13 B3
Carleton Rd N7 . . . . . 13 C3
Carlile Cl E3 . . . . 26 B3
Carlile Ho SE1 . . . . . 137 C1
Carlingford Rd
 . . . . 11 C4
Carlisle Ave EC3 . . . 110 C1
 London W3 . . . . 29 A3
Carlisle La SE1 . . . . 135 A2
Carlisle Pl SW1 . . . . 132 C1
Carlisle Rd NW6 . . . . 23 A4
 London N4 . . . . 5 C4
Carlisle St W1 . . . . . 105 B1
Carlisle Wlk ❽ E8 . . . 16 B2
Carlos Pl W1 . . . . . . 118 A3
Carlow St NW1 . . . . . 82 C2
Carlton Ct NW6 . . . . 78 B2
 London W9 . . . . 88 B4
Carlton Dr SW15 . . . 58 A2
Carlton Gdns SW1 . . 119 B1
Carlton Gr SE15 . . . . 50 A2
Carlton Hill NW8 . . . . 78 C2
Carlton Ho NW6 . . . . 23 B3
 ❷ NW6 . . . . 23 C3
 W11 . . . . 103 B2
Carlton House Terr
 SW1 . . . . 119 C2
Carlton Lo ❹ N4 . . . . . 5 C4
Carlton Mans W14 . . 126 B4
 W9 . . . . 88 B4
 London N16 . . . . 7 B3
Carlton Prim Sch
 NW5 . . . . 12 C3
Carlton Rd London N4 . . 5 C4
 ❶ London W4 . . . . . . 45 B3
Carlton Sq E1 . . . . . . 25 C1
Carlton St SW1 . . . . 119 B3

Carltons The ❺
 SW15 . . . . 58 A2
Carlton Tower Pl
 SW1 . . . . 131 A2
Carlton Vale NW6 . . . 23 C3
Carlton Vale Inf Sch
 NW6 . . . . 23 B2
Carlyle Cl NW10 . . . . 20 C4
Carlyle Ct SW6 . . . . 166 B3
Carlyle Ho ❸ SE5 . . . 48 B3
 SW3 . . . . 157 C3
 ❸ London N16 . . . . . . 7 A1
Carlyle Mans SW3 . . 158 A3
Carlyle Mews ❸ E1 . 25 C1
Carlyle Pl SW15 . . . . 57 C3
Carlyle's Ho★ SW3 . 158 A3
Carlyle Sq SW3 . . . . 143 C1
Carmalt Gdns SW15 . 57 B3
Carmarthen Ho ❻
 SW15 . . . . 69 B4
Carmarthen Pl
 SE1 . . . . .138 A4
Carmel Ct W8 . . . . . 128 A4
Carmelite St EC4 . . . 121 C4
Carmen St E14 . . . . . 34 A3
Carmichael Cl ❾
 . . . . 59 C4
Carmichael Ct ❺
 . . . . 46 B1
Carmichael Ho ❻
 E14 . . . . 34 B2
Carmichael Mews
 SW18 . . . . 71 C4
Carminia Rd SW17 . . 73 A2
Carnaby St★ W1 . . . 104 C1
Carnac St SE21,SE27 . 75 C1
Carnegie Ho NW3 . . . . 2 C1
Carnegie Pl SW19 . . . 69 C1
Carnegie St N1 . . . . . 85 A3
Carnicot Ho ❺
 SE15 . . . . 50 A2
Carnoustie Dr N1 . . . 14 B1
Carnwath Ho SW6 . . 59 A4
Carnwath Rd SW6 . . . 59 A4
 Streatham SW16 . . . .74 B1
Caroline Cl W2 . . . . 114 B3
 ❷ London W6 . . . . . 39 B1
Caroline Gdns E2 . . . 98 B4
Caroline Martyn Ho ❹
 N19 . . . . 4 C4
Caroline Ho W2 . . . 114 B3
 ❷ London W6 . . . . . 39 B1
Caroline Pl Mews
 W2 . . . . 114 B3
Caroline St E1 . . . . . 32 C3
Caroline Terr SW1 . . 145 B3
Caroline Wlk W6 . . . 154 A3
Carol St NW1 . . . . . . 82 C4
Caronia Ct ❹ SE16 . . 41 A2
Carpenter Ho
 ⑩ E14 . . . . 33 C4
 ❼ NW11 . . . . 1 C4
Carpenters Bsns Pk
 E15 . . . . 19 A1
Carpenters Ct NW1 . 82 C2
Carpenter's Pl SW4 . 61 C3
Carpenters Prim Sch
 E15 . . . . 27 B4
Carpenter's Rd E15 . . 19 A1
Carpenter St W1 . . . 118 A3
Carrara Wharf SW6 . 58 A4
Carrara Wlk ❼ SW9 . 63 A3
Carriage Dr E
 SW11 . . . . 159 C2
Carriage Drive E
 SW11 . . . . 159 B1

Carriage Drive N
 SW11,SW8 . . . . 159 C3
Carriage Dr N
 SW8,SW11 . . . . 158 C2
 SW8,SW11 . . . . 159 C3
Carriage Dr S
 SW11 . . . . 169 B2
Carriage Dr W
 SW11 . . . . 158 C1
Carrick Ho SE11 . . . 150 A2
 ❷ London N7 . . . . . 14 B2
Carrick Mews SE8 . . 51 C4
Carrington Ct SW11 . 60 A3
Carrington Ho W1 . . 118 A1
Carrington Lo ❸
 TW10 . . . . 54 A2
Carrington Rd
 TW10 . . . . 54 C3
Carrol Cl NW5 . . . . . 13 A4
Carroll Ho W2 . . . . . 115 B4
Carron Cl E14 . . . . . . 34 A3
Carroun Rd SW8 . . . 162 C2
Carr St E14 . . . . 33 A4
Carslake Rd SW15 . . 57 B1
Carson Rd E16 . . . . . 35 C4
 Dulwich SE21 . . . . . . 75 C2
Carter Ct EC4 . . . . . 108 B1
Carteret Ho ❸ W12 . 30 A2
Carteret St SW1 . . . 133 B3
Carteret Way SE8 . . 41 A2
Carter Ho E1 . . . . . . 110 C3
 ⓫ London SW2 . . . . 62 C2
Carter La EC4 . . . . . 108 B1
Carter Pl SE17 . . . . . 151 A1
Carters Cl ❷ NW5 . . 13 C2
Carter St SE17 . . . . . 150 C1
Carter's Yd SW18 . . . 58 C2
Carthew Rd W6 . . . . 39 A3
Carthew Villas W6 . . 39 A3
Carthusian St EC1 . . 108 C4
Carter Circ E14 . . . . 34 B2
Carting La WC2 . . . . 120 B3
Cartmel NW1 . . . . . . 92 C4
Carton Ho SE16 . . . . 139 B2
 ⑫ London W11 . . . . 30 C2
Cartwright Gdns
 WC1 . . . . 94 A3
Cartwright Ho SE1 . . 137 A1
Cartwright St E1 . . . 125 A3
Cartwright Way
 SW13 . . . . 47 A3
Carvel Ho E14 . . . . . 42 B1
Carver Cl ⑱ W4 . . . . 37 B3
Carver Rd SE24 . . . . 63 B1
Carville Cres TW8 . . 36 A2
Cary Ho ❼ SW9 . . . . 69 C3
Carysfort Rd N16 . . . 15 C4
Casby Ho SE16 . . . . 139 B2
Casella Rd SE14 . . . . 50 C3
Casey Cl NW8 . . . . . 90 B3
Casino Ave SE24 . . . 63 C2
Caspian Ho ⑫ E1 . . . 32 C4
Caspian St SE5 . . . . 48 C3
Cassandra Ct NW2 . . 9 B2
Cassell Ho SW9 . . . 172 B2
Casserley Ho W4 . . . 37 C3
Cass Ho ⑳ E9 . . . . . . 17 C2
Cassidy Rd SW6 . . . 155 B1
Cassinghurst SE24 . . 63 C2
Cassland Rd E9 . . . . 17 C2
Casson Ho E1 . . . . . 111 B4
Casson St E1 . . . . . . 111 B3
Castalia Sq ⑧ E14 . . 42 B4
Castellain Mans W9 . 88 B2
Castellain Rd W9 . . . 88 B2
Castell Ho ⓫ SE8 . . . 51 C3

Castello Ave SW15 . . .57 B2
Castelnau SW13 . . . . .47 A3
Casterbridge NW6 . . . .78 B4
 3 London W11 . . . . . .31 C3
Casterton St E8 . . . . . .17 A2
Castle Ave 102 A1
Castle Baynard St
EC4 . . . . .108 C1
Castlebrook Cl
SE11 . . . . .150 A4
Castle Cl London E9 . .18 A3
London W3 . . . . .37 A4
Wimbledon SW19 . . . .69 C1
Castlecombe Dr
SW19 . . . . .69 C4
Castle Ct EC3 . . . . . .109 C1
Castleden Ho NW6 . . .11 C1
Castleford Ho SE1 . . . .89 C2
Castlefrank Ho N1 . . . .98 B4
Castlegate TW9 . . . . . .54 B4
Castlehaven Rd
NW1 . . . . .13 A1
Castle Ho SE1 . . . . . .150 C4
SW8 . . . . .162 B2
Castle Ind Est
SE17 . . . . .150 C4
Castle La SW1 . . . . . .132 C2
Castlemaine SW11 . . . .169 A2
Castle Mead SE5 . . . . .48 B3
Castle Mews NW1 . . . .13 A2
Castlenau Gdns
SW13 . . . . .47 A4
Castlenau Mans
SW13 . . . . .47 A4
Castlenau Row
SW13 . . . . .47 A4
Castle Pl **8** W4 . . . . . .38 A2
London NW1 . . . . . . .13 A2
Castlereagh St W1 . . . .102 C2
Castleton Ho **2** E14 . . .42 B2
Castletown Rd
W14 . . . . .140 B1
Castleview Cl N4 . . . . .6 B2
Castle Way SW19 . . . .69 C1
Castle Yd SE1 . . . . . .122 B2
London N6 . . . . .3 C4
Castor La E14 . . . . . . .34 A2
Caterham Rd SE13 . . . .67 C4
Catesby Ho **25** E9 . . . . .17 B1
Catesby St SE17 . . . . .151 C3
Cathay Ho SE16 . . . . .40 A4
Cathay St SE16 . . . . . .40 A4
Cathcart Hill N19 . . . . .4 B1
Cathcart Rd SW10 . . .156 C4
Cathcart St NW5 . . . . .13 A2
Cathedral Ct EC4 . . . .108 B2
Cathedral Sch of St
 Saviour & St Mary
 Overie Prim Sch
SE1 . . . . .137 A4
Cathedral St SE1 . . . .123 B2
Catherall Rd N5,N16 . .6 B1
Catherine Baird Ct **2**
SW12 . . . . .72 B3
Catherine Dr TW9 . . . .54 A3
Catherine Gr SE10 . . . .52 A2
Catherine Griffiths Ct
EC1 . . . . .95 C2
Catherine Ho **16** N1 . . . .24 A4
Catherine Pl SW1 . . . .132 C2
Catherine St WC2 . . . .120 C4
Catherine Wheel Alley
E1 . . . . .110 B3
Catherine Wheel Yd
SW1 . . . . .118 C1
Catherwood Ct N1 . . . .87 B1
Cathles Rd SW12 . . . . .61 A1

Cathnor Rd W12 . . . . . .39 A4
Catlin St SE16 . . . . . . .40 A1
Catman Ho N4 . . . . .5 B3
Cato Rd SW4 . . . . .61 C3
Cator St SE15 . . . . . . .49 B3
 SE15 . . . . .49 B4
Cato St W1 . . . . .102 B2
Catton St WC1 . . . . . .106 C3
Caughley Ho SE11 . . . .135 B1
Caulfield Ct **12** NW1 . . .13 B1
Caulfield Rd SE15 . . . .50 A1
Causeway The
SW18 . . . . .59 A2
Causton Cotts **3**
E14 . . . . .33 A3
Causton Ho SE5 . . . . . .48 B3
Causton Rd N6 . . . . . . .4 A4
Causton St SW1 . . . . . .147 C2
Cautley Ave SW4 . . . . .61 B2
Cavalry Gdns SW15 . . .58 B2
Cavave Ho SW10 . . . . .157 A4
Cavaye Pl SW10 . . . . . .143 A1
Cavell Ho **8** N1 . . . . . .24 A4
Cavell St E1 . . . . .32 A4
Cavendish Ave NW8 . . .79 C1
Cavendish Cl NW8 . . . .89 C4
London NW6 . . . . . . .10 B2
3 Putney SW15 . . . . .58 A2
Cavendish Ct EC2 . . . .110 B2
Cavendish Gdns
SW4 . . . . .61 B1
Cavendish Ho NW8 . . . .79 C1
SW8 . . . . .172 A4
Cavendish Mans
EC1 . . . . .95 B1
London E5 . . . . .17 B3
 3 London NW6 . . . . .10 C3
 2 London SW12 . . . . .61 B1
Cavendish Mews N
W1 . . . . .104 B4
Cavendish Mews S
W1 . . . . .104 B3
Cavendish Par
SW12 . . . . .61 A1
Cavendish Pl W1 . . . . .104 B2
W4 . . . . .46 A3
Cavendish Prim Sch
Chiswick W4 . . . . . . .45 B2
London NW6 . . . . . . .10 C3
London W12 . . . . .61 B1
Cavendish Rd
London E5 . . . . .7 B4
Cavendish Sch The
NW1 . . . . .82 B4
Cavendish Sq W1 . . . .104 B2
Cavendish St N1 . . . . . .87 B1
Cavendish Terr **10**
E3 . . . . .26 B2
Cavendish The NW11 . .2 A4
Caversham Ho **7**
SE15 . . . . .49 C4
Caversham Rd NW5 . . .13 B2
Caversham St
SW3 . . . . .158 C4
Caverswall St W12 . . . .30 B3
Cavour Ho SE17 . . . . .150 B2
Caxton Gr E3 . . . . .26 C2
Caxton Hall SW1 . . . . .133 B2
Caxton Rd W12 . . . . . .39 C4
Caxton St N E16 . . . . .35 B3
Caxton St SW1 . . . . . .133 B2
Cayford Ho **1** NW3 . . . .12 B3
Cayley Prim Sch
E14 . . . . .33 A3
Cayton Pl EC1 . . . . . . .97 B3
Cayton St EC1 . . . . . . .97 B3
Cazenove Mans **1**
N16 . . . . .7 C2

Cazenove Rd N16 . . . . . .7 C2
Cecil Ct SW10 . . . . . . .156 C4
WC2 . . . . .120 A3
Cecilia Rd E8 . . . . .16 C3
Cecil Mans **2** SW17 . .72 C2
Cecil Rd
London NW10 . . . . . . .21 A4
London W3 . . . . .28 B4
Cecil Rhodes Ho
NW1 . . . . .83 B2
Cedar Cl Bow E3 . . . . . .26 B4
West Norwood SE21 . .75 B2
Cedar Ct SW1 . . . . . . .102 B2
London N1 . . . . .15 B1
Mortlake SW14 . . . . . .55 B3
Wimbledon SW19 . . . .69 C1
Cedar Gr W5 . . . . .36 A3
Cedar Ho **5** E14 . . . . . .42 B4
 16 SE16 . . . . .40 C4
London SE14 . . . . . . .50 C2
Cedar Lo SW6 . . . . . . .47 C2
Cedarne Rd SW6 . . . . .156 A1
Cedar Rd NW2 . . . . . . .9 B4
Cedars Cl SE13 . . . . . .67 C4
Cedars Ct SW15 . . . . . .56 C1
Cedars Ho **2** SW2 . . . . .62 B3
Cedars Mews SW4 . . . .61 A3
Cedars Rd
Barnes SW13 . . . . . . .46 C1
London SW4 . . . . .61 A3
London W4 . . . . .38 A1
Cedars The E9 . . . . . . .17 C1
Cedar Terr TW9 . . . . . .54 A3
Cedar Tree Ct SE8 . . . .48 B2
Cedar Way NW1 . . . . . .83 B4
Cedra Ct N16 . . . . .7 C3
Cedric Chambers
NW8 . . . . .89 B2
Celandine Cl E3,E14 . .33 C4
Celandine Dr E8 . . . . . .16 B1
Celbridge Mews
W2 . . . . .100 B2
Celestial Gdns SE13 . .67 C3
Celia Ct **7** TW9 . . . . . .44 B2
Celia Ho N1 . . . . .24 A3
Celia Rd N19 . . . . .13 B4
Celtic St E14 . . . . .34 A4
Cenacle Cl NW3 . . . . . .1 C1
Cenotaph* SW1 . . . . . .134 A4
Centaur Ct **8** TW8 . . . .36 A1
Centaur St SE1 . . . . . .135 A2
Central Ave SW11 . . . .159 A1
Central Bsns Ctr
NW10 . . . . .8 A3
Central Criminal Court
(Old Bailey)★
EC4 . . . . .108 B2
Central Foundation
 Lower Sch E3 . . . . . .26 A2
Central Foundation Sch
EC2 . . . . .97 C2
Central Foundation
 Upper Sch E3 . . . . . .26 A2
Central Middlesex Hospl
NW10 . . . . .20 B2
Central Par W3 . . . . . . .37 A4
Central Sch of Speech &
 Drama The NW3 . . . .11 C1
Central School of Ballet
EC1 . . . . .95 C1
Central St EC1 . . . . . . .96 C3

Central St Martins Coll
 of Art and Design (The
 London Inst)
WC1 . . . . .106 C3
Central St Martin's Sch
 of Art & Design
W1 . . . . .105 C1
Central Way NW10 . . . .20 B2
Centre Ave
London NW10 . . . . . . .22 B2
London W3 . . . . .28 C1
Centre Bldgs SE1 . . . .151 A4
Centre Hts **3** NW3 . . . .11 C1
Centre Point SE1 . . . . .153 B2
Centre St E2 . . . . .25 A3
Centurion Cl N7 . . . . . .14 B1
Centurion La E3 . . . . . .26 B3
Century Ho SE13 . . . . . .52 A1
Cephas Ave E1 . . . . . . .25 B1
Cephas Ho **5** E1 . . . . . .25 B1
Cephas St E1 . . . . .25 B1
Cerise Rd SE15 . . . . . .49 C2
Cerney Mews W2 . . . . .115 B4
Cervantes Ct W2 . . . . .100 B1
Ceylon Rd W14 . . . . . .126 A1
 6 London W14 . . . . . .39 C3
Chadacre Ho **3**
SW9 . . . . .63 A3
Chadbourn St E14 . . . .34 A4
Chadston Ho **21** N1 . . . .15 A1
Chadswell SE1 . . . . . . .94 B3
Chadwell St EC1 . . . . . .95 C4
Chadwick Cl SW15 . . . .68 B4
Chadwick Rd
London NW10 . . . . . . .21 B4
London SE15 . . . . . . .49 B1
Chadwick St SW1 . . . .133 B1
Chadworth Ho EC1 . . . .96 C3
London N4 . . . . .6 B3
Chagford Ho **38** E3 . . . .27 A2
London NW1 . . . . .90 C1
Chagford St NW1 . . . . .91 A1
Chalbury Ho **3**
SW9 . . . . .62 B3
Chalbury Wlk N1 . . . . . .85 B2
Chalcot Cres NW1 . . . .81 A4
Chalcot Gdns **3** NW3 . .12 B2
Chalcot Mews
SW16 . . . . .74 A1
Chalcot Rd NW1 . . . . . .81 B4
Chalcot Sch NW1 . . . . .13 A1
Chalcot Sq NW1 . . . . . .12 C1
Chaldon Rd SW6 . . . . .154 B2
Chale Rd SW2 . . . . . . .62 A1
Chalfont Ct NW1 . . . . . .91 A1
Chalfont Ho **2**
SE15 . . . . .49 C3
Chalford **7** NW3 . . . . . .11 B2
Chalford Ct **15**
SW15 . . . . .57 C1
Chalkers Cnr TW9 . . . . .55 A4
Chalk Farm Rd NW1 . . .82 B4
Chalk Farm Sta
NW3 . . . . .12 C1
Chalk Hill Rd W6 . . . . .39 C2
Chalkwell Ho **9** E1 . . . .32 C3
Challenge Cl NW10 . . .21 A4
Challenger Ho **7**
E14 . . . . .33 A2
Challice Way SW2 . . . .74 B3
Challoner Cres
W14 . . . . .140 C1
Challoner Mans
W14 . . . . .140 C1
Challoner St W14 . . . .140 C1
Chalmers Ho **19**

Chalmer's Wlk **14** . . .
SE17 . . . . .48 A4
Chalner Ho SW2 . . . . . .74 C3
Chaloner Ct SE1 . . . . .137 B4
Chalsey Rd SE4 . . . . . .66 B3
Chalton St NW1 . . . . . .83 B1
Chamberlain Cotts
SE5 . . . . .48 C2
Chamberlain Ho **5**
E1 . . . . .32 B2
Chamberlain St
NW1 . . . . .12 B1
Chamberlayne Mans **3**
NW10 . . . . .22 C2
Chamberlayne Rd
NW10 . . . . .22 B4
Chambers La NW10 . . . .9 B1
Chambers Rd N7 . . . . . .14 A4
Chambers St SE16 . . . .139 B3
Chamber St E1 . . . . . . .125 A4
Chambon Pl **6** W6 . . . .38 C2
Chambord Ho **2** E2 . . . .99 A3
Chambord St E2 . . . . . .99 A3
Champion Gr SE5 . . . . .63 C4
Champion Hill SE5 . . . .63 C4
Champion Pk SE5 . . . . .48 C1
Champlain Ho **26**
W12 . . . . .30 A2
Chancel St SE1 . . . . . .122 B1
Chancellor Gr SE21 . . .75 B1
Chancellor Ho
 2 E1 . . . . .32 A1
SW7 . . . . .129 A2
Chancellor Pas E14 . . .33 C1
Chancellors' Ct
WC1 . . . . .106 C4
Chancellor's Rd W6 . . .39 B1
Chancellors St W6 . . . .39 B1
Chancellors Wharf **21**
W6 . . . . .39 B1
Chancel St E1 . . . . . . .122 A1
Chancery Bldgs **13** . . .
E1 . . . . .32 B2
Chancery La EC4 . . . . .107 B2
Chancery Lane Sta
WC1 . . . . .107 B3
Chance St E2 . . . . .98 C2
Chandler Ave E16 . . . . .35 C4
Chandlers Mews
E14 . . . . .41 C4
Chandler St E1 . . . . . . .32 A1
Chandlers Way **11**
SE24 . . . . .74 D4
Chandler Way SE15 . . .49 B3
Chandos PC WC2 . . . .120 A3
Chandos Ct
London E15 . . . . .19 C3
London N10 . . . . .21 A1
London NW2 . . . . .9 B3
Chandos St W1 . . . . . .104 B3
Chandos Way NW11 . .2 A3
Change Alley EC3 . . . .109 C1
Channel Ho E14 . . . . . .33 A4
Channelsea Bsns Ctr
E15 . . . . .27 C3
Channing Sch N6 . . . . .4 A3
Chantrey Rd SW9 . . . . .62 B4
Chantry Cl W9 . . . . . . .23 B1
Chantry Cres NW10 . . .8 B2
Chantry Ct SW6 . . . . . .58 A4
Chantry Sq W8 . . . . . .128 A1
Chantry St N1 . . . . . . .86 B3
Chant Sq E15 . . . . .19 C1
Chant St E15 . . . . .19 C1
Chapel Cl NW10 . . . . . .8 B2

Chapel Ct EC2 . . . . .98 A3
SE1 . . . . .137 B4
Chapel House St
E14 . . . . .42 A2
Chapel Market N1 . . . . .85 B2
Chapel Pl EC2 . . . . .98 A3
N1 . . . . .85 C2
W1 . . . . .104 A1
Chapel Side W2 . . . . . . .114 A3
Chapel St NW1 . . . . .102 A3
SW1 . . . . .131 C2
Chapleton Ho SW2 . .62 C2
Chaplin Cl SE1 . . . . . . .136 A4
Chaplin Ho SW9 . . . . .62 C4
Chaplin Rd NW2 . . . . .8 C2
Chapman Ho E1 . . . . .32 A3
  West Norwood
  SE27 . . . . .75 A1
Chapman St E1 . . . . .32 A2
Chapone Pl W1 . . . . . . .105 B1
Chapter Cl W4 . . . . .37 B3
Chapter Rd SE17 . . . . . .150 B1
London NW2 . . . . .8 C3
Chapter St SW1 . . . . . .147 B3
Chara Pl W4 . . . . .45 C4
Charcot Ho
  SW15 . . . . .56 B1
Charcroft Ct [11]
  W14 . . . . .39 C4
Chard Ho [7] N7 . . . . .5 B2
Chardin Ho SW9 . . . . .173 C4
Chardin Rd [11] W4 . . .38 A2
Chardmore Rd N16 . . . .7 C3
Charcroft Way
  W12 . . . . .39 A4
Charfield Ct W9 . . . . .88 B1
Charford Rd E16 . . . . . . .35 C4
Chargrove Cl [22]
  SE16 . . . . .40 C4
Charing Cross
  SW1 . . . . .120 A2
Charing Cross Hospl
  W6 . . . . .39 C1
Charing Cross Rd
  WC2 . . . . .105 C1
Charing Cross Sta
  WC2 . . . . .120 B2
Charing Ho SE1 . . . . . .135 C4
Charlbert Ct NW8 . . . . . .80 A2
Charlbert St NW8 . . . . .80 A2
Charles Allen Ho
  EC1 . . . . .95 B4
Charles Auffray Ho [1]
  E1 . . . . .32 B4
Charles Barry Cl
  SW4 . . . . .61 B4
Charles Burton Ct
  E5 . . . . .18 A4
Charles Coveney Rd [4]
  SE15 . . . . .49 B2
Charles Darwin Ho [1]
  E2 . . . . .25 A2
Charles Dickens Ho [1]
  E2 . . . . .25 A2
Charles Dickens Prim
  Sch SE1 . . . . .136 C3
Charles Edward Brooke
  Sch SW9 . . . . .48 A2
Charles Haller St [3]
  SW2 . . . . .74 C4

Charles Harrod Ct
  SW13 . . . . .47 B4
Charles Hobson Ho
  NW10 . . . . .8 A1
Charles Hocking Ho [1]
  W3 . . . . .37 B4
Charles II Pl SW3 . . . . .144 C1
Charles II St SW1 . . . . .119 B2
Charles Lamb Ct NW8 .80 A2
Charles Lamb Prim Sch
  N1 . . . . .86 C4
Charles Mackenzie Ho
  SE16 . . . . .153 C4
Charles Pl NW1 . . . . .93 A3
Charles Rowan Ho
  WC1 . . . . .95 B3
Charles Sq N1 . . . . .97 C3
Charles St W1 . . . . .118 A2
  Barnes SW13 . . . . .46 A1
Charleston St
  SE17 . . . . .151 A3
Charlesworth Ho [3]
  EC1 . . . . .96 A2
Charlesworth Ho [2]
  E14 . . . . .33 C3
Charleville Ct SW5 . . .140 C1
Charleville Mans
  W14 . . . . .140 B1
Charleville Rd
  W14 . . . . .140 C1
Charlotte Ho [12] W6 .39 B1
Charlotte Mews
  W1 . . . . .104 A1
  W14 . . . . .140 A4
  London W10 . . . . .30 C3
Charlotte Pl SW1 . . . . .146 C3
Charlotte Rd
  EC2 . . . . .24 A1 98 A2
  Barnes SW13 . . . . .46 B2
Charlotte Sharman Prim
  Sch SE11 . . . . .136 A1
Charlotte Sq [6]
  TW10 . . . . .54 B1
Charlotte Terr N1 . . . . . .85 A3
Charlow Cl SW6 . . . . . .166 C1
Charlton Ct E2 [23] . . .24 B4
  [17] London N7 . . . . .13 C3
  Brentford TW8 . . . . .44 C4
Charlton King's Rd
  NW5 . . . . .13 C3
Charlton Pl N1 . . . . .86 A2
Charlton Rd NW10 . . . . .21 A4
Charlton Way SE10,
  SE3 . . . . .53 A2
Charlwood Ho
  SW1 . . . . .147 B3
  [1] Streatham SW2 . . . .74 B3
Charlwood Pl SW1 . . .147 A3
Charlwood Rd
  SW15 . . . . .57 C3
Charlwood St SW1 . . .147 A2
Charlwood Terr [5]
  SW15 . . . . .57 C3
Charman Ho SW8 . . . .162 C2
  [18] London SW2 . . . . . .62 C1
Charmian Ho [9] N1 . .24 A3
Charmouth Ct TW10 54 B2
Charmouth Ho
  SW8 . . . . .162 C2
Charnock Ho [22]
  W12 . . . . .30 A2
Charnwood Gdns
  E14 . . . . .41 C2

Charrington St NW1 . .83 B2
Charter Ct W1 . . . . .102 B3
London N4 . . . . .5 C4
Charter Ho W2 . . . . . . .106 B1
Charterhouse Bldgs
  EC1 . . . . .96 C1
Charterhouse Mews
  EC1 . . . . .96 C1
Charterhouse Rd
  E8 . . . . .16 C3
Charterhouse Sq
  EC1 . . . . .108 B4
Charterhouse Square
  Prim Sch The
  EC1 . . . . .108 B4
Charterhouse St
  EC1 . . . . .108 A4
Charteris Rd NW6 . . .23 B4
London N4 . . . . .5 C4
Charter Nightingale
  Hospl The NW1 . . . . . .102 B4
Charter Sch The
  SE24 . . . . .63 C2
Chartes Ho SE1 . . . . . .138 B2
Chartfield Ave
  SW15 . . . . .57 B2
Chartfield Sch
  SW15 . . . . .57 B2
Chartfield Sq SW15 .57 C2
Chartham Ct [8]
  SW9 . . . . .62 C4
Chartham Gr SE27 . . .75 A1
Chartham Ho SE1 . . .137 C2
Chartridge SE17 . . . . . .48 C4
Chart St N1 . . . . .97 C4
Chartwell [28] SW19 .69 C3
Chase Ct SW3 . . . . .130 C1
Chase Ctr The
  NW10 . . . . .20 C2
Chaseley Ct W4 . . . . . . .37 A1
Chaseley St E14 . . . . . . .33 A3
Chasemore Ho
  SW6 . . . . .154 B2
Chase Rd NW10 . . . . . . .20 C1
Chase Road Trad Est
  NW10 . . . . .20 C1
Chase The SW4 . . . . . . .61 A4
Chater Ho [6] E2 . . . . .25 C2
Chatfield Rd SW11 . . .59 B4
Chatham Ct SW11 . . . .60 B2
Chatham Ho [6]
  SE5 . . . . .49 A1
Chatham Pl E9 . . . . .17 B2
Chatham Rd SW11 . . . .60 B2
Chatham St SE17 . . . .151 C4
Chatsworth Ct W8 . .141 B4
London E5 . . . . .7 C1
Chatsworth Est E5 . . .17 C4
Chatsworth Gdns
  W3 . . . . .28 A1
Chatsworth Lo [1]
  W4 . . . . .37 C1
Chatsworth Rd
  Chiswick W4 . . . . .45 B4
  London E5 . . . . .17 C4
  London NW2 . . . . .9 C2
Chatsworth Way
  SE27 . . . . .75 B1
Chattenden Ho [8]
  N4 . . . . .6 C4
Chatterton Ct TW9 . .44 B1
Chatterton Rd N4 . . . .6 A1
Chatto Rd SW11 . . . . . . .60 B2
Chaucer Ave TW9 . . .44 C1
Chaucer Ct [9] N16 . . .16 A4
Chaucer Dr SE1 . . . . . .153 A3
Chaucer Ho SW1 . . . .146 C1

Chaucer Rd
  London SE24 . . . . .63 A2
  London W3 . . . . .28 B1
Chauldon Rd SW6 . . . . . .
Cheadle Ct NW8 . . . . . .89 C2
Cheadle Ho [9] E14 . . .33 B3
Cheam St [4] SE15 . . .65 A4
Cheapside EC2 . . . . . . .109 A1
Chearsley SE17 . . . . . .151 A4
Cheddington Ho [2]
  E2 . . . . .24 C4
Chedworth Cl E16 . . . . . .35 B1
Chedworth Ho [2] E5 .7 C2
Cheesemans Terr
  W14 . . . . .140 C1
Chelmer Rd E9 . . . . .17 C3
Chelmsford Cl W6 . . . .47 C4
Chelmsford Ho [3]
  N7 . . . . .14 B4
Chelmsford Sq
  NW10 . . . . .22 B4
Chelsea Barracks
  SW1 . . . . .145 C1
Chelsea Bridge
  SW1 . . . . .160 A4
Chelsea Bridge Rd
  SW1 . . . . .145 C1
Chelsea Cl NW10 . . . .20 C4
Chelsea Cloisters
  SW3 . . . . .144 B3
Chelsea Coll of Art &
  Design
  SW3 . . . . .144 A1
  London W12 . . . . .39 B4
Chelsea Cres
  SW10 . . . . .167 A3
Chelsea Ct SW3 . . . . . .159 B4
Chelsea Emb SW3 . . . .158 C3
Chelsea Est SW3 . . . . .158 B3
Chelsea Farm Ho
  SW10 . . . . .157 C3
Chelsea Gate SW1 . . .145 C1
Chelsea Gdns SW1 . . .145 C1
Chelsea Harbour Design
  Ctr SW10 . . . . .167 A4
Chelsea Harbour Dr
  SW10 . . . . .167 A4
Chelsea Harbour Pier
  SW10 . . . . .167 B3
Chelsea Lo SW3 . . . . . .159 A4
Chelsea Manor Ct
  SW6 . . . . .166 A4
Chelsea Manor Ct
  SW3 . . . . .158 B4
Chelsea Manor Gdns
  SW3 . . . . .144 B1
Chelsea Manor St
  SW3 . . . . .144 B1
Chelsea Manor Studios
  SW3 . . . . .144 B1
Chelsea Park Gdns
  SW3 . . . . .157 C3
Chelsea Physic Gdn*
  SW3 . . . . .158 C4
Chelsea Reach Twr
  SW10 . . . . .157 C2
Chelsea Sq SW3 . . . . .143 C1
Chelsea Twrs SW3 . . .158 B4
Chelsea & Westminster
  Hospl SW10 . . . . .157 A3
Chelsfield Ho
  SE17 . . . . .152 A3
Chelsfield Point [3]
  E9 . . . . .17 C1
Chelsham Ho [1]
  SW4 . . . . .61 C4
Chelsham Rd SW4 . . . .61 C4

Cheltenham Pl [1]
  W3 . . . . .37 A4
Cheltenham Rd
  SE15 . . . . .65 B3
Cheltenham Terr
  SW3 . . . . .145 A2
Chelverton Ct SW15 .57 C3
Chelverton Rd
  SW15 . . . . .57 C3
Chelwood Ho W2 . . . .101 C1
Chelwood Ho [4]
  W2 . . . . .114 A4
Chenies Ho W2 . . . . . .114 A4
Chenies Mews WC1 . .93 B2
Chenies Pl NW1 . . . . . .83 C2
Chenies St WC1 . . . . . .105 B4
Chenies The NW1 . . . .83 C2
Cheniston Gdns
  W8 . . . . .128 A2
Chepstow Cl SW15 . .58 A2
Chepstow Cres
  W11 . . . . .31 C2 113 B4
Chepstow Ct W11 . . . .113 A4
Chepstow Pl
  W2 . . . . .31 C2 113 C4
Chepstow Rd W2 . . . .31 C3
Chepstow Villas
  W11 . . . . .31 C2 113 B4
Chequers Ct EC1 . . . . . .97 C1
Chequers Ho NW8 . . . .90 A2
Chequer St EC1 . . . . .97 A1
Cherbury Ct N1 . . . . .87 C1
Cherbury St N1 . . . . .87 C1
Cheriton Ho [9] E5 . . .17 A3
Cheriton Sq SW17 . . . .72 C2
Cherry Cl [2] SW2 . . . .74 C4
Cherry Ct W3 . . . . .29 A1
Cherry Garden Ho [5]
  SE16 . . . . .40 A4
Cherry Garden Sch
  SE16 . . . . .153 C4
Cherry Garden St
  SE16 . . . . .40 A4
Cherry Laurel Wlk
  SW2 . . . . .62 B1
Cherry Tree Ct [17]
  E9 . . . . .25 B4
Cherry Tree Dr
  SW16 . . . . .74 A1
Cherrytree Ho [8]
  W10 . . . . .22 C2
Cherry Tree Ho
  SE14 . . . . .51 B1
Cherry Trees Sch The
  E3 . . . . .26 C2
Cherry Tree Terr
  SE1 . . . . .138 B4
Cherry Tree Wlk
  EC1 . . . . .97 A1
Cherrywood Cl E3 . . . .26 A2
Cherrywood Dr
  SW15 . . . . .57 C2
Chertsey St SW14 . . . .55 A4
Chertsey Ho E2 . . . . . . .98 C3
Cherwell Ho NW8 . . . .89 C1
Cheryls Cl SW6 . . . . . .166 B4
Chesham Cl SW1 . . . .131 B1
Chesham Ct SW18 . . . .71 C4
Chesham Flats W1 . .117 C4
Chesham Mews
  SW1 . . . . .131 B2
Chesham Pl SW1 . . . .131 B1
Chesham St NW10 . . . . . .
SW1 . . . . .131 B1

Cheshire St
E2 . . . . .24 C1 99 B2

Chesholm Rd N16 . . . . .7 A1
Cheshunt Ho NW6 . . . .78 A3
Chesil Ct 18 E2 . . . . . .25 B3
SW3 . . . . .158 C5
Chesilton Rd SW6 . . .164 C4
Chesney Ct W9 . . . . . .23 C1
Chesney Ho SE13 . . . . .67 C3
Chesney St SW11 . . . .169 B3
Chessington Ho
SW8 . . . . .171 B2
Chesson Rd W14 . . . . .154 A4
Chester Ave TW10 . . . .54 B1
Chester Cl SW1 . . . . . .132 A3
  1 Richmond TW10 . . . .54 B1
Barnes SW13 . . . . .57 A4
Chester Close N
NW1 . . . . .92 B4
Chester Close S
NW1 . . . . .92 B3
Chester Cres E8 . . . . . .16 B3
Chester Ct NW1 . . . . . .92 B3
  4 SE5 . . . . .48 C3
SE8 . . . . .40 C1
London NW5 . . . . .12 C4
Chesterfield Gdns
SE10 . . . . .52 C3
W1 . . . . .118 A2
Chesterfield Gr
SE22 . . . . .64 B2
Chesterfield Hill
W1 . . . . .118 A2
Chesterfield Ho
W1 . . . . .117 C2
Chesterfield Rd W4 . . .45 B4
Chesterfield St
W1 . . . . .118 A2
Chesterfield Way
SE15 . . . . .50 B3
Chesterford Gdns
NW3 . . . . .11 A4
Chester Gate NW1 . . . .92 B3
Chester Ho 1 SE8 . . . .51 B4
London N19 . . . . .4 A2
Chesterman Ct W4 . . . .46 B3
Chester Mews
SW1 . . . . .132 A2
Chester Pl NW1 . . . . . .92 A4
Chester Rd NW1 . . . . . .92 A4
London N19 . . . . .4 A2
Chester Row SW1 . . . .145 C4
Chester Sq SW1 . . . . .146 A4
Chester Sq Mews
SW1 . . . . .132 A1
Chester St E2 . . . . .24 C4
E2 . . . . .24 C1 99 B2
SW1 . . . . .131 C2
Chester Terr NW1 . . . . .92 A4
Chesterton Cl SW18 . . .58 C2
Chesterton Ho
  3 W10 . . . . .31 A4
  21 London SW11 . . . . .59 C4
Chesterton Prim Sch
SW11 . . . . .169 B3
Chesterton Rd W10 . . . .31 A4
Chesterton Sq W8 . . . .141 B3
Chester Way SE11 . . . .149 C3
Chestnut Alley
SW6 . . . . .155 A3
Chestnut Ave 11
SW14 . . . . .55 C4
Chestnut Cl
  5 London N16 . . . . . . .6 C2
London SE14 . . . . .51 B2
Chestnut Ct SW6 . . . . .155 A4
Chestnut Gr SW12 . . . .72 C3

Chestnut Grove Sch
SW12 . . . . .72 C3
Chestnut Ho
  7 London NW3 . . . . . .12 B2
London SE4 . . . . .66 B4
  1 London NW4 . . . . . . .1 A4
West Norwood SE27 . . .75 B1
Chestnut Rd SE21, . . .
SE27 . . . . .75 B1
Chestnuts The 1
N5 . . . . .15 A4
Chettle Cl SE1 . . . . . . .137 B2
Chetwode Ho NW8 . . . .90 A2
Chetwode Rd SW17 . . . .72 B1
Chetwynd Rd NW5 . . . . .4 A1
Cheval Ct SW15 . . . . . .57 A3
Cheval Pl SW7 . . . . . . .130 B2
Cheval St E14 . . . . .41 C3
Chevening Rd NW6 . . . . .23 A4
SE10 . . . . .43 B1
Cheverell Ho 3 E2 . . . .24 C3
Cheverton Rd N19 . . . . . .4 C3
Chevet St E9 . . . . .18 A3
Chevington NW2 . . . . . . .1 B1
Cheviot Ct 15 SE14 . . . .50 B3
Cheviot Gdns NW2 . . . . .1 A2
Cheviot Ho N16 . . . . . . .7 B3
Chevron Cl E16 . . . . . . .35 C3
Cheylesmore Ho
SW1 . . . . .146 A2
Cheyne Ct SW3 . . . . . .158 C4
Cheyne Gdns SW3 . . . .158 B3
Cheyne Mews SW3 . . . .158 B3
Cheyne Row SW3 . . . . .158 B3
Cheyne Wlk SW10 . . . .157 B2
Cheyney Ho 2 E9 . . . . .17 C2
Chichele Rd NW2 . . . . . .9 C3
Chicheley St SE1 . . . . .135 A4
Chichester Ho NW6 . . . .23 C3
Chichester Rd NW6 . . . .23 C3
NW6 . . . . .2 00 B4
Chichester Rents
WC2 . . . . .107 B2
Chichester St SW1 . . . .147 A1
Chichester Way E14 . . .42 C2
Chicksand St E1 . . . . . .111 A4
Chicksand St E1 . . . . . .111 B3
Chiddingstone SE13 . . .67 B2
Chiddingstone St
SW6 . . . . .165 C2
Chigwell Hill E1 . . . . . . .32 A2
Chiham Ho 6 SE15 . . . .50 B4
Chilcombe Ho 6
SW15 . . . . .68 C4
Chilcot Cl 15 E14 . . . . . .34 A3
Childebert Rd SW17 . . . .73 A2
Childeric Prim Sch
SE14 . . . . .51 A3
Childeric Rd SE14 . . . . .51 A3
Childerley St SW6 . . . .164 A4
Childers St SE8 . . . . . . .51 B4
Childers St 1 SE8 . . . . .41 B3
Child's Hill Prim Sch
NW2 . . . . .1 A1
Child's Pl SW5 . . . . . . .141 C3
Child's St SW5 . . . . . . .141 C3
Child's Wlk SW5 . . . . . .141 C3
Chilham Ct 14 SW9 . . . .62 C4
Chilham Ho SE1 . . . . . .137 C2
Chillingworth Rd
N7 . . . . .14 C3
Chiltern Ho SE17 . . . . . .48 C4
  5 W10 . . . . .31 A4
  5 London N16 . . . . . . .7 B3

Chiltern Rd E3 . . . . .26 C1
Chiltern St W1 . . . . . . .103 B4
Chilton Gr SE8 . . . . .41 A2
Chilton Rd TW9 . . . . . . .54 C4
Chilton St E2 . .24 B1 99 A2
Chilver St SE10 . . . . . . .43 B1
Chilworth Ct 5
SW19 . . . . .69 C3
Chilworth Mews
W2 . . . . .101 B1
Chilworth St W2 . . . . . .101 A1
China Ct 8 E1 . . . . .32 A1
China Mews 17 SW2 . . .74 B4
Chindit Ho 11 N16 . . . . .15 C4
Chinnocks Wharf
E14 . . . . .33 A2
Chipka St E14 . . . . .42 B4
Chipley St SE14 . . . . . . .51 A4
Chippendale Ho
SW1 . . . . .146 B1
Chippenham Gdns
NW6 . . . . .23 C2
Chippenham Mews
W9 . . . . .23 C1
Chippenham Rd W9 . . . .23 C1
Chip St SW4 . . . . .61 C3
Chipstead Ho 4
SW2 . . . . .74 A3
Chipstead St SW6 . . . .165 C2
Chisenhale Prim Sch
E3 . . . . .26 A3
Chisenhale Rd E3 . . . . . .26 A3
Chisholm Ct 6 W6 . . . . .38 C1
Chisholm Rd 13
TW10 . . . . .54 B1
Chisledon Wlk E9 . . . . .18 B2
Chislehurst Rd
TW10 . . . . .54 A2
Chislet 5 NW5 . . . . . . .12 C2
Chiswell St EC1 . . . . . .109 B4
Chiswick & Bedford
Park Prep Sch W4 . . .38 A2
Chiswick Common Rd
W4 . . . . .37 C2
Chiswick Com Sch
W4 . . . . .45 C3
Chiswick Green Studios
11 W4 . . . . .37 B2
Chiswick High Rd
W4 . . . . .38 A2
Chiswick High Road
(North Circular Rd)
W4 . . . . .36 C1
Chiswick Ho ★ W4 . . . . .45 C3
Chiswick La W4 . . . . . . .38 A1
Chiswick La S W4 . . . . .46 B4
Chiswick Mall W4 . . . . .46 B4
Chiswick Maternity
Hospl W4 . . . . .38 B1
Chiswick Park Sta
W4 . . . . .37 B2
Chiswick Pier W4 . . . . .46 B3
Chiswick Pk W4 . . . . . . .37 A2
Chiswick Plaza W4 . . . .45 B4
Chiswick Quay W4 . . . . .45 B2
Chiswick Rd W4 . . . . . . .37 B2
Chiswick Rdbt W4 . . . . .36 C1
Chiswick Sq W4 . . . . . . .46 A4
Chiswick Staithe
W4 . . . . .45 B2
Chiswick Terr 6
W4 . . . . .37 B2
Chiswick Village
W4 . . . . .45 A4
Chiswick Wharf W4 . . . .46 B4

Chitty St W1 . . . . .105 A4
Chivalry Rd SW11 . . . . .60 A2
Chivelston SW19 . . . . . .69 C3
Chobham Gdns
SW19 . . . . .69 C2
Chobham Rd E15 . . . . . .19 C3
Cholmeley Cres N6 . . . . .4 A4
Cholmeley Lo N6 . . . . . . .4 A3
Cholmeley Pk N6 . . . . . . .4 A4
Cholmley Gdns
NW6 . . . . .10 C3
Cholmondeley Ave
NW10 . . . . .21 C3
Chopin's Ct 15 E14 . . . .32 A1
Chopwell Cl E15 . . . . . . .19 C1
Choumert Gr SE15 . . . . .49 C1
Choumert Mews
SE15 . . . . .49 C1
Choumert Rd SE15 . . . . .49 B1
Choumert Sq 2
SE15 . . . . .49 C1
Chow Sq 2 E8 . . . . .16 B3
Chrisp Ho SE10 . . . . . . .53 A4
Chrisp St E14 . . . . .34 A3
Christchurch Ave
NW6 . . . . .10 A1
Christ Church Bentinck
CE Prim Sch NW1 . . .102 B4
Christ Church CE Prim
Sch
London N19 . . . . .4 B1
SW3 . . . . .158 C4
Christ Church CE Prim
Sch
SE10 . . . . .43 A1
London NW6 . . . . .10 B1
Christ Church CE Sch
E1 . . . . .110 C3
Christ Church Ct
London NW10 . . . . .21 A4
London NW6 . . . . .10 A1
Christchurch Hill
NW3 . . . . .11 C4
Christchurch Ho 2
SW2 . . . . .74 A3
Christchurch Pas
NW3 . . . . .2 B1
Christ Church Prim Sch,
Hampstead NW3 . . . .2 C1
Christchurch Rd
SW14 . . . . .55 B2
Christ Church Sch
NW1 . . . . .92 B4
Christ Church Sq 4
E9 . . . . .25 B4
Christchurch St
SW3 . . . . .158 C4
Christ Church
Streatham CE Prim Sch
SW2 . . . . .74 B3
Christchurch Terr
SW3 . . . . .158 C4
Christchurch Way
SE10 . . . . .43 A1
Christian Ct SE16 . . . . . .33 B1
Christian St E1 . . . . . . .111 C1
Christie Ct
  1 London N19 . . . . . . .5 A2
London NW3 . . . . .12 A3
Christie Ho 2 SE10 . . . .43 B1
Christie Rd E9 . . . . .18 A2
Christina Sq N4 . . . . .6 A3
Christina St EC2 . .97 C2 98 A2
Christopher Boone's
Almshouses SE13 . . .67 C3
Christopher Cl SE16 . . . .40 C4
Christopher Hatton Prim
Sch EC1 . . . . .95 C1

Christopher Lo 2 N6 . . . .4 C4
Christopher Pl NW1 . . . .93 C3
Christopher St EC2 . . . .97 C1
Christ's Coll SE3 . . . . . .53 C2
Christ's Sch (East Side)
TW10 . . . . .54 C2
Christ's Sch (West Side)
TW10 . . . . .54 B2
Christ the King RC Prim
Sch N4 . . . . .5 B2
Chryssell Rd SW9 . . . . .163 C1
Chubworthy St
SE14 . . . . .51 A4
Chudleigh Rd
London NW6 . . . . .9 C1
London SE4 . . . . .66 C2
Chudleigh St E1 . . . . . . .32 C3
Chumleigh Gdns
SE5 . . . . .49 A4
Chumleigh St SE5 . . . . .49 A4
Church App SE21 . . . . . .75 C1
Church Ave NW1 . . . . . .13 A2
Church Cl W8 . . . . .128 A4
Church Cres E9 . . . . . . .17 C1
Churchcroft Cl
SW12 . . . . .72 C4
Church Ct EC4 . . . . .107 C1
Churchdale Ct 1
W4 . . . . .37 A1
Church Entry EC4 . . . . .108 B1
Church Estate
Almshouses 8
TW9 . . . . .54 B3
Churchfield Ho W2 . . . . .89 B1
Churchfield Mans
SW6 . . . . .165 A1
Churchfield Rd W3 . . . . .28 B1
Churchfields SE10 . . . . .52 B4
Church Garth 3 N19 . . . .4 C2
Church Gate SW6 . . . . . .58 A4
Church Gn SW9 . . . . . . .173 C2
Church Gr SE13 . . . . . . .67 A2
Churchill Ct
London N4 . . . . .5 C4
London NW2 . . . . .9 A3
Churchill Gardens Prim
Sch SW1 . . . . .147 A1
Churchill Gdns
SW1 . . . . .160 C4
Churchill Gdns Rd
SW1 . . . . .160 C4
Churchill Pl E14 . . . . . . .34 A1
Churchill Rd
London NW2 . . . . .9 A2
London NW5 . . . . .13 A4
Churchill Wlk E9 . . . . . .17 B3
Church Mead SE5 . . . . . .48 B3
Churchmead Rd
NW10 . . . . .8 C2
Church Path W4 . . . . . . .37 B3
Church Pl SW1 . . . . . . .119 A3
Church Rd Acton W3 . . .37 B4
Barnes SW13 . . . . .46 C2
  21 London N1 . . . . . . .15 B2
London NW10 . . . . .8 A1
Richmond TW10,TW9 . .54 A2
Church Row NW3 . . . . . .11 B4
Church Row Mews
SW3 . . . . .90 A1
Churchward Ho
SE17 . . . . .48 A4
SW5 . . . . .141 A1

Churchway NW1 ....93 C4
Church Wlk
  Barnes SW13 ....46 C2
  London N16 ....15 C4
  London NW2 ....1 B1
Churchyard Row
  SE11 ....150 B4
Churnfield ■ N4 ....5 C2
Churston ⓱ SW2 ....74 C3
Churston Mans
  WC1 ....94 B1
Churton Pl SW1 ......147 A3
  Brentford W4 ....45 A4
Churton St SW1 ......147 A3
Chute Ho NW9 ....17 B1
Chuter Ede Ho
  SW6 ....155 A3
Cicada Rd SW18 ......59 B2
Cicely Ho NW8 ....79 C1
Cicely Rd SE15 ....49 C2
Cinnabar Wharf Central
  E1 ....125 C2
Cinnabar Wharf East
  E1 ....125 C2
Cinnabar Wharf West
  E1 ....125 C2
Cinnamon Cl ❽
  SE15 ....49 B3
Cinnamon Row ❸
  SW11 ....59 B4
Cinnamon St E1 ....32 A1
Cinnamon Wharf
  SE1 ....139 A4
Circle Ho ⑯ E14 .....34 C3
Circle The SE1 ......139 A4
Circus Lo NW8 ....89 B4
Circus Mews W1 .....102 C4
Circus Pl EC2 ....109 C3
Circus St SE10 ....52 B3
Cirencester St W2 ....100 A4
Cissbury Ho ❽
  SE26 ....76 C1
Citizen Ho N7 ....14 C4
Citizen Rd N7 ....14 C4
Citron Terr ❸ SE15 ..65 A4
Citrus Ho ❶ SE8 .....41 B1
City Airport Pier
  E16 ....35 B1
City and Islington Coll
  EC1 ....96 A4
City Banking Coll
  SE1 ....138 A4
City Bsns Ctr ❷❽
  SE16 ....40 B4
City Central Est EC1 .96 C3
City Forum EC1 ....96 C4
City Garden Row
  N1 ....86 B1
City Gate ❶
  E1 ....25 B1
City & Guilds of London
  Art Sch The SE1 ...149 C1
City Harbour E14 .....42 A3
City & Islington Coll
  N1 ....87 A4
City Literature Inst The
  WC2 ....106 B3
City of London Sch
  EC4 ....122 C4
City of London Sch for
  Girls EC2 ....109 A4
City of Westminster Coll
  NW1 ....102 A4
  W2 ....101 B4

City of Westminster
  Coll, Maida Vale Ctr
  W9 ....88 B3
City of Westminster
  Coll, Queens Park Ctr
  W9 ....23 C2
City Rd EC1 ....97 A4
City Thameslink Sta
  EC4 ....108 A1
Civil Service Coll
  SW1 ....146 C3
Clabon Mews SW1 ...144 C4
Clack St SE16 ....40 B4
Claire Ct NW2 ....10 B2
Claire Pl E14 ....41 C3
Clancarty Rd SW6 ...165 C1
Clandon Cl W3 ....37 A4
Clandon St SE8 ....51 C1
Clanfield Ho ⑫
  SW15 ....68 C3
Clanricarde Gdns
  W2 ....31 C2 113 C3
Clapham Common *
  SW4 ....61 B3
Clapham Common North
  Side SW4 ....60 C3
Clapham Common
  South Side SW4 ....61 A2
Clapham Common Sta
  SW4 ....61 B3
Clapham Common West
  Side
  London SW11 ....60 C2
  London SW4,SW11 ...60 B3
Clapham Court Terr ❷
  SW4 ....62 A2
Clapham Cres SW4 ...61 C3
Clapham Ct ❸ SW4 ..62 A2
Clapham High St
  SW4 ....61 C3
Clapham High Street Sta
  SW4 ....61 C3
Clapham Junction Est
  SW11 ....60 A4
Clapham Junction Sta
  SW11 ....60 A3
Clapham Manor Ct ❶
  SW4 ....61 B4
Clapham Manor Prim
  Sch SW4 ....61 B4
Clapham Manor St
  SW4 ....61 B4
Clapham Mans SW4 ..61 A1
Clapham North Sta
  SW4 ....62 A4
Clapham Park Rd
  SW4 ....61 C3
Clapham Park Terr ❹
  SW2 ....62 A2
Clapham South Sta
  SW4 ....61 A2
Clapham Comm E5 ....7 C2
Clapton Girls Tec Coll
  E5 ....17 B3
Clapton Pas E5 ....17 B3
Clapton Sq E5 ....17 B3
Clapton Terr E5 ......7 C3
Clapton Way E5 ....7 C1
Clara Grant Prim Sch
  The E14 ....26 C1
Clare Ct WC1 ....94 B3
Claredale Ho ❸ E2 ..25 A3
Claredale St E2 ......24 C3
Clare Gdns W11 ......31 A3
Clare Grant Ho ❽
  E14 ....41 C3

Clare Ho ❻ E3 ....26 B4
Clare La N1 ....15 B1
Clare Lawn Ave
  SW14 ....55 C2
Clare Mews SW6 .....156 A1
Clare Mkt WC2 ......107 A1
Claremont ❶ SW15 ..58 B2
Claremont Cl N1 .....85 C1
Claremont Ct ❷
  ❹ Streatham SW2 ..73 B3
Claremont Ct ❶ W9 .23 B3
Claremont Gr W4 .....46 A3
Claremont Rd
  London N6 ....4 B4
  London W9 ....23 B3
Claremont Sq N1 .....85 B1
Claremont St SE10 ...52 A4
Clorenco Ave SW4 ...61 C1
Clarence Ct ❿ W6 ...39 A2
Clarence Gate Gdns
  NW1 ....91 A1
Clarence Gdns NW1 ..92 B3
Clarence Ho W1 .....147 A1
Clarence Ho *
  SW1 ....119 A1
Clarence La SW15 ....56 B1
Clarence Mews
  ❶ SE16 ....32 C1
  Balham SW12 ....73 A4
  London E5 ....17 A3
Clarence PI ❷❺ E5 ..17 A3
Clarence Rd
  London E5 ....17 A4
  London N15 ....10 B1
  London NW6 ....10 B1
  Richmond TW9 ....44 C2
Clarence St ❼ TW9 ..54 A3
Clarence Terr NW1 ..91 A2
Clarence Way NW1 ...13 A1
Clarence Wlk SW4 ..172 A2
Clarendon Cl W2 ....116 A4
❼ Hackney E9 ....17 B1
Clarendon Cross
  W11 ....31 A2
Clarendon Ct ❶
  London NW2 ....10 A2
  ❶ Richmond TW9 ....44 C2
Clarendon Dr SW15 ..57 B3
Clarendon Flats
  W1 ....103 C1
Clarendon Gdns
  W9 ....89 A1
  London NW4 ....10 A3
Clarendon Ho NW1 ...83 A1
Clarendon Mews
  W2 ....116 A4
Clarendon PI W2 ....116 A4
Clarendon Rd
  W11 ....31 A1 112 B3
Clarendon Rise
  SE13 ....67 B3
Clarendon St SW1 ..146 B2
Clarendon Terr W9 ..89 A2
Clarendon Wlk ❿
  W11 ....31 A3
Clare PI SW15 ....68 B4
Clare Rd NW10 ....8 C1
Clare St E2 ....25 A3
Clareville Ct SW7 ..143 A3
Clareville Gr SW7 ..143 A3
Clareville Grove Mews
  SW7 ....143 A3
Clareville St SW7 ..143 A3
Clarewood Ct W1 ...102 C3
Clarewood Wlk
  SW9 ....62 C3

Clarges Ho W1 .....118 B2
Clarges Mews W1 ...118 A2
Clarges St W1 ......118 B2
Claribel Rd SW9 .....48 A1
Claridge Ct SW6 ...164 C3
Clarissa Ho ❼ E14 ..34 A3
Clarissa St E8 ....24 B4
Clarke Ho ❷ SW4 ...61 B4
Clarke Path N16 .....7 C3
Clarkes Mews W1 ...103 C4
Clark Lawrence Ct ❶
  SW11 ....59 C4
Clarkson Ho SW11 ...59 C3
Clarkson Rd E16 .....35 B3
Clarkson Row NW1 ..82 C1
Clarkson St E2 ....25 A2
Clark's PI EC2 .....110 A2
Clark St E1 ....32 A4
Classic Mans ❸❸ E9 .17 B1
Classinghall Ho ❹
  SW15 ....57 C1
Claude Rd SE15 ......50 A1
Claude St E14 ....41 C2
Claudia Jones Way
  SW2 ....62 A1
Claudia PI SW19 .....70 A3
Clavell St ❸ SE10 ...52 B4
Claverdale Rd SW2 ..74 C4
Clavering Ave SW13 ..47 A4
Clavering Ho SE13 ...67 C3
Claverton St ❶ SW1 147 A1
Clave St E1 ....32 B1
Claxton Gr W6 ....47 C4
Claybank Gr SE13 ...67 A4
Claybrook Rd W6 ....47 C4
Claydon SE17 ......150 C4
Clayhall Ct ❿ E3 ...26 B3
Claylands Pl SW8 ..163 B2
Claylands Rd SW8 ..163 A3
Claypole Rd E15 .....27 B3
Claypond Ave TW8 ..36 A2
Claypond's Hospl & Day
  Treatment Ctr
  TW8 ....36 A1
Claypond's La TW8 ..36 A1
Clays Ct N16 ....7 B3
Clays La E15 ....19 A3
Clays Lane Cl E15 ...19 A3
Clay St W1 ....103 A3
Clayton Ct N16 ....7 C4
Clayton Ho ❷ E9 ....17 B1
Clayton Mews SE10 .52 C2
Clayton Rd SE15 .....49 C2
Clayton St SE11 ...163 B4
Clearbrook Way ❶❸
  E1 ....32 B3
Clearwater Ho ❿
  TW10 ....54 A2
Clearwater Terr ❹
  W11 ....39 C4
Clearwell Dr W9 .....88 B1
Cleaver Ho ❾ NW3 ..12 B1
Cleaver Sq SE11 ...149 C1
Cleaver St SE11 ....149 C2
Cleeve Ho E2 ....98 B3
Cleeve Way SW15 ...68 B4
Clegg St ❶❸ E1 .....32 A1
Cleland Ho ❷❿ E2 ...25 B3
Clematis St W12 .....29 C2
Clem Attlee Ct
  SW6 ....155 A3
Clemence St E14 .....33 B4
Clement Attlee Ho
  NW10 ....8 B1
Clement Ave SW4 ....61 C3
Clement Cl
  London NW6 ....9 B1

Clement Cl continued
  London W4 ....37 C2
Clement Ho ❶❹ SE8 .41 A2
London W10 ....30 B4
Clements Ave ❶
  E16 ....35 C2
Clements Inn WC2 ..107 A1
Clements Inn Pas
  WC2 ....107 A1
Clement's La EC2,
  EC4 ....123 C4
Clemson Ho ❾ E8 ...24 B4
Clenham St SE1 .....137 A4
Clenston Mews
  W1 ....102 C2
Clent Ho ❶❸ N16 ....7 B3
Cleopatra's Needle *
  WC2 ....120 C2
Clephane Rd ❷ N1 ..15 B2
Clephane Rd N N1 ..15 B2
Clephane Rd S N1 ...15 C2
Clere PI EC2 ....97 C2
Clere St EC2 ....97 C2
Clerkenwell Cl EC1 ..95 C1
Clerkenwell Gn EC1 ..96 A1
Clerkenwell Parochial
  CE Prim Sch EC1 ..95 B4
Clerkenwell Rd EC1 ..96 A1
Clermont Rd E9 ......25 B4
Clevedon Ct SW11 ..168 A4
  Dulwich SE21 ....75 C1
Clevedon Mans
  NW5 ....12 C4
Cleve Ho NW6 ....11 A1
Cleveland Ave W4 ...38 B2
Cleveland Gdns
  W2 ....100 C1
  Barnes SW13 ....46 B1
Cleveland Gr ❸ E1 ..25 B1
Cleveland Mans
  SW9 ....163 B1
  W9 ....23 C1
  ❹ London NW6 .....10 B1
Cleveland Mews
  W1 ....104 C4
Cleveland Pl SW1 ..119 A2
Cleveland Rd
  Barnes SW13 ....46 B1
  London N1 ....15 C1
  ❶❹ London W4 .....37 B3
Cleveland Row
  SW1 ....119 A1
Cleveland Sq W2 ...100 C1
Cleveland St W1 .....92 C1
Cleveland Terr W2 ..101 A2
Cleveland Way E1 ...25 B1
Clevedon Cl N16 .....7 B1
Cleve Rd NW6 ....11 A1
Cleverly Cotts W12 ..29 B1
Cleverly Est W12 ....29 C2
Cley Ho SE4 ....65 C3
Clichy Ho ❷❼ E1 ...32 B4
Clifden Rd E5 ....17 C3
Cliff Ct ❶ NW1 .....13 C2
Cliffe Ho ❹ SE10 ...43 B1
Clifford Ave SW14 ..45 B1
Clifford Ct
  London NW10 ....8 A4
  London W2 ....100 A3
  Wandsworth SW18 ...71 C4
Clifford Dr SW9 .....63 A3
Clifford Gdns NW10 .22 B3
Clifford Haigh Ho
  SW6 ....47 C3
Clifford Ho W14 ...140 C3

Clifford's Inn Pas EC4 ....107 B1
Clifford St W1 ....118 C3
Clifford Way NW10 ...8 B4
Cliff Rd NW1 ....13 C2
Cliffsend Ho SW9 ....173 C1
Cliff Terr SE8 ....51 C1
Cliffview Rd SE13 ...66 C4
Cliff Villas NW1 ....13 C2
Clifton Ave W12 ...29 B1
Clifton Cres SE15 ...50 A3
Clifton Ct NW8 ....89 B2
SE15 ....50 A3
London N4 ....5 C2
Putney SW15 ....57 C2
Clifton Gate SW10 ...156 C4
Clifton Gdns W9 ....88 C1
London W4 ....37 C2
Clifton Gr E8 ....16 C2
Clifton Hill NW8 ...78 C3
Clifton Ho E2 ....98 C2
Clifton Mans 4
SW9 ....62 C3
Clifton Pl E16 ....80 B4
W2 ....101 C1
Clifton Rd E16 ....35 A4
W9 ....89 A2
London NW10 ....21 C3
Clifton Rise SE14 ...51 A3
Clifton St EC2 ...24 A1 98 A1
Clifton Terr N4 ....5 C2
Clifton Villas W9 ...100 C4
Clifton Way SE15 ...50 B3
Climsland Ho SE1 ...121 C2
Clinch Ct 11 E16 ...35 C4
Cline Ho SW15 ....56 C2
Clinger Ct N1 ....24 A4
Clink St SE1 ....123 B2
Clinton Rd E3 ....26 A2
Clipper Cl SE16 ...40 C4
Clipper Ho E14 ....42 B1
Clipper Way SE13 ...67 B3
Clipstone Ho 10
SW15 ....56 C2
Clipstone Mews
W1 ....104 C4
Clipstone St W1 ...104 C4
Clissold Cres N16 ...15 C4
Clissold Ct N4 ....6 C2
Clissold Ho 2 N16 ...6 C3
Clissold Rd N16 ....6 C1
Clitheroe Rd SW9 ...172 B1
Clive Ho W9 ....89 A2
Cliveden Pl SW1 ...145 B4
Clive Ho SE10 ....52 B4
London SW8 ....171 B2
Clive Rd SE21,SE27 ...75 C1
Cloak La EC4 ....123 B4
Clochar Ct NW10 ...21 B4
Clock Ho N16 ....7 B4
Clockhouse Cl
SW19 ....69 B2
Clockhouse Pl
SW15 ....58 A1
Clockhouse The
SW19 ....69 B1
Clock Tower Mews
N1 ....87 A3
Clock Tower Pl N7 ...14 A2
Cloister Rd
London NW2 ....1 B2
London W3 ....28 B4
Cloisters Ct N6 ....4 A3
Cloisters The SW9 ...173 C3
Clonbrock Rd N16 ...16 A4
Cloncurry St SW6 ...47 C1

Clone Ct 4 W12 ....38 A3
Clonmel Rd SW6 ...165 A4
Clonmore St SW18 ...70 B3
Clorane Gdns NW3 ...1 C1
Close The TW9 ....55 A4
Cloth Ct EC1 ....108 B3
Cloth Fair EC1 ....108 B3
Clothier St EC3 ...110 B2
Cloth St EC1 ....108 C4
Cloudesdale Rd
SW17 ....73 A2
Cloudesley Mans
N1 ....85 C3
Cloudesley Pl N1 ...85 C3
Cloudesley Rd N1 ...85 C3
Cloudesley Sq N1 ...85 C4
Cloudesley St N1 ...85 C3
Clove Cres E14 ....34 C2
Clovelly Ct NW2 ...9 B3
Clovelly Ho W2 ...100 C2
Clovelly Rd W4 ....37 C4
Clovelly Way E1 ...32 B3
Clover Mews SW3 ...159 A4
Clowes Ho 3 SW4 ...62 A3
Cloysters Gn E1 ...125 B2
Club Row E2 ...24 B1 98 C2
Clunbury St N1 ....87 C1
Clunie Ho SW1 ....131 A2
Cluny Mews SW5 ...141 B3
Cluny Pl SE1 ....138 A2
Cluse Ct N1 ....86 C2
Clutton St E14 ....34 A4
Clyde Ct N1 ....83 C2
Clyde Flats SW6 ...154 C2
Clyston St SW8 ...171 A2
Coach & Horses Yd
W1 ....118 C4
Coach House La
London N5 ....15 A4
Wimbledon SW19 ...69 C1
Coach House Mews
SE23 ....65 C1
Coach House Yd
NW3 ....11 C4
Coachmaker Mews 5
SW9 ....62 A4
Coalbrook Mans 3
SW12 ....73 A3
Coaldale Wlk SE21 ...75 B4
Coalecroft Rd SW15 ...57 B2
Coalport Ho SE11 ...149 B4
Coal Wharf Rd W12 ...30 C1
Coates Ave SW18 ...60 A1
Coates Ct NW3 ....12 A3
Coate St E2 ....24 C3
Coates Wlk TW8 ...36 A1
Cobbett St SW8 ...163 A1
Cobble La N1 ....15 A1
Cobble Mews N4,N5 ...6 B1
Cobbold Ct SW1 ...147 B4
Cobbold Ind Est
NW10 ....8 A4
Cobbold Mews W12 ...38 B4
Cobbold Rd
London NW10 ...8 A4
London W12 ...38 B4
Cobb's Hall 1 SW6 ...47 C4
Cobb St E1 ....110 C3
Cobden Bldgs WC1 ...94 C4

Cobden Ho E2 ....99 C4
NW1 ....82 C2
Cobham Cl SW11 ...60 A1
Cobham Mews 3
NW1 ....13 C1
Coborn Mews 6 E3 ...26 B2
Coborn Rd E3 ....26 B2
Coborn St E3 ....26 B2
Cobourg Prim Sch
SE5 ....49 B4
Cobourg Rd SE5 ...49 B4
Cobourg St NW1 ...93 A3
Coburg Cl SW1 ...147 A4
Coburg Cres SW2 ...74 C3
Coburg Dwellings 10
E1 ....32 B2
Cochrane Cl NW8 ...79 C1
Cochrane Mews
NW8 ....79 C1
Cochrane St NW8 ...79 C1
Cockburn Ho SW1 ...147 C1
Cock Hill E1 ....110 B3
Cock La EC1 ....108 B3
Cockpit Yd WC1 ...107 A4
Cockspur Ct SW1 ...119 C2
Cockspur St SW1 ...119 C2
Coda Ctr The SW6 ...164 B4
Code St E1 ....24 B1 99 A1
Codicote Ho 28 SE8 ...40 C2
Codicote Terr N4 ....6 B2
Codling Cl E1 ....125 C2
Codrington Ct SE16 ...33 A1
Codrington Ho 7
E1 ....25 A1
Codrington Mews
W11 ....31 A3
Cody Rd E16 ....27 C1
Coffey St SE8 ....51 C3
Cohen Lo E5 ....18 A3
Coin St SE1 ....121 B2
Coity Rd NW5 ....12 C2
Cokers La SE21 ....75 C3
Coke St E1 ....111 C2
Colas Mews 7 NW6 ...23 C4
Colbeck Mews
SW5 ....142 B3
Colberg Pl N16 ....7 B4
Colbert 1 SE5 ....49 B2
Colborne Ho 7 E14 ...33 C2
Colchester Ho
SE8 ....171 B4
Colchester St E1 ...111 A2
Coldbath Sq EC1 ...95 B2
Coldbath St SE13 ...52 A1
Coldblow La SE14 ...50 C4
Coldharbour E14 ...34 B1
Coldharbour Ind Est
SE5 ....48 B1
Coldharbour La
SW9 ....63 A4
Coldharbour Pl SE5 ...48 C1
Coldstream Gdns
SW18 ....58 B1
Colebeck Mews N1 ...15 A2
Colebert Ave E1 ...25 B1
Colebert Ho 20 E1 ...25 B1
Colebrook Cl SW19 ...34 A3
Colebrook Ct SW3 ...144 B3
Colebrooke Pl N1 ...86 B3
Colebrooke Row
N1 ....86 A4
N1 ....86 B2
Colebrooke Sch N1 ...86 B2
E14 ....34 A3
Coleby Path 21 SE5 ...48 C3

Colechurch Ho
SE1 ....153 B1
Coleford Rd SW18 ...59 B2
Colegrave Prim Sch
E15 ....19 C3
Colegrave Rd E15 ...19 C3
Colegrove Rd SE15 ...49 B4
Colehall Ct
SW10 ....142 B1
Coleherne Mans
SW10 ....142 B1
Coleherne Mews
SW10 ....142 A1
Coleherne Rd
SW10 ....142 A1
Colehill Gdns SW6 ...164 A3
Colehill La SW6 ...164 B3
Cole Ho SE1 ....135 C3
Coleman Ct SW18 ...70 C4
Coleman Fields N1 ...87 A4
Coleman Mans N19 ...5 A4
Coleman Rd SE5 ...49 A3
Coleman St EC2 ...109 B2
Coleman St Bldgs
EC2 ....109 B2
Colenso Rd E5 ....17 B4
Coleraine Rd SE3 ...53 B4
Coleridge Cl SW8 ...170 B1
Coleridge Ct W14 ...39 C3
Coleridge Gdns
NW6 ....11 B1
London NW6 ....11 B1
Coleridge Ho SE17 ...151 A2
SW1 ....147 A1
Coleridge Prim Sch
N8 ....5 A4
Coleridge Rd N4,N7 ...5 C2
Coles Ct SW11 ....167 C3
Coleshill Flats
SW1 ....145 C3
Cole St SE1 ....137 A3
Colestown St
SW11 ....168 B2
Colet Gdns W14 ...39 C2
Colet Ho SE17 ....150 B1
Colette Ct 5 SE16 ...40 C4
Coley St WC1 ....95 A1
Colfe & Hatchcliffe's
Glebe SE13 ....67 A2
Colgate Ho SE13 ...52 A1
Colin Blanchard Ho
SE4 ....51 C1
Colin Ct SW16 ....73 C2
Colinette Rd SW15 ...57 B3
Colin Rd NW10 ....8 C2
Colinsdale N1 ....86 A3
Colin Winter Ho 37
E1 ....25 B1
Coliston Pass SW18 ...70 C4
Coliston Rd SW18 ...70 C4
Collamore Ave
SW18 ....72 A3
Collard Pl NW1 ....13 A1
College App SE10 ...52 B4
College Cl E5 ....17 B3
College Cres NW3 ...11 C2
College Cross N1 ...14 C1
College Ct SW3 ....145 A1
London NW3 ....11 C2
London W6 ....39 B1
College Gdns
Dulwich SE21 ....76 A3
Upper Tooting SW17 ...72 A2
College Gr NW1 ....83 B4
College Hill EC4 ...123 A4
College La NW5 ....13 A4
College Park Cl
SE13 ....67 C3

College Park Sch
W2 ....100 A1
SW10 ....156 C2
College Pl NW1 ....83 A3
SW10 ....156 C2
College Rd
Dulwich SE19,SE21 ...76 A2
London NW10 ....22 B3
College Rd E24 ....123 A4
College Terr E3 ....26 B2
Collent Ho 12 E9 ...17 B2
Collent St E9 ....17 B2
Collerston Ho SE10 ...43 B1
Collette Ho N16 ....7 B3
Collett Rd SE16 ...139 C2
Colley Ho 17 N7 ....13 C3
Collier St N1 ....84 C1
Collingbourne Rd
W12 ....30 A1
Collingham Gdns
SW5 ....142 B3
Collingham Pl
SW5 ....142 B4
Collingham Rd
SW5 ....142 B3
Collingwood Ho 27
E1 ....25 A1
Collingwood St E1 ...25 A1
Collins Ct E8 ....16 C2
Collins Ho 4 E14 ...34 B2
6 SE10 ....43 B1
Collinson Ct 1 SE1 ...136 C3
Collinson Ho 13
SE15 ....49 C3
Collinson St SE1 ...136 C3
Collinson Wlk SE1 ...136 C3
Collins Rd N5,N16 ...15 B4
Collins Sq SE3 ....53 B1
Collins St SE3 ....53 A1
Collin's Yd N1 ....86 A3
Collyer Pl SE15 ....49 C2
Colmans Wharf 5
E14 ....34 A4
Colmar Cl 3 E1 ....25 C1
Colmore Mews
SE15 ....50 A2
Colnbrook St SE1 ...136 A2
Colne Ho NW8 ....89 C1
Colne Rd E5 ....18 A4
Cologne Rd SW11 ...59 C3
Colombo St SE1 ...122 A1
Colomb St SE10 ....43 A1
Colonades The 4
SE5 ....48 C2
Colonial Dr W4 ....37 B2
Colonnade WC1 ....94 B1
Colonnades The 6
E8 ....17 A2
Colonnade The 11
SE8 ....41 B2
Colstead Ho 52 E1 ...32 A3
Colston Rd SW14 ...55 B3
Colthurst Cres N4 ...6 B2
Coltman Ho 1 E14 ...33 A3
SE10 ....52 B4
Columba Ho SE14 ...51 B2
Columbas Dr NW3 ...2 C3
Columbia Ho E3 ....26 C2
Columbia Point 7
SE16 ....40 B3

Columbia Prim Sch
E2 ....98 C3
Columbia Rd
E2 ....24 B2 98 C4
Colverson Ho 11 ....E1 32 B4
Colvestone Cres E8 ..16 B3
Colvestone Prim Sch
E8 ....16 B3
Colville Gdns W11 ..31 B3
Colville Ho 12 E2 ....25 B3
W11 ....31 B3
Colville Mews W11 ..31 B3
Colville Pl W1 ......105 A3
Colville Prim Sch
W11 ....31 B3
Colville Rd W11 ......31 B3
London W3 ....37 A3
Colville Sq W11 ......31 B3
Colville Sq Mews 5
W11 ....31 B3
Colville Terr W11 ....31 B3
Colwall Ho SW9 ....173 A1
Colwell Rd SE22 ....64 B2
Colwick Cl N6 ....4 C4
Colwith Rd W6 ....47 B4
Colworth Gr SE17 ..151 A3
Colwyn Ho SE1 ......135 B1
Colyton Rd SE22 ....65 A2
Combe Ave SE3 ......53 B3
Combedale Rd SE10 43 C1
Combe Ho 30 W2 ....31 C4
Mortlake SW14 ....45 B1
Combemartin Rd
SW18 ....70 A3
Combe Mews 4
SE3 ....53 B3
Comber Gr SE5 ....48 B3
Comber Ho SE5 ......48 B3
Comber Grove Prim Sch
SE5 ....48 B3
Combermere Rd
SW9 ....62 B4
Combe The NW1 ......92 B3
Comeragh Mews
W14 ....140 B1
Comeragh Rd W14 ..140 B1
Comerford Rd SE4 ..66 B3
Comet Pl SE8 ....51 C3
Comet St SE8 ....51 C3
Commercial Rd
E1 ....32 B3 111 C2
Commercial St E1 ..110 C4
Commercial Way
SE15 ....49 C3
Wembley NW10 ....20 C3
Commerell Pl SE10 ..43 B1
Commerell St SE10 ..43 A1
Commodore Ct SE8 ..51 C2
Commodore Ho 7
E14 ....34 B2
Commodore St E1 ....26 A1
Commondale SW15 ..57 B4
Common Rd SW13 ..56 C4
Common View
SW15 ....57 C4
Commonwealth Ave 21
W12 ....30 A2
Community Coll The
E9 ....25 C4
E9 ....17 C3
Community Rd E15 ..19 C3
Compania Bldg 12
E1 ....32 C2
Compass Ct SE1 ....124 C1

Compass Ho
London SE8 ....52 A1
London W2 ....100 A1
Compass Point 9
E14 ....33 C2
Compayne Gdns
NW6 ....11 A1
Compton Ave
London N1 ....15 A2
London N6 ....3 A4
Compton Cl NW1 ....92 B3
E14 ....49 B3
Compton Cres W4 ..45 B4
Compton Ho SW11 168 A4
Compton Pas EC1 ....96 B2
Compton Pl WC1 ....94 A2
Compton Rd
London N1 ....15 A2
London NW10 ....22 C2
5 Richmond TW10 ......54 A1
Compton Sq W2 ......102 C1
Compton St EC1 ......96 B2
Comus Ho SE17 ......152 A3
Comus Pl SE17 ......152 A3
Comyn Rd SW11 ......60 A3
Comyns Cl E16 ....35 B2
Conant Ho SE11 ......48 A4
Conant Mews E1 ....125 B4
Concanon Rd SW2,
SW4 ....62 B3
Concert Hall App
SE1 ....121 A1
Concord Bsns Ctr
W3 ....28 A4
Concord Ctr W12 ....39 C4
Concordia Wharf
E14 ....34 B1
Concord Rd W3 ......28 A4
Condell Rd SW8 ....171 A3
Conder St E14 ....33 A3
Condray Pl SW11 ..158 A1
Conduit Ct WC2 ....120 A4
Conduit Ho SE10 ....52 C2
Conduit Mews W2 ..101 B1
Conduit Pas W2 ....101 B1
Conduit Pl W2 ......101 B1
Conduit St W1 ......118 C4
Conewood St N5 ......6 A1
Coney Acre SE21 ....75 B3
Coney Way SW8 ....163 A3
Congers Ho SE8 ......51 C3
Congreve Ho 10
N16 ....16 A3
Congreve St SE17 ..152 A3
Conifer Ct 28 SW19 69 C3
Conifer Gdns SW16 74 B1
Conifer Ho SE4 ......66 B3
Coniger Rd SW6 ....165 B2
Coningham Ct
SW10 ....157 A2
Coningham Mews
W12 ....29 C1
Coningham Rd W12 39 A4
Coningsby Rd N4 ....6 A4
Conington Rd SE13 ..52 B1
Conisbrough NW1 ..82 C3
Coniston NW1 ....92 C4
Coniston Cl
Barnes SW13 ....46 B3
Chiswick W4 ....45 B3
Coniston Ct 16 SE16 40 C4
W2 ....102 B1
Coniston Ho 6 E3 ..26 B2
13 SE5 ....48 B3
Coniston Wlk E9 ....17 B3
Conlan St W10 ....23 A1
Conley Rd NW10 ....8 A2

Conley St SE10 ....43 A1
Connaught Ave
SW14 ....55 B3
Connaught Cl W2 ..102 B1
Connaught Ho W1 ..118 A3
London NW10 ....22 A2
Connaught Lo N4 ....5 C4
Connaught Mans
SW11 ....168 B3
SW6 ....164 A4
15 London SW9 ....62 C3
16 London NW3 ....62 C3
Connaught Pl W2 ..102 C1
Connaught Rd
London N4 ....5 C4
London NW10 ....21 A3
5 Richmond TW10 ......54 B2
Connaught Sq W2 ..102 C1
Connaught St W2 ..102 B1
Connell Ct 6 SE14 ..50 C4
Connor Ct SW11 ....170 A3
Connor St E9 ....25 C4
Conrad Ho 8 SE16 ..33 A2
5 London N16 ....16 A3
SW8 ....162 A2
Consort Ho W2 ......114 B3
Consort Lo NW8 ......80 C3
Consort Rd SE15 ......50 A1
Cons St SE1 ....135 C4
Constable Ct 11
SE16 ....40 A1
Constable Ho NW3 ..12 B1
Constable Wlk SE21 76 A1
Constant Ho 21 E14 ..34 A2
Constantine Ho
SW2 ....74 C3
Constantine Rd
NW3 ....12 A4
Constitution Hill
SW1,W1 ....132 B4
London SW11 ....169 B3
Content St SE17 ....151 B3
Convent Gdns W11 ..31 B3
Convent of Jesus &
Mary Language Coll
NW10 ....21 B4
Convent of Jesus &
Mary RC Inf Sch
NW2 ....9 B2
Conway Gr W3 ....28 C4
Conway Ho 7 E14 ..42 A2
3 Streatham SW2 ......74 A3
Conway Mews W1 ..92 C1
Conway St W1 ....92 C1
Conybeare NW3 ......12 A1
Conyer St 19 E3 ......26 A3
Cookham Cres SE16 40 C4
Cookham Ho E2 ......98 C2
Cook's Rd E15 ....27 B3
SE17 ....150 B1
Coomassie Rd W9 ..23 B1
Coombe Ho 12 N7 ..13 C3
Coombe Rd W4 ....38 A1
Coomber Ho SW6 ....59 A4
Coombs St N1 ....86 B1
Coomer Mews
SW6 ....155 A3
Coomer Pl SW6 ....155 A3
Cooperage The
SE1 ....124 C1
Cooper Cl SE1 ....135 C3
Cooper Ct E15 ....76 B3
Cooper Ho NW8 ....89 B1
Cooper Rd NW10 ......8 B3
Coopersale Rd E9 ..17 C3
Coopers Cl E1 ....25 B1

Coopers Ct E3 ....26 B1
9 London W3 ....28 B1
Coopers La NW1 ....83 C1
Coopers Lodge
SE1 ....138 C2
Cooper's Rd SE1 ....153 A2
Cooper's Row EC3 124 C4
Cooper St 10 E16 ....35 B2
Cope Ho EC1 ....97 A3
Copeland Dr E14 ....41 C2
Copeland Ho SW11 135 A1
Copeland Rd SE15 ..50 A1
Copenhagen Gdns
W4 ....37 C4
Copenhagen Ho N1 85 B3
Copenhagen Pl E14 33 B3
Copenhagen Prim Sch
N1 ....84 C3
Copenhagen St N1 84 C3
Cope Pl W8 ....127 B1
Cope St SE16 ....40 C2
Cope Yd E1 ....125 C2
Copford Wlk N1 ......86 C4
Copleston Rd SE15 ..64 B4
Copley Cl 16 SE17 ..48 A4
Coppedhall 1 SE7 ..43 C1
Copperas St SE8 ......52 A4
Copper Beech N6 ......3 C4
Copperbeech Cl
NW3 ....11 C3
Copperfield Ho
SE1 ....139 B3
Copperfield Rd E3 ..33 A4
Copperfields Ct W3 36 C4
Copperfield St
SE1 ....136 C4
Coppice Dr SW15 ....57 A1
Coppin Ho SW2 ......75 A3
Coppock Cl SW11 ..168 A1
Copse Ct SW15 ....58 A2
Copthall Ave EC2 ..109 C2
Copthall Bldgs
EC2 ....109 C2
Copthall Cl EC2 ......109 B2
Copthorne Ave
SW12 ....73 C4
Coptic St WC1 ......106 A3
Copton Cl E3 ....33 C4
Coral Ho 6 E1 ....26 A1
Coral Row 18 SW11 59 B4
Coram Ho WC1 ....94 A3
1 London W4 ....38 A1
Coram St WC1 ....94 A1
Corbden Cl SE15 ....49 B2
Corbet Ct EC3 ....109 C1
Corbet Ho N1 ....85 B3
Corbet Pl E1 ....110 C4
Corbett Ho SW10 ..156 C4
Corbett's La SE16 ....40 B2
Corbidge Ct SE8 ......52 A4
Corbiere Ho 6 N1 ..24 A4
Corbin Ho 7 E3 ....27 A2
Corbridge Cres E2 ..25 A3
Corbyn St N4,N19 ....5 A3
Corby Rd NW10 ......20 C3
Corby Way E3 ....26 C1
Cordelia Cl SE24 ....63 A3
Cordelia Ho 31 N1 ..24 A3
Cordelia St E14 ....34 A3
Cording St E14 ....34 A4
Cordwainers Ct 13
E9 ....17 B1
Cord Way 7 E14 ....41 C3
Corfe Ho SW8 ....162 C2

Corfe Lo SE21 ....75 C2
Corfe Twr 6 W3 ......37 B4
Corfield St E2 ....25 A2
Coriander Ave E14 ..34 C3
Coriander Ct SE1 ..138 C2
Corinne Rd N19 ......13 B4
Cork Sq E1 ....32 A1
Cork St W1 ....118 C3
Cork St Mews W1 ..118 C3
Corlett St NW1 ......102 A4
Cormont Rd SE5 ......48 A2
Cormorant Ct
34 SE8 ....51 B4
12 Dulwich SE21 ....75 C2
Cornbury Ho 5 SE8 ..51 B4
Cornelia St N7 ....14 B2
Corner Fielde SW2 ..74 B3
Corner Gn SE3 ....53 C1
Corner House St
WC2 ....120 A2
Cornerways SW15 ..56 C3
Corney Rd W4 ....46 A4
Corney Reach Way
W4 ....46 A3
Cornflower Terr
SE22 ....65 A1
Cornford Gr SW12 ..73 A2
Cornhill EC3 ....109 C1
Cornick Ho 7 SE16 40 A3
Cornish Ho 8 SE17 48 A4
Brentford TW8 ....36 B1
Cornmill La SE13 ....67 B4
Cornmow Dr NW10 ..8 C3
Cornwall Ave E2 ......25 B2
Cornwall Cres W11 31 A3
Cornwall Gdns
SW7 ....128 B1
London NW10 ....22 B4
Cornwall Gdns Wlk
SW7 ....128 B1
Cornwall Gr W4 ......38 A1
Cornwall Ho NW1 ....91 A1
5 Putney SW15 ....69 B4
Cornwallis Ho 24
W12 ....30 A2
Cornwallis Rd N19 ..5 A2
Cornwallis Sq N19 ..5 A2
Cornwall Mans
NW1 ....91 A1
SW10 ....157 A2
Cornwall Mews S
SW7 ....128 C1
Cornwall Mews W
SW7 ....128 B1
Cornwall Rd SE1 ..135 C4
London N4 ....5 C4
London SE1 ....150 B2
Cornwall Sq SE11 ..150 B2
Cornwall St 4 E1 ....32 A2
Cornwall Terr NW1 ..91 A1
Cornwall Terr Mews
NW1 ....91 A1
Cornwood Dr E1 ....32 B3
Coronation Ave 1
N16 ....16 B4
Coronation Ct W10 30 B4
Coronet St N1 ....98 A3
Corporation Row
EC1 ....95 C2
Corporation St N7 ..14 A3
Corrance Rd SW2 ....62 A3
Corrigan Ct NW11 ..1 C4
Corringham Ho
E1 ....32 C3

Corringham Rd NW11 . . . . 1 C4
Corringham NW11 . . . 2 A4
Corry Dr SW9 . . . . .63 A3
Corry Ho **2** E14 . . . . . .34 A2
Corseley Way E9 . . . . .18 B2
Corsham St N1 . . . . . .97 C3
Corsica St N5 . . . . .15 A2
Cortayne Rd SW6 . . .164 C2
Cortis Rd SW15 . . . . . .57 A1
Cortis Terr SW15 . . . . .57 A1
Corunna Rd SW8 . . .171 A4
Corunna Terr SW8 . .171 A4
Corvette Sq **5** SE10 . .52 C4
Coryton Path W9 . . . . .23 B1
Cosbycote Ave SE24 . .63 B2
Cosgrove Ho **3** E2 . . . .24 C4
Cosmo Pl WC1 . . . . . .106 B4
Cosmur Cl W12 . . . . . .38 B3
Cossall Wlk SE15 . . . . .50 A2
Cosser Mews **10**
SW2 . . . . .74 B3
Cosser St SE1 . . . . . .135 B2
Costa St SE15 . . . . .49 C1
Coston Wlk **4** SE4 . . .65 C3
Cosway Mans NW1 . .102 B4
Cosway St NW1 . . . . .102 B4
Cotall St E14 . . . . .33 C4
Cotes Ho NW8 . . . . . . .90 A1
Cotham St SE17 . . . . .151 A3
Cotherstone Rd
SW2 . . . . .74 B3
Cotleigh Rd NW6 . . . . .10 C1
Cotman Cl SW15 . . . . .57 C2
Cotman Ho NW8 . . . . .80 A2
Cotswold Ct EC1 . . . . .96 C2
Cotswold Gate **2** NW2 . .1 A3
Cotswold Ho N16 . . . . . .7 B3
Cotswold Mews
SW11 . . . . .167 C3
Cottage Gn SE5 . . . . .48 C3
Cottage Gr SW9 . . . . . .62 A4
Cottage Pl SW3 . . . . .130 A1
Cottage St E14 . . . . . . .34 A2
Cottage Wlk **2** N16 . . .7 B1
Cottenham Ho **3**
N19 . . . . .5 A2
Cottesbrook St **9**
SE14 . . . . .51 A3
Cottesloe Ho NW8 . . . .90 A2
Cottesloe Mews
SE1 . . . . .135 C2
Cottesmore Ct W8 . .128 B2
Cottesmore Gdns
W8 . . . . .128 B2
Cottingham Rd
SW8 . . . . .163 A2
Cottington St SE11 . .150 A2
Cotton Ave W3 . . . . . . .28 C3
Cotton Ho
London W12 . . . . . . .38 B4
11 Streatham SW2 . . .74 B4
Cotton Row SW11 . . . .59 C4
Cotton's Gdn E2 . . . . . .98 B4
Cottons La SE1 . . . . . .123 C2
Cotton St E14 . . . . .34 B2
Cottrell Ct SE10 . . . . . .43 B3
Couchman Ho **8**
SW4 . . . . .61 B1
Coulgate St SE4 . . . . . .66 A4
Coulsdon Ho **5**
SW2 . . . . .74 A3
Coulson St SW3 . . . . .144 C2
Coulter Rd W6 . . . . . . .39 A3
Coults Cres NW5 . . . . . .3 C1
Councillor St SE5 . . . . .48 B3
Counters Ct W14 . . . .126 B2

Counter St SE1 . . . . . .124 A1
Countess Rd NW5 . . . .13 B3
Countisbury Ho
SE26 . . . . .76 C1
County Gr **5** SE5 . . . .48 B2
County Ho SW9 . . . . .173 B4
County St SE1 . . . . . .137 A1
Courier Ho **17** SW2 . .74 C4
Courland Gr SW8 . . . .171 C3
Courland St SW8 . . . .171 C3
Courtauld Galleries *
WC2 . . . . .120 C4
Courtauld Ho **11** E2 .24 C3
Courtauld Rd N19 . . . . .4 C3
Courtfield Gdns
SW5 . . . . .142 B3
Courtfield Ho EC1 . . .107 B4
Courtfield Mews
SW7 . . . . .142 C3
Courtfield Rd SW7 . .142 C3
Court Gdns N7 . . . . . . .14 C2
Courthill Rd SE13 . . . . .67 B3
Courthope Ho
SE16 . . . . .40 B3
SW8 . . . . .162 A1
Courthope Rd NW3 . . .12 B4
Court La SE21 . . . . .76 B4
Courtlands TW10 . . . . .54 C2
Courtlands Ave
TW9 . . . . .45 A1
Court Lane Gdns
SE21 . . . . .76 B4
Court Mans **8** W6 . . .38 C2
Courtmead Cl SE24 . . .63 B1
Courtnell St W2 . . . . . .31 C3
Courtney Ho N7 . . . . . .14 C2
Courtney Ho **9** W14 .126 B2
Courtney Rd N7 . . . . . .14 C2
Courtrai Rd SE23 . . . . .66 A1
Court Royal SW15 . . . .58 A2
Court St E1 . . . . .32 A4
Courtville Ho **11**
W10 . . . . .23 A2
Court Way W3 . . . . .28 B4
Courtyard The
Fulham SW6 . . . . . .164 A3
London N1 . . . . .14 B1
15 London SE1 . . . .59 C3
Cousin La EC4 . . . . . .123 B3
Couzens Ho **3** E3 . . . .33 B4
Coval Gdns SW14 . . . .55 A3
Coval La SW14 . . . . . . .55 A3
Coval Rd SW14 . . . . . .55 B3
Covell Ct **15** SE8 . . . .51 C3
Covent Garden Sta
WC2 . . . . .106 B1
Covent Gdn* WC2 . .120 B4
Coventry Cl NW6 . . . . .23 C4
Coventry Rd E1 . . . . . .25 A1
Coventry St W1 . . . . .119 B3
Coverdale Rd NW6 . . . .9 C1
Coverdale Rd
London NW2 . . . . . . .10 A2
London W12 . . . . . . .39 A4
Coverham Ho **6**
SE4 . . . . .65 C3
Coverley Cl E1 . . . . . .111 C4
Coverley Point
SE11 . . . . .148 C3
Cowcross St EC1 . . . .108 A4
Cowdenbeath Path
N1 . . . . .84 C4

Cowdray Hall Coll of
Nursing **3** W1 . . . .104 A2
Cowdray Ho **23**
SE22 . . . . .64 A4
Cowdry Rd E9 . . . . . . .18 B2
Cowley Rd
London SW9 . . . . . .173 C4
London W3 . . . . .29 B1
Mortlake SW14 . . . . .56 A4
Cowley St SW1 . . . . .134 A1
Cowling Cl W11 . . . . .112 A2
Cowper Rd
London N16 . . . . .16 A4
London W3 . . . . .28 C1
Cowper's Ct EC3 . . . .109 C1
Cowper St EC1,EC2 . . .97 C2
Cowper Terr W10 . . . . .30 C4
Cowthorpe Rd
SW8 . . . . .171 C4
Cox Ho W6 . . . . .154 A4
Cox's Ct E1 . . . . .110 C3
Coxson Way SE1 . . . .138 C3
Coysh Ct **3** SW15 . . .58 A2
Crabtree Cl E2 . . . . . . .24 B3
Crabtree Ct E15 . . . . . .19 A3
Crabtree Hall SW6 . . . .47 B3
Crabtree La SW6 . . . . .47 C3
Craddock St NW5 . . . .12 C2
Craigie Ho SE1 . . . . . .153 A3
Craigleith SW15 . . . . . .57 C1
Craignair Rd SW2 . . . .74 C4
Craig's Ct SW1 . . . . . .120 A2
Craik Ct NW6 . . . . .23 B3
Crail Row SE17 . . . . . .151 C3
Cramer St W1 . . . . . . .103 C3
Crammond Cl W6 . . . .154 A3
Crampton Sch
SE17 . . . . .150 B2
Crampton St SE17 . . .150 C2
Cranbourn Alley
WC2 . . . . .119 C4
Cranbourne Ct
SW11 . . . . .158 B2
Cranbourne Rd E15 . . .76 B4
Cranbourn Ho **6**
SE16 . . . . .40 A4
Cranbourn St WC2 . .119 C4
Cranbrook NW1 . . . . . .83 A3
Cranbrook Ho **5**
E5 . . . . .17 A3
Cranbrook Rd
London SE8 . . . . . . .51 C2
London W4 . . . . .38 A1
Cranbrook St E2 . . . . . .25 C3
Cranbury Rd SW6 . . .166 B1
Crandale Ho **8** E5 . . .17 A3
Crandley Ct SE8 . . . . . .41 A2
Crane Ave W3 . . . . .28 B2
Crane Ct EC4 . . . . . . .107 C1
7 London W12 . . . . .38 A4
Crane Gr N7 . . . . .14 C2
Crane Ho **23** E3 . . . . .26 A3
3 London SE15 . . . .49 B2
Crane Mead SE16 . . . .40 C2
Crane St SE10 . . . . . . .42 C1
5 London SE15 . . . .49 B2
Cranfield Ct NW1 . . . .102 B3
Cranfield Ho WC1 . . . .106 B4
Cranfield Rd SE4 . . . . .66 B4
Cranford Cotts **3**
E1 . . . . .32 C2
Cranford Lo SW19 . . . .69 C2
Cranford St E1 . . . . . . .32 C2
Cranhurst Rd NW2 . . . .9 B3
Cranleigh W11 . . . . . .112 C3

Cranleigh Ct
4 London N16 . . . . . . .7 A3
Richmond TW9 . . . . .54 C4
Cranleigh Hos NW1 . .83 A1
Cranleigh Mews
SW11 . . . . .168 B1
Cranleigh St NW1 . . . .83 A1
Cranley Gdns SW7 . .143 B2
Cranley Mews
SW7 . . . . .143 B2
Cranley Pl SW7 . . . . .143 B3
Cranmer Ct SW3 . . . .144 B3
Cranmer Ho SW11 . .168 A4
Cranmer Rd SW9 . . . .163 C2
Cranswick Rd SE16 . . .40 A1
Cranwell Cl E3 . . . . . . .27 A1
Cranwich Rd N16 . . . . .7 A4
Cranwood Ct EC1 . . . .97 C3
Cranwood St EC1 . . . .97 C3
Cranworth Gdns
SW9 . . . . .173 B4
Cranworth Ho **6**
N7 . . . . .14 B4
Craster Rd SW2 . . . . . .74 B4
Craston Ho **2** SE5 . . .49 A1
Craven Cl N16 . . . . .7 C4
Craven Cottage (Fulham
FC) SW6 . . . . .47 C2
Craven Ct NW10 . . . . .21 A4
Craven Hill W2 . . . . . .115 A4
Craven Hill Gdns
W2 . . . . .114 C4
Craven Hill Mews
W2 . . . . .115 A4
Craven Ho **2** SW14 .55 C4
Craven Lo W2 . . . . . . .115 A4
Fulham SW6 . . . . . . .47 C2
Craven Mews **6**
SW11 . . . . .60 C4
Craven Park Mews
NW10 . . . . .21 A4
Craven Park Rd
London N15 . . . . .21 A4
London NW10 . . . . . .21 A4
Craven Pas WC2 . . . .120 A2
Craven Pk NW10 . . . . .21 A4
Craven Rd W2 . . . . . .101 A1
London NW10 . . . . . .20 C4
Craven St WC2 . . . . . .120 A2
Craven Terr W2 . . . . .115 A4
Craven Wlk E5,N16 . . .7 C4
Crawford Bldgs
W1 . . . . .102 B3
Crawford Mews
W1 . . . . .102 C3
Crawford Pas EC1 . . . .95 C1
Crawford Pl W1 . . . . .102 B3
Crawford Place
Dwellings **1** W1 . .102 B3
Crawford Point **4**
E16 . . . . .35 B1
Crawford Prim Sch
SE5 . . . . .48 B2
Crawford Rd SE5 . . . . .48 B1
Crawford St W1 . . . . .102 C3
Crawshay Ct SW9 . . .173 C4
Crawshay Ho **13**
N16 . . . . .15 C4
Crawthew Gr SE22 . . .64 B3
Crayford Ho SE1 . . . .137 C3
London N7 . . . . .14 A4
Crayford Rd N7 . . . . . .14 A4
Crayle Ho EC1 . . . . . . .96 B2
Crealock St SW18 . . . .59 A1
Creasy Est SE1 . . . . . .138 A1
Crebor St SE22 . . . . . .64 C1
Credenhill Ho **2**
SE15 . . . . .50 A3

Crediton Hill NW6 . . . .11 A3
Crediton Rd E16 . . . . . .35 C3
London NW10 . . . . . .22 C4
Credon Rd SE16 . . . . . .40 A1
Creechurch La
EC3 . . . . .110 B1
Creechurch Pl EC3 . .110 B1
Creed Ho SE15 . . . . . . .65 A4
Creed La EC4 . . . . . . .108 B1
Creek Ho W14 . . . . . .126 B2
Creek Rd SE10,SE8 . . .52 A4
Creekside SE8 . . . . . . .52 A3
Crefeld Cl W6 . . . . . . .154 A3
Creighton Cl W12 . . . .30 A2
Creighton Rd NW6 . . .22 C3
Cremer Bsns Ctr **8**
E2 . . . . .24 B3
Cremer Ho **9** SE8 . . .51 C3
Cremer St E2 . . . . .24 B3
Cremorne Rd
SW10 . . . . .157 B2
Creon Ct SW9 . . . . . .173 B4
Crescent EC3 . . . . . . .124 C4
Crescent Court Bsns Ctr
E16 . . . . .27 C1
Crescent Ct SW4 . . . . .61 C2
Crescent Gdns
SW19 . . . . .70 C1
Crescent Gr SW4 . . . . .61 B3
Crescent La SW13 . . . .52 A1
Crescent La SW4 . . . . .61 C2
Crescent Mans
W11 . . . . .112 B4
London N5 . . . . .15 A3
Crescent Pl SW3 . . . .144 B4
Crescent Row EC1 . . . .96 C1
Crescent St N1 . . . . . . .14 B1
Crescent Stables
SW15 . . . . .58 A2
Crescent The
Barnes SW13 . . . . . .46 C1
London W3 . . . . .29 A3
Wimbledon SW19 . . .70 C1
Crescent Way SE4 . . . .66 C4
Crescent Wood Rd
SE21,SE26 . . . . .76 C1
Cresford Rd SW6 . . . .166 A3
Cressage Ho **9**
TW8 . . . . .44 A4
Cressall Ho **8** E14 . . .41 C3
Cresset Ho **9** E9 . . . .17 B2
Cresset Rd E9 . . . . . . .17 B2
Cresset St SW4 . . . . . .61 C4
Cressfield Cl NW5 . . . .12 C3
Cressida Rd N19 . . . . . .4 C3
Cressingham Rd
SE13 . . . . .67 B4
Cressington Cl **4**
N16 . . . . .16 A3
Cresswell Gdns
SW5 . . . . .142 C2
Cresswell Pl SW10 . .143 A2
Cressy Ct **6** E1 . . . . .32 B4
London W6 . . . . .39 A3
Cressy Hos **7** E1 . . .32 B4
Cressy Pl E1 . . . . .32 B4
Cressy Rd NW3 . . . . . .12 B4
Cresta Ho
7 Bow E3 . . . . .26 C1
London NW6 . . . . . . .11 C1
Crestfield St N1,
WC1 . . . . .94 B4
Crestview NW5 . . . . . . .4 A1
Crestway SW15 . . . . . .57 A1

Creswick Ct W3 .... .28 A2
Creswick Rd W3 .....28 B2
Creswick Wlk 6 E3 ..26 C2
Crewdson Rd SW9 .163 B1
Crewe Pl NW10 ......21 B2
Crewkerne Ct
SW11 ....167 C4
Crews St E14 ....41 C2
Crewys Rd
London SE15 ......65 B3
Crichton St SW8 ...170 C2
Cricketers Mews 4
SW18 ....59 A2
Cricketfield Rd E5 ..17 A4
Crickdale Ave SW2 ..74 B2
Cricklewood Broadway
NW2 ....9 C4
Cricklewood La NW2 ..1 B1
Cricklewood Sta
NW2 ....9 C4
Crieff Rd SW18 .....59 B1
Criffel Ave SW2 ....73 C3
Crimscott St SE1 ...138 B1
Crimsworth Rd
SW8 ....161 C1
Crinan St N1 ....84 B2
Cringle St SW8 ....160 C2
Cripplegate St
EC1 ....109 A4
Crispe Ho N1 ....85 A3
Crispian Cl NW10 ....8 A4
Crispin Ct SE17 ...152 A3
Crispin St E1 .....110 C3
Crisp Rd W6 ....39 B1
Cristowe Rd SW6 ...165 A1
Criterion Mews N19 ..4 C2
Crockerton Rd
SW17 ....72 B2
Croftdown Rd NW5 ...4 A1
Crofters Ct 8 SE8 ..41 A2
Crofters Way NW1 ...83 B4
Croft Ho
12 London W10 ....23 A2
Putney SW15 ......58 A1
Crofton Ave W4 ....45 C3
Crofton Gate Way
SE4 ....66 A2
Crofton L Ctr SE4 ..66 C1
Crofton Park Rd
SE4 ....66 B1
Crofton Park Sta
SE4 ....66 B2
Crofton Rd SE5 ....49 A1
Crofton Sch SE4 ....66 C1
Crofton Terr
London E5 ....18 A3
Richmond TW9 .....54 B3
Crofts Ho 10 E2 ...24 C3
Crofts St E1 ......125 B3
Croft St SE8 ......41 A2
Croft The NW10 ....21 C3
Crogsland Rd NW1 ..12 C1
Cromartie Rd N19 ...4 C4
Cromarty Ho 3 E1 ..33 A4
Crombie Mews
SW11 ....168 B2
Cromdale Ct N16 ....7 B4
Cromer Ct
Streatham SW16 ...74 A1
Wandsworth SW18 ..58 B1
Cromer St WC1 .....94 B3
Cromer Terr E8 ....16 C3
Cromer Villas Rd
SW18 ....58 B1

Cromford Path 6
E5 ....17 C4
Cromford Rd SW18 ..58 C2
Crompton Ct SW3 ..144 A4
Crompton Ho SE1 ..137 A1
SW8 ....171 A3
W2 ....89 B1
Crompton St W2 ....89 B1
London N6 ....4 B4
Cromwell Cl
London W3 ....28 B1
2 London W4 ......37 A1
Cromwell Cres
SW5 ....141 B4
Cromwell Ctr NW10 .20 C2
Cromwell Gdns
SW7 ....129 C1
Cromwell Gr W6 ....39 B3
Cromwell Ho
Putney SW15 ......56 C3
SW11 ....169 C3
Cromwell Hospl
SW5 ....142 A4
Cromwell Lo 50 E1 ..25 B1
Cromwell Mans
SW5 ....141 C4
Cromwell Mews
SW7 ....143 C4
Cromwell Pl N6 .....4 A3
SW7 ....143 C4
London W3 ....28 B1
Mortlake SW14 ....55 B4
Cromwell Rd SW7 ..142 C4
SW5 ....142 A4
London N10 ....4 A3
Cromwell Twr EC2 ..109 A4
Crondace Rd SW6 ..165 C3
Crondall Ct 7 N1 ..24 A3
Crondall Ho SW15 ..68 C3
Crondall Pl 8 N1 ..24 A3
Crondall St N1 .....24 A3
Crone Ct 8 NW6 ...23 B3
Cronin St SE15 ....49 B3
Crooked Billet Yd
E2 ....98 B4
Crooke Rd SE8 .....41 A1
Crookham Rd SW6 ..164 C3
Croom's Hill SE10 ..52 C3
Croom's Hill Gr
SE10 ....52 B3
Cropley Ct N1 .....87 B2
Cropley St N1 .....87 B2
Cropthorne Ct W9 ..89 A3
Crosby Ct SE1 ....137 B4
Crosby Row SE1 ...137 B4
Crosby Sq EC3 ....110 A2
Crosby Wlk
3 London E8 .....16 B2
Streatham SE24 ...74 C4
Crosfield Ct 3 W10 .30 C3
Crosfield Ho W11 ..112 A4
Crosland Pl 5
SW11 ....60 C4
Crossbow Ho 15 N1 .24 A4
Cross Cl SE15 .....50 A1
Cross Ct SE5 ......63 C4
Crossfield Rd NW3 ..11 C2
Crossfield St SE8 ..51 C3
Crossford St SW9 ..172 C1
Crossharbour & London
Arena E14 ....42 A3
Cross Keys Cl W1 ..103 C3
Cross Keys Cl E1 ..124 A3
Crosslet St SE17 ..151 C4
Crosslet Vale SE10 .52 A2

Crossley St N7 .....14 C2
Crossman Hos 18
SW12 ....74 A4
Crossmount Ho 13
SE5 ....48 B3
Cross St SE5 ......49 A1
Cross St N1 ....86 B4
Mortlake SW13 ....56 A4
Crosthwaite Ave
SE24,SE24 ....63 C3
Crosswall EC3 ....124 C4
Crossway E8,N16 ...16 A3
Crossway Ct SE4 ...51 A1
Croston St E8 ......24 C4
Crouch End Hill N8 ..4 C4
Crouch Hall Ct N19 ..5 A3
Crouch Hill N4,N8,
N10 ....5 A4
Crouchmans Cl
SE21,SE26 ....76 C1
Crowder St E1 .....32 A2
Crowfield Ho N5 ...15 B4
Crowfoot Cl E9 ....18 B3
Crowhurst Cl SW9 ..173 C2
Crowhurst Ho
SW9 ....173 A1
Crowland Ho NW8 ..78 C3
Crowland Terr N1 ..15 C1
Crowline Wlk 1 N1 .15 C2
Crown Cl E3 ....26 C4
London NW6 ......11 A2
E3 ....26 C4
Crown Close Bsns Ctr
E3 ....26 C4
Crown Ct EC4 .....109 A1
NW8 ....90 B3
WC2 ....106 B1
4 Putney SW15 ...57 C3
E14 ....34 B3
Crowndale Ct NW1 ..83 A2
Crowndale Rd NW1 ..83 A2
Crownfield Rd E15 ..19 C4
Crownhill Rd NW10 ..21 B4
Crownleigh Ct SW2 ..62 C2
Crown Lo SW3 ....144 B3
Crown Office Row
EC4 ....121 B4
Crown Pas SW1 ...119 A1
Crown Pl EC2 .....110 A3
London NW5 ....13 A2
Crown Reach SW1 ..147 C1
Crown St SE5 .....48 B3
Acton W3 ....28 A1
Crownstone Ct
SW2 ....62 C2
Crownstone Rd
SW2 ....62 C2
Crown Terr TW9 ...54 B3
Crows Rd E15 .....27 C2
Crowther Ave TW8 ..36 A2
Crowther Cl SW6 ..154 C4
Crowthorne Cl
SW18 ....70 B3
Crowthorne Rd
W10 ....30 C3
Croxley Rd W9 ....23 B2
Croxted Cl SE21 ...75 B4
Croxted Mews SE24 .63 B1
Croxted Rd SE21,
SE24 ....75 B4
Croxteth Ho SW8 ..171 B2
Croydon Ho SE1 ...135 C4
Crozier Ho SW8 ...162 C1
Crozier Terr E9 ....17 C3
Crucifix La SE1 ...138 A4
Cruden Ho 80 E3 ...26 A3
11 SE17 ....48 A4
Cruden St N1 ......86 B3

Cruickshank St
WC1 ....95 A4
Cruikshank Ho NW8 .80 B2
Crusoe House Sch
N1 ....97 B4
Crusoe Mews N16 ...6 C2
Crutched Friars
EC3 ....124 B4
Crystal Palace Rd
SE22 ....64 C2
Cuba St E14 ....41 C4
Cubitt Ho 8 SW4 ..61 B1
Cubitt St WC1 .....95 A3
Cubitt Terr SW4 ...61 B4
Cubitt Town Jun & Inf
Sch E14 ....42 B3
Cuddington SE17 ..151 A4
Cudworth Ho SW8 ..171 A3
Cudworth St E1 ....25 A1
Cuffley Ho W10 ....30 B4
Cuff Point 27 E2 ..98 C3
Culand Ho SE17 ...152 A3
Culford Gdns SW3 ..145 A3
Culford Gr N1 .....16 A2
Culford Mans SW3 ..145 A3
Culford Mews N1 ...16 A2
Culford Rd N1 .....24 A4
London N1 ....16 A2
Culham Ho 20
London E2 ....98 C3
21 W2 ....31 C4
Cullen Ho W9 ......23 B3
Cullen Way NW10 ..20 B1
Culling Rd SE16 ...40 B3
Cullingworth Rd
NW10 ....9 A3
Culloden Cl 20 SE16 153 C1
Culloden Prim Sch
E14 ....34 B3
Cullum St EC3 ....124 A4
Culmore Rd SE15 ..50 B3
Culmstock Rd SW11 .60 C2
Culpepper Ct SE11 .149 B4
Culross Bldgs NW1 ..84 A2
Culross St W1 .....117 B3
Culvert Ct SW11 ...59 A1
Culverden Rd SW12 .73 B2
Culverhouse 5
WC1 ....106 C3
Culverhouse Gdns
SW16 ....74 B1
Culvert Pl SW11 ...169 B2
Culvert Rd SW11 ..169 A2
Culworth Ho NW8 ..80 A2
Culworth St NW8 ...80 A1
Cumber Ho SW18 ..70 C3
Cumberland Ave
NW10 ....10 A3
Cumberland Bsns Pk
NW10 ....10 A3
Cumberland Cl E8 ..16 B2
Cumberland Cres
W14 ....140 B4
Cumberland Ct
W1 ....103 A1
Cumberland Gate
W1 ....117 A4
Cumberland Gdns
WC1 ....95 B4
Cumberland Ho
SW15 ....69 B4
Cumberland Mans
W1 ....102 C2
London NW6 ....10 C3
Cumberland Market
NW1 ....92 B4
Cumberland Mills Sq
E14 ....42 C1

Cumberland Park Ind
Est NW10 ....21 C2
Cumberland Pk NW10 28 B2
Cumberland Pl
NW1 ....92 A4
Cumberland Rd
Barnes SW13 ......46 C2
London W3 ....28 B2
Richmond TW9 ....44 C3
Cumberland Sch
E16 ....35 B2
Cumberland St
SW1 ....146 B2
Cumberland Terr
NW1 ....82 A1
Cumberland Terrace
Mews NW1 ....82 A1
Cumberland Villas
W3 ....28 B2
Cumbria Ho 2
SW15 ....58 B2
Cumbrian Gdns NW2 .1 A2
Cumming St N1 ....85 A1
Cumnor Cl SW9 ...173 A2
Cunard Pl EC3 ....110 B1
Cunard Rd NW10 ..20 C2
Cunard Wlk 2 SE16 .41 A2
Cundy St SW1 ....145 C3
Cunningham Ct 7
W9 ....89 B1
Cunningham Ho 16
SE5 ....48 C3
Cunningham Pl
NW8 ....89 B2
Cunnington St W4 ..37 B2
Cupar Rd SW11 ...169 C4
Cureton St SW1 ...147 C3
Curlew Ho
6 London SE15 ...49 B2
London SE4 ....66 A3
Curlew St SE1 ....139 A4
Curran Ho SW3 ...144 A3
Curricle St W3 .....29 A1
Currie Ho 28 SW12 .73 C4
Cursitor St EC4 ...107 B2
Curtain Pl EC2 .....98 B2
Curtain Rd
EC2 ....24 A1 98 B2
Curtis Dr W3 ......28 C3
Curtis Ho SE17 ...151 B2
Curtis St SE1 .....152 C4
Curtis Way SE1 ...152 C4
Curve The W12 ....29 C2
Curwen Rd W12 ...38 C4
Curzon Cres NW10 ..8 A1
Curzon Ct SW6 ...166 B3
Curzon Gate W1 ...117 C1
Curzon Pl W1 .....117 C1
Curzon St W1 .....118 A2
Custance Ho N1 ...87 B1
Custance St N1 ....97 B4
Custom House
EC3 ....124 A3
Custom House Reach
SE16 ....41 B3
Cutbush Ho N7 ....13 C3
Cutcombe Mans 22
SE5 ....48 B1
Cutcombe Rd SE5 ..48 B1
Cuthbert Harrowing Ho
EC1 ....96 C1
Cuthbert Ho W2 ...101 B4
Cuthbert St W2 ....89 B1
Cuthill Wlk 8 SE5 ..48 C2
Cutlers Gdns EC2 ..110 B2
Cutlers Sq E14 ....41 C2
Cutler St E1 ....110 B2
Cut The SE1 ......135 C4

Cutty Sark* SE10 .....52 B4
Cutty Sark Sta SE10 ..52 B4
Cuxton Ho SE17 .....152 B2
Cyclops Mews [9]
E14 ....41 C2
Cygnet St E1 ....99 A2
Cygnus Bsns Ctr
NW10 ....8 B2
Cynthia St N1 ....85 A1
Cypress Ct S E11 ...19 C4
Cypress Gdns SE4 ...66 A2
Cypress Ho SE14 ....50 C2
Cypress Pl W1 ....93 A1
Cyprus Pl E2 ....25 B3
Cyprus St E2 ....25 B3
Cyrena Rd SE22 .....64 B2
Cyril Jackson Prim Sch
(North Bldg) E14 ....33 B2
Cyril Jackson Prim Sch
(South Bldg) E14 ....33 B2
Cyril Mans SW11 ...169 A3
Cyril Thatcher Ho
SW6 ....165 C3
Cyrus Ho EC1 ....96 B2
Cyrus St EC1 ....96 B2
Czar St SE8 ....51 C4

D

Dabb's La EC1 ....95 C1
Dabin Cres SE10 ....52 B2
Dacca St SE8 ....51 B4
Dace Rd E3 ....26 C4
Dacre Ho SW3 ......157 C3
Dacre St SW1 ....133 B2
Daffodil St W12 .....29 B2
Dafforne Rd SW17 ..72 C1
Dagmar Ct E14 ......42 B3
Dagmar Gdns NW10 .22 C3
Dagmar Pas N1 ......86 B4
Dagmar Rd London N4 ..5 C4
London SE5 ....49 A2
Dagmar Terr N1 .....86 B4
Dagnall St SW11 ...169 B3
Dagnan Rd SW12 ...73 B4
Dagobert Ho S E1 ..32 B4
Daimler Ho S E3 ....26 C1
Dainton Ho W2 ......31 C4
Daintry Way E9 .....18 B2
Dairyman Cl NW2 ....1 A1
Daisy Dormer Ct [11]
SW9 ....62 B3
Daisy La SW6 ....58 C4
Dalberg Rd SW2 ....62 C2
Dalbury Ho S SW9 ..62 B3
Dalby Rd SW18 .....59 B3
Dalby St NW5 ....12 C2
Daleburry Rd SW17 .72 B2
Dale Croft N4 ....6 B1
Dalehead NW1 ......82 C1
Daleham Gdns NW3 .11 C2
Daleham Mews [13]
NW3 ....11 C2
Dale Ho NW8 ....78 C4
London SE4 ....66 A3
Dalemain Ho SW8 .171 C2
Dalemain Mews [15]
E16 ....35 C1
Dale Rd SE17 ....48 A4
London NW5 ....12 C3
Dale Row W11 ......31 A3
Dale St W4 ....38 A1
Daley Ho [1] W12 ..30 A3
Daley St E9 ....17 C2
Daley Thompson Way [5]
SW8 ....61 A4
Dalgarno Gdns W10 .30 B4

Dalgarno Way W10 ..22 B1
Daling Way E3 ....26 A3
Dalkeith Ct SW1 ...147 C3
Dalkeith Ho S SW9 .48 A2
Dalkeith Rd SE21 ..75 B4
Dalling Rd W6 ....39 A2
Dallington St EC1 ..96 B2
Dallington St EC1 ..96 B2
Dalmeny Ave N7 ....13 C4
Dalmeny Ct S W4 .172 A2
Dalmeny Rd N7 .....13 C4
Dalmeyer Rd NW10 .8 B2
Dalmore Rd SE21 ..75 B2
Dalrymple Rd SE4 ..66 A3
Dalston Jct E8 ......16 A2
Dalston Kingsland Sta
E8 ....16 B3
Dalston La E8 ....16 C3
Dalton Ho S E3 .....26 A3
S SE14 ....50 C4
Dalton St SE27 .....75 A1
Dalwood St SE5 ....49 A2
Dalyell Rd SW9 .....62 B4
Damascene Wlk
SE21 ....75 B3
Damer Ho S SE10 .52 C2
Damer Terr SW10 .157 A1
Dame St N1 ....86 C2
Damien Ct 20 E1 ...32 A3
Damien St E1 ....32 A3
Damory Ho S SE16 40 B2
Dan Bryant Ho S
SW12 ....73 B4
Danbury St N1 ......86 B2
Danby Ho
23 London E9 .....17 B1
S London W10 .....23 B2
Danby St SE15 .....64 B4
Dancer Rd
Fulham SW6 ....164 C3
Richmond TW9 ....54 C4
Dandridge Cl SE10 .43 B1
Dandridge Ho E1 ..110 C4
Danebury W11 ......31 A3
Danebury Ave SW15 56 B2
Danecroft Rd SE24 .63 C2
Dane Ho IE SE5 ....48 B1
Danehurst St SW6 164 A4
Danemere St SW15 57 B4
Dane Pl E3 ....26 B3
Danes Ct NW8 .....80 C3
Danesdale Rd E9 ...18 A2
Danesfield SE5 ......49 A4
Danes Ho W10 .....30 B4
Daneville Rd SE5 ..48 C2
Daniel Bolt Cl E14 .34 A4
Daniel Ct W3 ....29 A2
Daniel Gdns SE15 .49 B3
Daniell Ho N1 ....87 C2
Daniel's Rd SE15 ..65 B4
Dan Leno Wlk
SW6 ....156 A1
Dansey Pl W1 ......119 B4
Dante Rd SE11 ....150 A4
Danube Ct SE15 ...49 B3
Danube St SW3 ...144 B2
Danvers Ho E1 .....111 C1
Danvers St SW3 ..157 C3
Da Palma Ct SW6 .155 B3
Daphne St SW18 ..59 B1
Daplyn St E1 ....111 B4
D'arblay St W1 ....105 A1
Darcy Ho E8 ....25 A4
Darell Prim Sch
TW9 ....54 C4

Darell Rd TW9 ......54 C4
Daren Ct N7 ....14 A4
Daren Ho NW8 ....101 C4
Dareth Rd N16 ....7 B3
Darfield NW1 ....82 C3
Darfield Rd SE4 ....66 B2
Darfield Way W10 ..30 C3
Darfur St SW15 .....57 C4
Darien Ho S E1 .....32 C4
[17] London SW11 .59 C4
Darien Rd SW11 ...59 C4
Daring Ho S E3 .....26 A3
Darland Ct SW15 ..58 B2
Darlan Rd SW6 ....155 A1
Darley Ho SE11 ...148 C1
Darley Rd SW11 ...60 B1
Darling Ho S E5 ....64 C4
Darling Row E1 .....25 A1
Darlington Ho
SW8 ....161 C1
Darnay Ho S SE16 139 B2
Darnell Ho S SE10 52 B3
Darnley Ho S E14 .33 A3
Darnley Rd E9 ......17 B2
Darnley Terr S
W11 ....30 C1
Darrell Rd SE22 ....64 C2
Darren Cl N4 ....5 B4
Darsley Dr SW8 ...172 A4
Dartford Ho SE1 ...153 A4
Dartford St SE17 ..48 B4
Dartington Ho
S London E1 ......25 B1
London W2 ....100 A4
Dartle Ct S SE16 .139 C3
Dartmoor Wlk [17]
E14 ....41 C2
Dartmouth Cl W11 .31 C3
Dartmouth Ct SE10 52 B2
Dartmouth Gr SE10 52 B2
Dartmouth Hill
SE10 ....52 B2
Dartmouth Ho
Lewisham SE10 ....52 B1
London N19 ....4 A2
Dartmouth Park Ave
NW5 ....4 A1
Dartmouth Park Hill
N19 ....4 A2
Dartmouth Park Rd
NW5 ....4 A1
Dartmouth Pl W4 ..46 A4
Dartmouth Rd NW2 .9 C2
Dartmouth Row
SE10 ....52 B2
Dartmouth St SW1 133 C3
Dartmouth Terr
SE10 ....52 C2
Darton Ct W3 ....28 B1
Dartrey Twr SW10 157 B2
Dartrey Wlk SW10 157 A2
Dart St W10 ....23 B2
Darville Rd N16 .....7 B1
Darwen Pl E2 ....25 A4
Darwin Ct NW1 ....81 C4
Darwin St SE17 ...151 C4
Daryngton Ho
SW8 ....162 A1
Dashwood Ho SE21 76 B1
Data Point Bsns Ctr

Datchworth Ho S
N1 ....15 A1
Date St SE17 ....151 B1
Daubeney Prim Sch
E5 ....18 A4
Daubeney Rd E5 ...18 A4
Daubeney Twr S
SE8 ....41 B1
Dault Rd SW18 .....59 B1
Dauney Ho SE1 ...136 A3
Dave Adams Ho S
E3 ....26 B3
Davenant Rd London N19 ..4 C2
Davenant Rd N19 ...4 C2
Davenant St E1 ...111 C2
Davenport Ho
SE11 ....135 B1
Davenport Rd SE6 .67 B1
Daventry St NW1 .102 A4
Dave Porter Hts
SW19 ....70 A4
Daver Ct SW3 .....144 B1
Davern Cl SE10 ....43 B2
Davey Cl N7 ....14 B2
Davey Lo S N1 .....14 C1
Davey Rd E9 ....18 C1
Davey's Ct WC2 ..120 A4
Davey St SE15 .....49 B4
David Devine Ho S
E8 ....16 C3
Davidge Ho SE1 ..135 C3
Davidge St SE1 ...136 B3
David Ho S SW8 .162 A2
S Putney SW15 ...56 C2
David Mews W1 ..103 A4
Davidson Gdns
SW8 ....162 A2
Davidson Ho S N19 13 B4
David St E15 ....19 C3
Davies Mews W1 .118 A4
Davies St W1 ......118 A4
Da Vinci Ct S SE16 40 A1
Davina Ho 26 NW2 10 B2
S SW9 ....38 B4
Davis Ho S W12 ...30 A2
Davisville Rd W12 .38 C4
Dawes Ho SE17 ...151 B3
Dawes Rd SW6 ...154 C2
Dawes St SE17 ...151 C2
Dawlish Ave SW18 71 A2
Dawlish Rd NW2 ....9 C2
Dawnay Gdns SW18 71 C2
Dawnay Rd SW17,
SW18 ....71 C2
Dawn Cres E15 ....27 C4
Dawson Ho SE E2 25 B2
S London SE5 .....49 A2
Dawson Pl
W2 ....31 C2 113 C4
Dawson Rd NW4 ...9 A4
Daynor Ho S NW6 23 C4
Daysbrook Rd SW2 74 B3
Dayton Gr SE15 ....50 B2
Deacon Ho SE11 .149 A3
Deacon Mews N1 .15 C1
Deacon Rd NW2 ....8 C2
Deacon Way SE17 151 A4
Deal Ho SE15 ......50 C4
SE17 ....152 B2

Deal Porters Way
SE16 ....40 C2
Deal St E1 ....111 B4
Dealtry Rd SW15 ..57 B3
Deal Wlk SW9 ....163 C1
Dean Bradley St
SW1 ....134 A1
Dean Cl SE16 ....32 C1
London E9 ....17 B3
Deancross St E1 ..32 B3
Dean Ct SW8 ......162 A1
Deanery Mews W1 117 C2
Deanery St W1 ....117 C2
Dean Farrar St
SW1 ....133 C2
Deanhill Ct S
SW14 ....55 A3
Deanhill Rd SW14 55 A3
Dean Ho London E1 32 B3
London N4 ....6 B4
London SE14 ....51 B3
SW2 ....74 B4
Dean Rd NW2 ....9 B2
Dean Ryle St S SW1 148 A4
Dean's Bldgs SE17 151 C3
Deans Cl W4 ....45 A4
Dean's Ct EC4 ....108 B1
Deanshanger Ho S
SE8 ....40 C2
Dean's Mews W1 104 B2
Dean Stanley St
SW1 ....134 A1
Dean's Yd SW1 ...133 C2
Dean Trench St
SW1 ....134 A1
Dearmer Ho S
SW2 ....74 C4
Deason St E15 .....27 B4
Deauville Ct
S SE16 ....40 C4
London SW4 ....61 B1
Deauville Mans S
SW4 ....61 B1
De Barowe Mews
N1 ....15 A3
De Beauvoir Cres
N1 ....24 A4
De Beauvoir Pl S
N1 ....16 A2
De Beauvoir Prim Sch
N1 ....16 A1
De Beauvoir Rd N1 16 A1
De Beauvoir Sq N1 16 A1
Debenham Ct E8 ..24 C4
Debnams Rd SE16 40 B2
Decima St SE1 ....138 A2
Deck Cl SE16 ....32 C1
De Crespigny Pk
SE5 ....48 C1
Deeley Rd SW8 ...171 B4
Deepdale N1 ....6 A1
Deepdene Gdns
SW2 ....74 B4
Deepdene Ho N16 .6 C3
Deepdene Lo S
SW2 ....74 B4
Deepdene Mans
SW6 ....164 C4
Deepdene Rd SE5,
SE24 ....63 C3
Deerbrook Rd SE24,
SW2 ....75 A3

Dee Rd TW9 .....54 B3
Deerdale Rd SE24 ....63 B3
Deerhurst Ho **6**
SE15 .....49 C4
Deerhurst Rd NW2 ...9 C2
Deer Lo W6 .....58 A4
Deeside Rd SW17 ....71 C1
Dee St E14 .....34 B3
Defoe Ave TW9 .....44 C2
Defoe Ct E3 .....108 C4
6 London N16 .....7 A1
Defoe Pl EC2 .....108 C4
Defoe Rd SE16 .....41 B4
7 London N16 .....7 A1
De Gama Pl E14 .....41 C1
Dekker Ho **15** SE5 ..48 C3
Dekker Rd SE21 .....64 A1
Delafield Ho **1** E1 .111 C1
Delaford Rd SE16 ...40 A1
Delaford St SW6 ...154 B3
Delamere Ho **4** N4 ..6 C4
Delamere Rd W5 .....36 A4
Delamere St W2 .....100 C3
Delamere Terr W2 ..100 B4
Delancey Pas NW1 ..82 B3
Delancey St NW1 ...82 B3
Delancey Studios
NW1 .....82 B3
Delany Ho SE10 .....52 B4
Delarch Ho SE1 ....136 A3
De Laune St SE17 ..150 A1
Delaware Rd W9 .....88 A2
Delawyk Cres SE24 .63 C1
Delft Way **2** SE22 ..64 A2
Delhi St N1 .....84 B3
Delia St SW18 .....71 A4
Delius Gr E15 .....27 B3
Dellafield N4 .....5 C2
Dell Ct E15 .....27 C4
Dellow Ho **6** E1 ....32 A2
Dellow St E1 .....32 A2
Dell's Mews SW1 ...147 A3
Deloraine Ho SE8 ..51 C2
Deloraine St SE8 ..51 C2
Delorme St W6 .....47 C4
Delta Bldg **4** E14 ..34 B3
Delta Ho N1 .....97 C3
Delta Pk SW18 .....59 A3
Delta St **2** 99 B4
Delverton Ho SE17 .150 B2
Delverton Rd SE17 .150 B1
Delvino Rd SW6 ....165 C3
De Montfort Par **1**
SW16 .....74 A1
De Montfort Rd
SW16 .....74 A1
De Morgan Rd SW6 ..59 A4
Dempster Rd SW18 ..59 B2
Denbigh Cl
W11 .....31 B2 **113** A4
London NW10 .....8 A1
Denbigh Gdns TW10 54 B2
Denbigh Ho SW1 ...131 A2
W11 .....31 B2 **113** A4
7 W11 .....31 B3
Denbigh Mews
SW1 .....146 C3
Denbigh Pl SW1 ....146 C2
Denbigh Rd
W11 .....31 B2 **113** A4
Denbigh St SW1 ....147 A2
Denbigh Terr
W11 .....31 B2 **113** A4
Denbury Ho **48** E3 ..27 A2
Denby Ct SE11 .....149 A4

Dence Ho **22** 99 B3
Denchworth Ho
SW9 .....173 B1
Dendy St SW12 .....72 C3
Dene Cl **4** SE4 .....66 A3
Denehurst Gdns
Acton W3 .....28 A1
Richmond TW10 .....54 C3
Dene Mans **1** NW6 ..10 C2
Denesmead SE24 ....63 B2
Denewood Rd N6 .....3 B4
Dengie Wlk N1 .....86 C4
Denham Ho **10** W12 .30 A2
Denham St SE10 .....43 C1
Denholme Rd W9 ....23 B2
Denison Ho **6** E14 ..33 C3
Denland Ho SW8 ...163 A1
Denman Ho N16 .....7 A2
Denman Rd SE15 ....49 B1
Denman St W1 .....119 B3
Denmark Gr N1 .....85 B2
Denmark Hill SE5 ..48 C2
Denmark Hill Sta
SE5 .....48 B1
Denmark Mans **14**
SE5 .....48 B1
Denmark Pl WC2 ...105 C2
Denmark Rd NW6 ...23 B3
London SE5 .....48 B1
Denmark St WC2 ...105 C2
Denmead Ho **8**
SW15 .....56 B1
Denne Terr E8 .....24 B4
Dennett's Ct SE14 .51 C1
Dennett's Rd SE14 .50 B2
Denning Cl NW8 ....89 A3
Denning Point **1**
E1 .....111 A2
Denning Rd NW3 ....11 C4
Dennington Park Rd
NW6 .....10 C2
Dennis Ho **3** E3 ....26 B3
Dennison Point E15 .19 B1
Dennis Severs' Ho
E1 .....110 B4
Denny Cres SE11 ...149 C2
Denny St SE11 .....149 C2
Densham Ho NW8 ....79 C1
Denstone Ho **5**
SE15 .....49 C4
Dent Ho SE17 .....152 A3
Denton NW1 .....12 C2
Denton Ho N1 .....15 A1
Denton St SW18 ....59 A1
Dents Rd SW11 .....60 B1
Denver Rd N16 .....7 A4
Denyer Ho **5** NW3 ..12 B3
Denyer St SW3 .....144 B4
Denys Bldg EC1 ...107 C3
Denzil Rd NW10 .....8 B3
Deodar Rd SW15 ....58 A3
Depot App NW2 .....9 C4
Depot Rd W12 .....30 B2
Depot St SE5 .....48 C4
Deptford Bridge
SE8 .....51 C2
Deptford Bridge Sta
SE8 .....51 C2
Deptford Broadway
SE8,SE14 .....51 C2
Deptford Church St
SE8 .....51 C3
Deptford Ferry Rd **12**
E14 .....41 C2
Deptford Gn SE8 ...51 C3
Deptford Green Sch
SE14 .....51 B3
Deptford Green Sch
(Annexe) SE14 .....51 A3

Deptford High St
SE8 .....51 C3
Deptford Park Prim Sch
SE8 .....41 A1
Deptford Sta SE8 ..51 C2
Deptford Trad Est
SE8 .....51 A4
Deptford Wharf SE8 41 B2
Dept of Transport &
Environment
SW1 .....133 C2
De Quincey Mews **3**
E16 .....35 C1
Derby Ct **5** E5 .....17 C4
Derby Gate SW1 ....134 A4
Derby Ho SE11 .....149 B4
Derby Rd E9 .....25 C4
Mortlake SW14 .....55 A3
Derbyshire St
E2 .....24 C2 **99** C3
Derby St W1 .....117 C1
Dereham Ho **7** SE4 .65 C3
Dereham Pl EC2 ....98 B2
Derek Walcott Cl
SE24 .....63 A2
Dericote St E8 .....25 A4
Dering St W1 .....104 B1
Dermody Gdns
SE13 .....67 C2
Dermody Rd SE13 ..67 C2
Deronda Rd SE24,
SW2 .....75 A3
Derrick Ho **16** SW2 74 C3
Derrycombe Ho
W11 .....31 A3
18 W2 .....31 C4
Derry St W8 .....128 A3
Dersingham Rd NW2 .1 A1
Derwent NW1 .....92 C3
Derwent Ct **8** SE16 40 C4
2 London W6 .....39 B1
Derwent Gr SE22 ...64 B3
Derwent Ho **3** E3 ..26 B1
SW7 .....143 A4
Derwent St SE10 ...43 A1
Derwentwater Mans **3**
W3 .....28 B1
Derwentwater Prim Sch
W3 .....28 B1
Derwentwater Rd
W3 .....28 B1
Desborough Cl
W2 .....100 B4
Desborough Ho
W14 .....155 A4
Desenfans Rd SE21 .64 A1
Desmond St SE14 ...51 A4
Despard Ho SW2 ....74 C2
Despard Rd N19 .....4 B3
Dethick Ct E3 .....26 A4
Detling Ho SE17 ...152 A3
Devas St E3 .....27 A1
Deventer Cres **8**
SE22 .....64 A2
De Vere Cotts W8 .128 C2
De Vere Gdns W8 ..128 C3
Deverell St SE1 ...137 B1
De Vere Mews W8 ..128 C2
Devereux Ct WC2 ..107 B1
Devereux Ho **7**
SW15 .....56 C2
Devereux La SW13 ..47 A3
Devereux Rd SW11 .60 B1
Devitt Ho **4** E14 ...34 A2
Devizes St N1 .....87 C3
Devonhurst Pl **1**
W4 .....37 C1

Devonia Rd N1 .....86 B2
Devon Mans SE1 ...138 B4
Devonport W2 .....102 A2
Devonport Ho **23**
W2 .....31 C4
Devonport Rd W12 .39 A4
Devonport St E1 ...32 C3
Devonshire Cl W1 .104 A4
Devonshire Ct **6**
TW9 .....44 B2
Devonshire Dr SE10 52 A2
Devonshire Gdns
W4 .....45 B3
Devonshire Gr SE15 50 A3
Devonshire Hall **14**
E9 .....17 B2
Devonshire Ho
SE1 .....136 C2
SW1 .....147 C2
W2 .....101 C4
14 Balham SW12 ...73 A4
London NW6 .....10 B2
3 Putney SW15 .....69 B4
Devonshire Hospl
W1 .....103 C4
Devonshire House Prep
Sch NW3 .....11 C3
Devonshire House Sch
NW3 .....11 B3
Devonshire Mews **2**
W4 .....38 A1
Devonshire Mews N
W1 .....104 A4
Devonshire Mews S
W1 .....104 A4
Devonshire Mews W
W1 .....103 C4
Devonshire Pl W1 ..1 C1
W4 .....38 A1
W8 .....128 A1
Devonshire Place Mews
W1 .....103 C4
Devonshire Rd W4 ..38 A1
Devonshire Row
EC2 .....110 B3
Devonshire Row Mews
W1 .....92 B1
Devonshire Sq
EC2 .....110 B2
Devonshire St W1 ..104 A4
London W4 .....38 A1
Devonshire Terr
W2 .....101 A1
Devons Rd E3 .....27 A1
Devons Road Sta
E3 .....27 A1
Devon St SE15 .....50 A4
De Walden Ho NW8 ..80 A2
De Walden St W1 ..103 C3
Dewar St SE15 .....64 C4
Dewberry St E14 ...34 B4
Dewey Rd N1 .....85 B2
Dewhurst Rd W14 ..39 C3
Dewsbury Ct **5** W4 .37 B2
Dewsbury Rd NW10 ..8 C3
Dewsbury Terr NW1 .82 B4
D'eynsford Rd SE5 .48 C2
Dhonau Ho SE16 ...153 A4
Diadem Ct W1 .....105 B2
Dial Wlk The W8 ..128 A4
Diamond Est SW17 .72 A1
Diamond Ho **20** E3 .26 A3
Diamond St SE15 ...49 A3
Diamond Terr SE10 .52 B2
Diana Cl **20** SE8 ...51 B4
Diana Ho **4** SW2 ...62 B2

Diana, Princess of
Wales Mml Wlk
W2 .....114 C1
Dibden Ho **10** SE5 ..49 A3
Dibden St N1 .....86 C4
Dibdin Ho W9 .....78 A1
Dicey Ave NW2 .....9 B4
Dickens Ho NW8 ....89 C2
SE17 .....150 B1
W1 .....94 A2
London NW6 .....23 C2
Dickens House Mus
WC1 .....95 A1
Dickenson Rd N8 ....5 A4
Dickens Sq SE1 ....137 A2
Dickens St SW8 ....170 B2
Dickinson Ho E2 ...99 B3
Dicksee Ho NW8 ....89 B1
Dick Shepherd Ct **17**
SW2 .....62 C1
Dickson Ho **13** E1 ..32 A3
Didbin Ho N7 .....5 B2
Digby Bsns Ctr E9 .17 C2
Digby Cres N4 .....6 B2
Digby Mans W6 .....39 B1
Digby Rd E9 .....17 C2
Digby St E2 .....25 B2
Digby Stuart Coll
SW15 .....56 C2
Diggon St **10** E1 ...32 C4
Dighton Ct SE17 ...48 B4
Dighton Rd SW18 ..59 B3
Dignum St N1 .....85 B2
Digswell St N7 ....14 C2
Dilke St SW3 .....159 A4
Dilston Gr SE16 ...40 B2
Dilton Gdns SW15 ..69 A3
Dimes Pl **4** W6 .....39 A2
Dimson Cres E3 ....26 C2
Dinerman Ct NW8 ..79 A4
Dingle Gdns E14 ...33 C2
Dingley La SW16 ...73 C2
Dingley Pl EC1 ....97 A3
Dingley Rd EC1 ....96 C3
Dingwall Rd SW18 .71 B4
Dinmont Ho **20** E2 .24 C3
Dinmont St **1** E2 ..25 A3
Dinmore Ho **7** E9 ..25 B4
Dinnington Ho **1**
E1 .....25 A1
Dinsdale Rd SE3 ...53 B4
Dinsmore Rd SW12 73 A4
Dinton Ho NW8 .....90 A2
Dinwiddy Ho N1 ....84 C1
Disbrowe Rd W6 ...154 B3
Discovery Bsns Pk
SE16 .....139 C1
Discovery Ho **1**
E14 .....34 B2
Disney Pl SE1 .....137 A4
Disney St SE1 .....137 A4
Disraeli Cl **4** W4 ..37 C2
Disraeli Gdns SW15 58 B3
Disraeli Rd
Acton W3 .....20 C3
Putney SW15 .....58 A3
Diss St E2 .....98 C4
Distaff La EC4 ....122 C4
Distillery La W6 ..39 B1
Distillery Rd W6 ..39 B1
Distillery Wlk **14**
TW8 .....44 A4
Distin St SE11 ....149 B3
Ditchburn St E14 ..34 B2
Ditton Ho **10** E5 ...17 A3
Divis Way SW15 ....57 A1
Dixon Clark Ct N1 .15 A2

Dixon Rd SE14 ......51 A2
Dobree Ave NW10 ....9 A4
Dobson Cl NW6 ......11 C1
Dobson Ho 18 SE14 ..50 C4
SE5 ....48 C3
Doby Ct E1 ....123 A4
Dockers Tanner Rd 19
E14 ....41 C2
Dockhead SE1 ....139 A3
Dockhead Wharf
SE16 ....139 A4
Dock Hill Ave SE16 ..40 C4
Docklands Heritage Mus
SE16 ....139 B4
Dockley Rd SE16 .....139 B1
Dockley Road Ind Est
SE16 ....139 B1
Dock Offices 12
SE16 ....40 B3
Dock Rd E16 ....35 B2
Dock St E1 ....125 C4
Doctor Spurstowe
Almshs 8 E8 ....17 A2
Docura Ho N7 ....5 B2
Docwra's Bldgs 1 .16 A2
Dodbrooke Rd SE27 .75 A1
Dodd Ho 18 SE16 ....40 A2
Doddington Gr
SE17 ....150 B1
Doddington Pl 4
SE17 ....48 A4
Dodson St SE1 ....135 C3
Dod St E14 ....33 C3
Dog Kennel Hill
SE22 ....64 A4
Dog Kennel Hill Sch
SE22 ....64 A4
Dog La NW10 ....8 A4
Dolben Ct SE8 ....51 B4
Dolben St SE1 ....122 B1
Dolby Rd SW6 ....164 C1
Dolland Ho SE11 ....149 A1
Dolland St SE11 .....149 A1
Dollar Bay E14 ....42 B4
Dollis Hill Sta NW2 ..8 C3
Dolman Rd W4 ....37 C2
Dolman St SW4 ......62 B3
Dolphin Cl 2 SE16 ..40 C4
Dolphin Ct N7 ....13 C4
Dolphin La E14 ....34 A2
Dolphin Sch SW11 ..60 B2
Dolphin Sq SW1 .....147 B1
Dolphin Twr 21 SE8 .51 B4
Dombey Ho SE1 .....139 B3
4 London W11 ......30 C1
Dombey St WC1 .....106 C4
Domelton Ho SW18 .59 A1
Domett Cl SE5 ....63 C3
Domfe Pl E5 ....17 B4
Domingo St EC1 .....96 C1
Dominion St EC2 ....109 C4
Donaghue Cotts 5
E14 ....33 A4
Donaldson Rd NW6 .23 B4
Donegal Ho 2 E1 ....25 B1
Donegal St N1 ....85 A1
Donerale Ho SW18 ..146 A1
Donerale St SW6 ....47 C2
Dongola Rd E1 ....33 A4
Donkey Alley SE22 ..64 C1
Donkin Ho 15 SE16 .40 A2
Donne Ct SE24 ......63 B1
Donne Ho 7 E14 .....33 C3
SE14 ....50 C4
10 London N16 .....15 C4
Donnelly Ct SW6 ....154 B2
Donne Pl SW3 ....144 B4

Donnington Ct
London NW10 ....9 A1
11 London NW1 ....13 A1
Donnington Ho
SW8 ....171 B2
Donnington Prim Sch
NW10 ....22 A4
Donnington Rd
NW10 ....22 A4
Donovan Ct SW7 ....143 B1
Donovan Ho 3 E1 ...32 B2
Don Phelan Cl SE5 ..48 C2
Doon St SE1 ....121 B2
Doradus Ct 20
SW19 ....69 C3
Dora Ho 1 E14 ......33 B3
11 London W11 .....30 C2
Dorando Cl W12 ....30 A2
Doran Wlk E15 ....76 B1
Dora St E14 ....33 B3
Dorcas Ct 9 SW18 ..59 C3
Dorchester Ct
SW1 ....131 A1
1 London N1 ....16 A1
London SE24 ....63 B2
5 Streatham SW16 .74 A1
Dorchester Dr SE24 .63 B2
Dorchester Gr W4 ..38 B1
Dordrecht Rd W3 ...29 A1
Doria Rd SW6 ....165 A2
Doric Ho 7 E2 ....25 C3
Doric Way NW1 .....93 B4
Doris Emmerton Ct 3
SW11 ....59 B3
Dorking Cl SE8 ......51 B4
Dorking Ho SE1 .....137 C2
Dorlcote Rd SW18 ..72 A4
Dorleston Ct N1 .....87 C4
Dorman Way NW8 ..79 B4
Dormay St SW18 ....59 A2
Dormstone Ho
SE17 ....152 A3
Dornan Wlk E15 .....27 B4
Dornberg Cl SE3 .....53 C3
Dorncliffe Rd SW6 ..164 B2
Dorney NW3 ....12 A1
Dorney Ct SW6 .....58 A4
Dornfell St NW6 .....10 B3
Dornoch Ho 24 E3 ..26 B3
Dornton Rd SW12,
SW17 ....73 B2
Dorothy Charrington Ho
7 ....64 B1
Dorothy Rd SW11 ..60 B4
Dorrien Wlk SW16 ..73 C2
Dorrington Point 20
E3 ....27 A2
Dorrington St EC1 ..107 B4
Dorrit Ho 2 W11 ....30 C1
Dorrit St SE1 ....137 A4
Dorset Bldgs EC4 ...108 A1
Dorset Cl NW1 ......102 C4
Dorset Ct 3 N1 .....16 A1
Dorset Mans 2 W6 .47 C4
Dorset Mews SW1 ..132 A2
Dorset Pl E15 ....19 C2
Dorset Rd SW8 .....162 C2
Dorset Rise EC4 ....108 A1
Dorset Sq NW1 .....90 C1
Dorset St W1 ....103 A3
Dorton Cl 6 SE15 ...49 A3
Dorville Cres W6 ....39 A3
Doughty Ct 11 E1 ...32 A1
Doughty Mews WC1 .94 C1
Doughty St WC1 ....94 C1
Douglas Bldgs SE1 .137 A4
Douglas Ct 5 NW6 .10 C1

Douglas Gracey Ho
SW18 ....70 A4
Douglas Ho SW15 ..56 C1
Douglas Johnstone Ho
SW6 ....154 C2
Douglas Mews NW2 ..1 A1
Douglas Rd 5 E16 ..35 C4
London N1 ....15 B1
Douglas Rd N N1 ...15 B2
Douglas Rd S N1 ...15 B2
Douglas St SW1 ....147 B3
Douglas Waite Ho
NW6 ....11 C1
Douglas Way SE8 ..51 B3
Doulton Ho SE11 ...149 A4
Doulton Mews 4 ....11 A2
Dounesforth Gdns
SW18 ....71 A3
Douro Pl W8 ....128 B2
Douro St E3 ....26 C3
Douthwaite Sq 6 E1 .125 C2
Dovecote Gdns 4 ..55 C4
SW14
Dovedale Cotts
SW11 ....168 C2
Dovedale Ho N16 ...6 C4
Dovedale Rd SE22 ..65 A1
Dovehouse St
SW3 ....144 A1
Dove Mews SW7 ...143 A2
Dovercourt Rd SE22 .64 B1
Dover Ct EC1 ....96 A2
London SE10 ....52 A2
Dove Rd N1 ....15 C2
Doverfield Rd SW2 .74 A4
Dover Flats SE1 ....152 B3
Dover Ho 11 SE15 ..50 B4
London SE5 ....48 A2
Dover House Rd
SW15 ....57 A2
Dover Mans 11 SW9 .62 C1
Dover Row 2 ....24 C4
Dover Park Dr
SW15 ....57 A1
Dover St W1 ....118 C2
Dover Terr TW9 ....44 C1
Dover Yd W1 ....118 C2
Doves Yd N1 ....85 B3
Doveton Ho 6 E1 ...25 B1
Doveton St 5 E1 ....25 B1
Dove Wlk SW1 .....145 B2
Dowdeswell Cl
SW15 ....56 A3
Dowding Ho N6 .....3 C4
Dowell Ho SE21 ....76 B1
Dowes Ho 11 SW16 .74 A1
Dowgate Hill EC4 ..123 B4
Dowland St W10 ....23 A2
Dowlas St SE5 ......49 A3
Downbarton Ho
SW9 ....173 B4
Downbury Mews 18
SW18 ....58 C2
Downend Ct 8
SE15 ....49 A4
Downer's Cotts SW4 .61 B3
Downey Ho 6 E1 ...25 C1
Downfield Cl W9 ...88 A1
Downham Ct N1 ....15 C1
Downham Rd N1 ...15 C1
Downing Ho
11 London W10 ....30 C3
2 Putney SW15 ....56 C2
Down Pl W6 ....39 A1

Downs Ct 18 E8 .....17 A3
Downsell Jun & Inf Schs
E15 ....19 C4
Downsell Rd E15 ...19 C4
Downshire Hill
NW3 ....11 C4
Downside 2 SW15 .58 A2
Downside Cres
NW3 ....12 A3
Downs La 8 E5 ......17 A4
Downs Park Rd E5,
E8 ....16 C3
Downs Rd E5,N16 ..16 C4
Downs Side JMI Sch
E5 ....16 C4
Down St W1 ....118 A1
Down St Mews
W1 ....118 A1
Downsview Sch E5 .17 A4
Downton Ave SW2 .74 B2
Downtown Rd SE16 .41 A4
Dowrey St N1 ....85 B4
Dowson Cl SE5 .....63 C3
Dowson Ct SE13 ...67 C4
Dowson Ho 7 E1 ...32 C3
Doyce St SE1 ....136 C4
Doyle Gdns NW10 ..22 A4
Doyle Ho W3 ....37 A4
D'Oyley St SW1 ....145 B4
Doynton St N19 ....4 A2
Draco St SE17 ......48 B4
Dragon Rd SE15 ...49 A4
Dragon Yd WC1 ....106 B2
Dragoon Rd SE8 ...41 B1
Dragor Rd NW10 ...20 C1
Drake Ct 5 SE16 ...40 C4
Drake Croft N16 ....6 C2
Drake Ct 12 W12 ..39 A4
Drakefell Rd SE4,
SE14 ....65 C4
Drakefield Rd SW17 .72 C1
Drake Ho 17 E1 ....32 B4
2 London E14 ......33 A3
Drakeley Ct N5 .....15 A4
Drake Rd SE4 ......66 C4
Drakes Ctyd NW6 ..10 B1
Drake St WC1 ......106 C3
Draldo Ho 9 SW15 .58 A2
Draper Ho SE1 .....150 B4
Draper Pl N1 ....86 B4
Drapers Almshouses 4
E3 ....26 C2
Drapers Gdns EC2 ..109 C2
Drapers Rd E15 ....19 C4
Drapers Way
SE16 ....153 C4
Draycott Ave SW3 .144 B3
Draycott Ct SW3 ...144 C3
Draycott Ho SW3 ..144 C3
Draycott Pl SW3 ...144 C3
Draycott Terr SW3 .145 A3
Drayford Cl W9 .....23 B1
Dray Gdns SW2 ....62 B2
Draymans Ct 4 .....62 B4
Drayson Mews W8 .127 C3
Drayton Ct SW10 ..143 A1
Drayton Gdns
SW10 ....143 A1
Drayton Ho 1 SE5 ..48 C3
N5 ....15 A4
Drayton Park Prim Sch
N5 ....14 C3
Drayton Park Sta
N5 ....14 C3
Drayton Pk N5,N7 ..14 C3
Drayton Rd NW10 ..21 B4

Dreadnought St
SE10 ....43 A3
Dresden Cl NW6 ...11 A2
Dresden Ho SE11 ..149 A4
London SW11 ......169 B2
Dresden Rd N19 ...4 C3
Dressington Ave
SE4 ....66 C1
Drewett Ho E1 .....111 C1
Drew Ho 12 SW16 .74 A1
Drewstead Rd
SW16 ....73 C2
Driffield Rd E3 .....26 A3
Driftway Ho 15 E3 ..26 B3
Drinkwater Ho 11
SE5 ....48 C3
Drive Mans SW6 ..164 B2
Drive The London N7 ..5 A4
London NW11 ......1 A4
London SW19 ......2 B3
Dr Johnson Ave
SW17 ....73 A1
Dr Johnson's Ho
EC4 ....107 C1
Droitwich Cl SE26 ..76 C1
Dromore Rd SW15 ..58 A1
Dron Ho E1 ....32 B4
Droop St W10 ......23 A1
Drovers Ct SE13 ...67 B4
Drovers Pl SE15 ...50 A3
Druce Rd SE21 ....64 A1
Druid St SE1 ....138 C3
Drummer Lo N7 ....5 B1
Drummond Cres
NW1 ....93 B4
Drummond Gate
SW1 ....147 C2
Drummond Ho 12
E2 ....24 C3
Drummonds Pl TW9 .54 A3
Drummond PI TW9 ..54 A3
Drummond St NW1 .92 C2
Drum St E1 ....111 A2
Drury Ho SW8 ......170 C4
Drury La WC2 ......106 B1
Dryad St SW15 ....57 C4
Dryburgh Ho SW1 .146 B2
Dryburgh Mans
SW15 ....57 B4
Dryburgh Rd SW15 .57 B4
Dryden Ct SE11 ...149 C3
Dryden Ho
16 London N16 .....7 A1
6 London SE5 .....49 A2
Dryden St WC2 ....106 B1
Dryer's Bldgs EC1 ..107 B3
Dryfield Wlk 1 SE8 .51 C4
Drysdale Flats 3 ....16 B3
E8
Drysdale Ho 2 ......98 B4
Drysdale Pl N1 .....98 B4
Drysdale St N1 .....98 B4
Dublin Ave E8 ......24 C4
Ducal St E2 ....99 A3
Ducane Cl W12 ....30 B3
Du Cane Ct SW12 ..72 C3
Du Cane Rd W12 ..29 C3
Ducavel Ho SW2 ...74 B3
Duchess Mews W1 .104 B3
Duchess of Bedford Ho
W8 ....127 B4
Duchess of Bedford's
Wlk W8 ....127 B3
Duchess St W1 .....104 B3

Duchy St E1 .... 121 C2
Ducie Ho B SW15 .... 57 B2
Ducie St SW4 .... 62 A3
Duckett St E1 .... 33 A4
Duck La W1 .... 105 B1
Du Cros Rd W3 .... 29 A1
Dudden Hill La NW10 8 B3
Dudley Ct W1 .... 102 C1
   WC2 .... 106 A2
Dudley Ho W2 .... 101 B3
   London SW9 .... 173 B2
Dudley Mews
   SW2 ....
Dudley Rd NW6 .... 23 B3
   Richmond TW9 ..... 44 B1
Dudley St W2 .... 101 B3
Dudmaston Mews
   SW3 .... 143 C2
Duffell Ho SE11 .... 149 A1
Dufferin Ave EC1 ..... 97 B1
Dufferin Ct EC1 .... 97 B1
Dufferin St EC1 .... 97 A1
Duffield Ho N4 .... 6 B4
Duff St E14 .... 34 A3
Dufour's Pl W1 .... 105 A1
Dugdale Ho ID N7 ... 13 C3
Duke Humphrey Rd
   SE3 .... 53 A1
Duke of Wellington Pl
   SW1,W1 .... 131 C4
Duke Of York's Sq
   SW3 .... 144 C3
Duke of York St
   SW1 .... 119 A2
Duke Rd W4 .... 37 C1
Duke's Ave W4 .... 37 C1
Dukes Ct
   London SE13 .... 52 B1
   London SE22 .... 65 A2
   London SE22 .... 76 C3
Dukes Gate B W4 .. 37 B2
Dukes Head Yd N6 .. 4 A3
Duke's Ho E SW1 .. 147 C4
Duke Shore Wharf
   E14 .... 33 B2
Dukes La W8 .... 128 A4
Duke's Mews W1 .... 103 C2
Duke's Pl EC3 .... 110 B1
Dukes Point N6 .... 4 A3
Duke's Rd WC1 .... 93 C3
Duke St W1 .... 103 C1
Duke St Hill SE1 ..... 123 C2
Duke St Mans W1 ... 103 C1
Duke St St James's
   SW1 .... 119 A2
Duke's Yd W1 .... 117 C4
Dulas St N4 .... 5 B3
Dulford St
   W11 .... 31 A2 112 A4
Dulka Rd SW11 .... 60 B2
Dulverton NW1 .... 83 A3
Dulverton Mans
   W1 .... 95 A1
Dulwich Coll (Endowed)
   SE21 .... 76 A2
Dulwich Coll Picture
Gall SE21 .... 76 A4
Dulwich Coll Prep Sch
   SE21 .... 76 A3
Dulwich Comm
   SE21 .... 76 A3
Dulwich Hamlet Jun Sch
   SE21 .... 63 C1
Dulwich High Sch for
Boys SE24 .... 63 C2

Dulwich Hospl SE22 64 A3
Dulwich Mead SE24 .63 B1
Dulwich Mews B
   SE22 .... 64 B3
Dulwich Oaks The
   SE21 .... 76 B1
Dulwich Rd SE24 .... 63 A1
Dulwich Village
   SE21 .... 64 A1
Dulwich Village CE Inf
   Sch SE21 .... 64 A1
Dumain Ct SE11 .... 150 A3
Du Maurier Ho B
   NW3 .... 12 B3
Dumbarton Ct ID
   SW2 .... 74 A4
Dumbarton Rd SW2 .62 A1
Dumont Rd N16 .... 7 A1
Dumphreys Ho B
   SW4 .... 73 C4
Dumpton Pl NW1 .. 112 C1
Dunbar St SE27 ...... 75 B1
Dunbar Wharf B
   E14 .... 33 B2
Dunboyne Rd NW3 ...12 B3
Dunbridge Ho B
   SW15 .... 56 B1
Dunbridge St E2 .... 25 A1
Duncan Ct B E14 .....34 B4
Duncan Gr W3 .... 29 A3
Duncan Ho B NW3 ..12 B3
Duncannon Ho
   SW1 .... 147 C1
Duncannon St
   WC2 .... 120 A3
Duncan Rd E8 .... 25 A4
   Richmond TW9 ..... 54 A3
Duncan St N1 .... 86 A2
Duncan Terr N1 .... 86 A2
Dunch St B E1 .... 32 A3
Duncombe Ho B
   SW19 .... 69 C3
Duncombe Prim Sch
   N19 .... 4 C3
Duncombe Rd N19 ... 4 C3
Duncrievie Rd SE13 .67 C1
Dundalk Ho B E1 .... 32 B3
Dundalk Rd SE4 ...... 66 A4
Dundas Ho B E2 ..... 25 B3
Dundas Rd SE15 .... 50 B1
Dundee Ct B E1 ..... 32 A1
Dundee Ho W9 .... 88 C4
Dundee St E1 .... 32 A1
Dundee Wharf E14 .. 33 B2
Dundonald Rd
   NW10 .... 22 C4
Dundry Ho B SE26 ...76 C1
Dunelm Gr SE27 ...... 75 B1
Dunelm St E1 .... 32 C3
Dunford Rd N7 .... 14 B4
Dungarvan Ave
   SW15 .... 56 C3
Dungeness Ho
   SW18 .... 59 B3
Dunhill Point B
   SW15 .... 69 A3
Dunkeld Ho B E14 .34 C3
Dunlace Rd E5 .... 17 C4
Dunlin Ct E SE21 ..75 C2
Dunlin Ho E SE16 ... 40 C2
Dunloe Ct B E2 ...... 24 B3
Dunloe St E2 .... 24 B3
Dunlop Pl SE16 .... 139 A1
Dunmore Point B
   E2 .... 24 B2 98 C3
Dunmore Rd NW6 .. 23 A4
Dunmow Ho B SE11 149 A2
Dunmow Rd E15 .... 19 C4

Dunmow Wlk N1 ..... 86 C4
Dunnage Cres SE16 .41 A2
Dunnet Ho B E3 .... 26 B3
Dunnico Ho SE17 .. 152 A2
Dunn Mews SE21 .. 75 C2
Dunn's Pas WC1 ... 106 B2
Dunn St E8 .... 16 B3
Dunollie Pl NW5 ..... 13 B3
Dunollie Rd NW5 .... 13 B3
Dunoon Ho N1 .... 84 C3
Dunraven Ho B
   TW9 .... 44 B2
Dunraven Rd W12 .. 29 C1
Dunraven St W1 .... 117 A4
Dunraven Upper Sch
   SW16 .... 74 B1
Dunrobin Ct NW3 ... 11 A3
Dunsany Rd W14 .... 39 C3
Dunsfold Ho B
   SW2 .... 74 B4
Dunsford Way
   SW15 .... 57 A1
Dunsmure Rd N16 .... 7 A3
Dunstable Ct B
   SE3 .... 53 C3
Dunstable Mews
   W1 .... 103 C4
Dunstable Rd TW10,
   TW9 .... 54 A3
Dunstall Ho B SE15 .49 C2
Dunstan Ho SE4 ..... 51 B1
Dunstan Ho B
   E1 .... 111 C3
Dunstan's Gr SE22 .65 A1
Dunstan's Rd SE22 .64 C1
Dunster Ct EC3 .... 124 B4
Dunster Gdns NW6 ..10 B1
Dunsterville Way
   SE1 .... 137 C3
Dunston Rd E8 .... 24 B4
   London SW11 ..... 169 C1
Dunston St E8 .... 24 B4
Dunton Ho B
   SW16 .... 74 A1
Dunton Rd SE1 ..... 152 C3
Dunsthill Rd SW18 .. 71 A3
Dunworth Mews
   W11 .... 31 B3
Duplex Ride SW1 .. 131 A3
Durand Gdns SW9 173 A3
Durand Prim Sch
   SW9 .... 173 A3
Durant St E2 .... C2 99 B4
Durban Ho B W12 .. 30 A2
Durdans Ho B NW1 .13 B1
Durfey Ho SE5 .... 48 C3
Durford Cres SW15 .69 A3
Durham Ct SE11 .... 149 A2
Durham Ho NW8 .... 20 C3
Durham Hill B
   SW2 .... 90 B3
Durham House St
   WC2 .... 120 B3
Durham Pl SW3 .... 144 C1
Durham Rd N4,N7 ... 5 B2
Durham Row E1 ...... 33 A4
Durham St SE11 .... 162 C4
Durham Terr W2 ...... 100 A2
Durley Rd N16 .... 7 A4
Durlock Ho SW9 ... 173 B4
Durlston Rd E5 .... 7 C2
Durnford St B SE10 52 B4
Durnsford Ave
   SW18,SW19 .... 70 C2
Durnsford Rd SW18,
Durrell Rd SW6 .... 164 C3
Durrels Ho W14 .... 141 A4
Durrington Rd E5 .. 18 A4

Durrington Twr
   SW8 .... 171 A2
Durrisdeer Ho NW2 .10 B4
Durston NW5 .... 12 C3
Durward St E1 .... 32 A4
Durweston Mews
   W1 .... 103 A4
Durweston St W1 .. 103 A3
Dutch Yd SW18 ...... 58 C2
Dutton Ho SW2 ...... 75 A3
Dutton St SE10 ...... 52 B2
Dwight Ct SW6 .... 164 B2
Dycer Ho B E9 .... 17 C2
Dye House La E3 .... 26 C4
Dyer's La SW15 ...... 57 A3
Dykes Ct B SW2 .... 74 B3
Dylan Rd B SE24 .. 63 A3
Dylways SE5 .... 63 C3
Dymchurch Ho B
   E5 .... 17 A3
Dymes Path SW19 .. 69 C2
Dymock St SW6 ...... 59 A4
Dyne Rd NW6 .... 10 B1
Dynevor Rd
   London N16 .... 7 B1
   Richmond TW10 ... 54 A2
Dynham Rd NW6 .... 10 C1
Dyott St WC1 .... 105 C2
WC1,WC2 .... 106 A2
Dysart St EC2 .... 24 A1 98 A1
Dyson Ho B SE10 .. 43 B1

E

Eade Rd N4 .... 6 B4
Eagle Cl SE16 .... 40 B1
Eagle Ct EC1 .... 108 A4
   B Dulwich SE21 .. 75 C2
Eagle Dwellings
   EC1 .... 97 A4
Eagle Ho B EC1 ..... 96 A1
Eagle Hts ID SW11 ..60 A4
Eagle Mans N16 ..... 16 B3
Eagle Mews N1 ...... 16 A2
Eagle Pl SW1 .... 119 A3
   SW7 .... 143 A2
Eagle St WC1 .... 106 C3
Eagle Wharf SE1 .. 124 C1
Eagle Wharf Rd N1 .87 A2
Ealing,Hammersmith &
   West London Coll
   W14 .... 140 B2
Ealing Tertiary Coll
   W3 .... 28 A3
Eamann Casey Ho
   SW9 .... 173 C3
Eamont Ct NW8 ...... 80 B2
Eamont St NW8 ...... 80 B2
Eardley Cres SW5 . 141 C1
Earldom Rd SW15 .. 57 B3
Earlham St W2 .... 106 A1
Earlom Ho WC1 ...... 90 B1
Earlom Ho WC1 ...... 95 B3
Earl Rd SW14 .... 55 B3
Earl's Court Ex Ctr *
   .... 141 B2
Earl's Court Gdns
   SW5 .... 142 A3
Earl's Court Rd
   SW5,W8 .... 141 C4
Earl's Court Sq
   SW5 .... 142 A2
Earl's Court Sta
   SW5 .... 141 C3
Earlsferry Way N1 .. 14 A1

Earlsfield Prim Sch
   SW18 .... 71 B2
Earlsfield Rd SW18 .71 B4
Earlsfield Sta SW18 71 B3
Earlsmead Rd NW10 22 B2
Earl St EC2 .... 110 A4
Earl Terr W8 .... 127 A1
Earlsthorpe Mews B
   SW12 .... 60 C1
Earlstoke St EC1 .... 96 A4
Earlston Gr E9 .... 25 A4
Earls Wlk W8 .... 127 B1
Earlswood Cl B
   SE10 .... 43 A1
Earlswood Ho B
   SW2 .... 74 B3
Earlswood St SE10 .43 A1
Early Mews NW1 .... 82 B4
Earnshaw St WC1,
   .... 105 C2
Earsby St W14 ..... 140 B4
Eashing Point B
   SW15 .... 69 A3
Easleys Mews W1 . 103 C2
East Acton Arc W3 .29 B3
East Acton Ct W3 .. 29 A2
East Acton La W3 .. 29 A2
East Acton Prim Sch
   W3 .... 29 A2
East Acton Sta W12 29 B3
East Arbour St E1 .. 32 C3
East Bank N16 .... 7 A4
East Block B E1 .... 32 C2
Eastbourne Ave W3 28 C3
Eastbourne Gdns
   SW14 .... 55 B4
Eastbourne Mews
   W2 .... 101 A2
Eastbourne Rd W4 .45 B4
Eastbourne Terr
   W2 .... 101 A2
Eastbury Gr W4 ...... 38 A1
Eastbury Terr E1 ..... 25 C1
Eastcastle St W1 .. 105 A2
Eastcheap EC3 ..... 124 A4
East Churchfield Rd
   W3 .... 28 C1
Eastcote St SW9 .. 172 C1
East Cross Ctr E15 . 18 C2
East Cross Route
   E3 .... 26 C4
   London E9 .... 18 B3
Eastdown Ho E8 .... 16 C4
Eastdown Pk SE13 .67 C3
East Dulwich Gr
   SE22 .... 64 A2
East Dulwich Rd
   SE15,SE22 .... 64 C3
East Dulwich Sta
   SE22 .... 64 A4
Eastern Rd SE4 ...... 66 C3
East Ferry Rd E14 .. 42 A2
Eastfields Av W3 .... 28 B4
Eastfield St E14 ...... 33 A4
East Harding St
   EC4 .... 107 C2
East Heath Rd NW3 ..2 C1
East Hill SW18 .... 59 B2
East India Bldgs B
   .... 98 A1
East India Dock Basin
   E14 .... 35 A1
East India Dock Rd
   E14 .... 34 A2
East India Dock Road
   Tunnel ID E14 ..... 34 C3

East India Dock Wall Rd E14 ...34 C2
East India Sta E14 ...34 C2
East La SE16 ...139 B3
Eastlake Ho NW8 ...89 C1
Eastlake Rd SE5 ...48 B1
Eastlands Cres SE21 ...64 B1
Eastleigh Wlk 🄴
SW15 ...68 C4
East London Coll &
  Toynbee Centre
E1 ...111 A3
East London Stadium
E3 ...33 B4
Eastman Dental Hospl
WC1 ...94 C2
Eastman Ho 🄳 SW4 ...61 B2
Eastman Rd W3 ...37 C4
Eastmearn Rd SE21,
SE27 ...75 B2
East Mount St E1 ...32 A4
Eastney St SE10 ...42 C1
Easton Ho 🄸 SE27 ...75 A1
Easton St WC1 ...95 B2
East Parkside SE10 ...43 B4
East Pas EC1 ...108 C4
East Point SE1 ...153 B2
East Poultry Ave
  EC1 ...108 A3
East Putney Sta
SW15 ...58 A2
East Rd N1 ...97 C4
East Row W10 ...23 A1
Eastry Ho SW8 ...162 A1
East Sheen Ave
SW14 ...55 C3
East Sheen Prim Sch
SW14 ...56 A3
East Smithfield E1 ...125 A3
East Surrey Gr SE15 ...49 B3
East Tenter St E1 ...111 A1
Eastvale W3 ...29 B1
East View NW3 ...12 A4
Eastway E3,E9 ...26 C4
  London E9,E10 ...18 C4
Eastwell Ho SE1 ...137 C2
Eastwick Ct 🄯
SW19 ...69 C3
Eaton Cl SW1 ...145 B3
Eaton Dr SW9 ...63 A3
Eaton Gate SW1 ...145 B4
Eaton Ho SW11 ...167 C3
Eaton House The Manor
  Sch SW4 ...61 A3
Eaton La SW1 ...132 B1
Eaton Mans SW1 ...145 B3
Eaton Mews N
SW1 ...131 C1
Eaton Mews S
SW1 ...132 A1
Eaton Mews W
SW1 ...145 C4
Eaton Pl SW1 ...131 C1
Eaton Row SW1 ...132 A1
Eaton Sq SW1 ...131 C1
Eaton Square Sch
SW1 ...146 A3
Eaton Terr 🄴 E3 ...26 A2
SW1 ...145 C4
Eaton Terr Mews
SW1 ...145 B4
Eatonville Rd SW17 ...72 B2
Eatonville Villas
SW17 ...72 B2
Ebbisham Dr SW8 ...162 C3
Ebbsfleet Rd NW2 ...10 A3

Ebenezer Ho SE11 ...150 A3
Ebenezer Mussel Ho 🄵
E2 ...25 B3
Ebenezer St N1 ...97 B4
Ebley Cl SE15 ...49 B4
Ebner St SW18 ...59 A2
Ebony Ho 🔟 NW3 ...11 A2
Ebor Cotts SW15 ...68 A1
Ebor St E1,E2 ...98 C2
Eburne Rd N7 ...5 A1
Ebury Bridge Rd
SW1 ...145 C1
Ebury Mews 🄴
SW1 ...146 A4
Ebury Mews E
SW1 ...132 A1
Ebury Sq SW1 ...145 C3
Ebury St SW1 ...146 A4
Ecclesbourne Prim Sch
N1 ...15 C1
Ecclesbourne Rd
N1 ...15 B1
Eccles Rd SW11 ...60 B3
Eccleston Mews
SW1 ...131 C1
Eccleston Pl SW1 ...146 A4
Eccleston Sq SW1 ...146 B2
Eccleston Sq Mews
SW1 ...146 C2
Eccleston St SW1 ...146 A4
Eckersley St E2 ...99 A1
Eckford St N1 ...85 B2
Eckstein Rd SW11 ...60 A3
Edans Ct W12 ...38 B4
Edbrooke Rd W9 ...23 C1
Eddisbury Ho 🄴
SE26 ...76 C1
Eddiscombe Rd
SW6 ...165 A2
Eddystone Rd SE4 ...66 A2
Eddystone Twr SE8 ...41 A1
Edenbridge Cl 🕑
SE16 ...40 A1
Edenbridge Rd E9 ...17 C1
Eden Cl 🄰 W8 ...127 C2
  London NW3 ...1 C2
Edendale W3 ...28 A2
Eden Gr N7 ...14 B3
Edenham Way W10 ...31 B4
Eden Ho NW8 ...90 A1
 🔟 London SE16 ...40 A4
Eden Lodge NW6 ...9 C1
Eden Mews SW17 ...71 B1
Edensmuir Ct SE3 ...53 C3
Edensor Gdns W4 ...46 A3
Edensor Rd W4 ...46 A3
Edenvale St SW6 ...166 C1
Edgar Ho SW8 ...162 A2
  London NW3 ...1 C1
Edgarley Terr SW6 ...164 A3
Edgar Rd E3 ...27 A2
Edgcott Ho W10 ...30 B4
Edgecombe Ho
 🄴 London SE5 ...49 A1
  Putney SW19 ...70 A4
Edgecote Cl 🄾 W3 ...28 B1
Edgehill Ho 🄺 SW9 ...48 A1
Edgeley La SW4 ...61 C4
Edgeley Rd SW4 ...61 C4
Edgel St SW18 ...59 A3
Edge St W8 ...31 C1 113 C2
Edgeworth Ho NW8 ...78 C4
Edgson Ho SE1 ...146 A2

Edgware Rd W1,
  W2,NW1,NW8 ...102 A3
Edgware Road Sta
  (Bakerloo) NW1 ...102 A3
Edgware Road Sta
  (Ham,Distr,Circle)
  NW1 ...102 B3
Edinburgh Cl 🄵 E2 ...25 B3
Edinburgh Ct 🔟
SE16 ...32 C1
Edinburgh Ho W9 ...88 B4
Edington 🕗 NW5 ...12 C2
Edison Bldg 🄴 E14 ...41 C4
Edison Ct SE10 ...43 B3
Edis St NW1 ...81 C4
Editha Mans SW10 ...156 C3
Edith Cavell Cl 🄰
N19 ...5 A4
Edith Gr SW10 ...157 A2
Edith Ho 🄺 W6 ...39 B1
Edith Neville Prim Sch
NW1 ...83 B1
Edith Ramsay Ho 🄴
E1 ...33 A4
Edith Rd W14 ...140 B3
  London E15 ...19 C3
Edith Row SW6 ...166 B4
Edith St E2 ...24 C3
Edith Summerskill Ho
SW6 ...154 C2
Edith Terr SW10 ...156 C2
Edith Villas W14 ...140 C2
Edith Yd SW10 ...157 A2
Edmeston Cl E9 ...18 A2
Edmond Ct SE14 ...50 B2
Edmonton Ct 🄴
SE16 ...40 B3
Edmund Halley Way
SE10 ...43 A4
Edmund Ho SE17 ...150 B1
  London SE14 ...51 B2
Edmundsbury Ct Est 🔟
SW9 ...62 B3
Edmund St SE5 ...48 C3
Edmund Waller Prim
  Sch SE14 ...50 C1
Ednam Ho SE15 ...49 C4
Edred Ho E9 ...18 A4
Edrich Ho SW4 ...172 A3
Edric Ho SW1 ...147 C4
Edric Rd SE14 ...50 C3
Edridge Ho 🄴 SE27 ...75 A1
Edward Alleyn Ho
SE21 ...76 A4
Edward Ct 🔟 E16 ...35 C4
Edward Dodd Ct N1 ...97 C4
Edward Edward's Ho
SE1 ...122 A1
Edwardes Sq W8 ...127 B1
Edward Friend Ho 🄴
N16 ...7 A1
Edward Ho SE11 ...149 A2
  W10 ...89 B1
Edward Kennedy Ho 🄸
W10 ...23 A1
Edward Mann Cl 🕘
E1 ...32 C3
Edward Mews NW1 ...82 B1
Edward Pl SE8 ...51 B4
Edward Robinson Ho 🄳
SE14 ...50 C3
Edward's Cotts 🄸
N1 ...15 A1

Edward's La N16 ...7 A2
Edwards Mews
  W1 ...103 B1
  London N1 ...14 C1
Edward Sq N1 ...84 C3
SE16 ...33 A1
Edward St SE14 ...51 B3
Edward VII Mans
NW10 ...22 C2
Edward Wilson Prim Sch
W2 ...100 A4
Edwin Ho SE15 ...49 C3
Edwin's Mead E9 ...18 A4
Edwin St E1 ...25 B1
  E16 ...35 C4
Edwy Ho E9 ...18 B4
Edwyn Ho SW18 ...59 A1
Effie Pl SW6 ...155 C1
Effie Rd SW6 ...155 C1
Effingham Ho SW8 ...171 B1
Effra Ct SE2 ...62 B2
Effra Mans SW2 ...62 C2
Effra Par SW2 ...62 C2
Effra Rd SW2 ...62 C2
Effra Road Ret Pk
SW2 ...62 C2
Egbert Ho E9 ...18 A3
Egbert St NW1 ...81 B4
Egbury Ho SW15 ...56 B1
Egerton Ct 🕔 TW10 ...54 A2
Egerton Dr SE10 ...52 A2
Egerton Gdns SW3 ...130 A1
  Willesden NW10 ...22 B4
Egerton Gdns Mews
SW3 ...130 B1
Egerton Ho W4 ...45 B4
Egerton Pl SW3 ...130 B1
Egerton Rd N16 ...7 B4
Egerton Terr SW3 ...130 B1
Egham Cl SW19 ...70 A2
Eglantine Rd SW18 ...59 B2
Eglington Ct SE17 ...48 B4
Egliston Mews
SW15 ...57 B4
Egliston Rd SW15 ...57 B4
Egmont St SE14 ...50 C3
Egremont Ho SE13 ...52 A1
Egremont Rd SE27 ...74 C1
Egret Ho 🕕 SE16 ...40 C2
Eider Ct 🕙 SE8 ...51 B4
Ekarra Ho SW8 ...172 B4
Elaine Ct 🄴 NW3 ...12 B2
Elaine Gr NW5 ...12 C3
Elaine Ho N4 ...5 A3
Elam Cl SE5 ...48 A1
Elam St SE5 ...48 A1
Elan Ct E1 ...32 A4
Eland Rd SW11 ...60 B4
Elba Pl SE17 ...151 A4
Elbe St SW6 ...166 C2
Elborough St SW18 ...70 C3
Elbury Dr E16 ...35 C3
Elcho St SW11 ...158 B1
Elcot Ave SE15 ...50 A3
Elderberry Rd W5 ...36 A4
Elderfield Ho 🄳
E14 ...33 C2
Elderfield Rd E5 ...17 B4
Elder St E1 ...24 B1 98 C1
Elder Wlk N1 ...86 B4
Eldon Ct NW6 ...23 C4
Eldon Gr NW3 ...11 C3
Eldon Ho SW9 ...63 A4
Eldon Rd W8 ...128 B1
Eldon St EC2 ...109 C3
Eldon Way NW10 ...20 A3

Eldridge Ct SE16 ...139 B1
Eleanor Cl SE16 ...40 C4
Eleanor Ct 🄸 E2 ...24 C4
Eleanor Gr SW13 ...56 A4
Eleanor Ho
 🄸 London NW5 ...13 B3
  London W6 ...39 B1
Eleanor Palmer Prim
  Sch NW5 ...13 B4
Eleanor Rathbone Ho 🄸
N6 ...4 C4
Eleanor St E3 ...26 C2
Electric Ave SW9 ...62 C3
Electric Ho 🄸 E3 ...26 C2
Electric La 2 SW9 ...62 C3
Electric Mans 🄸
SW9 ...62 C3
Elephant & Castle
SE1 ...136 B1
SE1 ...150 B4
Elephant & Castle Sta
SE1 ...136 B1
SE17 ...150 C4
Elephant La SE16 ...40 B4
Elephant Rd SE17 ...150 C4
Elfindale Rd SE24 ...63 B2
Elford Rd N5 ...14 C4
Elf Row E1 ...32 B2
Elgar Ave W5 ...36 A4
Elgar Cl SE8 ...51 C3
Elgar Ct W14 ...126 A1
Elgar Ho NW6 ...78 A2
 🄸 London SW11 ...146 B1
  London NW6 ...11 B1
Elgar St SE16 ...41 A3
Elgin Ave W9 ...88 A2
  London W12 ...39 A3
Elgin Cres
W11 ...31 A2 112 B4
Elgin Cl W12 ...88 A2
Elgin Ct 🄴 E14 ...34 A3
Elgin Mans W9 ...88 A3
Elgin Mews W11 ...31 A3
Elgin Mews N W9 ...88 B4
Elgin Mews S W9 ...88 B4
Elgood Ho NW8 ...79 C1
Elham Ho 🔟 E5 ...17 A3
Elia Mews N1 ...86 A1
Elias Pl SW8 ...163 B3
Elia St N1 ...86 A1
Elim Est SE1 ...138 A2
Elim St SE1 ...138 A2
Eliot Ct SW18 ...59 A1
Eliot Gdns SW15 ...56 C3
Eliot Hill SE13 ...52 B1
Eliot Ho 🔟 TW10 ...54 B1
Eliot Mews NW8 ...78 C2
Eliot Pk SE13 ...52 B1
Eliot Pl SE3 ...53 A1
Eliot Vale SE3 ...52 C1
Elizabeth Ave N1 ...87 A4
Elizabeth Barnes Ct
SW6 ...166 B2
Elizabeth Cl 🄴 E14 ...34 A3
  W9 ...89 A1
Elizabeth Cotts 🄴
TW9 ...44 C2
Elizabeth Ct NW8 ...90 B1
SW10 ...157 C3
SW1 ...133 C1
  London SE22 ...64 C3
Elizabeth Finn Ho
W12 ...38 C3
Elizabeth Garrett
  Anderson Hospl
NW1 ...92 C1

Elizabeth Garrett
Anderson Language
Coll N1 ....84 C2
Elizabeth Gdns 41 29 B1
Elizabeth Ho 48 E3
SE11 ....39 A1
16 London W6 ....39 B1
Elizabeth Ind Est
SE14 ....50 C4
Elizabeth Kenny Ho
N1 ....15 B2
Elizabeth Mews
NW3 ....12 B2
Elizabeth Selby Inf Sch
E2 ....24 C2 99 C4
Elizabeth Sq 11
SE16 ....33 A2
Elizabeth St SW1 ..145 C4
Elkington Point
SE11 ....149 B3
Elkstone Rd 8 ....31 B4
Ellacombe Ho 11
SW2 ....74 C4
Ellaline Rd W6 ....47 C4
Ella Mews NW3 ....12 B4
Elland Ho 1 E14 .....33 B3
Elland Rd SE15 ....65 B3
Ella Rd N4,N8 ....5 A4
Ellenborough Ho 5
W12 ....30 A2
Ellenborough Pl
SW15 ....56 C3
Ellen St E1 ....111 C1
Ellen Wilkinson Ho
7 E2 ....25 C2
SW6 ....155 A3
Ellerby St SW6 ....47 C2
Ellerdale Cl 22 NW3 11 B4
Ellerdale Rd NW3 ....11 B3
Ellerdale St SE13 ....67 A4
Ellerslie Gdns
NW10 ....21 C4
Ellerslie Ind Est
SW2 ....62 A2
Ellerslie Rd W12 .....30 A1
Ellerton Ct SW13 .....37 A1
Ellerton Rd
Barnes SW13 ....46 C2
Wandsworth SW17,
SW18 ....71 C3
Ellery St SE15 ....50 A1
Ellery St SE15 ....50 A1
Ellesmere Ct W4 .....45 C4
Ellesmere Rd 3 ....26 A3
Chiswick W4 ....45 C4
London NW10 ....8 C3
Ellesmere St E14 ....34 A3
Ellingfort Rd E8 ....17 A1
Ellingham Rd
London E15 ....19 C4
London W12 ....38 C4
Ellington Ho SE1 ....137 A1
Ellington St N7 ....14 C2
Elliot Rd SW9 ....48 A3
Elliott Rd
London SW9 ....48 A2
London W4 ....38 A2
Elliott Sch SW15 .....57 C1
Elliott's Pl N1 ....86 B3
Elliott's Row SE11 ..150 B4
Ellis Cl NW10 ....9 B2
Ellisfield Dr SW15 ...68 C4

Ellis Franklin Ct
NW8 ....78 C2
Ellis Ho SE17 ....151 B2
Ellison Ho 1 SE13 ..52 B1
Ellison Rd SW13 ....46 B1
Ellis St SW1 ....145 B4
Ellsworth St E2 ....25 A2
Ellwood Ct W9 ....88 B1
Elm Bank Gdns
SW13 ....46 A1
Elm Bank Mans
SW13 ....46 A1
Elmbourne Rd
SW17 ....73 A1
Elmbridge Wlk E8 ...16 C1
Elm Cl N19 ....4 B2
Elmcourt Rd SE21,
SE27 ....75 A2
Elm Court Sch SE27 79 B2
Elm Cres W6 ....39 A4
Elmcroft N6 ....4 A4
Elmcroft Ave NW11 ...1 B4
Elmcroft Cres NW11 ..1 A4
Elmcroft St E5 ....17 B4
Elm Ct EC4 ....121 B4
London SE13 ....67 C4
London SW9 ....173 B4
25 London W2 ....31 C4
Elmer Ct SW4 ....164 A2
Elmer Ho NW1 ....102 A4
Elmfield Ho W9 ....23 C1
London N5 ....15 B3
Elmfield Mans 5
SW17 ....72 C2
Elmfield Rd SW17 ....73 A2
Elmfield Way W9 .....31 C4
Elm Friars Wlk
NW1 ....13 C1
Elm Gn W3 ....29 A3
Elm Gn NW2 ....2 C2
London SE15 ....49 C1
Elm Grove Rd
Barnes SW13 ....46 C1
London W5 ....36 A3
Elm Ho 1 E14 ....42 B4
Elmhurst Mans
SW4 ....61 C4
Elmhurst St SW4 .....61 C4
Elmhurst Villas
SE15 ....65 B3
Elmington Rd SE5 ....48 C3
Elmira St SE13 ....67 A4
Elm Lo SW6 ....47 C2
Elmore Ho SW9 ....48 A1
Elmore St N1 ....15 C1
Elm Park Gdns
SW10 ....143 B1
Elm Park Ho SW10 .143 B1
Elm Park La SW3 ...143 B1
Elm Park Mans
SW10 ....157 A4
Elm Park Rd SW3 ...157 B4
Elm Pk SW2 ....74 B4
Elm Pl SW7 ....143 B2
Elm Quay SW8 ....161 B3
Elm Rd SW14 ....55 B3
Elm Row NW3 ....2 B1
Elms Cres SW4 ....61 C1
Elmshaw Rd SW15 ...56 C2
Elmslie Point 2 E3 ...33 B4
Elms Mews W2 ....115 B4
Elms Rd SW4 ....61 C2
Elm St WC1 ....95 A1
Elmstone Rd SW6 ...165 B4

Elm Terr NW2 ....1 C1
Elmton Ct NW8 ....89 B2
Elmton Way E5 ....7 C1
Elm Tree Cl NW8 ......89 B4
Elm Tree Ct 5 ....89 B4
5 London SE5 ....48 B2
Elm Tree Rd NW8 .....89 B4
Elm Way NW10 ....8 A4
Elm Wlk NW3 ....1 C2
Elmwood Ct SW11 ..170 A4
Elm Wood Prim Sch
SE27 ....75 C1
Elmwood Rd
Chiswick W4 ....45 B4
London SE24 ....63 C2
Elmworth Gr SE21 ...75 C2
Elnathan Mews W9 ...88 B1
Elphinstone St N5 ...15 A4
Elrington Rd E8 ....16 C2
Elsa St E1 ....33 A4
Elsdale St E9 ....17 B2
Elsden Mews E2 ......25 B3
Elsenham St SW18,
SW19 ....70 B2
Elsham Rd W14 ......126 A3
Elsham Terr W14 ....126 A3
Elsie Lane Ct W2 .....31 C4
Elsiemaud Rd SE4 ...66 B2
Elsie Rd SE22 ....64 B3
Elsinore Gdns NW2 ...1 A1
Elsinore Ho N1 ....85 B3
London SE5 ....48 B1
Elsinore Way TW9 ...55 A4
Elsley Rd SW11 ....60 C4
Elsley Sch SW11 ......60 C4
Elspeth Rd SW11 .....60 B3
Elstead Ho 9 SW2 ...74 B4
Elsted St SE17 ....151 C3
Elstow Grange NW6 ..9 C1
Elswick Rd SE13 ......52 A1
Elswick St SW6 ....166 B2
Elsworthy Rd NW3 ...80 A4
Elsworthy Rise NW3 12 A3
Elsworthy Terr NW3 12 A3
Elsynge Rd SW18 .....59 C2
Elsynge Road Mans
SW18 ....59 C2
Elthiron Rd SW6 .....165 C3
Elthorne Rd N19 ....4 C2
Elthruda Rd SE13 .....67 C1
Eltham Ho 1 ....114 C3
Elton Ho 8 E3 ....26 B4
Elton Pl N16 ....16 A3
Elton St 6 N16 ....16 A3
Eltringham St SW18 59 B3
Elvaston Mews
SW7 ....129 A2
Elvaston Pl SW7 .....129 A1
Eveden Ho 17 SW9 ...62 B3
Elver Gdns 2 ....99 C4
Everson Rd SE8 ....51 B2
Everson Rd Sta
SE8 ....52 A1
Everton St SW1 ......147 B4
Elvin Ho 2 E9 ....17 B2
Elvis Rd NW2 ....9 B2
Elwin St 2 ......24 C2 99 C4
Elwood Ho N5 ....6 A1
Elwood St N4,N5 ....6 A1
Elworth Ho SW8 ......163 A1
Ely Cottages SW8 ...163 A1
Ely Court Flats
SW1 ....155 A2
Ely Ho 4 SE15 ....49 C3
Ely Pl EC1 ....107 C3
Elysium Gate 4
SW6 ....164 C3
Elysium Pl SW6 ......164 C1

Elysium St SW6 ......164 C1
Elystan Pl SW3 ....144 C2
Elystan St SW3 ......144 B3
Elystan Wlk N1 ....85 B3
Elyston Ct SW15 ....57 A2
Emanuel Ave W3 ......28 B3
Emanuel Ct W3 ....28 C3
Emanuel Sch SW11 ...60 A2
Emba St SE16 ....139 C3
Ember Ct 5 W12 ......38 A3
Emberton SE5 ....49 A4
Emberton Ct EC1 .....96 A3
Embleton Rd SE13 ...66 C3
Embley Point 2 E5 ...17 A4
Emden St SW6 ....166 B4
Emerald Sq SW15 ...56 C2
Emerson Ho N16 .....16 A3
Emerson St SE1 .....122 C2
Emery Hill St SW1 ..133 A1
Emery St SE1 ....135 C2
Emily Pl N7 ....14 C4
Emily St 7 E16 ....35 B1
Emlyn Gdns 1 W12 .38 A3
Emlyn Rd W12 ....38 B3
Emmanuel CE Prim Sch
NW6 ....10 C3
Emmanuel Ho
SE11 ....149 B3
Dulwich SE21 ....75 C1
Emmanuel Rd SW12 73 C3
Emma St E2 ....25 A3
Emminster NW6 ....78 A3
Emmott Cl E1 ....26 A1
Emperor's Gate
SW7 ....142 C4
Empingham Ho 20
SE8 ....40 C2
Empire Ho SW3 ....130 A1
Empire Sq N19 ....5 A1
Empire Wharf E3 .....26 A4
Empire Wharf Rd
E14 ....42 C2
Empress Mews 27
SE5 ....48 B1
Empress Pl SW5 .....141 B1
Empress St SE17 ....48 B4
Empson St E3 ....27 A1
Emsworth St SW2 ....74 B2
Emu Rd SW8 ....170 A1
Enard Ho 27 E3 ....26 B3
Enbrook St W10 ....23 A2
Enclave Ct EC1 ....96 A2
Endell St WC2 ....106 A1
Enderby St SE10 ......43 A1
Endlesham Ct 2
SW12 ....72 C4
Endlesham Rd
SW12 ....72 C4
Endsleigh Gdns
WC1 ....93 B2
Endsleigh Mans 4
SW16 ....74 A1
Endsleigh Pl WC1 ....93 C2
Endsleigh St WC1 ....93 C2
Endwell Rd SE4 ....51 A1

Elysium St SW6 ......164 C1
Endymion Rd
London N4 ....6 A4
London SW2 ....62 B1
Energen Cl
London NW10 ....8 A1
London NW10 ....8 A1
Enfield Cloisters 1
N1 ....98 A4
Enfield Ho 9 SW9 ...172 B2
Enfield Rd
London E8,N1 ....16 A1
London W3 ....37 A4
Enford St W1 ....102 C4
Engadine St SW18 ...70 C3
Engate St SE13 ....67 B3
England's La NW3 ....12 B2
Englefield NW1 ....92 C3
Englefield Rd N1 ......16 A1
Englewood
SW12 ....61 B1
English Gardening Sch
The SW3 ....158 C4
English Grounds
SE1 ....124 A1
English Martyrs RC Prim
Sch E1 ....110 C1
English St E3 ....26 B1
Enid St SE16 ....139 A2
Enid Stacy Ho 11
N19 ....5 A4
Enmore Ct SW14 .....55 C2
Enmore Gdns SW14 ..55 C2
Enmore Rd SW15 .....57 B2
Ennerdale Ho 3 N4 ...6 C4
Ennerdale Rd TW9 ...44 B1
Ennersdale Prim Sch
SE13 ....67 C2
Ennersdale Rd SE13 67 C2
Ennis Ho 16 E14 ......34 A3
Ennismore Ave W4 ..38 B2
Ennismore Gdns
SW7 ....130 A3
Ennismore Gdns Mews
SW7 ....130 A2
Ennismore Mews
SW7 ....130 A2
Ennismore St SW7 ..130 A2
Ennis Rd N4 ....5 C3
Ensbury Ho SW8 ....162 C2
Ensign Ct E1 ....125 C3
Ensign St E1 ....125 B4
Ensor Mews SW7 ...143 B2
Enterprise Way
London NW10 ....21 B2
London SW18 ....58 C3
Enterprize Way SE8 .41 B2
Epirus Mews SW6 ...155 B2
Epirus Rd SW6 ....155 A2
Epping Cl E14 ....41 C2
Epping Ho 5 ....7 C2
Epping Pl N1 ....14 C2
Epple Rd SW6 ....165 A4
Epworth St EC2 ....97 C2
Equity Sq E2 ....99 A3
Erasmus St SW1 .....147 C3
Erconwald St W12 ...29 B3
Eresby Ho SW7 ......130 B3
Eresby Pl NW6 ....10 C1

Erica Ct SW4 ....172 B3
Erica Ho SE4 ....66 B4
Erica St W12 ....29 C2
Ericcson Cl SW18 ....58 C2
Eric Fletcher Ct 7
N1 ....15 B1
Eric Macdonald Ho
SW6 ....165 C3
Eric Rd NW10 ....8 B2

Ericson Ho
London N16 ....7 B3
London SE13 ....67 C3
Eric St E3 ....26 B1
Eric Wilkins Ho
SE1 ....153 B1
Eridge Ho SE22 ....64 A4
Eridge Rd W4 ....37 C3
Erlanger Rd SE14 ....50 C1
Ermine Rd SE13 ....67 A3
Ernest Bevin Coll
SW17 ....72 A2
Ernest Ave SE14 ....45 A4
Ernest Simmonds Ho
SE14 ....50 B1
Ernest St E1 ....25 C1
Ernshaw Pl SW15 ....58 A2
Eros (Shaftesbury
Meml) W1 ....119 B3
Erpingham Rd
SW15 ....57 B4
Errington Rd W9 ....23 B1
Errol St EC1 ....97 A1
Erskine Ho SW1 ....146 C1
Erskine Rd NW3 ....12 B1
Escuan Lo N5 ....15 B3
Esher Gdns SW19 ....69 C2
Esher Ho SW8 ....171 C2
Eskdale NW1 ....82 C1
Esk Ho E3 ....26 B1
Esme Ho SW15 ....56 B3
Esmeralda Rd SE1 ....153 C3
Esmond Ct SW3 ....144 B3
Esmond Gdns W4 ....37 C2
Esmond Rd NW6 ....23 B4
London W4 ....37 C2
Esmond St SW15 ....58 A3
Esparto St SW18 ....71 A4
Essendine Mans
W9 ....23 C2
Essendine Prim Sch
W9 ....23 C2
Essendine Rd W9 ....23 C2
Barnes SW13 ....46 B1
London W6 ....39 B3
Essex Ho E14 ....34 A3
Essex Park Mews
W3 ....29 A1
Essex Pl W4 ....37 B2
Essex Place Sq W4 ....37 C2
Essex Rd N1 ....86 B4
London NW10 ....8 A1
London W3 ....28 B2
London W4 ....37 C2
Essex Road Sta N1 ....15 B1
Essex St WC2 ....121 B4
Essex Villas W8 ....127 B3
Essian St E1 ....33 A4
Essington SW15 ....58 A1
Estcourt Rd SW6 ....154 C2
Estella Ho W11 ....30 C2
Estelle Rd NW3 ....12 B4
Esterbrooke St
SW1 ....147 B3
Este Rd SW11 ....60 A4
Estoria Cl ② SW2 ....74 C4
Etal Ho N1 ....15 A1
Etchingham Rd E15 ....76 B4
Ethelbert Ho E9 ....18 A4
Ethelbert St SW12 ....73 A3
Ethelburga St
SW11 ....168 A4
Ethelburga Twr
SW11 ....168 A4
Ethelden Rd W12 ....30 A1

Ethel Rankin Ct
SW6 ....164 C2
Ethel St SE17 ....151 A3
Ethelworth Ct ④
SW2 ....74 C3
Etherow St SE22 ....76 C4
Ethnard Rd SE15 ....50 A4
Eton Ave NW3 ....12 A1
Eton Cl SW18 ....71 A4
Eton College Rd
NW3 ....12 B2
Eton Ct NW3 ....11 C1
Eton Garages ⑪
NW3 ....12 A2
Eton Hall NW3 ....12 B2
Eton Ho N5 ....15 A4
Eton Pl NW1 ....12 C1
Eton Rd NW3 ....12 B2
Eton Rise NW3 ....12 B2
Eton St TW10 ....54 A2
Eton Villas NW3 ....12 B2
Etta St SE8 ....51 A4
Ettrick St E14 ....34 B3
Eugene Cotter Ho
SE17 ....151 C3
Eugenia Rd SE16 ....40 B2
Euro Cl NW10 ....8 C2
Eurolink Bsns Ctr
SW2 ....62 C3
Europa Pl EC1 ....96 C3
Eustace Ho SE11 ....148 C4
Eustace Rd SW6 ....155 B2
Euston Rd NW1 ....93 A2
Euston Sq NW1 ....93 B3
Euston Square Sta
WC1 ....93 A2
Euston Sta NW1 ....93 B3
Euston Underpass
NW1 ....92 C2
Evandale Rd SW9 ....173 C2
Evangelist Rd NW5 ....13 A4
Evans Cl E8 ....16 B2
Evans Ho SW8 ....161 C1
⑭ London W12 ....30 A2
Evelina Mans ❸
SE5 ....48 C3
Evelina Rd SE15 ....50 B1
Eveline Lowe Prim Sch
SE1 ....153 C1
Evelyn Ct N1 ....87 B1
London W4 .... B1
Evelyn Denington Ct ②
N1 ....15 A1
Evelyn Fox Ct W10 ....30 B4
Evelyn Gdns SW7 ....143 B1
Richmond TW9 ....54 A3
Evelyn Ho
❸ London SW2 ....62 B2
London W12 ....38 B4
Evelyn Rd
London W4 ....37 C3
Richmond TW9 ....54 A4
Evelyn St SE8 ....41 A1
Evelyn Terr TW9 ....54 A4
Evelyn Wlk N1 ....87 B1
Evelyn Yd W1 ....105 B2
Evenwood Cl SW15 ....58 A2
Everard Ho E1 ....111 C1
Everatt Cl SW18 ....58 B2
Everdon Rd SW13 ....46 C4
Everest Pl E14 ....34 B4
Everett Ho SE17 ....151 B2
London N7 ....14 C4
Evergreen Sq ❸ E8 ....16 B1
Everilda St N1 ....85 A3

Evering Rd E5,N16 ....7 C1
Everington St W6 ....47 C4
Everitt Rd NW10 ....20 C2
Everleigh St N4 ....5 B3
Eversfield Rd TW9 ....44 B1
Evershed Ho E1 ....111 A2
Evershed Wlk W4 ....37 C2
Eversholt St N1 ....83 A1
Evershot Rd N4 ....5 B3
Eversleigh Rd
SW11 ....169 B1
Eversley Ho E2 ....99 B3
Everthorpe Rd SE15 ....64 B4
Everton Bldgs NW1 ....92 C3
Evesham Ct ❶
TW10 ....54 B1
Evesham Ho ❶ E2 ....25 B3
London SW1 ....146 B2
NW8 ....78 C3
Evesham St W11 ....30 C2
Evesham Way SW11 ....60 C4
Evesham Wlk
London SE5 ....48 C1
London SW9 ....173 B2
Ewald Rd SW6 ....164 C1
Ewart Pl ⑰ E3 ....26 B3
Ewe Cl N7 ....14 A2
Ewen Cres SW2 ....74 C4
Ewen Ho N1 ....84 C3
Ewer St SE1 ....122 C1
Ewhurst ⑲ SW15 ....57 C1
Ewhurst Cl E1 ....32 B4
Ewhurst Rd SE4 ....66 B1
Exbury Ho London E9 ....17 B2
❹ London SW9 ....62 B3
Excel Ct WC2 ....119 C3
Excelsior Gdns SE13 ....52 B1
Excelsior Ind Est
SE16 ....50 B4
Exchange Arc EC2 ....110 B4
Exchange Ct WC2 ....120 B3
Exchange Mans ❷
NW11 ....1 B4
Exchange Pl EC2 ....110 A4
Exeter Ct NW6 ....23 C3
Exeter Ho ⑪ SE15 ....49 C4
W2 ....100 C2
Putney SW15 ....57 B1
Exeter Mans NW2 ....10 A2
Exeter Mews NW6 ....11 A2
Exeter Rd E16 ....35 C4
London NW2 ....10 A2
Exeter St WC2 ....120 C4
Exeter Way SE14 ....51 B3
Exford Ct SW11 ....167 C4
Exhibition Cl W12 ....30 B2
Exhibition Rd SW7 ....129 C2
Exmoor Ho ❷❸ E3 ....26 A3
Exmoor St W10 ....30 C4
Exmouth Ho ❻ E14 ....42 A2
Exmouth Market
EC1 ....95 C2
Exmouth Mews
NW1 ....93 A3
Exmouth Pl E8 ....17 A1
Exmouth St E1 ....32 B3
Exonbury NW8 ....78 B3
Exon St SE17 ....152 A3
Exton St SE1 ....121 B1
Eynella Rd SE21 ....76 B4
Eynham Rd W12 ....30 B3
Eynsford Ho SE1 ....137 B4
❷ SE15 ....50 B4
❸ SE17 ....152 A3
Eyot Gdns W6 ....38 B1
Eyot Gn W6 ....38 B1
Eyre Ct NW8 ....79 B2

Eyre St Hill EC1 ....95 B1
Eythorne Rd SW9 ....173 C3
Ezra St E2 ....99 A4

F

Fabian Rd SW6 ....155 A2
Fabyc Ho TW9 ....44 C3
Fairacres SW6 ....56 C3
Fairbairn Gn ❶
London SW9 ....48 A2
Fairbridge Rd N19 ....4 C2
Fairburn Ct SW15 ....58 A2
Fairburn Ho SW5 ....141 A1
❸ London SW12 ....73 C4
Fairby Ho SE1 ....153 A4
Fairchild Cl SW11 ....167 C1
Fairchild Ho N1 ....98 A4
London SW1 ....147 A3
⑮ London E9 ....17 B1
Fairchild Pl EC2 ....98 B1
Fairchild St EC2 ....98 B1
Fairclough St E1 ....111 C1
Faircourt NW3 ....12 B2
Faircroft N16 ....6 C3
Fairdale Gdns SW15 ....57 A3
Fairdene Ct N7 ....14 A3
Fairfax Ho
London SW9 ....173 C1
❻ Putney SW15 ....56 C2
Fairfax Mews SW15 ....57 B3
Fairfax Pl NW6 ....11 B1
Fairfax Rd
London NW6 ....11 B1
London W4 ....38 A3
Fairfield ❹ E1 ....32 B4
NW1 ....82 C3
Fairfield Ct
London NW10 ....21 C4
❶ London SW18 ....59 A2
Fairfield Dr SW18 ....59 A2
Fairfield Rd ❶ E3 ....26 C3
Fairfield St SW18 ....59 A2
Fairfoot Rd E3 ....26 C1
Fairford Ho SE11 ....149 C3
Fairhazel Gdns
London NW6 ....11 B1
Fairheathe SW15 ....57 C1
Fairholme Rd W14 ....140 B1
Fairholt Cl N16 ....7 A3
Fairholt Rd N16 ....6 C3
Fairholt St SW7 ....130 B2
Fairhurst ❹ NW6 ....10 C1
Fairlawn Ave W4 ....37 B2
Fairlawn Ct ❸ W4 ....37 B2
Fairlawn Gr W4 ....37 B2
Fairlawn Mans SE14 ....50 C2
Fairlawns SW15 ....57 C2
Fairley House Sch
SW1 ....147 B3
Fairlie Ct ⑫ E3 ....27 A2
❶ London N7 ....13 C4
Fairlight Ave NW10 ....21 A3
Fairlight Ct NW10 ....21 A3
Fairlop Pl NW8 ....89 C3
Fairmead Ho E9 ....18 A4
Fairmead Rd N7,N19 ....5 A1
Fairmont Ho ❶ E3 ....26 C1
Fairmount Rd SW2 ....62 B1
Fair St SE1 ....138 C4
Fairstead Wlk N1 ....86 C4
Fairthorn Rd SE7,
SE10 ....43 C1
Fairview Ho ⑭ SW2 ....74 B4
Fairview Pl SW2 ....74 B4

Fairwall Ho ❻ SE5 ....49 A2
Fairway Cl NW11 ....2 B4
Fairway Ct ❸ SE16 ....40 C4
Fairway The ❸ W3 ....28 A4
Fairweather Ho N7 ....14 A4
Faith Ct NW2 ....9 A2
Faithfull Ho N5 ....15 B3
Fakruddin St
E1 ....24 C1 99 C1
Falconberg Ct W1 ....105 C2
Falconberg Mews
W1 ....105 C2
Falconbrook Inf Sch
SW11 ....59 C4
Falcon Cl SE1 ....122 B2
Chiswick W4 ....45 B4
Falcon Ct EC4 ....107 B1
N1 ....86 B1
❼ Dulwich SE21 ....75 C2
Falcon Gr SW11 ....60 A4
Falcon Ho ⓘ SE15 ....60 A4
Falcon La SW11 ....60 A4
Falcon Lo ❸ W9 ....31 C4
London NW3 ....11 A4
Falcon Pk Ind Est
NW10 ....8 A3
Falcon Point SE1 ....122 B3
Falcon Rd SW11 ....60 A4
Falcon Terr SW11 ....60 A4
Falcon Way E14 ....42 A2
Falconwood Ct SE3 ....53 B1
Falkener Ct SW11 ....169 C3
Falkirk Ct ⑰ SE16 ....32 C1
Falkirk Ho W9 ....88 B4
Falkirk St N1 ....24 A3
Falkland Ho W14 ....140 C2
W8 ....128 A1
Falkland Pl ❷ NW5 ....13 B3
Falkland Rd NW5 ....13 B3
Falladon Ho W11 ....31 B4
Fallodon Ho SW8 ....171 C2
Fallow Ct SE16 ....153 C1
Fallowfield N4 ....5 B2
Falmouth Ho SE11 ....149 C2
W2 ....116 A4
Falmouth Rd SE1 ....137 A1
Falmouth St E15 ....19 C3
Falstaff Ct SE11 ....150 A3
Falstaff Ho ❶ N1 ....24 A3
Fane St W14 ....155 A4
Fann St EC1 ....97 A1
Fanshaw St N1 ....98 A4
Fanthorpe St SW15 ....57 B4
Faraday Cl N7 ....14 B2
Faraday Ho ❸ E14 ....33 B2
W10 ....31 A4
❷ Balham SW12 ....73 A4
Faraday Lo SE10 ....43 B3
Faraday Rd W10 ....31 A4
London W3 ....28 B2
Fareham Ho ⑥
SW15 ....68 C3
Fareham St W1 ....105 B2
Farjeon Ho NW6 ....11 C1
Farleigh Pl N16 ....16 B4
Farleigh Rd N16 ....16 B4
Farley Ct NW1 ....91 B1
W14 ....126 C2
Farlington Pl SW15 ....69 A4
Farlow Rd SW15 ....57 C4
Farlton Rd SW18 ....71 A4
Farm Ave NW2 ....1 B1
Farm Cl SW6 ....155 C2

Farmdale Rd SE10 . . .43 C1
Farmer Ho 4 SE16 . . .40 A3
Farmers Rd SE5 . . . . .48 A3
Farmer St W8 . . . . . .113 C2
Farm La SW6 . . . . . . .155 C2
Farm Lane Trad Ctr
 SW6 . . . . .155 C2
Farmleigh Ho SW9 . . .63 A1
Farm Pl W8 . . . . .113 B2
Farm Rd NW10 . . . . . .20 C4
Farm St W1 . . . . .118 A3
Farnaby Ho 2 W10 . . .23 B2
Farnborough Ho 10
 SW15 . . . . .68 C3
Farnborough Way 10
 SE15 . . . . .49 A3
Farncombe St
 SE16 . . . . .139 C3
Farndale Ho NW6 . . . .78 A4
Farnell Mews SW5 . . .142 A2
Farnell Pl W3 . . . . . . .28 A2
Farnfield Ho 12
 SW2 . . . . .62 B2
Farnham Ct 2 N16 . . . .7 A3
Farnham Ho NW1 . . . .90 B1
 SE1 . . . . .122 C1
Farnham Pl SE1 . . . . .122 B1
Farnham Royal
 SE11 . . . . .149 A1
Farnhurst Ho
 SW11 . . . . .169 B2
Farningham Ho 8
 N4 . . . . .6 C4
Farnley Ho SW8 . . . . .171 B2
Farnworth Ho 6
 E14 . . . . .42 C2
Faroe Rd W14 . . . . . .39 C3
Farquhar Rd SW19 . . .70 C1
Farrance St E14 . . . . .33 C3
Farrant Ho 11 SW11 . .59 C4
Farrell Ho E1 . . . . . . .32 B3
Farrer Ho SE8 . . . . . . .51 C3
Farrier Mews SE15 . . .65 B4
Farrier St NW1 . . . . . .13 B1
Farrier Wlk SW10 . . . .156 C4
Farringdon La EC1 . . .95 C1
Farringdon Rd EC1 . . .95 C1
Farringdon St EC4 . . .108 A2
Farringdon Sta
 EC1 . . . . .108 A4
Farrins Rents SE16 . . .33 A1
Farrow La SE14 . . . . . .50 B3
Farrow Pl SE16 . . . . . .41 A3
Farthingale Wlk
 E15 . . . . .19 C1
Farthing Alley SE1 . . .139 B3
Farthing Fields 8
 E1 . . . . .32 A1
Fashion & Design
 Museum The*
 SE1 . . . . .138 B4
Fashion St E1 . . . . . . .111 A3
Fassett Rd E8 . . . . . . .16 C2
Fassett Sq E8 . . . . . . .16 C2
Fauconberg Ct W4 . . .45 B4
Fauconberg Rd W4 . . .45 B4
Faulkner Ho SW15 . . .47 B1
Faulkner's Alley
 EC1 . . . . .108 A4
Faulkner St SE14 . . . .50 B2
Faunce Ho 5 SE17 . . .48 A4
Faunce St SE17 . . . . .150 A1
Favart Rd SW6 . . . . . .165 C4
Faversham Ho NW1 . .83 A3
 SE17 . . . . .152 A1

Fawcett Cl SW11 . . . .167 C1
Fawcett Est E5 . . . . . . .7 C3
Fawcett Ho SW9 . . . . .172 B2
Fawcett Rd NW10 . . . . .8 B1
Fawcett St SW10 . . . .156 C4
Fawe Park Rd SW15 . .58 B3
Fawe St E14 . . . . .34 A4
Fawkham Ho SE1 . . . .153 A3
Fawley Ct SE27 . . . . .75 A2
Fawley Lo 2 E14 . . . . .42 B2
Fawley Rd NW6 . . . . . .11 A3
Fawnbrake Ave
 . . . . .63 B2
Fayetville Ho 24 N19 . .5 A4
Faygate Rd SW2 . . . . .74 B2
Fazerley Ct 4 W2 . . . .31 C4
Fearnley Ho SE5 . . . . .49 A1
Fearon St SE10 . . . . . .43 C1
Feathers Pl SE10 . . . . .52 C4
Featherstone St
 EC1 . . . . .97 B2
Featley Rd SW9 . . . . .63 A4
Felbridge Ho 20
 SE22 . . . . .64 A4
Felday Rd SE13 . . . . .67 A1
Felden St SW6 . . . . . .164 C3
Feldman Cl N16 . . . . . .7 C3
Felgate Mews 4
 W6 . . . . .39 A2
Felix St 19 E2 . . . . . . .25 A3
Felixstowe Rd
 NW10 . . . . .22 A2
Fellbrigg Rd SE22 . . . .64 B2
Fellbrigg St 6 E1 . . . .25 A1
Fellows Ct E2 . . . . . . .24 B3
Fellows Rd NW3 . . . . .12 A1
Fells Haugh 5 W3 . . . .28 B3
Felltram Way SE7 . . . .43 C1
Felmersham Cl 2
 SW4 . . . . .61 C3
Felsberg Rd SW2 . . . .74 A4
Felsham Ho SW15 . . .57 C4
Felsham Rd SW15 . . . .57 C4
Felstead St E9 . . . . . . .18 B2
Felstead Wharf E14 . .42 B1
Felton Ho N1 . . . . .87 C3
Felton St N1 . . . . .87 C3
Fenchurch 34 N1 . . . .24 A4
Fenchurch Ave
 EC3 . . . . .110 A1
Fenchurch Bldgs
 EC3 . . . . .110 B1
Fenchurch Pl EC3 . . .124 B4
Fenchurch St EC3 . . .124 B4
Fenchurch Street Sta
 EC3 . . . . .124 B4
Fen Ct EC3 . . . . .124 A4
Fendall St SE1 . . . . . .138 B1
Fender Ct SW4 . . . . . .172 A2
Fendt Cl 3 E16 . . . . . .35 B1
Fenelon Pl W14 . . . . .141 A3
Fenham Rd SE15 . . . .50 A3
Fenner Cl SE16 . . . . . .40 A2
Fenner Ho 20 E1 . . . . .32 A1
Fenner Sq 7 SW11 . . .59 C4
Fenning St SE1 . . . . . .138 A4
Fenn St E9 . . . . .17 B3
Fenstanton Prim Sch
 SW2 . . . . .74 C3
Fentiman Rd SW8 . . .162 C2
Fenton Cl London E8 . .16 B2
 London SW9 . . . . . . .172 C1
Fenton Ho SE14 . . . . .51 A3
Fentons SE3 . . . . .53 B3
Fenton St E1 . . . . .32 A3
Fenwick Gr SE15 . . . .64 C4

Fenwick Pl SW9 . . . . .62 A4
Fenwick Rd SE15 . . . .64 C4
Ferdinand Ho 1
 . . . . .13 A1
Ferdinand Pl NW1 . . . .12 C1
Ferdinand St NW1 . . . .12 C1
Ferguson Dr W3 . . . . .28 C3
Ferguson Ho SE10 . . .52 B2
Ferguson's Cl E14 . . . .41 C2
Fergus Rd N5 . . . . . . .15 A3
Fermain Ct E N1 . . . . .24 A4
Fermain Ct N N1 . . . . .24 A4
Fermain Ct W N1 . . . . .24 A4
Fermoy Rd W9 . . . . . .23 B1
Fernbank Mews
 SW12 . . . . .61 B1
Fern Cl 3 N1 . . . . .24 A3
Ferncliff Rd E8 . . . . . .16 C3
Ferncroft Ave NW3 . . .10 C4
Fern Ct SE14 . . . . . . .50 C1
Ferndale Ct 3 SE3 . . .53 B3
Ferndale Ho N16 . . . . .6 C3
Ferndale Rd SW4,
 SW9 . . . . .62 B3
Ferndene Rd SE24 . . .63 B3
Ferndown Lo 2 E14 . .42 B3
Fernhead Rd W9 . . . . .23 B2
Fernhill Ho E5 . . . . . . .7 C2
Fernholme Rd SE15 . .65 C2
Fernhurst Rd SW6 . . .164 B4
Fernie Ho SE22 . . . . . .64 B4
Fernlea Rd SW12 . . . .73 A3
Fernleigh Cl W9 . . . . .23 B2
Fernsbury St WC1 . . . .95 B3
Fernshaw Mans
 SW10 . . . . .156 C3
Fernshaw Rd
 SW10 . . . . .156 C3
Fernside Rd SW12 . . .72 C4
Fern St E3 . . . . .26 C1
Fentower Rd N5 . . . . . .15 C3
Fern Wlk SE16 . . . . . .153 C1
Fernwood SW19 . . . . .70 B3
Ferrey Mews SW9 . . .173 B1
Ferriby Cl N1 . . . . .14 C1
Ferrier Ind Est
 . . . . .59 A3
Ferrier Point 6
 E16 . . . . .35 C4
Ferrier St SW18 . . . . . .59 A3
Ferrings SE21 . . . . . . .76 A1
Ferris Rd SE22 . . . . . .64 C3
Ferrybridge Ho
 SE11 . . . . .135 A1
Ferry La
 Barnes SW13 . . . . . . .46 B4
 Brentford TW8 . . . . . .44 A4
 Richmond TW9 . . . . .44 B4
Ferry Rd SW13 . . . . . .46 C2
Ferry Sq 1 TW8 . . . . .44 A4
Ferry St E14 . . . . .42 B1
Festing Rd SW15 . . . .57 C4
Festival Pier SE1 . . . .120 C2
Festival Pleasure Gdns
 SW11 . . . . .158 C1
Fetter La EC4 . . . . . . .107 C2
Hetties Ho NW8 . . . . .79 C1
Ffinch St SE8 . . . . . . .51 C3
Field Ct WC1 . . . . . . .107 A3
 London N7 . . . . .5 A1
 Wimbledon SW19 . . . .70 C1
Fieldgate Mans E1 . . .111 C3
Fieldgate St E1 . . . . . .111 C2
Fieldhouse Rd
 SW12 . . . . .73 B3
Fielding Ho NW8 . . . .78 C4

Fielding Ho continued
 Chiswick W4 . . . . . . .46 A4
Fielding Mews NW6 . .23 C2
Fielding Rd
 SW13 . . . . .47 A4
Fielding St
 London W14 . . . . . . .39 C3
 London W4 . . . . .38 A3
Fielding St SE17 . . . . .48 B4
Field Rd W6 . . . . .154 A4
Fields Est E8 . . . . .16 C1
Field St WC1 . . . . .94 C4
Fieldsway Ho N5 . . . . .14 C3
Fieldview SW17,
 SW18 . . . . .71 C3
Fieldview Ct N5 . . . . .15 A3
N/W 14 C3
Fieldwick Ho 11 E9 . .17 C2
Fife Rd E16 . . . . .35 C4
 Mortlake SW14 . . . . . .55 B2
Fife Terr N1 . . . . .85 A2
Fig Tree Cl NW10 . . . .21 A4
Filey Ave N16 . . . . . . .7 C3
Filey Ho SW18 . . . . . .59 B3
Filigree Ct SE16 . . . . .33 B1
Filmer Ho SW6 . . . . . .164 B4
Filmer Rd SW6 . . . . . .154 C1
Filmer Road Studios
 SW6 . . . . .164 B4
Filton Ct 14 SE14 . . . .50 B3
Finborough Ho
 SW10 . . . . .156 C4
Finborough Rd
 SW10 . . . . .156 C4
Finchdean Ho SW15 . .68 B4
Finch Ho 11 SE8 . . . . .52 A3
Finch La EC2,EC3 . . . .109 C1
Finchley Pl NW8 . . . . .79 B2
Finchley Rd NW8 . . . .11 B2
 London NW3 . . . . .11 B2
Finchley Road & Frognal
 Sta
 NW3 . . . . .11 B3
Finchley Road Sta
 NW3 . . . . .11 B2
Finch Lo 13 W9 . . . . .31 C4
Finch Mews SE5 . . . . .48 B2
Finch's Ct 10 E14 . . . .34 A2
Findhorn St E14 . . . . .34 B3
Findon Cl SW18 . . . . .58 C1
Findon Rd W12 . . . . . .38 C4
Fineran Ct 10 SW11 . .59 C3
Fingal St SE10 . . . . . .43 B1
Fingest Ho NW8 . . . . .90 A2
Finland Rd SE4 . . . . . .66 A4
Finland St SE16 . . . . .41 A3
Finlay St SW6 . . . . . . .47 C2
Finley Ct 21 SE5 . . . . .48 B3
Finmere Ho 11 N4 . . . .6 B4
Finnemore Ho N1 . . . .86 C4
Finn Ho N1 . . . . .97 C4
Finnis St E2 . . . . .25 A1
Finsbury Ave EC2 . . . .109 C3
Finsbury Cir EC2 . . . .109 C3
Finsbury Ct EC2 . . . . .109 B4
Finsbury Market
 EC2 . . . . .110 A4
Finsbury Mkt EC2 . . . .98 A1
Finsbury Park N4,
 N5 . . . . .6 A2
Finsbury Park Sta
 N4 . . . . .5 C2
Finsbury Pavement
 EC2 . . . . .109 C4
Finsbury Sq EC2 . . . .109 C4
Finsbury St EC2 . . . . .109 B4

Finsen Rd SE5 . . . . . .63 B4
Finstock Rd W10 . . . . .30 C3
Finton House Sch
 SW17 . . . . .72 B2
Finucane Ct TW9 . . . .54 B4
Finwhale Ho E14 . . . . .42 A3
Fiona Ct 2 NW6 . . . . .23 B3
Firbank Rd SE15 . . . . .50 A1
Fircroft N1 . . . . .86 B4
Fircroft Prim Sch
 SW17 . . . . .72 B1
Fire Brigade Pier
 SE1 . . . . .148 B4
Firecrest Dr NW3 . . . . .2 A1
Firle Ho W10 . . . . . . .30 B4
Firmston Ho 5
 SW14 . . . . .55 C4
Firs Ave SW14 . . . . . .55 B3
Firsby Rd N16 . . . . . . .7 C3
First Ave W10 . . . . . . .23 A1
 London W3 . . . . .29 B1
 Mortlake SW14 . . . . .56 A4
First St SW3 . . . . .144 B4
Firth Gdns SW6 . . . . .164 A3
Fir Tree Ho 11 SE14 . .50 B3
Fir Trees Cl SE16 . . . . .33 A1
Fisher Ho 8 E1 . . . . . .32 B2
 N1 . . . . .85 B3
 2 N19 . . . . .4 B1
Fishermans Dr SE16 . .40 C4
Fisherman's Wlk
 E14 . . . . .33 C1
Fishers Cl SW16 . . . . .73 C1
Fishers Ct SE14 . . . . .50 C2
Fisher's La W4 . . . . . .37 C2
Fisher St E16 . . . . .35 C4
 WC1 . . . . .106 C3
Fisherton St NW8 . . . .89 C2
Fisherton Street Est
 NW8 . . . . .89 C1
Fishlock Ct SW4 . . . . .172 A2
Fish St Hill EC3 . . . . .123 C3
Fitch Ct SW2 . . . . .62 C2
Fitzalan St SE11 . . . . .149 B4
Fitzclarence Ho
 W11 . . . . .126 B4
Fitz-George Ave
 W14 . . . . .140 A3
Fitzgerald Ave
 SW14 . . . . .56 A4
Fitzgerald Ho
 E14 . . . . .34 A3
 London SW9 . . . . . . .173 B1
Fitzgerald Rd SW14 . .55 C4
Fitzhardinge Ho
 W1 . . . . .103 B2
Fitzhardinge St
 W1 . . . . .103 B2
Fitzherbert Ho 11
 TW10 . . . . .54 B1
Fitzhugh Gr SW18 . . .59 C1
Fitzjames Ave
 W14 . . . . .140 B3
Fitzjohn's Ave NW3 . .11 C3
Fitzjohns Mans
 NW3 . . . . .11 B2
Fitzjohns Prim Sch
 NW3 . . . . .11 B2
Fitzmaurice Ho 17
 SE16 . . . . .40 A2
Fitzmaurice Pl W1 . . .118 B2
Fitzneal St W12 . . . . .29 B3
Fitzroy Cl N6 . . . . .3 B3
Fitzroy Cres 4 W4 . . .45 C3
Fitzroy Ct W1 . . . . . . .93 A1

Fitzroy Ho 14 E14 ....33 B3
SE1 ....153 A2
Fitzroy Mews W1 .....92 C1
Fitzroy Pk N6 ....3 B3
Fitzroy Rd NW1 ......81 B4
Fitzroy Sq W1 ....92 C1
Fitzroy St W1 ....92 C1
Fitzroy Yd NW1 ......81 B4
Fitzsimmons Ct 1
NW10 ....20 C4
Fitzwarren Gdns N19 .4 B3
Fitzwilliam Ave
TW9 ....44 B1
Fitzwilliam Mews
E16 ....35 C1
Fitzwilliam Rd SW4 .61 B4
Fives Ct SE11 ......136 A1
Fiveways Rd SW9 ..173 C1
Flamborough Ho 11
SE15 ....49 C2
Flamborough St
E14 ....33 A3
Flamingo Ct 2 SE8 .51 C3
Flamsted Ho SE10 ...52 C4
Flanchford Rd W12 .38 B3
Flanders Mans 1
W4 ....38 B2
Flanders Rd W4 .....38 A2
Flanders Way 2 E9 .17 C2
Flank St 1 ....125 B4
Flansham Ho 2
E14 ....33 B3
Flask Wlk NW3 .....11 C4
Flavell Mews SE10 .43 A1
Flaxman Ct W1 .....105 B1
10 London W4 ....38 B2
Flaxman Ho SE5 .....48 A1
2 W4 ....38 A1
Flaxman Terr WC1 ..93 C3
Flecker Ho 5 SE5 ..48 C3
Fleece Wlk N7 ....14 A2
Fleet Ct 11 W12 .....38 A3
Fleetfield WC1 ....94 B4
Fleet Ho 6 E14 .....33 A2
6 London SW2 ......62 C2
Fleet Pl EC4 ....108 A2
Fleet Prim Sch NW3 12 B3
Fleet Rd NW3 ....12 B3
Fleet Sq WC1 ....95 A3
Fleet St EC4 ....107 C1
Fleet Street Hill 1
E1 ....99 B1
Fleetway WC1 ....94 B4
Fleet Wood Ho 14 ...8 C2
Fleetwood Rd NW10 .8 C3
Fleetwood St 16 ......7 A2
Fleming Cl 3 W9 ....23 C1
Fleming Ct W2 .....101 B4
Fleming Ho SE16 ...139 B3
London N4 ....6 B3
Fleming Rd SE17 ....48 A4
Fletcher Bldgs
WC2 ....106 B1
Fletcher Ho 17 NW5 13 A4
Fletcher Ho 21 N1 ..24 A4
16 London N16 ....16 A4
Fletcher Path 7
SE8 ....51 C3
Fletcher Rd W4 .....37 B3
Fletcher St E1 .....125 C4
Fleur Gates 7
SW19 ....69 C4
Flinders Ho 28 E1 ..32 A1
Flinton St SE17 .....152 B2
Flint St SE17 ....151 C3
Flitcroft St WC2 ....105 C1
Flitton Ho 7 N1 .....15 A1
Flock Mill Pl SW18 .71 A3

Flodden Rd SE5 .....48 B2
Flood St SW3 ....158 B4
Flood Wlk SW3 .....158 B4
Flora Cl E14 ....34 A3
Flora Gardens Prim Sch
W6 ....39 A2
Flora Gdns 2 W6 ....39 A2
Floral St WC2 ....120 A4
Florence Ct W9 ......89 A3
4 London E5 ....7 C1
Florence Gdns W4 ...45 B4
Florence Ho
20 SE16 ....40 A1
8 London SW18 .....59 C3
2 London SW2 ......62 B2
10 London W11 .....30 C2
Florence Mans
SW6 ....164 C4
Florence Nightingale
Ho 1 N1 ....15 B2
Florence Nightingale
Mus SE1 ....135 A3
Florence Rd
London N4 ....5 C4
London SE14 ....51 B2
London W4 ....37 C3
Florence St N1 ....15 A1
Florence Terr
Kingston st SW15 ...68 A1
London SE14 ....51 B2
Florence Way 72 B3
Flores Ho 10 E1 .....32 C4
Florfield Rd E8 ......17 A2
Florian SE5 ....49 A2
Florian Rd SW15 ....58 A3
Florida St E2 .24 C2 99 C3
Florin Ct E1 ....138 C2
Floris Pl 7 SW4 .....61 B4
Florys Ct 7 SW19 ...70 A3
Floss St SW15 ....47 B1
Flower & Dean Wlk
E1 ....111 A3
Flowersmead SW17 .72 C2
Flowers Mews 1
N19 ....4 B2
Flower Wlk The
SW7 ....129 A4
Flue De Lis St E1 ....98 C1
Flynn Ct 12 E14 .....33 C2
Foley Ho 10 E1 ......32 B3
Foley St W1 ....104 C3
Folgate St E1 ....110 C4
Foliot Ho N1 ....84 C2
Foliot St W12 ....29 B3
Follett Ho SW10 ....157 B2
Follett St E14 ....34 B3
Folly Wall E14 ....42 B4
Fontarabia Rd
SW11 ....60 C3
Fontenelle SE5 ......49 A2
Fontenoy Ho SE11 .150 A3
Fontenoy Rd SW12,
SW17 ....73 B2
Fonthill Ho SW1 ...146 B2
W14 ....126 B2
Fonthill Mews N4 ....5 B2
Fonthill Rd N4 ....5 C2
Fontley Way SW15 .68 C4
Footpath The SW15 .56 C2
Forber Ho 22 E2 .....25 B2
Forbes Ho 2 W4 .....36 C1
Forbes St E1 ....111 C1
Forburg Rd N16 ......7 C3
Ford Cl 11 E3 ....26 A3
Fordcombe SE1 ...NW5 12 C2
Fordham Ho 5 ...
Fordham St E1 .....111 C2
Fordingley Rd W9 ..23 B2

Ford Rd E3 ....26 B3
Fords Park Ho E16 ..35 C3
Ford Sq E1 ....32 A4
Ford St E16 ....35 B1
E3 ....26 A3
Fordwych Ct NW2 ...10 A2
Fordwych Rd NW2 ..10 A3
Fordyce Rd SE13 ....67 B2
Foreign, Commonwealth
& Home Offices
SW1 ....134 A4
Foreland Ho 1 W11 112 A4
Foreshore SE8 ....41 B2
Fore St EC2 ....109 B3
Fore St Ave EC2 ....109 B3
Forester Rd SE15 ...65 A4
Forest Dr E8 ....16 B2
Forest Gr E8 ....16 B2
Forest Hill Rd SE22 .65 A1
Forest Rd E8 ....16 B2
Richmond TW9 ....44 C3
Forfar Rd SW11 ....169 C4
Forman Ho SE4 ......66 A3
Forman Pl N16 ....16 B4
Formby Ct 1 N7 .....14 C3
Formosa Ho 1 E1 ...26 A1
Formosa St W9 ....88 B1
Formunt Cl E16 ......35 B2
Forrest Ho SW15 ....47 B1
Forset Ct W1 ....102 B2
Forset St W1 ....102 B2
Forster Rd SW2 .....74 A4
Forstick Wlk E1 ....111 A3
Forston St N1 ....87 A2
Forsyth Gdns SE17 48 A4
Forsyth Ho 2 E9 ....17 B1
Forsythia Ho 6 SE4 66 A4
Fortescue Ave 1
E8 ....17 A1
Fortess Gr NW5 .....13 B3
Fortess Rd NW5 .....13 B3
Fortess Wlk NW5 ...13 A3
Forthbridge Rd
SW11 ....60 C3
Forth Ho 28 E3 ......26 B3
Forties The 9 NW5 .13 B3
Fortior Ct N6 ....4 B4
Fortnam Rd N19 ......4 C2
Fort Rd SE1 ....153 A3
Fortrose Gdns
SW12,SW2 ....74 A3
Fort St E1 ....110 B3
London E16 ....35 C1
Fortuna Cl N7 ....14 B2
Fortune Gate Rd
NW10 ....21 A4
Fortune Green Rd
NW6 ....10 C4
Fortune Ho EC1 .....97 A1
SE11 ....149 B3
Fortune St EC1 ......97 A1
Fortune Way NW10 21 C2
Forty Acre La E16 ...35 C4
Forward Bsns Ctr The
E16 ....27 C1
Fosbroke Ho SW8 .162 A1
Fosbury Ho 7 SW9 .62 B3
Fosbury Mews W2 ..114 B3
Foscote Mews W9 ..31 C4
Foskett Rd SW6 ....165 A1
Fossil Rd SE13 ....66 C4
Foster Ct E16 ....35 B2
4 London NW1 ......13 B1
Foster Ho SE14 ......51 B2
Foster La EC2 ....108 C2

Foster Rd
London W3 ....29 A2
London W4 ....37 C1
Foubert's Pl W1 ....104 C1
Foulden Rd N16 ......16 B4
Foulden Terr N16 ...16 B4
Foulis Terr SW7 ....143 C2
Foulser Rd SW17 ...72 C1
Foundary Ho 6 E14 .34 A4
Founders Ct EC2 ...109 B2
Founders Ho 1 SW1 147 B2
Foundling Ct WC1 ..94 A2
Foundry Cl SE16 .....33 A1
Foundry Mews NW1 93 A2
Foundry Pl SW18 ...71 A4
E1 ....32 B4
Fountain Ct EC4 ....121 B4
SW1 ....146 A3
Fountain Green Sq
SE16 ....139 C3
Fountain Ho SE16 .139 C3
W1 ....117 B2
2 London NW6 ......10 A1
Fountains The
London N5 ....15 B4
London NW3 ....11 B2
Fountain Pl SW9 ...173 C3
Fountayne Rd N16 ...7 C2
Fount St SW8 ....161 C1
Fournier St E1 ......111 A4
Four Seasons Cl E3 26 C3
Fovant Ct SW8 .....170 C1
Fowey Cl E1 ....32 A1
Fowey Ho SE11 ....149 C2
Fowler Cl SW11 .....59 C4
Fowler Ho N1 ....86 B4
SW8 ....171 C3
5 London SE5 ....49 A1
Fowler Rd N1 ....86 B4
Fownes St SW11 ....60 A4
Foxberry Ct SE4 ....66 B3
Foxberry Rd SE4 ....66 A4
Foxborough Gdns
SE4 ....66 C2
Foxbourne Rd
SW17 ....72 C2
Fox Cl E1 ....25 B1
E16 ....35 C4
Foxcombe Rd 6
SW15 ....68 C3
Foxcote SE5 ....152 B1
Foxcroft N1 ....85 A1
Foxglove St W12 ....29 B2
Foxham Rd N19 ......4 C1
Fox Ho 2 SW11 .....59 C3
Fox & Knot St EC1 108 B4
Foxley Cl E8 ....16 C3
Foxley Ho 4 E3 ......27 A2
Foxley Rd SW9 ......48 A3
Foxley Sq 3 SW9 ...48 A2
Foxmore St SW11 .168 C3
Fox Prim Sch
W8 ....31 C1 113 B1
Fox's Yd E2 ....99 A2
Foxwell Mews SE4 .66 A4
Foxwell St SE4 ......66 A4
Foyle Rd SE3 ....53 B4
Fradel Lo N16 ....6 C2
Framfield Rd N5 .....15 A3
Frampton NW1 ....13 C1
Frampton Ct 3 W3 .37 B4
Frampton Ho NW8 ..89 C1
Frampton Park Rd
E9 ....17 B1
Frampton St NW8 ...89 C1
Francemary Rd SE4 66 C2

Frances Grey Ho 13 ....32 C4
Franche Court Rd
SW17 ....71 B1
Francis Chichester Way
SW11 ....169 C3
Francis Cl 6 E14 ....42 C2
Francis Ct 12 SE14 .50 C4
Francis Ho N1 ....24 A4
London NW10 ....21 B4
Francis Holland Sch
SW1 90
NW1 ....145 C3
Francis Snary Lo 1
SW18 ....58 C2
Francis St SW1 .....147 A4
Francis Terr N19 .....4 B1
Francis Wlk N1 ......84 C3
Franconia Rd SW4 ..61 C2
Frank Barnes Prim Sch
for Deaf Children
NW3 ....11 C1
Frank Beswick Ho
SW6 ....155 A3
Frank Dixon Cl
SE21 ....76 A3
Frank Dixon Way
SE21 ....76 A3
Frank Douglas Ct
W6 ....38 C2
Frankfurt Rd SE24 .63 B2
Frankham Ho 3
SE8 ....51 C3
Frankham St SE8 ...51 C3
Frank Ho SW8 .....162 A2
Frankland Cl SE16 .40 A2
Frankland Ho 4
SW12 ....73 A4
Frankland Rd SW7 129 B1
Franklin Bldg 6
E14 ....41 C4
Franklin Cl
London SE13 ....52 A2
West Norwood SE27 .75 A1
Franklin Ho 28 E1 ..32 A1
Franklin Sq SW5 ...141 A1
Franklin's Row
SW3 ....145 A3
Franklin St 15 E3 ...27 A2
Franklyn Rd NW10 ..8 B2
Frank Soskice Ho
SW6 ....155 A3
Frank Whymark Ho 4
SE16 ....40 B4
Frans Hals Ct E14 ..42 C3
Fraserburgh Ho 28
E3 ....26 B3
Fraser Ct SW11 ....168 A4
Fraser Ho
Brentford TW8 ......36 B1
London SW8 ....171 B1
Fraser Regnart Ct 5
NW5 ....12 B3
Fraser St W4 ....38 A1
Frazier St SE1 ......135 B3
Frean St SE16 ......139 B2
Frearson Ho WC1 ...95 A4
Freda Corbett Cl 1
SE15 ....49 C3
Frederica St 4 N7 ..14 B1
Frederick Cl W2 ....116 C4
Frederick Charrington
Ho 3 E1 ....25 B1
Frederick Cres SW9 48 A3

Frederick Ct SW6 .....58 A4
Frederick's PI EC2 .109 B1
Frederick Sq 11
SE16 ....33 A2
Frederick's Row
EC1 ....96 A4
Frederick St WC1 ...94 C3
Frederick Terr E8 ..16 B1
Frederic Mews
SW1 ....131 B3
Freedom St SW11 .169 A2
Freegrove Rd N7 ....14 A3
Freeling Ho NW8 ....79 B4
Freeling St 7 N1 ...14 B1
Freeman Ho 13
SW2 ....74 A4
Freemantle St
SE17 ....152 A2
Freemens Hos 1
SW9 ....62 B3
Freke Rd SW11 ....60 C4
Fremantle Ho 4 E1 .25 A1
Fremont St E9 ....25 B4
French Ordinary Ct
EC3 ....124 B4
French PI E1 ....98 B2
Frendsbury Rd SE4 ..66 A3
Frensham Ct N5 .....15 B3
Frensham Dr SW15 .68 C2
Frensham St SE15 ..49 C4
Frere St SW11 ......168 B2
Freshfield Ave E8 ..16 B1
Freshfield CI SE13 ..67 C3
Freshford St
SW18 ....71 B1
Freston Rd W10,
W11 ....30 C3
Freswick Ho 6 SE8 .41 A2
Freud Mus The
NW3 ....11 B2
Frewell Bldg WC1 ..107 C3
Frewin Rd SW18 .....71 C3
Friar Mews SE27 ....75 A1
Friars Ave SW15 ....68 B1
Friars CI SE1 ....122 B1
Friars Gdns W3 .....28 C3
Friars Mead E14 ....42 B3
Friars Place La
W3 ....28 C2
Friars Prim Sch
SE1 ....136 B3
Friars Stile PI 9
TW10 ....54 A1
Friars Stile Rd
TW10 ....54 A1
Friar St EC4 ....108 B1
Friars Way W3 ......28 C3
Friary Park W3 .....28 B3
Friary Rd SE15 .....49 C3
London W3 ....28 B3
Friday St EC4 ....122 C4
Frideswide PI NW5 ..13 B3
Friendly PI SE13 ....52 A2
Friendly St SE8 .....51 C2
Friendly Street Mews
SE8 ....51 C1
Friend St EC1 ....96 A4
Friern Rd SE22 ......64 C1
Frigate Ho 6 E14 ....42 B2
Frigate Mews SE8 ...51 C4
Frimley CI SW19 .....70 A2
Frimley Way E1 .....25 C1
Frinstead Ho
W10 ....30 C2
Friston St SW6 .....166 A1
Frith Ho E2 ....24 C2 99 B3

Frith Ho continued
NW8 ....89 C1
Frith Rd E11 ....19 C4
Frith St W1 ....105 B1
Frithville Ct W12 ...30 B1
Frithville Gdns W12 .30 B1
Frobisher Ct
1 SE10 ....52 C4
3 London W12 ....39 B4
Frobisher Ho 27 E1 .32 A1
Frobisher Pas E14 ..34 C1
Frobisher PI SE14 ..50 B2
Frobisher St SE10 ..53 A4
Froebel Coll SW15 ..56 B1
Frogley Rd SE22 ....64 B3
Frogmore SW18 .....58 C2
Frogmore Est NW10 .20 B2
Frogmore Ind Est
N5 ....15 B4
Frognal NW3 ....11 B3
Frognal CI NW3 ......11 B3
Frognal Ct NW3 .....11 B2
Frognal Gdns NW3 ..11 B4
Frognal La NW3 .....11 A3
Frognal Par NW3 ....11 B2
Frognal Rise NW3 ...11 B4
Frognal Way NW3 ...11 B4
Frome Ho SE15 .....65 B3
Frome St N1 ....86 C2
Frontenac NW10 ....9 A1
Froude St SW8 .....170 B1
Frye Ct E3 ....26 B2
Frying Pan Alley
E1 ....110 C3
Fry Rd NW10 ....21 B4
Fulbeck Ho N7 ......14 B2
Fulbourne St E1 .....32 A4
Fulbrook Rd N19 ...13 B4
Fulcher Ho 10 N1 ...24 A4
3 SE8 ....41 B1
Fulford Mans N19 ...5 A1
Fulford St SE16 .....40 A4
Fulham Broadway
SW6 ....155 C1
Fulham Broadway Sta
SW6 ....155 C2
Fulham Cross Sec Sch
SW6 ....154 B2
Fulham Ct SW6 .....165 B4
Fulham High St
SW6 ....164 B1
Fulham Palace★
SW6 ....164 A1
Fulham Palace Rd
SW6 ....47 C3 164 A3
Fulham Park Gdns
SW6 ....164 C2
Fulham Park Rd
SW6 ....164 C2
Fulham Prep Sch
SW6 ....154 B1
Fulham Prim Sch
SW6 ....155 B3
Fulham Rd SW10 ..157 A4
Fulham Sq SW6 ....165 A4
Fullarton Rd SW18 .59 B2
Fuller CI E2 ....99 B2
Fullers Ho 6 SW18 .58 C2
Fullerton Rd SW18 .59 B2
Fullwood's Mews
N1 ....97 C4
Fulmar Ct 5 SE21 ..75 C2
Fulmar Ho NW8 ....90 C2
2 SE16 ....40 C2
Fulmead St SW6 ..166 B3
Fulneck 1 E1 ....25 B1
Fulthorp Rd SE3 ...53 C1
Fulton Mews W2 ..114 C4

Fulwood PI WC1 ....107 A3
Fulwood Wlk SW19 .70 A3
Furber St W6 ....39 A3
Furley Ho 7 SE15 ..49 C3
Furley Rd SE15 .....49 C3
Furlong Rd N7 ......14 C2
Furmage St SW18 ..71 A4
Furness Ho SW1 ...146 A2
Furness Lo 4 SW14 .55 A3
Furness Rd
London NW10 ....21 C3
London SW6 ....166 B2
Furnival St EC4 ....107 B2
Furrow La E9 ....17 B3
Fursecroft W1 .....102 C2
Furze St E3 ....33 C4
Fyfield N4 ....5 C2
Fyfield Rd 6 SW9 ..62 C4
Fynes St SW1 ......147 B4

G

Gable Ho 13 W4 .....38 A2
Gabriel CI SE5 ......49 A2
Gabriel Ho 1 SE11 148 C4
Gabriel Mews NW2 .1 B2
Gabrielle Ct NW3 ..11 C2
Gabriel's Wharf
SE1 ....121 B2
Gaddesden Ho EC1 .97 C3
Gadsden Ho 8 W10 .23 A2
Gage Ho E16 ....27 C2
Gagarin Ho SW11 ..59 C4
Gage Rd E16 ....35 A4
Gage St WC1 ....106 B4
Gainford Ho 18 E2 .25 A3
Gainford St N1 .....85 B4
Gainsborough Ct
6 SE16 ....40 A1
Dulwich SE21 ....76 A2
London W12 ....39 B4
Gainsborough Gdns
London NW11 ....1 C4
London NW3 ....2 C1
Gainsborough Ho
E14 ....33 A2
SW1 ....147 C3
London N4 ....5 C4
2 London NW3 .....11 B4
Gainsborough Prim Sch
E9 ....18 C2
Gainsborough Rd
London W4 ....38 B2
Richmond TW9 ......54 B4
Gainsford St SE1 ..139 A4
Gairloch Ho 2
NW1 ....13 C1
Gairloch Rd SE5 ....49 A1
Gaisford St NW5 ...13 B2
Gaitskell Ct SW11 168 A2
Gaitskell Ho SE17 ..48 C4
Galata Rd SW13 ....46 C3
Galatea Sq SE15 ...65 A4
Galbraith St E14 ....42 B3
Gale Ho 10 SW2 ...62 B2
Galena Ho 8 W6 ....39 A2
Galena Rd W6 ......39 A2
Galesbury Rd SW18 59 B1
Gales Gdns E2 ......25 A2
Gale St E3 ....33 C4
Galgate CI 4 SW19 .70 A3
Galleon CI 7 SE16 ..40 C4
Galleon Ho 7 E14 ..42 B2
Gallery Ct SW10 ...156 C3

Gallery Rd SE21 ....75 C3
Galleywall Prim Sch
SE16 ....40 A2
Galleywall Rd SE16 40 A2
Galleywall Road Trad
Est 12 SE16 ....40 A2
Galleywood Ho W10 30 B4
Gallia Rd N5 ....15 A3
Gallions Rd SE7 ....43 C2
Galloway Rd W12 ..29 C1
Galsworthy Ave E14 33 A4
Galsworthy Ho 2
W11 ....31 A3
Galsworthy Rd NW2 .1 A1
Galton St W10 ......23 A2
Galveston Ho 2 E1 .26 A1
Galveston Rd SW15 58 B2
Galway Cl 3 SE16 ..40 A1
Galway Ho 6 E1 ....32 C4
EC1 ....97 A3
Galway St EC1 ......97 A3
Gambetta St SW8 .170 B1
Gambia St SE1 .....122 B1
Gambier Ho 5 EC1 ..97 A3
Gamlen Rd SW15 ...57 C3
Gandolfi St 5 SE15 .49 A4
Ganley Ct 18 SW11 59 C4
Gannet Ct 4 SE21 ..75 C2
Gannet Ho SE15 ...49 B2
Ganton St W1 .....105 A1
Garbett Ho 2 SE17 48 A4
Garbutt PI W1 .....103 C3
Garden CI SW15 ....69 A4
Garden Ct EC4 .....121 B4
4 Richmond TW9 ...44 B2
NW8 ....79 A4
12 London W4 ......37 B3
4 Richmond TW9 ...54 B4
Garden Flats SW16 74 A1
Garden Ho SW9 ...172 B2
Garden La SW2 .....74 B3
Garden Mews W2 .113 C3
Garden PI 22 E8 ....24 B4
Garden Rd NW8 ....89 A4
Richmond TW9 ......54 C4
Garden Row SE1 ..136 A2
Garden Royal 10
SW15 ....57 C1
Garden St E1 ....32 C4
Gardens The
London N16 ....7 B4
London SE22 ....64 C3
Garden Terr SW1 ..147 B2
SW7 ....130 B3
Garden Wlk
EC2 ..24 A2 98 A2
Gardiner Ave NW2 ..9 B3
Gardiner Ct NW10 ..20 C4
Gardiner Ho SW11 168 A4
Gardner Ct N5 ......15 B4
Gardners La EC4 ..122 C4
Gardnor Mans 19
NW3 ....11 B4
Gardnor Rd NW3 ...11 C4
Gard St EC1 ....96 B4
Garendon Rd SM4 ...1 C1
Gareth Ct SW16 ....73 C1
Garfield Rd SW11 ..60 C4
Garford St E14 .....33 C2
Garland Ho N16 .....6 C1
Garlinge Ho SW9 ..173 B4
Garlinge Rd NW2 ...10 B2
Garnault Mews EC1 95 C3
Garnault PI EC1 .....95 C3
Garner St E2 ....24 C3
Garnet Rd NW10 ....8 A2
Garnet St E1 ....32 B2
Garnett Ho 3 NW3 .12 B3

Garnett Rd NW3 ...12 B3
Garnham CI 2 N16 ..7 B2
Garnham St 1 N16 ..7 B2
Garnies CI SE15 ....49 B3
Garrad's Rd SW16 .73 C1
Garrard Wlk NW10 ..8 A2
Garratt Ho 8 N16 ...7 A3
Garratt La SW18 ...71 A3
Garratt Park Sch
SW18 ....71 B1
Garraway Ct SW13 47 B3
Garraway Ho SE21 76 B1
Garrett CI W3 ....28 C4
Garrett Ho W12 ....30 A3
Garrett St EC1 ......97 A2
Garrick CI SW18 ...59 B3
Garrick Ho W1 .....118 A1
Chiswick W4 ....46 A4
Garrick Rd TW9 ....44 C1
Garrick St WC2 ....120 A4
Garrick Yd WC2 ...120 A4
Garsdale Terr
SW5 ....140 C2
Garsington Mews
SE4 ....66 B4
Garson Ho W2 .....115 B4
Garston Ho 6 N1 ...15 A1
Garter Way SE16 ...40 C4
Garth Ct W4 ....45 C4
Garth Ho NW2 ....1 B2
Garth Rd London NW2 1 B2
London W4 ....45 B3
Gartmoor Gdns
SW19 ....70 B3
Garton Ho 6 N6 .....4 C4
Garton PI SW18 ....59 B1
Gartons Way SW11 59 B4
Garway Rd W2 ....100 A1
Gascoigne PI E2 ....98 C3
Gascony Ave NW6 ..10 C1
Gascoyne Ho 2 E9 .17 C1
Gascoyne Rd E9 ...17 C1
Gaselee St E14 .....34 B2
Gasholder PI SE11 149 A1
Gaskarth Rd SW12 61 A1
Gaskell St SW4 ....172 A2
Gaskin Ho N16 ......6 C1
Gaskin St N1 ....86 A4
Gaspar CI SW7 ....142 B4
Gaspar Mews SW5 142 B4
Gasson Ho 24 SE14 50 C4
Gastein Rd W6 .....47 C4
Gastigny Ho EC1 ...97 A3
Gaston Bell CI TW9 54 B4
Gaston Gate SW8 .172 C4
Gataker Ho 5 SE16 40 A3
Gataker St SE16 ...40 A3
Gatcliff CI SW1 ....145 C1
Gatcombe Ho 20
SE22 ....64 A4
Gatcombe Rd
9 E16 ....35 C1
London N19 ....4 C1
SE22 ....64 A4
Gatebeck Ho 21
SE22 ....64 A4
Gatefield Ct SE15 ..64 C4
Gateforth St NW8 ..90 A1
Gate Hill Ct W11 ..113 A2
Gatehouse Sch E2 ..25 C3
Gatehouse Sq SE1 123 A2
Gateley Ho 6 SE4 ..65 C3
Gateley Rd SW9 ....62 B4
Gate Mews SW7 ..130 B3
Gatesborough St
EC2 ....98 A2
Gates Ct SE17 ....150 C2
Gatesden WC1 .....94 B3

Gateside Rd SW17	.72 B1
Gate St WC2	.106 C2
Gateway SE17	.48 B4
Gateway Mews **4**	
E8	.16 B3
Gateway Prim Sch	
NW8	.89 C2
Gateways The	
SW3	.144 B3
Gateway Trad Est	
NW10	.21 B2
Gathorne St E2	.25 B3
Gatliff Rd SW1	.146 A1
Gatonby St SE15	.49 B2
Gatwick Ho **5** E14	.33 B3
Gatwick Rd SW18	.70 B4
Gauden Cl SW4	.61 C4
Gauden Rd SW4	.61 C4
Gaugin Ct **13** SE16	.40 A1
Gaunt St SE1	.136 C2
Gautrey Rd SE15	.50 B1
Gaverick Ho EC1	
Gavel St SE17	.151 C4
Gaviller Pl **4** E5	.17 A4
Gavrelle Ho EC1	
Gawber St **2**	.25 B2
Gawthorne Ct E3	.26 C3
Gay Cl NW2	.9 A3
Gaydon Ho W2	.100 A4
Gayfere St SW1	.134 A1
Gayford Rd W12	.38 B4
Gay Ho N16	.16 A3
Gayhurst SE17	.48 C4
Gayhurst Ho NW8	.90 B2
Gayhurst Rd E8	.16 C1
Gayhurst Sch E8	.17 A2
Gaymead NW8	.78 B3
Gay Rd E15	.27 C3
Gaysley Ho SE11	.149 B3
Gay St SW15	.57 C4
Gayton Cres NW3	.11 C4
Gayton Ho E3	.26 C1
Gayton Rd NW3	.11 C4
Gayville Rd	.60 B1
Gaywood Cl SW2	.74 C3
Gaywood St SE1	.136 B1
Gaza St SE17	.150 A1
Gaze Ho **10** E14	.34 C3
Gean Ct **3** E11	.19 C4
Geary Ho N7	.14 B3
Geary Rd NW10	.8 C3
Geary St N7	.14 B3
Gedling Ho SE22	.64 B4
Gedling Pl SE1	.139 A2
Gees Ct W1	.103 C1
Gee St EC1	.96 C2
Geffrye Ct N1	.24 A3
Geffrye Mus ★ E2	.24 B3
Geffrye St E2	.24 B3
Geldart Rd SE15	.50 A3
Geldeston Rd E5	.7 C2
Gellatly Rd SE14	.50 C1
Gemini Bsns Ctr	
E14	.27 C1
Gemini Ho NW8	.57 C3
General Wolfe Rd	
SE10	.52 C2
Geneva Ct London N16	.6 C3
1 NW3	.11 B4
Geneva Dr SW9	.62 C3
Genoa Ave SW15	.57 B2
Genoa Ho **11** E1	.25 C1
Geoffrey Chaucer Tech	
Coll SE1	.137 B1
Geoffrey Cl SE5	.48 B1
Geoffrey Ct SE4	.66 B4
Geoffrey Ho SE1	.137 C2

Geoffrey Jones Ct	
NW10	.21 C4
Geoffrey Rd SE4	.66 B4
Geological Mus	
SW7	.129 C1
George Beard Rd **10**	
SE8	.41 B2
George Beare Lo **8**	
SW4	.61 B2
George Belt Ho **8**	
George Ct WC2	.120 B3
George Downing Est	
N16	.7 B2
George Eliot Ho	
SW1	.147 A3
George Eliot Jun & Inf	
Sch NW8	.79 B4
George Elliot Ho	
SE17	.150 C2
George Elliston Ho	
SE1	.153 B1
George Eyre Ho	
NW8	.79 C1
George Green's Sec Sch	
E14	.42 B1
George Inn Yd SE1	.123 B1
George La SE13	.67 B1
George Lansbury Ho	
7 E3	.26 B2
London NW10	.8 A1
George Lashwood Ct **15**	
SW9	.62 B3
George Leybourne Ho	
E1	.125 C4
George Lindgren Ho	
SW6	.155 A2
George Loveless Ho	
E2	.99 A4
George Mews NW1	.92 C3
George Orwell Sch	
N4	.5 B3
George Peabody Ct	
NW1	.102 A4
George Row SE16	.139 B3
George's Rd N7	.14 B3
George's Sq SW6	.155 A4
George St **6** E16	.35 B1
W1	.103 A2
George Tingle Ho	
SE1	.139 A2
Georgette Pl SE10	.52 B3
George Vale Ho **2**	
E2	.24 C3
Georgiana St NW1	.83 A4
Georgian Ct **19** E9	.25 B4
Georgina Gdns **2**	
E2	.99 A4
Geraldine Rd	
Brentford W4	.44 C4
London SW18	.59 B2
Geraldine St SE11	.150 B1
Gerald Mews SW1	.145 C4
Gerald Rd SW1	.145 C4
Gerard Ct NW2	.9 C3
Gerard St W1	.44 B3
Gerards Cl SE16	.40 B1
Gernigan Ho SW18	.59 C1
Gernon Rd E3	.26 A3
Gerrard Ho **5** SE14	.50 C3
Gerrard Pl W1	.119 C4
Gerrard Rd N1	.86 B2

Gerrard St W1	.119 C4
Gerridge Ct SE1	.135 C2
Gerridge St SE1	.135 C2
Gerry Raffles Sq	
E15	.19 C2
Gertrude St SW10	.157 A3
Gervase St SE15	.50 A3
Ghent Way E8	.16 B2
Giant Arches Rd	
SE24	.63 B1
Gibbings Ho SE1	.136 B3
Gibbins Rd E15	.76 B1
Gibbon Ho NW8	.89 C1
Gibbon Rd	
London SE15	.50 B1
London W3	.29 A2
Gibbons Rd NW10	.8 A2
Gibbon Wlk SW15	.56 C3
Gibbs Gn W14	.141 A2
Gibbs Green Sch	
W14	.141 A2
Gibbs Ho **6** SW12	.73 A4
Gibraltar Ho NW10	.20 C3
Gibraltar Wlk E2	.99 A3
Gibson Cl E1	.25 B1
Gibson Gdns N16	.7 B2
Gibson Rd SE11	.149 A3
Gibson Sq N1	.85 C4
Gibson St SE10	.43 A1
Gideon Rd SW11	.60 C4
Giesbach Rd N19	.4 C2
Giffen Square Mkt	
SE8	.51 C3
Giffin St SE8	.51 C3
Gifford Ho SE10	.42 C1
London SW4	.61 C3
Gifford St N1	.14 A1
Gilbert Ho **5** E2	.25 C2
EC2	.109 A3
SE8	.51 C4
SW1	.146 B1
SW8	.162 A2
Gilbert Pl WC1	.106 A3
Gilbert Sheldon Ho	
W2	.101 C4
Gilbert St W1	.103 C1
Gilbeys Yd NW1	.12 C1
Gilby Ho **8** E9	.17 C2
Gilda Cres N16	.7 C3
Gildea St W1	.104 B3
Gilden Cres NW5	.12 C3
Giles Ho SE16	.139 B2
London W11	.31 C3
Gilesmead SE5	.48 C2
Gilkes Cres SE21	.64 A1
Gilkes Pl SE21	.64 A1
Gillam Ho **6** SE16	.40 B2
Gill Ave E16	.35 C3
Gillender St E3	.27 B1
Gillespie Prim Sch	
N5	.6 A1
Gillespie Rd N4,N5	.6 A1
Gillett Pl **2** E8	.16 A3
Gillett St E8,N16	.16 A3
Gillfoot NW1	.82 C1
Gillian St SE13	.67 A2
Gillies Ho NW6	.11 C1
Gilling Ct **5** NW3	.12 A2
Gillingham Mews	
SW1	.146 C4
Gillingham Rd NW2	.1 A1

Gillingham Row	
SW1	.146 C4
Gillingham St SW1	.146 C4
Gillison Wlk SE16	.139 C2
Gillman Ho **22** E2	.24 C3
Gillray Ho SW10	.157 B3
Gill St E14	.33 B2
Gilmore Ho SW4	.60 B3
Gilmore Rd SE13	.67 C3
Gilpin Ave SW14	.55 C3
Gilpin Cl W2	.100 C4
Gilpin Rd E5	.18 A4
Gilstead Rd SW6	.166 B2
Gilston Rd SW10	.143 A1
Giltspur St EC1	.108 B2
Gilwell Ct **5** E5	.17 A4
Gipsy Cnr W3	.28 C4
Gipsy La SW15	.57 C1
Gipsy Moth IV SE10	.52 B4
Giraud St E14	.34 A3
Girdlers Rd W14	.39 C3
Girdlestone Wlk N19	.4 B2
Girdwood Rd SW18	.70 A4
Girling Ho **9** N1	.24 A4
Gironde Rd SW6	.155 A1
Girton Ho SW15	.57 C1
Girton Villas **6**	
W10	.30 C3
Gissing Wlk N1	.14 C1
Glading Terr N16	.7 B1
Gladsmuir Rd N19	.4 B3
Gladstone Ct SW1	.147 C3
London NW2	.9 A3
Gladstone Ho **14**	
E14	.33 C3
Gladstone Park Sch	
NW10	.9 A3
Gladstone Rd W4	.37 C3
Gladstone St SE1	.136 A2
Gladstone Terr	
SW8	.170 B4
Gladwin Ho NW1	.83 A1
Gladwyn Rd SW15	.57 C4
Gladys Rd NW6	.10 C1
Glaisher St **4** SE10	.52 A3
Glamis Ct W3	.37 A4
Glamis Est **3** E1	.32 C2
Glamis Pl E1	.32 B2
Glamis Rd E1	.32 B2
Glanville Ho **2**	
SW2	.74 B4
Glanville Rd SW2	.62 B2
Glasbrook Rd SE9	.183 B2
Glaserton Rd N16	.7 A4
Glasgow Ho W9	.78 B1
Glasgow Terr SW1	.146 C1
Glasshill St SE1	.136 B4
Glasshouse Fields	
E1	.32 C2
Glasshouse St W1	.119 A3
Glasshouse Wlk	
SE11	.148 C2
Glasshouse Yd EC1	.96 C1
Glass St **8** E2	.25 A1
Glastonbury Ct **12**	
SE14	.50 B3
Glastonbury Ho	
SW1	.146 A2
Glastonbury Pl **22**	
E1	.32 B3
Glastonbury St NW6	.10 B3
Glazbury Rd W14	.140 B2
Glazebrook Cl SE21	.75 C2
Glebe Cl **1** W4	.38 A1

Glebe Ho **11** SE16	.40 A3
Glebelands Cl SE5	.64 A4
Glebe Pl SW3	.158 A4
Glebe Rd	
Barnes SW13	.47 A1
London E8	.16 B1
London NW10	.8 C2
London W4	.38 A1
Glebe St W4	.38 A1
Glebe Terr **15** E3	.27 A2
Glebow Gdns	
SW5	.142 C3
Gledstanes Rd	
W14	.140 B1
Glegg Pl **3** SW15	.57 C3
Glenaffric Ave E14	.42 C2
Glen Albyn Rd	
SW19	.69 C2
Glenalmond Ho **7**	
SW15	.57 C1
Glenarm Rd E5	.17 C4
Glenbrook Inf Sch	
SW4	.61 C1
Glenbrook Jun Sch	
SW4	.61 C1
Glenbrook Rd NW6	.10 C3
Glenburnie Rd	
SW17	.72 B1
Glencoe Mans	
SW9	.163 B1
Glendall St SW9	.62 B3
Glendarvon St	
SW15	.57 C4
Glendower Gdns **10**	
SW14	.55 C4
Glendower Pl SW7	.143 B3
Glendower Prep Sch	
SW7	.143 B3
Glendower Rd	
SW14	.55 C4
Glendown Ho **2** E8	.16 C3
Glendun Ct W3	.29 A2
Glendun Rd W3	.29 A2
Gleneagles Cl **9**	
SE16	.40 A1
Glenelg Rd SW2	.62 A2
Glenfield Rd SW12	.73 B3
Glenfinlas Way SE5	.48 A3
Glengall Gr E14	.42 B3
Glengall Pass **2**	
NW6	.23 C4
Glengall Rd NW6	.23 B4
Glengall Terr SE15	.49 B4
Glengarnock Ave	
E14	.42 B2
Glengarry Rd SE22	.64 B2
Glen Ho No1	.132 C2
Glenhurst Ave NW5	.12 C4
Glenilla Rd NW3	.12 A2
Glenister Rd SE10	.43 B1
Glenloch Ct **2** NW3	.12 A2
Glenloch Rd NW3	.12 A3
Glenluce Rd SE3	.53 C4
Glenmore SW15	.57 C1
Glenmore Ho **9**	
TW10	.54 A1
Glenmore Rd NW3	.12 A2
Glennie Ct SE21	.76 C3
Glennie Ho SE10	.52 B2
Glennie Rd SE27,	
Glenridding NW1	.83 A1
Glenrosa St SW6	.166 C2
Glenroy St W12	.30 B3

Glensdale Rd SE4 ....66 B4
Glenshaw Mans
 SW9 ....163 B1
Glentanner Way
 SW17 ....71 C1
Glen Terr E14 ......42 B4
Glentham Gdns
 SW13 ....47 A4
Glentham Rd SW13 ..47 A4
Glenthorne Mews
 W6 ....39 A2
Glenthorne Rd W6 ..39 A2
Glenthorpe SW15 ...56 C3
Glentworth St NW1 ..90 C1
Glenville Gr SE8 ....51 B3
Glenville Mews
 SW18 ....71 A4
Glenworth Ave E14 ..42 C2
Gliddon Rd W14 ...140 A2
Glifford Ho SW1 ...146 C1
Globe Pond Rd
 SE16 ....33 A1
Globe Prim Sch E2 ..25 B2
Globe Rd E1,E2 ....25 B1
Globe St SE1 ......137 B3
Globe Terr 9 E2 ....25 B2
Globe Theatre The*
 SE1 ....122 C3
Globe View EC4 ....122 C3
Globe Yd W1 ......104 A1
Gloucester Ave
 NW1 ....81 C4
Gloucester Cir SE10 .52 B3
Gloucester Cres
 NW1 ....82 A4
Gloucester Ct EC3 ..124 B3
 SE1 ....137 A2
 London NW11 .....1 B4
 London SE22 .....76 C3
 Richmond TW9 ...44 C3
Gloucester Dr N4 ....6 A2
Gloucester Gate
 NW1 ....82 A2
Gloucester Gate Mews
 NW1 ....82 A2
Gloucester Gdns
 W2 ....100 C2
 London NW11 .....1 B4
Gloucester Ho NW6 .23 C3
 Richmond TW10 ..54 C2
Gloucester Mews
 W2 ....101 A1
Gloucester Mews W
 W2 ....101 A1
Gloucester Pk
 SW7 ....142 C4
Gloucester Pl W1 ...103 A4
Gloucester Pl Mews
 W1 ....103 A3
Gloucester Prim Sch
 SE15 ....49 A3
Gloucester Rd
 SW7 ....142 C4
 Acton W3 ....37 B4
 Richmond TW9 ...54 C2
Gloucester Road Sta
 SW7 ....142 C4
Gloucester Sq
 6 E2 ....24 C4
 W2 ....101 C1
Gloucester St SW1 .146 C1
Gloucester Terr
 W2 ....101 A1

Gloucester Way
 EC1 ....95 C3
Gloucester Wlk
 W8 ....127 C4
Glover Ho
 2 London NW6 ...11 B1
 London SE15 ....65 A3
Glycena Rd SW11 ...60 B4
Glyn Ct SE27 ......74 C1
Glynde Mews SW3 .130 B1
Glynde Reach WC1 ..94 B3
Glynde St SE4 .....66 B1
Glynfield Rd NW10 ...8 A1
Glyn Mans W14 ....140 B4
Glyn Rd E5 ....17 C4
Glyn St SE11 ......148 C1
Goater's Alley
 SW6 ....155 A1
Goat Wharf TW8 ...44 A4
Godalming Rd E14 ..34 A4
Goddard Ho SW19 ..70 A3
Goddard Pl N19 .....4 B1
Godfrey Ho EC1 ....97 B3
Godfrey St E15 .....27 B3
 SW3 ....144 B2
Goding St SE11 ....148 B1
Godley Rd SW18 ...71 C3
Godliman St EC4 ..122 C1
Godman Rd SE15 ...50 A1
Godolphin Ho
 London NW3 .....12 A1
 7 Streatham SW2 .74 C3
Godolphin & Latymer
 Sch W6 ....39 A2
Godolphin Pl W3 ...28 C2
Godolphin Rd W12 ..39 A4
Godson St N1 ......85 B2
Godstone Ct 1 N16 ..7 A3
Godstone Ho SE1 ..137 C2
Godwin Cl N1 ......87 A2
Godwin Ho E2 .....24 B3
 NW6 ....78 A3
Goffers Ho SE3 ....53 A1
Goffers Rd SE3,SE13 .53 A1
Goffton Ho SW9 ...173 A1
Golborne Gdns W10 .23 B1
 5 W10 ....23 A1
Golborne Mews 9
 W10 ....31 A4
Golborne Rd W10 ..31 A4
Golden Cross Mews 8
 W11 ....31 B3
Golden Hind Pl 5
 SE8 ....41 B2
Golden La EC1 .....97 A2
Golden Plover Cl
 E16 ....35 C3
Golden Sq W1 .....119 A4
Golders Ct NW11 ....1 B4
Golders Gdns NW11 ..1 A4
Golders Green Coll
 NW11 ....1 C3
Golders Green Cres
 NW11 ....1 C4
Golders Green Rd
 NW11 ....1 A4
Golders Green Sta
 NW11 ....1 C3
Golders Hill Sch
 SE22 ....76 C4
Golderslea NW11 ....1 C3
Golders Park Cl
 NW11 ....1 C3
Golders Way NW11 ..1 A4
Goldhawk Ind Est The
 W6 ....39 A3

Goldhawk Mews 2
 W12 ....39 A4
Goldhawk Rd W12 ..38 C3
Goldhawk Road Sta
 W12 ....39 B4
Goldhurst Terr NW6 .11 B1
Goldie Ho N19 ......4 C4
Golding St E1 ......111 C1
Golding Terr E1 ....111 C2
Goldington Cres
 NW1 ....83 B2
Goldington St
 NW1 ....83 B2
Goldman Cl
 E2 ....24 C1 99 B2
Goldney Rd W9 ....23 C1
Goldsboro Rd SW8 .161 C1
Goldsborough Ho
 SW8 ....171 C3
Goldsmith Ave W3 ..28 C2
Goldsmith Ct WC1 .106 B2
Goldsmith Ho W3 ..28 C2
Goldsmith Rd
 London SE15 ....49 C2
 W3 ....28 C1
Goldsmiths Bldgs
 W3 ....28 C1
Goldsmith's Cl W3 ..28 C1
Goldsmiths Coll, Univ of
 London SE14 ....51 A2
Goldsmith's Pl NW6 .78 A3
Goldsmith's Row E2 .24 C3
Goldsmith's Sq 10
 E2 ....24 C3
Goldsmith St EC2 ..109 A2
Goldthorpe NW1 ...82 C3
Goldwell Ho SE22 ..64 A4
Goldwin Cl SE14 ...50 B2
Goldwing Cl E16 ...35 C3
Gomm Rd SE16 ....40 B3
Gondar Gdns NW6 ..10 B3
Gondar Mans NW6 .10 B3
Gonson St SE8 ....52 A4
Gonville Ho 6
 SW15 ....57 C1
Gonville St SW6 ....58 A4
Gooch Ho EC1 ....107 B4
Goodall Ho 10 SE4 ..65 C3
Goodfaith Ho 10
 E14 ....34 A2
Goodge Pl W1 .....105 A3
Goodge St W1 .....105 A3
Goodge Street Sta
 W1 ....105 B4
Goodhall St NW10 ..21 B2
Good Hart Pl E14 ..33 A2
Goodhope Ho 18
 E14 ....34 A2
Goodinge Cl N7 ....14 A2
Goodinge Rd N7 ...14 A2
Goodman Cres SW2 .73 C2
Goodman's Stile
 E1 ....111 B2
Goodman's Yd E1,
 EC3 ....124 C4
Goodrich Com Sch
 SE22 ....64 C1
Goodrich Ho 9 .....30 C5
 2 N19 ....4 C4
Goodrich Rd SE22 ..64 C1
Good Shepherd RC Prim
 Sch The W12 ....38 B4
Goodson Rd NW10 ...8 A1

Goodsway NW1 .....84 A2
Goodway Gdns E14 .34 C3
Goodwill Ho 19 E14 .34 A2
Goodwin Cl SE16 ..139 A1
Goodwin Ho 2
 SE15 ....65 A4
Goodwin Rd W12 ...38 C4
Goodwin St N4 .....5 C2
Goodwood Ct W1 ..104 B4
Goodwood Ho 3
 W3 ....37 B3
Goodwood Mans 4
 SW9 ....62 C4
Goodwood Rd SE14 .51 A3
Goose Green Trad Est
 SE22 ....64 C3
Gophir La EC4 .....123 B4
Gopsall St N1 ......87 C3
Gordon Ave SW13 ..56 A3
Gordonbrock Prim Sch
 SE4 ....66 C2
Gordonbrock Rd
 SE4 ....66 C2
Gordon Ct W12 ....30 B3
Gordon Gr SE5 .....48 A1
Gordon Ho E1 .....32 B2
 10 E1 ....32 B2
Gordon Hospl The
 SW1 ....147 B3
Gordon House Rd
 NW5 ....12 C4
Gordon Lo N16 .....6 C2
Gordon Pl W8 .....127 C4
Gordon Rd
 Chiswick W4 ....45 A4
 London E15 .....76 B4
 London SE15 ....50 A1
 Richmond TW9 ..44 B2
Gordon Sq WC1 ....93 C2
Gordon St WC1 ....93 C2
Gorefield Ho NW6 ..23 C3
Gorefield Pl NW6 ..23 C3
Gore Rd E9 ....25 B4
Gore St SW7 ......129 A2
Gorham Ho 13 SW4 .61 B1
Gorham Pl W11 ....112 A3
Goring St EC3 .....110 B2
Gorleston St W14 ..140 B4
Gorse Cl E16 ......35 C3
Gorsefield Ho 5
 E14 ....33 C2
Gorst Rd
 London NW10 ..20 C1
 London SW11 ...60 B1
Gorsuch Pl E2 .....98 C4
Gorsuch St E2 .....98 C4
Gosberton Rd SW12 .72 C3
Gosfield St W1 ....104 C3
Goslett Yd WC2 ...105 C1
Gosling Ho 1 E1 ...32 B2
Gosling Way SW9 ..173 B4
Gospel Oak Prim Sch
 NW5 ....12 C4
Gospel Oak Sta
 NW5 ....12 C4
Gosport Ho 9
 SW15 ....56 C2
Gosset St E2 .....24 C2 99 B4
Gosterwood St SE8 .51 A4
Goswell Pl EC1 ....96 B3
Goswell Rd EC1 ....96 B3
Gothic Ct 17 SE5 ..48 B3

Gottfried Mews
 NW5 ....13 B4
Gough Ho N1 ......86 B4
Gough Sq EC4 .....107 C2
Gough St WC1 .....95 A1
Gough Wlk 10 E14 ..33 C3
Goulden Ho SW11 .168 A2
Gouldman Ho 10 E1 .25 B1
Gould Terr 2 E8 ...17 A3
Goulston St E1 ....110 C2
Goulton Rd E5 .....17 A4
Govan St E2 ....24 C4
Gover Ct SW4 .....172 B2
Gowan Ave SW6 ...164 A4
Gowan Ho 2 ....99 A3
Gowan Rd NW10 ...9 A2
Gower Cl SW4 .....61 B1
Gower Ho SE17 ...151 A2
Gower Mews WC1 .105 C4
Gower St WC1 .....93 B1
Gower's Wlk E1 ...111 B1
Gowlett Rd SE15 ...64 C4
Gowrie Rd SW11 ...60 C4
Gracechurch St
 EC2,EC4 ....109 C1
Gracefield Gdns
 SW16 ....74 A1
Gracehill 2 E1 .....32 B4
Grace Ho SE11 ....163 A4
Grace Jones Cl E8 ..16 C2
Grace Pl E3 ....27 A2
Grace's Mews SE5 ..49 A1
Grace's Rd SE5 ....49 A1
Grace St E3 ....27 A2
Graemesdyke Ave
 SW14 ....55 A3
Grafton Cres NW1 ..13 A2
Grafton Ct 10 E8 ..16 C3
Grafton Ho 3 E3 ...27 A2
 12 SE8 ....41 B1
Grafton Mews W1 ..92 C1
Grafton Pl NW1 ....93 C3
Grafton Prim Sch N7 .5 A1
Grafton Rd
 London NW5 ....12 C3
 London W3 .....28 B2
Grafton Sq SW4 ...61 B4
Grafton St W1 .....118 B3
Grafton Terr NW5 ..12 C3
Grafton Way W1 ...93 A1
Grafton Yd NW5 ...13 A2
Graham Ct 5 SE14 ..50 C4
Graham Ho
 7 Balham SW12 .73 A4
 3 London N19 ...13 C4
Graham Mans 2 E8 .17 A2
Graham Rd
 London E8 ......16 C2
 London W4 .....37 C3
Graham St N1 .....86 B1
Graham Terr SW1 ..145 C3
Grainger Ct 22 SE5 .48 B3
Grampian Gdns NW2 .1 A3
Grampians The 10
 W14 ....39 C4
Granard Ave SW15 ..57 A2
Granard Ho 20 E9 ..17 C2
Granard Prim Sch
 SW15 ....57 A1
Granary Rd E1 .....25 A1
Granary Sq N1 .....83 B3
Granary St NW1 ....83 B3
Granby Pl SE1 .....135 B3

Granby St E1 . . . . .99 B2
Granby Terr NW1 . . . . . .82 C1
Grand Ave EC1 . . . . . .108 B4
Grandfield Ct W4 . . . . .45 C4
Grandison Rd SW11 . .60 B2
Grand Junction Wharf
N1 . . . . .86 C1
Grand Par SW14 . . . . . .55 B3
Grand Union Cl W9 . .31 B4
Grand Union Cres
E8 . . . . .24 C4
Grand Union Ind Est
NW10 . . . . .20 A3
Grand Vitesse Ind Est
SE1 . . . . .122 B1
Granfield St SW11 . .167 C3
Grangecourt Rd N16 . .7 A3
Grange Ct W2 . . . . . . .107 A1
London SE15 . . . . .49 B1
Grangefield N1 . . . . . . .14 A1
Grange Gdns NW3 . . . .2 A1
Grange Gr N1 . . . . .15 B2
Grange Ho SE1 . . . . . .138 C3
London NW10 . . . . . . .21 B3
Grange La SE21 . . . . . .76 B2
Grangemill [1] NW5 . . .12 C4
Grange Mills SW12 . . .73 B3
Grange Mus of
Community History The
NW10 . . . . .9 A4
Grange Pl NW6 . . . . . .10 C1
Grange Prim Sch
SE1 . . . . .138 A1
Grange Rd SE1 . . . . . .138 C1
Barnes SW13 . . . . .46 C2
London NW10 . . . . .9 A2
London W4 . . . . .37 A1
Grange St N1 . . . . .87 C3
Grange The SE1 . . . . .138 C1
W14 . . . . .140 C3
[10] London NW3 . . . . .12 B2
London W12 . . . . .39 A3
London W3 . . . . .37 A4
[7] London W4 . . . . . .37 A1
Grangeway NW6 . . . . .10 C1
Grange Wlk SE1 . . . . .138 C1
Grange Yd SE1 . . . . . .138 C1
Gransden Ave E8 . . . . .17 A1
Gransden Ho [1] SE8 .41 B1
Gransden Rd W12 . . . .38 B4
Grantbridge St N1 . . .86 B2
Grantham Ct [9]
SE16 . . . . .40 C4
Grantham Ho [12]
SE15 . . . . .49 C4
Grantham Pl W1 . . . .118 A1
Grantham Rd
Chiswick W4 . . . . .46 A3
London SW9 . . . . . . .172 B1
Grant Ho SW8 . . . . . .171 B1
Grantley Ho
[2] SE14 . . . . .50 C4
[1] Putney SW15 . . . . .69 C3
Grantley St E1 . . . . . . .25 C1
Grant Rd SW11 . . . . . . .60 A4
Grant St N1 . . . . .85 C2
Grantully Rd W9 . . . . .88 A3
Granville Ct [8]
SE14 . . . . .51 A3
Granville Gr SE13 . . . .67 B4
Granville Ho [5] E14 .33 C3
Granville Mans
WC1 . . . . .94 A2
Granville Pk SE13 . . . .67 C4
Granville Pl SW6 . .156 A1
W1 . . . . .103 B1

Granville Point NW2 . .1 B2
Granville Rd NW6 . . . .23 C3
London NW2 . . . . .1 B2
Wandsworth SW18 . . .70 B4
Granville Sq
[8] SE15 . . . . .49 A3
WC1 . . . . .95 A3
Granville St WC1 . . . . .95 A3
Grape St WC2 . . . . . .106 A2
Grasmere NW1 . . . . . .92 B3
Grasmere Ave W3 . . .28 C2
Grasmere Ct SW13 . . .47 A4
Grasmere Ho [10]
N16 . . . . .15 C4
Grasmere JMI Sch
SE15 . . . . .50 B3
Grasmere Point [2]
SE15 . . . . .50 B3
Grately Ho [10] SW15 .68 C3
Gratton Rd W14 . . . . .126 A1
Graveley Ho [7] SE8 .41 A2
Gravel La E1 . . . . .110 C2
Gravesend Rd W12 . . .29 C2
Grayfriars Pas EC1 . .108 B2
Gray Ho SE17 . . . . . . .151 A2
Grayland Ct WC1 . . . . .94 C3
Grayling Rd N16 . . . . . .6 C2
Grayling Sq
E2 . . . . .24 C2 99 C4
Grayshott Rd SW11 . .60 C4
Gray's Inn* WC1 . . . . .107 B4
Gray's Inn Pl WC1 . . .107 A3
Gray's Inn Rd WC1 . . .95 A2
Gray's Inn Sq WC1 . .107 B4
Grayson Ho EC1 . . . . .97 A3
Gray St SE1 . . . . .135 C3
Grayswood Point [14]
SW15 . . . . .68 C3
Gray's Yd W1 . . . . . . .103 C2
Grazebrook Prim Sch
N16 . . . . .7 A2
Grazebrook Rd N16 . .6 C2
Great Arthur Ho
EC1 . . . . .96 C1
Great Bell Alley
EC2 . . . . .109 B2
Great Castle St
W1 . . . . .104 C2
Great Central St
NW1 . . . . .102 C4
Great Chapel St
W1 . . . . .105 B2
Great Chertsey Rd
SW14,W4 . . . . .45 C2
Great Church La
W6 . . . . .39 C1
Great College St
SW1 . . . . .134 A2
Great Croft WC1 . . . . .94 B3
Great Cumberland Mews
W1 . . . . .102 C1
Great Cumberland Pl
W1 . . . . .103 A1
Great Dover St
SE1 . . . . .137 B2
Great Eastern Bldgs [10]
E8 . . . . .17 A2
Great Eastern Ent Ctr
E14 . . . . .42 A4
Great Eastern Pier
E14 . . . . .41 C1
Great Eastern Rd
E15 . . . . .19 C2
Great Eastern St
EC2 . . . . .24 A1 98 A2
Great Eastern Wharf
SW11 . . . . .158 B1

Great Field [1] NW5 .13 B3
Greatfield Cl
[4] London N19 . . . . .13 B4
London SE4 . . . . .66 C3
Great George St
SW1 . . . . .134 A3
Great Guildford Bsns Sq
SE1 . . . . .122 C1
Great Guildford St
SE1 . . . . .122 C1
Greatham Wlk [8]
SW15 . . . . .68 C3
Great James St
WC1 . . . . .106 C4
Great Marlborough St
W1 . . . . .104 C1
Great Mathers Rd
SE11 . . . . .150 A4
Great Maze Pond
SE1 . . . . .137 C4
Great Newport St
WC2 . . . . .120 A4
Great New St EC4 . . .107 C2
Greatorex Ho [1] E1 .111 B4
Greatorex St E1 . . . . .111 B4
Great Ormond St
WC1 . . . . .94 C1
Great Ormond St Hospl
for Children WC1 . . . .94 C2
Great Percy St WC1 . . .95 B4
Great Peter St
SW1 . . . . .133 C1
Great Portland St
W1 . . . . .104 B4
Great Portland Street
Sta W1 . . . . .92 B1
Great Pulteney St
W1 . . . . .119 A4
Great Queen St
WC2 . . . . .106 B2
Great Russell St
WC1 . . . . .106 A3
Great Scotland Yd
SW1,WC2 . . . . .120 A2
Great Smith St
SW1 . . . . .133 C2
Great Spilmans
SE22 . . . . .64 A2
Great St Helen's
EC3 . . . . .110 A2
Great St Thomas
Apostle EC4 . . . . .123 A4
Great Suffolk St
SE1 . . . . .122 B1
Great Sutton St EC1 .96 B1
Great Swan Alley
EC2 . . . . .109 B2
Great Titchfield St
W1 . . . . .104 C2
Great Tower St
EC3 . . . . .124 A4
Great Trinity La
EC4 . . . . .123 A4
Great Turnstile
WC2 . . . . .107 A3
Great Western Rd
W2,W9 . . . . .31 B4
Great West Rd W4,
W6 . . . . .45 C4
Great West Road Cedars
Rd W4 . . . . .45 B4
Great West Road
Hogarth La W4 . . . . . .46 A4
Great Winchester St
EC2 . . . . .109 C2
Great Windmill St
W1 . . . . .119 B4

Great Yd SE1 . . . . . . .138 B4
Greaves Cotts [12]
E14 . . . . .33 A4
Greaves Twr SW10 .157 A2
Grebe Ct [3] E14 . . . .42 B4
Greek Ct W1 . . . . .105 C1
Greek St W1 . . . . .105 C1
Greenacre Ct [8] 16 C3
Greenacre Sq [20]
SE16 . . . . .40 C4
Green Arbour Ct
EC1 . . . . .108 A2
Greenaway Gdns
NW3 . . . . .11 A4
Greenaway Ho NW8 .78 C4
SW11 . . . . .95 B3
Green Bank E1 . . . . . . .32 A1
Greenberry St NW8 . .80 A1
Green Cl NW11 . . . . . . .2 B4
Greencoat Pl SW1 . .147 A4
Greencoat Row
SW1 . . . . .133 A1
Greencourt Ho E1 . . .25 C1
Greencroft Gdns
NW6 . . . . .11 B1
Green Dale SE22 . . . . .64 A2
Greendale Cl SE22 . . .64 A2
Green Dragon Ct
SE1 . . . . .123 B1
Green Dragon Ho
WC1 . . . . .106 B2
Green Dragon Jun & Inf
Sch TW8 . . . . .44 A4
Green Dragon La
TW8 . . . . .36 B1
Green Dragon Yd
E1 . . . . .111 B3
Greene Ct [20] SE14 .50 C4
Greene Ho SE1 . . . . .137 B1
Greenend Rd W4 . . . .38 A4
Greener Ho [3] SW4 .61 C4
Greenfell Mans SE8 .52 A4
Greenfield Gdns
NW2 . . . . .1 A1
Greenfield Ho [20]
SW19 . . . . .69 C3
Greenfield Rd E1 . . . .111 C2
Greenham Cl SE1 . . .135 B3
Greenham Ho [6] E9 .25 B4
Greenheath Bsns Ctr [3]
E2 . . . . .25 A1
Greenhill NW3 . . . . . . .11 C4
Greenhill Pk NW10 . .21 A4
Greenhill Rd NW10 . .21 A4
Greenhill's Rents
EC1 . . . . .108 A4
Greenhills Terr [16]
N1 . . . . .15 C2
Green Ho The [5]
SW19 . . . . .70 A3
Green Hundred Rd
SE15 . . . . .49 C4
Greenland Ho [4] E1 .26 A1
London SE8 . . . . .40 C1
Greenland Mews
SE8 . . . . .40 C1
Greenland Pl NW1 . .82 B4
Greenland Quay
SE16 . . . . .40 C2
Greenland Rd NW1 . .82 C4
London NW1 . . . . .82 B4
Green Lanes N4,N8,
N15 . . . . .6 A4
Greenleaf Cl [8]
SW2 . . . . .74 C4
Greenman St N1 . . . . .86 C4

Greenmead Sch
SW15 . . . . .57 A2
Greenock Rd [3] W3 .37 B3
Green Park SW1,
W1 . . . . .132 B4
Green Park Sta
SW1 . . . . .118 C2
Greenroof Way
SE10 . . . . .43 B3
Green St W11 . . . . . . .119 B4
Green's Ct W11 . . . . .112 C1
Greenside Prim Sch
W12 . . . . .38 C4
Greenside Rd W12 . . .38 C4
Green St W1 . . . . .117 B4
Greenstead Gdns
SW15 . . . . .57 A2
Greenstreet Hill
SE4 . . . . .65 C4
Green Terr EC1 . . . . . . .95 C3
Green The W3 . . . . . . .29 A3
Green View Cl W3 . . .29 A1
Greenway Cl N4 . . . . . .6 B2
Greenwell St W1 . . . . .92 B1
Greenwich Academy
SE10 . . . . .52 A2
Greenwich Bsns Ctr
SE10 . . . . .52 A3
Greenwich Bsns Pk
SE10 . . . . .52 A3
Greenwich Church St
SE10 . . . . .52 B4
Greenwich Ct [8] E1 .32 A3
Greenwich District
Hospl SE10 . . . . .43 B1
Greenwich High Rd
SE10 . . . . .52 A3
Greenwich Ind Est
SE10 . . . . .52 A4
Greenwich Mkt [1]
SE10 . . . . .52 B4
Greenwich Park
SE10 . . . . .53 A3
Greenwich Park St
SE10 . . . . .52 C4
Greenwich South St
SE10 . . . . .52 B2
Greenwich Sta SE10 .52 A3
Greenwich View
E14 . . . . .42 A3
Green Wlk SE1 . . . . . .138 A1
Greenwood
SW19 . . . . .69 C4
Green Wood NW5 . . . .13 B3
Greenwood Ho WC1 .95 B3
[8] London SE4 . . . . . .65 C3
Greenwood Pl NW5 .13 A3
Greenwood Rd E8 . . .16 C2
Greenwood Terr
NW10 . . . . .20 C3
Green Yd WC1 . . . . . . .95 A2
Green Yd The SE1 . . .125 A4
Green St E1 . . . . .121 C5
Gregor Mews SE3 . . . .53 C3
Gregory Pl W8 . . . . . .128 A4
Greig Terr SE17 . . . . .48 A4
Grenada Ho [18] E14 .33 B2
Grenade St E14 . . . . . .33 B2
Grena Gdns TW9 . . . .54 B3
Grena Rd TW10,TW9 .54 B3
Grenard Cl SE15 . . . . .49 C3
Grendon Ho [5]
N1 . . . . .84 C1
[20] London E9 . . . . . .17 B1

Grendon St NW8 ....90 A2
Grenfell Ho SE5 ....48 B3
Grenfell Rd W11 ....30 C2
Grenfell Twr [1] W11 ....30 C2
Grenfell Wlk [4] 30 C2
Grenville Ho [2] SE3 ....26 B3
[4] SE8 ....51 C4
Grenville Lo [1] W1 ....30 C2
Grenville Mews SW7 ....143 A3
Grenville Pl SW7 ....142 C4
Grenville Rd N19 ....5 A3
Grenville St WC1 ....94 B1
Gresham Almshouses [9] SW9 ....62 C3
Gresham Coll EC1 ....107 C3
Gresham Gdns NW11 .1 A3
Gresham Rd SW9 ....62 C4
Gresham St EC2 ....109 A2
Gresham Way SW19 70 C1
Gresham Way Est SW19 ....70 C1
Gresley Ho SW8 ....171 C4
Gresley Rd N19 ....4 B4
Gressenhall Rd SW18 ....70 B4
Gresse St W1 ....105 B2
Greswell St SW6 ....47 C2
Gretton Ho [2] E2 ....25 B2
Greville Hall NW6 ....78 B2
Greville Ho SW1 ....131 B2
Putney SW15 ....57 C4
Greville Lo W2 ....100 A2
Greville Mews NW6 .78 A3
Greville Pl W9 ....78 B3
Greville Rd NW6 ....78 B3
Richmond TW10 ....54 B1
Greville St EC1 ....107 C3
Grey Coat Hospital CE Sch The SW1 ....133 B1
Grey Coat Hospital St Michaels The SW1 ....147 B3
Greycoat Pl SW1 ....133 B1
Greycoat St SW1 ....133 B1
Grey Eagle St E1 ....24 B1 99 A1
Greyfriars [18] SE26 ....76 C1
Greyfriars Ho SE3 ....53 B4
Grey Ho [27] W12 ....30 A2
Greyhound Ct WC2 121 B4
Greyhound Rd W6 154 A4
London NW10 ....22 A2
Greyladies Gdns SE10 ....52 B1
Greystoke Ho SE15 ..49 C4
Greystoke Pl EC4 ....107 C2
Grey Turner Ho W12 ....29 C3
Grice Ct N1 ....15 B2
Griffin Cl NW10 ....9 A3
Griffin Ct [4] Brentford TW8 ....44 A4
London W12 ....30 A1
London W4 ....38 B1
Griffin Gate SW15 ....57 C4
Grifton Ho [3] SW11 .60 A4
Grigg's Pl SE1 ....138 B1
Grimaldi Ho N1 ....84 C2
Grimsby St E2 ....99 A2
Grimsel Path SE5 ....48 A3
Grimshaw Cl N6 ....3 C4
Grimston Rd SW6 164 C1

Grimthorpe Ho EC1 ..96 A2
Grimwade Cl SE15 ....65 B4
Grindall Ho [18] E1 ....25 A1
Grindal St SE1 ....135 B3
Grindley Ho [3] E3 ....33 B4
Grinling Gibbons Prim Sch SE8 ....51 B4
Grinling Pl SE8 ....51 C4
Grinstead Rd SE8 ....41 A1
Grisedale NW1 ....92 C4
Grittleton Rd W9 ....23 C1
Grocers' Hall Ct EC2 ....109 B1
Groombridge Rd E9 ..17 C1
Groom Cres SW18 ....71 C4
Groome Ho SE11 ....149 A3
Groom Pl SW1 ....131 C2
Grosse Way SW15 ....57 A1
Grosvenor Ave London N5 ....15 B3
Mortlake SW14 ....56 A4
Richmond TW10 ....54 A2
Grosvenor Bridge SW1 ....160 B4
Grosvenor Cotts SW1 ....145 B4
Grosvenor Cres SW1 ....131 C3
Grosvenor Cres Mews SW1 ....131 B3
Grosvenor Ct London NW6 ....22 C4
London W4 ....37 A1
Putney SW15 ....58 A2
Grosvenor Ct Mans W2 ....102 C1
Grosvenor Gdns SW1 ....132 B1
London NW2 ....9 B3
Mortlake SW14 ....56 A4
Grosvenor Gdns Mews E SW1 ....132 B2
Grosvenor Gdns Mews N SW1 ....132 A1
Grosvenor Gdns Mews S SW1 ....132 B1
Grosvenor Hill W1 ....118 A4
Grosvenor Hill Ct W1 ....118 A4
Grosvenor Ho SE5 ....7 C3
Grosvenor Park SE5 ..48 B4
Grosvenor Pier SW1 ....161 B3
Grosvenor Pk SE5 ....48 B4
Grosvenor Rd SW1 161 A4
London W4 ....37 B1
Richmond TW10 ....54 A2
Grosvenor Residences [1] W14 ....39 C3
Grosvenor Sq W1 ....118 A4
Grosvenor St W1 ....118 A4
Grosvenor Terr SE5 ..48 B4
Grosvenor The NW11 ..1 A4
Grosvenor Wharf Rd E14 ....42 C2
Grote's Pl SE3 ....53 A1
Groton Rd SW18 ....71 A2
Grotto Ct SE1 ....136 B4
Grotto Pas W1 ....103 C4
Grove Crescent Rd E15 ....19 C2
Grove Ct NW8 ....89 B4
SW10 ....143 A1
London SW4 ....61 B4

Grovedale Rd N19 ....4 C2
Grove Dwellings E1 ..32 B4
Grove End Gdns NW8 ....79 A1
Grove End Ho NW8 ....89 B3
Grove End Rd NW8 ....89 B3
Grove Gdns NW8 ....90 B3
Grove Hall Ct [3] London N16 ....7 C3
NW8 ....89 A4
London N8 ....89 A4
Grove Hill Rd SE5 ....64 A4
Grove Ho SW3 ....158 B4
London SE3 ....53 B1
Grove La SE5 ....48 C1
Groveland Ct EC4 ....109 A1
Grovelands Cl SE5 ....49 A1
Grove Lane Terr SE5 ....48 C1
Groveley Ho [1] N4 ....6 B4
Grove Lo SW4 ....61 B3
Grove Mans [3] London N16 ....7 C3
London SW4 ....60 B3
[4] London W6 ....39 B3
Grove Mews W6 ....39 B3
W4 ....45 B3
Grove Park Bridge W4 ....45 B3
Grove Park Gdns W4 ....45 B3
Grove Park Mews W4 ....45 B3
Grove Park Prim Sch W4 ....45 B3
Grove Park Rd W4 ....45 A3
Grove Park Terr W4 ....45 A3
Grove Pk SE5 ....49 A1
Grove Pl Balham SW12 ....61 A1
London NW3 ....2 C1
London W3 ....28 B1
Grover Ct SE13 ....52 A1
Grove Rd E3 ....26 A3
Barnes SW13 ....46 B1
London NW2 ....9 B2
London W3 ....28 B1
Richmond TW10 ....54 B1
Grover Ho SE11 ....149 A1
[4] London SW4 ....61 B2
Groveside Ct SW11 ....167 B2
Grove St SE8 ....41 B1
Grove Terr NW5 ....13 A4
Grove The N6 ....3 C3
Dulwich SE21 ....76 C3
London N4 ....5 B4
London N8 ....4 C4 (?)
London NW11 ....1 A4
Grove Vale SE22 ....64 B3
Grove Vale Prim Sch SE22 ....64 B3

Guild Hall* EC2 ....109 A2
Guildhall Bldgs EC2 ....109 B2
Guildhall Sch Music & Drama EC2 ....109 A4
Guildhall Yd EC2 ....109 A2
Guildhouse St SW1 ....146 C3
Guilford Pl WC1 ....94 C1
Guilford St WC1 ....94 B1
Guillemot Ct [20] SE8 ..51 B4
Guinness Cl E9 ....18 A1
Guinness Ct E1 ....111 A1
EC1 ....97 A3
NW8 ....80 B3
SW3 ....144 C3
Guinness Sq SE1 ....152 A4
Guinness Trust Bldgs [7] 24 C3
SE11 ....138 A4
SE1 ....130 B4
SW3 ....144 C3
London W6 ....39 B1
Guion Rd SW6 ....165 A2
Gujarat Ho [1] N16 ....7 C1
Gulland Wlk [20] N1 ....15 B2
Gullane Ho [22] E3 ....26 B3
Gulliver St SE16 ....41 B3
Gulston Wlk SW3 ....145 A3
Gunmakers La E3 ....26 A4
Gunnersbury Avenue (North Circular Rd) W3 ....36 C3
Gunnersbury Cl [8] W4 ....37 A1
Gunnersbury Cres W3 ....36 C4
Gunnersbury Ct [3] W3 ....36 C4
Gunnersbury Dr W5 36 B4
Gunnersbury Gdns W3 ....36 C4
Gunnersbury La W3 36 C4
Gunnersbury Mews [6] W4 ....37 A1
Gunnersbury Park W3 ....36 C3
Gunnersbury Park Mus W3 ....36 C2
Gunners Rd SW18 ....71 C2
Gunpowder Sq EC4 ....107 C2
Gun St E1 ....110 C3
Gunstor Rd N16 ....16 A4
Gunter Gr SW6 ....156 C2
Gunterstone Rd W14 ....140 B2
Gunthorpe St E1 ....111 A2
Gunwhale Cl SE16 ....32 C1
Gun Wharf E1 ....32 B1
Gurdon Ho [3] E14 ....33 C3
Gurdon Rd SE7 ....43 C1
Gurney Ho [2] E2 ....24 C3
London W2 ....100 A2
Gurney Rd SW6 ....59 B4
Guthrie Ct SE1 ....135 C3
Guthrie St SW3 ....144 A2
Gutter La EC2 ....108 C2
Guyscliff Rd SE13 ....67 B2
Guy's Hospl SE1 ....137 C4
Guy's Hospl Sch SE1 ....123 B1

Guy St SE1 ....137 C4
Gwalior Rd SW15 ....57 C4
Gwendolen Ave SW15 ....57 C2
Gwendolen Cl SW15 57 C2
Gwendwr Rd W14 ....140 B2
Gwent Ct [13] SE16 ....32 C1
Gwilym Maries Ho [11] E2 ....25 A2
Gwyn Cl SW6 ....156 C1
Gwynne Cl W4 ....46 B4
Gwynne Ho EC1 ....95 B3
WC1 ....95 A3
[8] Streatham SW2 ....74 B3
Gwynne Pl WC1 ....95 A3
Gwynne Rd SW11 ....167 C2
Gye Ho [2] SW4 ....62 A3
Gylcote Cl SE5 ....63 C3

H

Haarlem Rd [12] W14 ....39 C3
Haberdasher Pl N1 ....98 A4
Haberdasher St N1 ....97 C4
Habington Ho [9] SE5 ....48 C3
Hackett Cl SE8 ....41 B2
Hackford Rd SW9 ....173 A4
Hackford Wlk SW9 ....173 B3
Hackney Central Sta E8 ....17 A2
Hackney Coll (Poplar Ctr) E3 ....27 A1
Hackney Com Coll N1 ....98 A4
London N1 ....6 B4
Hackney Downs Sch E5,E8 ....16 C3
Hackney Downs Sta E8 ....17 A3
Hackney Free & Parochial CE Sch (Secondary) E9 ....17 B2
Hackney Gr E8 ....17 A2
Hackney Hospl E9 ....18 A3
Hackney Rd E2 ....24 C3
Hackney Wick E9 ....18 B2
Hackney Wick Sta E9 ....18 B2
Hackworth Point [24] E3 ....27 A2
Haddington Ct [4] SE10 ....52 A3
Haddo Ho SE10 ....52 A4
London NW5 ....13 A4
Haddon Ct W3 ....29 B2
Haddo St SE10 ....52 A4
Haden Ct N4 ....5 C2
Hadfield Ho [6] E1 ....111 C1
Hadleigh Cl [18] E1 ....25 B1
Hadleigh Ho [16] E1 ....25 B1
Hadleigh St E2 ....25 B2
Hadley Ct N16 ....7 C3
Hadley Gdns W4 ....37 C1
Hadley St NW1 ....13 A2
Hadlow Ho [2] SE17 152 B2
Hadrian Cl SE4 ....66 C4
Hadrian Est [1] E2 ....24 C3
Hadrian St SE10 ....43 A1
Hadstock Ho NW1 ....93 C4
Hadyn Park Ct [13] W12 ....38 C4
Hadyn Park Rd W12 38 C4
Hafer Rd SW11 ....60 B3
Haggard Rd TW1 ....54 B1
Haggerston Rd E8 ....24 B4
Haggerston Sch E2 24 B3
Hague Prim Sch E2 ..25 A1
Hague St E2 ....123 B1

Haig Ho 4 E2 ....24 C3	
Hailsham Ave SW2 ....74 B1	
Hailsham Rd NW8 .....90 A1	
Hainford CI SE4 ......65 C3	
Haining CI 3 W4 ......36 C1	
Hainton CI E1 ....32 A3	
Halcomb St N1 ....24 A4	
Halcrow St E1 ....32 A4	
Halcyon Wharf E1 ...125 C2	
Haldane PI SW18 ......71 A3	
Haldane Rd SW6 .....155 A3	
Haldon Rd SW18 ......58 B1	
Hale Ho SW1 ....147 C2	
Hales Ho 8 SW12 .....73 A4	
Hales Prior N1 ....84 C1	
Hales St SE8 ....51 C3	
Hale St E14 ....43 B1	
Halesworth Rd	
SE13 ....67 A4	
Half Moon Ct EC1 ...108 C3	
Half Moon La SE24 ...63 B1	
Halfmoon Pas E1 ....111 A1	
Half Moon St W1 ....118 B1	
Halford Ho 9 SW15 ..57 C2	
Halford Rd SW6 .....155 B3	
Richmond TW10 .....54 A2	
Haliday Ho N1 ....15 C2	
Haliday Wlk 4 N1 .....15 C2	
Halidon CI E9 ....17 B3	
Haliwell Ho NW6 ......78 A3	
Halkett Ho 1 E2 ......25 B4	
Halkin Arc SW1 ......131 A2	
Halkin Mews SW1 ...131 B2	
Halkin PI SW1 ....131 B2	
Halkin St SW1 ....131 C3	
Hallam Ct W1 ....104 B4	
Hallam Ho N1 ....147 A1	
London SW9 ....173 B4	
Hallam Mews W1 .....104 B4	
Hallam Rd SW13 ......57 A4	
Hallam St W1 ....104 B4	
Halley Gdns SE13 .....67 C3	
Halley Ho 5 E2 ....24 C3	
8 E3 ....43 B1	
Halley Prim Sch	
E14 ....33 A4	
Halley St E14 ....33 A4	
Hallfield 92 ....100 C1	
Hallfield Jun & Inf Schs	
W2 ....100 A2	
Hall Gate NW8 ....89 A4	
Halliday Ho E1 ....111 C1	
Halliford St N1 ....15 C1	
Halling Ho SE1 ....137 C3	
Halliwell Ct 4 SE22 ..64 C2	
Halliwell Rd SW2 .....62 B1	
Hall Oak Wlk NW6 ....10 B2	
Hall PI W2 ....89 B1	
Hall Rd NW8 ....89 A4	
London E15 ....19 C4	
Hall Sch The NW3 ....11 C2	
Hall Sch Wimbledon	
SW15 ....68 C1	
Hallsville Prim Sch	
E16 ....35 C3	
Hallsville Rd E16 .....35 B3	
Hall Twr W2 ....101 C4	
Halpin PI SE17 ....151 C3	
Halsbury Ho 4 N7 ....14 B4	
Halsbury Rd W12 .....30 A1	
Halsey St SW3 ....144 C4	
Halsmere Rd SE5 .....48 A2	
Halstead Ct N1 ....87 C1	
Halston CI SW11 ......60 B1	
Halstow 7 NW5 ....12 C2	

Halstow Prim Sch	
SE10 ....43 C1	
Halstow Rd	
SE3,SE10 ....43 C1	
London NW10 ....22 C2	
Halton Cross St N1 ...86 B4	
Haltone Ho SW4 .....171 C1	
Halton Ho 23 N1 ......15 A1	
Halton Mans N1 ......15 A1	
Halton PI N1 ....86 C4	
Halton Rd N1 ....86 B4	
Halyard Ho E14 ....42 B3	
Hambalt Rd SW4 .....61 B2	
Hambledon SE17 ......48 C4	
Hambledon Chase	
N4 ....5 A4	
Hambledon Ho E5 ....17 A4	
Hambledon PI SE21 ..76 B3	
Hambledon	
SW18 ....70 B4	
Hamble St SW6 ....59 A4	
Hambley Ho 5	
SE16 ....40 A2	
Hamblyn Ct N16 ....7 B4	
Hambridge Way	
SW2 ....74 C4	
Hambrook Ct 12	
NW5 ....13 A4	
Hamers Ho 10 SW8 .162 B3	
Hamers Ho SW2 ......74 C4	
Hamilton CI NW8 ......89 B3	
SE16 ....41 A4	
Hamilton Ct W9 ....88 C4	
Hamilton Gdns	
NW8 ....89 A4	
Hamilton Hall NW8 ...78 C1	
Hamilton Ho 1 E14 ..33 B2	
19 E3 ....26 B2	
NW8 ....89 B4	
W8 ....128 A4	
Chiswick W4 ....46 A4	
Putney SW15 ....56 C2	
10 Richmond TW9 ..44 C2	
Hamilton La N5 ....15 A4	
Hamilton Lo 22 E1 ...25 B1	
Hamilton Mews	
W1 ....132 A4	
Hamilton Pk N5 ....15 A4	
Hamilton Pk W N5 ...15 A4	
Hamilton Rd N1 ......117 C1	
Hamilton Rd	
London NW10 ....8 C3	
London NW11 ....1 A4	
London W4 ....38 A4	
Hamilton Sq SE1 ....137 C4	
Hamilton St SE8 ......51 C4	
Hamilton Terr NW8 ...89 A4	
Hamlet Ct SE11 ......150 A2	
1 London W6 ......38 C2	
Hamlet (Day) Hospl The	
TW9 ....54 A4	
Hamlet Gdns W6 .....38 C2	
Hamlet Ind Est 19 ...18 C1	
Hamlets Way E3 ......26 B1	
Hamlet The SE5 ......63 C4	
Hamlet Way SE1 .....137 C4	
Hammelton Ho	
SW9 ....48 A2	
Hammersley Ho 3	
SE14 ....50 B3	
Hammersmith Bridge Rd	
W6,SW13 ....39 B1	
Hammersmith Broadway	
8 W6 ....39 B2	
Hammersmith Flyover	
W6 ....39 B1	

Hammersmith Gr	
W6 ....39 B3	
Hammersmith Hospl	
W12 ....30 A3	
Hammersmith Rd	
W14 ....140 B4	
London W6 ....39 C2	
Hammersmith Sta	
W6 ....39 B2	
Hammersmith Terr	
W6 ....38 C1	
Hammett St EC3 .....124 C4	
Hammond Ho E14 ....42 A3	
4 SE14 ....50 B3	
Hammond Lo 6	
W9 ....31 C4	
Hammond Sq N1 .....24 A3	
Hampden CI NW1 .....83 C2	
Hampden Gurney CE	
Prim Sch W1 ......102 B2	
Hampden Gurney St	
W1 ....102 C1	
Hampden Ho SW9 ...173 C1	
Hampden Rd N19 ......4 C2	
Hampshire Ct 6	
SW13 ....46 B1	
Hampshire Hog La 6	
W6 ....39 A2	
Hampshire Sch The	
SW7 ....130 A3	
Hampshire St NW5 ...13 C2	
Hampson Way	
SW8 ....172 C4	
Hampstead Gate	
NW3 ....11 B3	
Hampstead Gn NW3 ..12 A3	
Hampstead Gr NW3 ...2 B1	
Hampstead Heath* 2 C2	
Hampstead Heath Sta	
NW3 ....12 A4	
Hampstead High St	
NW3 ....11 C4	
Hampstead Hill Gdns	
NW3 ....12 A4	
Hampstead Hill Sch	
NW3 ....12 A4	
Hampstead La N6 ......3 A4	
Hampstead Parochial CE	
Prim Sch NW3 ......11 B4	
Hampstead Rd NW1 ..92 C4	
Hampstead Sch	
NW2 ....10 A4	
Hampstead Sq NW3 ...2 B1	
Hampstead Sta	
NW3 ....11 B4	
Hampstead West 4	
NW6 ....10 C2	
Hampstead Wlk 8	
E3 ....26 B4	
Hampton CI NW6 .....23 C2	
Hampton Ct 8	
17 SE16 ....32 C1	
1 London N1 ....15 A2	
Hampton St SE1 .....150 B3	
Ham Yd W1 ....119 B4	
Hanameel St 5 E16 ..35 C1	
Hana Mews E5 ....17 A4	
Hanbury Ho E1 ......111 B4	
Hanbury Rd W3 ....37 A4	
Hanbury St E1 ....111 B4	
Hancock Nunn Ho 9 ..12 B1	
Hancock Rd E3 ....27 B2	
Handa Wlk 3 N1 ......15 B2	
Hand Ct WC1 ....107 A3	

Handel Mans SW13 ..47 B3	
Handel St WC1 ....94 B2	
Handforth Rd SW9 ..163 B2	
Handley Rd E9 ....25 B4	
Hands Wlk E16 ....35 C3	
Hanford CI SW18 .....70 C3	
Hankey PI SE1 ....137 C3	
Hanley Gdns N4 ....5 B3	
Hanley Rd N4,N19 ....5 A3	
Hanmer Wlk N7 ....5 B2	
Hannah Mary Way	
SE1 ....153 C3	
Hannay La N8 ....4 C4	
Hannell Rd SW6 .....154 B2	
Hannen Ho SE5 ....63 C4	
Hannen Rd SE27 .....75 A1	
Hannibal Rd E1 ....32 B4	
Hannington Rd	
SW4 ....61 A4	
Hanover CE Prim Sch	
SW8 ....172 C4	
Hanover CI TW9 ......44 C3	
Hanover Ct	
London N16 ....7 B4	
London W12 ....29 C1	
Hanover Gate Mans	
NW1 ....90 B2	
Hanover Gdns	
SE11 ....163 B3	
Hanover Ho NW8 .....80 A1	
Hanover Mans 5	
SW2 ....62 C2	
Hanover Pk SE15 .....49 C2	
Hanover PI 4 E3 .....26 B2	
WC2 ....106 B1	
Hanover Prim Sch	
N1 ....86 C2	
Hanover Rd NW10 ....22 B4	
Hanover Sq W1 ......104 B1	
Hanover St W1 ....104 B1	
Hanover Steps W2 ..102 B1	
Hanover Terr NW1 ....90 C3	
Hanover Terr Mews	
NW1 ....90 B3	
Hanover West Ind Est	
NW10 ....20 C2	
Hansard Mews W14 ..39 C4	
Hanscomb Mews 3	
SW4 ....61 B3	
Hans Cres SW1 ......130 C2	
Hansler Rd SE22 .....64 B2	
Hanson CI	
Balham SW12 ....73 A4	
Mortlake SW14 ......55 B4	
Hanson Ho 12 E1 ...125 C4	
Hanson St W1 ....104 C4	
Hans PI SW1 ....130 C2	
Hans Rd SW3 ....130 C2	
Hans St SW1 ....131 A1	
Hanway Ho SW9 ....173 C4	
Hanway PI W1 ....105 B2	
Hanway St W1 ....105 B2	
Hanwell Ho 24 W2 ...31 C4	
Harben Rd NW6 ......11 B1	
Harberson Rd SW12 .73 A3	
Harberton Rd N19 .....4 B3	
Harbet Rd W2 ....101 C3	
Harbinger Prim Sch	
E14 ....42 A2	
Harbinger Rd E14 ....42 A2	
Harbin Ho 5 SW2 ....74 C3	
Harbledown Ho	
SE1 ....137 B3	
Harbledown Rd	
SW6 ....165 B4	

Harbord CI SE5 ....48 C1	
Harbord Ho 5 SE16 ..40 C2	
Harbord St SW6 ......47 C2	
Harborough Sch N19 ..4 C2	
Harbour Ave SW10 ..167 A3	
Harbour Exchange Sq	
E14 ....42 A4	
Harbour Rd SE5 ......63 B4	
Harbridge Ave	
SW15 ....68 C4	
Harbut Rd SW11 .....59 C3	
Harcombe Rd N16 .....7 A1	
Harcourt Ho W1 .....104 A2	
Harcourt Rd SE4 ....171 B2	
Harcourt St W1 ......102 B3	
Harcourt Terr	
SW10 ....142 B1	
Hardcastle Ho 8	
SE15 ....49 C2	
Hardel Rise SW2 .....75 A3	
Hardel Wlk SE24,	
Harden Ho SE5 ....49 A1	
Harders Rd SE15 .....50 A1	
Hardess St SE24 .....63 B4	
Hardham Ho 5	
SW2 ....62 C1	
Harding CI SE17 ......48 B4	
Hardinge Rd NW10 ..22 B4	
Hardinge St E1 ....32 B3	
Harding Ho SW13 ....47 A4	
Hardington 2 NW1 ...12 C1	
Hardwicke Ho 14	
E3 ....27 A2	
Hardwicke Mews	
WC1 ....95 A3	
Hardwicke Rd W4 ....37 C2	
Hardwick Ho NW8 ....90 B2	
London SW8 ....171 B2	
Hardwick St EC1 .....95 C3	
Hardwick's Way	
SW18 ....58 C2	
Hardy Ave 4 E16 .....35 C1	
Hardy CI SE16 ....40 C4	
Hardy Cotts 2 SE10 ..52 C4	
Hardy Ct SE3 ....53 B4	
Hardy Rd SE3 ....53 B4	
Hare & Billet Rd	
SE3 ....52 C1	
Harecourt Rd N1 .....15 B2	
Hare Ct EC4 ....107 B1	
Haredale Ho 24	
SE16 ....139 B3	
Haredale Rd SE24 ...63 B3	
Harefield Mews SE4 .66 B4	
Harefield Rd SE4 .....66 B4	
Hare Marsh	
E2 ....24 C1 99 B2	
Hare PI EC4 ....107 C1	
Hare Row E2 ....25 A3	
Hare Wlk N1 ....24 A3	
Harewood Ave NW1 ..90 B1	
Harewood PI W1 ....104 B1	
Harewood Row	
NW1 ....102 B2	
Harfield Gdns 1	
SE5 ....64 A4	
Harfleur Ct 4 SE11 .150 A3	
Harford Ho SE5 ......48 B4	
W11 ....31 B4	
Harford St E1 ....26 A1	
Hargrave Mans 2	
N19 ....4 C2	

Hargrave Park Prim Sch
N19 . . . . .4 B2
Hargrave Pk N19 . . . . .4 B2
Hargrave Pl N7 . . . . .13 C3
Hargrave Rd N19 . . . . .4 B2
Hargraves Ho **14**
W12 . . . . .30 A2
Hargwyne St SW9 . . .62 B4
Harkness Ho E1 . . . . .111 C1
Harlech Twr **8** W3 . . .37 B4
Harlescott Rd SE15 . .65 C3
Harlesden Gdns
NW10 . . . . .21 B4
Harlesden Plaza **2**
NW10 . . . . .21 A3
Harlesden Prim Sch
NW10 . . . . .21 A3
Harlesden Rd NW10 . .21 C4
Harlesden Sta
NW10 . . . . .20 C3
Harleyford Rd SW8 . .162 C4
Harleyford Manor **5**
W3 . . . . .28 B1
Harleyford Rd
SE11 . . . . .162 C4
Harleyford St SE11 . .163 B3
Harley Gdns SW10 . .143 A1
Harley Gr E3 . . . . . . .26 B2
Harley Ho NW1 . . . . .91 C1
Harley Pl W1 . . . . . .104 A3
Harley Rd
London NW10 . . . . . .21 A3
London NW3 . . . . . .11 C1
Harley St W1 . . . . . .104 A3
Harley Villas NW10 . .21 A3
Harling Ct SW11 . . . .168 C2
Harlowe Ho **18** E8 . . .24 B4
Harlynwood **19** SE5 .48 B3
Harman Cl E1 . . . . .153 B1
London NW2 . . . . . . .1 A1
Harman Dr NW2 . . . .10 A4
Harmon Ho **8** SE8 . .41 B2
Harmood Gr NW1 . . .13 A1
Harmood Ho **2**
NW1 . . . . .13 A1
Harmood St NW1 . . .13 A1
Harmsworth St
SE17 . . . . .150 A1
Harold Ct **14** SE16 . .40 C4
Harold Est SE1 . . . . .138 B1
Harold Ho **12** E2 . . .25 C3
Harold Laski Ho
EC1 . . . . .96 B3
Harold Maddison Ho
SE17 . . . . .150 B2
Harold Pl SE11 . . . . .149 B1
Harold Rd NW10 . . . .20 C2
Harold Wilson Ho
SW6 . . . . .155 A3
Harp Alley EC4 . . . .108 A2
Harpenden Rd SE27, .
SW16 . . . . .75 A2
Harpenmead Point
NW2 . . . . .1 B2
Harper Ho **5** SW9 . .63 A4
Harper Mews SW11 . .71 B1
Harper Rd SE1 . . . . .137 A2
Harp La EC3 . . . . . . .124 A3
Harpley Sq E1 . . . . . .25 C1
Harpsden St SW11 . .169 B3
Harpur Mews WC1 . .106 C4
Harpur St WC1 . . . . .106 C4
Harrier Ho **9** SW11 .60 A4
Harriet Cl E8 . . . . . .24 C4
Harriet Ho SW6 . . . .156 B1

Harriet St SW1 . . . . .131 A3
Harriet Tubman Cl **21**
SW2 . . . . .74 C4
Harriet Wlk SW1 . . . .131 A3
Harrington Ct
SW7 . . . . .143 C4
□ W9 . . . . .23 B2
Harrington Gdns
SW7 . . . . .142 C3
Harrington Ho NW1 . .92 C4
SW1 . . . . .147 C2
Harrington Rd
SW7 . . . . .143 B4
Harrington Sq NW1 . .82 C1
Harrington St NW1 . .92 C4
Harriott Cl SE10 . . . .43 B2
Harriott Ho **11** E1 . .32 B3
Harris Ho **10** E3 . . .26 C2
□ London SW9 . . . . .62 C4
Harrison Ho SE17 . . .151 B2
Harrisons Ct **1**
SE14 . . . . .50 C4
Harrison St WC1 . . . .94 B3
Harris St SE5 . . . . . .48 C3
Harrodian Sch The
SW13 . . . . .46 B3
Harrogate Ct **2**
SE26 . . . . .76 C1
Harrold Ho **1** NW3 . .11 B1
Harroway Rd
SW11 . . . . .167 C2
Harrowby St W1 . . . .102 B2
Harrowgate Ho **22**
E9 . . . . .17 C2
Harrowgate Rd E9 . .18 A1
Harrow La E14 . . . . . .34 B2
Harrow Pl E1 . . . . . .110 B2
Harrow Rd W2 . . . . .101 B3
W2,W9 . . . . .23 C1
Harrow St NW1 . . . .102 A4
Harry Gosling Prim Sch
E1 . . . . .111 B1
Harry Hinkins Ho
SE17 . . . . .151 A1
Harry Lambourn Ho **10**
SE15 . . . . .50 A3
Hartfield Terr **3** E3 . .26 C3
Hartham Cl N7 . . . . .14 A3
Hartham Rd N7 . . . . .14 A3
Hart Ho SW2 . . . . . .74 C3
Hartington Ct SW8 . .172 A4
Chiswick W4 . . . . . .45 A3
Hartington Rd
SW8 . . . . .162 A1
Chiswick W4 . . . . . .45 B3
Hartismere Rd
SW6 . . . . .155 A2
Hartlake Rd E9 . . . . .18 A2
Hartland Rd E15 . . . .19 B4
Hartland Rd NW6 . . .23 B4
London NW1 . . . . . . .13 A1
Hartley Ho SE1 . . . .153 A4
Hartley St E2 . . . . . .25 B2
Hartnoll Ho **4** N7 . .14 C3
Hartnoll St N7 . . . . .14 B3
Harton Lo **2** SE8 . . .51 C2
Harton St SE8 . . . . . .51 C2
Hartopp Ct N16 . . . . .7 A1
Hartopp Point
SW6 . . . . .154 B2
Hartshorn Alley
EC3 . . . . .110 B1
Hart's La SE14 . . . . . .51 A2
Hart St EC3 . . . . . . .124 B4
Hartswood Ho **10**
SW2 . . . . .74 A3

Hartswood Rd W12 . .38 B3
Hartwell St E8 . . . . . .16 B2
Harvard Ct NW6 . . . .11 A3
Harvard Hill W4 . . . . .45 A4
Harvard Ho **3** SE17 .48 A4
Harvard Mans **18**
SW11 . . . . .59 C3
Harvard Rd
London SE13 . . . . . .67 B2
London W4 . . . . .37 A1
London W4 . . . . .37 A1
Harvey Ct SW11 . . . .168 B4
Harvey Ho E1 . . . . . .25 A1
□ London N1 . . . . . .15 A1
Harvey Point **7** E16 .35 C4
Harvey Rd **15** SE5 . .48 C2
Harvey St N1 . . . . . . .87 C3
Harvington Wlk E8 . .16 C1
Harwood Ct N1 . . . . .87 C3
Harwood Ct **1**
SW15 . . . . .57 C3
Harwood Point
SE16 . . . . .41 B4
Harwood Rd SW6 . . .156 A1
Harwood Terr
SW6 . . . . .166 A4
Hascombe Ho **11**
SW15 . . . . .69 A3
Hascombe Terr **2**
SE5 . . . . .48 C1
Haslemere Rd SW4 . .61 C1
Hasker St SW3 . . . .144 B4
Haslam Cl N1 . . . . . .14 C1
Haslam Ho **1** N1 . . .15 B1
Haslam St SE15 . . . . .49 B2
Haslemere Ave
SW18 . . . . .71 A2
Haslemere Ct **5** N16 .7 A3
Haslemere Ind Est
SW18 . . . . .71 A2
Haslemere Rd N8 . . . .5 A4
Hassard St E2 . . . . . .24 B3
Hassett Rd E9 . . . . . .18 A2
Hassop Rd NW2 . . . . .9 C4
Hastings Cl **18** SE15 .49 C3
Hastings Ho **15** W12 .30 A2
Hastings Hos WC1 . . .94 A3
Hastings St WC1 . . . .94 A3
Hatcham Mews Bsns Ctr
SE14 . . . . .50 C2
Hatcham Park Mews
SE14 . . . . .50 C2
Hatcham Park Rd
SE14 . . . . .50 C2
Hatcham Rd SE15 . . .50 B4
Hatchard Rd N19 . . . .5 A2
Hatcliffe Almshouses **8**
SE10 . . . . .43 A1
Hatcliffe St SE10 . . . .43 B1
Hatfield Cl SE14 . . . .50 C3
Hatfield Ct SE3 . . . . .53 C3
Hatfield Ho EC1 . . . .96 C1
Hatfield Rd W4 . . . . .37 C4
Hatfields SE1 . . . . . .121 C2
Hathaway Ho N1 . . . .98 A4
Hatherley Ct W2 . . . .100 A2
Hatherley Gr W2 . . . .100 A2
Hatherley Rd TW9 . . .44 B2
Hatherley St SW1 . . .147 A3
Hathersage Ct N1 . . .15 C3
Hathersley Ho **3**
SW2 . . . . .74 C4

Hathorne Cl **3**
SE15 . . . . .50 A1
Hathway Ho **3**
SW15 . . . . .58 B2
Hathway St **4**
SW15 . . . . .58 B2
Hatley Rd N4,N7 . . . .5 B2
Hat & Mitre Ct EC1 . .96 B1
Hatteraick St **6**
SE16 . . . . .40 B4
Hatton Gdn EC1 . . . .107 C4
Hatton Ho E1 . . . . . .125 C4
Hatton Pl EC1 . . . . . .107 C4
Hatton Row NW8 . . .89 C1
Hatton St NW8 . . . . .89 C1
Hatton Wall EC1 . . . .107 C4
Haunch of Venison Yd
W1 . . . . .104 A1
Hautoville Court Gdns **2**
SE16 . . . . .40 B4
Havana Rd SW18,
SW19 . . . . .70 C2
Havannah St E14 . . .41 C4
Havelock Ct **13** SW12 .73 A4
Havelock St N1 . . . . .84 B4
Havelock Terr
SW8 . . . . .160 B1
Haven Cl SW19 . . . . .69 C1
Havenpool NW8 . . . .78 B3
Haven St **8** NW1 . . .13 A1
Haven The TW9 . . . .54 C4
Havercourt **3** NW3 .12 A2
Haverfield Gdns
TW9 . . . . .44 C3
Haverfield Rd E3 . . .26 A2
Haverhill Rd SW12 . .73 B3
Havering **8** NW1 . . .13 A1
Havering Ho N4 . . . . .6 B4
Havering St E1 . . . . . .32 C3
Haversham Pl N6 . . . .3 B2
Haversham Pl N6 . . . .3 B2
Haverstock Hill
NW3 . . . . .12 B2
Haverstock Rd NW5 .12 C3
Haverstock Sch
NW1 . . . . .12 C2
Haverstock St N1 . . . .86 B1
Havil St SE5 . . . . . . .49 A2
Havisham Ho SE16 . .139 C3
Hawarden Gr SE24 . .75 B4
Hawberry Ho N7 . . . .14 A2
Hawes St N1 . . . . . . .15 A1
Hawgood St E3 . . . . .33 C4
Hawke Ho **7** E1 . . . .25 C1
Hawke Pl **20** SE16 . .40 C4
Hawkesbury Rd
SW15 . . . . .57 A2
Hawkesworth Ho **5**
SW4 . . . . .61 B1
Hawke Twr **4** SE14 .51 A4
Hawk Ho **7** SW11 . .60 A4
Hawkins Ho **3** SE8 .51 C4
Hawkley Gdns SE27 .75 A2
Hawkridge **10** NW5 .12 C2
Hawkshaw Cl **24**
SW2 . . . . .74 A4
Hawkshead
London NW10 . . . . .8 C1
London W4 . . . . .38 A4
Hawkshead Rd
London NW10 . . . . .8 B1
London W4 . . . . .38 A3
Hawkslade Rd SE15 .65 C2
Hawksley Rd N16 . . . .7 A1
Hawks Mews **10**
SE10 . . . . .52 B3
Hawksmoor Mews
E1 . . . . .32 A2
Hawksmoor St **6**
W6 . . . . .47 C4
Hawkstone Rd SE16 .40 B2
Hawkwell Wlk N1 . . .87 A4

Hawley Cres NW1 . . .13 A1
Hawley Inf Sch
NW1 . . . . .13 A1
Hawley Mews **4**
NW1 . . . . .13 A1
Hawley Rd **3** NW1 . .13 A1
Hawley St NW1 . . . . .13 A1
Haworth Ct E15 . . . . .76 B3
Haworth Ho **7** SW2 .62 C1
Hawstead Rd SE6 . . .67 A1
Hawthorn Ave **2** E3 .26 B4
Hawthorn Ct
Putney SW15 . . . . . .57 A4
Richmond TW9 . . . . .45 A2
Hawthorne Ho
SW1 . . . . .147 A1
Hawthorn Rd NW10 . .8 C1
Hawthorn Wlk W10 . .23 A1
Hawtrey Rd NW3 . . . .12 A1
Haycroft Gdns
NW10 . . . . .22 A4
Haycroft Mans
NW10 . . . . .22 A4
Haycroft Rd SW2 . . .62 A2
Hay Currie St E14 . . .34 A3
Hayday Rd E16 . . . . .35 C4
Hayden's Pl W11 . . . .31 B3
Haydon St E1,EC3 . . .124 C4
Haydon Way SW11 . .59 C3
Haydon Wlk E1 . . . . .111 A1
Hayes Ct **28** SW2 . .74 A4
Stretham SW12 . . . .74 A3
Hayes Pl NW1 . . . . . .90 B1
Hayfield Pas E1 . . . . .25 B1
Hay Hill W1 . . . . . . .118 B3
Hayles Bldgs SE11 . .150 A4
Hayles St SE11 . . . . .150 A4
Hayling **20** N16 . . . .16 A4
Haymans Point
SE11 . . . . .148 C2
Haymarket SW1 . . . .119 B3
Haymerle Ho **6**
SE15 . . . . .49 C3
Haymerle Rd SE15 . .49 C4
Haymerle Sch SE15 . .49 C4
Hayne Ho W11 . . . . .112 A2
Haynes Ho **3** E9 . . .17 C2
Hayne St EC1 . . . . . .108 B4
Hay's Galleria SE1 . .124 A2
Hay's La SE1 . . . . . .124 A1
Hay's Mews W1J 118 A2
Hay St E2 . . . . .24 C4
Hayter Ho W12 . . . . .29 C2
Hayter Rd SW2 . . . . .62 B2
Haythorn Ho SW11 . .167 C3
Hayton Cl **11** E8 . . .16 B2
Hayward Ct SW4 . . . .172 B2
Hayward Gallery★ .
SE1 . . . . .121 A2
Hayward Gdns
SW15 . . . . .57 B1
Hayward Ho N1 . . . . .85 B2
Hayward's Pl EC1 . . .96 A2
Haywood Lo **2** N7 . .13 C3
Hazelbourne Rd
SW12 . . . . .61 A1
Hazel Cl London N19 .4 B2
London SE15 . . . . . .49 C1
Hazeldon Rd SE4 . . .66 A2
Hazel Ho
12 London NW3 . .12 B2
London SE4 . . . . . . .66 B4
Hazellville Rd N19 . . .4 C3
Hazelmere Ct **13**
SW2 . . . . .74 B3
Hazelmere Rd NW6 . .23 C4

Hazel Rd NW10 . . . .22 B2
Hazel Way SE1 . . . .152 C2
Hazelwood Cl W5 . .36 A4
Hazelwood Ho **1**
SE8 . . . . .41 A2
Hazelwood Mans
SW6 . . . . .164 C4
Hazlebury Rd SW6 .166 B2
Hazledene Rd W4 . . .45 B4
Hazlewell Rd SW15 .57 B2
Hazlewood Cres
W10 . . . . .23 A1
Hazlewood Twr
W10 . . . . .23 B1
Hazlitt Mews W14 .126 A1
Hazlitt Rd W14 . . . .126 A1
Headbourne Ho
SE1 . . . . .137 C2
Headcorn **10** NW5 . .12 C2
Headfort Pl SW1 . . .131 C3
Headington Rd
SW18 . . . . .71 B2
Headlam Rd SW4 . . .73 C4
Headlam St E1 . . . . .25 A1
Heads Mews W11 . . .31 C3
Head St E1 . . . . . . .32 C3
Heald St SE8,SE14 . .51 C2
Healey St NW1 . . . . .13 A2
Healy Ho **2**
E3 . . . . .26 C1 163 C1
Heanor Ct **4** E5 . . .17 C4
Hearne Rd W4 . . . . .44 C4
Hearn's Bldgs
SE17 . . . . .151 C3
Hearn St EC2 . .24 A1 98 B1
Hearnville Rd SW12 .72 C3
Heart Hospl The
W1 . . . . .103 B3
Heathbrook Prim Sch
SW4 . . . . .170 C1
Heath Brow NW3 . . . .2 B1
Heath Cl NW11 . . . . . .2 B4
Heathcote St WC1 . .94 C3
Heathcroft NW11 . . . .2 A3
Heath Ct London N16 . .6 C3
2 London NW3 . . . .12 B3
Heather Cl SW8 . . . .61 A4
Heather Ct SW4 . . . .172 B3
Heather Ho **7** E14 . .34 B3
Heatherley Ct N16 . . .7 C1
Heatherley Sch of Fine
Art SW10 . . . . . . .157 A1
Heather Lo N16 . . . . .7 A3
Heather Wlk W10 . . .23 A1
Heathfield Ave
SW18 . . . . .71 C4
Heathfield Ct
5 London W4 . . . . .37 C1
Wandsworth SW18 . . .71 C4
Heathfield Gdns
London SW18 . . . . . .59 C1
London W4 . . . . .37 B1
Heathfield Ho SE3 . . .53 A1
Heathfield Pk NW2 . . .9 B2
Heathfield Rd
London SW18 . . . . . .59 C1
London W3 . . . . .37 A4
Heathfield Sq SW18 .71 C4
Heathfield Terr W4 . .37 C1
Heathgate Pl NW3 . .12 B4
Heath Hurst Rd
NW3 . . . . .12 A4
Heath La SE3 . . . . . .52 C1
Heath Mead SW19 . . .69 C1

Heath Mans
4 London NW3 . . . .11 B4
Putney SW15 . . . . . .57 C1
Heathman's Rd
SW6 . . . . .165 A3
Heath Mead SW15 . .68 C2
Heathmere Prim Sch
SW15 . . . . .68 C3
Heath Park Gdns
NW3 . . . . .11 B4
Heathpool Ct **8** E1 . .25 A1
Heath Rd SW8 . . . .170 B1
Heath Rise SW15 . . .57 C1
Heath Royal SW15 . .57 C1
Heathshot **7** TW10 .54 A1
Heathside NW3 . . . .11 C4
Heathside Prep Sch
NW3 . . . . .11 B4
Heath St NW3 . . . . . .2 B1
Heathstan Rd W12 . .29 C3
Heathview **8** NW5 . .12 C4
Heath View NW5 . . .12 C4
Heathview Ct SW19 .69 C2
Heathview Gdns
SW15 . . . . .69 B4
Heathville Rd N4,N19 .5 A4
Heathwall St SW11 . .60 B4
Heathway **6** SE3 . . .53 B3
Greenwich SE3 . . . . .53 C3
Heathway Ct NW3 . . .1 B2
Heathwood Ct
SW12 . . . . .73 B3
Heaton Ho SW10 . . .157 A4
1 London SE15 . . . .50 A1
Heaton Rd SE15 . . . .50 A1
Heaver Rd **23** SW11 .59 C4
Hebden Ct **2** E2 . . .24 B4
Hebdon Rd SW17 . . .72 A1
Heber Prim Sch
SE22 . . . . .64 B1
Heber Rd NW2 . . . . . .9 C4
London SE22 . . . . . .64 B1
Hebron Rd W6 . . . . .39 A3
Heckfield Pl SW6 . . .155 B1
Heckford St E1 . . . . .32 C2
Hector Ct
London SW9 . . . . . .173 B4
Putney SW15 . . . . . .57 C2
Hector Ho **8** E2 . . .25 A3
Heddington Gr N7 . .14 B3
Heddon St W1 . . . . .118 C4
Hedger's Gr E9 . . . . .18 A2
Hedger St SE11 . . . .150 A4
Hedingham Cl **4**
N1 . . . . .15 B1
Hedley Cl SW15 . . . .57 C1
Hedley Ho E14 . . . . .42 B3
Hedley Row N5,N16 .15 C3
Hedsor Ho **2**
E2 . . . . .98 C2
Heidegger Cres
SW13 . . . . .47 A3
Heights The NW3 . . .11 B4
Heiron St SE17 . . . . .48 A4
Helby Rd SW4 . . . . .61 C1
Heldar Ct SE1 . . . . .137 C3
Helena Rd NW10 . . . . .9 A3
Helena Sq **15** SE16 . .33 A2
Helen Gladstone Ho
SE1 . . . . .136 A4
Helen Ho **9** E2 . . . .25 A3
Helen Mackay Ho **9**
E14 . . . . .34 C3
Helen Peele Cotts **10**
SE16 . . . . .40 B3
Helenslea Ave NW11 . .1 C3
Helen's Pl E2 . . . . . .25 B2
Helen Taylor Ho **6**
SE16 . . . . .153 B4

Heliport Est The
SW11 . . . . .167 B1
Helix Gdns SW2 . . . .62 B1
Helix Rd SW2 . . . . . .62 B1
Hellenic Coll of London
SW1 . . . . .130 C1
Hellings St E1 . . . . .125 C1
Helmet Row EC1 . . . .97 A2
Helmsdale Ho NW6 . .78 A1
Helmsley Pl E8 . . . . .17 A1
Helmsley St **7** E8 . .17 A1
Helperby Rd NW10 . . .8 A1
Helsby Ct NW8 . . . . .89 B2
Helston NW1 . . . . . .83 A2
Helston Ho SE11 . . .149 C2
Hemans St SW8 . . . .161 C1
Hemans St Est SW8 .161 C1
Hemberton Rd SW9 . .62 A4
Hemingford Rd N1 . .85 A4
Hemlock Rd W12 . . .29 B2
Hemming St
E1 . . . . .24 C1 99 C1
Hemp Wlk SE17 . . . .151 C4
Hemstal Rd NW6 . . .10 C1
Hemsworth Ct N1 . . .24 A3
Hemsworth St N1 . . .24 A3
Hemus Pl SW3 . . . .144 B1
Henchman St W12 . .29 B3
Henderson Ct
8 SE14 . . . . .50 C4
London NW3 . . . . . . .11 C3
Henderson Dr NW8 . .89 B2
Henderson Rd
SW18 . . . . .72 A4
Hendham Rd SW17 . .72 A4
Hendre Ho SE1 . . . .152 B3
Hendre Rd SE1 . . . .152 B3
Hendrick Ave SW12 . .72 B4
Heneage La EC3 . . . .110 B1
Heneage Pl EC3 . . . .110 B1
Heneage St E1 . . . . .111 A4
Henfield Cl N19 . . . . .4 C3
Henley Cl SE16 . . . . .40 B4
Henley Ct
London NW2 . . . . .9 C2
London SE15 . . . . . .64 C4
Henley Dr SE1 . . . . .153 A4
Henley Ho E2 . . . . . .99 A2
Henley Prior N1 . . . . .84 C1
Henley Rd NW10 . . . .22 B4
Henley St SW11 . . . .169 C2
Henniker Mews
SW3 . . . . .157 B4
Henniker Rd E15 . . . .19 C3
Henning St SW11 . . .168 A3
Henrietta Cl SE8 . . . .51 C4
Henrietta Ho **11** W6 .39 B1
Henrietta Mews
WC1 . . . . .94 B2
Henrietta Pl W1 . . . .104 A2
Henrietta St E15 . . . .76 B3
London WC2 . . . . . .120 B4
Henriques St E1 . . . .111 C1
Henry Cavendish Prim
Sch SW12 . . . . .73 B3
Henry Compton Sec Sch
SW6 . . . . .164 A4
Henry Dent Cl SE5 . . .63 C4
Henry Dickens Ct
W11 . . . . .112 A2
Henry Fawcett Prim Sch
SE11 . . . . .163 B4
Henry Ho NW8 . . . . .80 A2
SE1 . . . . .121 C1
SW8 . . . . .162 A2

Henry Jackson Ho
SW15 . . . . .57 C4
Henry Jackson Rd
SW15 . . . . .57 C4
Henry Rd N4 . . . . . . .6 B3
Henryson Rd SE4 . . .66 C2
Henry Wise Ho
SW1 . . . . .147 A3
Henshall Point **10**
E3 . . . . .27 A2
Henshall St N1 . . . . .15 C2
Henshaw St SE17 . . .151 B4
Henslowe Rd SE22 . .64 C2
Henslow Ho **11**
SE15 . . . . .49 C3
Henson Ave NW2 . . . .9 B3
Henson Ct **3** N5 . . .15 B4
Henty Cl SW11 . . . .168 B4
Henty Wlk SW15 . . .57 A2
Hepburn Mews
SW11 . . . . .60 B2
Hepplestone Cl
SW15 . . . . .57 A1
Hepscott Rd E8 . . . .18 C1
Hepworth Ct N1 . . . .86 B4
Hera Ct **2** E14 . . . . .41 C2
Heralds Pl SE11 . . . .150 A4
Herald St **5** E2 . . . .25 A1
Herbal Hill EC1 . . . . .95 C1
Herbert Chapman Ct
N5 . . . . .15 A4
Herbert Cres SW1 . . .131 A2
Herbert Gdns
Chiswick W4 . . . . . . .45 A4
London NW10 . . . . . .22 A3
Herbert Ho E1 . . . . .110 C2
Herbert Mews **13**
SW2 . . . . .62 C1
Herbert Morrison Ho
SW6 . . . . .154 C3
Herbert Morrison Prim
Sch SW8 . . . . .162 B1
Herbert St NW5 . . . .12 C2
Herbrand Est WC1 . . .94 A2
Herbrand St WC1 . . . .94 A2
Hercules Pl N7 . . . . . .5 A1
Hercules Rd SE1 . . . .135 A1
Hercules St N7 . . . . . .5 A1
Hereford Bldgs
SW3 . . . . .157 C4
Hereford Ho SW10 . .156 B2
SW3 . . . . .130 B2
28 London SE5 . . . .48 B1
London SW2 . . . . . . .62 C3
Hereford Mans **11**
W2 . . . . .31 C3
Hereford Mews **11**
W2 . . . . .31 C3
Hereford Pl SE14 . . . .51 B3
Hereford Rd
W2 . . . . . .31 C4 113 C4
London W3 . . . . .28 B2
Hereford Retreat **5**
SE15 . . . . .49 C3
Hereford Sq SW7 . . .143 A3
Hereford St E2 . . . . . .99 C3
Hereward House Sch
NW3 . . . . .11 C2
Hereward Rd SW17 . .72 B1
Heritage Cl SW9 . . . .63 A4
Heritage Ct SE8 . . . .40 C1
Heritage Ho **22**
SW19 . . . . .69 C3
Hermes Cl **9** W9 . . .23 C1
Hermes Ct SW9 . . . .173 B4
Hermes St N1 . . . . . .85 B1
Herm Ho **10** N1 . . . .15 B2

Hermitage Ct E1 . . .125 C1
2 NW2 . . . . .1 C1
Hermitage Gdns
NW2 . . . . .1 C1
Hermitage La NW2 . . .1 C1
Hermitage Prim Sch
E1 . . . . .125 C2
Hermitage Row **9**
E8 . . . . .16 C3
Hermitage St W2 . . .101 B3
Hermitage The
Barnes SW13 . . . . . .46 B2
Richmond TW10 . . . .54 A2
Hermitage Wall
E1 . . . . .125 C1
Hermit Pl NW6 . . . . .78 A3
Hermit Rd E16 . . . . . .96 A4
Herndon Rd SW18 . .59 B2
Herne Cl NW10 . . . . . .8 A3
Herne Hill SE24 . . . . .63 B3
Herne Hill Ho SE24 . .63 A1
Herne Hill Mans
SE24 . . . . .63 B1
Herne Hill Rd SE24 . .63 B3
Herne Hill Sta SE24 . .63 A1
Herne Hill Stad
SE24 . . . . .63 C1
Herne Pl SE24 . . . . . .63 A2
Heron Cl NW10 . . . . . .8 A2
Heron Ct **14** E14 . . .42 B3
6 Dulwich SE21 . . .75 C2
Herondale Ave
SW18 . . . . .72 A3
Heron Dr N4 . . . . .6 B2
Herongate N1 . . . . . .87 A4
Heron Ho NW8 . . . . .80 A1
SW11 . . . . .168 A4
London SE15 . . . . . .49 B2
Heron Ind Est E15 . .27 A3
Heron Pl SE16 . . . . .33 A1
W1 . . . . .103 C2
Heron Quays E14 . . .33 C1
Heron Quays Sta
E14 . . . . .33 C1
Heron Rd SE24 . . . . .63 B3
Heron Trad Est W3 . .28 A4
Herrick Ho **10** SE5 . .48 C3
1 London N16 . . . .15 C4
Herrick Rd N5 . . . . . .6 B1
Herrick St SW1 . . . .147 C3
Herries St W10 . . . . .23 A3
Hersant Cl NW10 . . .21 C4
Herschell's Mews
SE5 . . . . .63 B4
Hersham Cl SW15 . . .68 C4
Hershell Ct **1**
SW14 . . . . .55 A3
Hertford Ave SW14 . .56 A3
Hertford Ct **16**
SW11 . . . . .60 A4
Hertford Lo **10**
SW19 . . . . .70 A3
Hertford Pl W1 . . . . .93 A1
Hertford Rd N1 . . . . .24 A4
Hertford St W1 . . . .118 A1
Hertmitage The **4**
SE13 . . . . .52 B1
Hertslet Rd N7 . . . . . .5 B1
Hertsmere Rd E14 . .33 C2
Hesewall Ct SW4 . . .171 A1
Hesketh Pl W11 . . . .112 A3
Heslop Ct **3** SW12 . .72 C3
Heslop Rd SW12 . . . .72 B3
Hesper Mews SW5 . .142 A3
Hesperus Cres E14 . .42 A2
Hessel Rd W14 . . . . .140 B2
Hessel St E1 . . . . . . .32 A3

Hestercombe Ave
SW6 .... **164** B3
Hester Rd SW11 ..**158** A1
Hester Terr TW9 ....54 C4
Heston Ho
 5 London SE8 .....51 C2
 London W4 ....37 A1
Heston St SE14 .....51 C2
Hetherington Rd
SW2,SW4 ....62 A3
Hethpool Ho W2 ..**89** B1
Hethway Rd W12 ...39 A4
Hevelius Cl SE10 ...43 B1
Hever Ho SE15 ......50 C2
Heversham Ho SE15 50 C2
Hewer 5 SW4 ......61 B2
Hewer St W10 ......30 C4
Hewett St
EC2 ....24 A1 **98** B1
Hewison St E3 ......26 B3
Hewlett Rd E3 ......26 A3
Hewling Ho 5 N16 66 A4
Hewtt Ho SW15 ....47 B1
Hexagon The N6 ....3 B3
Hexham Rd SE27 ..75 B2
Hey Bridge 9 NW1 ..13 A2
Heydon Ho 5 SW8 50 B2
Heyford Ave SW8 ..162 B2
Heygate St SE17 ..**151** A4
Heylyn Sq E3 ......26 B2
Heysham La NW3 ...2 A1
Heythorp St SW18 .70 B2
Heywood Ho
 7 SE4 ....50 C4
 6 London SW2 ....62 C1
Heyworth Rd E5 ...17 A4
Hibbert St SW11 ....59 B4
Hichisson Rd SE15 .65 B2
Hickes Ho 6 NW6 .11 C1
Hickey's Almshouses 7
TW9 ....54 B3
Hickin 2 E14 ....42 B3
Hickleton NW1 .....**83** A3
Hickling Ho 9 SE16 40 A3
Hickmore Wlk SW4 61 B4
Hicks Cl SW11 ......60 A4
Hicks St SE8 ....41 A1
Hide Pl SW1 ....**147** B3
Hide Twr SW1 .....**147** B3
Hieover SE21 ....75 B2
Higgins Ho 7 N1 ..24 A4
Higginson Ho
NW3 ....12 B1
Higgs Ind Est 8
SE24 ....63 A4
Highbridge Ct 13
SE14 ....50 B3
High Bridge Wharf
SE10 ....42 C1
Highbury (Arsenal FC)
N5 ....7 B1
Highbury Cnr N5 ...15 A2
Highbury Corner
N5 ....15 A2
Highbury Cres N5 ..14 C3
Highbury Fields Sch
N5 ....15 A3
Highbury Gr N5 ...15 A3
Highbury Grange
N5 ....15 B4
Highbury Grove Ct
N5 ....15 A3
Highbury Grove Sch
N5 ....15 A4
Highbury Hill N5 ..15 A4

Highbury & Islington Sta
N1 ....15 A2
Highbury New Pk
N5 ....15 B4
Highbury Pk N5 ....15 A4
Highbury Pl N5 ....15 A3
Highbury Quadrant
N5 ....15 B4
Highbury Quadrant Prim
Sch N5 ....15 B4
Highbury Station Rd
N1 ....14 C2
Highbury Terr N5 ..15 A3
Highbury Terrace Mews
N5 ....15 A3
Highcliffe Dr SW15 .56 B1
Highcroft Rd N19 ...5 A4
Highcross Way 4
SW15 ....68 C3
Highdown Rd SW15 .57 A1
Highenden Ho NW8 **90** A2
Highfield Ave NW11 ..1 A4
Highfield Cl SE13 ...67 C1
Highfield Gr N6 .....3 B4
Highfield Rd W3 ...28 B3
Highfield Sch SW18 72 A4
Highgate Archway
N6 ....4 B3
Highgate Ave N6 ....4 A4
Highgate Cemetery★
N19 ....4 A2
Highgate Cl N6 .....3 C4
Highgate High St N6 4 A3
Highgate Hill N19 ..4 B3
Highgate Ho 3
SE26 ....76 C1
Highgate Jun Sch N6 3 B4
Highgate Rd NW5 ..13 A4
Highgate Sch N6 ....3 C4
Highgate West Hill
N6 ....3 C3
Highgrove Point 2
NW3 ....11 B4
High Holborn WC1 **106** C3
Highlands Ave W3 .28 B2
Highlands Cl N4 ....5 A4
Highlands Heath
SW15 ....69 B4
Highlever Rd W10 ..30 B4
Highmore Rd SE3 ..53 A3
High Park Ave TW9 44 C2
High Park Rd TW9 44 C2
High Par The SW16 .74 A1
High Point N6 ....3 C4
High Rd NW10 .....22 A3
Highshore Rd SE15 .49 B1
Highshore Sch SE15 49 B2
High St E15 ....27 B4
 Acton W3 ....28 A1
 Brentford TW8 .....44 A4
High Street Harlesden
NW10 ....21 B3
High Street Kensington
Sta W8 ....**128** A3
High The SW16 ....74 A1
High Timber St
EC4 ....**122** C4
High Trees SW2 ....74 C3
Hightrees Ho SW12 60 C1
Highview N8 ....5 A4
Highview Ct 2
SW19 ....70 A3
High View Prim Sch
SW11 ....59 C3
Highway Bsns Pk The 7
E1 ....32 C2

Highway The E1 ....32 B2
Highway Trad Ctr The 8
E1 ....32 C2
Highwood Rd N19 ...5 A1
Highworth St NW1 **102** B4
Hilary Cl SW6 ......**156** A2
Hilary Ho N1 ....**29** B2
Hilborough Ct 1
E8 ....24 B4
Hilborough Rd 1
E8 ....16 B1
Hilda Terr SW9 ....**173** C2
Hildreth Ho N1 ....**20** C2
Hildred Ho NW1 ...**146** A4
Hildreth St SW12 ..73 A3
Hildreth Street Mews 2
SW12 ....73 A3
Hildyard Rd SW6 ..**155** C4
Hiley Rd NW10 ....22 B2
Hilgrove Rd NW6 ..11 B1
Hillary Ho E14 .....34 B4
Hillbeck Cl SE15 ...50 B3
Hillbrow 7 N4 .....5 B4
Hillbury Rd SW17 ..73 A1
Hillcourt Rd SE22 ..65 A1
Hillcrest W11 ....**112** C3
 London N6 ....3 C4
 London SE24 ......63 C3
Hillcrest Ct NW2 ...10 A3
Hillcrest Rd W3 .....28 A1
Hill Ct London NW3 ..12 A4
 Putney SW15 ......57 C2
Hilldrop Cres N7 ..13 C3
Hilldrop Est 1 N7 ..13 C3
Hilldrop La N7 ......13 C3
Hilldrop Rd N7 .....13 C3
Hillersdon Ave
SW13 ....46 C1
Hillersdon Ho
SW1 ....**146** A2
Hillery Cl SE17 ....**151** C3
Hill Farm Rd W10 .30 C4
Hillfield Ct NW3 ...12 A3
Hillfield Ho N5 .....15 B3
Hillfield Mans NW3 12 A3
Hillfield Rd NW6 ...10 C3
Hillgate Pl
 W8 ....31 C1 **113** B2
 Balham SW12 .....73 A4
Hillgate St W8 ....**113** B2
Hill House Sch
SW1 ....**130** C2
Hilliard Ho 1 E1 ...32 A1
Hilliard's Ct 1 E1 ..32 B1
Hillier Ho 1 NW1 ..13 C1
Hillier Rd SW11 ....60 B1
Hillingdon St SE17 48 A4
Hill Lo SW11 ....59 C3
Hillman St E8 ....17 A2
Hillmarton Rd N7 ..14 A3
Hillmead Dr SW9 ..63 A3
Hill Mead Prim Sch
SW9 ....63 A3
Hillmore Ct SE13 ..67 C4
Hill Rd NW8 ....79 A1
Hillrise Mans N19 ..5 A4
Hillrise Rd N19 .....5 A4
Hillsboro Rd SE22 ..64 A2
Hillsborough Ct 6
NW6 ....78 A3
Hillside NW10 ......20 C4
 London NW8 ......78 B3
 London NW3 ......11 B3
Hillside Gdns SW2 .74 C2
Hillside Rd SW2 ...74 C2

Hillsleigh Rd
W14 ....31 B1 **113** A2
Hillstone Ct 3 E3 ..27 A1
Hilltop Ct
 London NW8 ....11 B1
 12 London SE18 ..59 C3
Hilltop Ho 7 N6 .....4 C4
Hilltop Rd NW6 ....10 C1
Hillway N6 ....3 C2
Hill Wood Ho NW1 83 A1
Hillworth Rd SW2 ..74 C4
Hillyard St SW9 ..**173** B3
Hillyfield Cl E9 .....18 A3
Hilly Fields Cres
SE4 ....66 C4
Hilsea Point 7
SW15 ....69 A3
Hilsea St E5 ....17 B4
Hilton Ho London N7 ..14 A4
 6 London SE4 ....65 C3
Hilversum Cres 10
SE22 ....64 A2
Hinckley Rd SE15 ..64 C3
Hind Ct EC4 ....107 C1
Hinde Mews 2 W1 103 C2
Hinde St W1 ....103 C2
Hind Gr E14 ....33 C3
Hindhead Point 6
SW15 ....69 A3
Hind Ho 19 SE14 ..50 C4
 London N7 ....14 C4
Hindle Ho E8 ......16 B3
Hindley Ho N7 .....5 B1
Hindlip Ho SW8 ...**171** B3
Hindmans Rd SE22 64 C2
Hindmarsh Cl E1 ..125 C4
Hindrey Rd E5 .....17 A3
Hinstock NW6 .....78 A4
Hinton Rd SE24 ....63 A3
Hippodrome Mews
W11 ....112 A3
Hippodrome Pl
W11 ....112 A3
Hitchin Sq E3 ......26 A3
Hitherfield Prim Sch
SW2 ....74 C2
Hitherfield Rd
SW16,SW27 ....74 C2
Hither Green La
SE13 ....67 C1
Hither Green Prim Sch
SE13 ....67 C1
Hitherlands SW12 ..73 A2
HM Prison Wormwood
Scrubs W12 ....29 C3
Hoadly Rd SW16 ..73 C2
Hobart Pl SW1 ....**132** A2
Hobbes Wlk SW15 57 A2
Hobb's Ct SE1 ....**139** A4
Hobbs' Pl N1 ....24 A4
Hobday St E14 .....34 A3
Hobsons Pl E1 ....111 B4
Hobury St SW10 ..157 B3
Hocker St E2 ......98 C3
Hockley Ho 4 E9 ..17 B2
Hockliffe Ho W10 ..30 B4
Hockney Ct 1 SE16 40 A1
Hockworth Ho 7
N16 ....6 C3
Hocroft Ave NW2 ...1 B1
Hocroft Ct NW2 .....1 B1
Hocroft Rd NW2 ....1 B1
Hocroft Wlk NW2 ...1 B1
Hodford Rd NW11 ...1 B3

Hodister Cl 20 SE5 .48 B3
Hodnet Gr SE16 ....40 C2
Hoffman Sq N1 .....97 C4
Hofland Rd W14 ..126 A2
Hogan Mews 2 W2 101 B4
Hogan Way E5 ......7 C2
Hogarth Bsns Pk
W4 ....46 A4
Hogarth Ct E1 ....111 C1
 EC3 ....124 B4
 6 London NW1 .....13 B1
Hogarth Ho SW1 .147 C3
Hogarth Ind Est
NW10 ....21 C1
Hogarth La W4 .....46 A4
Hogarth Pl SW5 ..142 A3
Hogarth Prim Sch
W4 ....38 A1
Hogarth Rd SW5 .142 A3
Hogarth Roundabout
W4 ....46 A4
Holbeach Mews 1
SW12 ....73 A3
Holbeach Rd SE6 ..49 C3
Holbein Ho SW1 .145 B2
Holbein Mews
SW1 ....145 B2
Holbein Pl SW1 ...145 B3
Holberton Gdns
NW10 ....22 A2
Holborn EC1 ......107 C3
Holborn Cir EC1 ..107 C3
Holborn Pl WC1 ..106 C3
Holborn Sta WC1 ..106 B3
Holbrook Cl N19 ....4 A3
Holbrooke Ct N7 ...14 A4
Holbrook Ho
 London W3 ....28 C4
 5 Streatham SW2 ..74 B3
Holburn 33 N1 ......24 A4
Holburn Viaduct
EC1 ....108 A3
Holcombe Ho SW9 62 A4
Holcombe St W6 ...39 A2
Holcroft Ct W1 ....104 C4
Holcroft Ho
 London SE10 ....52 B2
 London SW11 .....59 C4
Holcroft Rd E9 .....17 B1
Holden Ho N1 ......86 C3
 12 SE8 ....51 C3
Holden St SW11 ..169 B1
Holdernesse Rd 6
SW17 ....72 C2
Holderness Ho SE5 64 A4
Holdsworth Ho 5
SW2 ....74 C4
Holford Ho 6 SE16 40 A2
 WC1 ....95 A4
Holford Pl WC1 ....95 A4
Holford St WC1 ....95 A4
Holgate Ave SW11 59 C4
Holland Gr SW9 ..163 C1
Holland Park
 W11 ....31 B1 112 C1
Holland Park Ave
 W11 ....112 B2
 W14 ....126 B4
Holland Park Gdns
W14 ....126 A4
Holland Park Mews
W11 ....31 B1 112 C1

Holland Park Rd
W14 . . . .**127** A1
Holland Park Rdbt
W14 . . . .**39** C4
Holland Park Sch
W8 . . . .**127** A4
Holland Park Sta
W11 . . . .**B1 112** C1
Holland Pl W8 . . . .**128** A4
Holland Rd W14 . . . . . .**126** B2
London NW10 . . . .**22** A3
Holland Rise Ho
SW9 . . . .**163** A1
Holland St SE1 . . . .**122** B2
W8 . . . .**127** C4
Holland Villas Rd
W14 . . . .**126** A3
Holland Wlk N19 . . . .**4** C3
W8 . . . .**127** A3
Hollar Rd N16 . . . .**7** B1
Hollen St W1 . . . .**105** B2
Holles Ho SW9 . . . .**173** B2
Holles St W1 . . . .**104** B2
Holley Rd W3 . . . .**38** A4
Holliday Sq 7
SW11 . . . .**59** C4
Hollies Way 1
SW12 . . . .**72** C4
Hollingbourne Rd
SE24 . . . .**63** B2
Hollins Ho N7 . . . .**14** A4
Hollisfield WC1 . . . .**94** B3
Holloway Rd
London N19 . . . .**4** C2
London N7 . . . .**14** B4
Holloway Road Sta
N7 . . . .**14** B3
Holloway Rd N7 . . . .**13** C3
Holly Berry La 6
NW3 . . . .**11** B4
Hollybush Gdns E2 . . . .**25** A2
Holly Bush Hill 2
NW3 . . . .**11** B4
Hollybush Ho 23 E2 . . . .**25** A2
Holly Bush Vale 9
NW3 . . . .**11** B4
Holly Cl NW10 . . . .**8** A1
Hollycroft Ave NW3 . . . .**1** C1
Holly Dale Prim Sch
. . . .**50** B1
Hollydale Rd SE15 . . . . .**50** B1
Hollydene
London SE13 . . . .**67** C1
5 London SE15 . . . . . .**50** A2
Holly Gr SE15 . . . .**49** C1
Holly Hedge Terr
SE13 . . . .**67** C2
Holly Hill NW3 . . . .**11** B4
Holly Lo SE13 . . . .**67** C3
Holly Lodge Gdns N6 . . .**3** C3
Holly Lodge Mans
N6 . . . .**3** C2
Holly Mews SW10 . . . .**143** A1
Holly Mount NW3 . . . . . .**11** B4
Hollymount Cl 9
SE10 . . . .**52** B2
Holly Park Est N4 . . . . . .**5** B4
Holly Pk N4 . . . .**5** B4
Holly Pl NW3 . . . .**11** B4
Holly Rd W4 . . . .**37** C2
Holly St E8 . . . .**16** B1
Holly Terr N6 . . . .**3** C3
Hollytree Cl SW19 . . . . .**69** C3
Holly Tree Ho SE4 . . . . . .**66** B4
Holly Village N6 . . . .**4** A2

Hollwell Row
EC2 . . . .**24** A1 **98** A1
Holly Wlk NW3 . . . .**11** B4
Hollywood Mews
SW10 . . . .**156** C4
Hollywood Rd
SW10 . . . .**156** C4
Holman Ho 2 E2 . . . . . .**25** C2
Holman Hunt Ho
W14 . . . .**140** A1
Holmbrook NW1 . . . .**82** C2
Holmbury Ct SW17 . . . . .**72** B1
Holmbury Ho SW9 . . . . .**173** B2
Holmbush Rd SW15 . . . .**58** A1
Holmcote Gdns N5 . . . . .**15** B3
Holmdale Rd N16 . . . . . .**10** C3
Holmdene Ave SE24 . . . .**63** B2
Holmead Rd SW6 . . . . . .**156** B1
Holmefield Ho W10 . . . . .**23** A1
Holmes Ct
London SW4 . . . .**172** A2
17 London W4 . . . .**38** A2
Holmesdale Ave
SW14 . . . .**55** A3
Holmesdale Ho
London N6 . . . .**4** A4
Richmond TW9 . . . .**44** B2
Holmesdale Rd
London N6 . . . .**4** A4
Holmesley Rd SE23 . . . .**66** A1
Holmes Pl SW10 . . . . . .**157** A4
Holmes Rd NW5 . . . .**13** A3
Holmes Terr SE1 . . . . . .**135** B4
Holmewood Gdns
SW2 . . . .**74** B4
Holmewood Rd
SW2 . . . .**74** B4
Holmfield Ct 4
NW3 . . . .**12** A2
Holmhurst SE13 . . . .**67** C1
Holmleigh Prim Sch
N16 . . . .**7** A3
Holmleigh Rd N16 . . . .**7** A3
Holm Oak Cl SW15 . . . . .**58** B1
Holmsbury Ho 6
N7 . . . .**13** C3
Holmside Ct
E14 . . . .**34** A2
Holmside Ct SW12 . . . . .**60** C1
Holmside Rd SW12 . . . . .**60** C1
Holmsley Ho SW15 . . . . .**68** B4
Holm Wlk SE3 . . . .**53** C1
Holmwood Ct 3 N16 . . . .**7** B4
Holocaust Meml Gdn
W2 . . . .**130** C3
Holroyd Rd SW15 . . . . . .**57** B2
Holsgrove Ct W3 . . . .**29** A1
Holst Mans SW13 . . . . . .**47** B3
Holsworthy Ho 40
E3 . . . .**27** A2
Holt Ct E15 . . . .**76** B3
Holt Ho SW2 . . . .**62** C1
Holton St E1 . . . .**25** C1
Holwood Pl 7 SW4 . . . . .**61** C3
Holybourne Ave
SW15 . . . .**68** C4
Holy Cross RC Sch
SW6 . . . .**165** B3
Holy Family RC Prim
Sch **34** A2
Holy Ghost RC Prim Sch
. . . .**72** C1
Holyhead Cl E3 . . . .**26** C2
Holyoake Ct SE16 . . . . . .**41** B4
Holyoak Rd SE11 . . . . . .**150** B3
Holyport Rd SW6 . . . .**47** C3

Holyrood Ho N4 . . . .**6** A3
Holyrood Mews 11
E16 . . . .**35** C1
Holyrood St SE1 . . . . . .**124** A1
Holy Trinity CE Inf Sch
. . . .**77** B2
Holy Trinity CE JMI Sch
E8 . . . .**16** B2
Holy Trinity CE Jun Sch
TW10 . . . .**54** A2
Holy Trinity CE Prim Sch
SW1 . . . .**145** A4
SW1 . . . .**145** B4
London SW2 . . . .**74** B4
Streatham SW2 . . . .**74** B4
Holy Trinity & St Silas
CE Prim Sch NW1 . . . . . .**13** A1
Holywell Cl 3 SE16 . . . . .**40** A1
SE3 . . . .**53** C4
Holywell La EC2 . . . .**98** B2
Homan Ho 6 SW4 . . . . . .**73** C4
Homefield Ave W4 . . . . . .**38** B1
Homefield St 11 N1 . . . . .**24** A3
Homeleigh Ct 8
SW16 . . . .**74** A1
Homeleigh Rd SE15 . . . .**65** C2
Homemead SW12 . . . . . .**73** A2
Home Office SW1 . . . . . .**133** C2
Home Park Rd
SW19 . . . .**70** B1
Homer Dr E14 . . . .**41** C2
Homer Rd E9 . . . .**18** A2
Homer Row W1 . . . .**102** B3
Homer St W1 . . . .**102** B3
Homerton Coll of
Technology E9 . . . .**17** B3
Homerton Gr E9 . . . .**17** C3
Homerton High St
E9 . . . .**17** C3
Homerton Hospl E9 . . . .**17** C3
Homerton Rd E9 . . . .**18** B3
Homerton Row E9 . . . . . .**17** C3
Homerton Sta E9 . . . .**17** C2
Homerton Terr E9 . . . . . .**17** B2
Homestall Rd SE22 . . . . .**65** B2
Homestead Rd
SW6 . . . .**155** A1
Homewoods 2
SW12 . . . .**73** B4
Homildon Ho 10
SE26 . . . .**76** C1
Honduras St EC1 . . . .**96** C2
Honeybourne Rd
NW6 . . . .**11** A3
Honeybrook Rd
SW12,SW4 . . . .**73** B4
Honeyfield Ho 2 N4 . . . . .**6** B4
Honey La EC2 . . . .**109** A1
Honeyman Cl NW6 . . . . . .**9** C1
Honeywell Jun & Inf
Schs SW11 . . . .**60** B1
Honeywell Inf Sch SW11 .**60** B1
Honeywell Rd 5
SW11 . . . .**49** C2
Honeywood Rd
NW10 . . . .**21** B3
Honiton Gdns 1
SE15 . . . .**50** B1
Honiton Ho 30 SE5 . . . . .**48** B1
Honiton Rd NW6 . . . .**23** B3
Honor Oak Park Sta
SE23 . . . .**65** C1
Honor Oak Pk SE23 . . . .**65** C1
Honor Oak Rise
SE23 . . . .**65** B1
Honwell Ho W2 . . . .**31** C4

Hood Ave SW14 . . . .**55** B2
Hood Ct N7 . . . .**5** B1
Hood Ho 17 SE5 . . . .**48** C3
Hooke Ct SE10 . . . .**52** B2
Hooke Ho 30 E3 . . . .**26** A3
Hookham Ct SW8 . . . . . .**171** B4
Hooks Cl SE15 . . . .**50** A2
Hooper Ho 3 SW18 . . . . .**58** B2
Hooper Rd E16 . . . .**35** C3
Hooper St E1 . . . .**111** B1
Hooper's Mews 4
W3 . . . .**28** B1
Hoop La NW11 . . . .**1** C4
Hope Cl
2 Brentford TW8 . . . .**36** A1
London N1 . . . .**15** B2
Hopefield Ave NW6 . . . . .**23** A3
Hope St SW11 . . . .**59** C4
Hopetown St E1 . . . .**111** A3
Hopewell St SE5 . . . .**48** C3
Hop Gdns WC2 . . . .**120** A3
Hopgood St W12 . . . .**30** B1
Hopkins Ho 12 E14 . . . . .**33** C3
Hopkinson Ho
SW11 . . . .**169** B2
Hopkins's Pl NW1 . . . . . .**81** B4
Hopkins St W1 . . . .**105** B1
Hopping La N1 . . . .**15** A2
Hopton Ho 5 SW9 . . . . . .**48** A1
Hopton's Gdns SE1 . . . .**122** B2
Hopton St SE1 . . . .**122** B2
Hopwood Cl SW17 . . . . . .**71** B1
Hopwood Rd SE17 . . . . . .**48** C4
Hopwood Wlk E8 . . . .**16** C1
Horatio Ho 13 E2 . . . .**24** B3
Horatio Pl E14 . . . .**34** B1
Horatio St 12 E2 . . . .**24** B3
Horbury Cres
W11 . . . .**31** C2 **113** B3
Horbury Mews
W11 . . . .**31** B2 **113** A3
Horder Rd SW6 . . . .**164** B3
Hordle Prom E 14
SE15 . . . .**49** B3
Hordle Prom N 3
SE15 . . . .**49** B3
Hordle Prom S 7
SE15 . . . .**49** C3
Horizon Bldg 7
E14 . . . .**33** C2
Horizon Sch N16 . . . .**16** A4
Horle Wlk SE5 . . . .**48** A1
Hormead Rd W9 . . . .**23** B1
Hornbeam Cl SE11 . . . . .**149** B4
Hornbeam Ho 2
NW3 . . . .**12** B2
Hornblower Cl 2
SE16 . . . .**41** A2
Hornby Cl NW3 . . . .**11** C1
Hornby Ho 9 SE11 . . . . .**163** C4
Horndean Cl 3
SW15 . . . .**68** C3
Horner Hos 18 N1 . . . . . .**24** A4
Horne Way SW15 . . . .**47** B1
Horn La SE10 . . . .**43** C2
Horn La W3 . . . .**28** B2
Hornsby House Sch
SW12 . . . .**72** C3
Hornsey La N6 . . . .**4** B4
Hornsey Lane Gdns
N6 . . . .**4** B4
Hornsey La N7,N19 . . . . . .**5** B2

Hornsey Rise Gdns
N19 . . . .**5** A4
Hornsey St N7 . . . .**14** B3
Hornshay St SE15 . . . . . .**50** B4
Hornton Ct W8 . . . .**127** C3
Hornton Pl W8 . . . .**127** C3
Horrocks Ho SW15 . . . . .**57** A2
Horse & Dolphin Yd
W1 . . . .**119** C4
Horseferry Pl SE10 . . . . .**52** B4
Horseferry Rd E14 . . . . . .**33** A2
SW1 . . . .**147** C4
Horseferry Rd Est
SW1 . . . .**133** B1
Horseguards Ave
SW1 . . . .**120** A1
Horse Guards Par ★
SW1 . . . .**119** C1
Horse Guards Rd
SW1 . . . .**133** C4
Horsell Rd N5 . . . .**14** C2
Horselydown La
SE1 . . . .**124** C1
Horselydown Mans
SE1 . . . .**138** C4
Horsendon Ho 11
N7 . . . .**13** C3
Horseshoe Cl E14 . . . . . .**42** B1
Horse Shoe Yd W1 . . . . .**118** B4
Horse Yd N1 . . . .**86** B4
Horsfeld Gdns SE9 . . . . . .**2** B3
Horsfield Ho 9 N1 . . . . . .**15** B1
Horsford Rd SW2 . . . .**62** B2
Horsley St 5 SE17 . . . . . .**48** C4
Horsman Ho SE5 . . . .**48** B4
Horsman St SE5 . . . .**48** B4
Horsmonden Rd
SE4 . . . .**66** B1
Hortensia Ho
SW10 . . . .**156** C2
Hortensia Rd
SW10 . . . .**156** C2
Horticultural Pl 6
W4 . . . .**37** C1
Horton Ave NW2 . . . .**10** A4
Horton Ho 18 SE15 . . . . . .**50** B4
SW8 . . . .**162** C2
W14 . . . .**140** A1
Horton Rd E8 . . . .**17** A2
Horton St SE13 . . . .**67** A4
Horwood Ho 24 E2 . . . . . .**25** A2
NW8 . . . .**90** B2
Hosack Rd SW12,
SW17 . . . .**72** C2
Hosier La EC1 . . . .**108** B3
Hoskins St SE10 . . . .**42** C1
Hospl for Tropical
Diseases NW1 . . . .**83** B3
Hospl of St John and St
Elizabeth NW8 . . . .**79** B1
Hotham Prim Sch
SW15 . . . .**57** C3
Hotham Rd SW15 . . . .**57** B4
Hotfield Pl SE16 . . . .**40** B3
Hotspur St SE11 . . . .**149** B2
Houblon Rd TW10 . . . . . .**54** A2
Houghton Cl 11 E8 . . . . . .**16** B2
Houghton St WC2 . . . . . .**107** A1
Houndsditch EC3 . . . . . .**110** B2
Houseman Way 20
SE5 . . . .**48** C3
Houses of Parliament ★
SW1 . . . .**134** B2

Hoveden Ho NW2 . . . . . .10 A3
Howard Cl Acton W3 . . . . .28 A3
  London NW1 . . . . .92 C3
Howard Ho SE8 . . . . .51 B4
  W1 . . . . .92 B1
  7 London SW9 . . . . .62 C4
Howard Rd NW2 . . . . .9 C4
  London N16 . . . . .15 C4
Howard's La SW15 . . . . . .57 B3
Howbury Rd SE15 . . . . . . .65 B4
Howcroft Ho **3** 26 B2
Howden St SE15 . . . . .64 C4
Howell Ho **5** N7 . . . . .13 C3
Howell Wlk SE1 . . . . .150 B3
Howgate Rd SW14 . . . . . . .55 C4
Howick Pl SW1 . . . . .133 A1
Howie St SW11 . . . . .158 A1
Howitt Cl **5** NW3 . . . . . . .12 A2
Howitt Rd NW3 . . . . .12 A2
Howland Ho **9**
  SW16 . . . . .74 A1
Howland Mews E
  W1 . . . . .105 A4
Howland St W1 . . . . .105 A4
Howland Way SE16 . . . . . .41 A4
Howletts Rd SE24 . . . . . . .63 B1
Howley Pl W2 . . . . .101 A4
Howsman Rd SW13 . . . . . .46 C4
Howson Rd SE4 . . . . .66 A3
Howson Terr TW10 . . . . . . .54 A1
How's St E2 . . . . .24 B3
Hoxton Mkt N1 . . . . .98 A3
Hoxton Point EC1 . . . . . . .98 A4
Hoxton Sq N1 . . . . .98 A3
Hoxton St N1 . . . . .24 A3
Hoylake Rd W3 . . . . .29 A3
Hoyland Cl **4** SE15 . . . . .50 A3
Hoy St E16 . . . . .35 B1
Hub Buildings The **4**
  SW12 . . . . .72 C3
Huberd Ho SE1 . . . . .137 C2
Hubert Gr SW9 . . . . .62 A4
Hubert Ho NW8 . . . . .90 A1
Hucknall Ct NW8 . . . . .89 B2
Huddart St E3 . . . . .33 B4
Huddleston Cl E2 . . . . .25 B3
Huddlestone Rd NW2 . . . . .9 A2
Huddleston Rd N7 . . . . . . .13 B4
Hudson Cl **15** W12 . . . . . . .30 A2
Hudson Ct E14 . . . . .41 C1
Hudson Ho SW10 . . . . . . .156 C2
  5 W11 . . . . .31 A3
Hudsons Ho N1 . . . . .97 C3
Hudson's Pl SW1 . . . . . . .146 C4
Huggin Ct EC4 . . . . .123 A4
Huggin Hill EC4 . . . . .123 A4
Huggins Ho **3** E3 . . . . . . .26 C2
Huggins Pl SW2 . . . . .74 B3
Hughan Rd E15 . . . . .19 C3
Hugh Astor Ct SE1 . . . . . .136 B2
Hughenden Terr
  E15 . . . . .76 B4
Hughes Ho **26** E2 . . . . .25 B2
SE17 . . . . .150 B3
  18 SE8 . . . . .51 C4
  London SE5 . . . . .48 B2
Hughes Mans
  E1 . . . . .24 C1 99 C1
Hughes Terr **6** E16 . . . . . .35 B2
Hugh Gaitskell Cl
  SW6 . . . . .154 C3
Hugh Gaitskell Ho
  London N16 . . . . .7 B2
  London NW8 . . . . .8 B1

Hugh Mews SW1 . . . . . . .146 B3
Hugh Morgan Ho **5** 61 C4
Hugh Myddelton Prim
  Sch EC1 . . . . .95 C3
Hugh Platt Ho **28** 25 A3
Hugo Ho SW1 . . . . .131 A2
Hugo Rd N19 . . . . .13 B4
Hugon Rd SW6 . . . . .59 A4
Huguenot Pl SW18 . . . . . .59 B2
Huguenot Sq SE15 . . . . . .65 A4
Hullbridge Mews
  N1 . . . . .87 B4
Hull Cl SE16 . . . . .32 C1
Hull St EC1 . . . . .96 C3
Hulme Pl SE1 . . . . .137 A3
Humber Dr W10 . . . . .22 C1
Humber Rd SE3 . . . . .53 B4
Humberton Cl E9 . . . . .18 A3
Humbolt Rd W6 . . . . .154 A3
Hume Ct N1 . . . . .15 A1
Hume Ho **14** W11 . . . . .30 C1
Humphrey Ct
  SW11 . . . . .167 C3
Humphrey St SE1 . . . . . . .152 C2
Humphry Ho **10**
  SW15 . . . . .57 C2
Hungerford Bridge
  WC2 . . . . .120 C2
Hungerford Ho
  SW1 . . . . .161 A4
Hungerford Inf Sch
  N7 . . . . .14 A2
Hungerford Jun & Inf
  Schs N7 . . . . .13 C2
Hungerford La
  WC2 . . . . .120 B2
Hungerford Prim Sch
  N7 . . . . .14 A3
Hungerford Rd
  4 London N7 . . . . .14 A3
  London N7 . . . . .13 C2
Hungerford St **24** 32 A3
Hunsdon Rd SE14 . . . . . . .50 C3
Hunslett St **27** E2 . . . . . . .25 B3
Hunstanton Ho
  NW1 . . . . .102 B4
Hunt Cl W11 . . . . .30 C1
Hunter Cl
  2 London SE5 . . . . .63 C3
  2 Streatham SW12 . . . .74 C4
Hunter Ho N19 . . . . .4 B1
  SE1 . . . . .136 B3
  SW5 . . . . .141 C4
  SW8 . . . . .161 C1
  WC1 . . . . .94 B2
Hunter Lo **9** W9 . . . . .31 C4
Hunter St WC1 . . . . .94 B2
Huntingdon Ct
  SW14 . . . . .55 B4
Huntingdon Gdns
  W4 . . . . .45 B3
Huntingdon Ho
  SW5 . . . . .141 C4
  London N12 . . . . .14 B1
Huntingfield Rd
  SW15 . . . . .56 C2
Huntingford Ho
  SW15 . . . . .47 B1
Huntley St WC1 . . . . .93 B1
Huntly St E1 . . . . .111 B4

Hunts Cl SE3 . . . . .53 C1
Hunt's Ct WC2 . . . . .119 C3
Hunt's La E15 . . . . .27 B3
Hunt's La SE15 . . . . .152 A3
Huntspill St SW17 . . . . . . .71 B1
Hunts Slip Rd SE21 . . . . . .76 A2
Huntsworth Mews
  NW1 . . . . .90 C1
Hurdwick Ho NW1 . . . . . . .82 C2
Hurleston Ho **11**
  SE8 . . . . .41 B1
Hurley Cres SE16 . . . . .40 C4
Hurley Ho E2 . . . . .98 C3
  SE11 . . . . .149 C3
Hurlock St N5 . . . . .6 A1
Hurlock St N5 . . . . .6 A1
Huron Rd SW17 . . . . .72 C1
Hurstbourne Ho **8**
  SW15 . . . . .56 B1
Hurstdene Gdns N15 . . . . . .7 A4
Hurst Ho N1 . . . . .85 A1
Hurst St SE24 . . . . .63 A1
Hurstway Wlk **2**
  W11 . . . . .30 C2
Husbourne Ho **8**
  SE8 . . . . .41 A2
Huson Cl NW3 . . . . .12 A1
Hutching's St E14 . . . . .41 C4
Hutchins Cl E15 . . . . .76 B1
Hutchinson Ho **5**
  SW4 . . . . .73 C4
Hutchinson Ho **9**
  SE14 . . . . .50 B3
Hutton Ct **3** N4 . . . . .5 B3
Hutton Ho E2 . . . . .99 B3
Hutton St EC4 . . . . .107 C1
Huxbear St SE4 . . . . .66 B2
Huxley Ho NW8 . . . . .89 C1
  London SW9 . . . . .172 C2
Huxley St W10 . . . . .23 A2
Hyacinth Rd SW15 . . . . . . .68 C3
Hyde Farm Mews
  SW12 . . . . .73 C3
Hyde Ind Est **6**
  NW9 . . . . .1 A2
Hyde La SW11 . . . . .168 A4
Hyde Park* W2 . . . . .116 C2
Hyde Park Cnr
  SW1 . . . . .131 C4
Hyde Park Corner Sta
  SW1 . . . . .131 C4
Hyde Park Cres
  W2 . . . . .102 A1
Hyde Park Gate Mews
  SW7 . . . . .128 C3
Hyde Park Gdns
  W2 . . . . .101 C1
Hyde Park Gdns Mews
  W2 . . . . .116 A4
Hyde Park Mans
  NW1 . . . . .102 A3
Hyde Park Pl W2 . . . . . . .116 A3
Hyde Park Sq W2 . . . . . .102 A1

Hyde Park Square Mews
  W2 . . . . .102 A1
Hyde Park St W2 . . . . . . .102 A1
Hyde Park Twrs
  W2 . . . . .114 C3
Hyde Rd N1 . . . . .24 A4
  Richmond TW10 . . . . .54 B2
Hyde's Pl **12** N1 . . . . .15 A1
Hyde St SE8 . . . . .51 C4
Hydethorpe Rd
  SW12 . . . . .73 B3
Hyde Vale SE10 . . . . .52 B3
Hylda Ct NW5 . . . . .3 C1
Hyndman Ho **5**
  N7 . . . . .13 C4
Hyndman St SE15 . . . . . . .50 A4
Hyperion Ho **29** E3 . . . . . .26 A3
  streatham SW2 . . . . .74 B4
Hyson Rd SE16 . . . . .40 A1
Hythe Ho **7** SE16 . . . . . . .40 B4
Hythe Rd NW10 . . . . .21 C1
Hythe Road Ind Est
  NW10 . . . . .21 C1

I

Ian Hamilton Ho
  NW1 . . . . .93 C4
Ibberton Ho SW8 . . . . . . .162 C2
  W14 . . . . .126 B1
Ibbotson Ave E16 . . . . .35 B1
Ibbott St **2** E1 . . . . .25 B1
Iberia Ho **17** N19 . . . . .4 C4
Ibis Ct **18** SE8 . . . . .51 B4
Ibis La W4 . . . . .45 B2
Ibsley Gdns SW15 . . . . . . .68 C3
Ibstock Place Sch
  SW15 . . . . .56 A1
Icarus Ho **18** E3 . . . . .26 B2
Iceland Rd E3 . . . . .26 C4
Iceland Wharf SE16 . .41 A2
Ice Wharf NW1 . . . . .84 B1
Ida St E14 . . . . .34 B3
Idmiston Rd SE21,
  SE27 . . . . .75 B2
Idol La EC3 . . . . .124 A3
Idonia St SE8 . . . . .51 C3
Iffley Ho E2 . . . . .98 C3
Iffley Rd W6 . . . . .39 A3
Ifield Ho SE17 . . . . .152 B2
Ifield Rd SW10 . . . . .156 B4
Ifor Evans Pl E1 . . . . .25 C1
Ightham Ho SE17 . . . . . . .152 A3
Ilbert St W10 . . . . .23 A2
Ilchester Gdns W2 . . . . . .114 A4
Ilchester Mans W8 . . . . . .127 C2
Ilchester Pl W14 . . . . .127 A2
Ildersly Gr SE21 . . . . .75 C2
Ilderton Prim Sch
  SE16 . . . . .40 B1
Ilderton Rd SE15,
  SE16 . . . . .50 B4
Ilex Rd NW10 . . . . .8 B2
Ilford Ho **11** N1 . . . . .15 C2
Iliffe St SE17 . . . . .150 B2
Iliffe Yd SE17 . . . . .150 B2
Ilkeston Ct **7** E5 . . . . .17 C4
Ilminster Gdns
  SW11 . . . . .60 A3
Ilsley Ct SW8 . . . . .170 C1
Imber St N1 . . . . .87 B3
Imperial Ave **5** N16 . . . . . . .7 A1
Imperial College Rd
  SW7 . . . . .129 B2

Imperial Ct NW8 . . . . .80 B2
Imperial Ho **2** E14 . . . . . .33 B2
  E3 .26 A2
Imperial Mews **6**
  E6 .166 B3
Imperial Rd SW6 . . . . . . .166 B3
Imperial Sq SW6 . . . . . . .166 B3
Imperial St E3 . . . . .27 B2
Imperial Twrs **3**
  NW3 . . . . .11 B2
Imperial War Mus*
  SE1,SE11 . . . . .135 C1
Imre Ct W12 . . . . .30 A1
Independant PI E8 . . . . . . .16 B3
Indescon Ct E14 . . . . .42 A4
India St EC3 . . . . .110 C1
India Way W12 . . . . .30 A2
Indigo Mews N16 . . . . .6 C1
Indus Ct **15** SE15 . . . . . . .49 B3
Ingate Pl SW8 . . . . .170 C3
Ingelow Ho **8** 128 A4
Ingelow Rd SW8 . . . . .170 A1
Ingersoll Rd W12 . . . . .30 A1
Ingestre Pl W1 . . . . .105 A1
Ingestre Rd NW5 . . . . .13 A4
Ingham Rd NW6 . . . . .10 C4
Inglebert St EC1 . . . . .95 B4
Ingleborough St
  SW9 . . . . .173 B2
Ingleby Rd N7 . . . . .5 A1
Inglefield Sq **12** E1 . . . . . .32 A1
Ingle Ho SW12 . . . . .73 C3
Ingleshaw Wlk E9 . . . . . . .18 B2
Ingleside Gr SE3 . . . . .53 B4
Inglethorpe St SW6 . . . . . .47 C2
Ingleton St SW9 . . . . .173 B2
Inglewood Cl E14 . . . . .41 C2
Inglewood Mans **11**
  NW6 . . . . .10 C3
Inglewood Rd NW6 . . . . . .10 C3
Inglis Ho **1** SW1 . . . . .57 B2
Inglis St SE5 . . . . .48 A2
Ingram Ave NW11 . . . . .2 B4
Ingram Cl SE11 . . . . .149 A4
Ingram Ho E3 . . . . .26 A4
Ingram Lo **5** SW4 . . . . . . .61 C1
Ingrave St SW11 . . . . .60 A4
Ingrebourne Ho
  NW8 . . . . .101 C4
Ingress St **4** W4 . . . . .38 A1
Inigo Pl WC2 . . . . .120 A4
Inkerman Rd NW5 . . . . .13 A2
Inkerman Terr W8 . . . . . . .127 C1
Inkster Ho **9** SW11 . . . . . . .60 A4
Inman Rd
  London NW10 . . . . .21 A4
  Wandsworth SW18 . . . . . . .71 B4
Inner Circ NW1 . . . . .91 B4
Inner Park Rd SW19 . . . . . .69 C2
Inner Temple La
  EC4 . . . . .107 B1
Innes Gdns SW15 . . . . .57 A1
Innis Ho SE17 . . . . .152 A2
Insley Ho E13 . . . . .27 C2
Inst for Child Health
  WC1 . . . . .94 C1
Institute Pl E8 . . . . .17 A3
Instituto Espanol
  Vicente Canada Blanch
  W10 . . . . .31 A4
Inst of Ophthalmology
  EC1 . . . . .97 C2
Interchange The
  NW5 . . . . .13 A3
International Sch of
  London W3 . . . . .36 C2
Inveagh Cl E9 . . . . .25 C4

Inver Ct W2 ....100 B1
Inverforth CI NW3 .....2 B2
Inverforth Ho NW3 ....2 B2
Invergarry Ho NW6 ...78 A1
Inverness Gdns
  W8 ....114 A4
Inverness Mews
  W2 ....114 B4
Inverness PI W2 ......114 B4
Inverness St NW1 .....82 B4
Inverness Terr W2 ...114 B4
Inverton Rd SE15 ....65 C3
Invicta CI E3 ....33 C4
Invicta Plaza SE1 ...122 A2

Invicta Prim Sch
  SE3 ....53 C3
Invicta Rd SE3,SE7 ..53 C4
Inville Rd SE17 ......151 C1
Inwen Ct SE8 ....41 A1
Inwood Ct NW1 ....13 B1
Inwood Ho SE22 ......64 A4
Inworth St SW11 .....168 B2
Inworth Wlk N1 ......86 C4
Ion Ct E2 ....24 C3
Ionian Bldg E14 ......33 A2
Ionian Ho E2 ....25 C3
Ipsden Bldgs SE1 ....135 C4
Ipswich Ho SE4 ....65 C2
Irby Ho SW2 ....62 C1
Ireland Yd EC4 ......108 B1
Irene Rd SW6 ....165 C3
Ireton Ho SW9 ......173 C1
Ireton St E3 ....26 C1
Iroko Ho N7 ....13 C3
Iron Bridge CI NW10 ..8 A3
Iron Bridge Ho NW3 ..12 B1
Iron Mill PI SW18 ....59 A1
Iron Mill Rd SW18 ...59 A1

Ironmonger La
  EC2 ....109 B1

Ironmonger Pas
  EC1 ....97 A3

Ironmonger Row
  EC1 ....97 A3

Ironmonger's PI E14 ..41 C2
Ironside CI SE16 .....40 C4
Ironside Ho E9 ....18 A4
Irvine Ct W1 ....93 A1
Irvine Ho E2 E14 .....34 A4
  London N7 ....14 B2
Irving Gr SW9 ....172 C1
Irving Ho SE17 ......150 A1
Irving Mews N1 ....15 B2
Irving Rd W14 ....39 C3
Irving St WC2 ....119 C3
Irwell Est E16 SE16 ..40 B4
Irwin Gdns NW10 .....22 A4
Isabella Ct E3 TW10 .54 B1
Isabella Ho E1 ....150 A2
  E9 Isabella Mews E14 .18 B3
Isabella Rd E9 ....17 B3
Isabella St SE1 ......122 A1
Isabel St SW9 ....173 A4
Isambard Mews E14 ..42 B3
Isambard PI SE16 ....32 B1
Isel Way E9 SE22 ....64 A2
Isis CI SW15 ....57 B3
Isis Ct W4 ....45 A3
Isis Ho NW8 ....89 C1
Isis St SW18 ....71 B2

Islamia Girls' High Sch
  NW6 ....23 A4

Islamia Prim Sch
  NW6 ....23 A4

Islamic Coll for
Advanced Studies
  NW10 ....9 A2
Island Gardens Sta
  E14 ....42 B1
Island Row E14 ....33 B3
Isleden Ho N1 ....86 C4
Isledon Rd N4,N5 .....6 B4
Islington Est N1 .....86 C4
Islington Gn N1 ......86 A3

Islington Green Sch
  N1 ....86 C3

Islington High St
  N1 ....86 A2

Islington Park Mews
  N1 ....15 A1

Islington Park St
  N1 ....15 A1

Islington Sixth Form Ctr
  N7 ....14 C4
Islip St NW5 ....13 B3
Isokon Flats B
  NW3 ....12 B3
Ivanhoe Ho B Balham SW12 ..73 A4
  London E3 ....26 A3
Ivanhoe Rd SE5 ......64 B4
Ivatt PI W14 ....141 A1
Iveagh Ct EC3 ....110 C1
Iveagh Ho SW10 .....157 A2
Ivebury Ct W10 ......30 B3
Iveley Rd SW4 ......170 C1
Iver Ct N1 ....15 B2
Iverna Ct W8 ....127 C2
Iverna Gdns W8 .....127 C2
Iverson Rd NW6 .....10 C2
Ives Rd E16 ....35 A4
Ives St SW3 ....144 B4
Ivimey St E2 ....24 C2 99 C4
Ivinghoe Ho N7 .....13 C3
Ivor Ct NW1 ....90 C2
Ivories The N1 ....15 B1
Ivor PI NW1 ....90 C1
Ivor St NW1 ....13 B1
Ivory Ho E1 ....125 A2
  E6 London SW11 .....59 B4
Ivybridge Ho E8
  SE22 ....64 A4
Ivybridge La WC2 ...120 B3
Ivy Church La E1 ...153 A2
Ivy Cres W4 ....37 B2
Ivy Ct E8 SE16 .....153 C1
  London SE13 ....66 C2
Ivydale Prim Sch
  SE15 ....65 C3
Ivydale Rd SE15 ....65 C3
Ivyday Gr SW16 .....74 B1
Ivy Lo W8 ....113 B2
Ivymount Rd SE27 ..74 C1
Ivy Rd E16 ....35 C3
  NW2 ....9 B4
Ivy St N1 ....24 A3
Ixworth PI SW3 .....144 A3

Jack Taylor Sch
  NW8 ....78 C4
Jack Tizard Sch
  W12 ....41 A2
Jack Walker Ct N5 ...15 A4
Jacobin Lo N7 ....14 A3
Jacob Mans B E1 ....32 A3
Jacobson Ct SW11 ..168 B3
Jacobson Ho E1 ....110 C2
Jacob St SE1 ....139 B4
Jacob's Well Mews
  W1 ....103 C2
Jacotts Ho W10 .....22 B1
Jaggard Way SW12 ..72 B4
Jagger Ho SW11 ....168 C4
Jago Wlk SE5 ....48 C3
Jamahirya Sch
  SW3 ....158 A4
Jamaica Rd SE1 ....139 B2
  SE16 ....40 A3
Jamaica St E1 ....32 B4
James Allen's Girls' Sch
  SE22 ....64 A2
James Anderson Ct
  E2 ....24 A3
James Ave NW2 ....9 B3
James Brine Ho E2 ..99 A4
James Campbell Ho E2 ..25 B3
James Collins CI
  W9 ....23 B1
James Docherty Ho E2 ..25 B3
James Hammett Ho E2 ..24 B3
James Joyes Wlk E ..48 C3
James Leicester Hall of
Residence N7 ....14 A2
James Lind Ho E 41 B2
James Middleton Ho E2 ..25 A2
Jameson Ct E2 ......25 B3
Jameson Ho SE11 ..148 C2
Jameson PI TW1 W3 ..37 B4
Jameson St W8 .....113 C2
James St W1 ....103 C1
  WC2 ....120 B4
James Stewart Ho
  NW6 ....10 B1
James Stroud Ho
  SE17 ....151 A1
Jamestown Rd NW1 ..82 A4
Jamestown Way
  E14 ....34 C2
James Wolfe Prim Sch
  SE10 ....52 B3
Jamuna CI E14 ......33 A4
Jane St E1 ....32 A3
Janet St E14 ....41 C3
Janeway PI E2 SE16 ..40 A4
Janeway St SE16 ....139 C3
Jansen Wlk SW11 ...59 C3
Japan Cres N4 ....5 B3
Jardine Rd E1 ....32 C2
Jarman Ho B E1 .....32 B4
  SE16 ....40 C2
Jarrett Cl SW2 ....75 A3
Jarrow Rd SE16 .....40 B1
Jarrow Way E9 ......18 A4
Jarvis Ct B SE10 ...52 B3
Jarvis Ho B SE15 ...49 C2
Jarvis Rd SE22 ......64 A3

Jasmin SE1 ....125 A1
Jasmin Ho SE4 ......66 B4
Jasmin Lo D SE16 ..40 A1
Jason Ct W1 ....103 C2
  London SW9 ....173 B4
Jasper Wlk N1 ......97 B4
Java Wharf SE1 ....139 A4
Jay Ho SW15 ....47 B1
Jay Mews SW7 .....129 A3
Jean Darling Ho
  SW10 ....157 B3
Jean Pardies Ho E
  E1 ....32 B4
Jebb Ave SW2 ....62 A1
Jebb St E3 ....26 C3
Jedburgh St SW11 ..60 C3
Jeddo Mews W12 ...38 B4
Jeddo Rd W12 ......38 B4
Jefferson Bldg E
  E14 ....41 C4
Jeffrey's PI NW1 ....13 B1
Jeffrey's Rd SW4 ..172 A2
Jeffrey's St NW1 ...172 A2
  NW1 ....13 B1
Jeger Ave E2 ....24 B4
Jelf Rd SW2 ....62 C2
Jellicoe Ho E B E2 ..24 C3
  NW1 London SW15 ..57 C2
  SW8 Putney SW15 ..57 C2
Jemotts Ct B SE14 ..50 C4
Jenkins Ho SW8 ...171 B4
Jenkinson Ho E2 ...25 C2
Jenner Ave W3 .....28 C4
Jenner Ho SE3 .....53 A4
Jenner PI SW13 .....47 A4
Jenner Rd N16 ......7 B1
Jennifer Ho SE11 ..149 C3
Jennings Ho SE10 ..42 C1
Jennings Rd SE22 ..64 B1
Jensen Ho SE10 E3 ..26 C1
Jephson Ct SW4 ...172 B1
Jephson Ho B
  SE17 ....48 A4
Jephson St SE5 .....48 C2
Jephtha Rd SW18 ..58 C1
Jerdan PI SW6 .....155 B2
Jeremiah St E14 ...34 A3
Jeremy Bentham Ho
  E2 ....99 C3
Jermyn St SW1 ....119 A2
Jerningham Ct
  SE14 ....51 A2
Jerningham Rd
  SE14 ....51 A2
Jerome Cres NW8 ..90 A2
Jerome Ho NW1 ...102 B4
Jerome St E1 .24 B1 98 C1
Jerome Twr B W3 ..37 A4
Jerrard St SE13 .....67 A4
Jerrold Lo SW15 ...57 B4
Jerrold St E B N1 ..24 A3
Jersey Ho E Ho 15 B2
Jersey Rd E16 ......36 A2
  N1 ....15 B2
Jersey St E2 ....25 A2
Jerusalem Pas EC1 ..96 A1
Jervis Bay Ho B
  E14 ....34 C3
Jervis Ct W1 ....104 B1
Jessel Ho SW1 ....147 C4
  WC1 ....94 A3
Jessica Rd SW18 ...59 B2
Jessie Blythe La E
  N19 ....5 A4
Jessie Duffett Ho E
  SE5 ....48 B3
Jesson Ho SE17 ...151 B3
Jessop Ct N1 ....86 B1

Jessop Prim Sch
  SE24 ....63 B3
Jessop Sq E14 ......33 C1
Jessop St SE27 .....75 A1
Jethou Ho B N1 ....15 B2
Jevons Ho B NW8 ..11 C1
Jewell Ho B SW12 ..73 B4
Jewish Prep Sch The
  NW6 ....78 A1
Jewry St EC3 ....110 C1
Jews Free Sch N4 ..1 C2
Jews Row SW18 ....59 B3
Jeymer Ave NW2 ...9 B3
Jeypore Rd SW18 ..59 B1
Jim Griffiths Ho
  SW6 ....155 A3
Joanna Ho B W6 ...39 B1
Joan St SE1 ....122 A1
Jocelin Ho N1 ......85 A3
Jocelyn Rd TW9 .....54 A4
Jocelyn St SE15 ....49 C2
Jockey's Fields
  WC1 ....107 A4
Jodane St SE8 ......41 B2
Jodrell Rd E3 ....18 B1
Johanna Prim Sch
  SE1 ....135 B3
Johanna St SE1 ...135 B3
John Adam St
  WC2 ....120 B3
John Aird Ct W2 ...101 A4
John Archer Way
  SW18 ....59 C1
John Ashby CI SW2 ..62 A1
John Ball Prim Sch
  SE3 ....53 B1
John Barker Ct
  NW6 ....10 A1
John Betts Ho W12 ..38 C3
John Betts Prim Sch
  W6 ....39 B3
John Bond Ho E
  E3 ....26 B3
John Brent Ho B
  SE8 ....40 C2
John Buck Ho
  NW10 ....21 B4
John Burns Prim Sch
  SW11 ....169 C1
John Campbell Rd E4
  N16 ....16 A3
John Carpenter St
  EC4 ....122 A4
John Cartwright Ho E
  E2 ....25 A2
John Conwey Ho E
  SW2 ....62 C1
John Dee Ho B
  SW14 ....55 C4
John Donne Prim Sch
  SE15 ....50 A2
John Dwight Ho
  SW6 ....166 D5
John Felton Rd B
  SE16 ....139 B3
John Fielden Ho B
  E2 ....25 A2
John Fisher St E1 ..125 B4
John F. Kennedy Specl
  Sch E15 ....27 C4
John Glynes Ct E
  SW15 ....57 A3
John Harris Ho
  SE15 ....64 C4

John Harrison Way SE10 .....43 B3
John Islip St SW1 **SW1** .148 A3
John Keall Ho SW15 .....57 C4
John Keble CE Prim Sch NW10 .....21 B4
John Kennedy Ct **1** N1 .....15 C2
John Kennedy Ho **1** SE16 .....40 C2
John Kennedy Lo **2** N1 .....15 C2
John King Ct **8** N19 .4 C2
John Kirk Ho **22** SW11 .....59 C4
5 Streatham SW16 .74 A1
John Knight Lo SW6 .....155 C2
John Maurice Cl SE17 .....151 B4
John McDonald Ho **3** E14 .....42 B3
John McKenna Wlk SE16 .....139 C2
John Milton Prim Sch SW8 .....160 C1
John Nettleford Ho **14** E2 .....25 A2
John Orwell Sports Ctr E1 .....32 A1
John Parker Sq **8** SW11 .....59 C4
John Parry Ct **28** N1 .....24 A3
John Paul II Sch SW19 .....69 C4
John Penn St SE13 .52 A2
John Perryn Prim Sch W3 .....29 A3
John Prince's St W1 .....104 B2
John Pritchard Ho **1** E1 .....99 C1
John Ratcliffe Ho **6** NW6 .....23 C2
John Rennie Wlk **1** E1 .....32 B1
John Roan Sch The SE3 .....53 B3
John Roll Way SE16 .....139 C2
John Ruskin Prim Sch SE5 .....48 B4
John Ruskin St SE5 .48 B4
John Scurr Ho **20** E14 .....33 B3
John Scurr Prim Sch E1 .....25 B1
John Silkin La SE8 .40 C1
John's Mews WC1 .....95 A1
John Smith Ave SW6 .....154 C2
Johnson Cl E8 .....24 C4
Johnson Ct **10** SW18 .....59 C3
Johnson Ho E2 .....99 C3
NW1 .....145 C3
SW1 .....147 C1
Johnson Lo **12** W9 .31 C4
Johnson Rd NW10 .20 C4
Johnsons Ct EC4 .....107 C1
Johnson's Pl SW1 .146 C1
Johnson St E1 .32 B3

Johnsons Way NW10 .....20 A1
John Spencer Sq N1 .15 A1
John's Pl E1 .32 A3
John St WC1 .....95 A1
John Stainer Com Prim Sch SE4 .....66 A3
Johnston Cl SW9 .173 A3
Johnstone Ho **3** SE13 .67 C4
John Strachey Ho SW6 .....155 A3
John Trundle Ct EC2 .....108 C4
John Tucker Ho **2** E14 .41 C3
John Wesley's House & Mus **3** EC1 .97 C2
John Wheatley Ho SW6 .....155 A3
John Williams Cl SE14 .50 C4
Joiners Ho **8** SW15 .56 C2
Joiners Arms Yd **1** SE5 .....48 C2
Joiner St SE1 .....123 C1
Jolles Ho **9** E3 .27 A2
Jonathan Ct **9** W4 .38 A2
Jonathan St SE11 .148 C2
Jones Ho London N16 .7 A3
4 South Bromley E14 .....34 C3
Jones St W1 .....118 A3
Jones Wlk **6** TW10 .54 B1
Jonson Ho SE1 .....137 C1
10 London N16 .16 A4
Jordan Ct SW15 .57 C3
Jordan Ho **1** N1 .....87 C3
12 London SE4 .....65 C3
Jordans Ho NW8 .90 A1
Joscoyne Ho **4** E1 .32 A3
Joseph Ave W3 .28 C3
Joseph Conrad Ho SW1 .....147 A3
Joseph Ct **4** N16 .....7 A4
Josephine Ave SW2 .62 B2
Joseph Irwin Ho **1** E14 .....33 B2
Joseph Lancaster Prim Sch SE1 .....137 B1
Joseph Powell Cl **1** SW12 .....61 B1
Joseph Priestley Ho **2** E2 .....25 A2
Joseph St E3 .....26 B1
Joseph Trotter Cl EC1 .....95 C3
Joshua St E14 .34 B3
Joslings Cl W12 .29 C2
Josseline Ct **8** E3 .26 A3
Joubert Mans SW3 144 B2
Joubert St SW11 .169 A2
Jowett Ho **9** SW9 .172 B1
Jowett St SE15 .49 B3
Jubilee Bldgs NW8 .79 B2
Jubilee Cres E14 .42 B3
Jubilee Ho SE11 .149 C3
Jubilee Mans **10** E1 .32 B3
Jubilee Mkt **21** WC2 .120 B4
Jubilee Pl SW3 .144 B2
Jubilee Prim Sch
London N16 .7 C3
London SW2 .62 C1
Jubilee The **2** SE10 .52 A3

Jubilee Yd SE1 .....138 C4
Judd St WC1 .....94 A3
Jude St E16 .....35 B3
Juer St SW11 .....158 B1
Julian Ave W3 .28 A2
Julian Pl E14 .42 A1
Julia St NW5 .....12 C3
Juliet Ho **11** N1 .24 A3
Julius Ct TW8 .44 A3
Julius Nyerere Cl N1 .....84 C4
Junction App
London SE13 .....67 B4
London SW11 .....60 A4
Junction Mews W2 .....102 A2
Junction Pl W2 .....101 C2
Junction Rd N19 .....4 C1
Juniper Cres NW1 .12 C1
Juniper Ct N16 .....6 C2
Juniper Dr SW18 .59 B3
Juno Ct SW9 .163 B1
Juno Ho **3** E3 .26 C4
Juno Way SE14 .50 C4
Juno Way Ind Est SE14 .50 C4
Jupiter Ct SW9 .163 B1
Jupiter Way N7 .14 B2
Jupp Rd E15 .19 C1
Jupp Rd W E15 .27 C4
Jura Ho SE16 .41 A2
Jurston Ct SE1 .135 C3
Justice Wlk SW3 .158 A3
Jutland Cl N19 .5 A3
Jutland Ho **8** SE5 .48 B1
Juxon St SE11 .149 A4

K

Kambala Rd SW11 .59 C4
Kara Way NW2 .....9 C4
Karen Ct **2** SE5 .64 A4
Karen Ho **7** N16 .15 C4
Kasmin Ct NW10 .8 C1
Kassala Rd SW11 .169 A3
Katherine Cl **7** SE16 .....32 C1
Katherine Ho **13** W10 .....23 A1
Katherine Sq W11 .112 A2
Kathleen Ave W3 .28 B4
Kathleen Rd SW11 .60 C4
Kay Rd SW9 .172 C1
Kay St E2 .24 C3
Kean Ho **5** SE17 .48 A4
Kean St WC2 .106 C1
Keates Est N16 .7 B2
Keats Cl SE1 .152 C3
London NW3 .12 A4
Keats Gr NW3 .12 A4
Keats Ho **20** E2 .25 B2
SW1 .....161 A4
4 SE5 .48 B3
Keats House Mus* NW3 .12 A4
Keats Pl EC2 .109 B3
Keble Ho **4** SW15 .57 C1
Keble Pl SW13 .47 A4
Kedge Ho **10** E14 .41 C3
Kedleston Ct E5 .18 A4
Kedleston Wlk **21** E2 .....25 A2
Keel Cl SE16 .32 C1
Keeley St WC2 .106 C1
Keen's Yd N1 .15 A2
Keeper Wharf **1** E1 .32 C2

Keeper Wharf **18** E1 .....32 C2
Keep The SE3 .53 C1
Keeton's Rd SE16 .40 A3
Keevil Dr SW19 .70 A4
Keighley Cl N7 .14 A4
Keildon Rd SW11 .60 B3
Keir Hardie Ho
18 London N19 .4 C4
London NW10 .....8 B1
London W6 .47 C4
Keith Connor Cl **8** ...
Keith Gr W12 .29 C1
Keith Ho NW6 .78 A1
Kelby Ho N7 .14 B2
Kelfield Ct **1** W10 .30 C3
Kelfield Gdns W10 .30 C3
Kelfield Mews W10 .30 C3
Kellett Ho N1 .87 C3
Kellett Rd SW2 .62 C3
Kellow Ho SE1 .137 B4
Kell St SE1 .136 B2
Kelly Ave SE15 .49 B2
Kelly Ct **8** E14 .33 C2
Kelly St NW1 .13 A2
Kelman Cl SW4 .171 C1
Kelmore Gr SE22 .64 C3
Kelmscott Gdns W12 .38 C3
Kelmscott Rd SW11 .60 B2
Kelross Rd N5 .15 B4
Kelsey St E2 .24 C1 99 B2
Kelshall Ct N4 .6 B2
Kelson Ho E14 .42 B3
Kelso Pl W8 .128 B2
Kelvedon Ho SW8 .172 B4
Kelvedon Rd SW6 .155 A1
Kelvin Ct W11 .113 B3
Chiswick W4 .37 A1
Kelvington Rd SE15 .65 C2
Kelvin Rd N5 .15 A4
Kelyway Ho **20** SW2 .74 C4
Kember St N1 .14 B1
Kemble Ho SW9 .63 A4
Kemble St WC2 .106 C1
Kemerton Rd SE5 .63 B4
Kemey's St E9 .18 A3
Kemp Ct SW8 .162 A1
Kempe Ho SE1 .137 C1
Kempe Rd NW6 .22 C2
Kemp Ho **1** E2 .25 B3
Kempis Way **5** SE22 .64 A2
Kemplay Rd NW3 .11 C4
Kemp's Ct W1 .105 B1
Kemps Dr E14 .33 C2
Kempsford Gdns SW5 .141 C1
Kempsford Rd SE11 .149 C3
Kempson Rd SW6 .155 C1
Kempthorne Rd SE8 .41 B2
Kempton Ct E1 .32 A4
Kempton Ho **21** N1 .24 A4
Kemsford Rd SE11 .150 A3
Kemsing Ho SE1 .137 C3
Kemsing Rd SE10 .43 C1
Kemsley SE13 .67 A2
Kenbrook Ho W14 .127 A1
London NW5 .13 B3
Kenbury Gdns SE5 .48 B1
Kenbury Mans **19** SE5 .48 B1
Kenbury St SE5 .48 B1

Kenchester Cl SW8 .162 B1
Kendal NW1 .92 B4
Kendal Ave W3 .28 A4
Kendal Cl SE5 .48 A3
Kendal Ct NW2 .10 A3
Kendal Ho N1 .85 A2
22 London E9 .17 B1
Kendall Ct **8** SE22 .64 C2
Kendall Ho **3** ... .103 B3
Kendall Pl W1 .58 B2
Kendal Rd NW10 .8 C4
Kendal St W2 .102 B1
Kendal Steps W2 .102 B1
Kender Prim Sch SE14 .50 B2
Kender St SE14 .50 B2
Kendoa Rd **1** SW4 .61 C3
Kendrick Ct **11** SE15 .50 B2
Kendrick Mews SW7 .143 B3
Kendrick Pl SW7 .143 B3
Kenilworth Ct SW6 .58 A4
Kenilworth Rd E3 .26 A3
NW6 .23 B4
Kenley Wlk W11 .112 A3
Kenmare Mans NW6 .10 B3
Kenmont Gdns NW10 .22 A2
Kenmont Prim Sch
NW10 .....22 A2
Kenmure Rd E8 .17 A3
Kenmure Yd E8 .17 A3
Kennacraig Cl **7** E16 .35 C1
Kennard Ho **1** SW11 .169 C3
Kennard Rd E15 .19 C1
Kennard St **1** SW11 .169 B3
Kennedy Cox Ho **9** E16 .35 B2
Kennedy Ho SE11 .148 C2
Kennedy Wlk SE17 .151 C3
Kennet Cl SW11 .59 C3
Kennet Ct **27** W2 .31 C4
Kenneth Campbell Ho NW8 .89 C2
Kenneth Cres NW2 .9 A3
Kenneth Ct SE11 .149 C4
Kennet Ho NW8 .89 C1
Kenneth Younger Ho SW6 .155 A3
Kennet Rd W9 .23 B1
Kennet St E1 .125 C2
Kennet Wharf La EC4 .123 A4
Kenning Ho **6** N1 .24 A4
Kenning St **12** SE16 .40 B4
Kennings Way SE11 .149 C2
Kennington Gr SE11 .163 A4
Kennington La SE11 .149 B1
Kennington Oval SE11 .163 A3
Kennington Palace Ct SE11 .149 B2
Kennington Park Gdns SE17 .48 A4
Kennington Park Ho SE11 .149 C1
Kennington Park Pl

Kennington Park Rd
 SE11 . . . . .150 A2
Kennington Rd
 SE11 . . . . .149 B4
Kennington Sta
 SE17 . . . . .150 A3
Kennoldes SE21 . . . .75 C2
Kenrick PI W1 . . . .103 B3
Kensal Green Cemy (All
 Souls)★ W10 . . . . . .22 B2
Kensal Green Sta
 NW10 . . . . .22 C2
Kensal Ho W10 . . . . .22 C1
Kensal Rd W10 . . . . .23 A1
Kensal Rise Prim Sch
 NW6 . . . . .22 C2
Kensal Rise Sta
 W10 . . . . .22 C3
Kensington & Chelsea
 Coll
 SW10 . . . . .156 C2
 W10 . . . . .31 A4
Kensington Church Ct
 W8 . . . . .128 A3
Kensington Church St
 W8 . . . . .31 C1 113 C1
Kensington Church Wlk
 W8 . . . . .128 A3
Kensington Court Mans
 W8 . . . . .128 B3
Kensington Court Mews
 W8 . . . . .128 B3
Kensington Court PI
 W8 . . . . .128 B3
Kensington Ct W8 128 B3
Kensington Ct Gdns
 W8 . . . . .128 B2
Kensington Gardens
 W2 . . . . .115 A1
Kensington Gate
 W8 . . . . .128 C2
Kensington Gdns Sq
 W2 . . . . .114 A4
Kensington Gore
 SW7 . . . . .129 B3
Kensington Hall Gdns
 W14 . . . . .140 C2
Kensington High St
 W8 . . . . .127 C2
Kensington Ho 3
 NW5 . . . . .13 B3
Kensington Hts
 W8 . . . . .113 B1
Kensington Mall
 W8 . . . . .113 C2
Kensington Mans
 SW5 . . . . .141 C2
Kensington Olympia Sta
 W14 . . . . .126 A1
Kensington Palace★
 W8 . . . . .114 B1
Kensington Palace Gdns
 W11 . . . . . .31 B2 113 A3
Kensington Park Mews
 W11 . . . . .31 B3
Kensington Park Rd
 W11 . . . . . .31 B2 113 A4
Kensington PI
 W8 . . . . .31 C1 113 B2
Kensington Prep Sch
 SW6 . . . . .165 A4
Kensington Rd
 SW7 . . . . .129 B3
 W8 . . . . .112 A4

Kensington Sq W8 .128 A3
Kensington Village
 W14 . . . . .141 A3
Kensington W
 W14 . . . . .140 A4
Kensworth Ho EC1 . .97 C3
Kent Ct 3 E2 . . . . . .24 B3
Kent Ho SE1 . . . . . .153 A1
 SW1 . . . . .147 B1
 13 London W4 . . . . .38 A1
 Richmond TW10 . . . . .54 C2
Kentish Bldgs SE1 .123 B1
Kentish Town Rd
 NW1 . . . . .13 A2
Kentish Town Sta
 NW5 . . . . .13 B3
Kentish Town West Sta
 NW5 . . . . .13 A2
Kent Lo 5 SW19 . . . .69 C3
Kentmere Ho SE15 . .50 B4
Kenton Ct W14 . . . .126 C1
Kenton Ho 7 E1 . . . .25 B1
 London N5 . . . . .5 C1
Kenton Rd E9 . . . . . .17 C2
Kenton St WC1 . . . . .94 A2
Kent Pas NW1 . . . . . .90 C2
Kent Rd London W4 . .37 B3
 Richmond TW9 . . . . . .44 C3
Kent St E2 . . . . .24 B3
Kent Terr NW1 . . . . . .90 B3
Kentwell CI SE4 . . . . .66 A3
Kentwode Gn SW13 .46 C3
Kent Yard SW7 . . . .130 B3
Kenway Rd SW5 . . . .142 A3
Ken Wilson Ho 17
 E2 . . . . .24 C3
Kenwood CI NW3 . . . .2 C3
Kenwood Ho★ NW3 . .3 A3
 13 London E9 . . . . . .18 A2
Kenworthy Rd E9 . . .18 A2
Kenwrick Ho N1 . . . . .85 A3
Kenwyn Rd SW4 . . . .61 C3
Kenyon Ho 5 SE5 . . .48 B3
Kenyon St SW6 . . . . .47 C2
Kepler Ho 8 SE10 . . .43 B1
Kepler Rd SW2,SW4 .62 B3
Keppel Ho 5 SE8 . . . .41 B1
 SW3 . . . . .144 A3
Keppel Row SE1 . . . .122 C1
Keppel St WC1 . . . . .105 C4
Kerbela St 2 . . . . . . .99 B2
Kerbey St E14 . . . . . .34 A3
Kerfield Cres SE5 . . .48 C2
Kerfield PI SE5 . . . . .48 C2
Kerridge Ct N1 . . . . .16 A2
Kerrier Ho SW10 . . .157 A1
Kerrington Ct 7
 W12 . . . . .39 B4
Kerrin Point SE11 . .149 B3
Kerrison Rd E15 . . . . .27 C4
 London SW11 . . . . . . .60 A4
Kerry 4 N7 . . . . .14 A2
Kerry Ho 5 E1 . . . . . .32 B3
Kerry Path SE8 . . . . . .51 B4
Kerry Rd SE8 . . . . . . .51 B4
Kerscott Ho 30 E3 . . .27 A2
Kersfield Ho SW15 . .57 C1
Kersfield Rd SW15 . .57 C1
Kershaw CI SW18 . . .59 C1
Kershaw Ho 7
 SE27 . . . . .75 A1
Kersley Mews
 SW11 . . . . .168 C3
Kersley Rd N16 . . . . . .7 A1
Kersley St SW11 . . . .168 C2

Kerwick CI 1 N7 . . . . .14 B1
Keslake Mans
 NW10 . . . . .22 C3
Keslake Rd NW6 . . . .22 C3
Keston Ho SE17 . . . .152 B2
Keston Rd SE15 . . . . .64 C4
Kestral Ho EC1 . . . . . .96 C4
Kestrel Ave SE24 . . . .63 B2
Kestrel Ho 4 SW11 . .60 A4
Kestrel PI SE14 . . . . .51 A4
Keswick Ct 3 SE22 . .64 C2
Keswick Ho 5 SE5 . . .48 B2
Keswick Hts 9
 SW15 . . . . .58 A2
Keswick Lo E8 . . . . . .16 B2
Keswick Rd SW15 . . .58 A2
Kett Gdns SW2 . . . . . .62 B2
Kettleby Ho SW9 . . . .63 A4
Ketton Ho W10 . . . . . .22 B1
Kevan Ho SE5 . . . . . .48 B3
Kew Bridge TW8 . . . .36 B3
Kew Bridge Ct 8
 W4 . . . . .36 C1
Kew Bridge Distribution
 Ctr TW8 . . . . .36 B1
Kew Bridge Rd TW8 . .36 B1
Kew Bridge Sta
 TW8 . . . . .36 B1
Kew Bridge Steam Mus
★ TW8 . . . . .36 A1
Kew Foot Rd TW9 . . .54 A4
Kew Gardens Rd
 TW9 . . . . .44 C2
Kew Gardens (Royal
 Botanic)★ TW9 . . . . .44 A2
Kew Gardens Sta
 TW9 . . . . .44 C2
Kew Gn TW9 . . . . . . .44 C4
Kew Green TW9 . . . . .44 B4
Kew Lo 11 TW9 . . . . .44 B2
Kew Palace TW9 . . . .44 A3
Kew Pier TW9 . . . . . .44 A3
Kew Ret Pk TW9 . . . .45 A2
Key CI E1 . . . . .25 A1
Keyes Ct SE22 . . . . . .64 C2
Keyes Rd NW2 . . . . . . .9 C3
Keyham Ho 5 W2 . . . .31 C4
Key Ho SE11 . . . . . . .163 B4
Keymer Rd SW2 . . . . .74 B2
Keynsham Ho 2 N4 . . .6 B4
Keyse Rd SE1 . . . . . .138 C1
Keystone Cres N1 . . .84 B1
Keyworth CI E5 . . . . .18 A4
Keyworth PI SE1 . . . .136 B2
Keyworth Prim Sch
 SE17 . . . . .150 B2
Keyworth St SE1 . . . .136 B2
Kezia St SE8 . . . . .41 A1
Khyber Rd SW11 . . . .168 A1
Kibworth St SW8 . . . .162 C1
Kidbrooke Gdns
 SE3 . . . . .53 C2
Kidderpore Ave
 NW3 . . . . .10 C4
Kidderpore Gdns
 NW3 . . . . .10 C4
Kiffen St EC2 . . . . .97 C2
Kilbrennan Ho 5
 E14 . . . . .34 B3
Kilburn Bridge 14
 NW6 . . . . .23 C4
Kilburn Gate NW6 . . .78 A2
Kilburn High Rd
 NW6 . . . . .23 C4
Kilburn High Road Sta
 NW6 . . . . .78 A3

Kilburn Ho 13 W9 . . .23 B2
Kilburn La W10 . . . . .23 A3
Kilburn Park Jun Sch
 NW6 . . . . .23 C2
Kilburn Park Rd
 NW6 . . . . .23 C2
Kilburn Park Sta
 NW6 . . . . .23 C3
Kilburn PI NW6 . . . . . .23 C4
Kilburn Priory NW6 . .78 A3
Kilburn Sq NW6 . . . . .23 C4
Kilburn Sta NW2 . . . . .10 B2
Kilburn Vale NW6 . . . .78 A3
Kilburn Vale Est 13 . .23 C4
Kildare Ct
 W2 . . . . . . .31 C3 113 A4
Kildare Gdns
 W2 . . . . . . .31 C3 113 A4
Kildare Rd E16 . . . . . .35 C4
Kildare Terr
 W2 . . . . . . .31 C3 113 A4
Kildare Wlk E14 . . . . .33 C3
Kildoran Rd SW2 . . . .62 A2
Kilgour Rd SE23 . . . . .66 A1
Kilkie St SW6 . . . . . .166 C1
Killarney Rd SW18 . . .59 B1
Killieser Ave SW2 . . . .74 A2
Killip CI E16 . . . . .35 B1
Killoran Ho 2 E14 . . .42 B3
Killowen Rd E9 . . . . . .17 C2
Killyon Rd SW8 . . . . .171 B1
Kilmaine Rd SW6 . . .154 B1
Kilmarsh Rd W6 . . . . .39 B2
Kilmington Rd
 SW13 . . . . .46 C4
Kilmuir Ho SW1 . . . .145 C3
Kiln Ct E14 . . . . .33 B2
Kilner Ho SE11 . . . . .163 B4
Kilner St E14 . . . . . . .33 C4
Kiloh Ct 1 SW11 . . . .60 A4
Kilpatrick Ct N16 . . . . .7 B3
Kilpeck Ho 9 N4 . . . . .6 B4
Kilravock St W10 . . . .23 A2
Kilronan 3 W3 . . . . . .28 C3
Kimbell Gdns SW6 .164 A3
Kimber Ctr The
 SW18 . . . . .70 C4
Kimberley Ave SE15 . .65 B4
Kimberley Ho 7
 E14 . . . . .42 B3
Kimberley Rd NW6 . . .23 A4
 London SW9 . . . . .62 A4
 London E16 . . . . .35 B4
Kimble Ho NW8 . . . . .90 B2
 1 London N7 . . . . . . .14 A3
Kimbolton Row
 SW3 . . . . .144 A3
Kimpton Ct 12 SE5 . . .48 C2
Kimpton Ho SW15 . . .68 C4
Kimpton Rd SE5 . . . . .48 C2
Kinburn St SE16 . . . . .40 C4
Kincaid Rd SE15 . . . . .50 A3
Kincardine Gdns
 W9 . . . . .23 C1
Kindell Ho 4 SW14 . .55 C4
Kinder Ho N1 . . . . . . .87 C2
Kindersley Ho E1 . . .111 C1
Kinder St 9 E1 . . . . . .32 A3
Kinefold Ho N7 . . . . . .14 A2
Kinfauns Rd SW2 . . . .74 C2
King Alfred Sch
 NW11 . . . . .2 A3
King Arthur CI SE15 . .50 B3

King Charles Ho
 SW6 . . . . .156 B2
King Charles St
 SW1 . . . . .134 A4
King Charles Wlk 6
 SW19 . . . . .70 A3
King David La E1 . . . .32 B2
Kingdon Ho 6 E14 . . .42 B3
Kingdon Rd NW6 . . . .10 C2
King Edward Mans 12
 E8 . . . . .25 A4
King Edward Mews
 SW13 . . . . .46 C2
King Edwards Rd
 E9 . . . . .25 B4
King Edward The Third
 Mews 6 SE16 . . . . . .40 A4
King Edward St
 EC1 . . . . .108 C2
King Fahed Acad
 W3 . . . . .29 B2
Kingfield St E14 . . . . .42 B2
Kingfisher Ct
 12 E14 . . . . .42 B4
 4 London SW11 . . . . .60 A4
 Putney SW19 . . . . . . .70 A2
Kingfisher Ho
 W14 . . . . .126 C2
 3 London SW18 . . . . .59 B2
Kingfisher Mews
 SE13 . . . . .67 A2
Kingfisher Sq 10
 SE8 . . . . .51 B4
King Frederick IX Ct
 SE16 . . . . .41 B3
King George Sq
 TW10 . . . . .54 B1
King George St
 SE10 . . . . .52 B3
Kingham CI
 W11 . . . . .39 C4
 Wandsworth SW18 . . .71 B4
King Henry's Rd
 NW3 . . . . .12 A1
King Henry's Reach
 W6 . . . . .47 B4
King Henry St N16 . . .16 A3
King Henry's Wlk
 N1 . . . . .16 A2
King Henry's Yd 5
 N16 . . . . .16 A3
Kinghorn St EC1 . . . .108 C3
King James St SE1 . .136 B3
King John Ct EC2 . . . .98 B2
King John St E1 . . . . .32 C4
Kingly Ct W1 . . . . . . .119 A4
Kingly St W1 . . . . . . .118 C4
King & Queen St
 SE17 . . . . .151 A2
King's Arms Ct E1 . . .111 B3
King's Arms Yd
 EC2 . . . . .109 B2
Kings Ave SW4 . . . . . .62 A1
Kings Avenue Sch
 SW4 . . . . .62 A2
King's Bench St
 SE1 . . . . .136 B4
King's Bench Wlk
 EC4 . . . . .107 C1

Kingsbridge N16 .... 6 C3
Kingsbridge Ave
W3 .... 36 B4
Kingsbridge Ct E14 .41 C2
Kingsbridge Rd
W10 .... 30 B4
Kingsbury Rd N1 ...16 A2
Kingsbury Terr N1 ..16 A2
Kingsclere Cl SW15 .68 C4
Kingscliffe Gdns
SW19 .... 70 B3
King's Coll WC2 ...121 A4
  London SE24 .... 63 C1
Kings College Ct
NW3 .... 11 C3
King's College Hospl
SE5 .... 48 C1
King's College London
NW3 .... 11 C3
Kings College Rd
NW3 .... 11 C1
King's Coll London
W8 .... 127 B4
Kings Coll London
(Chelsea Campus)
SW3 .... 144 A1
Kingscote NW11 ....1 B3
Kingscote Rd W4 ...37 C3
Kingscote St EC4 ..122 A4
King's Court N
SW3 .... 144 A1
Kingscourt Rd
SW16 .... 74 A1
King's Court S
SW3 .... 144 A1
King's Cres N4,N5 ...6 B1
Kingscroft SW4 ......62 A1
Kingscroft Rd NW2 .10 B2
King's Cross WC1 ..94 B4
King's Cross Bridge
WC1 .... 94 B4
King's Cross Rd
WC1 .... 95 A3
King's Cross Sta N1 .94 B4
King's Cross, St Pancras
N1 .... 94 A4
King's Cross (Thames
Link) Sta WC1 ......94 B4
Kings Ct NW8 ....80 C3
  London N7 ....14 B1
  London SE22 .... 64 C3
  London W6 .... 39 B2
  Putney SW15 ....68 C4
Kingsdale Gdns
W11 .... 30 C1
Kingsdale Sec Sch
SE21 .... 76 A1
Kingsdown Ave W3 .29 A2
Kingsdown Cl
26 SE16 ....40 A1
  11 W11 ....31 A3
  London W10 ....30 C3
Kingsdown Ct SW11 .60 A1
Kingsdown Ho 1
E8 .... 16 C3
Kingsdown Rd
N19 .... 5 A2
Kings Farm Ave
TW10 .... 54 C3
Kingsfield Ho 16 N16 .7 A1
Kingsford St NW5 ..12 B3
Kingsgate Est N1 ...16 A2
Kingsgate Ho 173 .173 C4
Kingsgate Pl NW6 ..10 C1

Kingsgate Prim Sch
NW6 .... 10 C1
Kingsgate Rd NW6 .10 C1
King's Gdns 4 NW6 .10 C1
King's Gr SE15 ....50 A3
  London SE15 ....50 A2
Kings Hall Mews
SE13 .... 67 B4
King's Head Yd
SE1 .... 123 B1
Kingshill SE17 ......151 A4
Kings Ho SE14 ....33 B2
Kingshold Rd E9 ....17 B1
King's House Jun Sch
TW10 .... 54 B2
King's House Prep Sch
TW10 .... 54 B1
King's Keep 6
SW15 .... 57 C2
Kingsland NW8 .....80 B3
Kingsland Gn 1 E8 ..16 B2
Kingsland High St
E8 .... 16 C3
Kingsland Pas 2
E8 .... 16 A2
Kingsland Rd E2 ....24 A3
Kingsland Sch E8 ..16 B3
Kingslawn Cl SW15 .57 A2
Kingsley Ct NW2 ....9 A2
Kingsley Flats SE1 .152 B3
Kingsley Ho SW3 ..157 C3
  London SW4 ....171 C2
Kingsley Mews
W8 .... 128 B1
Kingsley Pl N6 ....3 C4
Kingsley Rd NW6 ...23 B4
Kingsley St SW11 ...60 B4
Kings Mall W6 ......39 B2
Kings Mans 3 ......158 A3
Kingsmead TW10 ...54 B1
Kingsmead Ct N6 ...4 C4
Kingsmead Ho E9 ..18 A4
Kingsmead Prim Sch
E9 .... 18 A4
Kingsmead Rd SW2 .74 C2
Kingsmead Way E5,
  E9 .... 18 A4
Kingsmere Cl SW15 .57 C4
Kingsmere Pl N16 ...6 C3
Kingsmere Rd
SW19 .... 69 C2
Kings Mews WC1 ...95 A1
  3 London SW4 ....62 A2
Kingsmill NW8 .....79 C2
Kingsmill Terr NW8 .79 C2
Kingsnorth Ho 12
W10 .... 30 C3
King's Par
  London W12 .... 38 C3
  Willesden NW10 ....22 B4
King's Pl SE1 ....136 C3
Kings Pl W4 ....37 B2
King Sq EC1 ....96 C3
King's Quay SW10 .167 A4
King's Rd SW10 ....156 B4
  SW3 .... 144 A1

King's Scholars' Pas
SW1 .... 146 C4
King St EC2 ....109 A1
  SW1 .... 119 A2
  WC2 .... 120 A4
  London W3 ....28 B1
  London W6 .... 38 C2
King Stairs Cl SE16 .40 A4
King's Terr NW1 ....82 C3
Kingston Ho 2
NW6 .... 10 A1
Kingston Ho E
SW7 .... 130 A3
Kingston Ho N
SW7 .... 130 A3
Kingston Ho S
SW7 .... 69 A3
Kingston Rd SW15,
  SW19 .... 69 A3
Kingston Univ
Roehampton Vale Ctr
SW15 .... 68 B1
Kingstown St NW1 .81 B4
King Street Cloisters 7
W6 .... 39 A2
King Street Coll
  London W12 .... 39 B4
  London W12 .... 39 B2
Kingswater Pl
SW11 .... 158 A1
Kingsway WC2 ......106 C2
  Mortlake SW14,TW9 ..55 C4
Kingsway Coll NW5 .13 A2
Kingsway PI EC1 ....96 A2
Kingsway Rd NW5 ...4 C1
Kingswood 2 E2 ....25 B3
Kingswood Ave
NW6 .... 22 C3
Kingswood Cl SW8 .162 B1
Kingswood Ct 7
TW10 .... 54 B2
Kings Wood Ct 4
NW6 .... 10 C1
Kingswood Rd
  London W3 .... 37 B3
  Streatham SW2 ....74 A4
Kingswood Terr W4 .37 B3
Kings Yd E15 ....19 A4
Kington Ho NW6 ....78 B3
Kingward Ho E1 ....111 B4
King William La 3
SE10 .... 43 A1
King William St
EC4 .... 123 C4
King William Wlk
SE10 .... 52 B4
Kingwood Rd SW6 .154 A1
Kinloch St N7 ....5 B1
Kinnaird Ave W4 ...45 B3
Kinnear Rd W12 ....38 B4
Kinnerton Pl N
SW1 .... 131 A3
Kinnerton Pl S
SW1 .... 131 A3
Kinnerton St SW1 .131 B3
Kinnerton Yd SW1 .131 B3
Kinnoull Mans 10
E5 .... 17 A4
Kinnoul Rd W6 .....154 A4
Kinross Ho N1 ....84 C4
Kinsale Rd SE15 ....64 C4
Kinsham Ho 2 ....99 C2
Kintore Way SE1 ...152 C4
Kintyre Ct 17 SW2 .74 A4
Kinver Ho N4 ....6 C4
Kipling Ho 20 SE5 ..48 B3

Kipling St SE1 ......137 C4
Kipling Twr 3 W3 ..37 B3
Kirby Est SE16 ......40 A3
Kirby Gr SE1 ....138 A4
Kirby St EC1 ....107 C4
Kirkeby Bldg EC1 ..107 C3
Kirkley Ho N16 ....7 A3
Kirkman Pl W1 .....105 B3
Kirkmichael Rd E14 .34 B3
Kirkside Rd SE3 .....53 C4
Kirk's Pl E3 ....33 B4
Kirkstall Gdns SW2 .74 A3
Kirkstall Ho SW1 ..146 A2
Kirkstall Rd SW2 ...74 A3
Kirkstead Ct E5 .....18 A4
Kirkstone NW1 ......92 C4
Kirkton Lo SW18 ...59 A1
Kirkwall Pl E2 ......25 B2
Kirkwood Rd SE15 ..50 A1
Kirtley Ho SW8 ....171 A4
Kirtling St SW8 ....160 C2
Kirton Cl W4 ....37 C2
Kirwin Way SE5 .....48 A3
Kitcat Terr E3 ....26 C2
Kite Ho 5 SW11 .....60 A4
Kitson Rd SE5 ....48 B3
  Barnes SW13 ....46 C3
Kittiwake Ct 28 SE8 .51 B4
Kitto Rd SE14 ....50 C1
Kiver Rd N19 ....5 A2
Klea Ave SW4 ....61 B1
Kleffens Ct 2 SE3 ...53 B3
Knapp Cl NW10 ......8 A2
Knapp Rd E3 ....26 C1
Knaresborough Dr
SW18 .... 71 A3
Knaresborough Ho 4
N4 .... 6 B4
Knaresborough Pl
SW5 .... 142 A4
Knatchbull Rd
  London NW10 ....20 C4
  London SE5 ....48 A2
Knebworth Ho
SW8 .... 171 C3
  2 London N16 ....16 A4
Knebworth Rd 3
N16 .... 16 A4
Kneller Ho SW3 ...133 A4
Kneller Rd SE4 ......66 A3
Knighten St E1 ....125 C2
Knighthead Point
E14 .... 41 C4
Knight Ho SE17 ....152 A3
Knightleas Ct NW2 ..9 B2
Knightrider Ct EC4 .122 C4
Knightrider St EC4 .122 B4
Knights Arc SW1 ..130 C3
Knight's Ave W5 .....36 A4
Knightsbridge
SW1,SW7 ....130 C3
Knightsbridge Ct
SW1 .... 131 A3
Knightsbridge Gn
SW1 .... 130 C3
Knights Cl E9 ....17 B3
Knights Ho SW8 ...162 B1
  SW5 .... 140 C2
  8 SE1 .... 138 C4
Knight's Ho SW10 .156 C2
Knights Rd E16 ....43 C4
Knight's Wlk SE11 .150 A3
Knightswood Ct N6 ..4 C4
Knivet Rd SW6 ....155 B3
Knobs Hill Rd E15 ..27 A4
Knoll Ho NW8 ......78 C2

Knoll Rd SW18 ......59 B2
Knolly's Cl SE27,
SW16 .... 74 C1
Knolly's Rd SE27,
SW16 .... 74 C1
Knot Ho SE1 ....124 C1
Knottisford St 2 ....25 B2
Knowlden Ho 4 E1 .32 B2
Knowle Cl SW9 .....62 C4
Knowles Hill Cres
SE13 .... 67 C2
Knowles Ho
  London NW10 ....21 C4
  Wandsworth SW18 ....59 A1
Knowles Wlk SW4 ..61 B4
Knowlton Ho SW9 .173 C4
Knowsley Rd
SW11 .... 168 C1
Knox Ct SW4 ....172 B2
Knox Ho SW15 ......47 B1
Knox St W1 ....102 C4
Knoyle Ho W14 ....126 B2
Knoyle St SE14 .....51 A4
Kobi Nazrul Prim Sch
E1 .... 111 C2
Kossuth St SE10 ...43 A1
Kotree Way SE1 ....153 C4
Kramer Mews
SW5 .... 142 A1
Kreedman Wlk 8
E8 .... 16 C3
Kreisel Wlk TW9 ...44 B4
Kylemore Ct 4
W12 .... 38 C4
Kylemore Rd NW6 .10 C1
Kylestrome Ho
SW1 .... 145 C3
Kynance Mews
SW7 .... 128 B1
Kynance Pl SW7 ..128 C1
Kynaston Ho 7
SW2 .... 74 B3
Kynaston Rd N16 ...7 A1
Kyrle Rd SW11 .....60 C1
Kyverdale Rd N16 ..7 B3

L

Laburnam Cl 5
SE15 .... 50 B3
Laburnum Cl NW2 ..1 B2
Laburnum Ho SE4 ..51 B1
Laburnum Ct 2 E2 .24 B4
Laburnum Ho 6 N1 .15 B2
Laburnum JMI Sch
E2 .... 24 B4
Laburnum St E2 ....24 B4
Lacey Ho 6 SE13 ..52 B1
Lacey Wlk E3 ....26 C3
Lacine Ct 12 SE16 ..40 C4
Lackington St EC2 .109 C4
Lackland Ho 1 ......153 A2
Lacland Ho SW10 .157 B2
Lacon Rd SE22 .....64 C3
Lacy Rd SW15 ......57 C3
Ladbroke Cres W11 .31 A3
Ladbroke Gdns
W11 .... 31 B2
Ladbroke Gr
  W10 .... 31 A4
  W11 .... 31 B2
Ladbroke Gr W11 ..112 C4
Ladbroke Grove Ho
W11 .... 31 B2
Ladbroke Grove Sta
W10 .... 31 A4
Ladbroke Mews
W11 .... 112 B1

Ladbroke Rd
W11 ....31 B1 **112** C2
Ladbroke Sq
W11 ....31 B1 **113** A3
Ladbroke Terr
W11 ....31 B1 **113** A2
Ladbroke Wlk
W11 ....31 B1 **113** A2
Ladlands SE22 ....76 C4
Ladybower Ct **6** E5 17 C4
Ladycroft Rd SE13 .67 A4
Lady Elizabeth Ho
SW14 ....55 B4
Lady Florence Ctyd **14**
SE8 ....51 C3
Lady Margaret Rd
NW5 ....13 B3
Lady Margaret Sch
SW6 ....**165** B3
Lady Somerset Rd
NW5 ....13 A4
Ladywell Cl SE4 ....66 C3
Ladywell Hts SE4 ....66 B1
Ladywell Rd SE13 ...67 A2
Ladywell Sch SE13 ...67 A2
Ladywell Water Twr
SE4 ....66 C2
Lafitte Ho **22** N19 ....4 C4
Lafone Ho **11** SW2 ...74 A4
Lafone St SE1 ....**138** C4
Lagado Mews .32 C1
Lagonda Ho **11** E3 ...26 C1
Lagonier Ho EC1 ....97 A3
Laing Ho SE5 ....48 B3
Lainson St SW18 .....70 C4
Lairdale Cl SE21 .....75 B4
Laird Ho SE5 ....48 B3
Lairs Cl N7 ....14 A2
Laitwood Rd SW12 ...73 A3
Lakanal **14** SE5 ....49 A2
Lake Ho SE1 ....**136** C3
Laker Ct SW4 ....**172** B2
Laker Ho **5** SE5 .....58 A1
Lakeside Ct N4 ....6 B3
Lakeside Rd W14 ...39 C3
Lakeview **22** E3 .....25 C3
Lake View Ct SW1 ...**132** B2
Lakis Cl NW3 ....11 B4
Laleham Ho **2** 98 C2
Lamb Ct **10** E14 ....33 A2
Lamberhurst Ho **14**
SE15 ....50 B4
Lambert Ave TW9 ....55 A4
Lambert Ho
10 N19 ....4 C4
London SW9 ....**173** B1
Lambert Rd SW2 .....62 B2
Lambert St N1 ....14 C1
Lambeth Coll (Brixton
Ctr) SW2 ....62 B2
Lambeth Coll (Clapham
Ctr) SW4 ....61 B2
Lambeth Coll (Tower
Bridge Ctr) SE1 ...**124** B1
Lambeth Coll (Vauxhall
Ctr) SW8 ....**171** B4
Lambeth Ct **8**
SW18 ....58 C2
Lambeth High St
SE1 ....**148** C4
Lambeth Hill EC4 ...**122** C4
Lambeth Hospl SW9 62 B4
Lambeth Inst Strand Ctr
SW2 ....74 B4
Lambeth North Sta
SE1 ....**135** B2

Lambeth Palace★
SE1 ....**134** C1
Lambeth Palace Rd
SE1 ....**134** C2
Lambeth Pier SE1 ...**134** B1
Lambeth Rd SE1 ....**135** B1
Lambeth Twrs
SE11 ....**135** B1
Lambeth Wlk SE11 ..**149** A4
Lambfold Ho N7 .....14 A2
Lamble St NW5 ....12 B4
Lambolle Pl NW3 .....12 A2
Lambolle Rd NW3 ....12 A2
Lambourn Cl **9**
NW5 ....13 B4
Lambourne Ho
NW8 ....**101** C4
SE16 ....40 C2
Lambourn Rd SW4 ...61 A4
Lambrook Ho **12**
SE15 ....49 C2
Lambrook Terr
SW6 ....**164** A4
Lamb's Bldgs EC1 ...97 B1
Lamb's Conduit Pas
WC1 ....**106** C4
Lamb's Conduit St
WC1 ....94 C1
Lamb's Mews N1 .....86 A3
Lamb's Pas EC1 .....97 B1
Lambs St E1 ....**110** C4
Lambton Ct **2** N19 ...5 A3
Lambton Pl W11 ....**113** A4
Lambton Rd N19 .....5 A3
Lamb Wlk SE1 ....**138** A3
Lamerton Lo **7**
TW9 ....44 B2
Lamerton St **8** SE8 ..51 C4
Lamington St **8**
W6 ....39 A2
Lamlash St SE11 ....**150** A4
Lamley Ho SE10 .....52 A3
Lammas Rd E9 ....17 C1
Lammermoor Rd
SW12 ....73 A4
Lamont Rd SW10 ....**157** B3
Lamont Rd Pas
SW10 ....**157** B3
Lampard Gr N16 .....7 B3
Lampern Sq **2** 99 C4
Lampeter Sq **6** **154** A3
Lamplighter Cl **8**
E1 ....25 B1
Lampson Ho **6** N19 13 B4
Lanark Ho SE1 ......**153** B1
Lanark Mans 89 A2
6 London W12 ...39 B4
Lanark Pl W9 ....89 A2
Lanark Rd W9 ....88 C3
Lanark Sq E14 ....42 A3
Lanbury Rd SE15 ...**118** B4
Lancaster Ave SE21,
SE27 ....75 B2
Lancaster Cl **2** **114** A3
9 London N1 ...16 A1
Lancaster Cotts **1**
TW10 ....54 A1
Lancaster Ct SW6 ...**155** A1
W2 ....**115** B4
West Norwood SE27 .75 A2
Lancaster Dr E14 ....34 B1
London NW3 ....12 A2

Lancaster Gate
W2 ....**115** A4
Lancaster Gate Sta
W2 ....**115** B4
Lancaster Gr NW3 ...12 A2
Lancaster Ho SW1 ..**132** C4
Lancaster Lo **2**
W11 ....31 A3
Lancaster Mews
W2 ....**115** A4
3 London SW18 ...59 A2
8 Richmond TW10 ...54 A1
Lancaster Pk TW10 ..54 A2
Lancaster Pl WC2 ...**120** C4
Lancaster Rd W11 ...31 A3
London N4 ....5 C4
London NW10 ....8 B2
Lancaster St SE1 ...**136** B3
Lancaster Stables **10**
NW3 ....12 A2
Lancaster Terr W2 ..**115** B4
Lancaster Wlk
W2 ....**115** A2
Lancefield Ho SE15 .65 A4
Lancefield St W10 ...23 B2
Lancell St N16 ....7 A2
Lancelot Pl SW7 ....**130** C3
Lancer Sq W8 ....**128** A4
Lanchester Ct W2 ..**102** C1
Lancing St NW1 .....93 B3
Lancresse Ct N1 ....24 A4
Landale Ho **15** SE16 40 B3
Landcroft Rd SE22 ..64 B1
Landells Rd SE22 ...64 C1
Landford Rd SW15 ..57 B4
Landin Ho **1** E14 ....33 C3
Landleys Field **2**
N7 ....13 C3
Landmann Ho **16**
SE16 ....40 A2
Landmann Way
SE14 ....40 C1
London SW1 ....**120** C2
Landons Cl E14 .....34 B1
London Wlk E14 ....34 A2
Landor Ct N16 ....16 A3
Landor Ho **7** SE5 ...48 C3
Landor Rd SW9 .....62 A4
Landor Wlk **11** W12 38 C4
Landrake NW1 ....83 A3
Landridge Rd SW6 .**164** C2
Landseer Ho NW8 ...89 C2
SW1 ....**147** C3
SW11 ....**169** C3
Landseer Rd N19 .....5 A2
Landulph Ho SE11 ..**149** C2
Landward Ct W1 ....**102** B2
Lane Ct SW11 ....72 B4
Lanercost Cl SW2 ...74 C2
Lanercost Rd SW2 ..74 C2
Lane The NW8 ....78 C1
Laneway SW15 ....57 A2
Laney Bldg EC1 .....**107** B4
Lanfranc Rd E3 .....26 A3
Lanfrey Pl W14 .....**140** C1
Langbourne Ave N6 ..3 C2
Langbourne Ho **7**
SW2 ....62 C2
Langbourne Mans
N6 ....3 C2
Langbourne Prim Sch
SE21 ....76 A1
Langdale NW1 ....92 C4

Langdale Cl SE17 ....48 B4
Mortlake SW14 ....55 A3
Langdale Ho SW1 ..**146** C1
Langdale Rd SE10 ...52 B3
Langdale St **1** E1 ....32 A3
Langdon Ct EC1 .....86 B1
London NW10 ....21 A4
Langdon Ho **6** E14 ..34 B3
Langdon Park Rd N6 ..4 B4
Langdon Park Sec Sch
E14 ....34 B3
Langdon Pl SW14 ...55 B4
Langdon Way **11** ...**153** C3
Langford Cl NW8 ....79 A2
London E8 ....16 C3
Langford Ct NW8 ....79 A1
Langford Gn SE5 ....64 A4
Langford Ho **6** SE8 .51 C4
Langford Pl NW8 ....79 A2
Langford Prim Sch
SW6 ....**166** B2
Langford Rd SW6 ...**166** B2
Langham Ct **4**
SW15 ....57 C2
Langham Ho SW4 ....61 B2
Langham Mans
SW5 ....**142** A1
Langham Pl W1 .....**104** B3
Chiswick W4 ....46 A4
Langham St W1 .....**104** B3
Lang Ho **3** N19 ......4 B1
SW8 ....**162** A1
Langholm Cl SW12 ..73 C4
Langhorne Ct **10**
NW8 ....11 C1
Langhorne Ho **4**
SW11 ....**169** B2
Langland Gdns
NW3 ....11 A3
Langland Ho **10** SE5 48 C3
Langler Rd NW10 ...22 B3
Langley Ct WC2 ....**120** A4
SW9 ....**173** B1
Langley Dr W3 .....37 A4
Langley Ho
11 London E5 .....17 A3
1 London W2 ....31 C4
Langley La SW8 ....**162** B4
Langley Mans SW8 **162** B4
Langley St WC2 ....**106** A1
Langmead Ho **24** E3 27 A2
Langmore Ho **2** **111** C1
Langport Ho **1** 48 A1
Langridge **18** NW5 ..12 C2
Langroyd Rd SW17 ..72 B2
Langside Ave SW15 .56 C3
Lang St E1 ....25 B1
Langston Hughes Cl **5**
SE24 ....63 A3
Langthorn Ct EC2 ..**109** C2
Langthorne St
SW6 ....47 C3
Langton Cl WC1 .....95 A3
Langton Ho SE11 ..**149** A4
Langton Pl SW18 ...70 C3
Langton Rd SW9 ....48 A3
Langton St SW10 ..**157** A3
Langton Way SE3 ...53 C3
Langtry Ct **6** W6 ....**154** C4
Langtry Pl SW6 .....**155** C4
Langtry Rd NW8 .....78 B3
Langtry Wlk NW8 ...78 C4
Lanhill Rd W9 ....23 C1
Lanier Ho **2** SE13 ...67 C1
Lanner Ho **9** SW11 .60 A4

Lannoy Point SW6 ..**154** B2
Lanrick Rd E14 ....34 C3
Lansbury Gdns **1**
E14 ....34 C3
Lanscombe Wlk
SW8 ....**162** A1
Lansdowne Cres
W11 ....31 A2 **112** B3
Lansdowne Dr E8 ...16 C1
Lansdowne Gdns
SW8 ....**172** A4
Lansdowne Gr NW10 ..8 A4
Lansdowne Hill
SE27 ....75 A1
Lansdowne Ho
W11 ....**112** C2
Lansdowne Mews
W11 ....**112** C2
Lansdowne Pl SE1 **137** C2
Lansdowne Rd
W11 ....31 A2 **112** B3
London E8 ....16 C2
Lansdowne Rise
W11 ....31 A2 **112** B3
Lansdowne Sch
SW2 ....62 B4
Lansdowne Terr
WC1 ....94 B1
Lansdowne Way
SW8,SW8 ....**172** B3
Lansdowne Wlk
W11 ....31 A2 **112** C2
Lansdowne Wood Cl **11**
SE27 ....75 A1
Lansdown Ho **20**
SE5 ....48 B1
Lantern Cl SW15 ....56 C3
Lanterns Ct E14 .....41 C3
Lant Ho SE1 ....**136** C3
Lantry Ct **1** W3 .....28 A1
Lant St SE1 ....**137** A3
Lanvanor Rd SE15 ..50 B1
Lanyard Ho **8** SE8 ..41 B2
Lapford Cl W9 ....23 B1
Lapsang SE1 ....**125** A1
Lapwing Twr **8** SE8 51 B4
Lapworth Ct W2 ....**100** B4
Lara Cl SE13 ....67 B1
Larch Ave W3 ....29 A1
Larch Cl **13** SE8 ....51 B4
Balham SW12 ....73 A2
7 London N19 ....4 B2
Larch Ct W9 ....31 C4
Larches Ave SW14 ..55 C3
Larchfield Ho **2** N5 15 B3
Larch Ho **17** SE16 ...40 B4
Larchmore Ct N19 ...5 A2
Larch Rd NW2 ....9 B4
Larcom St SE17 ....**151** A3
Larden Rd W3 ....38 A4
La Retraite RC Girls Sch
SW12 ....73 B4
Larissa St SE17 ....**151** C3
Larix Ct NW10 ....21 C4
Larkfield Rd TW9 ...54 A3
Lark Hall Inf Sch
SW4 ....**171** C1
Lark Hall Jun Sch
SW4 ....**172** A3
Larkhall La SW4 ...**172** A3
Larkhall Rise SW4 .**171** B1
Lark Row E2 ....25 B4

Larmenier & Sacred Heart RC Prim Sch W6 .....39 C2
Larnaca Ho SE1 .....134 C1
Larnach Rd W6 .....47 C4
Larpent Ave SW15 .....57 B2
La Saint Union RC Sec Sch NW5 .....3 C1
Lascelles Ho NW1 .....90 B1
Lassell St SE10 .....42 C1
Lasseter PI SE3 .....53 B4
Latchmere Rd SW11 .....168 C2
Latchmere St SW11 .....168 C2
Latham Ho E1 .....32 C3
Latimer SE17 .....152 A1
Latimer Ho W11 .....113 A3
11 London E9 .....17 C2
Latimer PI W10 .....30 B3
Latimer Rd W10 .....30 C3
Latimer Road Sta W10 .....30 C2
Latona Rd SE15 .....49 C4
Lattimer PI W4 .....46 A4
Latymer Ct W6 .....39 C2
Latymer Upper Sch W6 .....38 C1
Lauderdale Mans W9 .....88 B3
Lauderdale Rd W9 .....88 C3
Lauderdale Twr EC2 .....108 C4
Laud St SE11 .....148 C2
Laughton Ho 11 SW2 .....62 C1
Launcelot St SE1 .....135 B3
Launceston PI W8 .....128 C1
Launch St E14 .....42 B3
Laundress La N16 .....7 C1
Laundry La 15 N1 .....15 B1
Laundry Rd W6 .....154 A3
Laura PI E5 .....17 B4
Laurel Bank Gdns SW6 .....165 A2
Laurel CI 5 London N19 .....4 B2
5 Putney SW15 .....57 C2
Laurel Ho 9 SE8 .....51 B4
5 London NW3 .....11 A2
Laurel St E8 .....16 B2
Laurence Mews 7 W12 .....38 C4
Laurence Pountney Hill EC4 .....123 B4
Laurence Pountney La EC4 .....123 C4
Laurie Gr SE14 .....51 A2
Laurie Ho SE1 .....136 B1
W8 .....127 C1 B1
Laurier Rd NW5 .....4 A1
Lauriston Lo NW6 .....10 B2
Lauriston Rd E9 .....17 C1
Lauriston Sch E9 .....25 C4
Lausanne Rd SE15 .....50 B2
Lavell St N16 .....15 C4
Lavender CI SW3 .....157 C3
Lavender Ct SW4 .....172 B3
Lavender Gdns SW11 .....60 B3
Lavender Gr E8 .....16 C1
Lavender Hill SW11 .....60 C4
Lavender Ho 14 SE16 .....32 C1

Lavender Rd SE16 .....33 A1
London SW11 .....59 C4
Lavender Sweep SW11 .....60 B3
Lavender Terr 12 SW11 .....60 A4
Lavender Wlk SW11 .....60 B3
Lavendon Ho NW8 .....90 B2
Lavengro Rd SE27 .....75 B2
Lavenham Rd SW18 .....70 C3
Lavers Rd N16 .....7 A1
Laverstoke Gdns SW15 .....68 C4
Laverton Mews SW5 .....142 B3
Laverton PI SW5 .....142 B3
Lavina Gr N1 .....84 C2
Lavington CI E9 .....18 B2
Lavington St SE1 .....122 B1
Lawdale Jun Sch E2 .....24 C2 C3
Lawford Rd Chiswick W4 .....45 B3
London N1 .....16 A1
London NW5 .....13 B3
Lawford's Wharf 15 NW1 .....13 B1
Lawless Ho 5 E14 .....34 B2
Lawless St 11 E14 .....34 A2
Lawley St E5 .....17 B4
Lawman Ct 7 TW9 .....44 C3
Lawn Cres TW9 .....44 C1
Lawn House CI E14 .....42 B4
Lawn La SW8 .....162 C4
Lawn Rd NW3 .....12 B3
Lawns The N16 .....16 A3
Lawrence CI E3 .....26 C3
E12 .....47 C1
Lawrence Ct London N16 .....7 B1
4 London W3 .....37 B3
Lawrence Ho 15 SW1 .....147 C3
Lawrence La EC2 .....109 A2
Lawrence Mans SW3 .....158 A3
Lawrence PI N1 .....84 B4
Lawrence's Bldgs 7 N16 .....7 B1
Lawrence St E16 .....35 B2
SW3 .....158 A3
Lawrence Trad Est SE10 .....43 A2
Lawson CI SW19 .....69 C1
Lawson Ct 11 N4 .....5 B3
Lawson Ho 10 W12 .....30 A2
Law St SE1 .....137 C2
Lawton Rd E3 .....26 A2
Laxfield Ct E8 .....24 C4
Laxley CI SE5 .....48 A3
Laxton Path 1 SE4 .....65 C3
Laxton PI NW1 .....92 B2
Layard Rd SE16 .....40 A2
Layard Sq SE16 .....40 A2
Laycock Prim Sch N1 .....15 A2
Laycock St N1 .....14 C2
Layfield Ho 13 SE10 .....43 C1
Laystall Ct EC1 .....95 B1
Laystall St EC1 .....95 B1
Layton PI 3 TW9 .....44 C2
Lazar Wlk 2 N7 .....5 B2
Leabank Sq E9 .....18 C2
Leabourne Rd N16 .....7 C4
Leacroft Ave SW12 .....72 B4
Lea Ct 3 W12 .....38 A4

Leadenhall Mkt EC3 .....110 A1
Leadenhall PI EC3 .....110 A1
Leadenhall St EC3 .....110 A1
Leadenham Ct 19 E3 .....26 C1
Lea Ho NW8 .....90 A1
Lea Int E9 .....18 C3
Leake St SE1 .....135 A4
SE1 .....135 A3
Leamington Ct 4 Forest Hill SE26 .....76 C1
London W3 .....28 C4
Leamington Ho 3 W11 .....31 B4
Leamington Pk W3 .....28 C4
Leamington Rd Villas W11 .....31 B4
Leamore St W6 .....39 B2
Leamouth Rd E14 .....34 C3
Leander Ct 27 London E9 .....17 B1
London SE8 .....51 C2
Leander Rd SW2 .....62 C1
Leary Ho SE11 .....149 A1
Leatherdale St E1 .....25 B1
Leatherhead CI N16 .....7 B3
Leather La EC1 .....107 C4
Leathermarket Ct SE1 .....138 A3
Leathermarket St SE1 .....138 A3
Leathwaite Rd SW11 .....60 B2
Leathwell Rd SE8 .....52 A1
Lebanon Gdns SW18 .....58 C1
Lebanon Rd SW18 .....58 C2
Lebus Ho NW8 .....80 A1
Lechmere Rd NW2 .....9 A2
Leckford Rd SW18 .....71 B3
Leckhampton PI 22 SW2 .....74 C4
Lecky St SW7 .....143 B2
L'Ecole des Petits Sch SW6 .....166 B2
Leconfield Ave SW13,SW15 .....56 B4
Leconfield Ho SE5 .....64 A4
Leconfield Rd N5 .....6 C4
Leda Ct SW9 .....163 B1
Ledam Bldg EC1 .....107 B3
Ledbury Ho 22 SE22 .....64 A4
Ledbury Mews N W11 .....113 C4
Ledbury Mews W W11 .....113 B3
Ledbury Rd W11 .....31 C3 113 A4
Ledbury St SE15 .....49 C3
Ledo Ho 1 N16 .....15 C4
Lee Conservancy Rd E9 .....18 C3
Leeds Ct EC1 .....96 A2
Lee Ho 13 N19 .....13 C3
Leeke St WC1 .....94 C4
Leeland Way NW10 .....8 B4
Leerdam Dr E14 .....42 B3
Lees Ct W1 .....117 B4
Lees Ho SE17 .....151 C1
Leeson Rd 12 SE24 .....62 C3
Lees PI W1 .....117 B4
Lee St E8 .....24 B4
Leet Ct N16 .....6 C1
Lee Valley Sp Ctr E15 .....19 A4

Leeve Ho 7 W9 .....23 B2
Leeward Ct 1 E1 .....125 C2
Leeway SE8 .....41 B1
Lefevre Wlk 1 E3 .....26 B4
Leffern Rd W12 .....38 C4
Leff Ho 7 NW6 .....10 A1
Lefroy Ho SE1 .....136 C3
Lefroy Rd W12 .....38 B4
Legard Rd N5 .....6 A1
Leggatt Rd E15 .....27 B3
Legge St SE13 .....67 B2
Leghorn Rd NW10 .....21 C3
Legion Ct N1 .....54 C1
Legion Terr E3 .....26 C4
Leicester Ct 3 4 London W2 .....31 C4
Leicester Ho 4 London SW9 .....63 A4
5 Putney SW15 .....69 B4
Leicester PI WC2 .....119 C4
Leicester Sq* WC2 .....119 C3
Leicester Square Sta WC2 .....119 C4
Leicester St WC2 .....119 C4
Leigham Ave SW16 .....74 A1
Leigham Hall 3 SW16 .....74 A1
Leigham Hall Par 2 SW16 .....74 A1
Leigham Vale SE27, SW16,SW2 .....74 C2
Leigh Ct 2 SW2 .....62 C1
Leigh Gdns NW10 .....22 B3
Leigh Ho 5 SW15 .....56 C2
Leigh Orchard CI SW16 .....74 B1
Leigh PI EC1 .....107 B4
Leigh Rd N5 .....15 A4
Leigh St WC1 .....94 A3
Leighton Cres NW5 .....13 B3
Leighton Gdns NW10 .....22 B3
Leighton Gr NW5 .....13 B3
Leighton House (Art Gall & Mus) W14 .....127 A2
Leighton PI NW5 .....13 B3
Leighton Rd NW5 .....13 B3
Leinster Ave SW14 .....55 B3
Leinster Gdns W2 .....114 C4
Leinster Mews W2 .....114 C4
Leinster PI W2 .....100 C1
Leinster Sq W2 .....100 A1
Leinster Terr W2 .....114 C4
Leitch Ho 8 NW8 .....11 C1
Leithcote Path SW16 .....74 B1
Leith Ho 7 London N7 .....13 C3
17 Streatham SW2 .....74 A4
Leith Mans W9 .....88 A3
Leith Yd 3 NW6 .....23 C4
Letitia CI E8 .....24 C4
Leman St E1 .....111 A1
Lemmon Rd SE10 .....53 A4
Le Moal Ho 28 E1 .....32 B4
Lemsford Ct N4 .....6 B2
Lena Gardens Prim Sch W6 .....39 B3
Lena Gdns W6 .....39 B3
Lendal Terr 7 SW4 .....61 C4
Len Freeman PI SW6 .....154 C3
Lenham 11 NW5 .....12 C2
Lenham Ho SE1 .....137 C3

Lennon Rd NW2 .....9 B2
Lennox Gdns SW1 .....130 C1
SW1 .....144 C4
Lennox Gdns Mews SW1 .....144 C4
Lennox Ho 10 E9 .....17 B2
Lennox Rd N4,N7 .....5 C2
Lenthall Ho SW1 .....147 A1
Lenthall Rd E8 .....16 C1
Lenthorp Rd SE10 .....43 B2
Lenton Rise TW9 .....54 A4
Len Williams Ct NW6 .....23 C3
Leonard Ct W8 .....127 B2
WC1 .....94 A2
Leonard Day Ho 3 NW5 .....13 A4
Leonard PI 6 N16 .....16 A4
Leonard St EC2 .....97 C2
Leonora Ho W9 .....88 C2
Leontine CI SE15 .....49 C3
Leopards Ct EC1 .....107 B4
Leopold Bldgs E2 .....98 C4
Leopold Mews E9 .....25 B4
Leopold Prim Sch NW10 .....8 B1
Leopold Rd NW10 .....8 A1
Leopold St E3 .....33 B4
Leopold Wlk SE11 .....148 C1
Leo St SE15 .....50 A3
Leo Yd EC1 .....96 B1
Leppoc Rd SW4 .....61 C2
Leroy St SE1 .....152 A4
Lerry CI W14 .....155 A4
Lerwick Ho SW18 .....59 B3
Leslie Rd E11 .....19 C4
Lessar Ave SW4 .....61 B1
Lessar Ct SW4 .....61 B1
Lester Ct 42 E3 .....27 A2
Leswin PI N16 .....7 B1
Leswin Rd N16 .....7 B1
Letchford Gdns NW10 .....21 C2
Letchford Mews NW10 .....21 C2
Letchmore Ho W10 .....22 B1
Lethaby Ho 15 SW4 .....62 B3
Lethbridge CI SE13 .....52 B1
Letterstone Rd SW6 .....154 C1
Lettice St SW6 .....165 A3
Lett Rd E15 .....19 C1
Lettsom St SE5 .....49 A1
Leucha Rd E17 .....19 A4
Levana CI SW19 .....70 A3
Levant Ho 20 E1 .....25 C1
Leverhurst Way SW4,SW9 .....172 B2
Leven Rd E14 .....34 C3
Lever Ct 15 E9 .....17 C2
Leverett St SW3 .....144 B4
Leverington PI N1 .....97 C3
Lever St EC1 .....96 C3
Leverstock Ho SW3 .....144 B2
Leverton PI NW5 .....13 B3
Leverton St NW5 .....13 B3
Levison Way 2 N19 .....4 C3
Levita Ho NW1 .....93 C4
Levyne Ct EC1 .....95 B2
Lewesdon CI 13 SW19 .....69 C3
Lewes Ho E1 .....138 B4
SE15 .....49 C4
Leweston PI N16 .....7 B4
Lewin Rd SW14 .....55 C4
Lewis Ct 5 SE16 .....40 A1

Lewis Gr SE13 ......67 B4
Lewisham Bridge Prim
  Sch SE13 ....A7 A4
Lewisham Bsns Ctr
  SE14 ....50 C4
Lewisham Coll SE4 .51 C1
Lewisham Ctr SE13 ..51 B3
Lewisham High St
  SE13 ....67 A2
Lewisham Hill SE13 .52 B1
Lewisham Hospl
  SE13 ....67 A3
Lewisham Pk SE13 ..67 B1
Lewisham Pk Rd SE13 .67 B1
Lewisham St SW1 .133 C3
Lewisham Sta SE13 .67 B4
Lewisham Way SE4,
  SE14 ....51 B2
Lewis PI E8 ....16 C3
Lewis Silkin Ho 9
  SE15 ....50 B4
Lewis St NW1 ....13 A2
Lexden Ho 10 ....28 A1
Lexfield Ho N5 ....15 B4
Lexham Gardens Mews
  W8 ....142 A4
Lexham Gdns W8 ...142 A4
Lexham Mews W8 ..141 C4
Lexham Wlk W8 ......142 A4
Lexington St W1 .....119 A4
Lexton Gdns SW12 .73 C3
Leyborne Pk TW9 ...44 C2
Leybourne Ho
  E14 ....33 B3
  15 SE15 ....50 B4
Leybourne Rd 10
  NW1 ....13 A1
Leybourne St 5
  NW1 ....13 A1
Leyden Mans 3 N19 .5 A4
Leyden St E1 ....110 C2
Leydon Cl SE16 ....32 C1
Ley Ho SE1 ....136 C3
Leyland Ho 8 E14 ..34 A2
Leylands SW18 ....58 B1
Leylang Rd SE14 ....50 C3
Leys Ct SW9 ....173 B1
Leysdown 9 NW5 ....12 C2
Leysdown Ho SE17 152 B2
Leysfield Rd W12 ....38 C4
Leythe Rd W3 ....37 B4
Leyton Rd E15 ....19 C2
Liardet St SE14 ....51 A4
Liberia Rd N5 ....15 A2
Liberty Mews SW12 .61 A1
Liberty PI E1 ....125 C3
Liberty St SW9 ......173 A4
Libra Rd 6 E3 ....26 B3
Library Mans 4
  W12 ....39 B4
Library Par NW10 ...21 A4
Library PI E1 ....32 A2
Library St SE1 ....136 B3
Lichfield Ct SW9 .....54 A3
Lichfield Gdns
  TW10,TW9 ....54 A2
Lichfield Ho 28 SE5 .48 B1
Lichfield Rd E3 ....26 A2
  London NW2 ....10 A4
  Richmond TW9 ......44 B2
Lichfield Terr 1
  TW9 ....54 A2
Lichport Ct N4 ....6 A3
Lickey Ho W14 ....155 A4
Lidcote Gdns SW9 .173 A1
Liddell Gdns NW10 .22 B3
Liddell Rd NW6 ....10 C2

Lidfield Rd N16 ....15 C4
Lidgate Rd 21 SE15 .49 B3
Lidiard Rd SW18 ......71 B2
Lidlington PI NW1 ...83 A1
Lidyard Rd N19 ....4 B3
Liffords St SW13 ......46 B1
Lifford St SW15 ....57 C3
Lighter Cl 15 SE16 ..41 A2
Lighterman Mews 13
  E1 ....32 C3
Lighterman's Rd
  E14 ....42 A4
Lightermans Wlk
  SW18 ....58 C3
Ligonier St E2 ....98 C2
Lilac Ho SE4 ....66 B4
Lilac PI SE11 ....148 C3
Lilac St W12 ....29 C2
Lilburn Ct SW15 ......57 C4
Lilestone Est NW8 ..89 C2
Lilestone Ho NW8 ...89 C2
Lilestone St NW8 ....90 A2
Lilford Ho 20 SE5 ....48 B1
Lilford Rd SE5 ....48 A1
Lilian Baylis Ho N1 .15 B2
Lilian Baylis Sch
  SE11 ....148 C2
Lilley Cl E1 ....125 C1
Lillian Ave W3 ....36 C4
Lillian Cl 3 N16 ....7 A1
Lillian Rd SW13 ......47 A4
Lillie Ho N5 ....14 C3
Lillie Rd SW6 ....154 C3
Lilleshall Rd SW4 ...61 A4
Lillie Yd SW6 ....155 B4
Lillingston Ho N7 ....14 C4
Lily Cl W14 ....39 C2
Lily PI EC1 ....107 C4
Lilyville Rd SW6 .....164 C4
Limberg Ho 5 SE8 ..41 B2
Limborough Ho 4
  E14 ....33 C4
Limburg Rd SW11 ..60 A3
Limeburner La
  EC4 ....108 A2
Lime Cl E1 ....125 C2
Lime Ct SW15 ....57 A4
Lime Gr W12 ....39 B4
Limeharbour E14 ....42 A4
Limehouse Cswy
  E14 ....33 B2
Limehouse Cut 5
  E14 ....34 A4
Limehouse Fields Est
  SE16 ....33 A4
Limehouse Link
  (Tunnel) E14 ....33 B2
Limehouse Sta E14 .33 A3
Limekiln Wharf 21
  E14 ....33 B2
Limerick Cl SW12 ...73 B4
Limerick Ct 1
  SW12 ....73 A4
Limerston St
  SW10 ....157 A3
Limes Ave
  Barnes SW13 ....46 B1
  London NW11 ....1 A4
Limes Ct NW6 ....9 C1
Limes Field Rd
  SW14 ....56 A4
Limesford Rd SE15 .65 C3
Limes Gdns SW18 ..58 C1
Limes Gr SE13 ....67 B3
Lime St EC3 ....110 A1
Limes The W2 ....113 C3

Limes The continued
  London SE5 ....64 A4
  Lime St Pas E1 .....124 A4
Limes Wlk SE15 ......65 B3
Limetree Cl SW2 .....74 B3
Limpsfield Ave
  SW19 ....69 C2
Limscott Ho 35 E3 ..27 A2
Linacre Cl SE15 ......65 A4
Linacre Ct W6 ....39 C1
Linacre Rd NW2 ....9 A2
Linale Ho N1 ....87 B1
Linberry Wlk 8 SE8 .41 B2
Lincoln Ave SW19 ..69 C1
Lincoln Ct N16 ....6 C4
Lincoln Ho
  10 Finsbury Pk N5 .58 A2
  Lincoln Mews NW6 .23 B4
  Lincoln's Inn *
    WC2 ....107 A2
  Lincoln's Inn Fields
    WC2 ....107 A2
Lincoln St SW3 ......144 C3
Lindale SW19 ....70 A2
Lindal Rd SE4 ....66 B2
Linden Ave NW10 ...22 C3
Linden Ct
  8 London SE8 ....59 C3
  London W12 ....30 B1
Linden Gdns
  London W4 ....37 C1
  W2 ....34 C2 113 C3
Linden Gr SE15 ....65 B4
Linden Ho 10 SE8 ...51 B4
Linden Lodge Sch
  SW19 ....70 A3
Linden Mans N6 ....4 A3
Linden Mews
  London N1 ....15 C3
  London W12 ....30 B1
Lindens The W4 ....45 B2
Lindfield Gdns NW3 .11 B3
Lindfield Hts NW3 ..11 B3
Lindfield St E14 ......33 C3
Lindisfarne Way E9 .18 A4
Lindley Ho 6 SE15 .49 C3
Lindley PI TW9 ....44 C2
Lindley St E1 ....32 B4
Lindop Ho 7 E3 ....26 A1
Lindore Rd SW11 ....60 B3
Lindo St SE15 ....50 B1
Lindrop St SW6 .....166 C2
Lindsay Ct SW11 ...167 C3
Lindsay Sq SW1 ....147 C2
Lindsell St 6 SE10 .52 B2
Lindsey Ho *
  5 London SW10 ...157 C2
  Lindsey Mews 12
    N1 ....15 B1
Lindsey St EC1 ......108 B4
Lind St SE8 ....52 A1
Linfield WC1 ....94 C3
Linford Ho 17 E2 .....24 C4
Linford St SW8 ......170 C3
Lingard Ho 9 E14 ...42 B3
Lingards Rd SE13 ...67 B3
Lingfield Ho SE1 ....136 B3
  5 London W12 ....30 A2
Lingham St SW9 ....172 C1
Ling Rd E16 ....35 C4
Ling's Coppice SE21 .75 C2
Lingwell Rd SW17 ..72 A1
Lingwood Rd E5 ....7 C4
Linhope St NW1 ....90 C1
Linkenholt Mans 7
  W6 ....38 B2
Link St E9 ....17 B2
Links Yd E1 ....111 A4
Link The W3 ....28 A3

Linkway N4 ....6 B4
Linkwood Wlk NW1 .13 C1
Linnell Ho E1 ....110 C4
  NW8 ....78 C4
Linnell Rd SE5 ....49 A1
Linnet Mews SW12 .72 C4
Linom Rd SW4 ....62 A3
Linscott Rd E5 ....17 B4
Linsey St SE16 ......139 C1
  SE16 ....153 B4
Linslade Ho 10 E2 ...24 C4
  NW8 ....90 B2
Linstead St 1 NW6 ..10 C1
Lintaine Cl W6 ....154 B3
Linthorpe Rd N16 ....7 A4
Linton Ho 2 E3 ....33 C4
Linton St N1 ....87 A3
Linver Rd SW6 ....166 A2
Linwood Cl SE5 ....49 B1
Lion Cl SE4 ....66 C1
Lionel Ho 10 W10 ..31 A4
Lionel Mews 14
  W10 ....31 A4
Lion Mills 14 ....39 C3
Lionel Road Jun & Inf
  Sch TW8 ....36 A2
Lional Road N TW8 .36 A2
Lionel Road S TW8 .36 A1
Lion Gate Gdns
  TW9 ....54 B4
Lion Gate Mews
  SW18 ....70 C4
Lion Mills 21 E2 ......24 C3
Lion Yd SW4 ....61 C3
Lipton Rd 8 E1 ....32 C3
Lisburne Rd NW3 ...12 B4
Lisford St SE15 ....49 B2
Lisgar Terr W14 .....140 C4
Liskeard Gdns SE3 .53 C2
Liskeard Ho SE11 ..149 C2
Lisle Ct NW2 ....1 A1
Lisle St WC2 ....119 C4
Lismore Wlk 4 N1 ..15 B2
Lissenden Gdns
  NW5 ....12 C4
Lissenden Mans
  NW5 ....12 C4
Lisson Cotts NW1 ..102 B4
Lisson Gr NW1,NW8 .90 A2
Lisson Ho NW1 ......102 A4
Lisson St NW1 ....102 A4
Lister Cl W3 ....28 C4
Lister Ct N16 ....7 A2
Lister Ho E1 ....111 C4
  SE3 ....53 A4
Lister Hospl SW1 ..146 A1
Lister Mews N7 ......14 B4
Liston Rd SW4 ....61 B4
Listowel Cl SW9 ....163 C2
Listria Lo N16 ....7 B2
Listria Pk N16 ....7 B2
Litcham Ho 3 E1 .....25 C2
Litchfield Gdns
  NW10 ....8 C2
Litchfield St WC2 ...119 C4
Lithos Rd NW3 ....11 B2
Little Albany St
  NW1 ....92 B2
Little Argyll St W1 .104 C1
Little Boltons The
  SW10 ....142 B1
Little Britain EC1 ...108 C3
Little Chelsea Ho
  SW10 ....157 A3

Little Chester St
  SW1 ....132 A2
Little College St
  SW1 ....134 A2
Little Combe Cl 13
  SW15 ....57 C1
Littlecote Cl SW19 ..70 A4
Little Dimocks
  SW12 ....73 A2
Little Dorrit Ct
  SE1 ....137 A4
Little Edward St
  NW1 ....92 B4
Little Essex St
  WC2 ....121 B4
Littlefield Cl N19 .....13 B4
Little George St
  SW1 ....134 A3
Little Green St NW5 .13 A4
Little Marlborough St
  W1 ....104 C1
Little Newport St
  WC2 ....119 C4
Little New St EC4 ...107 C2
Little Portland St
  W1 ....104 B2
Little Road Mans
  SW6 ....154 B3
Little Russell St
  WC1 ....106 A3
Little Sanctuary
  SW1 ....134 A3
Little Smith St
  SW1 ....133 C2
Little Somerset St
  E1 ....110 C1
Little St James's St
  SW1 ....118 C1
Little St Leonards
  SW14 ....55 B4
Little Titchfield St
  W1 ....104 C3
Littleton St SW18 ....71 B2
Little Trinity La
  EC4 ....123 A4
Little Venice * W9 ..100 C4
Littlewood SE13 .....67 B1
Livermere Ct 3 E8 ..24 B4
Livermere Rd E8 .....24 B4
Liverpool Gr SE17 ..151 B1
Liverpool Ho N7 .....14 C2
Liverpool Rd E16 ...35 A4
  N1 ....85 C3
  N1,N7 ....14 C1
Liverpool St EC2 ....110 A3
Liverpool Street Sta
  EC2 ....110 A3
Livesey Mus SE15 ...50 A4
Livesey PI SE15 ......49 C4
Livingstone Ho 13
  W9 ....31 C4
Livingstone PI E14 .42 B1
Livingstone Rd E15 .27 B4
  SW11 ....59 C4
Livity Sch SW2 ....62 A2
Livonia St W1 ....105 A1
Lizard St EC1 ....97 A3
Llandovery Ho 10
  E14 ....42 B4
Llanelly Rd NW2 ......1 B2
Llanvanor Rd NW2 ...1 B2
Llewellyn St SE16 ..139 C3
Lloyd Baker St WC1 .95 B3

Lloyd Ct London SE13 .. **67** A2
6 West Norwood
SE27 .... **75** A1
Lloyd Ho N16 .... **6** C1
Lloyd's Ave EC3 ..... **110** B3
Lloyd's Bldg* EC3 .... **110** B3
Lloyd's Pl SE3 .... **53** A1
Lloyd Sq WC1 .... **95** B4
Lloyd's Row EC1 .... **96** A3
Lloyd St WC1 .... **95** B4
Lloyd Villas SE4 .... **51** C1
Loampit Hill SE13 .. **52** A1
Loampit Vale SE13 .. **67** B4
Loanda Cl E8 .... **24** B4
Loanda Ho SE15 .... **65** B4
Loats Rd SW2 .... **62** A1
Locarno Rd **6** W3 .. **28** B1
Lochbie N4 .... **5** A4
Lochinvar St SW12 .. **73** A4
Lochmore Ho SW1 .. **145** C3
Lochnagar St E14 ... **34** B4
Lockbridge Ct **8**
W9 .... **31** C4
Locke Ho SW8 ...... **170** C4
Lockesfield Pl E14 .. **42** A1
Lockgate Cl E9 ...... **18** B3
Lockhart Cl N7 ...... **14** B2
Lockhart St E3 ...... **26** B1
Lock Ho N16 .... **7** B3
Lockhurst St E5 ..... **17** C4
Lockington Rd
SW8 .... **170** B4
Lockmead Rd SE13 .. **67** B4
Lockside **17** E14 .... **33** A2
Locksley St E14 ..... **33** B4
Lock View Ct **9**
E14 .... **33** A2
Lockwood Ho
SE11 .... **163** B3
Lockwood Sq SE16 .. **40** A3
Lockyer Est SE1 .... **137** C3
Lockyer Ho **9** SE10 **43** B1
SW8 .... **162** A2
Lockyer St SE1 ..... **137** C3
Locton Gn **4** E3 ... **26** B4
Loddiges Ho **5** E9 **17** B1
Loddiges Rd E9 ..... **17** B1
Loddon Ho NW8 .... **89** C1
Loder St SE15 ...... **50** B3
Lodge Rd NW8 ..... **90** A3
Lodore St E14 ...... **34** B3
Lodsworth Ho
SW11 .... **169** B3
Loftie St SE16 ..... **139** C3
Lofting Rd N1 ...... **14** C1
Lofts on the Park **7**
E9 .... **17** C2
Loftus Rd W12 ...... **30** A1
**Loftus Rd (Queens Park
Rangers FC)** W12 .. **30** A1
Logan Mews W8 .... **141** B4
Logan Pl W8 .... **141** B4
Loggetts SE21 ...... **76** A2
Lohmann Ho SE11 . **163** B4
Lolesworth Cl E1 .. **111** A3
Lollard St SE11 .... **149** B3
Loman St SE1 ..... **136** B4
Lomas St E1 .... **111** C4
Lombard St EC3 ... **123** C4
Lombard Ho 4
SE10 .... **52** B3
Lombard Rd SW11 . **167** B2

Lombard St EC3 .... **109** C1
Lombardy Pl W2 ... **114** B3
Lomley Ho 10 SW2 . **62** C1
Lomond Gr SE5 .... **48** C3
Lomond Ho 10 SE5 **48** C3
Loncroft Rd SE5 .... **49** A4
Londale Ct SE10 .... **52** B2
Londesborough Ho 6
N16 .... **16** A4
Londesborough Rd
N16 .... **16** A4
London Aquarium* ...
SE1 .... **134** C3
London Bridge
EC3,SE1 .... **123** C2
London Bridge City Pier
SE1 .... **124** A2
London Bridge Hospl
SE1 .... **123** C2
London Bridge St
SE1 .... **123** C1
London Bridge Sta
SE1 .... **123** C1
London Business Sch
NW1 .... **90** C2
London Canal Mus
N1 .... **84** B2
London Central
Mosque* NW8 ..... **90** B3
London Chest Hospl
E2 .... **25** B3
London Clinic NW1 . **91** C1
London Coll of Fashion
EC2 .... **24** A1 **98** B2
London Coll of Fashion
The W1 .... **103** C1
**London Coll of
International Business
Studies** WC1 .... **106** B3
London Coll of Printing
SE11 .... **136** B1
London Ct 3 SW18 . **58** C2
**London Docklands
Visitor Ctr** E14 .... **42** B4
London Dungeon *
SE1 .... **123** C2
London Eye (Millennium
Wheel)* SE1 ...... **134** C4
London Fields East Side
E8 .... **17** A1
London Fields Prim Sch
E8 .... **17** A1
London Fields Sta
E8 .... **25** A4
London Fields West Side
E8 .... **16** C1
London Foot Hospl
W1 .... **92** C1
London Gas Mus The
E3,E16 .... **27** C1
London Ho NW8 .... **80** B2
**London Hospital Dental
Inst** E1 .... **32** A4
**London Independent
Hospl The** E1 ...... **32** C4
London Inst The
W1 .... **104** A1
**London International
Film Sch** WC2 .... **106** B2
London La E8 .... **17** A1
**London Metropolitan
Univ** E1 .... **110** C1
**London Metropolitan
Univ (Carleton Grange
Hall)** **2** N7 .... **13** C4

**London Metropolitan
Univ (Central Ho)**
E1 .... **111** B2
**London Metropolitan
Univ (Coll of Tech &
Design)** E1 .... **111** B2
**London Metropolitan
Univ (Commercial Rd)**
E1 .... **111** B2
**London Metropolitan
Univ (Ladbrook Ho)**
N5 .... **15** A3
**London Metropolitan
Univ (Moorgate)**
EC2 .... **109** C3
**London Metropolitan
Univ (North London
Campus)** **2** N7 ... **14** C3
**London Metropolitan
Univ (Tufnel Park Hall)**
N7 .... **4** B1
**London Metropolitan
Univ (Spring Ho)**
N1 .... **86** C3
London Mews 4 W2 **101** C2
London Nautical Sch
The SE1 .... **121** C2
London Oratory Sch The
SW6 .... **155** C2
London Peace Pagoda*
SW3 .... **159** A2
London Rd SE1 .... **136** B2
**London Sch of
Economics & Political
Science** WC2 .... **107** A1
London St EC3 ..... **124** B4
W2 .... **101** B1
London Stile 5 W4 . **36** C1
London Terr 1 E2 . **24** C3
**London Toy & Model
Mus** W2 .... **114** B4
London Transport Mus*
WC2 .... **120** B4
London Wall EC2 .. **109** A3
London Zoo * NW1 . **81** B2
Long Acre WC2 .... **106** B1
Longbeach Rd
SW11 .... **60** B4
Longberrys NW2 .... **1** B1
Longbow Ho 29 N1 **24** A4
Longbridge Way
SE13 .... **67** B2
Longcliffe Ho SW18 **59** A2
Longdale Sq N1 ..... **85** B4
Long Dr W3 .... **29** A3
Longfellow Way
SE1 .... **153** A3
Longfield Dr SW14 . **55** A2
Longfield Est SE1 . **153** A3
Longfield St SW18 . **70** C4
Longford Ct ....
2 London E5 ...... **17** C4
1 London W12 .... **30** B3
Longford Ho 7 E1 .. **32** B3
Longford St NW1 .. **92** B2
Longford Wlk **9**
SW2 .... **74** C4
Longhope Cl SE15 . **49** A4
Longhurst Ho **8**
W9 .... **23** B2
Long La EC1 .... **108** B4
SE1 .... **137** C3
Longland Ct SE1 .. **153** B2
London E9 .... **18** A3
Longlands Ct W11 . **31** B2 **3** A3

Longleat Ho SW1 . **147** B2
Longleigh Ho 6
SE5 .... **49** A2
Longlents Ho 1
NW10 .... **20** C4
Longley Ho **5** N19 . **13** B4
Longley St SE1 .... **153** B4
Longman Ho **9** E2 . **25** C3
10 E8 .... **24** B4
Long Meadow 20
N7 .... **13** C3
Longmoor Point 14
SW15 .... **69** A3
Longmore St SW1 . **146** C3
Longnor Rd E1 ...... **25** C2
Long Pond Rd SE3 . **53** A2
Long Rd SW4 .... **61** B3
Longridge Ho SE1 . **137** A1
Longridge Rd SW5 **141** C3
Long's Ct W1 ...... **119** C3
Longs Ct **2** TW9 .. **54** B3
Longshore SE8 ..... **41** B2
Long St E2 .... **98** C4
Longstaff Cres
SW18 .... **70** C4
Longstaff Rd SW18 **58** C1
Longstone Ave
NW10 .... **21** B4
Longthorne Ho 20
E3 .... **26** B2
Longville Rd SE11 . **150** B4
Long Wlk SE1 ..... **138** B2
Longwood Dr SW15 **56** C1
Long Yd WC1 ...... **94** C1
Lonsdale Ho ....
6 London N4 .... **6** B4
London SE6 .... **58** C4
Lonsdale Mews ......
W11 .... **31** B3
4 Richmond TW9 . **44** C2
Lonsdale Pl N1 ..... **14** C1
Lonsdale Rd NW6 .. **23** B4
W11 .... **31** B3
Barnes SW13 .... **46** C4
SW7 .... **38** B2
Lonsdell Ho 9 SW2 **62** C1
Lopez Ho 3 SW9 ... **62** A4
Loraine Rd
Chiswick W4 .... **45** A4
London N7 .... **14** B4
Lord David Pitt Ho 8
SE24 .... **63** A3
Lord Hills Rd W2 .. **100** B4
Lord Holland La 9
SW9 .... **173** C2
Lord Napier Pl 6 W6 **38** C1
Lord North St SW1 **134** A1
Lord Roberts Mews
SW6 .... **156** A1
Lords Cl SE21 .... **75** B2
Lord's Cricket Mus
NW8 .... **89** C3
Lordship Gr N16 ..... **6** C2
Lordship Ho 3 N16 . **6** C2
Lordship Ho 7 N16 . **6** C2
Lordship La SE22 .. **64** B1
N16 .... **6** C1
Lordship Park Mews
N16 .... **6** C2
Lordship Pk N16 .... **6** C2
Lordship Pl SW3 .. **158** A3
Lordship Rd N16 .... **6** C2
Lordship Terr N16 .. **6** C2
**Lord's Indoor Cricket
Sch**
NW8 .... **89** C4
SE8 .... **90** B3

Lord's (MCC &
Middlesex Cty Cricket
Ground)* NW8 .... **89** C4
Lord's View NW8 ... **89** C3
Loreburn Ho 2 N7 . **14** B4
Lorenzo St N1,WC1 **94** C4
Loris Rd W6 .... **39** B3
Lorn Ct SW9 ...... **173** B2
Lorne Cl NW8 ...... **90** B3
Lorne Ct SW15 ..... **57** C1
Lorne Gdns **6** W11 **39** C4
Lorne Ho **7** E1 .... **33** A4
Lorn Road N4 .. **5** B3
3 Richmond TW10 **54** B2
Lorn Rd SW9 ...... **173** B2
Lorraine Ct 10 NW1 **13** A1
Lorrimore Rd SE17 . **48** A4
Lorrimore Sq SE17 . **48** A4
Lorton Ho **9** NW6 . **23** C4
Lostock Ho SW8 .. **171** B2
Lothair Rd S N4 ...... **6** A4
Lothbury EC2 ..... **109** B2
Lothian Rd SW9 .... **48** A2
Lothrop St W10 ..... **23** A2
Lots Rd SW10 ..... **157** A1
Loudoun Rd NW8 ... **79** A3
Loughborough Ct 7
SW9 .... **63** A4
**Loughborough Junction
Sta** SW9 .... **63** A4
Loughborough Pk
SW9 .... **63** A3
Loughborough Prim Sch
SW9 .... **48** A1
Loughborough Rd
SE5,SW9 .... **48** A1
Loughborough St
SE11 .... **149** A1
Lough Rd N7 .... **14** B2
Louisa Cl E9 .... **25** C4
Louisa Gdns E1 .... **25** C1
Louisa Ho SW15 ... **56** B3
Louisa St E1 .... **25** C1
Louise Bennett Cl 9
SE24 .... **63** A3
**Louise De Marillac Ho
5** E1 .... **32** B4
Louise White Ho 1
N19 .... **4** C3
Louisville Rd SW17 **72** C1
Louvaine Rd SW11 . **59** C3
Lovat La EC3 ...... **124** A3
Lovatt Ct SW12 ..... **73** A3
Loveday Ho 2 SW2 **74** C3
Lovegrove St SE1 . **49** C4
Lovegrove Wlk E14 **34** B1
Love La EC2 ...... **109** A2
Lovelace Ho 12 E8 . **24** B4
Lovelace Rd SE21 .. **75** B3
Lovelinch Cl SE15 .. **50** B4
Lovell Ho E8 .... **24** C4
Lovell Pl SE16 ...... **41** A3
Loveridge Mews
NW6 .... **10** B2
Loveridge Rd NW6 . **10** B2
Lover's Wlk W1 ... **117** B1
Lovette Ho 3 E3 ... **26** C2
Love Wlk SE5 .... **48** C1
Low Cross Wood La
SE21 .... **76** B1
Lowden Rd SE24 ... **63** B3
Lowder Ho 6 E1 .... **32** A1
Lowe Ave E16 ...... **35** C4
Lowell Ho 10 SE5 . **48** B3
Lowell St E14 .... **33** A3
Lower Addison Gdns
W14 .... **126** A3

Lower Belgrave St SW1 ....132 A1
Lower Clapton Rd E5 ....17 B4
Lower Clarendon Wlk 12
  W11 ....31 A3
Lower Comm S SW15 ....57 A4
Lower Grosvenor Pl
  SW1 ....132 B2
Lower Grove Rd TW10 ....54 B2
Lower James St W1 ....119 A4
Lower John St W1 ....119 A4
Lower Lea Crossing
  E14,E16 ....35 B2
Lower Mall W6 ....39 A1
Lower Marsh SE1 ....135 B3
Lower Merton Rise
  NW3 ....12 A1
Lower Mortlake Rd
  TW9 ....54 B4
Lower Pk 5 SW15 ....57 C2
Lower Place Bsns Ctr
  NW10 ....20 B3
Lower Rd SE16 ....40 B4
Lower Richmond Rd
  Mortlake SW14,TW9 ....55 A4
  Putney SW15 ....57 B4
Lower Robert St
  WC2 ....120 B3
Lower Sloane St
  SW1 ....145 B2
Lower Terr NW3 ....2 B1
Lower Thames St
  EC3 ....124 A3
Lowerwood Ct W11 ....31 A3
Loweswater Ho E3 ....26 B3
Lowfield Rd
  London NW6 ....10 C1
  London NW6 ....28 B3
Lowlands NW3 ....12 A2
Lowman Rd N7 ....14 B4
Lowndes Cl SW1 ....131 C1
Lowndes Ct SW1 ....131 A2
Lowndes Pl SW1 ....131 B1
Lowndes Sq SW1 ....131 A3
Lowndes St SW1 ....131 B2
Lowood Ho 1 E1 ....32 B2
Lowood St E1 ....32 A3
Lowry Ct 3 SE16 ....40 A1
Lowther Ho 11 E8 ....24 B4
  SW1 ....147 A1
Lowther Prim Sch
  SW13 ....46 C4
Lowther Rd
  Barnes SW13 ....46 B2
  London N7 ....14 C3
Lowth Rd SE5 ....48 B1
Loxford Ho SW1 ....145 C3
Loxham St WC1 ....94 B3
Loxley Rd SW18 ....71 C3
Lubbock Ho 8 E14 ....34 A2
Lubbock St SE14 ....50 B3
Lucan Ho N1 ....87 C3
Lucan Pl SW3 ....144 B3
Lucas Ct SW11 ....169 C3
Lucas Ho SW8 ....171 A2
  London SW10 ....156 C2
Lucas St SE4,SE8 ....51 C2
Lucas Vale Prim Sch
  SE8 ....51 C2
Lucerne Mews W8 ....113 C2
Lucerne Rd N5 ....15 A4
Lucey Way SE16 ....153 C4
Lucien Rd SW18 ....71 A2

Lucraft Ho 5 SW2 ....74 A4
Lucy Ashe Ho SE17 ....150 B3
Lucy Brown Ho
  SE1 ....123 A1
Lucy Cres W3 ....20 B1
Ludgate Broadway
  EC4 ....108 B1
Ludgate Cir EC4 ....108 A1
Ludgate Hill EC4 ....108 B1
Ludgate Sq EC4 ....108 B1
Ludham NW5 ....12 B3
Ludlow Ct W3 ....37 B4
Ludlow St EC1 ....96 C2
Ludovick Wlk SW15 ....56 A3
Ludwell Ho W14 ....39 C4
Ludwick Mews SE14 ....51 A3
Lugard Ho 6 W12 ....30 A1
Lugard Rd SE15 ....50 A2
Luke Ho 15 E1 ....32 A3
Luke St EC2 ....24 A1 98 A2
Lukin St E1 ....32 B3
Lullingstone Ho 20
  SE15 ....50 B4
Lullingstone La
  SE13 ....67 C1
Lulot Gdns N19 ....4 A2
Lulworth SE17 ....151 B2
  NW1 ....83 A3
Lulworth Ho SW8 ....162 C1
Lulworth Rd SE15 ....50 A1
Lumiere Ct 1 SW17 ....72 C2
Lumley Ct WC2 ....120 B3
Lumley Flats SW1 ....145 B2
Lumley St W1 ....103 C1
Lumsden Ho NW8 ....78 B3
Lunan Ho 10 E3 ....26 B3
Lund Point E15 ....27 B4
Lupin Cl SW2 ....75 A2
Lupino Ct SE11 ....149 A4
Lupin Point SE1 ....139 A3
Lupton St NW5 ....13 B4
Lupus St SW1 ....147 A1
Luralda Gdns E14 ....42 C1
Lurgan Ave W6 ....47 C4
Lurline Gdns
  SW11 ....169 C4
Luscombe Ho SW18 ....58 B2
Luscombe Way
  SW8 ....162 A2
Lusher Ho SW15 ....57 C1
Lushington Rd
  NW10 ....22 A3
Lushington Terr 11
  E8 ....16 C3
Luton Pl SE10 ....52 B3
Luton St NW8 ....89 C1
Luttrell Ave SW15 ....57 A2
Lutyens Ho 2 SW1 ....146 C1
Luxborough Ho
  W1 ....103 A4
Luxborough St W1 ....103 A4
Luxborough Twr
  W1 ....103 A4
Luxemburg Gdns
  W6 ....39 C2
Luxford St SE16 ....40 C2
Luxmore St SE4 ....51 A2
Luxor St SE5 ....63 B4
Lyall Mews SW1 ....131 B1
Lyall Mews W SW1 ....131 B1
Lyall St SW1 ....131 B1
Lyal Rd E3 ....26 A3
Lycée Francais Charles
  de Gaulle (French Univ
  Coll) SW7 ....143 A4
Lycée The SE11 ....149 C1

Lycett Ho 10 SW2 ....74 A4
Lycett Pl 3 W12 ....38 C4
Lydden Gr SW18 ....71 A4
Lydden Rd SW18 ....71 A4
Lydford NW1 ....83 A3
Lydford Rd W9 ....23 B1
  London NW2 ....9 B2
Lydgate Ho 8 N16 ....16 A3
Lydhurst Ave SW2 ....74 B2
Lydney Cl SE15 ....49 A3
  Putney SW19 ....70 A2
Lydon Rd SW4 ....61 B4
Lydwell Ho SW8 ....171 B1
Lyford Rd SW18 ....72 A3
Lygoe Ho 10 N6 ....4 C4
Lygon Ho 2 ....99 B4
Lygon Pl SW1 ....132 A1
Lyham Cl SW2 ....62 A1
Lyham Rd SW2 ....62 A1
Lyly Ho SE1 ....137 C1
Lyme Gr 8 E9 ....17 B1
Lyme Grove Ho 2
Lyme St NW1 ....82 C4
Lyminge Gdns
  SW17,SW18 ....72 A3
Lymington Mans
  NW6 ....11 A2
Lymington Rd NW6 ....11 A2
Lympstone Gdns
  SE15 ....49 C3
Lynch Cl SE3 ....53 B3
Lynch Wlk 2 SE8 ....51 B4
Lyncott Cres SW4 ....61 A3
Lyncourt SE3 ....52 C1
Lyncroft Gdns NW6 ....10 C3
Lyncroft Mans NW6 ....10 C3
Lyndale NW2 ....1 B1
Lyndale Ave NW2 ....1 B1
Lyndale Cl SE3 ....53 B4
Lynde Ho 2 SW4 ....61 C4
Lynden Gate SW15 ....69 A3
Lyndhurst Gdns
  NW3 ....11 C3
Lyndhurst Gr SE5,
  SE15 ....49 B1
Lyndhurst Ho 2
  SW15 ....68 C4
Lyndhurst House Prep
  Sch NW3 ....11 C3
Lyndhurst Lo 3
  E14 ....42 C2
Lyndhurst Rd NW3 ....11 C3
Lyndhurst Sch SE5 ....48 C1
Lyndhurst Sq SE15 ....49 B2
Lyndhurst Terr
  NW3 ....11 C3
Lyndhurst Way SE15 ....49 B1
Lyneham Wlk E5 ....18 A3
Lynette Ave SW4 ....61 B1
Lynford French Ho
  SE17 ....150 C2
Lynmouth Rd N16 ....7 B3
Lynne Ct NW6 ....11 A1
Lynnett Ct E9 ....18 A2
Lynne Way NW10 ....8 A2
Lynns Ho N16 ....15 C4
Lynn Rd SW12 ....73 A4
Lynton Cl NW10 ....8 B3
Lynton Ct 2 W3 ....28 B3
Lynton Est SE1 ....153 B3
Lynton Ho 2 ....100 B1
Lynton Lo N5 ....15 A3
Lynton Mans SE1 ....135 B2
Lynton Rd NW6 ....23 B3

Lynton Rd continued
  SE1 ....153 A3
  Acton W3 ....28 A2
Lynton Terr 4 W3 ....28 B3
Lyon Ho NW8 ....90 A1
Lyon St N1 ....14 B1
Lyons Wlk W14 ....140 A4
Lyric Rd SW13 ....46 B2
Lysander Gr N19 ....4 C3
Lysander Ho 10 E2 ....25 A3
Lysander Mews N19 ....4 B3
Lysia St SW6 ....47 C3
Lysias Rd SW12 ....61 A1
Lysia St SW6 ....47 C3
Lytcott Gr SE22 ....64 B2
Lytham St SE17 ....151 B1
Lyttelton Cl NW3 ....12 A1
Lyttelton Ho 18 E9 ....17 B1
Lytten Ct 3 W12 ....29 C1
Lyttleton Ho 10 E9 ....17 B1
Lytton Ct WC1 ....106 B3
Lytton Gr SW15 ....58 A1

M

Mabel Thornton Ho 12
  N16 ....15 C4
Mableton Pl NW1,
  WC1 ....93 C3
Mablethorpe Rd
  SW6 ....154 A1
Mabley St E9 ....18 A3
MacArthur Ho 4
  SW2 ....74 A4
Macaulay CE Prim Sch
  SW4 ....61 A3
Macaulay Ct SW4 ....61 A4
Macaulay Ho
  2 W10 ....31 A4
  London N16 ....7 A1
Macaulay Rd SW4 ....61 A4
Macaulay Sq SW4 ....61 A3
McAuley Cl SE1 ....135 B2
Macbeth Ho N1 ....24 A3
Macbeth St W6 ....39 A1
McBride Ho 8 E3 ....26 B3
McCall Cl SW4 ....172 A2
McCall Ho N7 ....14 A4
McCarthy Ct SW11 ....168 B3
Macclesfield Rd
  EC1 ....96 C4
Macclesfield St
  W1 ....119 C4
McCoid Way SE1 ....136 C3
Mcconnell Ho
  SW8 ....171 B3
McCormick Ho 5
  SW2 ....74 C3
McCrone Mews 3
  NW3 ....11 C2
McCullum Rd E3 ....26 B4
McDermott Cl
  SW11 ....60 A4
McDermott Rd SE15 ....64 C4
Macdonald Ho 6
  SW11 ....169 B2
Macdonald Rd N19 ....4 B2
McDougall Ct TW9 ....44 C1
McDowall Cl E16 ....35 B2
McDowall Rd SE5 ....48 B2
Macduff Rd SW11 ....169 C4
Mace Cl E1 ....32 A1
Mace St E2 ....25 C3
McEwan Way E15 ....27 C4
Macey Ho 9 SE10 ....52 B4
  SW11 ....168 A3
Macfarlane Rd W12 ....30 B1

Macfarren Ho W10 ....23 A2
MacFarren Pl NW1 ....91 C1
McGlashon Ho E1 ....99 B1
McGregor Ct N1 ....98 B4
McGregor Ho 2 ....73 C3
McGregor Rd W11 ....31 B4
Machell Rd SE15 ....65 B4
McIndoe Ct N1 ....87 B4
McIntyre Ct SW4 ....172 B2
Mackay Ho 33 W12 ....30 A2
Mackay Rd SW4 ....61 A4
McKenna Ho 3 E3 ....26 B3
Mackennal St NW8 ....80 B2
McKerrell Ho 7
  W12 ....30 A2
Mackenzie Ho 3 ....14 C1
Mackenzie Wlk E14 ....33 C1
McKerrell Rd SE15 ....49 C2
Mackeson Rd NW3 ....12 B4
Mackie Ho 2 SW2 ....74 C4
Mackie Rd 18 SW2 ....74 C4
McKiernan Ct
  SW11 ....168 A2
McKinnon Wood Ho
  E2 ....99 C3
Mackintosh La E9 ....17 C3
Macklin St WC2 ....106 B2
Mackonochie Ho
  EC1 ....107 B4
Mackrow Wlk 11
  E14 ....34 B2
Macks Rd SE16 ....153 C4
Mackworth Ho NW1 ....92 C4
Mackworth St NW1 ....92 C4
Maclean Rd SE23 ....66 C1
Mcleod Ct SE21 ....76 C3
McLeod's Mews
  SW7 ....142 B4
Macleod St SE17 ....151 A1
Maclise Rd W14 ....126 A1
McManus Ho 3
  SW11 ....59 C4
Macmillan Ho NW8 ....90 B3
Macmillan Ho NW6 ....64 A4
Macmillan Ho NW4 ....9 A4
McMillan St SE8 ....51 C4
Mcmorran Ho N7 ....14 A4
Macnamara Ho
  SW10 ....157 B2
Mcneil Rd SE5 ....49 A1
McNicol Dr NW10 ....20 B3
Maconochies Rd
  E14 ....42 A1
Macquarie Way E14 ....42 A2
Macready Ho W1 ....102 B3
Macready Pl 2 N7 ....14 A4
Macroom Ho W9 ....23 B2
Macroom Rd W9 ....23 B2
Mac's Pl EC4 ....107 C2
Madame Tussaud's*
  NW1 ....91 B1
Maddams St E3 ....27 A1
Maddocks Ho 5 E1 ....32 A2
Maddock Way SE17 ....48 A4
Madison Ho W1 ....118 C4
Madinah Rd E8 ....16 C2
Madison Ho E3 ....27 B2
Madras Pl N7 ....14 C2
Madrid Rd SW13 ....46 C2
Madron St SE17 ....152 B2
Mafeking Ave TW8 ....44 A4

Magdala Ave N19 .....4 B2
Magdalene Cl 7
SE1 .....50 A1
Magdalene Ho 7
SW15 .....57 C1
Magdalen Pas E1 .125 A4
Magdalen St SE18 71 C3
Magdalen St SE1 .124 A1
Magee St SE11 .....163 B3
Magellan Ho 16 E1 .25 C1
Magellan Pl 10 E14 .41 C2
Magnin Cl 8 E8 .....24 C4
Magnolia Ct
Richmond TW9 .....45 A2
Magnolia Ho 11 SE8 .51 B4
Magnolia Pl SW4 .....62 A2
Magnolia Rd W4 .....45 A4
Magnolia Wharf
W4 .....45 A4
Magpie Ho 7 E3 .....26 B4
Magpie Pl SE14 .....51 A4
Maguire St SE1 .....139 A4
Mahatma Ganhi Ind Est
1 SE24 .....63 A3
Mahogany Cl SE16 .33 A1
Mahoney Ho SE14 .51 B2
Maida Ave W2 .....89 A1
Maida Vale W9 .....88 C3
Maida Vale Psychiatric
Hospl W9 .....89 A2
Maida Vale Sta W9 .88 B4
Maiden La SE1 .....123 A2
WC2 .....120 B4
London NW1 .....13 C1
Maidenstone Hill
SE10 .....52 B2
Maidstone Bldgs
SE1 .....123 B1
Maidstone Ho 4
E14 .....34 A3
Mail Coach Yd E2 .98 B2
Main Yd E9 .....18 C2
Maismore St SE15 .49 C4
Maitland Cl 5 SE10 .52 A3
Maitland Ct W2 .....115 B4
Maitland Ho 17 E2 .25 B3
SW1 .....160 C4
Maitland Park Rd
NW3 .....12 B2
Maitland Park Villas
NW3 .....12 B2
Maitland Pl E5 .....17 A4
Majestic Ct N4 .....6 A3
Major St SE16 .....139 C2
London E15 .....19 C3

Maldon Cl N1 .....87 A4
London E15 .....19 C1
London SE5 .....64 A4
Maldon Rd W3 .....28 B2
Malet Pl WC1 .....93 B1
Malet St WC1 .....105 C4
Maley Ave SE27 .....75 A2
Mallams Mews 1
SW9 .....63 A4
Mallard Cl NW6 .....23 C4
London E9 .....18 B2
Mallard Ho NW8 .....80 A1
7 London SE15 .....49 B2
Mallard Point 6 E3 .26 C2
Mallet Ho 11 SW15 .56 C2
Mallet Rd SE13 .....67 C1
Malling SE13 .....67 A2
Mallinson Rd SW11 .60 B2
Mallon Gdns E1 .....111 A3
Mallord St SW3 .....157 C4
Mallory Bldgs EC1 .96 A1
Mallory Ho E14 .....34 B3
Mallory St NW8 .....90 B2
Mallow St EC1 .....97 B2
Mall Rd W6 .....39 A1
Mall Studios 9
NW3 .....12 B3
Mall The SW1 .....119 B1
Mortlake SW14 .....55 B2
Malmesbury 31 E2 .25 B3
Malmesbury Prim Sch
E2 .....25 A3
Malmesbury Rd 85 E16 35 A4
London E3 .....26 B3
Malmesbury Terr
E16 .....35 B2
Malmsey Ho SE11 .149 A2
Malmsmead Ho E9 .18 A3
Maloress Jun & Inf Schs
NW6 .....9 C1
Malpas Rd
London SE4 .....51 B1
London E8 .....17 A2
Malta St EC1 .....96 B2
Maltby St SE1 .....138 C2
Malthouse Dr W4 .46 B4
Malthouse Pas
SW13 .....46 A1
Malting Ho E14 .....33 B2
Maltings W4 .....36 C1
Maltings Cl SW13 .46 A1
Maltings Lo W4 .....46 A3
Maltings Pl SE1 .138 B4
SW6 .....166 B3
Malt Mill SE1 .....124 C1
Malton Mews 1

Manaton Cl SE15 .....65 A4
Manbre Rd W6 .....47 B4
Manchester Dr W10 23 A1
Manchester Gr E14 .42 B1
Manchester Ho
SE17 .....151 A2
Manchester Mans
N19 .....5 A4
Manchester Mews
W1 .....103 B3
Manchester Rd E14 .42 B3
Manchester Sq
W1 .....103 C2
Manchester St W1 .103 B3
Manchuria Rd
SW11 .....60 C1
Manciple St SE1 .137 C2
Mandalay Ho 5
London N16 .....6 C2
Mandalay Rd SW4 .61 C2
Mandarin Ct 6 SE8 .51 C4
Mandela Cl 32 W12 .30 A2
Mandela Ho 2 .....98 C4
Mandela Rd E16 .....35 C3
Mandela St NW1 .....83 A4
SW9 .....163 B1
Mandela Way SE1 .152 B4
Manderville Ho
SE1 .....153 A2
Mandeville Cl 5
SE3 .....53 B3
Mandeville Ct NW3 .11 A3
Mandeville Ctyd
SW11 .....169 B3
Mandeville Ho 6
SW4 .....61 B2
Mandeville Pl W1 .103 C2
Mandrake Rd SW17 .72 B1
Mandrell Rd SW2 .62 A2
Manette St W1 .....105 C1
Manfred Ct 9
SW15 .....58 B2
Manfred Rd SW15 .58 B2
Manger Rd N7 .....14 A2
Manilla St E14 .....41 C4
Manitoba Ct 23
SE16 .....40 B4
Manley Ct N16 .....7 B1
Manley Ho SE11 .149 B2
Manley St NW1 .....81 B4
Mannebury Prior
N4 .....85 A1
Mannering Ho 16
SW2 .....62 B2
Manningford Cl EC1 96 A4
Manning Ho 3
W11 .....31 A3
Manning Pl W10 .54 B1
Manningtree Cl
SW19 .....70 A3
Manningtree St 11 E1 111 B2
Manny Shinwell Ho
SW6 .....155 A3
Manor Ave SE4 .....51 B1
Manor Circus TW9 .54 C4
Manor Ct Sw6 .....166 B3
London SE15 .....49 B2
7 London SW2 .....62 B2
2 London W3 .....36 C2
Streatham SW16 .74 A1
Manorfield Cl 3
N19 .....13 B4
Manorfield Prim Sch
E14 .....34 A4
Manor Gdns
London N7 .....5 A1
London SW4 .....171 A1

Manor Gdns continued
London W3 .....36 C2
6 London SW4 .....38 A1
Richmond TW10,TW9 .54 B3
Manor Gr SE15 .....50 B4
Richmond TW9 .....54 C4
Manor Gt SW2 .....58 A2
Manor Ho NW1 .....102 A4
Manor House Ct
W9 .....88 C1
Manor House Dr
NW6 .....9 C1
Manor Lodge NW2 .9 C2
Manor Mans
London N7 .....5 A4
7 London NW3 .....12 A2
Manor Mews NW6 .23 C3
London SE4 .....51 B1
Manor Oak Mans
SE22 .....65 A1
Manor Par N6 .....7 B2
Manor Park Rd
NW10 .....21 C4
Manor Pk TW9 .....54 B3
Manor Pl SE17 .....150 C2
Manor Rd London N16 .7 A3
Richmond TW9,TW10 .54 B3
Manor Sch NW10 .22 B4
Manor Street Est
SW3 .....158 B4
Manor The W1 .....118 A3
Manor Way SE3 .....36 C2
Manresa Rd SW3 .144 A1
Mansel Ct SW11 .168 B3
Mansell Ho SW8 .171 A4
Mansell Rd W3 .....37 C4
Mansell St E1 .....110 C1
Manse Rd N16 .....7 B1
Mansfield Ct 57 E2 .24 B4
Mansfield Ho SW15 .57 C1
Mansfield Mews
W1 .....104 A3
Mansfield Pl 11
NW3 .....11 B4
Mansfield Rd
Acton W3 .....20 A1
London W3 .....20 A1
1 London NW3 .....12 B3
Mansford St E2 .....24 C3
Mansion Cl SW9 .173 C4
Mansion Gdns NW3 .2 A1
Mansion House*
EC4 .....109 B1
Mansion House Pl
EC3,EC4 .....109 B1
Mansion House St
EC2 .....109 B1
Mansion House Sta
EC4 .....123 A4
Mansions The NW6 .10 B3
Manson Mews
SW7 .....143 B3
Manson Pl SW7 .143 B3
Manston NW1 .....13 B1
Manstone Rd NW2 .10 A3
Manston Ho W14 .126 B2
Mantell Ho SW4 .....61 B2
Mantle Rd SE4 .....66 A4
Manton Ho N16 .....6 C1
Mantua St 23 SW11 .59 C4
Mantus Cl E1 .....25 B1
Mantus Rd E1 .....25 B1
Manville Gdns
SW17 .....73 A1
Manville Rd SW17 .73 A2
Manwood Rd SE4 .66 B1
Many Gates SW12 .73 A2

Mapesbury Ct NW2 .10 A3
Mapesbury Rd NW2 .10 A2
Mapeshill Pl NW2 .9 B2
Mapes Ho 5 NW6 .10 A1
Mape St 2 .....25 A1
Maple Ave W3 .....29 A1
Maple Cl SW4 .....61 C1
Maple Ct NW2 .....9 C4
Mapledene Est E8 .16 C1
Mapledene Rd E8 .16 C1
11 London NW3 .....12 B2
Maple Leaf Sq 27
SE16 .....40 C4
Maple Lo SW15 .....58 A1
Maple Mews NW6 .78 A2
Maple Pl W1 .....93 A1
Maples Pl E1 .....32 A4
Maple St W1 .....93 A1
Maplestead Rd SW2 .74 B4
Mapleton Cres
SW18 .....59 A1
Mapleton Rd SW18 .59 A1
Maple Wlk W10 .....22 C1
Maplin St E3 .....26 B2
Marada Ho NW6 .....10 A1
Marais W4 .....45 B3
Marban Rd W9 .....23 B2
Marble Arch* W1 .117 A4
Marble Arch Sta
W1 .....103 A1
Marble Cl W3 .....28 A1
Marbleford Ct 4 N6 .4 C4
Marble Ho W9 .....23 B1
Marcella Rd SW9 .173 B1
Marchant Ct 1
SW2 .....153 A2
Marchant Ho 13
SW2 .....62 B2
Marchant St SE14 .51 A4
Marchbank Rd
W14 .....155 A4
March Ct SW1 .....57 A3
Marchmont Ho 1
TW10 .....54 B2
Marchmont St WC1 .94 A2
Marchwood Cl 17
SE5 .....49 A3
Marcia Rd SE1 .....152 B3
Marcilly Rd SW18 .59 C2
Marcon Ct 2 E8 .17 A3
Marcon Pl E8 .....17 A3
Marco Rd W6 .....39 B3
Marcus Ct 9 E15 .....19 C1
Marcus Garvey Mews
SE22 .....65 A2
Marcus Garvey Way 3
SE24 .....62 C3
Marcus Ho 15 SE15 .49 B2
Marcus St SW18 .59 A1
Marcus Terr SW18 .59 A1
Marden Ho 8 E8 .17 A3
Marden Sq SE16 .40 A3
Mardyke Ho SE17 .151 C4
Maresfield Gdns
NW3 .....11 B2
Mare St London E8 .....17 A2
London E8,E2 .....25 A4
Margaret Bondfield Ho
4 E3 .....26 A3
22 London N7 .....13 C3
Margaret Ct W1 .104 C2
Margaret Herbison Ho
SW6 .....155 A3
Margaret Ho 16 W6 .39 B1
Margaret Ingram Cl
SW6 .....154 C3

Margaret Mcmillan Ho
10 N19 ....A4
Margaret Rd N16 ....7 B3
Margaret's Ct SE1 ...123 B1
Margaret St W1 ......104 C2
Margaretta Terr
SW3 ....158 B4
Margaret White Ho
NW1 ....93 C4
Margate Rd SW2 .....62 A2
Margery Fry Ct N7 ....5 B1
Margery St WC1 .....95 B3
Margravine Gdns
W14 ....140 A2
London W6 ....39 C1
Margravine Rd
W6 ....154 A4
Marham Gdns SW17,
SW18 ....72 A3
Maria Cl SE1 ....153 C4
Maria Fidelis RC
Convent Sch NW1 ...93 C4
Marian Ct E9 ....17 B3
Marian Pl E2 ....25 A3
Marian Sq E2 ....25 A3
Marian St E2 ....25 A3
Marian Way NW10 ...8 B1
Maria Terr E1 ....25 C1
Maribor **13** SE10 ....52 B3
Marie Curie SE5 .....49 A2
Marie Lloyd Ct **6**
SW9 ....62 B3
N19 ....5 A4
Marie Lloyd Ho **1**
N1 ....87 A3
Marigold St SE16 ...40 A4
Marina Ct **11** E3 ....26 C2
Marinefield Rd
SW6 ....166 B2
Marinel Ho **28** SE5 ..48 B3
Marine St SE16 ....139 B2
Mariners Mews E14 .42 C2
Marine Twr **20** SE8 .51 B4
Marion Richardson Prim
Sch E1 ....32 C3
Marischal Rd SE13 .67 C4
Maritime Ho **5**
SW4 ....61 C4
Maritime Quay **6**
E14 ....41 C1
Maritime St E3 ....26 B1
Marius Mans **8**
SW17 ....72 C2
Marjorie Gr SW11 ..60 B3
Market Ct W1 ....104 C2
Market Mews W1 ...118 A1
Market Pl **8** SE16 ...40 A2
W1 ....104 C2
3 London W3 ....28 B1
Market Rd
London N7 ....14 A2
SW6 ....154 C4
Market Sq E14 ....34 A3
Market Way E14 ....34 A3
Market Yd Mews
SE1 ....138 A1
Markham Pl SW3 ...144 C2
Markham Sq SW3 ..144 C2
Markham St SW3 ..144 B2
Mark Ho **8** E2 ....25 C3
Mark La EC3 ....124 B4
Markland Ho W10 ..30 C2
Mark Mans W12 ....38 C4
Mark Sq EC2 ....98 A2
Mark St EC2 ....98 A2

Markstone Ho SE1 .136 A3
Markyate Ho W10 ...22 B1
Marland Ho SW1 ...131 A2
Marlborough **9**
4 Putney SW19 ....69 C3
Marlborough Ave **3**
E8 ....24 C4
Marlborough Cl
SE17 ....150 B3
Marlborough Cres
W4 ....38 A3
Marlborough Ct
W8 ....141 B4
Marlborough Day Hospl
NW8 ....78 C2
Marlborough Flats
SW3 ....144 B4
Marlborough Gr
SE1 ....153 B1
Marlborough Hill
NW8 ....79 A3
Marlborough Ho
NW8 ....78 C1
London N4 ....6 B3
Richmond TW10 ....54 C2
Wimbledon SW19 ..69 C1
Marlborough House
SW1 ....119 A1
Marlborough Mans **1**
NW6 ....10 C3
Marlborough Mews
SW2 ....62 B3
Marlborough Pl
NW8 ....79 A2
Marlborough Prim Sch
SW3 ....144 B3
Marlborough Rd
SW1 ....119 A1
London N19 ....5 A2
London W4 ....37 B1
Richmond TW10 ....54 B1
Marlborough St
SW3 ....144 B3
Marlborough Trad Est
TW9 ....45 A2
Marlborough Yd N19 .4 C2
Marlbury NW8 ....78 B3
Marley Ho **11** W11 ..30 C2
Marley Wlk NW2 .....9 B3
Marlin Ho SW15 ....58 A2
Marloes Rd W8 ....128 A1
Marlow Ct NW6 ......9 C1
Marlowe Bsns Ctr **2**
SE14 ....51 A3
Marlowe Ct **5** SW3 144 B3
Marlowe Ho **3** SE8 .41 B1
Marlowes The NW8 .79 B4
Marlow Ho E2 ....98 C3
SE1 ....138 C2
W2 ....100 B1
Marlow Studio
Workshops **2**
E2 ....98 C3
Marlow Way SE16 ..40 C4
Marl Rd SW18 ....59 B3
Marlston NW1 ....92 B3
Marlton St **3** SE10 .43 B1
Marmion Ho **13**
SW12 ....73 A4
Marmion Mews **4**
SW11 ....60 C3
Marmont Rd SE15 ..49 C3
Marmora Ho E1 .....33 A4
Marmora Rd SE22 .65 B1
Marner Prim Sch
E3 ....27 A1

Marne St W10 ....23 A2
Marney Rd SW11 ...60 C3
Marnfield Cres SW2 74 B3
Marnham Ave NW2 .10 A4
Marnock Ho SE17 .151 B2
Marnock Rd SE4 ...66 B2
Maroon St E14 ....33 A4
Marquess Rd N1 ...15 C2
Marquess Rd N N1 .15 C2
Marquess Rd S **17**
N1 ....15 B2
Marquis Ct N4 ....5 B3
Marquis Rd N4 ....6 A3
London N4 ....6 A3
London N19 ....5 A3
Marquis Rd N19 ......4 C3
Marrayat Sq SW6 .164 A4
Marrick Cl SW15 ...56 C3
Marrick Ho NW6 ....78 B3
Marriott Rd N4 ....5 B3
Marryat Ct **17** W6 ..39 A2
Marryat Ho SW1 ...146 C1
Marsala Rd SE13 ..67 A3
Marsalis Ho **2** E3 ..26 C2
Marsden Rd SE15 ..64 B4
Marsden St NW5 ...12 C2
Marshall Cl SW18 ..59 B1
Marshall Ho N1 ......87 C2
NW6 ....23 B3
SE17 ....151 B2
Marshall Rd E10 ...19 A4
Marshall's Pl SE16 139 A3
Marshall St W1 ....105 A1
Marshalsea Rd
SE1 ....137 A4
Marsham Ct SW1 ..147 C4
19 Putney SW19 ...69 C3
Marsham St SW1 .147 C4
Marsh Ct E8 ....16 C2
Marshfield St E14 ..42 B3
Marshgate Bsns Ctr **2**
E15 ....27 B3
Marshgate La E15 ..19 A1
Marsh Hill E9 ....18 A3
Marsh Ho SW1 ....147 C1
SW8 ....171 A4
Marsh St E14 ....42 A2
Marsh Wall E14 ....42 A4
Marshwood Ho **10**
NW6 ....23 C4
Marsland Cl SE17 .150 B1
Marsom Ho N1 ......87 B1
Marston Cl NW6 ....11 B1
Marston Ho SW9 ..173 C1
Marsworth Ho **8**
E2 ....24 C4
Martaban Rd N16 ...7 B2
Martello St E8 ....17 A1
Martello Terr E8 .....17 A1
Martell Rd SE21 ....75 C1
Martel Pl E8 ....16 B2
Martha's Bldgs EC1 97 C1
Martha St E1 ....32 B3
Martin Ct **10** E14 ..42 B4
Martindale SW14 ..55 B2
Martindale Ave **2**
E16 ....35 C2
Martindale Ho **20**
SW12 ....73 A4
Martindale Rd
SW12 ....73 A4
Martineau Ho SW1 146 C1
Martineau Mews
N5 ....15 A4

Martineau Rd N5 ...15 A4
Martin Ho SE1 .....137 A1
SW8 ....162 A2
Martin La EC4 ......123 C4
Martlett Ct WC2 ...106 B1
Martlett Lodge **3**
NW3 ....11 A4
Martley Ho SW8 ...171 A4
Martock Ct **10** SE15 .50 A2
Marton Rd **2** N16 ...7 A1
Marvel Ho **5** SW8 .162 C1
Marville Rd SW6 ..154 C1
Marville Rd SW6 ..154 C1
Marvin St **3** E8 .....17 A2
Mary Adelaide Cl
SW15 ....68 A1
Mary Adelaide Ho
W2 ....101 B4
Mary Ann Bldgs
SE8 ....51 C4
Mary Batchelor Sch
(Girls) SE5 ....48 C2
Mary Datcheler Cl
SE5 ....48 C2
Mary Datchelor Cl
SE5 ....48 C2
Mary Gn NW8 ....78 B4
Mary Ho
SW9 ....172 C1
W6 ....39 B1
Mary James Ho **29**
E2 ....24 C3
Mary Jones Ho **13**
E14 ....33 C2
Maryland Rd W9 ...23 C1
Maryland Wlk N1 ...86 C4
Mary Lawrenson Pl **3**
SE3 ....53 C3
Marylebone Flyover
NW1 ....102 A3
Marylebone High St
W1 ....103 C4
Marylebone La
W1 ....103 C2
Marylebone Mews
W1 ....104 A3
Marylebone Pas
W1 ....105 A2
Marylebone Rd
NW1 ....103 A4
Marylebone Sta
NW1 ....90 C1
Marylee Wy **1** SE11 149 A3
Mary Macarthur Ho
12 E2 ....25 C2
W14 ....154 A4
Mary McArthur Ho **12**
N19 ....4 C4
Maryon Mews NW3 .12 A4
Mary Pl
W11 ....31 A2 112 A3
Mary Secole Cl **6**
E8 ....24 B4
Mary's Ct NW8 .....90 B1
Mary St **5** E16 ......35 B2
N1 ....87 A3
Mary Terr NW1 .....82 C2
Mary Wharrie Ho **4**
NW3 ....12 B1
Masbro' Rd W14 ...39 C3
Mascotte Rd **2**
SW15 ....57 C3
Masefield Ct N5 ....15 C3
Masefield Ho **1**
NW6 ....23 C2
Mashie Rd W3 .....29 A3

Maskall Cl SW2 ....74 C3
Maskell Rd SW17 ..71 B1
Maskelyne Cl
SW11 ....168 B4
Mason Cl E16 ....35 C2
SE16 ....153 C3
Mason Ho **1**
E9 ....17 B1
W1 ....118 A4
Mason's Arms Mews
W1 ....104 B1
Mason's Ave EC2 ..109 B2
Mason's Pl EC1 .....96 C4
Mason's Yd SW1 ..119 A2
SW19 ....69 C1
Massie Rd E8 ....16 C2
Massinger St SE1,
SE17 ....152 A3
Massingham St E1 .25 C1
Masson Ho **1**
TW8 ....36 A1
Masterman Ho **6**
SE5 ....48 C3
Masters Dr SE16 ...40 A1
Masters Lo **22** E1 ..32 B3
Master's St **14** E1 ..32 C4
Mast House Terr
E14 ....41 C2
Mastin Ho SW18 ...70 C3
Mastmaker Rd E14 .41 C4
Matching Ct **13** E3 .26 C2
Matham Gr SE22 ..64 B3
Matheson Lang Ho
SE1 ....135 B3
Matheson Rd W14 140 C3
Mathieson Ct SE1 .136 B3
Matilda Ho E1 .....125 B2
Matilda St N1 ....85 A4
Matlock Cl SE24 ...63 B3
Matlock Ct NW8 ...78 C2
SE5 ....63 C3
Matlock St E14 .....33 A3
Maton Ho SW6 ....154 C2
Matson Ho **9** SE16 40 A3
18 London E9 ......17 C2
Matthew Parker St
SW1 ....133 C3
Matthews Ct N5 ...15 B4
Matthews Ho **3**
E14 ....33 C4
Matthews St SW11 168 C2
Matthias Ct **12**
TW10 ....54 A1
Matthias Ho **2** N16 .16 A3
Matthias Rd N16 ...16 A3
Mattingly Way **4**
SE15 ....49 B3
Maude Ho **8** E2 ....24 C3
Maude Rd SE5 .....49 A2
Maudlins Gn E1 ...125 B2
Maudsley Ho **1** TW8 36 A1
Maudsley Hospl The
SE5 ....48 C1
Maud St E16 ....35 B2
Maugham Ct **3** W3 .37 B3
Mauleverer Rd SW2 62 A2
Maundeby Wlk NW10 8 A2
Maunsel St SW1 ..147 B4
Mauretania Bldg **11**
E1 ....32 B2
Maurice Ho **12**
SW9 ....172 C2
Maurice St W12 ....30 A3
Mauritius Rd SE10 .43 A2
Maury Rd N16 ....7 C1
Maverton Rd E3 ....26 C4
Mavor Ho N1 ....85 A3

Mawbey Ho SE1 .....153 A1
Mawbey Pl SE1 .....153 A1
Mawbey Rd SE1 .....153 A1
Mawbey St SW8 .....162 A1
Mawdley Ho SE1 .....135 C3
Mawson Ho EC1 .....107 B4
Mawson La W4 .....46 B4
Maxden Ct SE15 .....64 C4
Maxted Rd SE15 .....64 B4
Maxwell Ct SE21 .....76 C3
Maxwell Ho SW1 .....156 A1
Maya Cl SE15 .....50 A2
Mayall Rd SE24 .....63 A2
Maybury Ct W1 .....103 C3
Maybury Gdns NW10 .....9 A2
Maybury Mews N6 .....4 B4
Maydew Ho SE16 .....40 B2
Maydwell Ho [6]
E14 .....119 C3
Mayers Ct E8 .....16 C3
Mayfair Pl W1 .....118 B2
Mayfield Ave W4 .....38 A2
Mayfield Cl
London E8 .....16 C1
London SW4 .....61 C2
Mayfield Ho [30] E2 .....25 A3
London N16 .....7 A4
Mayfield Mans
SW15 .....58 B2
Mayfield Rd
Acton W3 .....28 A2
London E8 .....16 B1
London W12 .....38 A4
Mayflower Cl SE16 .....40 C2
Mayflower Prim Sch
E14 .....34 A3
Mayflower St [1]
SE16 .....40 B4
Mayford NW1 .....83 A2
Mayford Cl SW12 .....72 B4
Mayford Rd SW12 .....72 C4
Maygood Ho N1 .....85 B2
Maygood St N1 .....85 B2
Maygrove Rd NW6 .....10 B2
Mayhew Ct [2] SE5 .....63 C3
Maylands Ho SW3 .....144 B3
Maynard Cl SW6 .....156 B1
Maynard Ho E1 .....26 A2
Maynards Quay E1 .....32 B2
Mayola Rd E5 .....17 B4
Mayo Ho [1] E1 .....32 B4
Mayo Rd NW10 .....8 A2
May's Buildings Mews
SE10 .....52 C3
Mays Ct WC2 .....120 A3
May's Ct SE10 .....52 C3
Maysoule Rd SW11 .....59 C3
Mayston Mews [3]
SE10 .....43 B1
Maythorne Cotts
SE13 .....67 C1
Mayton St N7 .....5 B1
May Tree Ho SE4 .....66 B4
Maytree Wlk SW2 .....74 C2
Mayward Ho [7] SE5 .....49 A2
Maze Hill SE10,SE3 .....53 A4
Maze Hill Lodge [6]
SE10 .....52 C4
Maze Hill Sta SE10 .....53 A4
Mazenod Ave NW6 .....10 C1
Maze Rd TW9 .....44 C3
Mead Cl [3] NW1 .....12 C1
Meadcroft Rd SE17 .....48 A4

Meade Cl W4 .....44 C4
Meader Ct SE14 .....50 C3
Mead Ho W11 .....112 C3
Mead Lo W4 .....37 C4
Meadowbank NW3 .....12 B1
Meadow Bank [7]
SW15 .....58 B2
Meadowbank Cl
SW6 .....47 B3
Meadow Cl E9 .....18 B3
Meadowcroft [9]
W4 .....36 C1
Meadowgate Sch
SE4 .....66 A4
Meadow Mews
SW8 .....162 C3
Meadow Pl SW8 .....162 B2
Meadow Rd SW8 .....162 C2
Meadow Row SE1 .....136 C1
Mead Pl E9 .....17 B2
Mead Row SE1 .....135 B2
Meadway The SE3 .....52 C1
Meakin Est SE1 .....138 A2
Meakin Ho N7 .....14 B3
Meard St W1 .....105 B1
Meath Cres E2 .....25 C2
Meath Ho SE24 .....63 A1
Meath St SW11 .....170 A4
Mecklenburgh Pl
WC1 .....94 C2
Mecklenburgh Sq
WC1 .....94 C2
Medburn St NW1 .....83 B2
Medcroft Gdns
SW14 .....55 A3
Medfield St SW15 .....69 A4
Medhurst Cl [7] E3 .....26 A3
Median Rd E5 .....17 B3
Medical Coll of St
Bartholomew's Hospl
The EC1 .....96 B1
Medina Ct N7 .....5 C1
Medina Gr N7 .....5 C1
Medina Ho SE15 .....65 B3
Medina Rd N7 .....5 C1
Medlar St SE5 .....48 B2
Medley Rd NW6 .....10 C2
Medora Rd SW2 .....74 B4
Medresco Rd SE6,SE13 .....67 A1
Medway Bldgs E3 .....26 A3
Medway Ct WC1 .....94 A3
Medway Ho NW8 .....102 A4
SE1 .....137 C3
London N16 .....15 C4
Medway Mews [33]
E3 .....26 A3
Medway Rd E3 .....26 A3
Medway St SW1 .....133 C1
Medwin St SW4 .....62 B3
Meecham Ct [1] SW11 .....168 A2
Meeson St E5 .....18 A4
Meeting House Alley [7]
E1 .....32 A1
Meeting House La
SE15 .....50 A3
Mehetabel Rd E9 .....17 B3
Melba Ct E15 .....76 C4
Melbourne Ct W9 .....89 A2
London E5 .....18 A4
Melbourne Gr SE22 .....64 B3
Melbourne Ho W8 .....113 B1
Melbourne Mews
SW9 .....173 B3
Melbourne Pl WC2 .....107 A1
Melbourne Sq
SW9 .....173 B3

Melbrook Ho [11]
SE22 .....64 A4
Melbury Ct W8 .....127 A2
Melbury Dr SE5 .....49 A3
Melbury Ho SW8 .....162 C2
Melbury Rd W14 .....127 A2
Melchester [3] W11 .....31 B3
Melchester Ho [1]
N19 .....4 C1
Melcombe Ct NW1 .....102 C3
Melcombe Ho
SW8 .....162 C1
Melcombe Pl NW1 .....102 C4
Melcombe Prim Sch
W6 .....47 C4
Melcombe St NW1 .....91 A1
Meldon Cl SW6 .....166 B4
Melford Ct SE22 .....76 C4
Melford Rd SE21,
SE22 .....76 C4
Melgund Rd N5 .....14 C3
Melina Ct NW8 .....89 B3
Putney SW15 .....56 C4
Melina Pl NW8 .....89 B3
Melina Rd W12 .....39 A4
Melior Pl SE1 .....138 A4
Melior St SE1 .....138 A4
Melisa Ct N6 .....4 C4
Mellington Ct [2] N16 .....7 C1
Mellis Ave TW9 .....45 A2
Mellish Ho [2] E1 .....32 A3
Mellish St E14 .....41 C3
Mellitus St W12 .....29 B3
Mell St [6] SE10 .....43 A1
Melody La N5 .....15 A3
Melody Rd SW18 .....59 B2
Melon Pl W8 .....127 C4
Melon Rd SE15 .....49 C2
Melrose Ave
London NW2 .....9 B3
Wimbledon SW19 .....70 C1
Melrose Ct SW18 .....58 B1
Melrose Gdns W6 .....39 B3
Melrose Ho NW6 .....23 C2
Melrose Rd
[1] Barnes SW13 .....46 B1
Wandsworth SW18 .....58 B1
Melrose Terr W6 .....39 B3
Melton Ct SW7 .....143 C3
Melton Ho E5 .....7 C2
Melton St NW1 .....93 B3
Melville Court Flats
W12 .....39 A4
Melville Ct SE8 .....41 A2
[4] London W4 .....36 C1
Melville Ho SE10 .....52 B2
Melville Pl [4] N1 .....15 B1
Melville Rd SW13 .....46 C2
Melville Villas Rd
W3 .....28 C1
Melvin Ct [3] TW9 .....44 C2
Melwood Ho [2] E1 .....32 A3
Melyn Cl N7 .....13 B4
Memel Ct EC1 .....96 C1
Memel St EC1 .....96 C1
Mendham Ho SE1 .....138 A2
Mendip Ct SE14 .....50 B3
[12] London SW11 .....59 B4
Mendip Dr NW2 .....1 A2
Mendip Ho [2] N4 .....6 C4
Mendip Hos [2] E2 .....25 B2
Mendip Rd SW11 .....59 B4
Mendora Rd SW6 .....154 C2
Menelik Rd NW2 .....10 B4
Menorah Gram Sch
NW11 .....1 A4

Menorah Prim Sch
NW11 .....1 C4
Menotti St E2 .....99 C2
Menteath Ho [5]
E14 .....33 C3
Mentmore Terr E8 .....17 A1
Mentone Ct SW8 .....172 B4
Meon Rd W3 .....37 B4
Mepham St SE1 .....121 B1
Merbury Cl SE13 .....67 C2
Mercator Pl E14 .....41 C1
Mercator Rd SE13 .....67 C3
Merceron Ho [3] E2 .....25 B2
Merceron St E1 .....25 A1
Mercers Cl SE10 .....43 B2
Mercer's Cotts [5]
E3 .....33 A3
Mercers Pl W6 .....39 C2
Mercers Rd N19 .....4 C1
Mercer St WC2 .....106 A1
Merchant Ct E1 .....32 B1
Merchant St E3 .....26 B2
Merchant Taylors Hall
EC3 .....109 C1
Merchon Ho N7 .....13 C3
Mercia Gr [3] SE13 .....67 B3
Mercia Ho [6] SE5 .....48 B1
Mercier Rd SW15 .....58 A2
Mercury Ct [2] E14 .....41 C2
London SW9 .....173 B4
Mercury Way SE14 .....50 C4
Mercy Terr SE13 .....67 A2
Mere Cl SW15,SW19 .....69 C4
Meredith Ho [2] N16 .....16 A3
Meredith Mews SE4 .....66 B3
Meredith St EC1 .....96 A3
Meredyth Rd SW13 .....46 C1
Meretone Cl SE4 .....66 A3
Mereworth Ho [5]
SE15 .....50 B4
Merganser Ct [7]
SE8 .....51 B4
Meridan Ct SE13 .....67 C3
Meriden Ct SW3 .....144 A1
Meriden Ho [2] N1 .....24 A4
Meridian Building
SE10 .....52 C3
Meridian Ho SE10 .....43 A2
Meridian Pl E14 .....42 B4
Meridian Prim Sch
SE10 .....52 C4
Meridian Sq E15 .....19 C1
Merivale Rd SW15 .....58 A3
Merlin Ho
London NW3 .....11 A4
[7] London W4 .....37 C1
Merlins Ct WC1 .....95 B3
Merlin St EC1 .....95 B3
Mermaid Ct SE1 .....137 B4
[6] London SE16 .....33 B1
Mermaid Ho [6] E14 .....34 B2
Mermaid Twr [8]
SE8 .....51 B4
Meroe Ct N16 .....7 A2
Merredene St SW2 .....74 B4
Merriam Ave [3] E9 .....18 B2
Merricks Ct [5]
SW14 .....55 A3
Merrick Sq SE1 .....137 B2
Merrington Rd
SW6 .....155 C4
Merritt Rd SE4 .....66 B2
Merrivale NW1 .....83 A3
Merrow St SE17 .....151 B1
Merrow Wlk SE17 .....151 C2
Merryfield SE3 .....53 B1

Mersey Ho [10] N7 .....14 C3
Merstone Ho SW18 .....59 A1
Merthyr Terr SW13 .....47 A4
Merton Abbey Mills
SW18 .....71 A3
Merton Ave W4 .....38 B2
Merton Ho SW18 .....70 C3
Merton La N6 .....3 B2
Merton Rd SW18 .....70 C4
Merton Rise NW3 .....12 A1
Merton Road Ind Est
SW18 .....70 C4
Merttins Rd SE15 .....65 C2
Meru Cl NW5 .....12 C3
Mervan Rd SW2 .....62 C3
Messaline Ave W3 .....28 B3
Messina Ave NW6 .....10 C1
Messiter Ho N1 .....85 A3
Metcalfe Ho [3] SW8 .....171 B2
Meteor St SW11 .....60 C3
Methley Ho [7] N7 .....5 B2
Methley St SE11 .....149 C1
Methodist Central Hall
SW1 .....133 C3
Methwold Rd W10 .....30 C4
Metropolitan Benefit
Societies Almshouses
[3] N1 .....16 A2
Metropolitan Cl [4]
E14 .....33 C4
Mews St E1 .....125 B2
Mexborough NW1 .....82 C3
Mexfield Rd SW15 .....58 B2
Meyer Ho [1] SW12 .....73 A4
Meymott St SE1 .....122 A1
Meynell Cres E9 .....17 C1
Meynell Gdns E9 .....17 C1
Meynell Rd E9 .....17 C1
Meyrick Ho [3] E14 .....33 C4
Meyrick Rd
London NW10 .....8 C2
London SW11 .....60 A4
Miah Terr [1] E1 .....125 C1
Micawber Ct N1 .....97 B4
Micawber Ho SE16 .....139 C3
Micawber St N1 .....97 B4
Michael Cliffe Ho
EC1 .....95 C3
Michael Faraday Ho
SE17 .....151 C1
Michael Faraday Sch
SE17 .....151 C1
Michael Rd SW6 .....166 B4
Michelangelo Ct [4]
SE16 .....40 A1
Michelle Ct W3 .....28 C2
Michels Almshouses [1]
TW10 .....54 A2
Michelsdale Dr [3]
TW9 .....54 A3
Michelson Ho
SE11 .....149 A3
Michel's Row [2]
TW9 .....54 A3
Michigan Ho E14 .....41 C3
Mickledore NW1 .....83 A1
Micklethwaite Rd
SW6 .....155 C3
Mickleton Ho [30]
W2 .....31 C4
Middlefield NW8 .....79 B4
Middle Row W10 .....23 A1
Middle Row Prim Sch
W10 .....23 A1
Middlesex Ct [5] W4 .....38 B2
Middlesex Hospl
W1 .....105 A3

Middlesex Hospl Annexe
W1 . . . . .105 A4
Middlesex Pas EC1 .108 B3
Middlesex Pl E9 . . . . .17 B2
Middlesex St E1 . . . .110 C2
Middle St EC1 . . . . . .108 C4
Middle Temple
EC4 . . . . .121 B4
Middle Temple La
EC4 . . . . .121 B4
Middleton Bldgs
W1 . . . . .104 C3
Middleton Dr SE16 . .40 C4
Middleton Gr N7 . . . .14 A3
Middleton Ho SE1 .137 B1
London E8 . . . . .16 B1
Middleton Mews
N7 . . . . .14 A3
Middleton Rd
London E8 . . . . .16 B1
London NW11 . . . . .1 C4
Middleton St E2 . . . .25 A2
Middleton Way
SE13 . . . . .67 C3
Midford Pl W1 . . . . . .93 A1
Midhope Ho WC1 . . . .94 B3
Midhope St WC1 . . . .94 B3
Midhurst Ct N8 . . . . . .5 A4
Midhurst Ho E14 . . . .33 B3
Midhurst Way E5 . . .16 C4
Midland Pl E14 . . . . . .42 B1
Midland Rd NW1 . . . .84 A1
Midland Terr NW10 . .21 A1
Midlothian Rd E3 . . .26 B1
Midmoor Rd SW12 . .73 B3
Midship Cl SE16 . . . .32 C1
Midship Point E14 . .41 C4
Midstrath Rd NW10 . .8 A4
Midway Ho EC1 . . . . .96 B4
Milborne Gr
SW10 . . . . .15 C3 143 A1
Milborne Ho E9 . . . . .17 B2
Milborne St E9 . . . . .17 B2
Milcote St SE1 . . . . .136 B3
Milday Gr N N1 . . . . .15 C2
Mildmay Ave N1 . . . .15 C2
Mildmay Gr N N1 . . .15 C3
Mildmay Gr S N1 . . .15 C3
Mildmay Ho E
SW15 . . . . .57 B2
Mildmay Mission Hospl
E2 . . . . .98 C3
Mildmay Pk N1 . . . . .15 C3
Mildmay Rd N1 . . . . .16 A3
Mildmay St N1 . . . . . .15 C3
Mile End Pl E1 . . . . . .25 C1
Mile End Rd E1,E3 . .25 C1
Mile End Sta E3 . . . .26 B2
Miles Bldgs NW1 .102 A4
Miles Coverdale Prim
Sch W12 . . . . .39 B4
Miles Ct E1 . . . . .32 A3
Miles Ho E SE10 . . . .43 A1
Miles Lo E15 . . . . .19 C3
Miles Pl NW8 . . . . . . .101 C4
Miles St SW8 . . . . . .162 B3
Milestone Green
SW14 . . . . .55 C3
Milfoil St W12 . . . . . . .29 C2
Milford Ct S N16 . . . . .7 A3
Milford La WC2 . . . .121 B4
Milford Mews SW16 .74 B1
Milk St E C4 . . . . .109 A1
Milkwell Yd SE5 . . . .48 B2
Milkwood Rd SE24 . .63 A3
Milk Yd E1 . . . . .32 B2
Millais Rd E11 . . . . . . .19 C4

Milland Ho E SW15 .68 C3
Millard Cl E2 N16 . . .16 A3
Millard Ho SE8 . . . . . .41 B1
Millbank SW1 . . . . . .148 A3
Millbank Prim Sch
SW1 . . . . .147 C3
Millbrooke Ct E7
SW15 . . . . .58 A2
Millbrook Ho 4
SE15 . . . . .49 C4
Millbrook Rd SW9 . . .63 A4
Millender Wlk SE16 .40 B2
Millennium Bridge★
SE1,EC4 . . . . .122 C3
Millennium Dome★
SE10 . . . . .35 A1
Millennium Dr E14 . .42 C2
Millennium Harbour
E14 . . . . .41 C4
Millennium Pl E
E2 . . . . .25 A3
Millennium Prim Sch
SE10 . . . . .43 B3
Millennium Sq
SE1 . . . . .139 A4
Millennium Way
SE10 . . . . .43 A3
Miller Ho E SW2 . . . .74 A4
Miller's Ave E8,N16 .16 A3
Miller's Ct 4 W4 . . . .38 B1
Miller St NW1 . . . . . . .82 C2
Miller's Terr 1 E8 . .16 B3
Millers Way 6 W6 . .39 B4
Millers Wharf Ho
E1 . . . . .125 B1
Miller Wlk SE1 . . . . .121 C1
Millfield N4 . . . . .5 C2
Millfield La N6 . . . . . . .3 B2
Millfield Pl N6 . . . . .3 C2
Millfields Com Sch
E5 . . . . .17 B4
Millgrove St SW11 .169 B2
Millharbour E14 . . . . .42 A4
Mill Hill SW13 . . . . . .56 C4
Mill Hill Gr I3 W3 . . .28 A1
Mill Hill Rd
Barnes SW13 . . . . . . .46 C1
London W3 . . . . .37 A4
Mill Hill Terr I W3 . .28 A1
Milligan St E14 . . . . . .33 B2
Millington Ho N16 . . . .6 C1
Mill La NW6 . . . . .10 C3
Millman Ct WC1 . . . .94 C1
Millman Mews WC1 .94 C1
Millman Pl WC1 . . . .95 A1
Millman St WC1 . . . .94 C1
Millmark Gr SE14 . . .51 A1
Millner Ct SE4 . . . . . .51 B1
Mill Pl E14 . . . . .33 A3
Mill Pond Cl SW8 . .161 C2
Millpond Est SE16 . .40 A4
Mill Row N1 . . . . .24 A4
Mills Ct EC2 . . . . .98 A3
Mills Gr E E14 . . . . . .34 B4
Mills Ho SW8 . . . . . .171 A4
Millshot Cl SW6 . . . .47 B2
Mills Row 4 W4 . . . .37 C2
Mill St SE1 . . . . .139 A4
W1 . . . . .118 C4
Millstream Rd SE1 .138 C3
Mill Trad Est The
NW10 . . . . .20 B2
Millwall Dock Rd
E14 . . . . .41 C3
Millwood St W10 . . . .31 A4
Mill Yd E1 . . . . .125 B4
Milman Rd NW6 . . . .23 A3
Milman's Ho SW10 .157 B3

Milman's St SW10 .157 B3
Milner Ho E SW11 . . .59 C4
Milner Pl N1 . . . . .85 C4
Milner Sq N1 . . . . . . .15 A1
Milner St SW3 . . . . .144 C4
Milnthorpe Rd W4 . .45 C4
Milo Rd SE22 . . . . . . .64 B1
Milrood Ho 4 E1 . . . .32 C4
Milroy Wlk SE1 . . . .122 A2
Milson Rd W14 . . . .126 A2
Milsted Ho 22 E5 . . .17 A3
Milton Ave London N6 .4 B4
London NW10 . . . . . . .20 C4
Milton Cl SE1 . . . . . .152 C3
Milton Court Rd
SE14 . . . . .51 A4
Milton Ct EC2 . . . . . .109 B4
SE14 . . . . .51 A4
Fulham SW6 . . . . .58 A4
I London SW18 . . . .58 C2
Milton Gr N16 . . . . .6 C1
Milton Ho IB E2 . . . .25 B2
SE5 . . . . .48 C3
Milton House Mans
E8 . . . . .16 B4
Milton Pk N6 . . . . .4 B4
Milton Pl N7 . . . . .14 C3
Milton Rd London N6 . .4 B4
London SE24 . . . . .63 A2
London W3 . . . . .28 C1
Mortlake SW14 . . . . . .55 C4
Milton St EC1,EC2 .109 B4
Milverton NW5 . . . . . .12 C3
Milverton Rd NW6 . . .9 B1
Milverton St SE11 . .149 C1
Milward St E1 . . . . . . .32 A4
Mimosa St SW6 . . . .164 C3
Mina Rd SE17 . . . . . .152 A1
Minchin Ho S E14 . .33 C3
Mincing La EC3 . . . .124 A4
Minera Mews SW1 .145 C4
Minerva Cl SW9 . . .163 C2
Minerva Rd NW10 . . .20 C2
Minerva St E2 . . . . . .25 A3
Minerva Wlk EC1 . . .108 B1
Minet Ave NW10 . . . .21 A3
Minet Gdns NW10 . .21 A3
Minet Rd SE5,SW9 . .48 A1
Minford Gdns W14 . .39 C4
Mingard Wlk N7 . . . . .5 B1
Ming St E14 . . . . .33 C2
Minnow Wlk SE17 . .152 B3
Minories EC3 . . . . . .124 C4
Minshull St SW8 . . .171 B3
Minson Rd E9 . . . . . . .25 C4
Minstead Gdns
SW15 . . . . .68 B4
Minster Rd NW2 . . . .10 A3
Mint Bsns Pk E16
E16 . . . . .35 C4
Mintern St N1 . . . . . . .87 C2
Minton Ho SE11 . . . .149 B4
Minton Mews
NW6 . . . . .11 A2
Mint St SE1 . . . . .137 A4
Mirabel Rd SW6 . . . .155 A2
Miranda Cl IB E1 . . .32 B4
Miranda Ho IB N1 . .24 A3
Miranda Rd N19 . . . . .4 B3
Missenden SE17 . . . .151 C1
Missenden Ho NW8 .90 A2
Mission Pl SE15 . . . .49 C2
Mission Sq I9 TW8 . .44 A4
Misterton Ct SW11 .167 C4
Mistral SE5 . . . . .49 A2
Mitali Pas E1 . . . . . . .111 B1

Mitcham Ho S SE5 . .48 B2
Mitchell Brook Prim Sch
NW10 . . . . .8 A2
Mitchell Ho
I London W12 . . . . . .30 A2
London W4 . . . . .37 B1
Mitchell's Pl SE21 . . .76 A4
Mitchell St EC1 . . . . .97 A2
Mitchison Rd N1 . . . .15 C2
Mitford Rd N19 . . . . . . .5 A2
Mitre Bridge Ind Pk
W10 . . . . .22 A1
Mitre Ct EC2 . . . . . . .109 A2
EC4 . . . . .135 C4
Mitre Rd SE1 . . . . . .135 C4
Mitre Sq EC3 . . . . . .110 B1
Mitre St EC3 . . . . . . .110 B1
Mitre The S E14 . . . .33 B2
Mitre Way W10 . . . . . .30 A4
Moatfield NW6 . . . . . .10 A1
Moat Pl Acton W3 . . .28 A3
London SW9 . . . . .62 B4
Moberly Rd SW4 . . . .73 C4
Mobey Ct SW4 . . . . .172 A3
Mocatta Ho I E1 . . .111 B4
Modbury Gdns NW5 .12 C2
Modder Pl SW15 . . . .57 C3
Model Cotts SW14 . .55 B4
Modling Ho E2 . . . . . .25 C3
Moelwyn Hughes Ct
N7 . . . . .13 C3
Moffat Ho 22 SE5 . . .48 B3
Mohawk Ho E9 E3 . . .26 A3
Moira Ct SW17 . . . . . .72 C2
Moira Ho SW9 . . . . .173 B4
Moland Mead SE16 . .40 C1
Molasses Ho I
SW11 . . . . .59 B4
Molasses Row E
SW11 . . . . .59 B4
Mole Ct E W12 . . . . .38 A4
Mole Ho NW8 . . . . . . .89 C1
Molesey Ho E2 . . . . .98 C2
Molesford Rd SW6 .165 B3
Molesworth Ho E
SE17 . . . . .48 A4
Molesworth St SE13 .67 B4
Molly Huggins Cl
SW12 . . . . .73 B4
Molton Ho N1 . . . . . . .85 A3
Molyneux St W1 . . . .102 B3
Mona Pl SE15 . . . . . . .50 B1
Mona St E16 . . . . .35 B2
Monck's Row SW18 . .58 B1
Monck St SW1 . . . . . .133 C1
Monclar Rd SE5 . . . . .63 C3
Moncorvo Cl SW7 . .130 A3
Moncrieff St SE15 . . .49 C1
Mondragon Ho
SW8 . . . . .172 B4
Monet Ct IB SE16 . . .40 A1
Moneyer Ho N1 . . . . .97 B4
Monica Shaw Ct
NW1 . . . . .83 C1
Monier Rd E3 . . . . . . .18 C1
Monkbretton Ho
E2 . . . . .99 B3
Monk Dr E16 . . . . .35 C2
Monkridge 3 N8 . . . .4 C4
Monksfield N4 . . . . . . .5 C2
Monkton Ct W14 . . .126 C2
Monkton Ho
I SE16 . . . . .40 C4
London E5 . . . . .17 A3
Monkton St SE11 . . .149 C4
Monkwell Sq EC2 . .109 A3
Monmouth Cl W4 . . .37 C3
Monmouth Gr TW8 . .36 A2

Monmouth Ho
S London NW5 . . . .13 A2
London SW18 . . . . . . .58 C1
Monmouth Pl W2 . . .100 A1
Monmouth Rd W2 . .31 C3
Monmouth St WC2 .106 A1
Monnery Rd N19 . . . .4 B1
Monnow Rd SE1 . . . .153 B3
Monro Dr SW1 . . . . . .55 A2
Monro Ho I SW15 . .57 A2
IB London N19 . . . . . .4 C4
Monro Ho
21 London SW1 . . . .11 B4
Putney SW15 . . . . .57 A2
Monro way E5 . . . . . .16 C4
Monsal Ct E5 . . . . . . .18 A4
Monsell Rd N4,N5 . . .6 A1
Monson Prim Sch
SE14 . . . . .50 C3
Monson Rd SE14 . . . .50 C3
London NW10 . . . . . . .22 A2
Montagu Ct W1 . . . .103 A3
Montague Ave SE4 . .66 C3
Montague Cl SE1 . . .123 B2
Montague Pl WC1 . .105 C4
Montague Rd
London E8 . . . . .16 C3
Richmond TW10 . . . . .54 A1
Montague Sq SE15 . .50 B3
Montague St WC1 . .106 A4
Montagu Mans
W1 . . . . .103 A3
Montagu Mews N
W1 . . . . .103 A3
Montagu Mews S
W1 . . . . .103 A2
Montagu Mews W
W1 . . . . .103 A2
Montagu Pl W1 . . . .103 A3
Montagu Row W1 . .103 A3
Montagu Sq W1 . . . .103 A3
Montagu St W1 . . . .103 A2
Montana Rd SW17 . .72 C1
Montcalm Ho E14 . . .41 C2
Montclare St
E2 . . . . .24 B1 98 C2
Monteagle Ct 27 N1 .24 A3
Monteagle Way
London E5 . . . . .7 C1
I London SE15 . . . . .65 A4
Montefiore Ct 2 N16 .7 B3
Montefiore St
SW8 . . . . .170 B1
Montem Prim Sch
N7 . . . . .5 B1
Montem St N4 . . . . . . .5 B3
Montesquieu Terr S
E16 . . . . .35 B1
Montford Pl SE11 . . .149 B1
Montfort Ho E14 . . . .42 B3
I E2 . . . . .25 B2
Montfort Pl SW19 . . .69 C3
Montgomery Ct I0 W4 .45 B4
Montgomery Ho S
SW14 . . . . .55 C4
Montgomery Lo 34
E1 . . . . .25 B1
Montgomery Rd W4 .37 B2
Montholme Rd
SW11 . . . . .60 B1
Monthorpe Rd E1 . .111 B3
Montolieu Gdns
SW15 . . . . .57 A2
Montpelier Gr NW5 .13 B3

Montpelier Mews
SW7 . . . . 129 B1
Montpelier Pl 2 E1 . 32 B3
SW7 . . . . 130 B2
Montpelier Rd SE15 .50 A2
Montpelier Rise
NW11 . . . . .1 A4
Montpelier Row
SE3 . . . . .53 B1
Montpelier Sq
SW7 . . . . 130 B2
Montpelier St SW7 130 B2
Montpelier Terr
SW7 . . . . 130 B3
Montpelier Vale
SE3 . . . . .53 B1
Montpelier Way
NW11 . . . . .1 A4
Montpelier Wlk
SW7 . . . . 130 B2
Montreal Pl WC2 . .120 C4
Montrose Ave NW6 . 23 A3
Montrose Ct SW7 . . 129 C3
Montrose Ho E14 . . .41 C3
SW1 . . . . 131 C3
Montrose Pl SW1 . . 131 C3
Montrose Villas W6 . 38 C1
Montserrat Rd
SW15 . . . . .58 A3
Monument Gdns
SE13 . . . . .67 B2
Monument St EC3 . 124 A3
Monument Sta
EC3 . . . . 123 C4
Monument The ★
EC3 . . . . 123 C4
Monza St E1 . . . . . .32 B2
Moodkee St SE16 . . .40 B4
Moody Rd SE15 . . . .49 B2
Moody St E1 . . . . . .25 C2
Moon St N1 . . . . . . .86 A4
Moorcroft Rd SW16 .74 A1
Moore Cl SW14 . . . .55 B4
Moore Ct N1 . . . . . .86 B4
Moore Ho E1 . . . . . .32 A1
16 E2 . . . . 25 B2
5 SE10 . . . . .43 B1
Wandsworth SW17 . 71 C1
Moore Park Ct
SW6 . . . . 156 B2
Moore Park Rd
SW6 . . . . 156 B2
Moore St SW3 . . . 144 C4
Moorfields EC2 . . . .109 B3
Moorfields Eye Hospl
EC1 . . . . .97 B3
Moorfields Highwalk
EC2 . . . . 109 B3
Moorfields Prim Sch
EC1 . . . . .97 B3
Moorgate EC2 . . . . 109 B3
Moorgate Pl EC2 . . 109 B2
Moorgate Sta EC2 . 109 B3
Moorgreen Ho EC1 . 96 A4
Moorhouse Rd W2 . 31 C3
Moor La EC2 . . . . . 109 B3
Moorland Rd SW9 . . 63 A3
Moor Pl EC2 . . . . . .109 B3
Moor St W1 . . . . . .105 C1
Morant Ho SW9 . . . 172 C2
Morant St E14 . . . . .33 C2
Mora Prim Sch NW2 . .9 B4
Mora Rd NW2 . . . . . .9 B4
Mora St EC1 . . . . . .97 A3

Morat St SW9 . . . .173 A4
Moravian Cl SW10 .157 C3
Moravian Pl SW10 .157 C3
Moravian St 2
E2 . . . . .25 B2
Moray Ho E1 . . . . . .26 A1
Moray Mews N4,N7 . .5 B2
Moray Rd N4,N7 . . . .5 B2
Mordaunt Ho
4 London NW10 . . 20 C4
8 London SW8 . . .171 B1
Mordaunt Rd NW10 . 20 C4
Mordaunt St SW9 . . 62 B4
Morden Hill SE13 . . 52 B1
Morden Ho 6 SW2 . .62 C1
Morden La SE13 . . .52 B2
Morden Mount Prim Sch
SE13 . . . . .52 A1
Morden Rd SE3 . . . .53 C1
Morden Road Mews
SE3 . . . . .53 C1
Morden St SE13 . . . 52 A2
Morden Wharf Rd
SE10 . . . . .43 A3
Mordern Ho NW1 . . .90 B1
Morecambe Cl
E1 . . . . .32 C4
Morecambe St
SE17 . . . . .151 A2
More Cl E16 . . . . . .35 B1
W14 . . . . 140 A3
Moredown Ho 3
E8 . . . . .16 C3
More House Sch
SW1 . . . . 131 A1
Moreland Ct 3 NW2 . 1 C1
Moreland Prim Sch
EC1 . . . . .96 B3
Moreland St EC1 . . .96 B4
Morella Rd SW11,
SW12 . . . . .72 B4
Morell Ho SW9 . . . .173 A1
Moresby Wlk SW8 . 170 B1
More's Gdn SW3 . . 157 C3
Moreton Ho SE16 . . 40 A3
Moreton Pl SW1 . . .147 A2
Moreton St SW1 . . .147 B2
Moreton Terr SW1 . 147 A2
Moreton Terr Mews N
SW1 . . . . 147 A2
Moreton Terr Mews S
SW1 . . . . 147 A2
Moreton Twr 3 W3 . 28 A1
Morgan Ct SW11 . . 167 C2
Morgan Ho SW1 . . .147 A3
SW8 . . . . 171 A4
Morgan Rd W10 . . . 31 B4
London N7 . . . . . . 14 C3
Morgan St E16 . . . . 35 B2
E3 . . . . .26 A2
Morgan's Wlk
SW11 . . . . .158 A1
Moriatry Cl N7 . . . . .14 A4
Morie St SW18 . . . .59 A2
Morkyns Wlk SE21 . 76 A1
Morland Cl NW11 . . .2 A3
Morland Est E8 . . . .16 C1
Morland Ho NW1 . . .83 A1
NW6 . . . . 23 C4
SW1 . . . . 148 A4
W11 . . . . .31 A3
Morland Mews N1 . . 14 C1
Morley Coll SE1 . . . 135 C2
Morley Ho
London N16 . . . . . .7 C2
Streatham SW2 . . . 74 A4
Morley St SE13 . . . .67 B3

Morley St SE1 . . . . .135 C3
Morna St SE5 . . . . . 48 B1
Morning La E9 . . . . .17 B2
Morningside Prim Sch
E9 . . . . .17 B2
Mornington Ave
W14 . . . . 140 C3
Mornington Avenue
Mans W14 . . . . . . 140 C3
Mornington Cres
NW1 . . . . 82 C2
Mornington Crescent
Sta NW1 . . . . 82 C2
Mornington Ct NW1 . 82 C2
Mornington Gr E3 . . 26 C2
Mornington Mews 2
SE5 . . . . .48 B2
Mornington Pl NW1 . 82 C2
4 SE8 . . . . .51 B3
Mornington Rd
SE14,SE8 . . . . 51 B3
London N7 . . . . . . 14 B2
Mornington St NW1 . 82 B2
Mornington Terr
NW1 . . . . 82 B2
Morocco St SE1 . . .138 A3
Morpeth Gr E9 . . . . 25 C4
Morpeth Rd E9 . . . . 25 C4
Morpeth Sec Sch
E2 . . . . .25 B2
Morpeth St E2 . . . . 25 C2
Morpeth Terr SW1 . 146 C4
Morrel Ct 10 E2 . . . 24 C3
Morris Blitz Ct 2
N16 . . . . 16 B4
Morris Ct 3 E1 . . . . 25 C1
Morris Gdns SW18 . 70 C4
Morris Ho 11 E2 . . . 25 B2
NW8 . . . . 90 A1
10 London N19 . . . 13 C4
1 London SW4 . . . 62 A3
Morrish Rd SW2 . . . 74 A4
Morrison Bldgs 11 . .111 B2
Morrison Ho 2 SW2 .74 C3
Morrison St SW11 . . 60 C4
Morris Pl N4 . . . . . . 5 C2
Morriss Ho 7 SE16 . 40 A4
Morris St E1 . . . . . .32 A3
E14 . . . . .33 A2
Morshead Mans W9 . 23 C2
Morshead Rd W9 . . .23 C2
Mortain Ho 3 SE16 . 40 A2
Morten Cl SW4 . . . . 61 C1
Mortimer Cl
London NW2 . . . . . 1 A1
Streatham SW16 . . 73 C2
Mortimer Cres NW6 . 78 B3
Mortimer Ct NW8 . . .79 A1
Mortimer Est NW6 . . 78 A3
Mortimer Ho W11 . . .30 C1
6 W14 . . . . .30 C1
Mortimer Lo 11
SW19 . . . . .70 A3
Mortimer Market
WC1 . . . . 93 A1
Mortimer Pl NW6 . . .78 A3
Mortimer Rd
London N1 . . . . . . 16 A1
London NW10 . . . . 22 B2
Mortimer Sq W11 . . 30 C2
Mortimer St W1 . . .105 A3
Mortimer Terr NW5 . 13 A4
Mortlake High St
SW14 . . . . .55 C4
Mortlake Sta SW14 . 55 B4
Mortlock Cl SE15 . . 50 A2

Morton Ho SE17 . . . 48 A4
Morton Mews
SW5 . . . . 142 A3
Morton Pl SE1 . . . .135 B1
Morton Rd N1 . . . . . 15 B1
Morval Rd SW2 . . . .62 C2
Morven Rd SW17 . . 72 B1
Morville Ho SW18 . . 59 C1
Morville St E3 . . . . . 26 C3
Morwell St WC1 . . .105 C3
Moscow Pl W2 . . . .114 A4
Moscow Rd W2 . . . 114 A4
Mosedale NW1 . . . . 92 B3
Moseley Way SE10 . 43 B3
Mosque La E11 . . . . .19 C4
Mosque Tower E1 . .111 B3
Mossbury Rd SW11 . 60 A4
Moss Cl E1 . . . . . . .111 C4
Mossford St E3 . . . . 26 B1
Mossington Gdns
SE16 . . . . .40 B2
Mossop St SW3 . . . 144 B4
Mostyn Gdns NW10 . 22 C3
Mostyn Gr E3 . . . . . 26 C3
Mostyn Lo N5 . . . . . 15 B4
Mostyn Rd SW9 . . . 173 C3
SW19 . . . . .69 C1
Motcomb St SW1 . . 131 B2
Mothers Sq The 13
E5 . . . . .17 A4
Motley Ave 2 EC2 . . 98 A2
Motley St SW8 . . . .170 C2
Moules Ct SE5 . . . . 48 B3
Moulins Rd E9 . . . . .17 B1
Moulsford Ho
2 W2 . . . . .31 C4
6 London N7 . . . . 14 A3
Mounsey Ho 10
W10 . . . . 23 A2
Mount Adon Pk
SE21,SE22 . . . . . . 76 C4
Mountague Pl 2
E14 . . . . .34 B2
Mountain Ho SE11 . 148 C2
Mount Angelus Rd
SW15 . . . . .68 B4
Mount Ararat Rd
TW10 . . . . .54 A2
Mountbatten Ho N6 . .3 C4
Mountbatten Mews
SW18 . . . . .71 B3
Mount Carmel RC Coll
N19 . . . . 4 C3
Mount Carmel RC Sec
Sch N7 . . . . 5 A1
Mountcarrel Gdns
SW16,SW17 . . . . . 74 B1
Mount Ephraim La
SW16 . . . . .73 C1
Mount Ephraim Rd
SW16 . . . . .73 C1
Mountfield NW2 . . . .1 B2
Mountfield Ct SE13 . 67 C1
Mountford Ct E1 . . .111 B2
Mountfort Cres N1 . . 14 C1
Mountfort Terr 1
N1 . . . . .14 C1
Mountgrove Rd N5 . . 6 B1
Mountjoy Ho EC2 . .108 C3
Mount Lodge SW4 . . 62 A3
Mount Mills EC1 . . . 96 B3
Mount Nod Rd
SW16,SW2 . . . . . . 74 B1
Mount Pl 7 W3 . . . .28 A1
Mount Pleasant
WC1 . . . . 95 B1
Mount Pleasant Cres
N4 . . . . .5 B4

Mount Pleasant Rd
London SE13 . . . . . 67 B1
Willesden NW10 . . 22 B4
Mount Pleasant Villas
N4 . . . . 5 B4
Mount Rd SW18,
SW19 . . . . .71 A2
Mount Row W1 . . . .118 A3
Mounts Pond Rd
SE3,SE13 . . . . 52 C1
Mount Sq The NW3 . .2 B1
Mount St W1 . . . . . 117 C3
Mount Terr E1 . . . . . 32 A4
Mount The NW3 . . . . 2 B1
W8 . . . . 113 B1
Mount Tyndal NW3 . .2 C3
Mount Vernon NW3 . 11 B4
Mountview 3 SW16 . 74 B1
Mountview Cl NW11 . 2 B3
Mount Villas SE27 . . 75 A1
Mourne Ho NW3 . . . 11 B2
Mowatt Cl N19 . . . . . 4 C3
Mowbray Rd NW6 . . 10 A1
Mowlem Prim Sch
E2 . . . . .25 B3
Mowlem St E2 . . . . 25 A3
Mowll St SW9 . . . . 163 B1
Moxon St W1 . . . . .103 B3
Moye Cl 1 E2 . . . . . 24 C3
Moylan Rd W6 . . . . 154 B3
Moyle Ho 1 SW1 . . 161 A4
Moyne Ho 10 SW9 . .63 A3
Mozart St W10 . . . . 23 B2
Mudchute Sta E14 . . 42 A2
Mudie Ho 3 SW2 . . 74 A4
Muir Cl SW18 . . . . . 60 A1
Muirdown Ave
SW14 . . . . .55 C3
Muirfield W3 . . . . . .29 A3
Muirfield Cl 28
SE16 . . . . .40 A1
Muirfield Cres E14 . . 42 A3
Muir Rd E5 . . . . .7 C1
Mulberry Bsns Ctr
SE16 . . . . .40 C4
Mulberry Cl SW3 . . 157 C3
London NW3 . . . . . 11 C4
London SE22 . . . . 64 C1
Mulberry Ct EC1 . . . 96 B3
10 W9 . . . . .23 B2
1 London E11 . . . . 19 C4
London N5 . . . . . . 15 A3
Mulberry Ho 5 E2 . . 25 B2
6 SE8 . . . . .51 B4
Mulberry House Sch
NW2 . . . . 10 A3
Mulberry Mews
SE14 . . . . .51 B2
Mulberry Pl W6 . . . .38 C1
8 E8 . . . . .16 B1
Mulberry Sch for Girls
E1 . . . . .32 A3
Mulberry St 1 E1 . .111 B2
Mulberry Wlk SW3 . 157 C4
Mulgrave Rd W14 . .154 C4
London NW10 . . . . .8 B4
Mulkern Rd N19 . . . . 4 C3
Mullard Ho WC1 . . .105 B4
Mullens Ho 7
SW15 . . . . .57 B2
Mullen Twr EC1 . . . .95 B1
Mullet Gdns E2 . . . . 24 C2
Mull Ho 8 E3 . . . . . 26 B3
Mullins Path SW14 . 55 C4
Mulready St NW8 . . 90 A1

Multi Way W3 .....38 A4
Multon Ho E1 .....17 B1
Multon Rd SW18 .....71 C4
Mulvaney Way SE1 137 C3
Mumford Rd SE24 .....63 A2
Muncaster Rd SW11 60 C2
Mundania Ct SE22 .....65 A1
Mundania Rd SE21 .....65 B1
Munday Ho SE1 .....137 B1
Munday Rd E16 .....35 C2
Munden Ho E3 .....27 A2
Munden St W14 .....140 A4
Mundy Ho E9 .....W10 .....25 A1
Mundy St N1 .....98 B4
Munro Ho SE1 .....135 B3
      SE1 .....136 C3
Munro Mews W10 .....31 A4
Munster Ct SW6 .....164 C2
Munster Rd SW6 .....154 B1
Munster Residences
      SW6 .....164 B4
Munster Sq NW1 .....92 B3
Munton Rd SE17 .....151 A4
Murchison Ho E1
      W10 .....31 A4
Murdoch Ho E5
      SE16 .....40 B3
Murdock Cl E16 .....35 B3
Murdock St SE15 .....50 A4
Murfett Cl SW19 .....70 A2
Muriel St N1 .....85 A2
Murphy Ho SE1 .....136 B2
Murphy St SE1 .....135 B3
Murray Gr N1 .....87 B1
Murray Mews NW1 .....13 C1
Murray St NW1 .....13 C1
Murray Terr NW3 .....11 C4
Musard Rd W6 .....154 B4
Musbury St E1 .....32 B3
Muscal W6 .....154 A4
Muscatel Pl SE5 .....49 A2
Muschamp Rd SE15 64 B4
Muscott Ho E2 .....24 C4
Muscovy St EC3 .....124 B4
Museum E E2 .....25 B2
Museum in Docklands*
      E14 .....33 C2
Museum St WC1 .....106 A2
Musgrave Cres
      SW6 .....165 C4
Musgrave Ct SW11 168 B4
Musgrove Ho E9 .....17 C2
Musgrove Rd SE14 .....51 A2
Musical Mus The
      TW8 .....44 A4
Musjid Rd SW11 .....167 C1
Mus of Garden History
      SE1 .....134 C1
Mus of London*
      EC2 .....108 C3
Mustow Pl SW6 .....165 A2
Mutrix Rd NW6 .....23 C4
Mutton Pl NW1 .....12 C2
Myatt Ct SE4 .....51 A1
Myatt Garden Prim Sch
      SE4 .....51 B1
Myatt Ho SE5 .....48 A1
Myatt Rd SW9 .....48 A2
Myatts Field Ct SE5 .....48 B2
Mycenae Rd SE3 .....53 C3
Myddelton Pas EC1 .....95 C4
Myddelton Sq EC1 .....95 C4
Myddelton St EC1 .....95 C3
Myddleton Ave N4 .....6 B2
Myers Ho E5 .....48 B3

Myers La SE14 .....50 C4
Mylius Cl SE14 .....50 B2
Mylne Cl W6 .....38 C1
Mylne St EC1 .....85 B1
Mynterne Ct
      SW19 .....69 C3
Myrdle Ct E1 .....111 C2
Myrdle St E1 .....111 C2
Myron Pl SE13 .....67 B4
Myrtle Ho SE14 .....50 C2
Myrtle Rd W3 .....28 B1
Myrtle Wlk E N1 .....24 A3
Mysore Rd SW11 .....60 B3
Mytton Ho SW8 .....162 C1

N

N1 Shopping Ctr
      N1 .....85 C1
Nags Head N7 .....14 B4
Nags Head Ct EC1 .....97 A1
Nairne Gr SE5,SE24 .....63 C3
Nairn St E14 .....34 B4
Naish Ct N1 .....84 B4
Nalton Ho E NW6 .....11 B1
Nankin St E14 .....33 C3
Nansen Rd SW11 .....60 C4
Nant Ct NW2 .....1 B2
Nant Ct E1 .....25 C1
Naoroji St WC1 .....95 B3
Napier Ave E14 .....41 C1
      Fulham SW6 .....58 B4
Napier Cl SE14,SE8 .....51 B3
      W14 .....126 C2
Napier Ct N1 .....87 B2
      Fulham SW6 .....58 B4
Napier Gr N1 .....87 A2
Napier Pl W14 .....126 C1
Napier Rd W14 .....126 C1
Napier Terr N1 .....15 A1
Narbonne Ave SW4 .....61 B2
Narborough St
      SW6 .....166 A1
Narcissus Rd NW6 .....10 C3
Narford Rd E5 .....7 C2
Narrow St E14 .....33 A2
      E Acton W3 .....28 A1
Nascot St W12 .....30 B3
Naseby Cl NW6 .....11 B1
Nashe Ho SE1 .....137 B1
Nash Ho SW1 .....146 B1
Nash Rd SE4 .....66 A2
Nash Street E1 .....92 B4
Nasmyth St W6 .....39 A3
Nassau Rd SW13 .....46 B2
Nassau St W1 .....104 C3
Nassington Rd NW3 .....12 B4
Nathan Ho SE11 .....149 C3
Nathaniel Cl E1 .....111 A3
National Army Mus*
      SW3 .....159 A4
National Film Theatre
      SE1 .....121 A2
National Gallery*
      W1 .....119 C3
National Hospl The
      WC1 .....94 B1
National Maritime
      Mus* SE10 .....52 C4

National Portrait
      Gallery* W1 .....119 C3
National Portrait Gallery
      (Annex)* W1 .....119 C3
National Postal Mus
      EC1 .....108 C2
National Theatre
      SE1 .....121 A2
Natural History Mus*
      SW7 .....129 B1
Nat West Twr*
      EC2 .....110 A2
Nautilus Bldg The
      N1 .....95 B4
Naval Row E14 .....34 B2
Navarino Gr E8 .....16 C2
Navarino Mans E8 .....16 C2
Navarre St E2 .....98 C2
Navenby Wlk E E3 .....26 C1
Navy St SW4 .....61 C4
Naylor Ho SE17 .....151 C2
Naylor Rd SE15 .....50 A3
Nazareth Cl SE15 .....50 A1
Nazrul St E2 .....98 C3
Nealden St SW9 .....62 B4
Neal St WC2 .....106 A1
Neal's Yd WC2 .....106 A1
Neasden Cl NW10 .....8 A3
Neasden Junc NW10 .....8 A4
Neasden La NW10 .....8 A3
Neasden Sta NW10 .....8 A3
Neate St SE5 .....49 A4
      SE5 .....49 B4
Neathouse Pl SW1 146 C4
Nebraska St SE1 .....137 B3
Neckinger SE16 .....139 A2
Neckinger Est
      SE16 .....139 A2
Neckinger St SE1 .....139 A2
Nectarine Way SE13 52 A1
Nedahall Ct E NW11 .....1 B4
Needham Ho SE11 149 B3
Needham Rd W11 .....31 C3
Needleman St SE16 .....40 C4
Needwood Ho N4 .....6 B3
Neilson-Terry Ct E
      SW9 .....62 B3
Neil Wates Cres E
      SW2 .....74 C3
Nella Rd W6 .....47 C4
Nelldale Rd SE16 .....40 B2
Nell Gwynn Ho
      SW3 .....144 B3
Nelson Cl E NW6 .....23 C2
Nelson Ct SE16 .....33 B1
Nelson Gdns
      E2 .....24 C2 99 C4
Nelson Pas EC1 .....97 A4
Nelson Pl N1 .....86 B1
Nelson Rd SE10 .....52 B4
Nelson's Monument*
      WC2 .....120 A2
Nelson Sq SE1 .....136 A4
Nelsons Row SW4 .....61 C3
Nelson St E1 .....32 A3
      E16 .....35 B2
Nelson Terr N1 .....86 B1
Nemoure Rd W3 .....28 B2
Nepaul Rd SW11 .....60 A4
Nepean St SW15 .....68 C4
Neptune Ct E14 .....41 C2
Neptune Ho E SE16 40 B3
      E4 London N16 .....16 A3
Neptune St SE16 .....40 B3

Nesham Ho E1 N1 .....24 A4
Nesham St E1 .....125 B2
Ness St SE16 .....139 B2
Nestor Ho E2 .....25 A3
Netheravon Rd W4 .....38 B1
Netheravon Rd S
      W4 .....38 B1
Netherby Ho SW8 171 B1
Nethercombe Ho E
      SE3 .....53 C4
Nethercott Ho E
      E3 .....27 A2
Netherfield Rd
      SW17 .....72 C1
Netherford Rd
      SW4 .....171 A1
Netherhall Gdns
      NW3 .....11 B3
Netherhall Way
      NW3 .....11 B3
Netherleigh Cl N6 .....4 A3
Netherton Gr
      SW10 .....157 A3
Netherwood Rd
      W14 .....39 C4
Netherwood St
      NW6 .....10 C2
Netley E SE5 .....49 A2
Netley Prim Sch
      NW1 .....92 C3
Netley Rd TW8 .....44 A4
Netley St NW1 .....92 C3
Nettlecombe Ho E
      London SW3 144 B3
Nettleden Ho SW3 .....144 B3
Nettlefold Pl SE27 .....75 A1
Nettleton Rd SE14 .....50 C2
Nevada St SE10 .....52 B4
Nevena Ct E SW2 .....62 C2
Nevern Mans SW5 141 B2
Nevern Pl SW5 .....141 C3
Nevern Rd SW5 .....141 B3
Nevern Sq SW5 .....141 C3
Nevil Ho E SW9 .....48 A1
Nevill Ct SW10 .....156 C2
Neville Cl NW1 .....83 C1
      NW6 .....23 B3
      E1 SE15 .....49 C3
      Acton W3 .....37 B4
      London SE15 .....49 C3
Neville Gill Cl SW18 .....59 A1
Neville Rd NW6 .....23 B3
Neville Terr SW7 .....143 B2
Nevill Rd N16 .....7 A1
Nevinson Cl SW18 .....59 C1
Nevis Rd SW17 .....72 C2
Nevitt Ho N1 .....87 C1
Newall Ho SE1 .....137 A2
Newark Cres NW10 .....20 C2
Newark Ho E SW9 .....48 A1
Newark St E1 .....32 A4
Newbery Ho N1 .....15 B1
Newbold Cotts E
      E1 .....32 B3
Newbolt Ho SE17 .....151 B2
New Bond St W1 .....118 B4
New Bridge St
      EC4 .....108 A1
New Broad St EC2 .....110 A3
New Bsns Ctr The
      NW10 .....21 B2
Newburgh Rd W3 .....28 B1
Newburgh St W1 .....105 A1

New Burlington Mews
      W1 .....118 C4
New Burlington Pl
      W1 .....118 C4
New Burlington St
      W1 .....118 C4
Newburn Ho SE11 149 A2
Newburn St SE11 .....149 A2
Newbury Ct E5 .....18 A3
Newbury Ho
      London SW9 .....48 A1
      W2 .....100 B1
Newby NW1 .....92 C4
Newby Pl E14 .....34 B2
Newby St SW8 .....61 A4
New Caledonian Wharf
      SE16 .....41 B3
New Campden Ct E
      NW3 .....11 B4
Newcastle Cl EC4 .....108 A2
Newcastle Ct EC4 .....123 C4
Newcastle Ho NW1 103 B4
Newcastle Pl W2 .....101 C4
Newcastle Row EC1 .....95 C1
New Cavendish St
      W1 .....104 A3
New Change EC4 .....108 C1
New Charles St EC1 .....96 B4
New Church Rd SE5 .....48 C4
      SE5 .....48 B3
New College Ct E
      NW3 .....11 B2
New College Mews E
      N1 .....14 C1
New College Par E
      NW3 .....11 C1
Newcombe Ho N5 .....15 B3
Newcombe St W8 .....113 C2
Newcome Rd E
      SW11 .....59 C4
New Compton St
      WC2 .....106 A1
New Concordia Wharf
      SE1 .....139 A4
Newcourt Ho E E2 .....25 A2
Newcourt St NW8 .....80 A1
New Covent Garden
      Flower Market
      SW8 .....162 A3
New Covent Garden
      Fruit & Vegetable Mkt
      SW8 .....161 B1
New Crane Pl E1 .....32 B1
New Crescent Yd E
      NW10 .....21 B3
New Cross SE14 .....51 B3
New Cross Gate
      SE14 .....50 C2
New Cross Gate Sta
      SE14 .....51 A3
New Cross Hospl
      SE14 .....50 B3
New Cross Rd SE14 51 A2
New Cross Sta SE14 .....51 B3
New Ct EC4 .....107 B1
London N16 .....6 C3
      E1 London SW2 .....62 C2
New Den (Millwall FC)
      The SE16 .....40 B1

234 New – Nor

Newdigate Ho 5
E14 .....33 B3
Newell St E14 .....33 B3
New End NW3 .....11 B4
New End Prim Sch
NW3 .....11 B4
New End Sq NW3 .....11 B4
Newent Cl SE15 .....49 A3
New Fetter La EC4 .....107 C2
Newfield Prim Sch
.....8 B1
New Furness Prim Sch
The NW10 .....21 C3
Newgate St EC1 .....108 B2
New Globe Wlk
SE1 .....122 B2
New Goulston St
E1 .....110 C2
Newham Sch of Nursing
E7 .....27 A1
Newham's Row
SE1 .....138 B3
Newhaven La
E16 .....35 C4
Newington Barrow Way
N7 .....5 B1
Newington Butts
SE1,SE11 .....150 B3
Newington Cswy
SE1 .....136 C2
Newington Green Mans
N16 .....15 C3
Newington Green Prim
Sch N16 .....15 C3
Newington Green Rd
N1 .....15 C3
Newington Ind Est
SE17 .....150 C3
New Inn Broadway
EC2 .....98 B2
New Inn Pas WC2 .....107 A1
New Inn Sq EC2 .....98 B2
New Inn St EC2 .....98 B2
New Inn Yd
EC2 .....24 A1 98 B2
New James Ct SE15 .....65 A4
New Kent Rd SE1 .....151 A4
New King's Prim Sch
SW6 .....164 C2
New King's Rd 165 C3
New King St SE8 .....51 C4
Newland Ho 17
SE14 .....50 C4
Newlands NW1 .....92 C4
Newlands Quay E1 .....32 B2
New London St
EC3 .....124 B4
Newlyn NW1 .....83 A3
Newman Pas W1 .....105 A3
Newman's Ct EC3 .....109 C1
Newman's Row
WC2 .....107 A3
Newman St W1 .....105 A3
Newmill Ho 3 E3 .....27 B1
Newmount NW3 .....11 C3
New Mount St E15 .....19 C1
Newnes Path SW15 .....57 A3
Newnham Ho 9
SW15 .....57 C1
Newnham Terr
SE1 .....135 B2
New North Pl EC2 .....98 A2
New North St WC1 .....87 B3

New North Road Bridge
N1 .....87 B3
New North St WC1 .....106 C4
Newnton Cl N4 .....6 C4
New Oxford St
WC1 .....106 A2
New Palace Yd
SW1 .....134 A3
New Park Ct 28
SW2 .....74 A4
New Park Par 18
SW2 .....74 A4
New Park Rd SW2 .....74 A4
New Place Sq SE16 .....40 A3
Newport Ave E14 .....34 C2
Newport Ct WC2 .....119 C4
Newport Ho 2 E3 .....26 A2
Newport Pl WC2 .....119 C4
Newport Rd SW13 .....46 C2
Newport St SE11 .....149 A4
New Priory Ct 9
NW6 .....10 C1
Newquay Ho SE11 .....149 B2
New Quebec St
W1 .....103 A1
New Rd E1 .....32 A4
New River Ct N5 .....15 C4
New River Way N4 .....6 C4
New Row WC2 .....120 A4
New Scotland Yard*
SW1 .....133 B2
New Spring Gdns Wlk
SE11 .....148 B1
New Sq WC2 .....107 A2
New Sq Pas WC2 .....107 A2
New St EC2 .....110 B3
New St Sq EC4 .....107 C2
Newton Ave W3 .....37 B4
Newton Gr W4 .....38 A2
Newton Ho NW8 .....78 C4
London SW8 .....171 B2
1 Stepney E1 .....32 A2
Newton Pl E14 .....41 C2
Newton Point 1
E16 .....35 C3
Newton Prep Sch
SW8 .....170 B4
Newton Rd
London E15 .....19 C3
London W2 .....100 A1
Newton St WC2 .....106 B2
Newton's Yd 14
SW18 .....58 C2
New Tower Bldgs 21
E1 .....32 A1
New Union Cl E14 .....42 B3
New Union St EC2 .....109 B3
New Wharf Rd N1 .....84 B2
Niagara Cl N1 .....87 A2
Niagara Ct 6 SE16 .....40 B3
Nicholas Ct W4 .....45 B3
Nicholas Ho 2
SW6 .....56 C2
Nicholas La EC2,
EC4 .....123 C4
Nicholas Pas EC3 .....123 C4
Nicholas Rd E1 .....25 B1
Nicholay Rd N19 .....4 C3
Nicholl Ho N4 .....6 B3
Nicholl St E2 .....24 C4
Nichols Cl N4 .....5 C2
Nichols Ct E2 .....24 B3
Nicholson Ho SE17 .....151 B2
Nicholson St SE1 .....122 A1
Nickleby Ho SE1 .....139 B3

Nickleby Ho *continued*
7 London W11 .....30 C1
Nicoll Ct NW10 .....21 A4
Nicoll Rd NW10 .....21 A4
Nicosia Rd SW18 .....72 A4
Nigel Bldg EC1 .....107 C3
Nigel Playfair Ave
W6 .....39 A1
Nigel Rd SE15 .....64 C4
Nightingale Cl W4 .....45 B4
Nightingale Ct
12 E14 .....42 B3
5 .....166 B3
Nightingale Gr SE13 67 C2
Nightingale Ho E1 125 B2
2 E1 .....24 A4
London W12 .....30 B3
Nightingale La
SW11,SW12 .....60 C1
Nightingale Lo 5
W9 .....31 C4
Nightingale Mews
3 .....150 A1
Nightingale Pl
SW10 .....156 C4
Nightingale Rd
London N1 .....15 B2
Nightingale Sch
SW17 .....71 C1
Nightingale Sq
SW12 .....72 C4
Nightingale Wlk
SW18,SW4 .....61 A1
Nile Cl N16 .....7 B1
Nile Ho N1 .....97 B4
Nile St N1 .....97 B4
Nile Terr SE1,SE15 .....153 A1
Nimegen Way 9
SE22 .....64 A2
Nimrod Pas 6 N1 .....16 A2
Nine Elms La SW8 .....161 B3
Nisbet Ho 2 E9 .....17 C3
Niton Rd TW9 .....54 C4
Niton St SW6 .....47 C3
Nobel Ho 8 SE5 .....48 B1
Noble Ct 1 .....32 A2
Noble St EC2 .....108 C2
Noel Coward Ho
SW1 .....147 A3
Noel Ho 3 NW3 .....11 C1
Noel Rd N1 .....86 B2
Acton W3 .....28 A3
Noel St W1 .....105 A1
Nolan Way E5 .....16 C4
Noll Ho N7 .....5 B2
Norbiton Rd E14 .....33 B3
Norbroke St W12 .....29 B2
Norburn St W10 .....31 A4
Norcombe Ho 2 N19 4 C1
Norcott Rd N16 .....7 C1
Norcroft Gdns SE22 .....76 C4
Norden Ho 28 E2 .....25 A2
Nore Ct NW10 .....21 A3
Norfolk Cres W2 .....102 B2
Norfolk Ho EC4 .....122 C4
SE3 .....53 A4
SW1 .....147 C4
London E8 .....16 B4
London SE8 .....51 C4
4 Putney SW15 .....69 B4
Richmond TW10 .....54 C2
Norfolk House Rd
SW16 .....74 A1
Norfolk Mans
SW11 .....169 A3
10 London SW18 .....58 C2

Norfolk Mews 13
W10 .....31 A4
Norfolk Pl W2 .....101 C2
Norfolk Rd NW8 .....79 C3
London NW10 .....8 A1
Norfolk Row SE1,
SE11 .....148 C4
Norfolk Sq W2 .....101 C1
Norfolk Sq Mews
W2 .....101 C1
Norgrove St SW12 .....72 C4
Norland Ho 11 W11 .....30 C1
Norland Pl
W11 .....31 A1 112 B1
Norland Place Sch
W11 .....31 A1 112 A1
Norland Rd W11 .....30 C1
Norland Sq W11 .....112 A1
Norley Vale SW15 .....68 C3
Norman Butler Ho 11
W10 .....23 A1
Normanby Cl SW15 .....58 B2
Normanby Rd NW10 .....8 B3
Norman Ct NW10 .....22 A3
Dulwich SE22 .....76 C4
London N4 .....6 B4
Normand Mews
W14 .....154 B4
Normand Park Prim Sch
W14 .....155 A4
Normand Rd W14 .....154 C4
Normandy Ho 5 SW9 173 B3
Normandy Rd SW9 .....173 B3
Norman Gr E3 .....26 A3
Norman Ho SW8 .....162 A2
Normanhurst Rd
SW2 .....74 B2
Norman Rd SE10 .....52 A3
Norman St EC1 .....97 A3
Normanton Ave
SW18,SW19 .....70 C2
Normanton Ho 4
SW4 .....61 B1
Norman Way W3 .....28 A3
Norris Ho 29 E9 .....25 B4
19 N1 .....24 A4
Norris St SW1 .....119 B3
Norroy Rd SW15 .....57 C3
Norse Ho 19 SE5 .....48 B1
Norstead Pl SW15 .....68 C2
North Acton Rd
NW10 .....20 C2
North Acton Sta
NW10 .....21 A2
Northampton Gr N1 .....15 C3
Northampton Pk
N1 .....15 C2
Northampton Rd
EC1 .....95 C2
Northampton Sq
EC1 .....96 A3
Northampton St N1 .....15 B1
North Audley St
W1 .....117 B4
North Ave 13 TW9 .....44 C2
Northaw Ho 10 W10 .....22 B1
North Bank NW8 .....90 A3
North Block 18 E1 .....32 B2
Northbourne Ho 21
E5 .....17 A3
Northbourne Rd
SW4 .....61 C2
North Branch Ave
NW10 .....22 B2
Northburgh St EC1 .....96 B2
North Carriage Dr
W2 .....116 B4

Northchurch SE17 .....151 C2
North Church Ho 19
E2 .....24 C4
Northchurch Rd N1 .....15 C1
Northchurch Terr
N1 .....16 A1
North Circular Rd
London NW10 .....8 A3
London NW2 .....8 A3
North Colonnade
E14 .....33 C1
Northcote Lodge Sch
SW11 .....60 B1
Northcote Rd
London NW10 .....8 B1
London SW11 .....60 B2
Northcourt W1 .....105 A4
North Cres E16 .....27 C1
WC1 .....105 B4
Northcroft Ct 8
W12 .....38 C4
North Cross Rd
SE22 .....64 C2
Northdown St N1 .....84 C1
North Dulwich Sta
SE21 .....63 C2
North End Ave NW3 .....2 B2
North End Cres
W14 .....140 C3
North End Ho W14 .....140 B3
North End Par
W14 .....140 B3
North End Rd W14 .....141 A1
London NW11 .....2 A2
North End Way NW3 .....2 B2
Northern Hts N8 .....4 C4
Northesk Ho 6 E1 .....25 A1
North Eyot Gdns 5
W6 .....38 B1
Northey St E14 .....33 A2
Northfield Hall N6 .....3 C4
Northfield Ho 5
SE15 .....49 C4
Northfield Rd W3 .....28 B4
Northfields SW18 .....58 C3
Northfields Prospect
SW18 .....58 C3
Northfields Rd W3 .....28 B4
Northfleet Ho 1 SE1 137 B4
North Flower Wlk
W2 .....115 B3
North Gate NW8 .....80 A1
Northgate Ct 15
SW9 .....62 C4
North Gower St
NW1 .....93 A3
North Gr N6 .....3 C4
North Greenwich Sta
SE10 .....43 A4
North Hill Ct N6 .....3 C4
North Ho 8 SE8 .....41 B1
Northiam WC1 .....94 B3
Northiam St E9 .....25 B4
Northington St WC1 .....95 A1
Northlands St SE5 .....48 B1
Northleigh Ho 38
E3 .....27 A2
North Lodge Cl
SW15 .....57 C2
North London Boys Sch
N16 .....6 C3
North Mews WC1 .....95 A1
Northolme Rd N5 .....15 B4
North Pas SW18 .....58 C2
North Pole Rd W10 .....30 B4

Northport St N1 . . . . .87 C3
North Rd
  Brentford TW8 . . . . .44 A4
  London N6 . . . . .3 C4
  London N7 . . . . .14 A2
  Richmond TW9 . . . . .44 C1
North Ride W2 . . . . . .116 A3
North Rise W2 . . . . . .102 B1
North Row W1 . . . . . .117 B4
North Sheen Sta
  TW10 . . . . .54 C3
North St SW4 . . . . . . .61 B4
Northstead Rd SW2 . . .74 C2
North Tenter St
  E1 . . . . .111 A1
North Terr SW3 . . . . .130 A1
Northumberland Alley
  EC3 . . . . .110 B1
Northumberland Ave
  WC2 . . . . .120 A2
Northumberland Ho
  NW5 . . . . .13 B2
Northumberland Mews
  W6 . . . . .38 C1
Northumberland Pl
  W2 . . . . .31 C3
Northumberland St
  WC2 . . . . .120 A2
Northumbria St E14 . .33 C3
North Verbena Gdns
  W6 . . . . .38 C1
Northview N7 . . . . .5 A1
Northview Cres
  NW10 . . . . .8 B3
Northview Prim Sch
  NW10 . . . . .8 B3
North Villas NW1 . . . .13 C2
Northway Rd SE5 . . . .63 B4
Northways Par B
  NW3 . . . . .11 C1
North Westminster Com
  Sch
  W2 . . . . .101 B4
  W9 . . . . .23 C1
Northwest Pl N1 . . . . .85 C2
North Wharf Rd
  W2 . . . . .101 B3
Northwick Cl NW8 . . .89 B2
Northwick Ho NW8 . . .89 A2
Northwick Terr
  NW8 . . . . .89 B2
North Wlk W2 . . . . . .114 C3
Northwold Prim Sch
  E5 . . . . .7 C2
Northwold Rd E5,N16 . .7 C2
North Wood Ho
  NW3 . . . . .11 A4
Northwood Rd N6 . . . .4 B4
North Worple Way
  SW14 . . . . .55 C4
Norton Folgate E1 . . .110 B4
Norton Ho B E1 . . . . .32 A3
  E2 . . . . .25 A3
  London SW9 . . . . . .173 A1
Norval Gn SW9 . . . . .173 C2
Norvic Ho B E5 . . . . .48 B1
Norway Gate SE16 . . .41 A3
Norway Pl E14 . . . . . .33 B3
Norway St SE10 . . . . .52 A4
Norwich Ho E14 . . . . .34 A3
Norwich St EC4 . . . . .107 B2
Norwood Ho E14 . . . .34 A2
Norwood Rd SE24,
  SE27 . . . . .75 B3
Notley St SE5 . . . . . . .48 C3

Notre Dame RC Girls
  Sch SE1 . . . . .136 B2
Notting Barn Rd
  W10 . . . . .22 C1
Nottingdale Sq
  W11 . . . . .31 A1 112 A2
Nottingham Ct
  WC2 . . . . .106 A1
Nottingham Ho
  London N4 . . . . .6 B4
  B4 London SE5 . . . .48 B1
Nottingham Pl W1 . . .103 B4
Nottingham Rd
  SW17 . . . . .72 B3
  Wimbledon SW19 . . .69 C1
Nottingham St W1 . . .103 B4
Nottingham Terr
  NW1 . . . . .91 B1
Notting Hill Gate
  W11 . . . . . . .31 C1 113 B2
Notting Hill Gate Sta
  W11 . . . . .113 B2
Nottingwood Ho
  W11 . . . . .112 A4
Nova Bldg B E14 . . . .41 C2
Novello St SW6 . . . . .165 B4
Nowell Rd SW13 . . . . .46 C4
Noyna Rd SW17 . . . . .72 B1
Nuding Cl SE13 . . . . . .66 C4
Nuffield Lo B W9 . . . .31 C4
Nugent Rd N19 . . . . . .5 A3
Nugent Terr NW8 . . . .79 A1
Nun Ct EC2 . . . . .109 B2
Nunhead Cres SE15 . .65 A4
Nunhead Gr SE15 . . . .65 A4
Nunhead La SE15 . . . .65 A4
Nunhead Sta SE15 . . .50 B1
Nursery Cl
  London SE4 . . . . . . .51 B1
  Putney SW15 . . . . . .57 C3
Nursery La E2 . . . . . . .24 B4
  London W10 . . . . . . .30 B4
Nursery Rd
  London E9 . . . . .17 B2
  London SW9 . . . . . . .62 B3
Nursery Row SE17 . . .151 C3
Nutbourne St W10 . . .23 A2
Nutbrook St SE15 . . . .64 C4
Nutcroft Rd SE15 . . . .50 A3
Nutfield Rd
  London E15 . . . . . . .76 B4
  London SE22 . . . . . .64 B3
Nutford Pl W1 . . . . . .102 C2
Nuthurst Ave SW2 . . .74 B2
Nutley Terr NW3 . . . . .11 C2
Nutt La E14 . . . . .34 C3
Nuttall St N1 . . . . .24 A3
Nutt St SE15 . . . . .49 C3
NW London Jewish Day
  Sch NW6 . . . . .10 A1
Nye Bevan Ho
  SW6 . . . . .154 C2
Nye's Wharf SE1 . . . . .49 C4
Nylands Ave TW9 . . . .44 C1
Nynehead St SE14 . . .51 A3
Nyton Cl N19 . . . . .5 A3

Oakden St SE11 . . . . .149 C4
Oake Ct SW15 . . . . . . .58 A2
Oakeford Ho W14 . . . .126 B2
Oakend Ho B N4 . . . .6 C4
Oakeshott Ave N6 . . . .3 C2
Oakey La SE1 . . . . . . .135 B2
Oakfield Ct London NW2 . .1 A2
  London N8 . . . . .5 A4
Oakfield Prep Sch
  SE21 . . . . .75 C2
Oakfield Rd
  London N4 . . . . .5 C4
  Wimbledon SW19 . . .69 C1
Oakfield St SW10 . . . .156 C4
Oak Gr NW2 . . . . .10 A4
Oakham Ho W10 . . . . .22 B1
Oakhill Ave NW3 . . . . .11 A4
Oakhill Ct
  London SE23 . . . . . . .65 B1
  Putney SW15 . . . . . .58 B2
Oak Hill Lo SW15 . . . .11 A4
Oak Hill Park Mews
  NW3 . . . . .11 B4
Oak Hill Pk NW3 . . . . .11 A4
Oak Hill Way NW3 . . .11 B4
Oak Ho B E14 . . . . . . .42 B4
  London N2 . . . . .1 C4
  B London NW3 . . . . .11 A2
Oakhurst Gr SE22 . . . .64 C3
Oakington Rd W9 . . . .23 C1
Oakington Way N8 . . .5 A4
Oakland Ct CW10 . . . .21 A4
Oaklands Gr W12 . . . .29 C1
Oaklands Ho SE4 . . . .66 B4
Oaklands Mews NW2 . .9 C4
Oaklands Pas B NW2 . .9 C4
Oaklands Pl B SW4 . .61 C3
Oaklands Rd
  London NW2 . . . . . . .9 C4
  Mortlake SW14 . . . . .55 C4
Oaklands Sec Sch
  E2 . . . . .25 A2
Oakley Cres EC1 . . . . .86 B1
Oakley Dr SE13 . . . . . .67 C1
Oakley Gdns SW3 . . .158 B4
Oakley Ho SW1 . . . . .145 A4
Oakley Pl SE1 . . . . . . .152 C1
Oakley Rd London N1 . .15 C1
Oakley Sq NW1 . . . . . .83 A2
Oakley St SW3 . . . . . .158 A4
Oakley Wlk W6 . . . . . .47 C4
Oak Lodge Sch
  SW12 . . . . .72 C4
Oakman Ho E9
  SW19 . . . . .69 C3
Oakmead Rd SW12 . . .73 A3
Oak Park Gdns
  SW19 . . . . .69 C3
Oak Park Mews N16 . .7 B1
Oakshaw Rd SW18 . . .71 A4
Oakshott Ct NW1 . . . . .83 B1
Oaks Sh Ctr The
  W3 . . . . .28 B1
Oaks The
  London NW10 . . . . . .9 A1
  London NW6 . . . . . . .9 C1
Oak Tree Ct
  Acton W3 . . . . .28 A2
  B London W5 . . . . . .36 A4
Oak Tree Ho W9 . . . . .88 A2
Oak Tree Rd NW8 . . . .90 A3
Oakview Lo NW11 . . . .1 B4
Oak Village NW5 . . . . .12 C4
Oak Way W3 . . . . .29 A1

Oakwell Ho SW8 . . . .171 B1
Oakwood Ct W14 . . . .126 C2
Oakwood La W14 . . . .126 C2
Oakworth Rd W10 . . . .30 C4
Oast Ct B E14 . . . . . . .33 B2
Oat La EC2 . . . . .109 A2
Oatlands Ct B
  SW19 . . . . .69 C3
Oatwell Ho SW3 . . . . .144 B3
Oban Ho E14 . . . . .34 C3
Oban St E14 . . . . .34 C3
Oberon Ho B N1 . . . . .24 A3
Oberstein Rd B
  SW11 . . . . .59 C3
Oborne Cl SE24 . . . . . .63 A2
O'Brian Ho B E1 . . . . .25 C2
Observatory Gdns
  W8 . . . . .127 C4
Observatory Mews
  E14 . . . . .42 C2
Observatory Rd
  SW14 . . . . .55 B3
Occupation Rd
  SE17 . . . . .150 C2
Ocean Est E1 . . . . .25 C1
Ocean Wharf E14 . . . .41 C4
Ockbrook B E1 . . . . . .32 B4
Ockendon Rd N1 . . . . .15 C2
Ockley Rd SW16 . . . . .74 A1
Octagon Arc EC2 . . . .110 A3
Octagon The W3 . . . . .28 B1
Octavia Ho W10 . . . . .23 A1
Octavia St SW11 . . . .168 B3
Octavius St SE8 . . . . .51 C3
Odeon Ct B E16 . . . . .35 C4
Odessa Rd NW10 . . . .21 A4
Odessa St SE16 . . . . . .41 B3
Odette Duval Ho B
  E1 . . . . .32 B4
Odger St SW11 . . . . . .169 A2
Odhams Wlk WC2 . . .106 B1
Odin Ho B SE5 . . . . . .48 B1
O'Donnell Ct WC1 . . . .94 B2
O'Driscoll Ho W12 . . . .30 A3
Offa's Mead E9 . . . . . .18 A4
Offenbach Ho B E2 . . .25 C3
Offerton Rd SW4 . . . . .61 B4
Offham Ho SE17 . . . . .152 A3
Offley Ho B E9 . . . . . .17 C2
Offley Rd SW9 . . . . . .163 B2
Offord Rd N1 . . . . .14 B1
Offord St N1 . . . . .14 B1
Ogilvie Ho B E1 . . . . .32 C3
Oglander Rd SE15 . . . .64 B4
Ogle St W1 . . . . .104 C4
O'Gorman Ho
  SW10 . . . . .157 A2
Oil Mill La W6 . . . . . . .38 C1
Okehampton Rd
  NW10 . . . . .22 C4
Okeover Manor
  SW4 . . . . .61 A3
Olaf St W11 . . . . .30 C2
Old Bailey EC4 . . . . . .108 B1
Old Barrack Yd
  SW1 . . . . .131 B3
Old Bellgate Wharf
  E14 . . . . .41 C3
Old Bethnal Green Rd
  E2 . . . . .25 A2
Old Bldgs WC2 . . . . . .107 B2
Old Brewery Mews
  NW3 . . . . .11 C4
Old Broad St EC2 . . . .109 C2

Old Brompton Rd
  SW5,SW7 . . . . .143 A3
Old Burlington St
  W1 . . . . .118 C3
Oldbury Ct E9 . . . . . . .18 A3
Oldbury Pl W1 . . . . . .103 C4
Old Castle St E1 . . . . .111 A2
Old Cavendish St
  W1 . . . . .104 A1
Old Change Ct
  EC4 . . . . .108 C2
Old Chiswick Yd
  W4 . . . . .46 A4
Old Church Rd E1 . . . .32 C3
Old Church St
  SW3 . . . . .157 C4
Old Compton St
  W1 . . . . .105 B1
Old County Hall
  SE1 . . . . .134 C4
Old Court Ho W8 . . . .128 A3
Old Court Pl W8 . . . . .128 A3
Old Covent Garden
  WC2 . . . . .120 B4
Old Dairy Mews
  B Balham SW12 . . . .72 C3
  London NW5 . . . . . . .13 A2
Old Deer Park Gdns
  TW9 . . . . .54 A4
Old Devonshire Rd
  SW12 . . . . .73 A4
Old Dock Cl TW9 . . . .44 C4
Oldfield Gr SE16 . . . . .40 C2
Oldfield Ho B W4 . . . .38 A1
Oldfield Mews N6 . . . .4 B4
Oldfield Rd
  London N16 . . . . .7 A1
  London NW10 . . . . . .8 B1
  London W3,W12 . . . .38 B4
Old Fish St Hill
  EC4 . . . . .122 C4
Old Fleet La EC4 . . . . .108 A2
Old Ford Prim Sch
  E3 . . . . .26 B3
Old Ford Rd E2,E3 . . . .25 C3
Old Ford Trad Ctr
  E3 . . . . .26 C4
Old Forge Mews
  W12 . . . . .39 A4
Old Gloucester St
  WC1 . . . . .106 B4
Oldham Terr W3 . . . . .28 B1
Oldhill St N16 . . . . .7 C3
Old Hospital Cl
  SW12,SW17 . . . . . . .72 B3
Old Jamaica Bsns Est
  SE16 . . . . .139 B1
Old Jamaica Rd
  SE16 . . . . .139 B2
Old James St SE15 . . .65 A4
Old Jewry EC2 . . . . . .109 B1
Old Kent Rd SE1 . . . . .152 B2
  SE1,SE15 . . . . .50 B3
Old Laundry The B
  SW18 . . . . .59 C3
Old Manor Yd
  SW5 . . . . .142 A3
Old Market Sq E2 . . . .99 A4
Old Marylebone Rd
  NW1 . . . . .102 B3
Old Mitre Ct EC4 . . . . .107 C1
Old Montague St
  E1 . . . . .111 B3

Old Nichol St
E2 . . . . 24 B1 98 C2
Old North St WC1 . . . . .106 C4
Old Oak Common La
NW10 . . . . .21 B2
Old Oak La NW10 . . . . .21 B2
Old Oak Prim Sch
W12 . . . . .29 B2
Old Oak Rd W3 . . . . . . .29 B2
Old Orch The W3 . . . . .12 B4
Old Palace Prim Sch
E3 . . . . .27 A2
Old Paradise St
SE11 . . . . .148 C4
Old Park Ave SW12 . . . .60 C1
Old Park La W1 . . . . . .118 A1
Old Pye St SW1 . . . . . .133 B2
Old Pye Street Est
SW1 . . . . .133 B1
Old Quebec St W1 . . . .103 A1
Old Queen St SW1 . . . .133 C3
Oldridge Rd SW12 . . . . .73 A4
Old Royal Free Pl
N1 . . . . .85 C3
Old Royal Free Sq
N1 . . . . .85 C3
Old Royal Observatory
Greenwich (National
Maritime Mus
Annexe)★ SE10 . . . .52 C3
Old School Sq E14
E14 . . . . .33 C3
Old School La
WC1 . . . . .106 C4
Old Seacoal La
EC4 . . . . .108 A1
Old South Lambeth Rd
SW8 . . . . .162 B2
Old Spitalfields Mkt
E1 . . . . .110 C3
Old Sq WC2 . . . . .107 B2
Old Stable Mews N5 . . . .6 B1
Old Street Sta EC1 . . . . .97 C2
Old Sun Wharf E14 . . . .33 A2
Old Swan Wharf
SW11 . . . . .167 C4
Old Theatre Ct
SE1 . . . . .123 A2
Old Town SW4 . . . . . . .61 B3
Old Woolwich Rd
SE10 . . . . .42 C1
Old York Rd SW18 . . . . .59 A2
O'Leary Sq E1 . . . . . . .32 B4
Olga Prim Sch E3 . . . . .26 A3
Olga St E3 . . . . .26 A3
Oliphant St W10 . . . . . .23 A2
Olive Blythe Ho E4
W10 . . . . .23 A1
Oliver Bsns Pk
NW10 . . . . .20 A3
Oliver Cl W4 . . . . .45 A4
Oliver Ho SE17 . . . . .2 B4
Oliver Goldsmith Prim
Schs SE5 . . . . .49 B2
Oliver House Sch
SW4 . . . . .139 B3
Oliver Mews SE15 . . . . .49 C1
Oliver's Yd EC1 . . . . . . .97 C2
Olive Tree Ho 7
SE15 . . . . .50 B4
Olivette St 1 SW15 . . . .57 C3
Olive Waite Ho
NW6 . . . . .11 A1

Ollerton Gn E3 . . . . . . .26 B4
Olligar Cl W12 . . . . . . .29 B1
Olliffe St E14 . . . . .42 B3
Olmar St SE1 . . . . .49 C4
Olney Ho NW8 . . . . . . .90 B2
Olney Rd SE17 . . . . . . .48 B4
Olympia Ex Ctr★
W14 . . . . .126 B2
Olympian Ct 1 E14 . . . .41 C2
Olympia Way W14 . . . .126 B1
Olympia Yd W2 . . . . . .114 B3
Olympic Ho W10 . . . . . .30 B3
Olympus Sq 5
Oman Ave NW2 . . . . . . .9 B4
Oman Ct NW4 . . . . .9 A4
Ombersley Ho N4 . . . . . .6 B4
Omeara St SE1 . . . . . .123 A1
Omega Cl E14 . . . . . . .42 A3
Omega Ho SW10 . . . . .157 A2
Omega Pl N1 . . . . .84 B1
Omega St SE14 . . . . . . .51 C2
Ommaney Rd SE14 . . . .51 A2
Ondine Rd SE15 . . . . . .64 B3
Onedin Point E1 . . . . .125 C3
Ongar Ho 15 N1 . . . . . .15 C2
Ongar Rd SW6 . . . . . .155 C4
Onslow Ave TW10 . . . . .54 A2
Onslow Avenue Mans 4
TW10 . . . . .54 A2
Onslow Cl SW10 . . . . .143 A1
Onslow Gdns SW7 . . . .143 B2
Onslow Lo 3 SW7 . . . . .74 C4
Onslow Mews E
SW7 . . . . .143 B3
Onslow Mews W
SW7 . . . . .143 B3
Onslow Rd TW10 . . . . . .54 A2
Onslow Sq SW7 . . . . . .143 C3
Onslow St EC1 . . . . . . .95 C1
Ontario St SE1 . . . . . .136 B2
Ontario Way E14 . . . . . .33 C2
Opal St SE11 . . . . .150 A2
Open Air Theatre,
Regent's Park (30)
NW1 . . . . .91 B3
Openview SW17,
SW18 . . . . .71 C2
Operating Theatre Mus
& Herb Garret
SE1 . . . . .123 C1
Ophelia Gdns NW2 . . . . .1 A1
Ophir Terr SE15 . . . . . .49 C2
Opie Ho NW8 . . . . .80 B1
Oppenheim Rd SE13 . . .52 B1
Oppidans Rd NW3 . . . .12 B1
Orange Pl SE16 . . . . . . .40 B3
Orange St WC2 . . . . . .119 C3
Orange Yd WC2 . . . . . .105 C1
Oratory La SW3 . . . . . .143 C2
Oratory RC Prim Sch
SW3 . . . . .144 A2
Oratory The★
SW7 . . . . .130 A1
Orbain Rd SW6 . . . . . .154 B1
Orbel St SW11 . . . . . . .168 A3
Orb St SE17 . . . . .151 B3
Orchard Cl W10 . . . . . . .31 A4
London N1 . . . . .15 B1
London SE23 . . . . .65 B1
Orchard Ct W1 . . . . . .103 B2
Barnes SW13 . . . . .56 B4
Orchard Dr SE3 . . . . . . .53 A1
Orchard Hill SE13 . . . . .52 A2

Orchard Ho 11 SE16 . . .40 B3
London SE5 . . . . .48 B2
London N1 . . . . .87 A3
Orchard Mead Ho
N1 . . . . .1 C2
Orchard Mews N1 . . . . .15 C1
Orchard Pl E14 . . . . . . .35 A1
Orchard Prim Sch
E9 . . . . .17 B1
Orchard Rd
London N6 . . . . .4 A4
Richmond TW9 . . . . . . .54 C4
Orchard Rise TW10 . . . .55 A3
Orchardson Ho
NW8 . . . . .89 C1
Orchardson St NW8 . . . .89 C1
Orchard Sq W14 . . . . .140 C1
Orchard St W1 . . . . . .103 C2
Orchard The
London SE3 . . . . .52 C1
London W4 . . . . .37 C2
Orchid St W12 . . . . . . .29 C2
Orde Hall St WC1 . . . .106 C4
Orde Ho 16 N16 . . . . . .15 C4
Ordell Ct 51 E3 . . . . . .26 B3
Ordell Rd E3 . . . . .26 B3
Ordnance Cres
SE10 . . . . .43 A4
Ordnance Hill NW8 . . . .79 C3
Ordnance Mews
NW8 . . . . .79 C2
Ordnance Rd E16 . . . . . .35 C2
Oregano Dr E14 . . . . . . .34 C3
Orestes Mews 1
NW6 . . . . .10 C3
Orford Ct SE27 . . . . . . .75 A2
Oriana Ho 3 E14 . . . . . .33 B2
Oriel Ct NW3 . . . . .11 B4
Oriel Dr SW13 . . . . . . .47 B4
Oriel Rd London E9 . . . .17 C2
London E9 . . . . .18 A2
Orient St SE11 . . . . . .150 A4
Orion Bsns Ctr SE14 . . .40 C1
Orion Ho 20 E1 . . . . . . .25 A1
Orkney Ho N1 . . . . .84 C4
Orkney St SW11 . . . . .169 B2
Orlando Rd SW4 . . . . . .61 B4
Orleston Mews N7 . . . . .14 C2
Orleston Rd N7 . . . . . . .14 C2
Orlop St SE10 . . . . .43 A1
Orme Ct W2 . . . . .114 A3
Orme Court Mews 3
W2 . . . . .114 B3
Orme Ho 8 E8 . . . . . . .24 B4
Orme La W2 . . . . .114 A3
Ormeley Rd SW12 . . . . .73 A3
Orme Sq W2 . . . . .114 A3
Ormiston Gr W12 . . . . . .30 A1
Ormiston Rd SE10 . . . . .43 C1
Ormond Cl WC1 . . . . .106 B4
Ormonde Ct SW15 . . . .57 B3
Ormonde Gate
SW3 . . . . .145 A1
Ormonde Pl SW1 . . . . .145 C3
Ormonde Terr NW8 . . . .80 C3
Ormond Ho 2 N16 . . . . .6 C2
Ormond Mews WC1 . . .94 B1
Ormond Rd N4,N19 . . . . .5 A3
Ormond Yd SW1 . . . . .119 A2
Ormrod Ct W11 . . . . . . .31 B3
Ormsby Lo 2 W4 . . . . . .38 A3
Ormsby Pl N16 . . . . .7 C1
Ormsby St E2 . . . . .24 B3
Ormside St SE15 . . . . . .50 B4
Ornan Rd NW3 . . . . . . .12 A3
Oronsay Rd 16 N1 . . . . .15 B2
Orpheus Ho 29 N19 . . . .4 C4

Orpheus St SE5 . . . . . .48 C2
Orsett Mews W2 . . . . .100 C2
Orsett St SE11 . . . . . . .149 B2
Orsett Terr W2 . . . . . .100 C2
Orsman Rd N1 . . . . .24 A4
Orton St E1 . . . . .125 B1
Orville Rd SW11 . . . . . .167 C2
Orwell Ct E8 . . . . .24 C4
London N5 . . . . .15 B4
Orwell Ho W12 . . . . . . .29 C2
Osbaldeston Rd N16 . . . .7 C3
Osbert St SW1 . . . . . . .147 B3
Osborn Cl E8 . . . . .24 C4
Osborne Rd
London E9 . . . . .18 B2
London N4 . . . . .5 C3
London NW2 . . . . .9 A2
London W3 . . . . .37 A4
Osborn St E1 . . . . .111 A3
Osbourne Ho 5 TW10 . .54 C2
Oscar Faber Pl 3
N1 . . . . .16 A1
Oscar St SE8 . . . . .51 C2
Oseney Cres NW5 . . . . .13 C2
O'Shea Gr E3 . . . . .26 B4
Osier Ct E1 . . . . .25 C1
Osier Mews W4 . . . . . . .46 B4
Osiers Rd SW18 . . . . . .58 C3
Osier St E1 . . . . .25 B1
Oslo Ct NW8 . . . . .80 A1
Oslo Ho 2 SE5 . . . . . . .48 B1
Oslo Sq SE16 . . . . .41 A3
Osman Prim Sch
E3 . . . . .111 B4
Osman Rd W6 . . . . .39 B3
Osmington Ho
SW8 . . . . .163 A1
Osmund St W12 . . . . . .29 B4
Osnaburgh St NW1 . . . .92 B2
Osnaburgh Terr
NW1 . . . . .92 B2
Osprey Ct NW3 . . . . . . .11 A3
Osprey Ho 3 E14 . . . . . .33 A2
London SE15 . . . . .49 B2
Ospringe Ho SE1 . . . . .121 C1
Ospringe Rd NW5 . . . . .13 B4
Osram Ct W6 . . . . .39 B3
Osric Path 8 N1 . . . . . .24 A3
Ossian Rd N4 . . . . .5 B4
Ossington Bldgs
W1 . . . . .103 B3
Ossington Cl W2 . . . . .113 C3
Ossington St W2 . . . . .114 A4
Ossory Rd SE1 . . . . . . .49 C4
Ossulston St NW1 . . . . .83 C2
Ostade Rd SW2 . . . . . . .74 B4
Osten Mews SW7 . . . . .128 B1
Osterley Ho 5 E14 . . . . .34 A3
Osterley Rd N16 . . . . . .16 A4
Oswald's Mead E9 . . . . .18 A4
Oswald Rd SW12,
SW17 . . . . .72 B2
Oswell Ho 9 E1 . . . . . . .32 A1
Oswin St SE11 . . . . . . .150 B4
Oswyth Rd SE5 . . . . . . .49 A1
Otford Cres SE4 . . . . . .66 B1
Otford Ho SE1 . . . . . . .137 C3
SE15 6 . . . . .50 B4
Otha Ho SW9 . . . . .172 B2
Othello Cl SE11 . . . . . .150 A2
Otis St E3 . . . . .27 B2
Otley Ho N5 . . . . .6 A1
Ottaway Ct E5 . . . . .7 C1
Ottaway St E5 . . . . .7 C1
Otterburn Ho 12
SE5 . . . . .48 B3
Otto St SE17 . . . . .48 A4

Our Lady of Dolours RC
Prim Sch W2 . . . . . .100 A3
Our Lady of Lourdes RC
Prim Sch SE13 . . . . .67 C4
Our Lady of Lourdes RC
Sch NW10 . . . . .20 B1
Our Lady of the
Assumption RC Prim
Sch E2 . . . . .25 B3
Our Lady of the Sacred
Heart RC Prim Sch
(Annexe) N7 . . . . . . .14 B2
Our Lady of the Sacred
Heart RC Sch N7 . . . .14 B3
Our Lady of Victories RC
Prim Sch
SW7 . . . . .143 A3
Putney SW15 . . . . .57 C3
Our Lady Queen of
Heaven RC Sch
SW19 . . . . .69 C4
Our Lady RC Prim Sch
E14 . . . . .33 B3
NW1 . . . . .82 C3
Our Lady's Convent High
Sch N15,N16 . . . . .7 A4
Our Lady & St Joseph
RC Prim Sch N1 . . . .16 A2
Ouseley Rd SW12 . . . . .72 B3
Outer Circ NW8 . . . . . .80 B1
Outgate Rd NW10 . . . . .8 B1
Outram Pl N1 . . . . .84 B4
Outwich St EC3 . . . . . .110 B2
Outwood Ho 3
SW2 . . . . .74 B4
Oval Mans SE11 . . . . .163 A4
Oval Pl SW8 . . . . .163 A2
Oval Rd NW1 . . . . .82 A4
Oval Sta SE11 . . . . . . .163 B3
Oval The E2 . . . . .25 A3
Oval The (Surrey Cnty
Crkt Gd) SE11 . . . . .163 A4
Oval Way SE11 . . . . . . .149 A1
Overbury St E5 . . . . .17 C4
Overbury St E5 . . . . . . .17 C4
Overcliff Rd SE13 . . . . .66 C4
Overhill Rd SE21,
SE22 . . . . .76 C4
Overlea Rd E5 . . . . .7 C4
Oversley Ho 17 W2 . . . .31 C4
Overstone Ho
E14 . . . . .33 C3
Overstone Rd W6 . . . . .39 B2
Overstrand Mans
SW11 . . . . .169 B3
Overton Ho SW15 . . . . .68 B4
Overton Rd SW9 . . . . .173 C1
Overy Ho SE1 . . . . . . .136 A3
Ovex Cl E14 . . . . .42 B4
Ovington Ct SW3 . . . . .130 B1
Ovington Gdns
SW3 . . . . .130 B1
Ovington Mews
SW3 . . . . .130 B1
Ovington Sq SW3 . . . .130 B1
Ovington St SW3 . . . . .144 B4
Owen Ho 11 N19 . . . . . .13 B4
Owen's Ct EC1 . . . . . . .96 A4
Owen's Row EC1 . . . . . .96 A4
Owen St EC1 . . . . .86 A1
Owgan Cl SE5 . . . . .48 C3
Oxberry Ave SW6 . . . .164 B2
Oxbridge Ct 4 W4 . . . .37 A1
Oxendon St SW1,
W1 . . . . .119 B3
Oxenford St SE15 . . . . .64 B4
Oxenham Ho 13 SE8 . . .51 C4

Oxenholme NW1 ....83 A1
Oxestalls Rd SE8 ....41 A1
Oxford Ave NW10 ....20 B1
Oxford & Cambridge
Mans NW1 ....102 B3
Oxford Cir W1 ....104 C1
Oxford Circus Ave
W1 ....104 C1
Oxford Circus Sta
W1 ....104 C1
Oxford Ct EC4 ....123 B4
  48 London W4 ....31 C4
  London W4 ....37 A1
Oxford Dr SE1 ....124 B1
Oxford Gardens Prim
Sch 30 C3
Oxford Gate W6 ....39 C2
Oxford Gdns
  Brentford W4 ....44 B4
  London W10 ....30 C3
Oxford Ho NW6 ....22 C3
  London E15 ....19 C2
  London N4 ....5 C3
  Putney SW15 ....58 A3
Oxford Rd N W4 ....37 A1
Oxford Rd S W4 ....37 A1
Oxford Sq W2 ....102 B1
Oxford St W1 ....104 B1
Oxley Cl SE1 ....153 A2
Oxonian St SE22 ....64 B3
Oxo Tower Wharf
SE1 ....121 C3
Oxted Ct N16 ....7 A3
Oyster Row E1 ....32 B3
Ozolins Way E16 ....35 C3

P

Pablo Neruda Cl
SE24 ....63 A3
Pace Pl E1 ....32 A3
Pacific Ho 15 E1 ....25 C1
Pacific Rd E16 ....35 C4
Pacific Wharf SE16 ....32 C1
Packenham Ho 2 ....99 A4
  24 London N19 ....4 C4
Packington Ho
SW9 ....172 B2
Packington Sq N1 ....86 E3
Packington St N1 ....86 B3
Padbury SE17 ....152 B1
Padbury Ct E2 ....99 A3
Padbury Ho NW8 ....90 B2
Paddenswick Rd
W6 ....39 A3
  ....38 C3
Paddington Com Hospl
W9 ....31 C4
Paddington Gn
W2 ....101 B4
Paddington Green Prim
Sch NW8 ....89 B1
Paddington St W1 ....103 B4
Paddington Sta
W2 ....101 B2
Paddock Cl SE3 ....53 C1
Paddock Sch SW15 ....56 B3
Padfield Rd SE5 ....63 B4
Padstow Ho 14 E14 ....33 B2
Pagden St SW8 ....170 B4
Pageant Cres SE16 ....33 B1
Pageantmaster Ct
EC4 ....108 A1
Page Ho SE10 ....52 B4
Page St SW1 ....147 C4

Page's Wlk SE1 ....138 B1
Page's Yd W4 ....46 A4
Paget Ho 12 E2 ....25 B3
Paget Rd N16 ....6 C3
Paget St EC1 ....96 A4
Pagham Ho W10 ....22 B1
Pagnell St SE14 ....51 B3
Pagoda Ave TW9 ....54 B4
Pagoda Gdns SE3 ....52 C1
Paine Ct SE3 ....53 B4
Painsthorpe Rd 3
N16 ....7 A1
Painswick Ct 1
SE15 ....49 B3
Painters Mews
SE16 ....153 C4
Pakeman Ho SE1 ....136 B4
Pakeman Prim Sch
N7 ....5 B1
Pakeman St N7 ....5 B1
Pakenham Cl SW12 ....72 C3
Pakenham St WC1 ....95 A2
Palace Ave W8 ....128 B4
Palace Ct W2 ....114 A3
  London NW3 ....11 A3
  Streatham SW2 ....74 C2
Palace Garden Mews
W8 ....113 C2
Palace Gate W8 ....128 C3
Palace Gdns Mews
W8 ....114 B3
Palace Gn W8 ....114 A1
Palace Mans W14 ....140 B4
Palace Pl SW1 ....132 C2
Palace St SW1 ....132 C2
Palatine Ave N16 ....16 A4
Palatine Rd N16 ....16 A4
Palemead Cl SW6 ....47 C2
Palermo Rd NW10 ....21 C3
Palewell Common Dr
SW14 ....55 C2
Palewell Pk SW14 ....55 C2
Palfrey Pl SW8 ....163 A2
Palgrave Gdns NW1 ....90 B1
Palgrave Ho 7 SE5 ....48 B3
  4 London NW3 ....12 B3
Palgrave Rd W12 ....38 B3
Palissy St 21 E2 ....98 C3
Palliser Ct W14 ....140 A1
Palliser Ho 2 E1 ....25 C1
  3 SE10 ....52 C4
Palliser Rd W14 ....140 A1
Pallister Terr SW15 ....68 B1
Pall Mall SW1 ....119 B1
Pall Mall E SW1 ....119 C2
Pall Mall Pl SW1 ....119 A1
Palm Ct 15 SE15 ....49 B3
  London N16 ....6 C2
Palmer Ct NW10 ....20 C4
Palmer Ho 5 N19 ....4 B1
  4 NW5 ....13 B4
  6 SE14 ....50 C3
Palmer Pl N7 ....14 C3
Palmers Rd E2 ....25 C3
  Mortlake SW14 ....55 B4
Palmer St SW1 ....133 B2
Palmerston Ct 22
E3 ....25 C3
Palmerston Ho
SW11 ....169 C3
  W8 ....113 B1

Palmerston Rd
  London NW6 ....10 B1
  London W3 ....37 B3
  Mortlake SW14 ....55 B3
Palmerston Way
SW8 ....160 B1
Palm Gr 5 W5 ....36 A3
Palm Tree Ho 2
SE14 ....50 C3
Pamela Ct N10 ....8 C1
Pamela Ho 4 E8 ....24 B4
Pamlion Ct N4 ....5 A4
Panama Ho 6 E1 ....32 C4
Pancras La EC2 ....109 B1
Pancras Rd N1 ....83 C2
Pandora Rd NW6 ....10 C2
Pangbourne W1 ....92 C3
Pangbourne Ave
W10 ....30 B4
Pangbourne Ho 4
N7 ....14 A3
Pankhurst Cl 7
SE14 ....50 C3
Panmure Cl N5 ....15 A4
Pansy Gdns W12 ....29 C2
Panton St SW1 ....119 B3
Panyer Alley EC2 ....108 C2
Paper Mill Wharf
E14 ....33 A2
Papworth Gdns N7 ....14 B3
Papworth Way SW2 ....74 C4
Parade Mans 19
SE5 ....48 B1
  London SW4 ....61 C3
Parade Mews SE27,
SW2 ....75 A2
Parade The SW11 ....159 A2
Paradise Pas 14
N7 ....14 C3
Paradise Rd
  London SW4 ....172 A2
  Richmond TW10 ....54 A2
Paradise Row E2 ....25 A2
Paradise St SE16 ....40 A4
Paradise Wlk SW3 ....159 A4
Paragon Cl E16 ....35 C3
Paragon Mews
SE1 ....151 C4
Paragon Pl SE3 ....53 B1
Paragon Rd E9 ....17 B2
Paragon The SE17 ....151 C3
  SE3 ....53 C1
Paragon
  London E9 ....17 B1
  London N4 ....6 A2
Parbury Rd SE23 ....66 A1
Pardoner St SE1 ....137 C2
Pardon St EC1 ....96 B2
Parfett St 11 E1 ....111 C2
Parfitt Cl NW3 ....2 B3
Parfrey St W6 ....47 B4
Paris Gdns SE1 ....122 A2
Paris Ho 12 E2 ....25 A3
Park Ave
  London NW2 ....1 A3
  London NW11 ....1 C4
  London NW2 ....9 B2
  Mortlake SW14 ....55 C3
Park Ave N NW10 ....9 A3
Park Bsns Ctr 4
NW6 ....23 C2
Park Cl 20 E9 ....25 B4
  SW1 ....130 C3
  W14 ....127 A2
Park Cres W1 ....92 A1
Park Cres Mews E
W1 ....92 B1

Park Cres Mews W
W1 ....92 A1
Park Ct SW11 ....170 A4
  Dulwich SE21 ....75 C1
  London SW4 ....61 C2
  Upper Tooting SW17 ....72 B2
Park Dr Acton W3 ....36 C3
  London NW11 ....1 C3
Park Dwellings 7
NW3 ....12 B3
Park End NW3 ....12 A4
Parker Ct N1 ....87 A4
  SW4 ....172 A3
Parker Mews WC2 ....106 B2
Parkers Row SE1 ....139 B3
Parker's Row SE1 ....139 A3
Parker St WC2 ....106 B2
Parkfield Ave SW14 ....56 A3
Parkfield Ind Est
SW11 ....169 C2
Parkfield Rd
  London NW10 ....9 A1
  London SE14 ....51 B2
Parkfields SW15 ....57 B3
Parkfield St N1 ....85 C2
Park Flats N6 ....3 A4
Parkgate Gdns
SW14 ....55 C2
Parkgate House Sch
SW11 ....60 C3
Parkgate Mews N6 ....4 B4
Park Hall SE21 ....75 C1
Park Hall Road Trad Est
SE21 ....75 C1
Parkham St SW11 ....168 A3
Park Hill
  London SW4 ....61 C2
  Richmond TW10 ....54 B1
Park Hill Ct SW17 ....72 B1
Parkhill Rd NW3 ....12 B3
Park Hill Wlk 12
NW3 ....12 B3
Park Ho 5 E9 ....17 B1
  London N4 ....6 A2
  8 London SE5 ....48 C2
Parkholme Rd E8 ....16 C2
Parkhouse St SE5 ....48 C3
Parkhurst Ct N7 ....14 A4
Parkhurst Rd N7 ....14 A4
Parkinson Ct EC1 ....97 C3
  N1 ....97 C4
Parkinson Ho 6 E9 ....17 B1
Park La E15 ....27 C4
  N1 ....117 B3
Parkland Ct W14 ....126 A4
Parkland Gdns 12
SW19 ....69 C3
Parklands London N6 ....4 A4
  London SE22 ....65 A2
Parklands London W4 ....55 B2
Parklands Cl SW14 ....55 B2
Park Lea Ct N16 ....7 A4
Park Lo E14 ....41 C2
  NW8 ....79 A1
  11 London NW8 ....11 C1
Park Lofts 5 SW4 ....62 A2
Park Lorne NW8 ....90 B3
Park Mans NW8 ....80 A1
  SW1 ....130 C3
  SW8 ....162 B2
  SW11 ....168 C3

Parkmead SW15 ....57 A1
Park Mews SW10 ....23 A3
Park Par Acton W3 ....36 C3
  London NW10 ....21 B3
Park Pl E14 ....33 C1
  SW1 ....118 C2
  London W3 ....36 C2
Park Place Dr W3 ....36 C2
Park Place Villas
W2 ....101 A4
  Chiswick W4 ....37 C1
  London W10 ....21 A4
  Richmond TW10 ....54 B1
Park Rd E W3 ....37 B4
Park Rd N
  London W3 ....37 A4
  London W4 ....37 C1
Park Row SE10 ....52 C4
Park Royal NW10 ....20 A4
Park Royal Bsns Ctr
NW10 ....20 B1
Park Royal Metro Ctr
NW10 ....20 A1
Park Royal Rd
NW10,W3 ....20 B1
Park S SW11 ....169 B3
Park Sheen 3
SW14 ....55 A3
Parkshot TW9 ....54 A3
Parkside SE3 ....53 B3
Park Side NW2 ....9 A4
Parkside Cres N7 ....5 C1
Parkside Est E9 ....25 C4
Parkside St SW11 ....169 B3
Park Sq E NW1 ....92 B2
Park Sq Mews NW1 ....92 A1
Park Sq W NW1 ....92 A1
Park St SE1 ....123 A2
  W1 ....117 B3
Park Steps W2 ....116 B4
Park St James 10
NW8 ....80 C3
Parkstone Rd 3
SE15 ....49 C1
Park The NW11 ....2 A3
Parkthorne Rd
SW12 ....73 C4
Park Twrs W1 ....118 A1
Park View NW2 ....9 B4
  London N5 ....15 B4
  London W3 ....28 B4
Parkview Ct SW6 ....164 B1
Park View Ct SW18 ....58 C1
Park View Ho SE24 ....63 A1
Park View Mews
SW9 ....172 C2
Park View Rd NW10 ....8 C4
Park Village E NW1 ....82 B1
Park Village W
NW1 ....82 A2
Parkville Rd SW6 ....154 C1
Park Vista SE10 ....52 C4
Park Walk Prim Sch
SW10 ....157 B3
Parkway NW1 ....82 B3
Park Way W3 ....36 C2
Park West 2 W2 ....102 B1
Park West Pl W1,
W2 ....102 B2
Park Wlk SW10 ....157 B4
Parkwood Prim Sch
N4 ....6 A2
Parliament Ct NW3 ....12 A4

Parliament Hill
NW3 ....12 A4

Parliament Hill Mans
NW5 ....12 C4

Parliament Hill Sch
NW5 ....12 C4

Parliament Mews
SW14 ....45 B1

Parliament Sq
SW1 ....134 A3

Parliament St
SW1 ....134 A3

Parliament View Apartments SE11 ..148 C3

Parma Cres SW11 ....60 B3

Parmiter Ind Est E2 ....25 C3

Parmiter St E2 ....25 A3

Parmoor Ct EC1 ......96 C2

Parnell Cl W12 ....39 A3

Parnell Rd E3 ....26 B4

Parnham St E14 ......33 A3

Paroles Ho N19 ....4 B3

Parr Ct N1 ....87 B2

Parrington Ho 1 SW4 ....61 C1

Parr Pl W4 ....38 B2

Parr St N1 ....87 B2

Parry Ho 23 E1 ....32 A1

Parry Rd W10 ....23 A2

Parry St SW8 ....162 B4

Parsifal Coll NW3 ....10 C4

Parsifal Ho NW3 ......10 C4

Parsifal Rd NW6 ......10 C3

Parsonage St E14 ...42 B2

Parson Ct SE13 ....67 A4

Parsons Gn SW6 ....165 B3

Parsons Green La SW6 ....165 B3

Parsons Green Sta SW6 ....165 B3

Parsons Ho W2 ....89 B1
21 Streatham SW12 ...74 A4

Parsons Lo NW6 ......11 A1

Parthenia Rd SW6 ..165 C3

Partington Cl N19 ......4 C3

Partridge Ct EC1 ......96 A2

Partridge Ho 2 E3 ....26 B3

Pascall Ho SE17 ......48 B4

Pascal St SW8 ....161 C2

Pascoe Rd SE13 ......67 C2

Pasley Cl SE17 ....150 C1

Passfield Dr E14 ......34 A4

Passfields W14 ....140 C1

Passing Alley EC1 ....96 B1

Passmore St SW1 ...145 B2

Pastor St SE1,SE11 ..150 B4

Patcham Terr SW8 ..170 B4

Patent Ho E14 ....34 A4

Paternoster Row EC2,EC4 ....108 C1

Paternoster Sq EC4 ....108 B2

Pater St W8 ....127 B1

Patience Rd SW11 ..168 A1

Patio Cl SW4 ....61 C1

Patmore Ho 5 N16 ...16 A3

Patmore St SW8 .....171 A4

Paton Cl E3 ....26 C2

Paton Ho SW9 ....172 C2

Paton St EC1 ....96 C3

Patrick Coman Ho EC1 ....96 A3

Patrick Connolly Gdns 41 E3 ....27 A2

Patriot Sq E2 ....25 A3

Patrol Pl SE6 ....67 A1

Pat Shaw Ho 2 E1 ...25 C1

Patshull Pl NW5 ......13 B2

Patshull Rd NW5 .....13 B2

Patten Ho N4 ....6 C3

Patten Rd SW18 ......72 A4

Patterdale NW1 ....92 B3

Patterdale Rd SE15 ..50 B3

Pattina Wlk SE16 .....33 A1

Pattison Point 10 E16 ....35 C4

Pattison Ho 1 E1 .....32 C3
SE1 ....137 A4

Pattison Rd NW2 ......1 C1

Paulet Rd SE5 ....48 A2

Paul Ho 13 W10 ......23 A1

Pauline Ho 4 E1 .....111 C4

Paul Julius Cl E14 ....34 C2

Paul's Ho E3 ....33 C4

Paul St EC2 ......24 A1 98 A2

Paultons Ho 3 SW3 .157 C4

Paultons Sq SW3 ....157 C4

Paultons St SW3 .....157 C3

Pauntley Ho 6 N19 ...4 B3

Pauntley St 4 N19 ....4 B3

Pavan Ct 25 E2 ....25 B2

Paveley Dr SW11 ....158 A1

Paveley Ho N1 ....25 A4 84 C1

Paveley St NW8 ....90 B2

Pavement The London SW4 ....61 B3
London W5 ....36 A3

Pavilion Ct 6 NW6 ..23 C2
London NW3 ....11 C3
4 London NW3 ....11 B4

Pavilion Mans 10 SW9 ....62 B3

Pavilion Rd SW1 .....131 A1

Pavilion St SW1 ......131 A1

Pavilion Terr W12 ....30 B3

Paxton Cl TW9 ....44 B1

Paxton Ho SE17 .....151 A2

Paxton Rd W4 ....46 A4

Paxton Terr SW1 ....160 B4

Payens Wlk W6 ......154 A3

Paymal Ho 23 E1 ....32 B4

Payne Ho N1 ....85 A3

Payne Rd E3 ....27 A3

Paynesfield Ave SW14 ....55 C4

Payne St SE8 ....51 B4

Peabody Ave SW1 ..146 B1

Peabody Bldgs
SE17 ....151 B3
London SE1 ....122 C1
2 London SE5 ....48 C2
4 E1 ....111 C1
12 E2 ....25 A3
EC1 ....95 C1
SE1 ....121 C1
SW3 ....122 C1
4 SW1 ....147 A4
SW6 ....155 A4
WC2 ....106 C1
London W10 ....30 B4
17 London N6 ....39 B1
Streatham SE24 ....75 C4

Peabody Hill SE21 ....75 B3

Peabody Sq SE1 ....136 A3

Peabody Twr EC1 ....96 C1

Peabody Yd N1 ....86 C4

Peach Rd W10 ....23 A2

Peacham Rd SE3 ......53 B4

Peach Walk Mews 3 E3 ....26 A3

Peacock St SE17 ....150 B3

Peacock Yd SE17 ....150 B3

Peak Ho N4 ....6 B3

Pearce Ho N19 ....4 B1
4 Streatham SW2 ......74 A4

Pear Cl SE14 ....51 A3

Pear Ct 20 SE15 ......49 B3

Peardon St SW8 .....170 B1

Pearfield Ho 1 N5 ...15 B3

Pearl St E1 ....32 A1

Pearman St SE1 .....135 C3

Pearscroft Ct SW6 ..166 B3

Pearscroft Rd SW6 ..166 B3

Pearse St 8 SE5 ......48 A4

Pearson Ho SW15 ....47 B1

Pearson's Ave SE8,
SE14 ....51 C2

Pearson St E2 ....24 B3

Peartree Ave SW17 ..71 B1

Pear Tree Cl 21 E2 ...24 B4

Pear Tree Ct EC1 .....95 C1
Putney SW15 ....57 A3

Pear Tree Ho SE4 ....66 B3

Peartree La E1 ....32 B2

Peartree St EC1 ....96 C2

Peary Pl E2 ....25 B2

Peckarmans Wood SE21,SE26 ....76 C1

Peckett Sq 5 N5 ......15 B4

Peckford Pl SW9 .....173 C1

Peckham Gr SE15 ....49 A3

Peckham High St SE15 ....49 C2

Peckham Hill St SE15 ....49 C3

Peckham Park Prim Sch SE15 ....49 C3

Peckham Park Rd SE15 ....49 C3

Peckham Rye London SE22 ....64 C3
Peckham SE15,SE22 ..65 A3

Peckham Rye Prim Sch SE15 ....49 C1

Peckham Rye Sta SE15 ....49 C1

Peckwater St NW5 ...13 B3

Pedlars Wlk N7 ....14 A3

Pedley St E1 ....24 C1 99 A1

Pedro St E5 ....17 C4

Pedworth Gdns 4 SE16 ....40 B2

Peel Gr E2 ....25 B3

Peel Pass W8 ....113 B1

Peel Prec NW6 ....23 C3

Peel Rd NW6 ....23 C2

Peel St W8 ....31 C1 113 B1

Peerless St EC1 ....97 B3

Pegasus Ct Brentford TW8 ....36 B1
London NW10 ....22 A2

Pegasus Ho 6 E1 ....25 C1

Pegwell Ho 5 E5 .....17 A3

Pekin St E14 ....33 C3

Pekoe SE1 ....125 A1

Peldon Ct TW10 ......54 B2

Pelham Cl SE5 ....64 A4

Pelham Cres SW7 ..144 A3

Pelham Ct SW3 ....144 A3

Pelham Ho W14 ......140 C3

Pelham Pl SW7 ......144 A3

Pelham St SW7 ....143 C3

Pelican Ho 5 SE8 .....41 B2

Pelier St SE17 ....48 B4

Pella Ho SE11 ....149 A2

Pellant Rd SW6 ......154 B2

Pellatt Rd SE22 ....64 B2

Pellerin Rd N16 ....16 A3

Pellew Ho 10 E1 ......25 A1

Pelling St E14 ....33 C3

Pelter St E2 ....98 C4

Pelton Rd SE10 ....43 A1

Pember Rd NW10 ....22 C2

Pemberton Ct 18 E1 ....25 C2

Pemberton Gdns N19 ....4 B1
8 E17 ....8 B1

Pemberton Pl 8 E8 ..17 A1

Pemberton Row EC4 ....107 C2

Pemberton Terr N19 ..4 B1

Pembridge Cres W11 ....31 C2 113 B4

Pembridge Gdns W2 ....31 C2 113 B3

Pembridge Mews W11 ....31 C2 113 B4

Pembridge Pl W2 ....31 C2 113 C4
1 London SW15 ....58 C2

Pembridge Rd W11 ....31 C2 113 B4

Pembridge Sq W2 ....31 C2 113 C3

Pembridge Villas W11 ....31 C2 113 B4

Pembroke 4 W14 ....140 C4

Pembroke Bldgs NW10 ....21 C2

Pembroke Cl SW1 ...131 C3

Pembroke Gdns W8 ....141 A4

Pembroke Gdns Cl W8 ....127 B1

Pembroke Ho Acton W3 ....37 B4
London W2 ....100 B1
Putney SW15 ....56 C2

Pembroke Mews 4 E3 ....26 A2
W8 ....127 B1

Pembroke Pl W8 .....127 B1

Pembroke Rd W8 ....141 B4
8 London N8 ....5 A4

Pembroke Sq W8 ....127 B1

Pembroke St N1 ....84 B4

Pembroke Studios W8 ....127 A1

Pembroke Terr NW8 ....79 B3

Pembroke Villas W8 ....141 B4

Pembroke Wlk W8 ..141 B4

Pembrook Lo 2 SW16 ....74 B1

Pembury Cl E5 ....17 A3

Pembury Ho SE5 ......49 A1

Pembury Pl 15 E5,
E8 ....17 A3

Pembury Rd E5 ....17 A3

Pemell Cl 27 E1 ....25 B1

Pemell Ho 28 E1 ......25 B1

Penally Pl N1 ....87 C4

Penang St E1 ....32 A1

Penarth St SE15 ....50 B4

Pencombe Mews W11 ....113 A4

Pencraig Way SE15 ..50 A4

Penda's Mead E9 .....18 A4

Pendennis Ho 15 SE8 ....41 A2

Penderyn Way N7 ....13 C4

Pendle Ho 16 SE26 ..76 C1

Pendley Ho 18 E2 ....24 C4

Pendrell Ho WC2 .....105 C1

Pendrell Rd SE4 ....51 A1

Penelope Ho SW9 ..173 B3

Penfield Lo 9 W9 .....31 C4

Penfields Ho N7 ....14 A2

Penfold Ct NW8 ....89 C1

Penfold Pl NW1 ....102 A4

Penfold St NW8 ....89 C1

Penford St SE5 ....48 A1

Penhurst Mans SW6 ....164 C4

Peninsula Ct E14 ......42 A3

Peninsular Park Rd SE7 ....43 C2

Penmayne Ho SE11 ....149 C2

Pennack Rd SE15 .....49 B4

Penn Almshouse 1 SE10 ....52 B2

Pennant Mews W8 ....142 A4

Pennard Mans 5 W12 ....39 B4

Pennard Rd W12 ......39 B4

Penner Cl SW19 ....70 A2

Pennethorne Cl E9 ...25 B4

Pennethorne Ho SW11 ....59 C4

Pennethorne Rd SE15 ....50 A3

Penn Ho NW8 ....90 A1

Pennine La NW2 ....1 A2

Pennine Mans NW2 ...1 A2

Pennine Par NW2 ......1 A2

Pennington Ct E1 ...125 C3
SE16 ....33 A1

Pennington St E1 ......32 A2

Penn Rd N7 ....14 A4

Penn St N1 ....87 C3

Pennyfields E14 ....33 C2

Pennyford Ct NW8 ....89 B2

Penny Mews SW12 ..73 A4

Pennymore Wlk W9 ..23 B1

Penny Rd NW10 ....20 A2

Penpoll Rd E8 ....17 A2

Penrhyn Cres SW14 ..55 B3

Penrith Cl SW15 ....58 A2

Penrith Pl SE27 ....75 A2

Penrose Gr SE17 ....150 C1

Penrose Ho SE17 ....150 C1

Penrose St SE17 .....150 C1

Penryn Ho SE11 .....150 A2

Penryn St NW1 ....83 B2

Penry St SE1 ....152 B3

Pensbury Pl SW8 ....171 A2

Pensbury St SW8 ....171 A2

Pensford Ave TW9 ...44 C1

Penshurst 3 NW5 ....12 C2

Penshurst Ho 16 SE15 ....50 B4

Penshurst Rd E9 ......17 C1

Pentland Cl NW11 .....1 A2

Pentland Ho 17 NW5 ....12 C2
7 London N16 ....7 B3

Pentland St SW18 ....59 B1

Pentlow St SW15 .....57 B4

Pentney Rd SW12 ....73 B3

Penton Gr N1 ....85 B1

Penton Ho N1 ....85 B1

Penton Pl SE17 ....150 B2

Penton Rise WC1 .....95 A4

Penton St N1 ....85 B1

Pentonville Rd N1 ...... .85 A1
Pentridge St SE15 ....49 B3
Penwith Rd SW18 ...71 A2
Penwood Ho **4**
SW15 ....56 B1
Penywern Rd SW5 .141 C2
Penzance Pl
W11 ....31 A1 **112** B2
Penzance St
W11 ....31 A1 **112** B2
Peony Gdns W12 ....29 C2
Peperfield WC1 ......94 C3
Pepler Ho **17** W10 ...23 A1
Pepler Mews SE1 .152 C1
Peploe Rd NW6 ......22 C3
Peppermead Sq
SE13 ....66 C2
Pepper St E14 .....42 A3
SE1 ....136 C4
Pepys Ct **2** E16 ..35 C1
Pepys Ent Ct **2**
SE8 ....41 B2
Pepys Ho **14** E2 ...25 B2
London SW4 ....61 C3
Pepys Rd SE14 ......50 C1
Pepys St EC3 ....124 B4
Percheron Ct **3**
SW9 ....62 B4
Perch St E8 ....16 B4
Percival Rd SW14 ..55 B3
Percival St EC1 ....96 B3
Percy Cir WC1 .....95 A4
Percy Mews W1 ....105 B3
Percy Pas W1 .....105 B3
Percy Rd E16 ....35 A4
London W12 ....38 C4
Percy St W1 ....105 B3
Peregrine Ho **1** EC1 ..96 B4
6 London SW11 .60 A4
Perham Rd W14 ...140 B1
Perifield SE21 ......75 B3
Perkins Ho **15** E14 ...33 B4
Perkins Rents
SW1 ....133 B1
Perkins Sq SE1 ....123 A2
Perley Ho **16** E3 ...33 B4
Perotti Ho SW6 ...54 A2
Perran Rd SE24,SW2 .75 A2
Perren St NW5 ......13 A2
Perrers Rd W6 .....39 A2
Perring Est **2** E3 ...33 C4
Perrin's Ct **21** NW3 .11 B4
Perrin's La NW3 ....11 B4
Perrin's Wlk NW3 ...11 B4
Perronet Ho SE1 ..136 B1
Perry Ave W3 ......28 C3
Perry Ct **23** E14 ...41 C1
Perry Ho **32** SW2 ..74 A4
Perrymead St SW6 .166 A3
Perryn Ho W3 ....29 A2
Perryn Rd **1** SE16 .40 A3
London W3 ....28 C2
Perry's Pl W1 .....105 B2
Perrywood Ho **17**
E5 ....17 A3
Perseverance Pl
SW9 ....163 B1
Perseverance Works
E2 ....98 B4

Peter Ave NW10 ......9 A1
Peter Best Ho **41** E1 ..25 C1
Peterboat Cl SE10 ..43 A2
Peterborough Ct
EC4 ....107 C1
Peterborough Mews
SW6 ....165 B2
Peterborough Prim Sch
SW6 ....166 C1
Peterborough Rd
SW6 ....58 C4
Peterborough Villas
SW6 ....166 A4
Peter Butler Ho
SE1 ....139 B3
Peter Hills Ho
SE16 ....153 B4
Peter Hills with St
Mary's & St Paul's CE
Prim Sch SE16 ....32 C1
Peter Ho SW8 .....162 A2
Peterley Bsns Ctr
E2 ....25 A3
Peters Ct W2 .....100 B2
Peter's Ct SW4 ....62 A1
Petersfield Rd W3 .37 B4
Petersfield Rise
SW15 ....69 A3
Petersham Ho
SW7 ....143 B4
Petersham La
SW7 ....129 A1
Petersham Mews
SW7 ....129 A1
Petersham Pl SW7 .129 A2
Peter's La EC1 .....108 B4
Peter St W1 ....119 B4
Peterstow Cl SW19 .70 A2
Petherton Ct NW10 .22 C4
Petherton Ho **2** N4 ..6 B3
Petherton Rd N5 ..15 B3
Petiver Cl **28** E9 ....17 B1
Petley Rd W6 ....47 C3
Peto Pl NW1 ....92 B2
Peto St N E16 ......35 B3
Petrel Ct **7** SE21 ..75 C2
Petrie Cl NW2 ......10 A2
Petros Gdns **1**
NW3 ....11 B2
Petticoat Lane Mkt*
EC2 ....110 C3
Petticoat Sq E1 ...110 C2
Petticoat Twr E1 ..110 C2
Pettiward Cl SW15 .57 B3
Petty France SW1 .133 B2
Petworth Ho **16**
SE22 ....64 A4
Petyt Pl SW3 .....158 A3
Petyward SW3 ....144 B3
Pevensey Ct
4 London W3 ...37 A4
West Norwood SE27 .74 C1
Pevensey Ho **5** E1 .33 A4
Peverill Ho SE1 ...137 C1
Pewsham Ho N4 ...6 B3
Peyton Pl SE10 ....52 B3
Pharamond NW2 ...9 C2
Phelps Ho SW15 ..57 C4
Phelp St SE17 ......48 C4
Phene St SW3 ....158 B4
Philadelphia Ct
SW10 ....157 A1

Philbeach Gdns
SW5 ....141 B2
Phil Brown Pl **3**
SW8 ....61 A4
Philchurch Pl E1 ..111 C1
Philia Ho **1** NW1 ..13 B1
Philip Ct W2 ....101 B4
Philip Ho NW6 .....78 A3
Philip St E15 ....64 C4
Philip Turner Est **28**
E9 ....17 B1
Philip Wlk SE15 ....64 C4
Phillimore Ct W8 .127 C3
Phillimore Gardens Cl
W8 ....127 B2
Phillimore Gdns
W8 ....127 B3
Willesden NW10 ...22 B4
Phillimore Pl W8 .127 B3
Phillimore Terr
W8 ....127 C2
Phillimore Wlk
W8 ....127 C2
Phillip Ho E1 ....111 A3
Phillipp St N1 ......24 A4
Philpot La EC3 .....124 A4
Philpot Sq SW6 ....59 A4
Philpot St E1 ....32 A3
Phipps Ho **16** W12 .30 A2
Phipp St EC2 ....24 A1 98 A2
Phoebeth Rd SE4 ..66 C2
Phoenix Bsns Ctr
E3 ....33 C4
Phoenix Ct **18** E14 .41 C2
2 SE14 ....51 A4
Brentford TW8 .....36 A1
Phoenix High Sch
W12 ....29 C2
Phoenix Lodge Mans
W6 ....39 B2
Phoenix Pl WC1 ....95 A2
Phoenix Rd NW1 ...93 B4
Phoenix Sch **3** E3 ..26 B2
Phoenix Sch The
NW3 ....11 B2
Phoenix St WC2 ..105 C1
Phoenix Wharf Rd
SE1 ....139 A3
Phyllis Hodges Ho
NW1 ....83 B1
Physic Pl SW3 ....158 C4
Piccadilly W1 .....118 C2
Piccadilly Arc
SW1 ....118 C2
Piccadilly Cir*
W1 ....119 B3
Piccadilly Circus Sta
SW1 ....119 B3
Piccadilly Pl W1 ..119 A3
Pickard St EC1 .....96 B4
Pickering Ho
London N4 ....6 C4
2 London W2 ....100 B1
Pickering Mews
W2 ....100 A2
Pickering Pl SW1 .119 A2
Pickering St N1 ...86 B4
Pickets St **3** SW12 .73 A4
Pickfords Wharf N1 .86 C1
Pickwick Ho SE16 .139 B3
Pickwick Rd SE21 .76 A4
Pickwick St SE1 ..136 C3
Picton Ho **8** SW4 ..74 A4
Picton Pl W1 ......103 C1

Picton St SE5 ....48 C3
Pied Bull Ct WC1 .106 B3
Pied Bull Yd WC1 .106 B3
Pier Ho SW3 ......158 B3
Piermont Rd SE22 .65 A2
Pierpoint Bldg **5**
E14 ....41 C4
Pierrepont Rd W3 .28 A2
Pier St E14 ....42 B2
Pier Terr SW18 ......59 B3
Piggott Ho **2** E2 ..25 C3
Pigott St E14 ....33 C3
Pilgrimage St SE1 .137 B3
Pilgrim Ho SE1 ....137 C1
Pilgrims Cloisters **18**
SE5 ....49 A3
Pilgrims Ct SE3 ....53 C2
Pilgrim's La NW3 ..11 C4
Pilgrims Mews **14** E14 .34 C2
Pilgrims Way N19 ..4 C3
SE15 ....50 B4
Pilgrims Way Prim Sch
SE15 ....50 B4
Pilkington Rd **4**
SE15 ....50 A1
Pilot Ind Ctr NW10 .21 A1
Pilsden Cl SW19 ...69 C3
Pilton Pl SE17 .....151 A2
Pimlico Rd SW1 ...145 C2
Pimlico Sta SW1 ..147 A1
Pimlico Wlk N1 ....98 A4
Pinchin St E1 ......125 C4
Pincombe Ho SE17 .151 B2
Pincott Pl SE4 ......65 C4
Pindar St EC2 .....110 A4
Pindock Mews W9 .88 B1
Pine Apple Ct
SW1 ....132 C2
Pine Ave E15 ....19 C3
Pine Cl **8** N19 .....4 B2
Pinedene **2** SE15 ..50 A2
Pinefield Cl E14 ....33 C2
Pine Gr N4,N19 ......5 B2
Pine Ho SE16 ......40 B4
4 London W10 .23 A2
Pinelands Cl **7** SE3 .53 B3
Pine Lo SW15 ......58 A1
Pine Rd NW2 ....9 C4
Pines The SW19 ...69 C3
Pine St EC1 ....95 B2
Pine Tree Ho SE14 .50 C3
Pinewood Ct SW4 .61 C1
Pinkham Mans W4 .36 C1
Pinnacle Ho EC3 ..124 A3
Pinner Ho **35** SE5 ..48 B1
Pintail Ct **40** SE8 ..51 B4
Pinter Ho **9** SW9 .172 B1
Pioneer Cl W12 ....30 A3
Pioneer St SE15 ...49 C2
Pioneer Way W12 .30 B3
Piper Cl N7 ....14 B2
Pirbright Rd SW18 .70 C3
Pitcairn Ho **1** E9 ..17 B1
Pitfield Ho N5 ......15 B3
Pitfield St N1 ....24 A3
Pitman Ho **4** SE8 ..51 C2
Pitman St SE5 ......48 B3
Pitmaston Ho **2**
SE13 ....52 B1
Pitsea Pl E1 ....32 C3
Pitsea St E1 ....32 C3
Pitt Ho **4** SW11 ...59 C3

Pitt's Head Mews
W1 ....117 C1
Pitt St W8 ....127 C4
Pixley St E14 ....33 B3
Planetarium The*
NW1 ....91 B1
Planetree Ct W6 ...39 C2
Plane Tree Ho SE8 .51 A4
Plantain Pl SE1 ...137 B4
Plantation The SE3 .53 C1
Platina St EC2 ......97 C2
Plato Pl **5** SW6 ...165 A2
Plato Rd SW2 ....62 A3
Platt's La NW3 ......1 C1
Platt St NW1 ....83 B2
Plaxdale Ho SE17 .152 A3
Playfair St W6 ......39 B1
Playfield Cres SE22 .64 B2
Playford Rd
London N4 ....5 B2
London N4 ....5 C2
Playhouse Yd EC4 .108 A1
Pleasance Rd SW15 .57 A2
Pleasance The
SW15 ....57 A3
Pleasant Pl N1 .....15 A1
Pleasant Row NW1 .82 B3
Plender Ct NW1 ....83 A3
Plender St NW1 ....83 A3
Pleshey Rd N7 ......13 C4
Plevna St E14 ....42 B3
Pleydell Ave E16 ..98 A2
Pleydell Ct EC4 ...107 C1
Pleydell St EC4 ...107 C1
Plimsoll Cl E14 ....34 A3
Plimsoll Rd N4 ......6 A1
Plough Ct EC3 .....123 C4
Plough La SE22 ....64 B1
Ploughmans Cl
NW1 ....83 B4
Plough Pl EC4 .....107 C2
Plough Rd SW11 ..59 C3
Plough St **9** E1 ...111 B2
Plough Terr SW11 .59 C3
Plough Way SE16 .41 A2
Plough Yd EC2 ......98 B1
Plover Ho SW9 ....163 B2
Plover Way SE16 ..41 A3
Plowman Ho SW19 .69 C2
Plumbers Row E1 .111 C2
Plumbridge St **7**
SE10 ....52 B2
Plume Ho SE10 ....52 A4
Plummer Ct SE13 .67 A1
Plummer Rd SW4 .73 C4
Plumtree Ct EC4 ..108 A2
Plymouth Ho **16** .35 C4
Plymouth Wharf
E14 ....42 C2
Plympton Ave NW6 .10 B1
Plympton Pl NW1 ..90 A1
Plympton Rd NW6 .10 B1
Plympton St NW1 ..90 A1
Pocklington Ct
SW15 ....68 C3
Pocock St SE1 ....136 B4
Podmore Rd SW18 .59 B3
Poets Corner SW1 .134 A2
Poet's Rd N5 ....15 C3
Point Cl SE10 ....52 B2
Pointer Sch The
SE3 ....53 C3
Pointers Cl E14 ....42 A1
Point Hill SE10 .....52 B2

Point Pleasant SW10 .....58 C3
Poland St W1 .....105 A1
Polesworth Ho 10 W2 .....31 C4
Polish Univ Abroad W6 .....38 C2
Pollard Cl E16 .....35 C2
 London N7 .....14 B4
Pollard Ho N1 .....84 C1
Pollard Row E2 .....24 C2 99 C4
Pollard St E2 .....24 C2 99 C4
Pollen St W1 .....104 B1
Pollitt Dr NW8 .....89 C2
Pollock Ho W10 .....23 A1
Polperro Mans 8 NW6 .....10 C3
Polperro Mews SE11 .....150 A3
Polygon Rd NW1 .....83 B1
Polygon The NW8 .....79 C4
 1 London SW4 .....61 B3
Pomell Way E1 .....111 A2
Pomeroy Ct W11 .....31 A3
Pomeroy Ho 5 E2 .....25 C3
Pomeroy St SE14 .....50 B2
Pomfret Rd SE5 .....63 A4
Pomoja La N19 .....5 A2
Pomona Ho 10 SE8 .....41 A2
Pond Cl SE3 .....53 C1
Pond Cotts SE21 .....76 A3
Ponder St 5 N7 .....14 B1
Pondfield Ho 4 N5 .....15 B3
Pond Ho SW3 .....144 A3
Pond Mead SE21 .....63 C1
Pond Pl SW3 .....144 A3
Pond Rd SE3 .....53 B1
Pond Sq N6 .....3 C3
Pond St NW3 .....12 A3
Ponler St E1 .....32 A3
Ponsard Rd NW10 .....22 A2
Ponsford St E9 .....17 B2
Ponsonby Ho 12 E2 .....25 B3
Ponsonby Pl SW1 .....147 C2
Ponsonby Rd SW15 .....69 A4
Ponsonby Terr SW1 .....147 C2
Ponton Ho 2 .....74 C3
Ponton Rd SW8 .....161 C3
Pont St Mews 131 A1
Pont St Mews SW1 .....130 C1 131 A1
Pontypool Pl SE1 .....136 A4
Poole Ct N1 .....16 A1
Poole Ho SE11 .....135 A1
Poole Rd E9 .....17 C2
Pooles Bldgs EC1 .....95 B1
Pooles La SW10 .....156 C1
Pooles Park Prim Sch N4 .....5 B2
Pooles Pk N4 .....5 C2
Poole St N1 .....87 B3
Pool Ho NW8 .....101 C4
Poolmans St SE16 .....40 C4
Poonah St E1 .....32 B3
Pope Ho 7 SE16 .....40 A2
 8 SE5 .....48 C3
Pope John RC Prim Sch W12 .....30 A2
Pope's Head Alley EC3 .....109 C1
Pope's La W5 .....36 A3
Pope's Rd SW9 .....62 C4
Pope St SE1 .....138 B3

Popham Ct N16 .....7 A1
Popham Gdns TW9 .....45 A1
Popham Rd N1 .....86 C4
Popham St N1 .....86 B4
 N1 .....86 C4
Poplar Bath St 10 E14 .....34 A2
Poplar Bsns Pk E14 .....34 B2
Poplar Ct 19 .....18 B3
Poplar Ct 4 SW16 .....74 B1
Poplar Gr W6 .....39 B4
Poplar High St E14 .....34 A2
Poplar Ho 2 SE16 .....40 C4
 London SE4 .....66 B3
Poplar Mews W12 .....30 B1
Poplar Pl W2 .....114 B4
Poplar Rd SE24 .....63 B3
Poplar Sta E14 .....34 A2
Poplars The NW5 .....13 B3
Poplar Wlk SE24 .....63 B3
Poppins Ct EC4 .....108 A1
Porchester Ct W2 .....114 B4
Porchester Gate W2 .....114 C3
Porchester Gdn Mews W2 .....100 B1
Porchester Gdns W2 .....114 B4
Porchester Mews W2 .....100 B2
Porchester Pl W2 .....102 B1
Porchester Rd W2 .....100 B2
Porchester Sq W2 .....100 B2
Porchester Terr W2 .....114 C4
Porchester Terr N W2 .....100 B2
Porden Rd SW2 .....62 B3
Porland Ct SE1 .....137 B1
Porlock Ho 5 SE26 .....76 C1
Porlock St SE1 .....137 C4
Portal Cl SE27 .....74 C1
Portbury Cl 15 SE15 .....49 C2
Portelet Ct 1 N1 .....24 A4
Portelet Rd E1 .....25 C2
Porten Hos W14 .....126 A1
Porten Rd W14 .....126 A1
Porter Sq N19 .....5 A3
Porter St SE1 .....123 A2
 W1 .....103 A4
Porteus Rd W2 .....101 A4
Portgate Cl W9 .....23 B1
Portia Way E3 .....26 B1
Porticos The SW3 .....157 B3
Portinscale Rd SW15 .....58 B2
Portishead Ho 59 .....31 C4
Portland Ave N16 .....7 B4
Portland Ct 1 SE14 .....51 A4
 7 London N1 .....15 B2
Portland Gr SW8 .....172 C4
Portland Ho 2 SW2 .....74 C3
Portland Hospl for Women & Children The W1 .....92 B1
Portland Mews W1 .....105 A1
Portland Pl W1 .....104 B3
Portland Rd W11 .....31 A3
 W11 .....31 A1 112 B2
Portland Rise N4 .....6 B3
Portland Sq 4 E1 .....32 A1
Portland St SE17 .....151 B1

Portland Village W6 .....39 B3
Portman Ave SW14 .....55 C4
Portman Cl W1 .....103 B2
Portman Gate NW1 .....90 B1
Portman Hts 1 .....1 C1
Portman Mews S W1 .....103 B1
Portman Pl E2 .....25 B2
Portman Sq W1 .....103 B2
Portman St W1 .....103 B1
Portman Twrs W1 .....103 A2
Portnall Rd W9 .....23 B2
Portobello Ct Est W11 .....31 B3
Portobello Mews W11 .....113 B3
Portobello Rd W11 .....31 A4 113 A4
Portobello Road Mkt* W10 .....31 A4
Portpool La EC1 .....107 B4
Portree St E14 .....34 C3
Port Royal Pl 3 N16 .....16 A3
Portsea Hall W2 .....102 B1
Portsea Ho 3 SW15 .....69 A3
Portsea Mews W2 .....102 B1
Portsea Pl W2 .....102 B1
Portslade Rd SW8 .....170 C2
Portsmouth Rd SW15 .....69 A4
Portsmouth St WC2 .....107 A1
Portsoken St E1, EC3 .....124 C4
Portswood Pl 10 SW15 .....56 B1
Portugal St WC2 .....107 A1
Poseidon Ct 8 E14 .....41 C2
Postal Ct SE1 .....137 C4
Post Office Way SW8 .....161 B2
Potier St SE1 .....137 C1
Potterne Cl 5 SW19 .....69 C4
Potters Fields SE1 .....124 B1
Potters Lo E14 .....42 B1
Potters Rd SW6 .....166 C1
Pottery La W11 .....31 A1 112 B2
Pottery Rd TW8 .....44 A4
Pottery St SE16 .....40 A4
Pott St E2 .....25 A2
Poullett Ho SW2 .....75 A3
Poulton Cl E8 .....17 A2
Poultry EC2 .....109 B1
Pound La NW10 .....8 C2
Pountney Rd SW11 .....60 C4
Povey Ho SE17 .....152 A3
 London SW2 .....62 C1
Powell's Wlk W4 .....46 B4
Powergate Bsns Pk NW10 .....20 C2
Power Ho 12 TW9 .....44 C2
Power Ho The W4 .....38 A2
Power Rd W4 .....36 C2
Powerscroft Rd E5 .....17 B4
Powis Gdns W11 .....31 B3
 London NW11 .....1 B4
Powis Ho WC2 .....106 B2
Powis Mews W11 .....31 B3
Powis Pl WC1 .....94 B1
Powis Rd E3 .....27 A2
Powis Sq W11 .....31 B3

Powis Terr W11 .....31 B3
Powlesland Ct 28
Powlett Ho E2 .....25 B3
Powlett Pl NW1 .....13 A2
Pownall Rd E8 .....24 C4
Powrie Ho SW11 .....167 C2
Poynder Ct 9 N7 .....14 A3
Poynders Ct 7 SW4 .....61 B1
Poynders Gdns SW12 .....73 B4
Poynders Rd SW12 .....61 A1
Poynter Ho NW8 .....89 B2
 10 London W11 .....30 C1
Poyntz Rd SW11 .....168 C1
Poyser St E2 .....25 A3
Praed Mews W2 .....101 C2
Praed St W2 .....101 C2
Prague Pl SW2 .....62 A2
Prah Rd N4 .....5 C2
Prairie St SW8 .....170 A1
Pratt Mews NW1 .....82 C3
Pratt St NW1 .....82 C4
Pratt Wlk SE11 .....149 A4
Prebend Gdns SW4, W6 .....38 B2
Prebend Mans 4 W4 .....38 B2
Prebend St N1 .....86 C4
The Precinct N1 .....86 C3
 London N5 .....15 A3
Preedy Ho N1 .....85 A2
Premier Park Rd NW10 .....20 A3
Premier Pl 14 E14 .....33 C2
Prendergast Ho 7 SW4 .....61 B3
Prendergast Sch SE4 .....66 C3
Prescot St E1 .....125 A4
Prescott Ho 16 SE17 .....48 A4
Prescott Pl SW4 .....61 C3
Presentation Mews SW2 .....74 B3
President Dr E1 .....32 A1
President Ho EC1 .....96 B3
President St EC1 .....96 C4
Prestage Way E14 .....34 B2
Prested Rd SW11 .....60 A3
Preston Cl SE1 .....152 A4
Preston Gdns NW10 .....8 A2
Preston Ho SE1 .....138 C2
 London N1 .....24 A4
 SE1 .....152 A4
Preston Pl London NW2 .....8 C2
 Richmond TW10 .....54 A2
Preston's Rd E14 .....34 B1
Prestwich Terr SW4 .....61 C2
Prestwood Ho 3 SE16 .....40 A3
Prestwood St N1 .....87 A1
Priam Ho 10 E2 .....25 A3
Price Cl SW17 .....72 B1
Price Ho N1 .....86 C3
Prices Ct SW11 .....59 C4
Price's St SE1 .....122 B2
Price's Yd N1 .....85 A3
Prichard Ct N1 .....167 C3
 London N7 .....14 B3
Prideaux Ho WC1 .....95 A4
Prideaux Pl WC1 .....95 A4
 W4 .....62 A4
Prideaux Rd SW9 .....62 A4
Priestley Cl N16 .....7 B4

Priestley Ho EC1 .....97 A1
 2 London NW5 .....13 A2
Priestman Point 28 E3 .....27 A2
Priests Bridge SW14 .....56 A4
Priest's Ct EC2 .....108 C2
Prima Rd SW9 .....163 B2
Primrose Ct 11 SW12 .....73 C4
Primrose Gdns NW3 .....12 A2
Primrose Hill EC4 .....107 C1
Primrose Hill Ct NW3 .....12 B1
Primrose Hill Rd NW1,NW3 .....80 C4
Primrose Hill Sch NW1 .....81 B3
Primrose Hill Sta NW1 .....81 B3
Primrose Hill Studios NW1 .....81 B4
Primrose Ho 7 London SE15 .....49 C2
 1 Richmond TW9 .....44 B2
Primrose Mans SW11 .....169 B4
Primrose Mews 1 NW1 .....12 B1
Primrose Sq E9 .....25 B4
Primrose St EC2 .....110 B4
Primrose Wlk 2 SE14 .....51 A3
Primula St W12 .....29 C3
Prince Albert Ct NW8 .....80 C3
Prince Albert Rd NW8 .....80 C3
Prince Arthur Ct 18 NW3 .....11 B4
Prince Arthur Mews 20 NW3 .....11 B4
Prince Arthur Rd NW3 .....11 B3
Prince Charles Rd SE3 .....53 B2
Prince Consort Rd SW7 .....129 B2
Princedale Rd W11 .....31 A1 112 B2
Prince Edward Mans W2 .....113 C4
Prince Edward Rd E9 .....18 B2
Prince George Rd N16 .....16 A4
Princelet St E1 .....111 A4
Prince of Orange La 3 SE10 .....52 B3
Prince of Wales Dr SW11 .....169 B4
Prince of Wales Mans SW11 .....169 C4
 London SW4 .....61 A2
Prince of Wales Pas NW1 .....92 C3
Prince of Wales Rd NW5 .....12 C2
 London SE3 .....53 B2
Prince of Wales Terr W8 .....128 B3
 London W4 .....38 A1
Prince Regent Ct SE16 .....33 A1
Prince Regent Mews NW1 .....92 C3

Princes Arc SW1 ....119 A2
Princes Ave W4 .....36 C3
Princes Cir WC2 ...106 A2
Princes Cl N4 ......6 A3
Prince's Ct SE16 ....41 B3
Princes Ct
London NW2 ......10 A3
London NW11 .....11 C4
Stepney E1 ....32 A2
Princes Gate SW7 129 C3
Princes Gate Ct
SW7 ....130 A3
Princes Gate Mews
SW7 ....129 C2
Princes Gdns SW7 .129 C2
Princes Ho W11 ....113 B3
Prince's Mews W2 .114 A4
London N6 ....39 A1
Princes Pl SW1 ....119 A2
W11 ....31 A1 112 A2
Princes Rd
Richmond TW10 ....54 B2
Richmond TW9 .....44 B2
Prince's Rd SW14 ...55 C4
Prince Rise SE13 ...52 B1
Princes Riverside Rd **7**
SE16 ....32 C1
Princess Alexandra
School of Nursing The
E1 ....32 A4
Princess Alice Ho
W10 ....22 B1
Princess Beatrice Ho
SW10 ....142 A1
Princess Christian Coll
WC1 ....106 B4
Princess Cres N4 ....6 A2
Princess Ct N1 ....102 C3
W2 ....114 B4
London NW6 .....10 C1
Princess Frederica CE
Prim Sch NW10 ...22 B3
Princess Grace Hospl
The 91 B1
Princess Louise Cl
W2 ....101 B4
Princess Louise Hospl
W10 ....30 B4
Princess Mary Ho
SW1 ....147 C3
Princess May Prim Sch
N16 ....16 B4
Princess May Rd
N16 ....16 A4
Princess Mews
NW3 ....11 C2
Princess Rd NW1 ...81 C4
NW6 ....23 C3
Princess St SE1 ...136 B1
Prince St SW11 ....160 B3
Prince's St EC2 ....109 B1
Richmond TW10,TW9 ...54 A2
Prince St SE8 ......51 B4
Princes Way
Acton W3 ....36 C3
Putney SW15,SW19 ...70 A3
Princes Yd N11 ....112 B1
Princethorpe Ho
W2 ....100 A4
Princethorpe Rd
SE26 ....23 C4
Princeton Mans
WC1 ....106 C3
Princeton St WC1 106 C4
Printers Mews E3 ...26 A4
Printer St EC4 .....107 C2

Printing House Yd
E2 ....98 B3
Printon Ho **3** E3 ....33 B4
Print Village Ind Est
SE15 ....49 B1
Prior Bolton St N1 ...15 A2
Prioress Ho **2** E3 ....27 A2
Prioress Rd SE27 ...75 A1
Prioress St SE1 ....137 C1
Priors Lo **4** TW10 ..54 A1
Prior St SE10 ......52 B3
Priority Ct SE15 ....65 B3
Prior Weston Prim Sch
EC1 ....97 A1
Priory Ave W4 ......38 A3
Priory Ct London E17 ...108 B1
London E9 ....17 C3
London SW8 .....171 C4
Putney SW15 ......56 B3
Roehampton SW15 ...56 B3
Priory Gdns
Barnes SW13 ......56 B4
London W4 ....38 A2
Priory Gn N1 ......84 C2
Priory Gr SW8 ....172 A3
Priory Heights N1 ...84 C2
Priory Ho E1 ......110 C4
EC1 ....96 A2
SW1 ....147 B2
Priory Hospl The
SW15 ....56 B3
Priory La SW15 ....56 B2
Priory Lo **17** W4 ...36 C1
Priory Mans SW10 143 A1
17 London NW3 ....11 C2
Priory Park Rd NW6 23 B4
Priory Rd
London N8 ....5 A4
London W4 ....37 C3
Richmond TW9 .....44 C3
Priory St **18** E3 ...27 A2
Priory Terr NW6 ...78 A4
Priory The SE1 ....136 A3
Priory Wlk SW10 ..143 A1
Pritchard Ho **34** E2 ..24 C3
Pritchard's Rd E2 ...24 C3
Priter Rd SE16 ....139 C1
Priter Road Hostel
SE16 ....139 C1
Probert Rd SW2 ....62 C2
Probyn Ho SW1 ....147 C4
Probyn Rd SW2 ....75 A2
Procter Ho **16** SE5 ..48 C3
Procter St WC1 ....106 C3
Proctor Ho SE1 ....153 B1
Prome Ho **3** N16 ..15 C4
Promenade Approach
Rd W4 ....46 A3
Promenade The W4 46 A2
Prospect Cotts
SW18 ....58 C3
Prospect Ho N1 ....85 B1
1 London E8 ....16 B2
16 London W10 ....30 C3
Prospect House Sch
SW15 ....69 C4
Prospect Pl **1** E1 ...32 B1
8 SE8 ....51 B4
3 London NW2 .....1 B1
24 London NW3 ....11 B4
2 London W4 ......37 C1
Prospect Quay
SW18 ....58 C3
Prospect Rd NW2 ...1 C1
Prospect St SE16 ...40 A4
Prospect Wharf E1 .32 B2

Prospero Rd N19 ....4 C3
Prothero Rd SW6 ..154 C2
Prout Gr NW10 .....8 B4
Provence St N1 .....86 C2
Providence Ct W1 ..117 C4
Providence Ho E9 ..25 C4
Providence Pl N1 ...86 A3
Providence Row N1 ..84 C1
Providence Sq **3** SE1 ..139 B4
Providence Twr
SE16 ....139 B4
Provost Ct NW3 ....12 B2
Provost Rd NW3 ...12 B1
Provost St N1 ......97 B4
Prowse Pl NW1 ....13 B1
Prudent Pas EC2 ..109 A1
Prusom's Island **8** ..
E1 ....32 B1
Prusom St E1 .....32 A1
Pryors The NW3 ....2 C1
Public Record Office
EC4,WC2 ....107 B2
Richmond TW9 .....44 C3
Public Record Office
Mus EC4,WC2 ....107 B1
Pudding La EC3 ...123 C4
Pudding Mill La
E15 ....27 A4
Pudding Mill Lane Sta
E15 ....27 A4
Puddle Dock EC4 ..122 B4
Pugin Ct N1 ....14 C1
Pulborough Rd
SW18 ....70 B4
Pulham Ho SW8 ...162 C1
Pullman Ct SW2 ...74 B3
Pullman Gdns SW15 57 B1
Pulross Rd SW9 ...62 B4
Pulteney Cl **13** E3 ..26 B4
Pulteney Terr N1 ...85 A4
Pulton Ho SE4 .....66 A3
Pulton Pl SW6 ....155 B1
Puma Ct E1 ....110 C4
Pump Ct EC4 ......107 B1
Pump House Cl
SE16 ....40 B4
Pumping Station Rd
W4 ....46 A4
Pump La SE14 .....50 B3
Punderson's Gdns
E2 ....25 A2
Purbeck Ho SW8 ..162 C1
Purbrook Est SE1 ..138 B3
Purbrook Ho **2** ...
SW15 ....69 A3
Purbrook St SE1 ..138 B2
Purcell Cres SW6 ..154 A2
Purcell Ho **10** SW10 ..157 B3
Purcell Mews NW10 ...8 A1
Purcell St N1 ......24 A3
Purchese St NW1 ...83 C1
Purday Ho **4** W10 ..23 B2
Purdon Ho **10** SE15 ..49 C2
Purdy St E3 ....27 A1
Purley Ave NW2 .....1 A2
Purley Pl N1 ......15 A1
Purser Ho **3** SW2 ..62 C1
Pursers Cross Rd
SW6 ....165 A4
Purves Rd NW10 ...22 B3
Pusey Ho **16** E14 ...33 C3
Puteaux Ho **2** E2 ...25 C3
Putney Bridge App
SW6 ....58 A4
Putney Bridge Rd
SW15 ....58 B3

Putney Bridge Sta
SW6 ....58 B4
Putney Comm SW15 57 B4
Putney Heath SW15 57 B1
Putney Heath La
SW15 ....57 C1
Putney High Sch
SW15 ....58 A3
Putney High St
SW15 ....58 A3
Putney Hill SW15 ...57 C2
Putney Hospl SW15 57 B4
Putney Park Ave
SW15 ....56 C3
Putney Park La
SW15 ....57 A2
Putney Pier SW15 ..58 A4
Putney School of Art &
Design SW15 .....58 A3
Putney Sta SW15 ...58 A3
Putney Wharf Twr
SW15 ....58 B4
Pylon Trad Est E16 ..34 C4
Pymers Mead SE21 75 B3
Pynfolds SE16 .....40 A4
Pynnersmead SE24 63 B2
Pyrford Ho **17** SW9 ..63 A3
Pyrland Rd
London N5 ....15 C3
Richmond TW10 ....54 B1
Pyrmont Gr SE27 ...75 A1
Pyrmont Rd W4 ....44 C4
Pytchley Rd SE22 ..64 A4

Q

Quadrangle Cl SE1 152 A4
Quadrangle The
SW10 ....167 A4
SW6 ....154 A1
W2 ....102 A2
London SE24 .....63 B2
Quadrant Arc W1 ..119 A3
Quadrant Bsns Ctr
NW6 ....23 A4
Quadrant Gr NW5 ..12 B2
Quadrant The
1 London W2 ....102 C2
Richmond TW9 .....54 A3
Quaker Ct EC1 .....97 A2
Quaker St E1 ..24 B1 98 C1
Quality Ct WC2 ....107 B1
Quantock Ho N16 ...7 B3
Quarenden St
SW6 ....165 C2
Quarry Rd SW18 ...59 B1
Quarterdeck The
E14 ....41 C4
Quartermile La E10, ...
E15 ....19 A4
Quayside Ct **6** ...
SE16 ....32 C1
Quebec & Crown
Wharves E14 .....33 B3
Quebec Ind Est
SE16 ....41 A3
Quebec Mews W1 ..103 A1
Quebec Way SE16 ..41 A4
Quedgeley Ct **3** ...
SE15 ....49 B4
Queen Alexandra Mans
WC1 ....94 A3
Queen Anne Mews
W1 ....104 B3
Queen Anne Rd E9 .17 C2

Queen Anne's Gate
SW1 ....133 B3
Queen Anne's Gdns
London W4 ....38 A3
London W5 ....36 A4
Queen Anne's Gr
London W4 ....38 A3
London W5 ....36 A4
Queen Anne St
W1 ....104 A3
Queen Caroline St
W6 ....39 B1
Queen Charlotte's &
Chelsea Hospl
W12 ....29 C3
Queen Elizabeth College
18 SE10 ....52 B3
Queen Elizabeth Hall &
Purcell Room
..............121 A2
Queen Elizabeth
Hospital for Children
The E2 ....24 C3
Queen Elizabeth II Con
Ctr SW1 ....133 C3
Queen Elizabeth II
Jubilee Sch W9 ...23 B1
Queen Elizabeth's Cl
N16 ....6 C2
Queen Elizabeth's Ct
SE1 ....138 C4
Queen Elizabeth's Wlk
N16 ....6 C2
Queen Elizabeth Wlk
SW13 ....47 A2
Queenhithe EC4 ...123 A4
Queen Margaret Flats **2**
E2 ....25 A2
Queen Margaret's Gr
N1 ....16 A3
Queen Margaret's Gr
N1 ....16 A3
Queen Mary's Gdns
NW1 ....91 B3
Queen Mary's Hospl
NW3 ....2 A1
Queen Mary's Univ
Hospl SW15 .....56 C1
Queen Mary, Univ of
London E1 ....26 A1
Queen of Denmark Ct
SE16 ....41 B3
Queensberry Mews W
SW7 ....143 B4
Queensberry Pl
SW7 ....143 B4
Queensberry Way
SW7 ....143 B4
Queensborough Mews
W2 ....114 C4
Queensborough Pas
W2 ....114 C4
Queensborough Terr
W2 ....114 C4
Queensbridge Ct **1**
E2 ....24 B3
Queensbridge Inf Sch
E8 ....16 B1
Queensbridge Rd
E2,E8 ....16 B1
Queensbury St N1 ..15 B1

Queen's CE Prim Sch The TW9 ....44 C3
Queen's Cir SW11 ...160 A1
Queen's Club Gdns W14 ....154 B4
Queen's Club The W14 ....154 B1
Queen's Coll W1 ......104 A3
Queen's Cres NW5 ...12 C2
Queen's Cres TW10 ...54 B2
Queen's Ct E14 ....33 B2
SW11 ....170 A4
Queen's Ct NW8 ......79 C2
W2 ....114 B3
Queens Ct SE5 ....49 A4
Queen's Ct Barnes SW13 ....56 C4
3 Richmond TW10 ...54 B1
Queensdale Cres W11 ....30 C1
Queensdale Pl W11 ....112 A1
Queensdale Rd W11 ....31 A1 112 A1
Queensdale Wlk W11 ....112 A1
Queens Down Rd E5 ....17 A4
Queen's Dr N4 ....6 A2
Queen's Elm Sq SW3 ....143 C1
Queen's Gallery The SW1 ....132 B3
Queen's Gate SW7 ...129 A3
Queen's Gate Gdns SW7 ....129 A2
Queensgate Gdns SW15 ....57 A3
Queen's Gate Mews SW7 ....129 A2
Queen's Gate Pl SW7 ....129 A2
Queensgate Pl NW6 ....10 C1
Queen's Gate Pl Mews SW7 ....129 A2
Queen's Gate Terr SW7 ....129 A2
Queen's Gate Villas E9 ....18 A1
Queen's Gdns W2 ...114 C4
Queen's Gr NW8 ......79 C3
Queen's Head Pas EC2 ....108 C2
Queen's Head St N1 ...86 B3
Queen's Head Yd SE1 ....123 B1
Queens Ho 5 SE17 ...48 C4
Queensland Ho 7 E16 ....76 C1
Queensland Pl N7 ....14 C4
Queensland Rd N7 ...14 C4
Queens Manor Prim Sch SW6 ....47 C4
Queen's Mans NW6 ...11 A3
Queen's Mans W6 ....39 C2
Queensmead NW8 ...79 C4
Queensmere Cl SW19 ....69 C2
Queensmere Ct SW13 ....46 C4
Queensmere Rd SW19 ....69 C2
Queen's Mews W2 ...114 A4
Queensmill Sch SW6 ...47 C3

Queensmill Sch SW6 ....166 B1
Queens Par NW2 ....9 B2
Queens Park Com Sch NW6 ....22 C4
Queen's Park Ct 5 W10 ....22 C2
Queen's Park Prim Sch W10 ....23 A1
Queen's Park Sta NW6 ....23 B3
Queen Sq WC1 ....106 B4
Queen Sq Pl WC1 ....94 B1
Queen's Quay EC4 ...123 A4
Queen's Rd London SE14,SE15 .....50 B2
Mortlake SW14 ....55 C4
Richmond TW10 ....54 B1
Queen's Ride SW13 ...57 A4
Queen's Rise TW10 ...54 B1
Queen's Road Sta SE15 ....50 B2
Queen's Row SE17 ...48 C4
Queen St EC4 ....123 A4
W1 ....118 A2
Queens Terr NW8 .....79 B2
Queenstown Rd SW8 ....160 A2
Queenstown Road Sta SW8 ....160 A1
Queen St Pl EC4 .....123 A4
Queensville Rd SW12,SW4 ....73 C4
Queensway W2 ....114 B4
Queensway Sta W2 ....114 B3
Queen's Wlk SW1 ...118 C1
Queen's Wood Ct 5 SW4 ....62 A2
Queens Yd W1 ....93 A1
Queen's Yd SE5 ....49 B1
Queen Victoria Mon SW1 ....132 C4
Queen Victoria St EC4 ....122 C4
Quelch Ho 3 N19 .....13 C3
Quemerford Rd N7 ...14 B3
Quendon Ho W10 .....22 B1
Quenington Ct 5 SE15 ....49 B4
Quennel Ho 7 SW12 ....73 B4
Quentington Mans SW6 ....164 C4
Querrin St SW6 ......166 C1
Quested Ct 27 E8 .....17 A3
Quex Mews NW6 .....23 C4
Quex Rd NW6 ....23 C4
Quick Rd W4 ....38 A1
Quick St N1 ....86 B1
Quickswood NW3 ...12 A1
Quill La SW15 ....57 C3
Quilt St N1 ....5 C1
Quilp St SE1 ....136 C4
Quilter St W9 ....23 B2
Quilter St E2 ....24 C2 B3
Quilting Ct 21 SE16 ...40 C4
Quintin Ct W4 ....45 B3
Quintock Ho 2 TW9 ....44 C2
Quinton Ho SW8 ....162 A2
Quinton Kynaston Sch NW8 ....79 B3
Quinton St SW18 .....71 B2
Quixley St E14 ....34 C2
Quorn Rd SE22 ....64 A4

Rabbit Row W8 ......113 C2
Raby St E14 ....33 A3
Rachel Point E5 ....16 C4
Racine 15 SE5 ....49 A2
Racton Rd SW6 ......155 B3
Radbourne Cl E5 ....17 C4
Radbourne Rd SW12 ....73 C3
Radcliff Bldg EC1 ...107 C3
Radcliffe Ave NW10 ...21 C3
Radcliffe Ho 10 SE16 ....40 A2
Radcliffe Path SW8 ....170 B1
Radcliffe Rd SE1 ....138 C2
Radcliffe Sq SW15 ...57 C1
Radcot St SE11 ......149 C1
Raddington Rd W10 ...31 A4
Radford Ho 3 E14 ...34 A3
London N7 ....14 B3
Radford Rd SE13 .....67 B1
Radipole Rd SW6 ...164 C4
Radland Rd E16 ....75 B1
Radlett Pl NW8 ....80 A4
Radley Ct 23 SE16 ...40 C4
Radley Ho NW1 ......90 C2
Radley Lo 35 SW19 ...69 C3
Radley Mews W8 ...127 C1
Radley Terr 1 E16 ...35 B2
Radnor Lo 27 W2 ...101 C1
Radnor Mews W2 ...101 C1
Radnor Pl W2 ....102 A1
Radnor Rd NW6 ......23 A4
SE15 ....49 C3
Radnor St EC1 ....97 A3
Radnor Terr W14 ....140 C4
Radnor Way NW10 ...20 A1
Radnor Wlk 11 E14 ...41 C2
SW3 ....144 C1
Radstock St SW11 ...158 A1
Radway Ho 58 W2 ...31 C4
Radwell Ho SW2 .....62 C2
Raebarn Ct 6 SW16 ....74 A1
Raeburn St SW2 ....62 A3
Ragate Ho 5 E5 ....16 C4
Ragged School Mus The E3 ....33 A4
Raglan Ct SW9 ....62 C4
Raglan St NW5 ....13 A2
Ragley Cl W3 ....37 B4
Rahere Ho EC1 ....96 C4
Railey Mews NW5 ...13 B3
Railton Rd SE24 ......63 A2
Railway App SE1 ....123 C2
Railway Ave SE16 ...40 B4
Railway Cotts W6 ...39 B4
Railway Gr SE14 .....51 B3
Railway Rise SE22 ...64 A3
Railway Side SW13 ...56 A4
Railway St N1 ....84 B1
Railway Terr SE13 ...67 A2
Rainbow Ave E14 .....42 A1
Rainbow Ct 3 SE14 ...51 A4
Rainbow Quay SE16 ...41 A3
Rainbow St SE5 ....49 A3
Raine's Foundation Sch E2 ....25 A2
Raines Foundation Sec Sch E2 ....25 B2
Raine St E1 ....32 A1
Rainford Ho 3 N7 .....5 B2
Rainham Cl SW11 .....60 A1
Rainham Ho NW1 .....83 A3
Rainham Rd NW10 ...22 B2

Rainhill Way E3 ....26 C2
Rainsborough Ave SE8 ....41 A2
Rainsford Ct NW10 ...19 C3
Rainsford Ho 14 SW2 ....62 B2
Rainsford Rd NW10 ...20 A3
Rainsford St W2 ....102 A2
Rainton Rd SE7 ....43 C1
Rainville Rd W6 ....47 B4
Raleigh Ct 2 SE16 ...32 C1
SE16 ....40 A4
Raleigh Gdns SW2 ...62 B1
Raleigh Ho SW8 .....171 B2
Raleigh Mews N1 .....86 B3
Raleigh Rd TW9 ....54 B4
Raleigh St N1 ....86 B3
Ralph Ct W2 ....100 B2
Ralston St SW3 ......144 C1
Ramar Ho E1 ....111 B4
Ramilies Cl SW2 ......62 A1
Ramillies Pl W1 ......104 C1
Ramillies Rd W4 ....37 C3
Ramillies St W1 ......104 C1
Rampart St E1 ....32 A3
Rampayne St SW1 ...147 B2
Ramsay Ho NW8 ......80 A2
Ramsay Rd W3 ....37 B4
Ramsdean Ho 1
SW1 ....147 C3
Ramsden Rd SW12 ...72 C4
Ramsey Ho SW9 .....163 C1
Ramsey St E2 ....24 C1
Ramsey St 24 C1 99 C2
Ramsfort Ho 4
SE16 ....40 A2
Ramsgate St E8 ....16 B2
Ram St SW18 ....59 A2
Randal Cremer JMI Sch E2 ....24 B3
Randall Cl SW11 ....168 A4
Randall Pl SE10 ......52 B3
Randall Rd SE11 ....148 C3
Randall Row SE11 ...148 C3
Randell's Rd N1 ....84 B4
Randolph Ave W9 .....88 C3
Randolph Cres W9 ...88 C2
Randolph Gdns NW6 ....78 A1
Randolph Mews W9 ...89 A1
Randolph Rd W9 ......89 A1
Randolph St NW1 ....13 B1
Ranelagh Ave Barnes SW13 ....46 C1
Fulham SW6 ....58 B4
Ranelagh Gardens Mans SW6 ....58 B4
Ranelagh Gardens (site of Chelsea Flower Show) SW1 ...145 C1
Ranelagh Gdns Chiswick W4 ....45 B3
London SW6 ....58 B4
3 London W6 ....38 B3
Ranelagh Gr SW1 ...145 C2
Ranelagh Ho SW3 ...144 C2
Ranelagh Mans SW6 ....165 A2
Ranelagh Rd E11 ....19 C4
London SW1 ....21 B3
Rangdon St EC3 .....110 C1
Rangers Sq SE10 .....52 C2
Rangoon Ho 6 E16 ...76 B4
Rankine Ho SE1 .....136 C1
Ranmere St SW12 ...73 A3
Rann Ho 1 SW14 ...55 C4
Rannoch Rd W6 ....47 C4
Ranston St NW1 ....102 A4
Ranulf Rd NW2 ....10 B4

Ranwell Cl 11 E3 .....26 B4
Ranwell Ho 10 E3 ...26 B4
Raphael Ct 5 SE16 ...40 A1
Raphael St SW7 .....130 C3
Rapley Ho 2 E2 ....99 B3
Rashleigh Ct 3
SW8 ....61 A4
Rashleigh Ho WC1 ...94 A3
Rastell Ave SW2 ......73 C3
Ratcliffe Cross St
E1 ....32 C3
Ratcliffe Ho 10 E14 ...33 A3
Ratcliffe La 13 E14 ...33 A3
Ratcliffe Orch 3
E1 ....32 C2
Rathbone Ho 5 E16 ...35 B1
NW6 ....23 C4
Rathbone Mkt 2
E16 ....35 B2
Rathbone Pl W1 .....105 B2
Rathbone Point E5 ...16 C4
Rathbone St E16 .....35 B1
W1 ....105 A3
Rathgar Rd SW9 ......63 A4
Rathmell Dr SW4 .....61 C1
Rattray Rd SW2 ......62 C2
Raul Rd SE15 ....49 C2
Raveley St NW5 ......13 B4
Ravenet St SW11 ...170 A3
Ravenfield Rd SW17 ...72 B1
Raven Ho 10 SE16 ...40 C2
Ravenna Rd SW15 ...57 C2
Raven Row E1 ....32 A4
Ravensbourne Ho
NW8 ....102 A4
Ravensbourne Pl
SE13 ....52 A1
Ravensbury Rd
SW18 ....71 A2
Ravensbury Terr
SW18 ....71 A2
Ravenscar NW1 ....82 C3
Ravenscourt 1 N16 ...7 C1
Ravenscourt Ave
W6 ....38 C2
Ravenscourt Gdns
W6 ....38 C2
Ravenscourt Park Mans
W6 ....39 A3
Ravenscourt Park Prep Sch W6 ....38 C2
Ravenscourt Park Sta
W6 ....39 A2
Ravenscourt Pk W6 ...39 A2
Ravenscourt Pl W6 ...39 A2
Ravenscourt Rd W6 ...39 A2
Ravenscourt Sq W6 ...38 C3
Ravenscourt Theatre Sch W6 ....39 A2
Ravenscroft Ave
NW11 ....1 B4
Ravenscroft Cl 4
E16 ....35 C4
Ravenscroft Ct NW11 ...1 B4
Ravenscroft Rd
Acton W4 ....37 B2
Ravenscroft St E2 .....99 A4
Ravensdon St
SE11 ....149 C1
Ravenshaw St NW6 ...10 B3
Ravenslea Rd SW11,
SW12 ....72 B4
Ravensmede Way
W4 ....38 B2
Ravenstone SE17 ....152 B1

Ravenstone Prim Sch SW12 ....72 C2
Ravenstone St SW12 ....72 C2
Ravenswood Rd SW12 ....73 A4
Ravensworth Ct SW6 ....155 B1
Ravensworth Rd NW10 ....22 A2
Raven Wharf SE1 ....138 C4
Ravey St EC2 ....24 A1 98 A2
Rav Pinter Cl N16 ....7 A4
Rawlings St SW3 ....144 C4
Rawlinson Ho SE13 ....67 C3
Rawlinson Point 8
E16 ....35 B2
Rawreth Wlk N1 ....87 A4
Rawson Ct SW11 ....169 C3
Rawson St SW11 ....170 A3
Rawstorne Pl EC1 ....96 A4
Rawstorne St EC1 ....96 A4
Rayburne Ct W14 ....126 A2
Raydon St N19 ....4 A2
Ray Ho 8 W10 ....30 C3
Raymede Twr W10 ....30 C3
Raymouth Rd SE16 ....40 A2
Raynald Ho 15
SW16 ....74 A1
Rayne Ct SE1 ....138 C4
Rayne Ho W9 ....88 A2
1 London SW12 ....60 C1
Rayner Ct 10 W12 ....39 B4
Rayner's Rd SW15 ....58 A2
Raynes Ct NW2 ....10 A4
Raynham W2 ....102 A2
Raynham Ho 1 E1 ....25 C1
Raynham Rd W6 ....39 A2
Raynor Pl N1 ....87 A4
Ray St EC1 ....95 C1
Ray Wlk N7 ....5 B2
Reachview Cl 14
NW1 ....13 B1
Reade Ct 3 W3 ....37 B3
Reade Ho 7 SE10 ....52 C4
Reade Wlk 6 NW10 ....8 A1
Read Ho 5 SE11 ....163 B4
Reading Ho SE15 ....49 C4
W2 ....100 C1
Reading La E8 ....17 A2
Reardon Ho 5 E1 ....32 A1
Reardon Path 51 E1 ....32 A1
Reardon St E1 ....32 A1
Reaston St SE14 ....50 C3
Reay Prim Sch
SW9 ....163 A1
Reckitt Rd W4 ....38 A1
Record St SE16 ....50 B4
Rector St N1 ....86 C3
Rectory Gdns SW4 ....61 B4
Rectory Gr SW4 ....61 B4
Rectory Rd
Barnes SW13 ....46 C1
London N16 ....7 B1
1 London W3 ....28 B1
Rectory Road Sta
N16 ....7 B1
Rectory Sq E1 ....32 C4
Reculver Ho 2
SE15 ....50 B4
Reculver Rd SE16 ....40 C1
Red Anchor Cl
SW3 ....158 A3
Redan Pl W2 ....100 A1
Redan St W14 ....39 C3
Redan Terr SE5 ....48 A1

Redbourne Ho 7
E14 ....33 B3
Redburn Ho W10 ....23 B2
Redbridge Gdns
SE5 ....49 A3
Redburn St SW3 ....158 C4
Redcar St SE5 ....48 B3
Redcastle Cl E1 ....32 B2
Redchurch St
E2 ....24 B1 98 C2
Redcliffe Cl 5
SW10 ....142 A1
Redcliffe Gdns
SW10 ....156 B4
London W4 ....45 A3
Redcliffe Mews
SW10 ....142 B1
Redcliffe Pl SW10 ....156 C3
Redcliffe Rd SW10 ....157 A4
Redcliffe Sch
SW10 ....156 C4
Redcliffe Sq SW10 ....142 B1
Redcliffe St SW10 ....156 B4
Redclyf Ho 10 E1 ....25 B1
Redcroft 6 NW6 ....11 A2
Redcross Way SE1 ....123 A1
Reddins Rd SE15 ....49 C4
Rede Pl W2 ....31 A2 113 C4
Redesdale St SW3 ....158 C4
Redfern Rd NW10 ....8 A1
Redfield La SW5 ....142 A4
Redfield Mews
SW5 ....141 C4
Rediff Est SE14 ....41 B3
Redford Wlk N1 ....86 C4
Redgate Terr SW15 ....57 C1
Redgrave Rd SW15 ....57 C4
Redhill Ct SW2 ....74 C2
Redhill St NW1 ....92 B4
Redington Gdns
NW3 ....11 A4
Redington Ho N1 ....85 A2
Redington Rd NW3 ....11 A4
Redlands Prim Sch

Redlands Way SW2 ....74 B4
Red Lion Cl 9 SE17 ....48 C4
Red Lion Ct EC4 ....107 C1
Red Lion Row SE17 ....48 B4
Red Lion Sq WC1 ....106 C3
Red Lion St WC1 ....106 C3
Red Lion Yd W1 ....117 C2
Redlynch Ct W14 ....126 B3
Redlynch Ho SW9 ....173 C4
Redman Bldg EC1 ....107 C3
Redman Ho N1 ....137 A3
Redman's Rd E1 ....32 B4
Redmayne Ho
SW9 ....173 A2
Redmead La E1 ....125 B1
Redmill Ho 24 E1 ....25 A1
Redmond Ho N1 ....85 A3
Redmore Rd W6 ....39 A2
Red Pl W1 ....117 B4
Red Post Hill SE21,
SE24 ....63 C2
Redriff Prim Sch
SE16 ....41 A4
Redriff Rd SE16 ....41 A3
Red Rover SW13 ....56 C4
Redrup Ho 24 SE14 ....50 C4
Redruth Rd E9 ....25 B4
Red Sq The N16 ....6 C1
Redstart Ct SE14 ....51 A3
Redvers St E2 ....98 B4
Redwood Cl SE16 ....33 A1
Redwood Ct
London N19 ....4 C4

Redwood Ct continued
London NW6 ....10 A1
Redwood Mews 2
SW4 ....61 A4
Redwoods SW15 ....68 C3
Reece Mews SW7 ....143 B4
Reed Cl E16 ....35 C4
Reedham St SE15 ....64 C4
Reed Ho SW15 ....56 C1
Reedholm Villas
N16 ....15 C4
Reed's Pl NW1 ....13 B1
Reedworth St
SE11 ....149 C3
Reef Ho E14 ....42 B3
Rees St N1 ....87 A3
Reeves Ho SE1 ....135 B3
W1 ....117 B3
Reeves Mews W1 ....117 C3
Reeves Rd E3 ....27 A1
Reform St 5 SW11 ....169 A2
London SW11 ....168 C2
Regal Cl E1 ....111 B4
Regal La NW1 ....81 C3
Regal Pl 6 E3 ....26 B2
SW6 ....156 B1
Regan Way N1 ....24 A3
Regatta Point TW8 ....44 B4
Regency Ct 3 E9 ....25 B4
Regency Lo NW3 ....11 C1
Regency Mews 3
NW10 ....8 C2
Regency St SW1 ....147 C3
Regency Wlk 6
TW10 ....54 A2
Regent Cl NW4 ....90 A3
1 London N16 ....7 A1
Regent Ho W14 ....140 A4
Regent Lo 9 SW2 ....74 B3
Regent Pl W1 ....119 A4
Regent Rd SE24 ....63 A2
Regents Bridge Gdns
SW8 ....162 B2
Regents Canal Ho 2
E14 ....33 A3
Regent's Coll NW1 ....91 B2
Regents Ct 8
E14 ....24 C4
Regents Gate Ho 20

Regents Mews NW8 ....79 A2
Regent's Park 3
NW1 ....81 B1
Regent's Park Barracks
NW1 ....82 B1
Regent's Park Rd
NW1 ....81 B4
Regent's Park Sta
NW1 ....92 A1
Regent's Park Terr
NW1 ....82 A4
Regents Pl SE3 ....53 C1
Regents Plaza NW6 ....78 A2
Regent Sq 2 E3 ....27 A2
London WC1 ....94 B3
Regent's Row 8 ....24 C4
Regent St W1 ....118 C4
London W4 ....36 C1
Regents Wharf
3 E2 ....25 A4
N1 ....84 C2
Reginald Pl 6 SE8 ....51 C3
Reginald Rd SE8 ....51 C3
Reginald Sq SE8 ....51 C3
Regina Point SE16 ....40 B3
Regina Rd N4 ....5 B3
Regis Ct NW1 ....102 C4
Regis Pl 17 SW2 ....62 B3
Regis Rd NW5 ....13 A3

Regnart Bldgs NW1 ....93 A3
Reid Ct SW14 ....45 B1
Reighton Rd E5 ....7 C2
Reizel Cl N16 ....7 B3
Relay Rd W12 ....30 B1
Relf Rd SE15 ....64 C4
Reliance Sq E2 ....98 B2
Relton Mews SW7 ....130 B2
Rembrandt Cl E14 ....42 C3
Rembrandt Ct 10
SE16 ....40 A1
Remington St N1 ....86 B1
Remnant St WC2 ....106 C2
Remsted Ho NW6 ....78 A3
Remus Rd E3 ....18 C1
Renbold Ho 5 SE10 ....52 B2
Rendlesham Ho 3
E5,N16 ....7 C1
Rendlesham Rd E5 ....7 C1
Renforth St SE16 ....40 B4
Renfrew Ho NW6 ....78 A1
Renfrew Rd SE11 ....150 A3
Rennell Ho 19 E9 ....17 C2
Rennell St SE13 ....67 B4
Rennie Cotts 2 E1 ....25 B1
Rennie Ct SE1 ....122 A2
Rennie Ho SE1 ....136 C1
Rennie St SE1 ....122 A2
Renoir Ct 7 SE16 ....40 A1
Renton Cl SW2 ....62 B1
Rephidim St SE1 ....138 A1
Replingham Rd
SW18 ....70 C3
Reporton Rd SW6 ....154 B1
Repton Ho 2 E14 ....33 A3
SW1 ....147 A3
Repton St E14 ....33 A3
Re Sassoon Ho
SE15 ....50 B3
Reservoir Rd SE4 ....51 A1
Restell Cl SE3 ....53 A4
Reston Pl SW7 ....128 C3
Restoration Sq
SW11 ....167 C3
Retcar Pl N19 ....4 A2
Retford St N1 ....24 A3
Retreat Ho 6 E9 ....17 B2
Retreat Pl E9 ....17 B2
Retreat The SW14 ....56 A4
Reunion Row E1 ....32 A2
Reveley Sq SE16 ....41 A4
Revelon Rd SE4 ....66 A4
Revelstoke Rd
SW18,SW19 ....70 C2
Rewell St SW6 ....156 C2
Rex Pl W1 ....117 C2
Reynard Cl SE4 ....66 A4
Reynard Pl SE14 ....51 A4
Reynolds Cl NW11 ....2 A4
Reynolds Ho 19 E2 ....25 B3
NW8 ....79 C1
SW1 ....147 C4
London N4 ....5 A3
Reynolds Pl 2
TW10 ....54 B1
Reynolds Rd
London SE15 ....65 B3
London W4 ....37 B3
Rheidol Mews N1 ....86 C2
Rheidol Terr N1 ....86 C3
Rhoda St 2 E2 ....24 A1 99 A2
Rhodes Ho N1 ....97 B4
W12 ....30 A1
Rhodesia Rd SW9 ....172 B1
Rhodes St N7 ....14 B3
Rhodeswell Rd E14 ....33 A4

Rhondda Gr E3 ....26 B2
Rhyl Prim Sch NW5 ....12 C2
Rhyl St NW5 ....12 C2
Ribblesdale Ho 3
NW6 ....23 C4
Ribbon Dance Mews
SE5 ....48 C2
Ribstone Ho 12 E9 ....17 C2
Ricardo St E14 ....34 A3
Riceyman Ho WC1 ....95 B3
Richard Anderson Ct
7 SE14 ....50 C3
Richard Atkins Prim Sch
SW2 ....74 A4
Richard Burbidge Mans
SW13 ....47 B4
Richard Cloudesley Sch
EC1 ....96 C1
Richard Cobden Prim
Sch NW1 ....83 A3
Richard Fox Ho N4 ....6 B1
Richard Ho 8 SE16 ....40 B2
Richard Knight Ho
SW6 ....165 C4
Richard Neale Ho 2
E1 ....32 A2
Richardson Cl 8 E8 ....24 B4
Richardson Ct
SW4 ....172 B2
Richardson's Mews
W1 ....92 C1
Richard's Pl SW3 ....144 B4
Richard St 10 E1 ....32 A3
Richbell Pl WC1 ....106 C4
Richborne Terr
SW8 ....163 A2
Richborough Ho
SE15 ....50 B4
14 London E5 ....17 A4
Richborough Rd
NW2 ....10 A4
Richford Gate W6 ....39 B3
Richford St W6 ....39 B3
Rich La SW5 ....142 A2
Richman Ho 10 SE8 ....41 B1
Richmond Ave N1 ....85 A4
NW10 ....9 B2
Richmond Bldgs
W1 ....105 B1
Richmond Circus
TW9 ....54 A3
Richmond Coll W8 ....128 B2
Richmond Cres N1 ....85 B4
Richmond Ct SW1 ....131 A3
Richmond Gr N1 ....15 A1
Richmond Hill
TW10 ....54 A1
Richmond Hill Ct 5
TW10 ....54 A1
Richmond Ho NW1 ....82 B1
12 Forest Hill SE23 ....76 C1
Richmond International
Bsns Ctr 18 TW9 ....54 B3
Richmond Mans
SW5 ....142 A2
Putney SW15 ....58 A4
Richmond Mews
W1 ....105 B1
Richmond Park Rd
SW14 ....55 C3
Richmond Rd
London E8 ....16 C1

Richmond Rd continued
London W5 ....36 A4
Richmond Sta W4 .....54 A3
Richmond Terr
SW1 ....134 A4
Richmond Way
W12,W14 ....39 C4
Rich St E14 ....33 B2
Rickard Cl SW2 ....74 C3
Rickett St SW6 ...155 C4
Rickman St 🔟 E1 ...25 B1
Rickman St 🔟 E1 ...25 B1
Rick Roberts Way
E15 ....27 C3
Rickthorne Rd 🔟
N19 ....5 A2
Riddell Ct SE1 ....152 C2
Ridgdale St E3 ....27 A3
Ridge Hill NW11 ......1 A3
Ridge Rd NW2 ....1 C1
Ridgeway 🔟 TW10 ..54 A1
Ridgeway Dr W3 ....36 C3
Ridgeway Gdns N6 ...4 B4
Ridgeway The
Acton W3 ....36 C3
London NW11 ....1 B3
Ridgewell Cl N1 ...87 A4
Ridgmount Gdns
WC1 ....105 B4
Ridgmount Pl WC1 105 B4
Ridgmount Rd
SW18 ....59 A2
Ridgmount St WC1 105 B4
Ridgway Rd SW9 ...63 A4
Riding House St
W1 ....104 C3
Ridings Cl N6 ....4 B4
Riding The NW11 ......1 B4
Ridley Ho 🔟 SW11 ..60 A4
Rigo Ho 🔟 E1 ....32 C4
Riley Ho SW10 ....157 B3
🔟 Bow E3 ....26 C1
🔟 Streatham SW4 .....73 C4
Riley Rd SE1 ....138 C2
Riley St SW10 .....157 B2
Rill Ho 🔟 SE5 ....49 A3
Rimini Ct SW12 .....72 B3
Rinaldo Rd SW12 ...73 A4
Ringcroft St N7 .....14 C3
Ring Cross Prim Sch
N7 ....14 B3
Ringford Ho SW18 ..58 B2
Ringford Rd SW18 ...58 C1
Ring Ho 🔟 E1 ....32 B2
Ringmer Ave SW6 .164 B3
Ringmer Gdns 🖪
N19 ....5 A2
Ringmer Ho 🔟
SE22 ....64 A4
Ringsfield Ho
SE17 ....151 A1

Ringwood Gdns
🔟 E14 ....41 C2
Roehampton SW15 ...68 C3
Ripley Gdns SW14 ...55 C4
Ripley Ho 🔟 SW1 ..160 C4
Mortlake SW14 ....56 A4
Riplington Ct SW15 .69 A4
Ripplevale Gr N1 ....14 C1
Risborough SE17 ...150 C4
Risborough Ho
NW8 ....90 B2
Risborough St SE1 .136 B4
Risdon Ho 🔟 SE16 ..40 B4
Risdon St 🔟 SE16 ...40 B4
Riseholme Ho 🖪
SE22 ....64 A4
Riseldine Rd SE23 ..66 A1
Risinghill St N1 .....85 B2
Rising Sun Ct EC1 ..108 B3
Risley Ho 🖪 E9 ......17 C2
Rita Rd SW8 ....162 C2
Ritchie Ho 🖪 SE16 ..40 B3
London N19 ....4 C2
🔟 South Bromley
E14 ....34 C3
Ritchie St N1 ....85 C2
Ritherdon Rd SW17 .73 A2
Ritson Ho N1 ....85 A2
Ritson Rd E8 ....16 C2
Rivaz Pl E9 ....17 B2
Riven Ct 🖪 W2 ....100 A2
Riverains The
SW11 ....167 B3
River Barge Cl E14 ..42 B4
Rivercourt Rd W6 ...39 A1
River Ct SE1 ....122 A3
Riverdale Dr SW18 ..71 A3
Riverfleet WC1 ......94 B4
Riverford Ho SW2 ...62 B2
River Ho SW13 ......46 A1
Rivermead Ct SW6 ..58 B4
Rivermead Ho E9 ...18 A3
River Pl N1 ....15 B1
Riversdale Prim Sch
N5 ....15 A4
Riversdale Rd N5 ....6 B1
Riversdene N5 ....6 B1
Rivers Ho 🔟 TW8 ...36 C1
Riverside SW11 ....158 B2
WC1 ....94 B4
Riverside Bsns Ctr
SW18 ....71 A3
Riverside Ct SW8 ..161 C4
Barnes SW13 ....46 A4
Dartford W4 ....46 A2
Riverside Gdns W6 ..39 A1
Riverside Mans 🔟
E1 ....32 B1
Riverside Prim Sch
SE16 ....139 C3
Riverside Rd E15 ...27 B3
SW17 ....71 B1
Wandsworth SW17,
SW19 ....71 B1
Riverside West
SW18 ....59 A3
Riverside Workshops
SE1 ....123 A2
River St EC1 ....95 B4
River Terr W6 ....39 B1
Riverton Cl 🔟 W9 ...23 B2
Riverview Gdns
SW13 ....47 A4
Riverview Gr W4 ....45 A4
Riverview Rd W4 ....45 A4
River Way SE10 .....43 B3
Rivet Ho SE1 ....153 A2
Rivington Ct NW10 ..21 C4

Rivington Pl EC2 .....98 B3
Rivington St EC2 .....98 A3
Rivington Wlk 🖪
E8 ....24 C4
Rixon St N7 ....5 C1
Roach Rd E3 ....18 C1
Roach Works 🖪 E3 ..18 C1
Roads Pl N19 ....5 A2
Roan St SE10 ....52 B4
Robert Adam St
W1 ....103 B2
Roberta St 🖪
E2 ....24 C2 99 C3
Robert Bell Ho
SE16 ....153 B4
Robert Blair Prim Sch
N7 ....14 A2
Robert Browning Prim
Sch SE17 ....151 B2
Robert Cl W9 ....89 A1
Robert Dashwood Way
SE17 ....150 C3
Robert Gentry Ho
W14 ....140 B1
Robert Jones Ho
SE16 ....153 B4
Robert Keen Cl 🖪
SE15 ....49 C2
Robert Lowe Cl
SE14 ....50 C3
Robert Owen Ho 🖪
E2 ....99 A4
Fulham SW6 ....47 C2
Robert Owen Lo 🖪
E8 ....25 A4
Roberts Ct N1 ....86 B4
London NW10 ....8 A2
Roberts Ho 🖪 SE27 ..75 A1
Roberts Mews
SW1 ....131 B1
Robertson Ho 🔟
E14 ....41 C3
Robertson Rd E15 ..27 B4
Robertson St SW8 ..170 B1
Robert's Pl EC1 ......95 C2
Robert St NW1 ....92 B3
WC2 ....120 B3
Robert Sutton Ho 🖪
E1 ....32 B3
Robeson St 🖪 E3 ....33 B4
Robin Ct 🖪 E14 ......42 B3
Robin Gr N6 ....3 C2
Robin Ho NW8 ....80 A1
Robin Hood SW15 ..68 A1
Robin Hood Gdns 🖪
E14 ....34 B2
Robin Hood La E14 ..34 B2
Robinscroft Mews
SE10 ....52 A2
Robins Ct TW10 .....54 A3
Robin's Ct SW4 ......62 A1
Robinsfield Inf Sch
NW8 ....80 A2
Robinson Ct N1 ......86 B4
🖪 Richmond TW9 .....54 B3
Robinson Ho 🔟 E14 ..33 C4
🖪 London W10 ....30 C3
Robinson Rd E2 .....25 B3
Robinson St SW3 ...158 C4
Robsart St SW9 ....173 B2
Robson Ave NW10 ...8 C1
Robson Rd SE21,
SE27 ....75 B1
Roby Ho 🔟 EC1 ......96 C2
Rochdale Way 🖪
SE8 ....51 C3
Roche Ho 🔟 E14 ....33 B2
Rochelle Cl SW11 ...59 C3

Rochelle Ct 🔟 E1 ...32 B3
Rochelle St 🖪
E2 ....98 C3
Rochemont Wlk 🖪
E8 ....24 C4 99 A4
Rochester Ct 🖪 E2 ..25 A1
🔟 London NW1 ......13 B1
Rochester Ho 🔟 SE1 137 C3
🔟 SE15 ....50 B4
Rochester Mews
NW1 ....13 B1
Rochester Pl NW1 ..13 B1
Rochester Rd NW1 ..13 B2
Rochester Row
SW1 ....147 A4
Rochester Sq NW1 ..13 B1
Rochester St SW1 ..133 B1
Rochester Terr
NW1 ....13 B2
Rochester Wlk
SE1 ....123 B2
Rochford Wlk 🖪 E8 ..16 C1
Rochfort Ho 🖪 SE8 ..41 B1
Rock Ave 🔟 SW14 ...55 C4
Rockefeller Ho E3 ...26 C3
Rockell's Pl SE22 ...65 A1
Rockfield Ho SE10 ..52 B4
Rock Grove Way
SE16 ....153 C4
Rockhall Rd NW2 ....9 C4
Rockingham Cl
SW15 ....56 B3
Rockingham St
SE1 ....136 C1
Rockland Rd SW15 ..58 A3
Rockley Ct 🖪 W14 ..39 C4
Rockley Rd W14 ....39 C4
Rocks La SW13 ......56 C4
Rock St N4 ....5 C2
Rockstraw Ho 🖪
NW3 ....12 B1
Rockwood Ct N16 ....7 C4
Rocliffe St N1 ....86 B1
Rocque Ho 🔟 SW6 ..154 C2
Rodborough Rd
NW11 ....1 C3
Rodenhurst Ct SW4 ..61 C2
Rodenhurst Rd SW4 ..61 C1
Roden St N7 ....5 B1
Roderick Ho 🖪
SE16 ....40 B2
Roderick Rd NW3 ...12 B4
Rodgers Ho 🖪 SW4 ..73 C4
Rodin Ct N1 ....86 B4
Roding Ho 🔟 N1 .....85 B3
Roding Mews E1 ...125 C2
Roding Rd E5 ....18 A3
Rodmarton St W1 ..103 A3
Rodmell WC1 ....94 B3
Rodmere St 🖪 SE10 ..43 A1
Rodmill La SW2 .....74 A4
Rodney Ct NW8 .....89 A2
Rodney Ho 🖪 E14 ...42 A2
N1 ....85 A1
🔟 London W11 ......113 B4
Rodney Pl SE17 ....151 A4
Rodney Rd SE17 ...151 B3
Rodney St N1 ....85 A1
Rodway Rd SW15 ...69 B4
Rodwell Rd SE22 ....64 B1
Roebuck Ho 🔟 SW1 132 C2
Roedean Cres SW15 ..56 A2
Roehampton CE Prim
Sch SW15 ....56 C3
Roehampton Cl
SW15 ....56 C3
Roehampton Ct
SW13 ....56 C4

Roehampton Gate
SW15 ....56 A1
Roehampton High St
SW15 ....68 C4
Roehampton La
Putney SW15 ....56 C1
Roehampton SW15 ..69 A3
Roehampton Vale
SW15 ....68 B2
Roffey St E14 ....42 B4
Roger Dowley Ct 🖪
E2 ....25 B3
Roger's Almshouses 🖪
SW9 ....62 B3
Rogers Est 🖪 E2 .....25 B2
Rogers Ho SW1 ....147 C4
Rogers Rd E16 ....35 B3
Roger St WC1 ....95 A1
Rokeby Ho WC1 .....94 C1
🖪 Balham SW12 .....73 A4
Rokeby Rd SE4 ......51 B1
Rokeby Sch E15 .....19 C1
Rokeland Ho SE4 ...66 A3
Roland Gdns SW7 ..143 A2
Roland Mews 🔟 E1 ..32 C4
SW7 ....143 A2
Rollins St SE15 ....50 B4
Rollit Ho N7 ....14 C3
Rollit St N7 ....14 C3
Rollo St SW11 ......170 A3
Rolls Bldgs EC4 ....107 C2
Rollscourt Ave SE24 ..63 B2
Rolls Pas EC4 ....107 B2
Rolls Rd SE1 ....153 A2
Rolt St SE8 ....51 A4
Roman Cl W3 ....37 A4
Romanfield Rd SW2 ..74 B4
Roman Rd E2,E3 ....25 C3
🖪 E6 ....35 A3
🔟 London W4 ....38 B2
Roman Square Mkt 🖪
E3 ....26 B3
Roman Way N7 .....14 B2
London N7 ....14 B2
Roma Read Cl
SW15 ....69 A4
Romayne Ho SW4 ...61 C4
Romberg Rd SW17 ..72 C1
Romborough Gdns
SE13 ....67 B2
Romborough Way
SE13 ....67 B2
Romer Ho
🔟 London W10 ....23 A2
🖪 London W10 ....23 B2
Romero Cl SW9 ......62 B4
Romeyn Rd SW16 ...74 B1
Romford Ho 🔟 N1 ...15 C2
Romford St E1 ....32 A4
Romilly Rd N4 ....6 A2
Romilly St W1 ......119 C4
Romily Ct SW6 .....164 B2
Romney Cl 🔟 SE14 ..50 B3
N17 ....14 B2
Romney Ct
🖪 London NW3 ......12 A2
🔟 London W12 ....39 B4
Romney Mews W1 ..103 B4
Romney Rd SE10 ...52 C4
Romney St SW1 ....134 A1
Romola Rd SE24,
SW2 ....75 A3
Romsey Ho 🖪
SW11 ....59 C3
Ronald Ross Prim Sch
SW19 ....70 A4

Ronaldshay N4 . . . . .5 C3
Ronalds Rd N5 . . . . .114 C3
Ronald St E1 . . . . .32 B3
Rona Rd NW3 . . . . .12 C4
Rona Wlk 7 N1 . . . . .15 C2
Rondu Rd NW2 . . . . .10 A3
Road La EC3 . . . . .124 A4
Rookery Rd SW4 . . . . .61 A3
Rooke Way SE10 . . . . .43 B1
Rookwood Rd N16 . . . . . . .7 C4
Rootes Dr W10 . . . . .30 C4
Ropemaker Rd
  SE16 . . . . .41 A3
Ropemaker's Fields 7
  E14 . . . . .33 B2
Ropemaker St EC2 . .109 B4
Roper La SE1 . . . . .138 B3
Roper's Orchard
  SW3 . . . . .58 A3
Ropers Wlk 14 SE24 74 C4
Ropery St E3 . . . . .26 B1
Rope St SE16 . . . . .41 A3
Ropewalk Gdns E1 111 C2
Ropley St 2 E2 . . . . . . .24 C3
Rosa Alba Mews N5 15 B4
Rosalind Ho 20 N1 . . . .24 A3
Rosaline Rd SW6 . . . . . .154 B1
Rosaline Terr SW6 . .154 B1
Rosa Parks Ho
  SW9 . . . . .172 C1
Rosary Gdns SW7 . .143 A3
Rosary RC Prim Sch
  NW3 . . . . .11 C3
Rosaville Rd SW6 . . .154 C1
Roscoe St EC1 . . . . .97 A1
Roscommon Ho 2
  NW3 . . . . .11 C3
Rose Alley EC2 . . . . . . .110 B3
SE1 . . . . .123 A2
Rosebank
  London SW6 . . . . .47 B3
  2 London W3 . . . . . . .28 C3
Rosebank Gdns E3 . .26 B3
  11 London W3 . . . . . .28 C3
Rosebank Way W3 . . .28 C3
Rosebank Wlk NW1 . .13 C1
Roseberry Pl E8 . . . . . .16 B2
Roseberry St SE16 . .40 A2
Rosebery Ave EC1 . . . .95 C3
  W1 . . . . .118 A2
Rosebery Ho 22 E2 . .25 B3
Rosebery Sq EC1 . . . . .95 B1
Rose Bruford Coll
  SE8 . . . . .51 C4
Rosebury Rd SW6 .166 B1
Rose Bush Ct NW3 . . .12 B3
Rosecroft Ave NW3 . . .1 C1
Rose & Crown Ct
  EC2 . . . . .108 C2
Rose & Crown Yd
  SW1 . . . . .119 A2
Rose Ct E1 . . . . .111 A3
  N1 . . . . .86 B4
Rosedale Ct N5 . . . . . . .15 A4
Rosedale Ho N16 . . . . . .6 C3
Rosedale Rd TW9 . . .54 A3
Rosedale Terr W6 . . .39 A3
Rosedene Ave
  SW16 . . . . .74 B1
Rosedew Rd W6 . . .47 C4
Rosefield Gdns E14 .33 C2
Rosehart Mews 3
  W11 . . . . .31 C3

Rosehill Rd SW18 . . .59 B2
Roseland Ho SW6 . . .58 A4
Roseleigh Ave N5 . . .15 A4
Rosemary Branch
  Bridge N1 . . . . .87 B3
Rosemary Ct 8 SE8 51 B4
E14 . . . . .34 C3
Rosemary Dr 13
  E14 . . . . .34 C3
Rosemary Gdns
  SW14 . . . . .55 C3
Rosemary Ho N1 . . . .87 C3
Rosemary La SW14 . .55 B4
Rosemary Mews N1 .87 C4
Rosemary Rd SE15 . .49 B3
  Wandsworth SW17 . . .71 B1
Rosemary Works Sch
  N1 . . . . .87 B3
Rosemead Prep Sch
  SE27 . . . . .75 B2
Rosemont Mans 11
  NW3 . . . . .11 A2
Rosemont Rd
  Acton W3 . . . . .28 A2
  London NW3 . . . . .11 C2
  Richmond TW10 . . . .54 A1
Rosemoor St SW3 . .144 C3
Rosemount Ct 2
  W3 . . . . .28 A2
Rosemount Lo W3 . .28 A2
Rosenau Cres
  SW11 . . . . .168 C3
Rosenau Rd SW11 .168 C4
Rosendale Prim Sch
  SE24 . . . . .75 B3
Roseneath Rd SW11 .60 C1
Rosenthal Rd SE6 . .67 B1
Rosenthorpe Rd
  SE15 . . . . .65 C2
Roserton St E14 . . . .42 B4
Rose Sq SW7 . . . . . . .143 C2
Rose St EC4 . . . . .108 B1
  WC2 . . . . .120 A4
Rosethorn Cl SW12 .73 C4
Rosetta Cl SW8 . . . .162 B1
Roseway SE21 . . . . . . .63 C1
Rosewood Ct 2
  E11 . . . . .19 C4
Rosewood Sq W12 .29 C3
Rosher Cl E15 . . . . . . .19 C1
Rosina St E9 . . . . .17 C2
Roskell Rd SW15 . . .57 C4
Roslin Ho 2 E1 . . . . .32 C2
Roslin Rd W3 . . . . . . .37 A3
Rosmead Rd
  W11 . . . . . .31 A2 112 B4
Rosoman Pl EC1 . . . . .95 C2
Ross Ct 4 SW15 . . .69 C4
Rossdale Rd SW15 . .57 B3
Rossendale Way
  NW1 . . . . .83 A4
Rossetti Ct W1 . . . . .105 B4
Rossetti Ho SW1 . . .147 C3
Rossetti Mews NW8 .79 C3
Rossetti Rd SE16 . . . .40 A1
Ross Ho 13 E1 . . . . . . .32 A1
Rossington St E5 . . . . .7 C2
Rossiter Rd SW12 . . .73 A3
Rosslyn Ave SW13 .56 A4
Rosslyn Ct NW3 . . . . .12 A3
Rosslyn Hill NW3 . . . .11 C3
Rosslyn Ho 9 TW9 .44 B2
Rosslyn Mans NW6 .11 B2

Rosslyn Park Mews
  NW3 . . . . .11 C3
Rossmore Ct NW1 . . .90 C2
Rossmore Rd NW1 . .90 B2
Rostrevor Mans
  SW6 . . . . .164 C4
Rostrevor Rd SW6 .164 C4
Rotary St SE1 . . . . . .136 B2
Rothay NW1 . . . . .92 B4
Rothbury Rd E9 . . . .18 C1
Rotherfield Ct 1 N1 .87 B4
Rotherfield Prim Sch
  N1 . . . . .87 A4
Rotherfield St N1 . . .87 A4
Rotherham Wlk
  SE1 . . . . .122 A1
Rotherhithe SE16 . . .33 A1
Rotherhithe Holiday Inn
  Pier SE16 . . . . .33 B1
Rotherhithe New Rd
  SE16 . . . . .40 A1
SE16 . . . . .40 C2
Rotherhithe Old Rd
  SE16 . . . . .40 C2
Rotherhithe Prim Sch
  SE16 . . . . .40 C2
Rotherhithe St SE16 40 A4
  10 SE16 . . . . .40 A4
Rotherhithe Sta
  SE16 . . . . .40 B4
Rotherhithe Tunnel
  SE16 . . . . .32 C1
Rother Ho SE15 . . . .65 A3
Rotherwick Rd NW11 .1 C4
Rothery St N1 . . . . . . .86 B4
Rothesay Ave SW14,
  TW10 . . . . .55 A3
Rothesay Ct SE11 . .163 B3
Rothley Ct NW8 . . . . .89 B2
Rothsay St SE1 . . . . .138 A1
Rothsay Wlk 14 E14 .41 C2
Rothschild Rd W4 . .37 B3
Rothwell St NW1 . . .81 A4
  12 London NW1 . . . . .12 B1
Roth Wlk N7 . . . . .5 B2
Rotten Row SW1 . . .130 C4
Rotterdam Dr E14 . .42 B3
Rouel Rd SE16 . . . . .139 B1
SE16 . . . . .153 B4
Roundacre SW19 . . .69 C2
Roundel Cl SE4 . . . . .66 B3
Roundwood Rd
  NW10 . . . . .8 B1
Rounton Rd E3 . . . . .26 C1
Roupell Rd SW2 . . . .74 B3
Roupell St SE1 . . . . .121 C1
Rousden St NW1 . . . .13 B1
Routh Rd SW18 . . . .72 A4
Rover Ho 27 N1 . . . . .24 A4
Rowallan Rd SW6 . .154 A1
Rowan Cl W5 . . . . . . .36 A4
Rowan Ct SW11 . . . .49 B3
  London W1 . . . . .60 B1
Rowan Ho
  London NW10 . . . . . . .21 A1
  8 London W3 . . . . . . .12 B2
Rowan Rd W6 . . . . . .39 C2
Rowan Terr W6 . . . . .39 C2
Rowan Wlk N19 . . . . .4 B2
Rowberry Cl SW6 . .47 B3
Rowcross St SE1 . . .153 A2
Rowditch La SW11 .169 B2
Rowdon Ave NW10 . .9 A1
Rowe La E9 . . . . .17 B3

Rowena Cres
  SW11 . . . . .168 B1
Rowfant Rd SW12,
  SW17 . . . . .72 C2
Rowhill Mans 1 E5 .17 A4
Rowhill Rd E5 . . . . . .17 A4
Rowington Cl W2 .100 A4
Rowland Hill Ho
  SE1 . . . . .136 A4
Rowland Hill St
  NW3 . . . . .12 A3
Rowley Gdns N4 . . . .6 B4
Rowley Ho SE8 . . . . .51 C4
Rowley Ind Pk W3 .37 A3
Rowley Way NW8 . . .78 C4
Rowntree Cl NW6 . . .10 C2
Rowse Cl E15 . . . . . . .27 B4
Rowstock 1 NW5 . . .13 C2
Rowstock Gdns N7 . .13 C3
Roxford Ho 2 E3 . . .27 A1
Roxley Rd SE13 . . . . .67 A1
Roxwell 10 NW1 . . .13 A2
Roxwell Rd W12 . . . .38 C4
Royal Academy of
  Dramatic Art*
  WC1 . . . . .105 C3
Royal Acad of Arts*
  W1 . . . . .118 C3
Royal Acad of Dance
  SW11 . . . . .167 C3
Royal Acad of Music
  NW1 . . . . .91 C1
Royal Albert Hall*
  SW7 . . . . .129 B3
Royal Ave SW3 . . . .144 C2
Royal Army Medical Coll
  SW1 . . . . .148 A2
Royal Avenue Ho
  SW3 . . . . .144 C2
Royal Ballet Sch The
  WC2 . . . . .106 B2
Royal Brompton School
  SW3 . . . . .143 C2
Royal Cir SE27 . . . . .75 A1
Royal Cl SE8 . . . . . . .51 B4
  London N16 . . . . .7 A3
  Putney SW19 . . . . . . .69 C2
Royal College St
  NW1 . . . . .83 A4
Royal Coll of
  Anaesthetists
  WC1 . . . . .106 B3
Royal Coll of Art
  SW7 . . . . .129 B3
Royal Coll of Art
  Sculpture Sch
  SW11 . . . . .158 A1
Royal Coll of Midwives
  W1 . . . . .104 A3
Royal Coll of Music
  SW7 . . . . .129 B2
Royal Coll of
  Obstetricians &
  Gynaecologists
  NW1 . . . . .90 C2
Royal Coll of Physicians
  NW1 . . . . .92 B2
Royal Coll of Science
  SW7 . . . . .129 B2
Royal Coll of Surgeons
  WC2 . . . . .107 A2
Royal Courts of Justice
  WC2 . . . . .107 B1
Royal Cres
  W11 . . . . . .31 A1 112 A1

Ron – Roy 245

Royal Crescent Mews
  W11 . . . . .30 C1
Royal Ct SE16 . . . . . .41 B3
Royal Duchess Mews
  SW12 . . . . .73 A4
Royal Exchange*
  EC3 . . . . .109 C1
Royal Exchange Ave
  EC3 . . . . .109 C1
Royal Exchange Bldgs
  EC3 . . . . .109 C1
Royal Festival Hall*
  SE1 . . . . .121 A1
Royal Free Hospl
  NW3 . . . . .12 A3
Royal Geographical
  Society SW7 . . . . . .129 C3
Royal Hill SE10 . . . . .52 B3
Royal Horticultural
  Society (Lawrence Hall
  & Conf Ctr) SW1 . .133 C2
Royal Horticultural
  Society (Lindley Hall)
  SW1 . . . . .147 C4
Royal Hospital (Army
  Pensioners) SW1 .145 B1
Royal Hospital Rd
  SW3 . . . . .145 A1
Royal Hospl and Home
  SW15 . . . . .58 A1
Royal Langford
  NW6 . . . . .78 A2
Royal London Est The
  NW10 . . . . .20 C3
Royal London
  Homeopathic Hospl
  The WC1 . . . . .106 B4
Royal London Hospl
  (Mile End) The E1 .25 C2
Royal London Hospl (St
  Clements) The E3 .26 B2
Royal London Hospl
  (Whitechapel) The
  E1 . . . . .32 A4
Royal Marsden Hospl
  SW3 . . . . .143 C2
Royal Mews The
  SW1 . . . . .132 B2
Royal Mint Pl E1 . . .125 B4
Royal Mint St E1 . .125 A4
Royal National
  Orthopaedic Hospl
  W1 . . . . .92 B1
Royal National TNE
  Hospl The WC1 . . .94 C4
Royal Naval Pl SE14 .51 B3
Royal Oak Ct 1 N1 . . .98 A4
Royal Oak Pl SE22 .65 A1
Royal Oak Rd 8 E8 .17 A2
Royal Oak Sta W2 .100 B3
Royal Opera Arc
  SW1 . . . . .119 B2
Royal Orchard Cl
  SW18 . . . . .70 A4
Royal Par SW6 . . . . .154 A2
  London SE3 . . . . .53 B1
Royal Pl 11 SE10 . . .52 B3
Royal Rd SE17 . . . . . .48 A4
Royal Sch Hampstead
  The NW3 . . . . .11 C4
Royal St SE1 . . . . . .135 A2
Royalty Mews W1 .105 C2
Royalty Studios
  W11 . . . . .31 A3

Royal United Services
Mus SW1 . . . . **120** A1
Royal Veterinary Coll
NW1 . . . . **83** B3
Royal Victoria Ste
E16 . . . . **35** C3
Royal Victor Pl E3 . . **25** C2
Roycroft Cl SW2 . . . **74** C3
Roydon Cl SW11 . . **168** C2
Roy Ho N1 . . . . **87** C3
Roy Ridley Ho 5
SW4 . . . . **61** C4
Roy Sq E14 . . . . **33** A2
Royston Ct E13 TW9 . **44** B2
Royston Ho E14 SE15 . **50** A4
Royston Rd TW10 . . . **54** A2
Royston St 25 E2 . . . **25** B3
Rozel Cl 5 N1 . . . . . **24** A4
Rozel Rd SW4 . . . . . . **61** B4
Ruby St SE15 . . . . . . **50** A4
Ruby Triangle SE15 . . **50** A4
Rucklidge Ave
NW10 . . . . **21** C3
Rudall Cres NW3 . . . . **11** C4
Rudbeck Ho 10
SE15 . . . . **49** C3
Ruddington Cl E5 . . . **18** A4
Rudge Ho SE16 . . . . . **40** A3
Rudgwick Terr NW8 . . **80** B3
Rudhall Ho 4 SW2 . . **62** C1
Rudloe Rd SW12 . . . . **73** B4
Rudolf Pl SW8 . . . . **162** B3
Rudolph Rd NW6 . . . **23** C3
Rudstone Ho 10 E3 . . **27** A2
Rudyard Ct SE1 . . . **137** C3
Rufford St N1 . . . . . . **84** B4
Rufford Street Mews
N1 . . . . **14** A1
Rufford Twr 5 W3 . . . **28** A1
Rufus Bsns Ctr
SW18 . . . . **71** A2
Rufus Ho SE1 . . . . . **139** A2
Rufus St N1 . . . . **98** A3
Rugby Mans W14 . . . **140** B4
Rugby Rd W4 . . . . . . **38** A4
Rugby St WC1 . . . . . . **94** C1
Rugg St E14 . . . . **33** C2
Rugless Ho 2 E14 . . . **42** B4
Rugmere 4 NW1 . . . . **12** C1
Rumball Ho 22 SE5 . . **49** A3
Rumbold Rd SW6 . . **156** B1
Rum Cl E1 . . . . **32** B2
Rumford Ho SE1 . . . **136** C1
Rumsey Rd SW9 . . . . **62** B4
Runacres Ct SE17 . . **150** C1
Runcorn Pl W11 . . . . **112** A4
Rundell Twr SW8 . . . **172** C4
Running Horse Yd 2
TW8 . . . . **44** A4
Runnymede Ho
London E9 . . . . **18** A4
Richmond TW10 . . . . **54** C2
Rupack St 3 SE16 . . . **40** B4
Rupert Ct W1 . . . . . **119** B4
Rupert Gdns SW9 . . . **48** A1
Rupert Ho SE11 . . . . **149** C3
Rupert Rd NW6 . . . . . **23** C3
London N19 . . . . **4** C2
London W4 . . . . **38** A3
Rupert St W1 . . . . . **119** B4
Rusbridge Cl E8 . . . . **16** C3
Ruscoe Rd E16 . . . . . **35** B1
Rusham Rd SW12 . . . **72** B4
Rushbrook Ho 6
SW8 . . . . **171** B2

Rushby Ct SW4 . . . . **172** A3
Rush Common Mews 18
E1 . . . . **24** A2
Rushcroft Rd SW2,
SW9 . . . . **62** C3
Rushcutters Ct 18
SE16 . . . . **41** A2
Rushey Mead SE4 . . . **66** C2
Rushford Rd SE4 . . . . **66** B1
Rush Hill Mews 3
SW11 . . . . **60** C4
Rush Hill Rd SW11 . . **60** C4
Rushlake Ho SW11 . . **169** B2
Rushmead 5 E2 . . . . **25** A2
Rushmere Ho 2
SW15 . . . . **68** C3
Rushmore Cres 5
E5 . . . . **17** C4
Rushmore Ho W14 . . **126** B2
9 London N7 . . . . **13** C3
Rushmore Prim Sch
E5 . . . . **17** C4
Rushmore Rd
London E5 . . . . **17** C4
E5 . . . . **18** A4
Rusholme Rd SW15 . . **58** A1
Rushton Ho SW8 . . . **171** B1
Rushton St N1 . . . . . . **87** C2
Rushworth St SE1 . . **136** B3
Ruskin Ave TW9 . . . . **44** C3
Ruskin Ct SE5 . . . . . . **63** C4
Ruskin Ho SW1 . . . . **147** C3
Ruskin Park Ho SE5 . . **63** C4
Ruskin Wlk SE24 . . . . **63** B2
Rusper Ct SW9 . . . . **172** B1
Russell Cl W4 . . . . . . **46** B4
Russell Ct SW1 . . . . **119** A1
SW11 . . . . **169** C3
5 London SE15 . . . . . **50** A1
Russell Gdns W14 . . **126** A2
Russell Gdns Mews
W14 . . . . **126** A2
Russell Gr SW9 . . . . **173** C4
Russell Ho 19 E14 . . . **33** C3
SW1 . . . . **146** C2
Russell Kerr Cl W4 . . . **45** B3
Russell Lodge SE1 . . **137** B1
Russell Mans WC1 . . **106** B3
Russell Pickering Ho 2
SW4 . . . . **61** C4
Russell Pl SE16 . . . . . **41** A3
London NW3 . . . . **12** A3
Russell Rd W14 . . . . **126** B1
Russell Sq WC1 . . . . **94** A1
Russell Square Mans
WC1 . . . . **94** A1
Russell Square Sta
WC1 . . . . **94** A1
Russell St WC2 . . . . **120** B4
Russell's Wharf 1
W9 . . . . **23** B1
Russell Wlk 4
TW10 . . . . **54** B1
Russet Cres N7 . . . . . **14** B3
Russet Way SE13 . . . . **52** A2
Russia Ct EC2 . . . . . **109** A2
Russia Dock Rd
SE16 . . . . **33** A1
Russia La E2 . . . . **25** B3
Russia Row EC2 . . . **109** A1
Rusthall Ave W4 . . . . **37** C3
Rusthall Mans W4 . . . **37** C2
Ruston Mews W11 . . . **31** A3
Ruston St E3 . . . . **26** B4
Rust Sq SE5 . . . . **48** C3
Ruth Ct 14 E3 . . . . . . **26** A3

Rutherford Ho 12
E1 . . . . **25** A1
Rutherford St SW1 . . **147** B4
Ruth Ho W10 . . . . . . **23** A1
Ruthin Rd SE3 . . . . . . **53** C4
Ruthven St E9 . . . . . . **25** C4
Rutland Cl SW14 . . . . **55** B4
Rutland Ct SW7 . . . . **130** B3
London SE5 . . . . **63** C3
Rutland Gate SW7 . . **130** B3
Rutland Gate Mews
SW7 . . . . **130** A3
Rutland Gdns SW7 . . **130** B3
W6 . . . . **39** C2
Rutland Gdns Mews
SW7 . . . . **130** A3
Rutland Gr W6 . . . . . . **39** A1
Rutland Ho W8 . . . . **128** A1
10 Putney SW15 . . . . **69** B4
Rutland Mews E
SW7 . . . . **130** A2
Rutland Mews S
SW7 . . . . **130** A2
Rutland Mews W
SW7 . . . . **130** A2
Rutland Park Gdns
NW2 . . . . **9** B2
Rutland Park Mans
NW2 . . . . **9** B2
Rutland Pk NW2 . . . . . **9** B2
Rutland Pl EC1 . . . . . **108** B4
Rutland Rd E9 . . . . . . **25** C4
Rutland St SW7 . . . . **130** B2
Rutland Studios
NW10 . . . . **21** C2
Rutley Cl SE11 . . . . . . **48** A4
Rutt's Terr SE14 . . . . . **50** C2
Ruvigny Gdns SW15 . . **57** C4
Ruvigny Mans SW15 . . **57** C4
Rycott Path SE22 . . . . **76** C4
Rycroft Sq SE3 . . . . . **53** B1
Rydal Ho SW8 . . . . . **171** B1
Rydal Water NW1 . . . . **92** C3
Ryde Ho 1 NW6 . . . . . **23** C4
Ryder Ct SW1 . . . . . **119** A2
Ryder Dr SE16 . . . . . . **40** A1
Ryder Ho 10 E1 . . . . . **25** B1
Ryder St SW1 . . . . . **119** A2
Ryder's Terr NW8 . . . . **78** C2
Ryde Vale Rd SW12 . . **73** B2
Rydon St N1 . . . . **87** A4
Rydston Cl 2 N7 . . . . **14** B1
Ryecotes Mead
SE21 . . . . **76** A3
Ryecroft Rd SE13 . . . . **67** B2
Ryecroft St SW6 . . . **166** A3
Ryedale SE22 . . . . **65** A1
Ryefield Path 7
SW15 . . . . **68** C3
Ryegates 2 SE15 . . . . . **50** A1
Rye Hill Pk SE15 . . . . . **65** B3
Rye La SE15 . . . . **49** C1
Rye Rd SE15 . . . . **65** C3
Rye Wlk SW15 . . . . . . **57** C2
Ryfold Rd SW19 . . . . . **70** A1
Ryland Rd NW5 . . . . . **13** A2
Rylett Cres W12 . . . . . **38** B3
Rylett Rd W12 . . . . . . **38** B3
Rylston Rd SW6 . . . . **154** C2
Rymer St SE24 . . . . . . **63** A1
Rysbrack St SW1 . . . **130** C2

S

Saatchi Gallery★
SE1 . . . . **134** C3

Sabbarton St 9
E16 . . . . **35** B1
Sabella Ct E3 . . . . **26** B3
Sabine Rd SW11 . . . . **60** C4
Sable St N1 . . . . **15** A1
Sacketts Ho SW9 . . . **173** C4
Sackville Ho 16
SW16 . . . . **74** A1
Sackville St W1 . . . . **119** A3
Sacred Heart High Sch
W6 . . . . **39** B2
Sacred Heart Jun Sch
W6 . . . . **39** C2
Sacred Heart RC Prim Sch,
Battersea SW11 . . . . **60** C4
Sacred Heart RC Prim
Sch SW15 . . . . **56** C2
Sacred Heart RC Sch
The SE5 . . . . **48** B2
Saddlers Mews
SW8 . . . . **172** B4
Sadler Ho 5 E3 . . . . . **27** A2
EC1 . . . . **96** A4
Saffron Ave E14 . . . . . **34** C2
Saffron Ct N1 . . . . **86** A4
Saffron Hill EC1 . . . . **107** C4
Saffron St EC1 . . . . . **107** C4
Saffron Wharf SE1 . . **139** A4
Sage Mews SE22 . . . . **64** B2
Sage St E1 . . . . **32** B2
Sage Way WC1 . . . . . . **94** C3
Sailmakers Ct SW6 . . **59** B4
Sail St SE11 . . . . **149** A4
Sainfoin Rd SW17 . . . **72** C2
St Agnes Cl E9 . . . . . . **25** B4
St Agnes Pl SE11 . . . . **48** A4
St Agnes RC Prim Sch
E3 . . . . **27** A1
St Agnes RC Sch
NW2 . . . . **1** A1
St Aidan's Prim Sch
N4 . . . . **5** C4
St Aidan's Rd SE22 . . **65** A2
St Alban's CE Prim Sch
EC1 . . . . **108** B4
St Alban's Cl NW11 . . . **1** C3
St Alban's Gr W8 . . . **128** B2
St Albans La NW11 . . . **1** C3
St Alban's Mans
W8 . . . . **128** B2
St Alban's Pl N1 . . . . . **86** A3
St Alban's Rd
London NW10 . . . . . . **21** A4
London NW5 . . . . **4** A1
St Alban's St SW1 . . . **119** B3
St Albans Studios
W8 . . . . **128** B2
St Albans Terr W6 . . . **154** A4
St Alban's Villas NW5 . **3** C1
St Alfege Pas SE10 . . . **52** B4
St Alfege with St Peter's
CE Prim Sch SE10 . . **52** B4
St Aloysius RC Inf Sch
NW1 . . . . **93** B4
St Aloysius RC Jun & Inf
Sch NW1 . . . . **93** A4
St Aloysius RC Jun Sch
NW1 . . . . **83** B1
St Alphage Gdn
EC2 . . . . **109** A3
St Alphage Highwalk
EC2 . . . . **109** A3
St Alphonsus Rd
SW4 . . . . **61** C3

St Andrew's CE Prim
Sch
N1 . . . . **85** A4
London SW9 . . . . . . **172** B1
St Andrews Ct 23
SE16 . . . . **40** A1
St Andrews Ct W4 . . . **45** B2
St Andrew's Ct
SW18 . . . . **71** B2
St Andrew's Gr N16 . . **6** C3
St Andrew's Greek Sch
NW1 . . . . **13** B1
St Andrew's Hill
EC4 . . . . **108** B1
St Andrews Ho 11
SE16 . . . . **40** A3
St Andrews Hospl
E3 . . . . **27** A1
St Andrew's Mans
W1 . . . . **103** B3
St Andrews Mews
Greenwich SE3 . . . . . **53** C3
4 Streatham SW12 . . **73** C3
St Andrew's PI NW1 . **92** B2
St Andrew's Rd
W14 . . . . **154** B4
London NW2 . . . . **9** A2
London W3 . . . . **29** A3
St Andrew's Sq
W11 . . . . **31** A3
St Andrew St EC4 . . . **107** C3
St Andrew & St Francis
CE Prim Sch NW2 . . **8** C2
St Andrews Way E3 . . **27** A1
St Andrew's Wharf
SE1 . . . . **139** A4
St Anne RC Prim Sch
E1 . . . . **99** B1
St Anne's CE Prim Sch
SW18 . . . . **59** A2
St Anne's Cl N6 . . . . . . **3** C1
St Anne's Ct NW6 . . . **23** A4
W1 . . . . **105** B1
St Anne's Flats NW1 . **93** B4
St Anne's Pas E14 . . . **33** B3
St Anne's RC Prim Sch
SE11 . . . . **162** C4
St Anne St E14 . . . . . . **33** B3
St Anne's Trad Est
E14 . . . . **33** B3
St Ann's Cres SW18 . . **59** B1
St Anns Gdns NW5 . . **12** C2
St Ann's Hill SW18 . . . **59** B1
St Ann's Ho WC1 . . . . **95** B3
St Ann's La SW1 . . . . **133** C1
St Ann's Park Rd
SW18 . . . . **59** B1
St Anns Rd SW13 . . . . **46** B2
St Ann's Rd W11 . . . . **30** C2
St Ann's St SW1 . . . . **133** C2
St Ann's Terr NW8 . . . **79** C2
St Ann's Villas
W11 . . . . **112** A1
St Anselm's Pl W1 . . **118** A4
St Anselm's RC Prim Sch
SW17 . . . . **72** C1
St Anthony's Cl E1 . . **125** B2
St Anthonys Cl
SW17 . . . . **72** A2
St Anthony's Ct
2 London SW17 . . . . **60** C1
Upper Tooting SW17 . **72** C2
St Anthony's Flats
NW1 . . . . **83** B1

St Anthony's RC Prim
Sch SE22 . . . . .64 C1
St Asaph CI SE4 . . . .65 C4
St Asaph Rd SE4 . . . .65 C4
St Aubins CI N1 . . . .87 C4
St Augustine's CE High
Sch NW6 . . . . .23 C3
St Augustine's CE Prim
Sch NW6 . . . . .78 A1
St Augustine's RC Prim
Sch W6 . . . . .154 B3
St Augustine's Rd
NW1 . . . . .13 C1
St Austell Rd SE13 . .52 C1
St Barnabas CE Prim
Sch SW1 . . . . . . .145 C2
St Barnabas CI 11 . . .
SE22 . . . . .64 A2
St Barnabas St
SW1 . . . . .145 C2
St Barnabas & St
Philip's CE Prim Sch W8 .127 C1
St Barnabas Terr
E9 . . . . .17 C3
St Barnabas Villas
SW8 . . . . .172 B4
St Bartholomew's Hospl
EC1 . . . . .108 B3
St Bede's RC Inf Sch
SW12 . . . . .73 C3
St Benets CI SW17 . .72 A2
St Benet's PI EC3 . .123 C4
St Bernadette RC Jun
Sch SW12 . . . . . . .73 B4
St Bernard Ho 6
E14 . . . . .42 B3
St Botolph St E1,
EC3 . . . . .110 C2
St Brelades CI SW17 .87 C4
St Bride's Ave EC4 . .108 A1
St Bride's Pas EC4 . .108 A1
St Bride St EC4 . . . .108 A2
St Catherines CI
SW17 . . . . .72 A2
St Catherines CI 6
W4 . . . . .38 A3
St Catherine's Dr
SE14 . . . . .50 C1
St Catherines Mews
SW3 . . . . .144 C4
St Chad's PI WC1 . . .94 C4
St Chad's St WC1 . . .94 C4
St Charles' Hospl
W10 . . . . .30 C4
St Charles PI W10 . .31 A4
St Charles RC Prim Sch
W10 . . . . .30 C4
St Charles RC Sixth
Form Coll W10 . . . .30 C4
St Charles Sq W10 . .30 C4
St Christina's Sch
NW8 . . . . .80 A2
St Christopher's Ho
NW1 . . . . .83 B1
St Christopher's PI
W1 . . . . .103 C2
St Christopher's Sch
NW3 . . . . .11 C3
St Clair Ho 14 E3 . . .26 B2
St Clare St EC3 . . . .110 C1
St Clement Danes CE
Prim Sch WC2 . . . .106 C1
St Clements CI 7 . . .
SE14 . . . . .50 C4
St Clement's Ct . . .
EC3 . . . . .123 C4

St Clements Ct
London N7 . . . . . . .14 B2
St London NW1 . . . .30 C2
St Clement's La
WC2 . . . . .107 A1
St Clements Mans 3
SW6 . . . . .47 C4
St Clements St N7 . .14 C1
St Clement & St James
CE Prim Sch
W11 . . . . . .31 A1 112 A1
St Columb's Ho 11
W10 . . . . .31 A4
St Crispins CI NW3 . .12 A4
St Cross St EC1 . . . .107 C4
St Cuthbert's Rd
NW2 . . . . .10 B2
St Cuthbert with St
Matthias Prim Sch
SW5 . . . . .142 A2
St Davids CI 27
SE16 . . . . .40 A1
St David's Sq E14 . . .42 A1
St Dionis Rd SW6 . .165 A2
St Dominic RC Prim Sch
NW5 . . . . .12 B3
St Dominics Prim
Sch E9 . . . . .18 A2
St Donatt's Rd SE14 .51 B2
St Dunstan's Alley
EC3 . . . . .124 A3
St Dunstan's Ave
W3 . . . . .28 C2
St Dunstan's Ct . . .
EC4 . . . . .107 C1
St Dunstan's Gdns
W3 . . . . .28 C2
St Dunstan's Hill
EC3 . . . . .124 A3
St Dunstan's La
EC3 . . . . .124 A3
St Dunstan's Rd W6 .39 C1
St Edmund RC Sch
E14 . . . . .41 C2
St Edmund's CI
NW8 . . . . .80 C3
SW17 . . . . .72 A2
St Edmund's Sq
SW13 . . . . .47 B4
St Edmund's Terr
NW8 . . . . .80 C3
St Edward's RC Prim
Sch NW1 . . . . .90 B1
St Elizabeth's RC Prim
Sch TW10 . . . . . . .54 B1
St Elmo Rd W12 . . . .38 B4
St Elmos Rd SE16 . . .41 A4
St Ermin's Hill
SW1 . . . . .133 B2
St Ervan's Rd W10 . .31 B4
St Eugene de Mazenod
RC Prim Sch NW6 . .23 C4
St Faith's CE Prim Sch
SW11 . . . . .59 B2
St Francesca Cabrini
Prim Sch SE23 . . . .65 B1
St Francis' Ho NW1 . .83 B1
St Francis of Assisi RC
Prim Sch W11 . . . .30 C2
St Francis RC Prim Sch
SE15 . . . . .49 C3
St Francis Rd SE22 . .64 A3

St Francis Xavier Sixth
Form Coll SW12 . . . .61 A1
St Gabriel's CE Prim Sch
SW1 . . . . .146 C1
St Gabriel's Rd NW2 .9 C3
St George Ho
SW11 . . . . .169 C3
St George's Ave N7 .13 C4
St George's Battersea
CE Prim Sch SW8 . .161 A1
St George's Cath
NW1 . . . . .92 B4
St George's Cath RC Jun
& Inf Sch SE1 . . . .136 A2
St George's Cath RC Prim
Sch SE1 . . . .
SE5 . . . . .49 A3
St George's Circ
SE1 . . . . .136 A2
St George's Ct SE1 .136 A1
SW3 . . . . .144 A4
SW7 . . . . .128 C1
St Georges Ct SW15 .58 B3
St George's Dr
SW1 . . . . .146 B2
St George's Field
W2 . . . . .102 B1
St George's Gr
SW17 . . . . .71 C1
St Georges Hanover Sq
Sch W1 . . . . .117 C3
St George's Ho
NW1 . . . . .83 A1
St George's La
EC3 . . . . .124 A4
St George's Mews 11
SE1 . . . .
St George's Mews
SE1 . . . . .135 C2
St George's RC Cath
SE1 . . . .
St George's RC Sec Sch
W9 . . . . .78 B1
St George's Rd
SE1 . . . . .136 A1
St George's Rd W4 . .37 C4
St George's Rd TW9 .54 B4
St George's Residences
4 SW2 . . . . .62 C2
St George's Sq . . . .
EC4 . . . . .108 A2
St Georges Sq 1 . . .
E14 . . . . .33 A2
St George's Sq SE8 .41 B2
SW1 . . . . .147 B1
St George's Square
Mews SW1 . . . . . .147 B1
St George St W1 . . .118 B4
St Georges Terr
NW1 . . . . .12 B1
St George's Way
SE15 . . . . .49 A4
St George the Martyr CE
Prim Sch WC1 . . . . .95 A1
St Gerards CI SW4 . .61 B2
St German's PI SE3 . .53 C2
St Giles Cir WC1 . . .105 C2
St Giles Coll W10 . .104 B4
St Giles Ct WC2 . . .106 A2
St Giles High St
WC2 . . . . .105 C2
St Giles Hospl SE5 . .49 A2
St Giles Pas WC2 . .105 C1
St Giles Rd SE5 . . . .49 A3
St Giles Twr 3 SE5 . .49 A2
St Gilles Ho 16 E2 . .25 C3
St Helena Ho WC1 . .95 B3
St Helena Rd SE16 . .40 C2

St Helena St WC1 . . .95 B3
St Helen's Gdns . . . .
W10 . . . . .30 C3
St Helen's PI EC3 . .110 A2
St Helier's RC Prim Sch
SW9 . . . . .62 C4
St Helier Ct 11 N1 . .24 A4
St Hildas CI SW17 . .72 A2
St Hilda's Rd SW13 . .9 C1
St Hilda's Rd SW13 . .47 A4
St Hildas Wharf 1 . .
E1 . . . . .32 B1
St Hubert's Ho 1 . . .
E14 . . . . .41 C3
St Hughes CI SW17 . .72 A2
St James Ct E2 . . . . .99 C3
St James' Ct SW1 . .133 A2
St James's Ave E2 . .25 B3
St James' Ct SW1 . . .
St James' Ct W4 . . . .37 C3
St James Hatcham CE
Prim Sch SE14 . . . .51 A2
St James Independent
Schs W14 . . . . . . .140 B4
St James Ind Mews
SE1 . . . . .153 C1
St James' Mans 5 . .
NW6 . . . . .10 C1
St James Mews E14 .42 B3
St James's St SE1 . .153 C2
St James's App EC2 .98 A1
St James's Ct SW1 . .
St James's CE Prim Sch
SE16 . . . . .139 B2
St James School Flats
5 N7 . . . . .14 C3
St James's CI NW8 . .80 C3
St James's CI . . . . . .
Upper Tooting SW17 .72 B2
St James's Cloisters 2
SE22 . . . . .64 B3
St James's Cres
SW9 . . . . .62 C4
St James's Dr . . . . . .
Balham SW12,SW17 .72 B4
Upper Tooting SW17 .72 B4
St James's Gdns . . . .
W11 . . . . . .31 A1 112 A2
St James's Gr
SW11 . . . . .169 A2
St James's Market
SW1 . . . . .119 B3
St James's Palace
SW1 . . . . .119 A1
St James's Park
SW1 . . . . .133 B3
St James's Park Sta
SW1 . . . . .133 B2
St James's Pas . . . . .
EC3 . . . . .110 B1
St James's PI SW1 . .118 C1
St James's Rd SE1, . .
SE16 . . . . .153 C4
St James's Sq . . . . .
SW1 . . . . .119 A2
St James's St SW1 . .118 C2
St James's & St
Michael's CE Prim Sch
W2 . . . . .114 C4
St James St W6 . . . .39 B1
St James's Terr . . . .
NW8 . . . . .80 C3
St James's Terrace
Mews NW8 . . . . . . .80 C3
St James's Wlk EC1 . .96 A2
St James The Great RC
Prim Sch SE15 . . . .49 B2

St Joan of Arc RC Prim
Sch N5 . . . . .15 B4
St John CE Prim Sch
SE17 . . . . .151 A3
St John CI SW6 . . . .155 B2
St John Evangelist RC
Prim Sch N1 . . . . . .86 A2
St John of Jerusalem CE
Prim Sch E9 . . . . . .17 B1
St John's Angell Town
CE Prim Sch SW9 . .173 B1
St John's Ave . . . . . .
London NW10 . . . . .21 B4
Putney SW15 . . . . . .57 C2
St John's CE Prim Sch
E2 . . . . .25 B3
Fulham SW6 . . . . . .164 B3
St John's Church Rd
E9 . . . . .17 B3
St Johns Concert Hall
SW1 . . . . .134 A1
St John's Cres SW9 .62 C4
St John's Ct E1 . . . .32 A1
St John's Ct . . . .
London NW3 . . . . . . .6 A2
London N5 . . . . . . .15 A4
5 London NW3 . . . .11 B2
London SE13 . . . . . .52 B1
London W6 . . . . . . .39 A2
St John's Dr SW18 . .71 A3
St John's Est SE1 . .138 C3
St Johns Gdns . . . . .
W11 . . . . . .31 B2 112 C3
St John's Gr . . . .
6 Barnes SW13 . . . .46 B1
London N19 . . . . . . .4 B2
11 Richmond TW9 . .54 A3
St John's (Highbury
Vale) CE Prim Sch
N5 . . . . .6 A1
St John's Hill SW11 .59 C3
St John's Hill Gr
SW11 . . . . .59 C3
St Johns Ho 6 . . . . .
SE17 . . . . .48 C4
St John's La EC1 . . .108 B4
St John's Mans 5 . . .
N19 . . . .
St John's Park Mans
N19 . . . . .4 B1
St John's Path EC1 . .96 A1
St John's Pk SE3 . . .53 C3
St John's PI EC1 . . . .96 A1
St John's RC Prim Sch
SE16 . . . .
St John's Rd E16 . . .35 C3
London SW11 . . . . . .60 A3
Richmond TW9 . . . . .54 A3
St John's Sq EC1 . . .96 A1
St Johns Sta SE13 . .67 C1
St John's & St Clements
CE Prim Sch SE15 . .64 C4
St John St EC1 . . . . .96 A2
St John's Terr W10 . .22 C1
St John & St James CE
Prim Sch E9 . . . . . .17 B3
St John's (Upper
Holloway) Prim Sch
N19 . . . . .4 C2
St John's Vale SE8 . .51 C1
St John's Villas . . . . .
W8 . . . . .128 B3
London N19 . . . . .4 C2
St John's Way N19 . . .4 C3
St John's Wood Ct
NW8 . . . . .89 C3

St John's Wood High St
NW8 ....**80** A1
St John's Wood Park
NW8 ....**79** B4
St John's Wood Prep
Sch NW8 ....**90** B3
St John's Wood Rd
NW8 ....**89** C3
St John's Wood Sta
NW8 ....**79** C2
St John's Wood Terr
NW8 ....**80** A1
St John the Baptist CE
Prim Sch N1 ....**87** C4
St John the Divine CE
Jun & Inf Schs SE5 ....**48** A3
St Joseph's CE W10 ....**31** A4
St Josephs Ct 🔢
NW10 ....**21** B3
St Joseph's Flats
NW1 ....**93** B4
St Josephs Ho NW6 ....**39** C2
St Joseph's Hospice
E9,E8 ....**25** A4
St Joseph's RC Jun & Inf
Sch
SE16 ....**139** B3
SE16 ....**40** B3
St Joseph's RC Jun Sch
SE5 ....**48** B3
St Joseph's RC Prim Sch
SE10 ....**43** A1
SE8 ....**51** C3
SW3 ....**144** C3
W9 ....**88** C3
WC2 ....**106** B2
London N19 ....**4** A3
London NW10 ....**8** A1
London SW18 ....**58** C2
St Joseph's St
SW8 ....**170** B4
St Joseph's Vale
SE3 ....**67** C4
St Jude's CE Prim Sch
SE24 ....**63** A2
St Judes Ho 🔢 W10 ....**23** B2
St Jude's Prim Sch
SE1 ....**136** A1
St Jude's Rd E2 ....**25** A3
St Jude's & St Paul's
Prim Sch N1 ....**24** A4
St Jude St N16 ....**16** A3
St Julian's Rd NW6 ....**23** C4
St Katharine's Ho
N1 ....**85** B2
St Katharine's Way
E1 ....**125** B3
St Katherine's Prec
NW1 ....**82** C4
St Katherine's Row
EC3 ....**110** B1
St Katherine's Wlk 🔢
W11 ....**30** C1
St Kilda's Rd N16 ....**7** A3
St Laurence's Cl
NW6 ....**22** C4
St Lawrence Ct N1 ....**87** C4
St Lawrence Ho
SE1 ....**138** A2
St Lawrence St E14 ....**34** B1
St Lawrence Terr
W10 ....**31** A4
St Lawrence Way
SW9 ....**173** C2
St Leonard's Ct N1 ....**97** C4

St Leonards Ct
SW14 ....**55** B4
St Leonards Hospl
N1 ....**24** A3
St Leonard's Rd E14 ....**34** B4
St Leonards Rd
SW14 ....**55** B4
St Leonard's Rd
NW10 ....**20** C1
St Leonard's Sq
NW5 ....**12** C2
St Leonard's St E3 ....**27** A2
St Leonard's Terr
SW3 ....**145** A1
St Loo Ave SW3 ....**158** B4
St Loo Ct SW3 ....**158** C4
St Luke's Ave SW4 ....**61** C3
St Luke's CE Prim Sch
E14 ....**42** C2
St Luke's CE Prim Sch
EC1 ....**96** C3
Richmond TW9 ....**44** C2
St Luke's CE WC1 ....**97** A2
St Luke's Cl EC1 ....**97** A2
St Luke's Hospl W1 ....**92** C1
St Luke's Mews
W11 ....**31** B3
St Luke's Prim Sch
E16 ....**35** B1
St Luke's Rd W11 ....**31** B4
St Luke's Sq E16 ....**35** B1
St Luke's St SW3 ....**144** B2
St Margaret's Cres
SW15 ....**57** A2
St Margaret's Ct
SW15 ....**57** A3
St Margaret's La
W8 ....**128** A1
St Margaret's Lo
W3 ....**37** A4
St Margaret's Rd
London NW10 ....**22** B2
London SE4 ....**66** B3
St Margaret's Sch
NW3 ....**11** A4
St Margaret St
SW1 ....**134** A3
St Mark's CE Prim Sch
SE11 ....**163** A4
St Mark's Cl 🔢 SE10 ....**52** B3
St Mark's Cres NW1 ....**81** C4
St Marks Gate E9 ....**18** B1
St Mark St E1 ....**111** A1
St Mark's Rd SW10 ....**156** B2
St Marks Ho 🔢
SE17 ....**48** C4
St Mark's Hospl EC1 ....**96** B4
St Mark's Pl W11 ....**31** A3
St Mark's Prim Sch
N19 ....**5** A2
St Mark's Rd W11 ....**31** A3
London W10 ....**30** C4
St Mark's Rise E8 ....**16** B3
St Mark St E1 ....**111** A1
St Martin-in-the-Fields
High Sch for Girls
SW2 ....**74** C3
St Martin's Almshouses
NW1 ....**82** C4
St Martins Cl NW1 ....**82** C4
St Martins Ct WC2 ....**120** A4
West Norwood SE27 ....**75** A2
St Martin's La
WC2 ....**120** A3

St Martin's Le Grand
EC1 ....**108** C2
St Martin's Pl WC2 ....**120** A3
St Martin's Rd
SW9 ....**172** C2
St Martin's St WC2 ....**119** C3
St Martin's Way
SW17 ....**71** B1
St Mary Abbots CE Prim
Sch W8 ....**128** A3
St Mary Abbot's Ct
W14 ....**126** C1
St Mary Abbot's Pl
W8 ....**127** A1
St Mary Abbots Terr
W14 ....**127** A1
St Mary at Hill
EC3 ....**124** A3
St Mary Axe EC3 ....**110** B2
St Marychurch St
SE16 ....**40** B4
St Mary Graces Ct
E1 ....**125** A3
St Marylebone CE Sch
The W1 ....**103** B3
St Mary le Bow
Church EC2 ....**108** C2
St Mary- le-Park Ct
SW11 ....**158** B1
St Mary Magdalene CE
Prim Sch
W2 ....**100** B4
London N7 ....**14** C2
London SE15 ....**50** A1
St Mary Magdalene RC
Prim Sch SE4 ....**66** A3
St Mary Magdalen's RC
Prim Sch SW14 ....**55** C4
St Mary Magdalen's RC
Jun Sch NW2 ....**9** A2
St Mary Newington CE
Prim Sch
SE17 ....**152** B2
St Mary of the Angels
RC Prim Sch
W2 ....**31** C3
St Mary RC Prim Sch
W10 ....**23** A1
St Mary's Bryanston
Square CE Sch
W1 ....**102** C4
St Mary's CE Prim Sch
N1 ....**86** B4
London NW10 ....**21** A2
Putney SW15 ....**57** C4
St Mary's Ct W6 ....**38** B3
St Mary's Est 🔢
SE16 ....**40** B4
St Mary's Flats NW1 ....**93** B4
St Mary's Gate W8 ....**128** A1
St Mary's Gdns
SE11 ....**149** C4
St Mary's Gr
Barnes SW13 ....**57** A4
Chiswick W4 ....**45** A4
London N1 ....**15** A2
Richmond TW10,TW9 ....**54** B3
St Mary's Ho N1 ....**86** B4
St Mary's Hospl
W2 ....**101** C2
St Mary's Kilburn CE
Prim Sch NW6 ....**23** C4
St Mary's Lewisham CE
Prim Sch SE13 ....**67** A2
St Mary's Mans
W2 ....**101** B4
London NW10 ....**21** A4

St Mary's Medical Sch
W2 ....**101** C2
St Mary's Mews
NW6 ....**11** A1
St Mary's Path N1 ....**86** B4
St Mary's Pl W8 ....**128** A1
St Mary's Rd
London N8 ....**4** C4
Chiswick W4 ....**46** A4
London SW8 ....**61** B2
London NW10 ....**170** B4
London N19 ....**5** A3
London W5 ....**39** C3
St Mary's Rd
London NW10 ....**21** A4
London NW11 ....**1** A4
London SE15 ....**50** B1
St Mary's Rd
Hampstead NW3 ....**11** C3
St Mary's Sq W2 ....**101** B4
St Mary's Stoke
Newington CE Prim
Sch N16 ....**7** A2
St Mary's Terr W2 ....**101** B4
St Mary & St Michael
Prim Sch E1 ....**32** B3
St Mary & St Pancras CE
Prim Sch NW1 ....**83** B1
St Mary's Twr EC1 ....**97** A1
St Mary's Wlk
SE11 ....**149** C4
St Matthews CE
SE1 ....**136** C1
St Matthew's Ct
SE1 ....**137** B1
St Matthew's Lo
NW1 ....**83** A2
St Matthew's Rd
SW2 ....**62** B2
St Matthew's Row
E2 ....**99** B2
St Matthews Sch
Westminster
SW1 ....**133** C2
St Matthew St
SW1 ....**133** B1
St Matthias CE Prim Sch
E2 ....**98** C2
St Matthias's CE Prim
Sch N16 ....**16** A4
St Maur Rd SW6 ....**165** A3
St Michael's Alley
EC3 ....**109** C1
St Michael's CE Prim
Sch
NW1 ....**82** C3
London N6 ....**3** C4
Wandsworth SW18 ....**58** C2
St Michaels Cl E14 ....**34** B4
St Michael's Ct NW11 ....**1** B4
St Michael's Flats
NW1 ....**83** B1
St Michael's Gdns
W10 ....**31** A4
St Michaels RC Sch
SE16 ....**139** B3
London SW9 ....**173** B2
St Michael's St
W2 ....**102** A2
St Mildred's Ct
EC2 ....**109** B1
St Monica's RC Prim Sch
N1 ....**98** A4
St Nicholas' Flats
NW1 ....**83** B1
St Nicholas Ho SE8 ....**51** C4
St Nicholas Rd SE8 ....**51** C4

St Norbert Gn SE4 ....**66** A3
St Norbert Rd SE4 ....**66** A3
St Olaf's Rd SW6 ....**154** B1
St Olaves Ct W2 ....**109** B1
St Olave's Ct EC2 ....**109** B1
St Olave's Est SE1 ....**138** B4
St Olave's Gdns
SE11 ....**149** B4
St Olave's Mans
SE11 ....**149** B4
St Olav's Sq 🔢 SE16 ....**40** B4
St Osmund's RC Prim
Sch SW13 ....**46** B2
St Oswald's Pl
SE11 ....**148** C1
St Oswulf St SW1 ....**147** C3
St Owen Ho SE1 ....**138** A2
St Pancras Almshouses
🔢 NW1 ....**12** B3
St Pancras Commercial
Ctr NW1 ....**83** A3
St Pancras Hospl
NW1 ....**83** B3
St Pancras Sta WC1 ....**94** A4
St Pancras Way
NW1 ....**83** A4
St Patrick's RC Inf Sch
E1 ....**32** A1
St Patrick's RC Prim Sch
NW5 ....**13** A3
St Paul's Ave SE16 ....**32** C1
London NW2 ....**9** B2
St Paul's Cath ⭐
EC4 ....**108** C2
St Paul's Cath Sch
EC4 ....**108** C2
St Paul's CE Prim Sch
SE17 ....**150** C2
London NW3 ....**12** B1
London W6 ....**39** B1
St Paul's Church Yd
EC4 ....**108** C2
St Pauls Cl W5 ....**36** B4
St Pauls Cres NW1 ....**13** C1
St Paul's Ct
🔢 London W12 ....**5** A2
London SW4 ....**61** C3
St Paul's Dr E15 ....**19** C3
St Paul's Girls' Sch
W6 ....**39** C3
St Pauls Mews NW1 ....**13** C1
St Pauls Pl N1 ....**15** C2
St Pauls Rd TW9 ....**54** B4
St Paul's Rd N1 ....**15** B2
St Paul's Sch SW13 ....**39** C1
St Paul's Sta EC2 ....**108** C2
St Paul St N1 ....**87** A3
St Paul's Terr SE17 ....**48** A4
St Pauls View WC1 ....**95** B3
St Paul's Way E3 ....**33** C4
St Paul's Way Com Sch
E3 ....**33** C4
St Paul's Whitechapel
CE Prim Sch E1 ....**125** C3
St Paul's with St
Michael's Prim Sch
E8 ....**24** C4
St Paul on St Luke CE
Prim Sch E3 ....**33** B4
St Peter's Alley
EC3 ....**109** C1
St Petersburgh Mews
W2 ....**114** A4
St Petersburgh Pl
W2 ....**114** A3
St Peter's CE Prim Sch
SE17 ....**151** C1

St Peter's CE Prim Sch
continued
W9 ....23 C1
St Peter's Church Ct
N1 ....86 B4
St Peters Cl E2 ....24 C3
St Peters Cl SW17 ...72 A2
St Peters Ct SE1 .....54 A1
St Peter's Eaton Square CE Sch SW1 ...132 B1
St Peter's Gdns
SE27 ....74 C1
St Peters Gr W6 .....38 C2
St Peters Ho WC1 ...94 B3
St Peter's Ho
■ SE17 ....48 C4
London N16 ....7 A4
St Peter's London Docks CE Prim Sch E1 ...32 B1
St Peter's Pl W9 ......88 A1
St Peter's Prim Sch
W6 ....38 C1
St Peter's Rd W6 ....38 C1
St Peter's Sq E2 .....24 C3
London W6 ....38 B1
St Peter's St N1 ......86 B3
St Peters St N1 ....86 B3
St Peters & St Pauls RC Prim Sch EC1 ......96 B2
St Peter's Street Mews
N1 ....86 B2
St Peter's Terr
SW6 ....154 B1
St Peter's Villas ■
W6 ....38 C2
St Peter's Way N1 ...16 A1
St Philip Ho WC1 .....95 B3
St Philip Sq SW8 ....170 A1
St Philip's Rd E8 .....16 C2
St Philip's Sch
SW7 ....142 C4
St Philip St SW8 .....170 A1
St Philip's Way N1 ...87 A3
St Quentin Ho
SW18 ....59 C1
St Quintin Ave W10 ..30 C4
St Quintin Gdns
W10 ....30 B4
St Regis Hts NW3 ......2 A1
St Richard of Chichester RC Sec Sch NW1 ...13 B1
St Rule St SW8 ......170 C1
St Saviours SW4 .....61 A3
St Saviour's CE Prim Sch
E14 ....34 A4
W9 ....88 B3
London SE24 ....63 B4
St Saviours Ho
SE1 ....139 B3
St Saviour's RC Prim Sch SE13 ....67 B3
St Saviour's Rd SW2 .62 B2
St Saviours St Olaves CE Sch SE1 ....137 C1
St Saviour's Wharf
SE1 ....139 A4
St Scholastica's RC Prim Sch E5 ....7 C1
St Silas Pl NW5 ......12 C2
St Simon's Ave
SW15 ....57 B2
St Stephen's Ave
W12 ....39 A4
St Stephen's CE Prim Sch
SW8 ....162 C2
W2 ....31 C4
London SE8 ....51 C1

St Stephen's CE Prim Sch continued
London W12 ....39 B1
St Stephen's Cl
NW8 ....80 B3
London NW5 ....12 B3
St Stephen's Cres
W2 ....31 C3
St Stephen's Gdns
W2 ....31 C3
₿ Putney SW15 ....58 B2
St Stephen's Gr
SE13 ....67 B4
St Stephen's Ho ■
SE17 ....48 C4
St Stephen's Mews ◪
W2 ....31 C4
St Stephen's Rd E3 ..26 B3
St Stephen's Row
EC4 ....109 B1
St Stephen's Terr
SW8 ....162 C1
St Swithin's La
EC4 ....123 B4
St Swithun's Rd
SE13 ....67 C2
St Thomas' CE Prim Sch
W10 ....23 A1
London N16 ....7 C3
St Thomas' Gdns
NW5 ....12 C2
St Thomas Ho ■
E1 ....32 C3
St Thomas More RC Sch
SW3 ....144 C3
St Thomas of Canterbury RC Prim Sch SW6 ....154 C2
St Thomas' Rd E16 ..35 C3
St Thomas' Rd W4 ..45 B4
St Thomas' Hospl
SE1 ....134 C2
St Thomas' Hospl Medical Sch SE1 ..134 C1
St Thomas's Pl ⅓
E9 ....17 B1
St Thomas's Rd
London N4,N5 ....5 C1
London N16 ....21 A4
St Thomas's Sq E9 ..17 B1
St Thomas St SE1 ..123 C1
St Thomas's Way
SW6 ....155 A2
St Thomas the Apostle Coll The SE15 ....50 B2
St Ursula's Convent Sch
SE10 ....52 C2
St Vincent De Paul Ho ◪ E1 ....32 B4
St Vincent De Paul RC Prim Sch SW1 ....132 C1
St Vincent Ho SE1 ..138 C2
St Vincent's RC Prim Sch
W1 ....103 C3
Acton W3 ....28 A2
St Vincent St W1 ....103 C3
St William of York RC Sec Boys Sch (Upper)
N1 ....14 A1
Salamanca Pl SE1 ..148 C3
Salamanca St SE1, SE11 ....148 C3
Salcombe Gdns
SW4 ....61 A3
Salcombe Lo NW5 ...12 C4

Salcombe Rd ◪
N16 ....16 A3
Salcombe Villas ◪
TW10 ....54 A2
Salcot N4 ....5 B2
Salcott Rd SW11 .....60 B2
Salehurst Rd SE4 ....66 B1
Salem Ho ◪ E9 ....17 C2
Salem Rd W2 ....114 B4
Sale Pl W2 ....102 A2
Salesian Coll
SW11 ....168 A3
Sale St E2 ...24 C1 99 B2
Salford Ho E14 ....42 B2
Salford Rd SW12 ....73 C3
Salisbury Cl SE17 ...151 B4
Salisbury Ct EC4 ....108 A1
SE16 ....139 C1
London E9 ....18 A3
London W4 ....38 A2
Salisbury Ho ◪ E14 ..34 A3
London N1 ....86 A4
SW1 ....147 C2
Wimbledon SW19 ....69 C1
Salisbury Mews
SW6 ....154 C1
Salisbury Pl SW9 ....48 A3
W1 ....102 C4
Salisbury Rd TW9 ....54 A3
Salisbury Sq EC4 ...107 C1
Salisbury St NW8 ....90 A1
◪ Acton W3 ....37 B4
Salisbury Terr SE15 ..65 B4
Salisbury Wlk N19 ....4 B2
Salmon La E14 ....33 A3
Salmon St ◪ E14 ....33 B3
Saltcoats Rd W4 .....38 A4
Saltdene 5 B3
Salter Rd SE16 ....33 A1
Salters Hall Ct
EC4 ....123 B4
Salters Rd W10 ......22 C1
Salter St ◪ E14 ....33 C2
London E14 ....33 C2
Saltoun Rd SW2 .....62 C3
Saltram Cres W9 .....23 C2
Saltwell St E14 ....33 C2
Saltwood Gr SE17 ...151 B1
Salusbury Prim Sch
NW6 ....23 B4
Salusbury Rd NW6 ..23 B4
Salutation Rd SE10 ..43 A2
Salvin Rd SW15 ......57 C4
Salway Ho SW8 .....172 B4
Salway Rd E15 ....19 C2
Salween Ho ◪ N16 ..7 A1
Samaritan Hospl for Women W1 ....102 C4
Sambrook Ho ◪ E1 ..32 B4
Samels Ct W6 ....38 C1
Samford Ho N1 ....85 B3
Samford St NW8 .....90 A1
Sam Manners Ho ◪
SE10 ....43 A1
Sam March Ho ◪
E14 ....34 C3
Sampson St E1 ......125 C1
Samuel Cl E8 ....24 B4
SE14 ....50 C4
Samuel Ho ◪◪ E8 ..24 B4
Samuel Jones Ind Est ◪
SE15 ....49 A3
Samuel Lewis Bldgs
N1 ....14 C2

Samuel Lewis Trust Dwellings
SW3 ....144 A3
SW6 ....155 C2
SW14 ....140 B4
◪ London SE5 ....48 B2
Samuel Rhodes Sch
N1 ....85 B4
Samuel Richardson Ho
W14 ....140 C3
Samuel's Cl ◪ W6 ...39 B2
Samuel St SE15 .....49 B3
Sancroft Ct SW11 ...168 B4
Sancroft St SE11 ....149 A2
Sanctuary St SE1 ...137 A4
Sanctuary The
◪ SE1 ....32 A1
SW1 ....133 C2
Sandale Cl N16 ....6 C1
Sandall Ho ◪ E3 .....26 A3
Sandall Rd NW5 .....13 B2
Sandalwood Cl ◪
E1 ....26 A1
Sandalwood Ho ◪
NW3 ....11 A2
Sandbourne ◪ W11 ...31 C3
Sandbourne Rd SE4 ..51 A1
Sandbrook Rd N16 ..7 A1
Sandby Ho ◪ NW6 ..23 C4
◪ London SE5 ....49 A2
Sandcroft Ho SE11 ..149 A2
Sandell St SE1 ....135 B4
Sanderling Ct ◪
SE8 ....51 B4
Sanders Ho WC1 .....95 B4
Sanderson Cl NW5 ..13 A4
Sanderson Ho ◪
SE8 ....41 B1
Sanderstead Ave
NW2 ....1 A2
Sanderstead Cl
SW12 ....73 B4
Sandfield WC1 ....94 B3
Sandford Ct N16 ......7 A3
Sandford Row
SE17 ....151 C2
Sandford St SW6 ....156 B1
Sandford Wlk SE14 ..51 A4
◪ London SE5 ....49 B2
Sandgate Ho ◪ E5 ..17 A4
Sandgate La SW17, SW18 ....72 A3
Sandgate St ◪ SE15 ..50 A4
Sandgate Trad Est ◪
SE15 ....50 A4
Sandham Ct SW4 ...172 B3
Sandhills The
SW10 ....157 A4
Sandhurst Ct SW2 ...62 A3
Sandhurst Ho ◪ E1 ..32 B4
Sandilands Rd
SW6 ....166 A3
Sandison St SE15 ....64 C4
Sandland St WC1 ...107 A3
Sandlings Cl SE15 ..50 A1
Sandmere Rd SW4 ..62 A3
Sandon Ho ◪ SW2 ..74 A4
Sandown Ho ◪ W4 ..37 B1
Sandpiper Cl SE16 ..41 B4
Sandpiper Ct
◪ E14 ....42 B3
◪ SE8 ....51 C3
Sandridge Cl N4 ......6 B2
Sandridge St ◪ N19 ..4 B2

Sandringham Cl ■
SW19 ....69 C3
Sandringham Ct
◪ SE16 ....32 C1
W1 ....105 A1
W9 ....89 A3
Putney SW15 ....57 C1
Sandringham Flats
WC2 ....119 C4
Sandringham Ho
W14 ....140 A4
London NW2 ....54 C2
Sandringham Rd
London E8 ....16 B3
London NW11 ....1 A4
London NW2 ....9 A2
Sands End La SW6 ..166 C4
Sandstone ◪ TW9 ....44 C3
Sandstone Pl N19 ....4 C2
Sandways ◪ TW9 ....44 C2
Sandwell Cres ◪
NW6 ....10 C2
Sandwell Mans ◪
NW6 ....10 C2
Sandwich Ho
◪ SE16 ....40 B4
WC1 ....94 A3
Sandwich St WC1 ....94 A3
Sandycombe Rd
TW9 ....44 C1
Sandy Ho ◪ N1 ....24 A4
Sandy Rd NW3 ....2 A2
Sandy's Row E1 .....110 B3
Sanford La N16 ....7 B2
Sanford St SE14,SE8 ..51 A4
Sanford Terr N16 ......7 B1
Sangora Rd ◪
SW11 ....59 C3
Sankey Ho ◪◪ E2 ...25 B3
Sansom St ◪ SE5 ...48 C3
London SE5 ....48 C2
Sans Wlk EC1 ....96 A2
Santley Ho SE1 ......135 C3
Santley St SW4 ....62 B3
Santos Rd SW18 .....58 C2
Sapcote Trad Ctr
NW10 ....8 B2
Saperton Wlk
SE11 ....149 A4
Sapperton Ct EC1 ....96 C2
Sapphire Ct E1 ....125 B4
Sapphire Rd SE8 .....41 A2
Saracen St E14 ....33 C3
Sarah Ho ◪ E1 ....32 A3
Roehampton SW15 ..56 B3
Sarah Swift Ho
SE1 ....137 C4
Sara Lane Ct ◪ N1 ..24 A3
Saratoga Rd E5 ....17 B4
Sardinia St WC2 .....106 C2
Sarjant Path SW19 ..69 C2
Sark Ho ◪ N1 ....15 B2
Sarnersfield Ho
SE15 ....50 A4
Sarratt Ho ◪ W10 ....30 B4
Sarre Rd NW2 ....10 B3
Sarsden Bldgs W1 ..103 C1
Sarsfeld Rd SW12, SW17 ....72 B3
Sartor Rd SE15 ....65 C3
Sarum Hall Sch
NW3 ....12 A1
Sarum Ho W11 ....113 A3
Satchwell Rd ◪ E2 ..24 C2

Saul Ct 4 SE15 .....49 B4
Saunders Cl 6 E14 .33 D2
Saunders Ho 10
  SW2 ....7 C4
Saunders Ness Rd
  E14 ....149 B4
Saunders St SE11 .149 B4
Savage Gdns EC3 .124 B4
Savana N16 ....7 A2
Savannah Ct 6
  SE15 ....49 B3
Savernake Ho N4 ....6 C4
Savernake Rd NW3 .12 B4
Saville Rd W4 ......37 C3
Saville Row W1 ....118 C4
Savill Ho 6 SW4 ...61 C1
Savona St SW8 ....160 C1
Savoy Bldgs W12 ..39 B2
Savoy Circus W3 ...29 B2
Savoy Ct SW5 .....142 A1
  WC2 ....120 B3
Savoy Hill WC2 ....120 C3
Savoy Pier WC2 ...120 C3
Savoy Pl WC2 .....120 C3
Savoy Row WC2 ...120 C3
Savoy St WC2 .....120 C3
Savoy Steps WC2 .120 C3
Savoy Way WC2 ...120 C3
Sawkins Cl SW19 ..70 A2
Sawley Rd W12 ....29 C1
Sawmill Yd E3 .....26 A4
Sawyer St SE1 ....136 C4
Saxby Rd SW2 .....74 A4
Saxonbury Ct
  2 London N7 ....14 A3
  16 London N7 ...14 A3
Saxoncroft Ho
  SW16 ....73 C1
Saxon Dr W3 ......28 A4
Saxonfield Cl SW2 .74 B4
Saxon Hall W2 ....114 A3
Saxon Ho 6 SW4 .61 C3
Saxon Rd E3 ......26 B3
Saxton Cl SE13 ...67 C4
Sayer Ho SE4 .....66 A3
Sayes Court St SE8 51 B4
Sayes Ct SE8 .....51 B4
Scafell NW1 ....92 C4
Scala St W1 ....105 A4
Scampston Mews 6
  W10 ....30 C3
Scandrett St 6 E1 .32 A1
Scarba Wlk N1 ....15 C2
Scarborough Rd N4 .5 C4
Scarborough St
  E1 ....111 A1
Scarlette Manor Wlk 10
  SE24 ....74 C4
Scarsbrook Ho 2
  SW2 ....62 C1
Scarsdale Pl W8 ..128 A2
Scarsdale Villas
  W8 ....127 C1
Scarth Rd SW13 ...56 B4
Scawen Rd SE8 ...41 A1
Scawfell St E2 ....24 B3
Sceptre Ho 8 E1 ..25 B1
Sceptre Rd E2 ....25 B2
Schofield Wlk SE3 .53 C3
Sch of Nursing
  W1 ....104 C4
Sch of Pharmacy
  WC1 ....94 B2
Scholars Rd SW12 .73 B3
Scholefield Rd N19 .4 C2

Scholey Ho SW11 ..60 A4
Schomberg Ho
  SW1 ....147 C4
Schonfeld Sq N16 ..6 C3
School App E2 .....98 B4
Schoolbank Rd
  SE10 ....43 B3
School Bell Cloisters 11
  E3 ....26 A3
Schoolbell Mews 16
  E3 ....26 A3
School Flats SW8 .172 A3
School Ho SE1 ....152 B4
Schoolhouse La E1 .32 C2
School of Finance &
  Management N7 ..14 B2
School Rd NW10 ..20 C1
School Sq SE10 ...43 B3
Schooner Cl E14 ..42 C3
  1 SE16 ....40 C4
Schubert Rd SW15 .58 B2
Science Mus ★
  SW7 ....129 B1
Sclater St E1 .....99 A2
Scoles Cres SW2 ..74 C3
Scoresby St SE1 ..122 A1
Scorton Ho 2 N1 ..24 A3
Scotch Ho SW1 ...130 C3
Scoter Ct 23 SE8 .51 B4
Scotia Bldg 10 E1 .32 C2
Scotia Ct 3 SE16 .40 C3
Scotia Rd 3 SW2 .74 C4
Scotland Pl SW1 ..120 A1
Scotson Ho SE11 .149 B3
Scotswood St EC1 .95 C2
Scott Ct
  17 London N16 ...7 A1
  London SW11 ...170 B1
  London W4 ......37 C4
Scott Ellis Gdns
  NW8 ....89 B3
Scott Ho N1 ......87 B1
  NW8 ....90 A1
  London N7 ......14 B2
Scott Lidgett Cres
  SE16 ....139 C3
Scotts Ct 6 W12 ..39 A4
Scott's Pl W12 ....39 A4
Scott's Sufferance
  Wharf SE1 ......139 A3
Scott St E1 ....25 A1
Scott's Yd EC4 ....123 B4
Scoulding Ho 6
  E14 ....41 C3
Scoulding Rd E16 .35 C3
Scouler St E14 ....34 C2
Scout App NW10 ..8 A4
Scriven Ct 8 E8 ...24 B4
Scriven St E8 .....24 B4
Scrooby St SE6 ...67 A1
Scrope Bldg 1 EC1 107 C3
Scrubs La NW10,
  W10,W12 ....22 A2
Scrutton Cl SW12 .73 C4
Scrutton St
  EC2 ....24 A1 98 A1
Scutari Rd SE22 ..65 A2
Scylla Rd SE15 ...65 A4
Seabright St 27 E2 .25 A2
Seacole Cl W3 ....28 C4
Seaford Ho 8 SE16 40 B4
Seaford St WC1 ..94 B3
Seaforth Cres N5 .15 B3

Seaforth Lo 2
  SW13 ....46 B1
Seaforth Pl SW1 ..133 A2
Seager Pl E3 ......33 B4
Seagrave Lo SW6 155 C4
Seagrave Rd SW6 155 C4
Seagrove Cl E1 ...32 C4
Seal Ho SE1 ......137 C2
Seal St E8 ....16 B4
Searle Pl N4 ......5 B3
Searles Cl SW11 ..158 B1
Searles Rd SE1 ...151 C4
Searson Ho SE17 .150 B3
Sears St SE5 .....48 C3
Seasalter Ho 6 SW9 173 B4
Seaton Cl
  SW15 ....69 A3 150 A2
Seaton Point 6
  E5 ....16 C4
Sebastian Ho 22 N1 24 A3
Sebastian St EC1 .96 B3
Sebbon St N1 .....15 A1
Sebright Ho 2 E2 .24 C3
Sebright Sch E2 ..24 C3
Secker Ho SW9 ...48 A1
Secker St SE1 ....121 B1
Second Ave W10 .23 A1
  London W3 ......29 B1
  Mortlake SW14 ..56 A4
Sedan Way SE17 .152 A2
Sedding St SW1 ..145 B4
Seddon Ho 2 EC2 108 C4
Seddon St WC1 ...95 A3
Sedgeford Rd W12 29 B1
Sedgewick Ho
  SW19 ....69 C2
Sedgley Ho N4 ...5 B2
Sedgmoor Pl SE5 .49 A3
Sedgwick St E9 ...17 C3
Sedleigh Rd SW18 58 B1
Sedlescombe Rd
  SW6 ....155 B4
Sedley Ho SE11 ..149 A2
Sedley Pl W1 .....104 A1
Seething La EC3 ..124 B4
Sefton St SW15 ..57 B4
Sekforde St EC1 ..96 A2
Selbie Ave NW10 .8 B3
Selborne 2 SW11 .60 C4
Selborne Ho SE1 .137 B3
Selborne Rd 1 SE5 48 C1
Selby Ho
  10 London SW4 .61 B1
  10 London W10 .23 A2
Selby St E1 .24 C1 99 C1
Selden Ho 2 SE15 50 B1
Selden Rd SE15 ..50 B1
Selden Wlk N7 ...5 B2
Seldon Ho SW1 ..146 C1
  SW8 ....160 C1
Selfridges ★ W1 ..103 C1
Selhurst Cl SW19 .69 C3
Selina Ho NW8 ...89 C2
Selkirk Ho N1 ....84 C4
  8 London N16 ..7 A3
Sellons Ave NW10 21 B4
Selma Ho W12 ...30 A3
Selman Ho 3 E9 ..18 A2
Selsdon Way E14 .42 A3
Selsea Pl N16 ....16 A3
Selsey St E14 ....33 C4
Selwood Ho 1 N4 .6 B4
Selwood Pl SW7 .143 B2
Selwood Terr SW7 143 B2
Selworthy Ho
  SW11 ....167 C4

Selwyn Ave TW9 ..54 B4
Selwyn Ct 5 E3 ...26 B3
Selwyn Ho 5 SW15 57 C1
Selwyn Rd E3 .....26 B3
  London NW10 ...8 A1
Semley Gate E9 ..18 B2
Semley Ho SW1 ..146 A3
Semley Pl SW1 ...146 A3
Senate St SE15 ..50 B1
Senators Ct 20 E3 26 A4
Sendall Ct 13 SW11 59 C4
Senior St W2 .....100 A4
Senrab St E1 .....32 C3
Seraph Ct EC1 ...96 C4
Serenaders Rd
  SW9 ....173 B1
Sergeant Ind Est The
  SW18 ....59 A1
Serica Ct 14 SW2 74 B4
Serjeants' Inn EC4 107 C1
Serlby Ct W14 ....126 C2
Serle St WC2 .....107 A2
Sermon La EC4 ...108 C1
Serpentine Ct 6
  SE16 ....40 C4
Serpentine Gallery ★
  W2 ....129 C4
Serpentine Rd W2 116 C1
Serpentine The ★
  W2 ....116 B1
Service Route No 1
  E15 ....19 C1
Service Route No 2
  E15 ....19 C1
Service Route No 3
  E15 ....19 C1
Servite Ho SE13 ..52 A2
Servite RC Prim Sch
  SW10 ....156 C4
Setchell Rd SE1 ..152 C4
Setchell Way SE1 152 C4
Seth St 18 SE16 .40 B4
Settlers Ct 2 E14 .34 C2
Settles St E1 .....111 C2
Settrington Rd
  SW6 ....166 A1
Seven Dials WC2 106 A1
Seven Mills Prim Sch
  E14 ....41 C4
Sevenoaks Rd SE4 66 A1
Seven Sisters Rd N4,
  N7,N15 ....5 C2
Seven Stars Cnr
  W12 ....38 C3
Severnake Cl E14 .41 C2
Severn Way NW10 8 B3
Severus Rd SW11 60 A3
Seville Ho 2 E1 ..125 C1
Seville Mews N1 ..16 A1
Seville St SW1 ...131 A3
Sevington St W9 .88 A1
Seward St EC1 ...96 C3
Sewardstone Rd E2 25 B3
Sextant Ave E14 .42 C2
Sexton's Ho 3 SE13 52 B4
Seymour Ct
  London N16 .....7 C3
  Putney SW15 ....57 A3
Seymour Gdns SE4 66 A4
Seymour Ho NW1 .93 C2
  WC1 ....94 A2
  London SW8 ....171 A2
Seymour Mews
  W1 ....103 B2
Seymour Pl W1 ..102 C2

Seymour Rd
  Acton W4 ....37 B2
  Wandsworth SW18 58 B1
  Wimbledon SW19 69 C1
Seymour St W1 ...103 A1
Seymour Wlk
  SW10 ....156 C4
Seyssel St E14 ...42 B2
Shaa Rd W3 ......28 C2
Shackleton Ct
  2 Dulwich SE21 .75 C2
  4 London W12 ..39 A4
  4 Millwall E14 ..41 C1
Shackleton Ho 5
  E1 ....32 B1
Shacklewell Ho 8
  E8 ....16 B4
Shacklewell La E8 .16 B3
Shacklewell Prim Sch
  E8 ....16 B4
Shacklewell Rd N16 16 B4
Shacklewell Row
  E8 ....16 B4
Shacklewell St 2 .99 A3
Shad Thames SE1 139 A4
Shadwell Gdns E1 .32 B2
Shadwell Pierhead
  E1 ....32 B2
Shadwell Sta E1 ..32 A2
Shaftesbury Ave
  W1 ....119 C4
Shaftesbury Ct N1 .87 B1
  1 London SE5 ...137 B1
  1 London SW5 ..141 C1
Shaftesbury Gdns
  NW10 ....21 A1
Shaftesbury Ho
  W2 ....114 B4
  13 London N16 ..7 A3
Shaftesbury Lo 9
  E14 ....34 A3
Shaftesbury Mews
  W8 ....127 C1
Shaftesbury Park
  Chambers 1
  SW11 ....60 C4
Shaftesbury Rd
  London N4,N19 .5 A3
  Richmond TW9 ..54 A4
Shaftesbury St N1 .87 B1
Shaftesbury Way
  SW17 ....72 B1
Shafto Mews SW1 131 A1
Shafts Ct EC3 ....110 A1
Shahjalal Ho 10 E2 24 C3
Shakespeare Ave
  NW10 ....20 C4
Shakespeare Cres
  NW10 ....20 C4
Shakespeare Ho 3
  E9 ....17 B1
Shakespeare Rd
  London SE24 ...63 A3
  London W3 ......28 B1
Shakespeare's Globe
  Theatre (site of)
  SE1 ....123 A2
Shakespeare Twr
  EC2 ....109 A4
Shakspeare Mews 7
  N16 ....16 A4

Shakspeare Wlk		
N16	16	A4
Shalbourne Sq E9	18	B2
Shalcomb St SW10	157	A3
Shalden Ho 6		
SW15	56	B1
Shalfleet Dr W10	30	C2
Shalford Ct N1	86	A2
Shalford Ho		
SE1	137	C2
Shalimar Gdns W3	28	B2
Shalimar Lo W3	28	B2
Shalimar Rd W3	28	B2
Shalstone Rd SW14,		
TW9	55	A4
Shamrock St SW4	61	C4
Shandon Rd SW4	61	B1
Shand St SE1	138	B4
Shandy St E1	25	C1
Shannon Ct		
London N16	7	A1
London NW10	8	C2
Shannon Gr SW9	62	B3
Shannon Pl NW8	80	B2
Shanti St SW18	70	C3
Shapla Prim Sch		
E1	125	C3
Shardcroft Ave		
SE24	63	A2
Shardeloes Rd SE14	51	B1
Shard's Sq SE15	49	C4
Sharebourne Ho		
SW2	62	C2
Sharnbrook Ho		
W6	155	B4
Sharon Gdns E9	25	B4
Sharon Rd W4	37	C1
Sharpe Way SW4	61	A4
Sharples Hall St 2		
NW1	12	B1
Sharpness Ct 2		
SE15	49	B3
Sharratt St SE14	50	B4
Sharsted St SE17	150	A1
Sharwell Ho SW18	59	A1
Sharwood WC1	85	A1
Shaver's Pl SW1	119	B3
Shawbury Ct SE22	64	B2
Shawbury Rd SE22	64	B2
Shaw Ct London NW19	5	A2
12 London SW11	59	C4
6 London W3	37	B3
Shawfield St SW3	144	B1
Shawford Ct 3		
SW15	68	C4
Shaw Rd SE22	64	A3
Shearling Way N7	14	A2
Shearsmith Ho E1	125	C4
Shearwater Ct 24		
SE8	51	B4
Sheen Common Dr		
SW14,TW10	54	C2
Sheen Court Rd		
TW10	54	C3
Sheen Ct TW10	54	C3
Sheendale Rd TW9	54	B3
Sheen Gate Gdns		
SW14	55	B3
Sheen La SW14	55	B3
Sheen Mount JMI Sch		
SW14	55	C2
Sheen Pk TW10,TW9	54	A3
Sheen Rd TW10,TW9	54	A3
Sheen Wood SW14	55	B2
Sheepcote La		
SW11	169	A1

Sheep La E8	25	A4
Sheffield Ho 14		
SE15	49	B2
Sheffield Sq 2 E3	26	B2
Sheffield St WC2	106	C1
Sheffield Terr		
W8	31 C1 113 C1
Shelbourne Ho 20		
N19	4	C4
Shelburne Ct SW15	57	C2
Shelburne Rd N7	14	B4
Shelbury Rd SE22	65	A2
Sheldon Ct SW8	162	A1
Sheldon Ho 6		
N1	87	C2
Sheldon Rd NW2	9	C4
Sheldrake Ho 18		
SE16	40	C2
Sheldrake Pl W8	127	B4
Shelduck Ct 33 SE8	51	B4
Shelford Pl N16	6	C1
Shelgate Rd SW11	60	B2
Shell Ctr SE1	121	A1
Shelley Cl SE15	50	A1
Shelley Ct SW3	159	A4
London N4	5	B3
Shelley Ho	11	40	C2
6 London N16	16	A4
Shelley NW10	20	C4
Shelley Sch SE11	149	C3
Shellgrove Rd N16	16	A3
Shellness Rd E5	17	A3
Shell Rd SE13	67	A4
Shellwood Rd		
SW11	168	C1
Shelmerdine Cl E3	33	C4
Shelton St WC2	106	A1
Shene Bldg EC1	107	C3
Shene Int Sch SW14	56	A3
Shenfield St N1	24	A3
Shenley Rd SE5	49	A2
Shepard Cl W1	117	B4
Shepherdess Pl N1	97	A4
Shepherdess Wlk		
N1	87	A1
Shepherd Ho		
10 E14	34	A3
London N7	14	A2
Shepherd Mkt W1	118	A1
Shepherd's Bush		
(Central Line) Sta		
W12	39	C4
Shepherd's Bush Gn		
W12	39	B4
Shepherd's Bush (Hamm		
& City) Sta W12	30	B1
Shepherd's Bush Market		
W12	39	B4
Shepherd's Bush Pl		
W12	39	C4
Shepherd's Bush Rd		
W6	39	B3
Shepherds Ct 8		
W12	39	C4
Shepherd's La E9	17	C2
Shepherds Path 4		
SW11	117	B4
Shepherd St W1	118	A1
Shepherd's Wlk		
NW3	11	C4
Sheppard Ho		
1 SE16	40	A1
Sheppard Ho 28 E2	24	C4
18 London SW11	59	C4
6 Streatham SW2	74	C3
Shepperton Rd N1	87	B4
Sheppey Ho E5	17	A4
Sheppey Wlk N1	15	B1

Shepton Ct SW11	167	C4
Shepton Ho 15 E2	25	B2
Sherard Ct N19	5	A1
Sherard Ho 24 E9	17	B1
Sheraton St W1	160	B4
Sheraton St W1	105	B1
Sherborne Ho		
SW1	146	B2
SW8	162	C1
Sherborne La EC4	123	C4
Sherborne St N1	87	B4
Sherbrooke Ho 6		
E2	25	B3
Sherbrooke Rd		
SW6	154	B1
Sherbrooke Terr		
SW6	154	B1
Shere Ho SE1	137	B2
Sherfield Gdns		
SW15	56	B1
Sheridan Bldgs		
WC2	106	B1
Sheridan Ct SW9	172	C4
Sheridan Ho	11	B1
Sheridan Ho 16 E1	32	B3
SE11	149	C3
7 London N16	7	A1
Sheridan Pl SW13	56	B4
Sheridan St 22 E1	32	A3
Sheringdale Prim Sch		
SW18	70	B3
Sheringham Ave		
NW8	79	C4
Sheringham Ho		
NW1	102	B4
Sheringham Rd N7	14	C2
Sherlock Ct NW8	79	B4
Sherlock Holmes Mus		
NW1	91	A1
Sherlock Mews		
W1	103	B4
Sherrick Green Rd		
NW10	9	A3
Sherriff Ct NW6	10	C2
Sherriff Rd NW6	10	C2
Sherrin Rd E10	19	A4
Sherston Ct SE1	150	B4
WC1	95	B3
Sherwin Ho SE11	163	B4
Sherwin Rd SE14	50	C2
Sherwood NW6	10	A1
Sherwood Cl SW13	57	A4
Sherwood Ct W1	102	C3
London SE13	52	A1
11 London SW11	59	B4
Sherwood Gdns		
E14	41	C2
SE16	40	A1
Sherwood Ho N4	6	B4
Sherwood St W1	119	A4
Shetland Rd E3	26	B3
Shillaker Ct W3	29	B1
Shillibeer Pl W1	102	B3
Shillingford Ho 40		
E3	27	A2
Shillingford St 22		
N1	15	A1
Shillingstone Ho		
W14	126	B2
Shipka Rd SW12	73	A3
Ship La SW14	45	B1
Shiplake Ho 2 E2	98	C3
Shipley Ho SW8	171	B1
Ship & Mermaid Row		
SE1	138	A4
Ship St SE8	51	C2

Ship Tavern Pas		
EC3	124	A4
Shipton Ho 14 E2	24	B3
7 NW5	12	C2
Shipton St E2 24 C3 99		A4
Shipwright Rd SE16	41	A4
Shipwright Yd SE1	124	A1
Shirbutt St E14	34	A2
Shire Pl SW18	71	B4
Shirland Mews W9	23	B2
Shirland Rd W9	23	C1
Shirley Gr SW11	60	C4
Shirley Ho 18 SE5	48	C3
Shirley Rd W4	37	C4
Shirley St E16	35	B1
Shirlock Rd NW3	12	B4
Shoe La EC4	107	C2
Shooters Hill Rd		
SE3,SE10	53	A2
Shoot-Up Hill NW2	10	A2
Shore Bsns Ctr 31		
E9	25	B4
Shoreditch Ct 8 E8	16	B1
Shoreditch High St		
7 E1 24 A1 98		B2
Shoreditch Sta		
E1	25	A1
Shoreham Cl SW18	59	A2
Shore Ho SW8	61	A4
Shore Mews 40 E9	17	B1
Shore Pl E9	17	B1
Shore Rd E9	17	B1
Shorncliffe Rd		
SE1	152	C2
Shorrold's Rd SW6	155	A2
Shortcroft Mead Ct		
NW10	8	C3
Shorter St 2	125	A4
Shortlands W6	39	C2
Short Rd W4	46	A4
Shorts Gdns WC2	106	A1
Short St SE1	135	C4
Shottendane Rd		
SW6	165	B4
Shottfield Ave		
SW14	56	A3
Shottsford 1 W11	31	C3
Shoulder of Mutton		
Alley 13 E14	33	A2
Shouldham St W1	102	B3
Shreveport Ho 23		
N19	4	C4
Shrewsbury Ave		
SW14	55	C3
Shrewsbury Cres		
NW10	20	C4
Shrewsbury Ho		
SW3	158	A3
W2	100	A2
Shrewsbury Mews 33		
W2	31	C4
Shrewsbury Rd W2	31	C3
Shropshire Pl WC1	93	A1
Shroton St NW1	102	B4
Shrubland Rd E8	24	C4
Shrubs Ho SW1	147	C3
Shubbery Cl N1	87	A3
Shurland Gdns SE15	49	B3
Shuttle St E1	24	C1 99	B1
Shuttleworth Rd		
SW11	168	A2
Sibella Rd SW4	171	C1
Sicilian Ave WC1	106	B3
Sidbury St SW6	164	A4
Siddons Ct WC2	106	C1

Siddons Ho W2	101	C3
6 London NW3	12	B3
Siddons La NW1	91	A1
Sidford Ho SE1	135	A1
Sidford Pl SE1	135	A1
Sidgwick Ho SW9	172	B1
Sidings Mews N7	14	C4
Sidlaw Ho N16	7	B3
Sidmouth Ho		
18 SE15	49	C3
W1	102	B2
20 Streatham SW2	74	C4
Sidmouth Par NW2	9	B1
Sidmouth Rd NW2	9	B1
Sidmouth St WC1	94	C3
Sidney Boyd Ct		
NW6	11	C1
Sidney Godley (VC) Ho		
9 E2	25	B2
Sidney Gr EC1	86	A1
Sidney Ho 2 E2	25	C3
Sidney Miller Ct 8		
W3	28	A1
Sidney Rd SW9	173	A1
Sidney Sq E1	32	B4
Sidney St E1	32	B4
Sidworth St 6 E8	17	A1
Siebert Rd SE3	53	C4
Siege Ho 21 E1	32	A3
Sigdon Rd E8	16	C3
Signmakers Yd		
NW1	82	B3
Silbury Ho 5 SE26	76	C1
Silbury St N1	97	B4
Silchester Rd W10	30	C3
Silesia Bldgs E8	17	A1
Silex St SE1	136	B3
Silk Mills Path SE13	67	B4
Silk Mills Sq E9	18	B2
Silk St EC2	109	A4
Sillitoe Ho N1	87	C3
Silsoe Ho NW1	82	B1
Silverbirch Wlk 6		
NW3	12	C2
Silverburn Ho 4		
SW9	48	A2
Silver Cl SE14	51	A3
Silver Cres W4	37	A2
Silver Ct N19	4	B1
Silverdale NW1	92	C4
Silverdale Ct EC1	96	A2
Silvermere Rd SE6	67	A1
Silver Pl W1	119	A4
Silver Rd W12	30	C2
Silverthorn NW6	78	B3
Silverthorne Rd		
SW8	170	B1
Silverton Rd W6	47	C3
Silvertown Way E16	35	C1
Silver Wlk SE16	33	B1
Silvester Ho 17 E1	32	A3
7 W11	31	B3
2 W11	31	B3
Silvester Rd SE22	64	B2
Silvester St SE1	137	B3
Silwood St SE16	40	B1
Simla Ho SE1	137	C3
Simmonds Ho 2		
TW9	99	B3
London N7	5	B1
Simms Ho SW6	58	A4
Simms Rd SE1	153	C3
Simon Cl		
W11	31 A2 113	A4
Simon Ct W9	23	C2
Simon Lo 31 SW19	69	C3

Simon Marks (Jewish) Prim Sch N16 .... 7 B2
Simons Wlk E15 .... 19 C3
Simpson Dr W3 .... 28 C3
Simpson Ho NW8 .... 90 A3
Simpson St SW11 .... 148 C1
Simpson's Rd E14 .... 34 A2
Simpson St SW11 .... 168 A1
Sinclair Ct N5 .... 15 B2
Sinclair Gdns W14 .... 39 C4
Sinclair Ho [1]
SW12 .... 73 C3
Sinclair Mans [1]
W12 .... 39 C4
Sinclair Rd W14 .... 126 A2
Sinclairs Ho E14 .... 26 B3
Singer St EC2 .... 97 C3
Sion-Manning RC Sch for Girls
W10 .... 31 A4
London W10 .... 30 C4
Sir Abraham Dawes Cotts SW15 .... 58 A3
Sir Alexander Cl W3 .... 29 B1
Sir Alexander Rd W3 .... 29 B1
Sirdar Rd
W11 .... 31 A2 112 A3
Sir Francis Drake Prim Sch SE8 .... 41 A1
Sirinham Point SW8 .... 163 A3
Sir James Barrie Prim Sch SW8 .... 171 A3
Sirius Bldg [13] E1 .... 32 C2
Sir John Cass Foundation & Redcoat CE Sec Sch E1 .... 32 C4
Sir John Cass's Prim Sch EC3 .... 110 B1
Sir John Kirk Cl [3] SE5 .... 48 B3
Sir John Lillie Prim Sch SW6 .... 154 B3
Sir Oswald Stoll Foundation The SW6 .... 156 A2
Sir Thomas Abney Sch N16 .... 6 C3
Sir Thomas More Est SW3 .... 157 C3
Sir William Burrough Prim Sch E14 .... 33 A3
Sir William Powell's Almshos SW6 .... 58 A4
Sise La EC4 .... 109 B1
Siskin Ho [14] SE16 .... 40 C2
Sispara Gdns SW18 .... 58 B1
Sissinghurst Ho [17] SE15 .... 50 B4
Sister Mabel's Way [2] SE15 .... 49 C3
Sisters Ave SW11 .... 60 B3
Sistova Rd SW12 .... 73 A3
Sisulu Pl SW9 .... 62 C4
Site of Changing of the Guard SW1 .... 132 C3
Sivill Ho E2 .... 99 A4
Siward Rd SW17 .... 71 B1
Six Bridges Ind Est SE1 .... 153 C1
Sixth Ave W10 .... 23 A2
Skardu Rd NW2 .... 10 A3

Skeena Hill SW18 .... 70 A4
Skeggs Ho [5] E14 .... 42 B3
Skegness Ho [3] N7 .... 14 B1
Skelbrook St SW18 .... 71 B2
Skelgill Rd SW15 .... 58 B3
Skelton Cl [8] E8 .... 16 B2
Skelton Ho N16 .... 16 A3
Skelwith Rd W6 .... 47 B4
Skenfrith Ho SE15 .... 50 A4
Sketchley Gdns SE16 .... 40 C1
Skiffington Cl SW2 .... 74 C3
Skinner Pl SW1 .... 145 B3
Skinners Company Sch (Upper) N16 .... 7 B4
Skinner St EC1 .... 95 C2
Skipsea Ho SW18 .... 59 C1
Skipton Ho SE4 .... 66 A3
Skipwith Bldg EC1 .... 107 C3
Skipworth Rd E9 .... 25 B4
Skua Ct [26] SE8 .... 51 B4
Skyline Ct SE1 .... 138 C2
Skylines E14 .... 42 B4
Slade Ct NW2 .... 10 A3
Sladen Pl [8] E5 .... 17 A4
Slade Wlk SE17 .... 48 B4
Slagrove Pl SE13 .... 67 A2
Slaidburn St SW10 .... 157 A3
Slaithwaite Rd SE13 .... 67 B3
Slaney Pl [1] N7 .... 14 C3
Sleaford Ho [3] E3 .... 26 C1
Sleaford Ind Est SW8 .... 161 A1
Sleaford St SW8 .... 161 A1
Slievemore Cl [1] SW4 .... 61 C4
Sligo Ho [6] E1 .... 25 C1
Slingsby Pl WC2 .... 120 A4
Slippers Pl SE16 .... 40 A3
Sloane Ave SW3 .... 144 B3
Sloane Avenue Mans SW3 .... 144 C3
Sloane Ct E SW3 .... 145 C2
Sloane Ct W SW3 .... 145 C2
Sloane Gate Mans SW1 .... 145 B4
Sloane Gdns SW1 .... 145 B3
Sloane Ho [7] E9 .... 17 B1
Sloane Sq SW1 .... 145 A3
Sloane Square Sta SW1 .... 145 A3
Sloane St SW1 .... 131 A1
Sloane Terr SW1 .... 145 B4
Sloane Terr Mans SW1 .... 145 B4
Slocum Cl SW2 .... 62 B1
Sly St [7] E1 .... 32 A3
Smallbrook Mews W2 .... 101 B1
Smalley Cl N16 .... 7 B1
Smart's Pl WC1, WC2 .... 106 B2
Smart St E2 .... 25 C2
Smeaton Ct SE1 .... 136 C1
Smeaton Rd SW18 .... 70 C4
Smeaton St E1 .... 32 A1
Smedley St SW4 .... 171 C2
Smeed Rd E3 .... 18 C1
Smiles Pl SE13 .... 52 B1
Smith Cl SE16 .... 32 C1
Smithfield Mkt EC1 .... 108 A3
Smithfield St EC1 .... 108 A3

Smithies Ct E15 .... 76 B3
Smith's Ct W1 .... 119 B4
Smith Sq SW1 .... 134 A1
Smith's Yd SW18 .... 71 B2
Smith Terr SW3 .... 144 C1
Smithwood Cl SW19 .... 70 A2
Smithy St E1 .... 32 B4
Smithy Street Sch E1 .... 32 B4
Smugglers Way SW18 .... 59 A3
Smyrk's Rd SE17 .... 152 B1
Smyrna Mans [8] NW6 .... 10 C1
Smyrna Rd NW6 .... 10 C1
Smythe St E14 .... 34 A2
Snarsgate St W10 .... 30 B4
Sneath Ave NW11 .... 1 B4
Sneyd Rd NW2 .... 9 B4
Snowberry Cl E11 .... 19 C4
Snowbury Rd SW6 .... 166 B1
Snowden St EC2 .... 24 A1 98 A1
Snow Hill EC1 .... 108 A3
Snow Ho SE27 .... 75 A1
Snowman Ho NW6 .... 78 B4
Snowsfields Prim Sch SE1 .... 138 A4
Snowsfields SE1 .... 137 C4
Soames St SE15 .... 64 B4
Soane Ct [3] NW1 .... 13 B1
Soane Ho SE17 .... 151 C1
Soane Mus WC2 .... 106 C2
Soaphouse La TW8 .... 44 A4
Soho Parish CE Prim Sch [1] W1 .... 119 B4
Soho Sq W1 .... 105 B2
Soho St W1 .... 105 B2
Sojourner-Truth Cl [1] E8 .... 17 A2
Solander Gdns E1 .... 32 B2
Stepney E1 .... 32 A2
Soldene Ct N7 .... 14 B2
Solebay St E1 .... 26 A1
Solent Ho [1] E1 .... 33 A4
Solent Rd NW6 .... 10 C3
Soley Mews WC1 .... 95 B4
Solna Ave SW15 .... 57 B2
Solomon's Pas SE15 .... 65 A3
Solon New Rd SW4 .... 62 A3
Solon Rd SW2 .... 62 A3
Solway Ho [1] E1 .... 25 C1
Solway Rd SE22 .... 64 C3
Somali Rd NW2 .... 10 B3
Somborne Ho SW15 .... 68 C4
Sombrook Ho SE11 .... 149 B3
Somer Ct SW6 .... 155 B3
Somerfield Ho SE16 .... 40 C1
Somerfield Rd N4 .... 6 A2
Somerford Gr N16 .... 16 B4
Somerford Grove Est N16 .... 16 B4
Somerford St E1 .... 25 A1
Somerford Way SE16 .... 41 A4
Somerleyton Rd SW9 .... 62 C3
Somers Cl NW1 .... 83 B2
Somers Cres W2 .... 102 A1
Somerset Gdns
London N6 .... 3 C4
London SE13 .... 52 A1

Somerset Ho WC2 .... 121 A4
Wimbledon SW19 .... 69 C3
Somerset Lo SW15 .... 57 A3
Somerset Rd
London W4 .... 37 C3
Wimbledon SW19 .... 69 C1
Somers Pl SW2 .... 74 B4
Somers Rd SW2 .... 62 B1
Somers Town Est NW1 .... 83 A1
Somerton Ave TW9 .... 55 A4
Somerton Rd
London NW2 .... 1 A1
London SE15 .... 65 A3
Somerville Ave SW13 .... 47 B4
Somerville Ho [11] SW15 .... 57 C1
Somerville Point SE16 .... 41 B4
Sonderburg Rd [1] N7 .... 5 B2
Sondes St SE17 .... 48 C4
Sonia Gdns NW10 .... 8 B4
Sonning Ho [2] E2 .... 98 C3
Sophia Cl N7 .... 14 B2
Sophia Ho [1] W6 .... 39 B1
Sophia Sq [16] SE16 .... 33 A2
Sopwith Way SW11 .... 160 A2
Sorrel La E14 .... 34 C3
Sorrell Cl SE14 .... 51 A3
London SW9 .... 173 C2
Sotheby Rd N5 .... 15 B4
Sotheran Cl E8 .... 24 C4
Sotheron Pl SW6 .... 156 B1
Soudan Rd SW11 .... 168 C3
Souldern Rd [1] W14 .... 39 C3
South Acton Sta W3,W4 .... 37 B3
South Africa Rd W12 .... 30 A2
Southall Pl SE1 .... 137 B3
Southam Ho [1] W10 .... 23 A1
Southampton Bldgs WC2 .... 107 B3
Southampton Pl WC1 .... 106 B3
Southampton Rd NW5 .... 12 B3
Southampton Row WC1 .... 106 B4
Southampton St WC2 .... 120 B4
Southampton Way SE5 .... 49 A3
Southam St W10 .... 23 A1
South Audley St W1 .... 117 C2
South Ave TW9 .... 44 C1
South Bank Bsns Ctr SW8 .... 161 C3
South Bank Univ SE1 .... 136 B1
South Bermondsey Sta SE16 .... 40 B1
South Black Lion La W6 .... 38 C1
South Block [1] SW1 .... 134 B1
South Block [10] E1 .... 32 B2
South Bolton Gdns SW10 .... 142 B2

Southborough Ho SE17 .... 152 B2
Southborough Rd E9 .... 25 C4
South Building SE10 .... 52 C3
Southbury NW8 .... 79 A4
South Camden Com Sch NW1 .... 83 B1
South Carriage Dr SW1,SW7 .... 130 C3
South Colonnade E14 .... 33 C1
Southcombe St W14 .... 140 A4
Southcote Rd N19 .... 13 B4
Southcott Ho [8] E3 .... 27 A2
W9 .... 89 A1
South Cres E16 .... 27 C1
WC1 .... 105 B3
South Ct [17] SW15 .... 57 C1
Southdean Gdns SW19 .... 70 B2
Southdown N7 .... 14 A2
South Eaton Pl SW1 .... 145 C4
South Edwardes Sq W8 .... 127 B1
South End W8 .... 128 B2
South End Cl NW3 .... 12 A4
South End Gn NW3 .... 12 A4
South End Rd NW3 .... 12 A4
South End Row W8 .... 128 B2
Southgate Gr N1 .... 15 C1
Southgate Gr [1] N1 .... 15 C1
Southgate Rd N1 .... 87 C4
South Gr N6 .... 3 C3
South Grove Ho N6 .... 3 C3
South Hampstead High Sch NW3 .... 11 C2
South Hampstead Jun Sch NW3 .... 11 B2
South Hampstead Sta NW8 .... 11 B1
South Hill Pk NW3 .... 12 A4
South Hill Pk Gdns NW3 .... 12 A4
Southill St E14 .... 34 A3
South Island Pl SW9 .... 163 B1
South Kensington Sta SW7 .... 143 C4
South Lambeth Pl SW8 .... 162 A4
South Lambeth Rd SW8 .... 162 B2
Southlands Coll SW15 .... 56 C1

Southlands Dr
SW19 ...... .69 C2
South Lo NW8 ...89 B4
South London Montessori Sch
SW11 ...... .168 A4
Southmead Prim Sch
SW19 ...... .70 A3
Southmead Rd
SW19 ...... .70 A3
South Molton La
W1 ...... .104 A1
South Molton Rd
E16 ...... .35 C3
South Molton St
W1 ...... .104 A1
Southmoor Way E9 .18 B3
South Par W4 ...... .37 C2
South Parade SW3 143 C2
South Park Mews
SW6 ...... .59 A4
South Pl EC2 ...... .109 C3
South Pl Mews
EC2 ...... .109 C3
South Quay Plaza
E14 ...... .42 A4
South Quay Sta E14 .42 A4
South Rise W2 ...... .116 B3
South Row SE3 ...... .53 B1
South Sea St SE16 ...41 B3
Southside N7 ...... .13 C4
South Side W6 ...... .38 B3
Southside Ind Est
SW8 ...... .170 C4
Southside Quarter
SW11 ...... .168 C2
South Sq WC1 ...... .107 B3
South St W1 ...... .117 C2
South Tenter St
E1 ...... .111 A1
South Terr SW7 ...... .144 A4
South Thames Coll
London SW18 ...... .59 A2
Putney SW15 ...... .57 C2
Southvale Rd SE3 ...53 A1
Southview Ave NW10 .8 B3
South Villas NW1 ...13 C2
Southville SW8 ...... .171 C3
Southwark Bridge
SE1,EC4 ...... .123 A3
Southwark Bridge Office Village SE1 ...... .123 A1
Southwark Bridge Rd
SE1 ...... .123 A2
Southwark Cath ★
SE1 ...... .123 B2
Southwark Coll
SE1 ...... .136 A4
SE15 ...... .50 A3
Southwark Coll (Blackfriars Ctr)
SE1 ...... .122 A1
Southwark Coll (Camberwell Ctr)
SE5 ...... .49 A3
Southwark Coll (Grange Ctr) SE1 ...... .138 B1
Southwark Coll (Surrey Docks Ctr) SE16 ...40 A3
Southwark Park Est 11
SE16 ...... .40 A3
Southwark Park Prim Sch SE16 ...... .40 A3
Southwark Park Rd
SE16 ...... .153 B4
Southwark St SE1 .122 C1

Southwater Cl 8
E14 ...... .33 B3
Southwell Gdns
SW7 ...... .142 C3
Southwell Ho
8 SE16 ...... .40 A2
11 London N16 ...16 A3
Southwell Rd SE5 ...63 B4
South Wharf Rd
W2 ...... .101 C2
Southwick Mews
W2 ...... .101 C2
Southwick Pl W2 ...102 A1
Southwick St W2 ...102 A2
Southwick Yd W2 ...102 A1
Southwold Mans
W9 ...... .23 C2
Southwood Ave N6 ...4 A4
Southwood Ct EC1 ...96 A3
Southwood Ho
W11 ...... .112 A4
Southwood Hospl (Geriatric) N6 ...... .3 C4
Southwood Hts N6 ...4 A4
Southwood La N6 ...... .3 C4
Southwood Lawn Rd
N6 ...... .4 A4
Southwood Park N6 ...3 C4
Southwood Smith Ho 8
E2 ...... .25 A2
Southwood Smith St
N1 ...... .86 A3
South Worple Way
SW14 ...... .55 C4
Southwyck Ho SW9 .62 C3
South Yd EC1 ...... .109 B4
Sovereign Cl E1 ...... .32 A2
Sovereign Cres
SE16 ...... .33 A2
Sovereign Ct
3 Richmond TW9 ...54 B3
Stepney E1 ...... .32 A2
Sovereign Ho 22 E1 .25 A1
Sovereign Mews 6
...... .24 B3
Sovereign Pk NW10 .20 A1
Spa Ct SE16 ...... .139 B1
Spafield St EC1 ...... .95 B2
Spalding Ho SE4 ...66 A2
Spanby Rd E3 ...... .26 C1
Spaniards Cl NW11 ...2 C3
Spaniards End NW3 ...2 C3
Spaniards Rd NW3 ...2 B2
Spanish Pl W1 ...... .103 C2
Spanish Rd SW18 ...59 B2
Spa Rd SE16 ...... .139 A1
Sparke Terr 2 E16 .35 B1
Sparkford Ho
SW11 ...... .167 C4
Sparks Cl W3 ...... .28 C3
Sparsholt Rd N19 ...5 A3
Sparta St SE10 ...... .52 B2
Spa Sch SE1 ...... .153 B4
Spa View 5 SW16 ...74 B1
Speakers' Corner ★
W1 ...... .117 A4
Speakman Ho SE4 ...66 A4
Spear Mews SW5 ...141 C3
Spears Rd N19 ...... .5 A3
Spectrum Ho NW5 ...12 C4
Spedan Cl NW3 ...... .2 A1
Speechly Mews E8 ...16 B3
Speed Ho EC2 ...... .109 A4
Speedwell St 5
SE8 ...... .51 C3
Speedy Pl WC1 ...... .94 A3

Speldhurst Rd
London E9 ...... .17 C1
London W4 ...... .37 C3
Spellbrook Wlk N1 .87 A4
Spelman Ho 6 E1 ...111 B3
Spelman St E1 ...... .111 B4
Spence Cl SE16 ...... .41 B4
Spencer Gdns SW14 .55 B2
Spencer Ho
3 London SW8 ...171 B1
24 Putney SW19 ...69 C3
Wimbledon SW19 ...69 C1
Spencer Mews W6 .154 A4
Spencer Park Ct
SW18 ...... .59 C2
Spencer Pk SW18 ...59 C2
Spencer Pl SW1 ...133 A1
Spencer Rd
3 London N8 ...... .5 A4
Chiswick W4 ...... .45 B3
London SW18 ...... .59 C2
London W3 ...... .28 B1
Spencer Rise NW5 ...4 A1
Spencer St EC1 ...... .96 A3
Spenlow Ho 16 SE16 139 C2
Spenser Gr N16 ...... .16 A4
Spenser Mews SE21 .75 C2
Spenser Rd SE24 ...63 A2
Spenser St SW1 ...133 A2
Spens Ho WC1 ...... .94 C3
Spensley Wlk N16 ...6 C1
Spert St E14 ...... .33 A2
Spey St E14 ...... .34 B4
Spezia Rd NW10 ...21 C3
Spice Ct 1 ...... .125 C2
10 London SW11 ...59 B4
Spice Quay Heights
SE1 ...... .124 C1
Spicer Cl SE5,SW9 .48 A1
Spindrift Ave E14 ...42 A2
Spinnaker Ho 8 E14 .41 C4
Spinney The
Barnes SW13 ...... .47 A4
Streatham SW16 ...73 C1
Spire Ct 13 TW10 ...54 A1
Spire Ho W2 ...... .115 A4
Spirit Quay E1 ...... .32 A1
Spital Sq E1 ...... .110 B4
Spital St E1 ...... .99 B1
Spital Yd E1 ...... .110 B4
Splendour Wlk
SE16 ...... .40 B1
Spode Ho SE11 ...135 B1
Spode Wlk NW3 ...11 A3
Sporle Ct 13 SW11 ...59 C4
Sprewell SW15 ...... .58 A1
Spriggs Ho 11 N1 ...15 A1
Sprimont Pl SW3 ...144 C2
Springall St 9 SE15 .50 A3
Springalls Wharf
SE16 ...... .139 B4
Springbank Wlk
NW1 ...... .13 C1
Spring Cott 10 W12 .38 C4
Springdale Rd N16 .15 C4
Springett Ho 3
SW2 ...... .62 B2
Springfield Ho
1 London SE5 ...49 A1
London W3 ...... .28 B1

Springfield Hospl
SW17 ...... .72 A1
Springfield La NW6 .78 A3
Springfield Rd NW8 .79 A3
Springfield Wlk
NW6 ...... .78 A3
Spring Gdns SW1 ...120 A2
London N5 ...... .15 B3
Spring Gr W4 ...... .44 C4
Spring Grove Rd
TW10 ...... .54 B2
Spring Hill E5 ...... .7 C4
Springhill Cl SE5 ...63 C4
Spring Ho WC1 ...... .95 B3
Spring Mews W1 ...103 A4
Springpark Dr N4 ...6 B3
Spring Pl NW5 ...... .13 A3
Springrice Rd SE13 .67 C1
Spring St W2 ...... .101 B1
Spring Terr TW10 ...54 A2
Springvale Ave TW8 .36 A1
Springvale Terr 5
W14 ...... .39 C3
Springwater WC1 ...106 C4
Springwell Ave
NW10 ...... .21 B4
Spruce Ct W5 ...... .36 A3
Spruce Ho 13 SE16 .40 C4
Sprules Rd SE4 ...... .51 A1
Spurgeon St SE1 ...137 B2
Spurling Rd SE22 ...64 B3
Spur Rd SE1 ...... .135 B4
Spurstow Rd E8 ...17 A2
Spurstowe Terr E8 .17 A3
Square Rigger Row 7
SW11 ...... .59 B4
Squarey St SW17 ...71 B1
Squire Gdns NW8 ...89 B3
Squires Ct SW4 ...172 B3
Squire's Mount NW3 .2 C1
Squirrels The SE13 .67 C4
Squirries St
E2 ...... .24 C2 99 C3
Stables End SE11 .149 B2
Stable Way W10 ...30 B3
Stable Yd Rd SW1 .133 A4
Stacey St WC2 ...... .105 C1
London N7 ...... .5 C1
Stack Ho SW1 ...... .145 C3
Stackhouse St
SW1 ...... .130 C2
Stacy Path SE5 ...49 A3
Stadium St SW10 ...157 A1
Stafford Cl NW6 ...23 C2
Stafford Cripps Ho
SW6 ...... .25 B2
London SW9 ...... .155 A3
Stafford Ct SW8 ...172 A4
W8 ...... .127 C2
Stafford Ho SE1 ...153 A2
Stafford Mans
SW11 ...... .158 C2
13 London SW4 ...62 A3
11 London W14 ...39 C3
Stafford Pl SW1 ...132 C2
Stafford Rd E3 ...... .26 B3
London NW6 ...... .23 C2
Staffordshire St
London SE15 ...... .49 C2
London SE15 ...... .50 A2
Stafford St W1 ...118 C2
Stafford Terr W8 ...127 B2

Stagshaw Ho 17
SE22 ...... .64 A4
Stainer St SE1 ...... .123 C1
Staining La EC2 ...109 A2
Stainsby Pl E14 ...33 C3
Stainsby Rd E14 ...33 C3
Stalbridge Ho NW1 .82 C1
Stalbridge St NW1 .102 B4
Stalham St SE16 ...40 A3
Stambourne Ho
SW8 ...... .172 B4
Stamford Bridge Stadium (Chelsea FC)
SW6 ...... .156 A2
Stamford Brook Ave
W6 ...... .38 B3
Stamford Brook Gdns 1
W6 ...... .38 B3
Stamford Brook Mans 2
W6 ...... .38 B3
Stamford Brook Rd
W6 ...... .38 B3
Stamford Brook Sta
W6 ...... .38 B2
Stamford Cl 2 NW3 ...2 B1
Stamford Ct W6 ...38 C2
Stamford Grove E 1
N16 ...... .7 C3
Stamford Grove W 4
N16 ...... .7 C3
Stamford Hill N16 ...7 B3
Stamford Hill Mans 1
N16 ...... .7 B3
Stamford Hill Sta
N16 ...... .7 A2
Stamford Hospl W6 .38 C2
Stamford Lo 2 N16 .7 B4
Stamford Mans 2
N16 ...... .7 C3
Stamford Rd N1 ...16 A2
Stamford St SE1 ...121 C2
Stamp Pl E2 ...... .98 C3
Stanard Cl N16 ...... .7 A4
Stanborough Ho 4
E3 ...... .27 A1
Stanborough Pas
E8 ...... .16 B2
Stanbridge Mans
SW15 ...... .57 B4
Stanbridge Rd
SW15 ...... .57 B4
Stanbury Ct 1 ...... .118 C2
Stanbury Rd
London SE15 ...... .50 A1
London SE15 ...... .50 B1
Standard Pl EC2 ...98 B3
Standard Rd NW10 .20 C1
Standen Rd SW18 ...70 C4
Standish Ho 6 W6 .38 C2
Standish Rd W6 ...38 C2
Stanesgate Ho 20
SE5 ...... .48 B3
Stanfield Ho NW8 ...89 C2
Stanfield Rd 13 E3 .26 A3
Stanford Ct SW6 ...166 B3
W8 ...... .128 B1
Stanford Pl SE1 ...152 A3
Stanford Rd W8 ...128 B2
Stanford St SW1 ...147 B3
Stanhope Cl 26
SE16 ...... .40 C4
Stanhope Gate
W1 ...... .117 C2

Stanhope Gdns
SW7 . . . . .143 A4
Stanhope Ho SE8 . . . .51 B3
4 Putney SW15 . . . . . .57 B2
Stanhope Mews E 5
SW7 . . . . .143 A4
Stanhope Mews S
SW7 . . . . .143 A3
Stanhope Mews W
SW7 . . . . .143 A4
Stanhope Pl W2 . . . .102 C1
Stanhope Rd N6 . . . . . .4 B4
Stanhope Row W1 . . .118 A1
Stanhope St NW1 . . . .92 C3
Stanhope Terr W2 . . .115 C4
Stanier Cl SW5 . . . . .141 A1
Staniake Rd W12 . . . .30 B1
Stanlake Villas W12 .30 B1
Stanley Bldgs NW1 . .84 A1
Stanley Cl SW8 . . . . .162 C3
Stanley Cres
W11 . . . . . . .31 B2 112 C4
Stanley Gdns NW1 . .112 C4
London NW2 . . . . .9 B3
Richmond TW9 . . . . . .54 A3
Stanley Gr SW11 . . . .169 C1
Stanley Ho 9 E14 . . . .33 C3
London SW8 . . . . . . .171 B1
Stanley Mans
SW10 . . . . .157 A4
Upper Tooting SW17 .72 B2
Stanley Rd E15 . . . . . .27 C4
London W3 . . . . .37 B3
Mortlake SW14 . . . . . .55 A3
Stanley St SE14,SE8 .51 B3
Stanley Studios
SW10 . . . . .157 A4
Stanley Terr 7 N19 . . .5 A2
Stanmer St SW11 . . .168 B2
Stanmore Gdns
TW9 . . . . .54 B4
Stanmore Ho SW8 .171 C2
Stanmore Pl NW1 . . .82 B4
Stanmore Rd TW9 . . .54 B4
Stanmore St N1 . . . . .84 C4
Stannard Cotts 22
E1 . . . . .25 B1
Stannard Mews E8 . .16 C2
Stannard Rd E8 . . . . .16 C2
Stannary Pl SE11 . . .149 C1
Stannary St SE11 . . .149 C1
Stansbury Ho 3
W10 . . . . .23 A2
Stansfeld Ho SE1 . . .153 A3
Stansfield Rd SW9 . .62 B4
Stanstead Ho 3 E3 . .27 B1
Stanswood Gdns
SE5 . . . . .49 A3
Stanton Ct N16 . . . . . .6 C4
Stanton Ho 8 SE10 . .52 B4
Stanton Rd SW13 . . . .46 B1
Stanway Ct 22 N1 . . .24 A3
Stanway St N1 . . . . . .24 A3
Stanwick Rd W14 . . .140 C3
Stanworth St SE1 . . .139 A3
Stapelhurst Ho 10
E5 . . . . .17 A3
Staplefield Cl 3
SW2 . . . . .74 A3
Stapleford Cl SW19 .70 A4
Staplehurst Ct
SW11 . . . . .60 B1
Staple Inn WC2 . . . .107 B3
Staple Inn Bldgs
WC2 . . . . .107 B3

Staples Cl SE16 . . . . . .33 A1
Staple St SE1 . . . . . .137 C3
Stapleton Hall N4 . . . .5 B4
Stapleton Hall Rd N4 .5 B4
Stapleton Ho 10 E2 . .25 A2
Stapleton Rd SW17 . .72 C1
Star Alley EC3 . . . . . .124 B4
Starboard Way E14 . .41 C3
Starcross St NW1 . . .93 A3
Starfield Rd W12 . . . .38 C4
Star & Garter Mans
SW15 . . . . .57 C4
Starliner Ct N7 . . . . . .14 C2
Starling Ho NW8 . . . .80 A2
Star Pl E1 . . . . .125 C3
Star Rd W14 . . . . . . .140 C1
Star St W2 . . . . .102 A2
Star Works NW10 . . .21 C2
Star Yd WC2 . . . . . .107 B2
Statham Gr N16 . . . . . .6 C1
Statham Ho SW8 . . .170 C4
Stathard Ho 18 E1 . .25 B1
Station App
Fulham SW6 . . . . . . .58 C4
London NW10 . . . . . .21 B2
Richmond TW9 . . . . . .44 C2
Station App Rd
SE1 . . . . .135 B4
Station Approach Rd
W4 . . . . .45 B3
Station Ave
5 London SW9 . . . . . .63 A4
19 Richmond TW9 . . .44 C2
Station Cres SE3 . . . .43 C1
Station Ct 5 SE15 . . .50 B1
Stationers Hall Ct
EC4 . . . . .108 B1
Station Gdns W4 . . . .45 B3
Station Par
Richmond TW9 . . . . . .44 C2
4 Upper Tooting
SW12 . . . . .72 C3
Station Pas SE15 . . .50 B2
Station Rd SE13 . . . . .67 B4
Station Rd N19 . . . . . .4 B1
Barnes SW13 . . . . . . .46 B1
London NW10 . . . . . .21 B3
London SE13 . . . . . . .67 B4
Station Rise SE27 . . .75 A2
Station St E15 . . . . . .19 C1
Station Terr
London NW10 . . . . . .22 C3
London SE5 . . . . .48 B2
Staunton Ho SE17 .152 A3
Staunton St SE8 . . . .51 B4
Staveley NW1 . . . . . .92 C4
Staveley Cl
London E9 . . . . .17 B3
London N7 . . . . .14 A4
London SE15 . . . . . . .50 B2
Staveley Gdns W4 . . .45 C2
Staveley Rd W4 . . . . .45 C3
Staverdale Lo W14 .127 A2
Stavers Ho 8 E3 . . . .26 B3
Staverton Rd NW2 . . .9 B1
Stave Yard Rd SE16 .33 A1
Stavordale Rd N5 . . .15 A4
Stayner's Rd E1 . . . . .25 C1
Steadman Ct EC1 . . .97 A2
Stead St SE17 . . . . . .151 B3
Stean St E8 . . . . .24 B4
Stebbing Ho 6
W11 . . . . .30 C1
Stebondale St E14 . .42 B2

Stebon Prim Sch
E14 . . . . .33 C4
Stedham Pl WC1 . . . .106 A2
Steedman St SE17 . .150 C3
Steele Rd
London NW10 . . . . . .20 B3
London W4 . . . . .37 B3
Steele's Mews N
NW3 . . . . .12 B2
Steele's Mews S
NW3 . . . . .12 B2
Steele's Rd NW3 . . . .12 B2
Steen Way 7 SE22 . .64 A2
Steep Hill SW16 . . . . .73 C1
Steeple Cl SW6 . . . .164 B1
Steeple Ct 11 E1 . . . .25 A1
Steeple Wlk N1 . . . . .86 C3
Steerforth St SW18 .71 B2
Steers Way SE16 . . . .41 A4
Stelfax Ho WC1 . . . . .95 A4
Stellman Cl E5 . . . . . . .7 C1
Stephan Cl E8 . . . . . .24 C4
Stephen Ct 18 SW19 .69 C3
Stephendale Rd
SW6 . . . . .166 C1
Stephen Fox Ho 7
W4 . . . . .38 A1
Stephen Hawking Sch
E14 . . . . .33 A3
Stephen Mews W1 . .105 B3
Stephen Pl SW4 . . . . .61 B4
Stephen Saunders Ct
SW11 . . . . .60 A2
Stephens Ct SE4 . . . .66 A4
Stephenson Ho
SE1 . . . . .136 C2
2 London SE8 . . . . . .12 B3
6 London NW5 . . . . . .13 A4
Stephenson St E16 . .35 A4
London NW10 . . . . . .21 B2
Stephenson Way
NW1 . . . . .93 A2
Stephen St W1 . . . . .105 B3
Stepney Cswy E1 . . . .32 C3
Stepney Day Hospl
E1 . . . . .32 B4
Stepney Green Ct 3
E1 . . . . .32 C4
Stepney Green Sch
E1 . . . . .32 C4
Stepney Green Sta
E1 . . . . .25 C1
Stepney High St E1 . .32 C4
Stepney Way E1 . . . . .32 B4
Sterling Cl NW10 . . . .8 C1
Sterling Gdns SE14 .51 A4
Sterling Pl W5 . . . . . .36 A2
Sterling St SW7 . . . .130 B2
Sterndale Rd W14 . . .39 C3
Sterne St W12 . . . . . .30 C1
Sternhall La SE15 . . .64 C4
Sternhold Ave
SW12,SW7 . . . . .73 C2
Sterry St SE1 . . . . . .137 B3
Steve Biko Ct W10 . .22 C1
Steve Biko Rd N7 . . . .5 C1
Stevedore St 3 E1 . .32 A1
Stevenage Rd SW6 . .47 C2
Stevens Ave E9 . . . . .17 B2
Stevenson Cres
SE16 . . . . .40 A1
Stevenson Ho NW8 . .78 C4
London SW11 . . . . . .168 C1

Stevens St SE1 . . . . .138 B2
Steventon Rd W12 . .29 B2
Steward St E1 . . . . . .110 B4
Stewart Headlam Prim
Sch E1 . . . . .25 A1
Stewart Ho SE1 . . . .138 A1
Stewart Rd E15 . . . . .19 C4
Stewart's Gr SW3 . .144 A3
Stewart's Rd SW8 . .170 C4
Stewart St E14 . . . . . .42 B4
Stew La EC4 . . . . . . .122 C4
Steyne Rd W3 . . . . . .28 A1
Stifford Ho E1 . . . . . . .32 B4
Stile Hall Gdns W4 . .36 C1
Sileman Ho 6 E3 . . . .33 B4
Stilingfleet Rd
SW13 . . . . .46 C4
Stillington St SW1 .147 A4
Stillness Jun & Inf Schs
SE23 . . . . .66 B1
Stillness Rd SE23 . . .66 B1
Stirling Ct EC1 . . . . . .96 A2
WC2 . . . . .106 C1
Stirling Mans NW6 . .11 B2
Stirling Rd
London SW9 . . . . . . .172 B1
London W3 . . . . .37 A3
Stoatley Ho 10
SW15 . . . . .68 C3
Stockbeck N1 . . . . . .83 A1
Stock Exchange
EC2 . . . . .109 C1
Stockfield Rd SW16 .74 B1
Stockholm Ho E1 . .125 C4
Stockholm Rd SE16 .40 B1
Stockholm Way E1 .125 B2
Stockhurst Cl SW15 .47 C1
Stockleigh Hall
NW8 . . . . .80 B2
Stock Orchard Cres
N7 . . . . .14 B3
Stock Orchard St
N7 . . . . .14 B3
Stocks Ct 5 E1 . . . . . .25 C1
Stocks Pl 10 E14 . . . .33 B2
Stockton Ho 10 E2 . .25 A2
Stockwell Ave SW9 . .62 B4
Stockwell Gdns
SW9 . . . . .172 C3
Stockwell Gn SW9 .172 C1
Stockwell La SW9 . .172 C3
Stockwell Park Cres
SW9 . . . . .173 A2
Stockwell Park Rd
SW9 . . . . .173 A3
Stockwell Park Sch
SW9 . . . . .172 C3
Stockwell Park Wlk
SW9 . . . . .62 C4
Stockwell Prim Sch
SW9 . . . . .62 B4
Stockwell Sta SW9 . .172 B3
Stockwell St SE10 . .52 B4
Stockwell Terr
SW9 . . . . .173 A3
Stoddart Ho SW8 . .163 A3
Stodmarsh Ho
SW9 . . . . .173 C4
Stoford Cl SW19 . . . .70 A4
Stokenchurch St
SW6 . . . . .166 A3
Stoke Newington
Church St N16 . . . . . .7 A2
Stoke Newington Comm
N16 . . . . .7 B2

Stoke Newington High
St N16 . . . . .7 B1
Stoke Newington Rd
N16 . . . . .16 B4
Stoke Newington Sch
N16 . . . . .6 C1
Stoke Pl NW10 . . . . . .21 B2
Stokesley St W12 . . .29 B3
Stondon Pk SE23 . . . .66 A1
Stone Bldgs WC2 . . .107 A3
Stonebridge Sch The
NW10 . . . . .20 C4
Stonebridge Sh Ctr 6
NW10 . . . . .20 C4
Stone Cl SW4 . . . . . .171 A1
Stonecutter St
EC4 . . . . .108 A2
Stonefield N4 . . . . . . .5 B2
Stonefield Mans N1 .85 B3
Stonefield St N1 . . . .85 C4
Stone Gate 8 NW5 .12 C2
Stonehill Cl SW14 . . .55 C2
Stonehill Rd
London W4 . . . . .36 C1
Mortlake SW14 . . . . . .55 C2
Stonehills Ct SE21 . .76 A1
Stonehill's Mans 3
SW16 . . . . .74 A2
Stonehouse NW1 . . . .83 A3
Stonehouse Ct
EC2 . . . . .110 B2
Stonehouse Ho 27
W2 . . . . .31 C4
Stoneleigh Lo 13
TW9 . . . . .44 B2
Stoneleigh Pl W11 . .30 C2
Stoneleigh St W11 . .30 C2
Stoneleigh Terr N19 . .4 A2
Stonell's Rd SW11 . .60 B2
Stonenest St N4 . . . . .5 B3
Stones End St SE1 .136 C3
Stoneyard La E14 . . .34 A2
Stoney La E1 . . . . . .110 B2
Stoney St SE1 . . . . .123 B2
Stonhouse St SW4 . .61 C3
Stonor Rd W14 . . . . .140 C3
Stopes St SE15 . . . . .49 B3
Stopford Rd SE17 . .150 B1
Stopher Ho SE1 . . . .136 B3
Storace Ho 6 SW4 . .62 A3
Storers Quay E14 . . .42 C2
Store St
London E15 . . . . .19 C3
London WC1 . . . . . . .105 B4
Storey Ct NW8 . . . . . .89 B3
Storey Ho 11 E14 . . . .34 A2
Storey's Gate SW1 .133 C3
Stories Rd SE5 . . . . . .64 A4
Storks Rd SE16 . . . . .139 C1
Stormont House Sch
E5 . . . . .17 A4
Stormont Rd
London N6 . . . . .3 B4
London SW11 . . . . . . .60 C3
Storrington WC1 . . . . .94 B3
Story St N1 . . . . .14 B1
Stothard Pl E1 . . . . . .110 B4
Stothard St 11 E1 . . .25 B1
Stott Cl SW18 . . . . . .59 C1
Stoughton Cl SE11 .149 A3
Roehampton SW15 . .68 C3
Stourcliffe Cl W1 . . .102 C2
Stourcliffe St W1 . . .102 C1
Stourhead Cl 6
SW19 . . . . .69 C4
Stour Rd E3 . . . . .18 C1

Stowage SE8 . . . . .52 A4
Stowe Ho 11 N16 . . . . . . .17 A2
Stowe Rd W12 . . . . .39 A4
Stracey Rd N5 . . . . .15 B4
Stradbroke Rd N5 . . . . . . .15 B4
Stradella Rd SE24 . . . . . . .63 B1
Straffan Lo 8 SW3 . .12 A2
Strafford Ho 9 SE8 . . . . .41 B1
Strafford Rd W3 . . . . .37 B4
Strafford St E14 . . . . .41 C4
Strahan Rd E3 . . . . .26 A2
Straightsmouth
SE10 . . . . .52 B3
Straker's Rd SE15 . . . . . . .65 A3
Strale Ho 17 N1 . . . . .24 A4
Strand WC2 . . . . .120 C4
Strand La WC2 . . . . .121 A4
Strand-on-the-Green
W4 . . . . .44 C4
Strand-on-the-Green
Sch W4 . . . . .44 C4
Strang Ho N1 . . . . .86 C3
Strangways Terr
W14 . . . . .126 C1
Stranraer Way N1 . . . . . . .14 A1
Strasburg Rd
SW11 . . . . .170 B4
Stratford Bus Sta
E15 . . . . .19 C1
Stratford Cir E15 . . . . . . .19 C2
Stratford Ctr E15 . . . . . . .19 C1
Stratford Gr SW15 . . . . . .57 C3
Stratford Pl W1 . . . . .104 A1
Stratford Rd W8 . . . . .127 C1
Stratford Sta E15 . . . . . . .19 C1
Stratford Studios
W8 . . . . .128 A1
Stratford Villas
NW1 . . . . .13 C1
Stratford Workshops
E15 . . . . .27 A4
Strathan Cl SW18 . . . . . . .58 A1
Strathblaine Rd
SW11 . . . . .59 C3
Strathdon Dr SW17 . . . . .71 C1
Strathearn Ho W2 . . . . . .116 A4
Strathearn Pl W2 . . . . . . .116 A4
Stratheden Par SE3 . . . . . .53 C3
Stratheden Rd SE3 . . . . . .53 C3
Strathleven Rd SW2 . . . . .62 A2
Strathmore Ct NW8 . .90 A4
Strathmore Gdns
W8 . . . . .113 C2
Strathmore Rd
SW19 . . . . .70 C1
Strathnairn St SE1 . . . . . .153 C3
Strathray Gdns
NW3 . . . . .12 A2
Strath Terr SW11 . . . . .60 A3
Strathville Rd SW18 . . . . .71 A2
Stratton Ct 4 N16 . . . . . .16 A1
Strattondale St E14 . . . . . .42 B3
Stratton St W1 . . . . .118 B2
Strauss Rd W4 . . . . .37 C4
Streamline Mews
SE22 . . . . .76 C3
Streatham Cl SW16 . . . . . .74 A2
Streatham & Clapham
High Sch SW16 . .73 C1
Streatham Ct SW16 . . . . . .74 A2
Streatham Hill SW2 . . . . . .74 A3
Streatham Hill &
Clapham High Sch
SW2 . . . . .74 B3
Strcothim Hill Sta
SW16 . . . . .74 A1
Streatham Pl SW2 . . . . . . .74 A4

Streatham St WC1 . . .106 A2
Streatham & Tooting
Adult Inst SW16 . . .74 B2
Streathbourne Rd
SW17 . . . . .72 C1
Streatham Wells Prim
Sch SW2 . . . . .74 B3
Streatleigh Par 8
SW16 . . . . .74 A2
Streatley Pl
12 London NW3 . . . . . .11 C4
5 London NW3 . . . . . . .11 B4
Streatley Rd NW6 . . . . . .10 B1
Streimer Rd E15 . . . . .27 B3
Strelley Way W3 . . . . .29 A2
Stretton Mans 16
SE8 . . . . .51 C4
Strickland Ct SE15 . . . . . .64 C4
Strickland Ho E2 . . . .99 A3
Strickland Row
SW18 . . . . .71 C4
Strickland St SE8 . . . . . . .51 C2
Stringer Hos 11 N1 . . . . . .24 A4
Strode Ho 8 SW2 . . . . .74 C3
Strode Rd SW6 . . . . .154 A2
Stroma Ct SW6 . . . . .8 C2
Strome Ho NW6 . . . . .78 A1
Stronsa Rd W12 . . . . .38 B4
Strood Ho SE1 . . . . .137 C3
Stroud Cres SW15 . . . . . .68 C1
Stroud Green JMI Sch
N4 . . . . .5 C4
Stroud Green Rd N4 . .5 C2
Stroudley Ho SW8 . . . . .171 A4
Stroudley Wlk E3 . . . . . . .27 A2
Stroud Rd SW19 . . . . .70 C1
Strout's Pl E2 . . . . .24 B3
Strudwick Ct SW4 . . .172 B3
Strutton Ground
SW1 . . . . .133 B1
Strype St E1 . . . . .110 C3
Stuart Ave W5 . . . . .36 B4
Stuart Ho W14 . . . . .140 A4
1 London E9 . . . . .17 C1
3 London SW4 . . . . .62 A3
Stuart Mill Ho N1 . . . . . . .84 C1
Stuart Rd
London NW6 . . . . .23 C2
London SE15 . . . . .65 B3
London W3 . . . . .28 B1
Wimbledon SW19 . . . . .70 C1
Stubbs Dr SE16 . . . . .40 A1
Stubbs Ho 1 E2 . . . .25 C2
London N4 . . . . .5 B3
Stucley Pl 15 NW1 . . . . . .13 A1
Studdridge St
SW6 . . . . .165 C2
Studd St N1 . . . . .86 A4
Studholme Ho W11 . . . . .10 C4
Studholme St SE15 . . . . . .50 A3
Studio Pl SW1 . . . . .131 A3
Studios The SW8 . . . .171 C3
4 London SW4 . . . . .61 B3
Studland Ho E14 . . . . .33 A3
Studland St W6 . . . . .39 A2
Studley Cl E5 . . . . .18 A3
Studley Ct 13 E14 . . . . . .34 C2
Studley Rd SW4 . . . . .172 B2
Stukeley St WC2 . . . . . . .106 B2
Stunnell Ho 21 SE14 . . . .50 C4
Sturdee Ho 2 E2 . . . . .24 C3
Sturdy Ho 2 E3 . . . . .26 A3
Sturdy Rd SE15 . . . . .50 A1
Sturgeon Rd SE17 . .150 C1
Sturge St SE1 . . . . .136 C4
Sturmer Way N7 . . . . .14 B3

Sturminster Ho
SW8 . . . . .163 A1
Sturry St E14 . . . . .34 A3
Sturt St N1 . . . . .87 A1
Stutfield St E1 . . . . .111 C1
Stuttle Ho E1 . . . . .99 B1
Styles Gdns SW9 . . . . .63 A4
Styles Ho SE1 . . . . .122 A1
Sudbourne Prim Sch
SW2 . . . . .62 B2
Sudbourne Rd SW2 . . . . .62 B2
Sudbrooke Rd
SW12 . . . . .60 C1
Sudbury Ct SW8 . . . . . . .171 C4
London E5 . . . . .18 A4
Sudbury Ho SW18 . . . . . .59 A2
Sudeley St N1 . . . . .86 B1
Sudlow Rd SW18 . . . . . . .58 C2
Sudrey St SE1 . . . . .136 C3
Suffield Ho SE17 . . . .150 B2
Suffolk Ho 5 . . . . .123 B4
Suffolk Pl SW1 . . . . .119 C2
Suffolk Rd
Barnes SW13 . . . . .46 C3
London SW11 . . . . .8 A1
Suffolk St SW1 . . . . .119 C2
Sugar House La E15 . . . . .27 B3
Sugar Loaf Wlk 6
E2 . . . . .25 B2
Sugden Rd SW11 . . . . . . .60 C3
Sulby Ho SE4 . . . . .66 A3
Sulgrave Gdns 11
W6 . . . . .39 B4
Sulgrave Rd W6 . . . . .39 B3
Sulina Rd SW2 . . . . .74 A4
Sulivan Ct SW6 . . . . . .165 B1
Sulivan Ent Ctr
SW6 . . . . .58 C4
Sulivan Prim Sch
SW6 . . . . .165 C1
Sulivan Rd SW6 . . . . .58 C4
Sulkin Ho 11 E2 . . . . .25 C2
Sullivan Cl SW11 . . . . .60 A4
Sullivan Ct SW5 . . . . .141 C4
London N16 . . . . .7 B3
Sullivan Ho SW1 . . . .160 B4
SE11 . . . . .149 A3
Sullivan Rd SE11 . . . . . . .149 C4
Sultan St SE5 . . . . .48 B3
Sumatra Rd NW6 . . . . . . .10 C2
Sumburgh Rd SW12 . . . . .60 C1
Summercourt Rd
E1 . . . . .32 B3
Summerfield Ave
NW6 . . . . .23 A3
Summer Ho SE13 . . . . . . .67 C3
Summerhouse Rd
N16 . . . . .7 A2
Summerlands Ave
W3 . . . . .28 B2
Summerley St
SW18 . . . . .71 A2
Summers St EC1 . . . . .95 B1
Summit Ct NW2 . . . . .10 A3
Summit Est N16 . . . . .7 C4
Sumner Ave SE15 . . . . . . .49 B2
Sumner Bldgs SE1 . . .122 C2
Sumner Ct SW8 . . . . .172 A4
Sumner Ho 1 E3 . . . . .34 A4
Sumner Pl SW7 . . . . .143 C3
Sumner Place Mews
SW7 . . . . .143 C3
Sumner Rd SE15 . . . . .49 B3
Sumner St SE1 . . . . .122 C2
Sumpter Cl NW3 . . . . .11 B2
Sun Alley 6 TW9 . . . . . . .54 A3
Sunbeam Cres W10 . . . . .22 B1

Sunbeam Rd NW10 . . . . .20 C1
Sunbury Ave SW14 . . . . . .55 C3
Sunbury Ct 8 SE14 . . . . . .50 C4
Sunbury Ho E2 . . . . .99 A3
Sunbury La SW11 . . . . . .167 C4
Sunbury Workshops
E2 . . . . .98 C3
Sun Ct EC3 . . . . .109 C1
Sunderland Ct SE22 . .76 C4
Sunderland Ho 28
W2 . . . . .31 C4
Sunderland Terr
W2 . . . . .100 A2
Sundew Ave W12 . . . . . . .29 C2
Sundridge Ho 4 E9 . . . . . .17 C1
Sunlight Sq 2 E2 . . . . .25 A2
Sunningdale Ave
W3 . . . . .29 A2
Sunningdale Cl 22
SE16 . . . . .40 A1
Sunningdale Gdns
W8 . . . . .127 C1
London W3 . . . . .37 B4
Sunninghill Ct 8
W3 . . . . .37 B4
Sunninghill Rd
SE13 . . . . .52 A1
Sunnyhill Cl E5 . . . . .18 A4
Sunnymead Rd
SW15 . . . . .57 A2
Sunnyside 3 NW2 . . . . . . .1 B1
Sunnyside Ho 3
NW2 . . . . .1 B1
Sunnyside Rd N19 . . . . . . .4 C4
Sun Pas SE16 . . . . .139 B2
Sunray Ave SE5,
SE24 . . . . .63 C3
Sun St EC2 . . . . .109 C4
Sun St Pas EC2 . . . . .110 A3
Sunwell Cl SE15 . . . . .50 A2
Surma Cl E1 . . . . .24 C1
Surrendale Pl W9 . . . . . . .23 C1
Surrey Canal Rd
SE14,SE16,SE8 . . . . . . .50 C4
Surrey Cres 1 W4 . . . . . . .36 C1
Surrey La SW11 . . . . .168 B3
Surrey Quays Rd
SE16 . . . . .40 C4
Surrey Quays Sh Ctr
SE16 . . . . .40 C3
Surrey Quays Sta
SE16 . . . . .40 C2
Surrey Rd SE15 . . . . .65 C2
Surrey Row SE1 . . . . .136 B4
Surrey Sq SE17 . . . . .152 B2
Surrey Square Inf Sch
SE17 . . . . .152 A2
Surrey Square Jun Sch
SE17 . . . . .152 A2
Surrey St WC2 . . . . .121 A4
Surrey Terr SE17 . . . . . . .152 B2
Surrey Water Rd
SE16 . . . . .32 C1
Surridge Ct SW9 . . . .172 B2
Surr St N7 . . . . .14 A3
Susan Constant Ct 3
E14 . . . . .34 C2
Susan Lawrence Prim
Schs E14 . . . . .34 B3
Susannah St E14 . . . . .34 B3
Sussex Cl N19 . . . . .5 A2
Sussex Ct SE10 . . . . .52 B3

Sussex Ct continued
W2 . . . . .101 B3
4 Barnes SW13 . . . . . . .46 B1
Sussex Gdns W2 . . . .101 C1
Sussex Ho
London NW3 . . . . .12 A2
Richmond TW9 . . . . .44 B1
Sussex House Sch
SW3 . . . . .144 C3
Sussex Lo W2 . . . . .101 C1
Sussex Mans SW7 . . .143 B3
WC2 . . . . .120 B4
Sussex Mews E
W2 . . . . .101 C1
Sussex Mews W
W2 . . . . .115 C4
Sussex Pl NW1 . . . . .90 C2
W2 . . . . .101 C1
22 London W6 . . . . . . .39 B1
Sussex Sq W2 . . . . .115 C4
Sussex St SW1 . . . . .146 B2
Sussex Way N19 . . . . .4 C3
London N7,N19 . . . . .5 A2
Sutherland Ave W9 . .88 B2
Sutherland Ct
W9 . . . . .23 C1
London N16 . . . . .6 C1
Sutherland Gdns
SW14 . . . . .56 A4
Sutherland Gr SW18,
SW19 . . . . .70 B4
Sutherland Ho W8 . . .128 A1
9 London NW6 . . . . . . .11 B2
7 Putney SW15 . . . . . . .69 B4
Sutherland Pl W2 . . . . . . .31 C3
Sutherland Point 1
E5 . . . . .17 A4
Sutherland Rd E3 . . . . . . .26 B3
Chiswick W4 . . . . .46 A4
Sutherland Row
SW1 . . . . .146 B2
Sutherland Sq
SE17 . . . . .150 C1
Sutherland St SW1 . .146 B2
Sutherland Wlk
SE17 . . . . .151 A1
Sutterton St N7 . . . . .14 B2
Sutton Court Rd
W4 . . . . .45 B4
Sutton Ct
Chiswick W4 . . . . .45 A4
9 London E5 . . . . .17 A4
Sutton Est SW3 . . . . .144 B2
Sutton Est The W10 . . . . .30 B4
Sutton La N4 . . . . .37 B2
Sutton La N SW4 . . . . .45 B4
Sutton La S W4 . . . . .45 B4
Sutton Pl E9 . . . . .17 B3
Sutton Row W1 . . . . .105 C2
Sutton Sq E9 . . . . .17 B3
Sutton St E1 . . . . .32 B3
Suttons Way EC1 . . . . . . .97 A1
Sutton Way W10 . . . . .30 B4
Sutton Wlk SE1 . . . . .120 C2
Swaby Rd SW17,
SW18 . . . . .71 B2
Swaffield Prim Sch
SW18 . . . . .71 B4
Swaffield Rd SW18 . .71 B4
Swain's La N6 . . . . .4 A2
Swainson Rd W3 . . . . .38 B4
Swallow Cl SE14 . . . . .50 C2
Swallow Ct 9 W9 . . . . . . .31 C4
Swallowfield NW1 . .92 B3
Swallow Ho NW8 . . . .80 A2

Swallow Pl W1 ....**104** B1
Swallow St W1 ....**119** A3
Swanage Ct 🔢 N1 ......**16** A1
Swanage Ho SW8 .....**162** C1
Swanage Rd SW18 ....**59** B1
Swanbourne SE17 ....**150** C3
Swanbourne Ho
  NW8 ....**90** A2
Swan Ct E14 ....**33** B2
  SW3 ....**144** B1
  SW6 ....**155** C1
Swan Ctr SW17 ....**71** B1
Swandon Way
  SW18 ....**59** A3
Swanfield St E2 ....**99** A3
Swan Ho N1 ....**15** C1
Swan La E14 ....**123** C3
Swan Lane Pier
  EC4 ....**123** C3
Swanlea Sec Sch
  E1 ....**25** A1
Swanley Ho SE17 .....**152** B2
Swan Mead SE1 ....**138** A1
Swan Mews SW9 ......**172** C2
Swanmore Ct SW18 ....**59** B1
Swanne Ho 🔢 SE10 ....**52** B3
Swan Pas E1 ....**125** C3
Swan Rd SE16 ....**40** B4
Swanscombe Ho 🔢
  W11 ....**30** C1
Swanscombe Point 🔢
  E16 ....**35** B2
Swanscombe Rd
  London W11 ....**30** C1
  🔢 London W4 ....**38** A1
Swan St SE1 ....**137** A3
Swanton Gdns
  SW19 ....**69** C3
Swanwick Cl SW15 ....**68** A4
Swan Wlk SW3 ....**158** C4
Swan Yd N1 ....**15** A2
Swaton Rd E3 ....**26** C1
Swaythling Ho 🔢
  SW15 ....**56** B1
Swedenborg Gdns
  E1 ....**32** A2
Sweden Gate SE16 ....**41** A2
Swedish Sch The
  SW13 ....**46** B4
Sweeney Cres SE1 ...**139** A3
Sweyn Pl SE3 ....**53** C1
Swift Ho 🔢 E1 ....**32** B3
  SW9 ....**163** C2
  🔢 London N16 ....**6** C3
Swift St SW6 ....**164** C4
Swinbrook Rd W10 ....**31** A4
Swinburne Ct 🔢
  SE5 ....**63** C3
Swinburne Ho 🔢
  E2 ....**25** B2
Swinburne Rd
  SW15 ....**56** C3
Swindon St W12 ....**30** B1
Swinford Gdns SW9 ...**63** A4
Swingfield Ho 🔢
Swinley Ho NW1 ....**92** B4
Swinnerton St E9 ....**18** A3
Swinton Ho 🔢 E2 ....**25** B2
Swinton Pl WC1 ....**94** C4
Swinton St WC1 ....**94** C4
Swiss Cottage NW3 ...**11** C1
Swiss Cottage
  NW8 ....**79** C4

Swiss Cottage Sta
  NW3 ....**11** C1
Swiss Re Building★
  EC2 ....**110** B3
Swiss Terr 🔢 NW3 .....**11** C1
Sybil Phoenix Cl
Sybil Thorndike Casson
  SW5 ....**141** C1
Sybil Thorndike Ho 🔢
  N1 ....**15** B2
Sycamore Ave E3 ......**26** B4
Sycamore Cl W3 ....**29** A1
Sycamore Ct NW6 .....**23** C4
  🔢 London SE5 ....**48** B2
Sycamore Gdns W6,
  W12 ....**39** A3
Sycamore Gr SE6 .....**67** B1
Sycamore Ho
  🔢 SE16 ....**40** C4
  🔢 London N16 ....**6** C2
  🔢 London NW3 ....**12** B2
  🔢 London W6 ....**39** B3
Sycamore Lo SW15 ...**57** A4
Sycamore Mews
  SW4 ....**61** B4
Sycamore St EC1 ......**96** C1
Sycamore Wlk 🔢
  W10 ....**23** A1
Sydenham Hill SE21,
  SE22,SE23,SE26,SE19 .**76** C1
Sydenham Hill Sta
  SE21 ....**76** B1
Sydner Mews N16 .....**16** B4
Sydner Rd N16 ....**16** B4
Sydney Cl SW3 ....**143** C3
Sydney Ho 🔢 W4 ......**38** A2
Sydney Mews SW3 ...**143** C3
Sydney Pl SW7 ....**143** C3
Sydney Rd TW10,
  TW9 ....**54** A3
Sydney St SW3 ....**144** A2
Sylva Ct 🔢 SW15 ......**69** C4
Sylvan Gr NW2 ....**9** C4
  SE15 ....**50** A4
Sylvester Ho 🔢 E8 ...**17** A2
Sylvester Path 🔢
Sylvester Rd E8 ....**17** A2
Sylvia Cotts 🔢 SE8 ...**51** C2
Sylvia Ct N1 ....**87** B1
Sylvia Pankhurst Ho 🔢
  E2 ....**25** C2
Sylvia Young Theatre
  Sch NW1 ....**90** B1
Symes Mews NW1 ....**82** C2
Symington Ho SE1 ...**137** B1
Symington Mews
  E9 ....**17** C3
Symister Mews N1 .....**98** A4
Symons St SW3 ....**145** A3
Symphony Mews 🔢
  W10 ....**23** A2
Syringa Ho SE4 ....**66** B4

T

Tabard Ct 🔢 E14 ....**34** B3
Tabard Ho 🔢 SE1 ....**137** C2
Tabard St SE1 ....**137** B2
Tabernacle St EC2 .....**97** C2
Tableer Ave SW4 ....**61** C2
Tabley Rd N7 ....**14** A4
Tabor Rd W6 ....**39** A3
Tachbrook Est
  SW1 ....**147** C1

Tachbrook Mews
  SW1 ....**146** C4
Tachbrook St SW1 ...**147** A3
Tack Mews SE4 ....**66** C4
Tadema Ho NW8 ....**89** C1
Tadema Rd SW10 ....**157** A1
Tadmor St W12 ....**30** C1
Tadworth Ho 🔢
Taeping St E14 ....**42** A2
Taft Way 🔢 E3 ....**27** A2
Tailworth St E1 ....**111** B3
Tait Ct 🔢 E3 ....**26** B4
  London N19 ....**4** C1
Takhar Mews
  SW11 ....**168** B2
Talacre Rd NW5 ....**12** C2
Talbot Ct EC3 ....**123** C4
Talbot Grove Ho 🔢
  W11 ....**31** A3
Talbot Ho 🔢 E14 ....**34** A3
  London N7 ....**5** B2
Talbot Pl SE3 ....**53** A1
Talbot Rd W11 ....**31** B3
  W2 ....**31** C3
  London Sq 🔢 **101** B1
Talbot Wlk W11 ....**31** A3
  London NW10 ....**8** A2
Talbot Yd SE1 ....**123** B1
Talcott Path 🔢
Talford Pl SE15 ....**49** B2
Talfourd Rd SE15 ....**49** B2
Talgarth Rd W14 ......**140** B2
  W6 ....**39** C1
Talia Ho E14 ....**42** B3
Talina Ctr SW6 ....**166** C3
Talleyrand Ho SE5 .....**48** B1
Tallis St EC4 ....**121** C4
Talma Rd SW2 ....**62** C3
Talmudical Coll N16 ....**6** C4
Talmud Torah Sch
Talwin St E3 ....**27** A2
Tamar Cl E3 ....**26** B4
Tamar Ho SE11 ....**149** C2
  🔢 E14 ....**42** B3
Tamarind Ct 🔢 W3 ...**28** B3
Tamarind Ho 🔢
Tamarind Yd E1 ....**125** C2
Tamarisk Sq W12 ....**29** B2
Tamworth N7 ....**14** A2
Tamworth St SW6 ....**155** B3
Tangley Gr SW15 ....**68** B4
Tangley Rd SW11 ....**167** B3
Tangmere WC1 ....**94** C3
Tanhurst Ho 🔢
Tankerton St WC1 ......**94** B3
Tanner Ho SE1 ....**138** B3
Tanner's Hill SE8 ....**51** C2
Tanners Yd 🔢 E2 ....**25** A3
Tannery Ho 🔢 E1 .....**111** B4
Tannington Terr N5 .....**5** C1
Tansley Cl N7 ....**13** C3
Tanswell St SE1 ....**135** B3
Tantallon Rd SW12 ....**72** C3
Tant Ave E16 ....**35** B1
Tanza Rd NW3 ....**12** B4
Tapley Ho SE1 ....**139** B3
Taplow NW3 ....**11** C1
Taplow Ho 🔢 E2 ....**98** C3
Taplow St N1 ....**87** A1

Tachbrook Rd
  SW1 ....**65** B4
Taranto Ho 🔢 E1 ....**32** C4
Tarbert Rd SE22 ....**64** A2
Tarbert Wlk E1 ....**32** B2
Tarling Ho 🔢 E1 ....**32** B3
Tarling Rd E16 ....**35** B1
Tarling St E1 ....**32** B3
Tarnbrook Ct SW1 ...**145** B3
Tarn St SE1 ....**136** C1
Tarns The NW1 ....**92** C4
Tarplett Ho 🔢 SE14 ...**50** C4
Tarragon Cl SE14 .....**51** A3
Tarranbrae NW6 ....**10** A1
Tarrant Ho E2 ....**25** B2
Tarrant Pl W1 ....**102** C3
Tarrantt Ho W14 ......**126** B2
Tarriff Cres SE8 ....**41** B2
Tarrington Cl SW16 ...**73** C1
Tartan Ho 🔢 E14 ....**34** B3
Tarver Rd SE17 ....**150** B2
Tarves Way SE10 ......**52** A3
Tasker Ho 🔢 E14 ....**33** B4
Tasker Rd NW3 ....**12** B3
Tasman Ct 🔢 E14 .....**42** A2
Tasman Ho 🔢 E1 ....**125** C2
Tasman Rd SW9 ....**62** A4
Tasso Rd W6 ....**154** A4
Tasso Yd W6 ....**154** A3
Tatchbury Ho 🔢
  SW15 ....**56** B1
Tate Britain★ SW1 ...**148** B3
Tate Ho 🔢 E2 ....**25** C3
Tate Modern★
  EC4 ....**122** B4
Tatham Pl NW8 ....**79** C2
Tatnell Rd SE23 ....**66** A1
Tatton Cres E5,N16 ....**7** B4
Tatum St SE17 ....**151** C3
Tauheed Cl N4 ....**6** B2
Taunton Ho 🔢 W2 ...**100** C1
Taunton Mews NW1 ...**90** C1
Taunton Pl NW1 ....**90** C2
Taverner Ho N16 ....**6** C1
Taverners Cl W11 .....**112** A1
Taverner Sq 🔢 N5 .....**15** B4
Tavern La SW9 ....**173** C2
Tavistock Cl N16 ....**16** A3
Tavistock Cres W11 ...**31** B4
  🔢 W11 ....**31** B4
Tavistock Ct WC2 ....**93** C2
Tavistock Ho 🔢
  W11 ....**31** B3
Tavistock Pl WC1 ....**94** A2
Tavistock Rd W11 ....**31** B4
Tavistock Sq WC1 ......**93** C2
Tavistock St WC2 .....**120** B4
Tavistock Terr N19 .....**4** C1
Taviton St WC1 ....**93** B2
Tavy Cl SE11 ....**149** C2
Tawny Way SE16 ....**40** C2
Taybridge Rd SW11 ...**60** C3
Tayburn Cl E14 ....**34** B3
Tay Ho 🔢 E3 ....**26** B3
Tayler Ct NW8 ....**79** B4
Taylor Ave TW9 ....**45** A1
Taylor Ct E15 ....**76** B3
Taylor Ho 🔢 SW2 ......**74** C3
Taylor's Gn W3 ....**29** A3
Taylor's La NW10 ....**8** A2
Tayport Cl N1 ....**14** A1
Tayside Ct 🔢 SE5 .....**63** C3
Teak Cl SE16 ....**33** A1

Tealby Ct N7 ....**14** B2
Teal Ct 🔢 SE8 ....**51** B4
Teale St E2 ....**24** C3
Teather St 🔢 SE5 .....**49** A3
Tebbs Ho 🔢 SW2 ......**74** C4
Ted Roberts Ho 🔢
  E2 ....**25** A3
Tedworth Gdns
  SW3 ....**144** C1
Tedworth Sq SW3 ...**144** C1
Teesdale Cl E2 ....**25** A3
Teesdale St E2 ....**25** A3
Teesdale Yd 🔢 E2 .....**25** A3
The The W3 ....**29** A3
Teignmouth Cl 🔢
Teignmouth Rd NW2 ...**9** C3
Telegraph Hill NW3 ...**1** C1
Telegraph Pl E14 ....**42** A2
Telegraph Rd SW15 ...**69** B4
Telegraph St EC2 .....**109** B2
Telfer Cl 🔢 W3 ....**37** B4
Telfer Ho EC1 ....**96** B3
Telferscot JMI Sch
  SW12 ....**73** C3
Telferscot Rd SW12 ...**73** C3
Telford Ave SW12,
  SW2 ....**74** A3
Telford Avenue Mans 🔢
Telford Ho 🔢 SE1 ....**136** C2
  🔢 W10 ....**31** A4
Telford Parade Mans 🔢
  SW2 ....**74** A3
Telford Rd W10 ....**31** A4
Telford Terr SW1 ......**146** C4
Telford Way W3 ....**29** A4
Tell Gr SE22 ....**64** B3
Telscombe Ho
  SW11 ....**169** B3
Temair Ho 🔢 SE10 ...**52** B3
Temeraire St SE16 .....**40** B4
Temperley Rd SW12 ...**72** C4
Templar Ho 🔢 NW2 ...**10** B2
Templars Ho E15 ....**19** A3
Templar St SE5 ....**48** A1
Temple Ave EC4 ......**121** C4
Temple Ct 🔢
  E9 ....**25** A4
Temple Ct SW8 ....**162** A1
Temple Dwellings 🔢
  E2 ....**25** A3
Temple Ho
  London N7 ....**4** B1
  🔢 London SW11 .....**60** A4
Temple La EC4 ....**107** C1
Templemead Cl W3 ...**29** A3
Templemead Ho E9 ...**18** A4
Temple Mills La
  E10,E15 ....**76** B4
Temple Mills Rd E9 ...**18** C4
Temple Pl WC2 ....**121** A4
Temple Rd
  London W4 ....**37** B3
  Richmond TW9 ....**54** B4
Temple Sheen
  SW14 ....**55** B2
Temple Sheen Rd
  SW14 ....**55** A3
Temple St E2 ....**25** A3
Temple Sta WC2 ......**121** B4
Templeton Cl 🔢
  N16 ....**16** A3
Templeton Pl SW5 ...**141** C3

Temple West Mews SE11 ....136 A1
Templewood Ave NW3 ....2 A1
Templewood Gdns NW3 ....2 A1
Templewood Point NW2 ....1 B2
Tenbury Ct SW12 ....73 C3
Tenby Ho W7 ....100 C1
  London N7 ....14 C4
Tench St E1 ....32 A1
Tenda Rd SE16 ....40 A2
Tendring Ho SW2 ....62 C1
Tenham Ave SW2 ....73 C2
Tenison Ct W1 ....118 C4
Tenison Way SE1 ....121 B1
Tenniel Cl W2 ....114 B4
Tennis St SE1 ....137 B4
Tennyson Ct SW6 ....166 B3
Tennyson Ho SE17 ....150 C2
Tennyson Rd NW6 ....23 B4
Tennyson St SW8 ....170 A1
Tensing Ho N1 ....15 A2
Tenterden Ho
  SE17 ....152 B1
Tenterden St W1 ....104 B1
Tent Ground E1 ....110 C3
Tent St E1 ....25 A1
Terborch Way 6
  SE22 ....64 A2
Terling Ho W10 ....30 B4
Terling Wlk N1 ....86 C4
Terminus Pl SW1 ....132 B1
Terrace Ave NW10 ....22 B2
Terrace Gdns SW13 ....46 B1
Terrace La TW10 ....54 A1
Terrace Rd E9 ....17 B1
Terrace The EC4 ....107 C1
  NW6 ....23 C4
  9 SE8 ....41 B2
  SW13,SW14 ....46 A1
Terrapin Ct SW17 ....73 A1
Terrapin Rd SW17 ....73 A1
Terrick St W12 ....30 A3
Territorial Ho
  SE11 ....149 C3
Terry Ho SW2 ....74 C3
Tersha St TW9 ....54 B3
Tessa Sanderson Pl 6
  SW8 ....61 A4
Testerton Wlk 3
  W11 ....30 C2
Tetcott Rd SW10 ....156 C1
Teversham La
  SW8 ....172 B4
Teviot St E14 ....34 B4
Teyham Ct SW11 ....60 B1
Thackeray Ct SW3 ....144 C2
  W14 ....126 A1
Thackeray Ho WC1 ....94 A2
Thackeray Mews 8 E8 ....16 C2
Thackeray Rd SW8 ....170 B1
Thackeray St W8 ....128 B2
Thalia Cl SE10 ....52 C4
Thame Rd SE16 ....40 C4
Thames Ave SW10 ....167 A4
Thames Bank SW14 ....45 B1
Thames Circ E14 ....41 C2
Thames Cres W4 ....46 A3
Thames Ct SE15 ....49 B3
Thames Hts SE1 ....138 C4
Thameside Ctr TW8 ....44 B4
Thames Link Ho 7
  TW9 ....54 A3
Thames Pl SW15 ....57 C4

Thames Quay E14 ....42 A4
  SW10 ....167 A3
Thames Rd W4 ....44 A4
Thames Reach W6 ....47 B4
Thames St SE10 ....52 A4
Thames Village W4 ....45 B2
Thames Wlk SW11 ....158 A2
Thane Mans N7 ....5 B1
Thanet Ho WC1 ....94 A3
  1 West Norwood
  SE27 ....75 A1
Thanet Lo NW2 ....10 A2
Thanet St WC1 ....94 A3
Thane Villas N7 ....5 B1
Thane Works N7 ....5 B1
Thavie's Inn EC4 ....107 C2
Thaxted Ct N1 ....87 C1
Thaxted Ho SE16 ....40 B2
Thaxton Rd W14 ....155 A4
Thayer St W1 ....103 C2
Theatre Mus WC2 ....120 B4
Theatre Sq E15 ....19 C2
Theatre St SW11 ....60 B4
Theberton St N1 ....86 A4
Theed St SE1 ....121 C1
Thelbridge Ho 28
  E3 ....27 A2
Theobalds Ct N4 ....6 B2
Theobald's Rd
  WC1 ....106 C4
Theobald St SE1 ....137 B1
Theodore Ho 1
  SW15 ....56 C2
Theodore Rd SE13 ....67 C1
Therapia Rd SE22 ....65 B1
Theresa Rd W6 ....38 C2
Therfield Ct N4 ....6 B2
Thermopylae Gate
  E14 ....42 A2
Theseus Ho 2 E14 ....34 C3
Theseus Wlk N1 ....86 B1
Thessaly Ho SW8 ....160 C1
Thessaly Rd SW8 ....171 A4
Thessus Ho 2 E14 ....34 C3
Thetford Ho SE1 ....138 C2
Thetis Terr TW9 ....44 C4
Third Ave
  London W10 ....23 A2
  London W3 ....29 B1
Thirleby Rd SW1 ....133 A1
Thirlmere NW1 ....92 B4
Thirlmere Ho 20
  N16 ....15 C4
Thirsk Rd SW11 ....60 C3
Thistle Gr SW7 ....143 A1
Thistle Ho 15 E14 ....34 B3
Thistlewood Cl 3 N7 ....5 B2
Thistly Ct SE8 ....52 A4
Thomas Baines Rd
  SW11 ....59 C4
Thomas Burt Ho 9
  E2 ....25 A2
Thomas Buxton Jun &
  Inf Sch E1 ....24 C1 V9
Thomas Doyle St
  SE1 ....136 B2
Thomas Fairchild Comm
  Sch N1 ....86 C2
Thomas Ho
  1 London E9 ....17 B2
  4 London SW4 ....62 A3
Thomas Hollywood Ho
  3 E2 ....25 B3
Thomas Jones Prim Sch
  W11 ....31 A3
Thomas More Ho
  EC2 ....108 C3

Thomas More Sq
  E1 ....125 B3
Thomas More St
  E1 ....125 B2
Thomas North Terr 3
  E16 ....35 B2
Thomas Pl W8 ....128 A1
Thomas Rd E14 ....33 C4
Thomas Road Ind Est
  E14 ....33 C3
Thomas's London Day
  Schs SW11 ....167 C3
Thomas's Prep Sch
  Clapham SW11 ....60 A2
Thompson Ave TW9 ....54 C4
  10 London N7 ....23 A1
Thompson Ho SE14 ....50 C4
  10 W10 ....23 A1
Thompson's Ave 6
  SE5 ....48 B3
Thomson Ho SE17 ....152 A3
  SW1 ....147 C1
Thorburn Ho SW1 ....131 B3
Thorburn Sq SE1 ....153 B3
Thoresby Ho N16 ....6 C1
Thoresby St N1 ....97 A4
Thornaby Ho 15 E2 ....25 A2
Thornbill Ho 5
  SE15 ....49 C3
Thornbury Cl N16 ....16 A3
Thornbury Ct W11 ....113 B4
Thornbury Ho N6 ....4 B3
Thornbury Rd SW2 ....62 A1
Thornbury Sq N6 ....4 B3
Thorncliffe Ho SW1 ....146 C2
Thorncliffe Rd SW2 ....62 A1
Thorncombe Rd
  SE22 ....64 A2
Thorncroft St SW8 ....162 A1
Thorndale Ho 10 ....7 A3
Thorndean St SW18 ....71 B2
Thorndike Cl
  SW10 ....156 C2
Thorndike Ho SW1 ....147 B2
Thorndike Rd 2 N1 ....15 B2
Thorndike St SW1 ....147 C3
Thorne Cl E16 ....35 C3
Thorne Ho 4 E14 ....42 B3
  24 E2 ....25 B2
Thorne Pas 7
  SW13 ....46 B1
Thorne Rd SW8 ....162 B1
Thorness Ct SW18 ....59 B1
Thorne St SW13,
  SW14 ....56 A4
Thornewill Ho 6
  E1 ....32 B2
Thorney Cres
  SW11 ....157 C1
Thorneycroft Ho 11
  W4 ....38 A1
Thorney Ct W8 ....128 C3
Thorney Hedge Rd
  W4 ....37 A2
Thorney St SW1 ....148 A4
Thornfield Ho 4
  E14 ....33 C2
Thornfield Rd W12 ....39 A4
Thornford Rd SE13 ....67 B2
Thorngate Rd W9 ....23 C1
Thornham Gr E15 ....19 C3
Thornham St SE10 ....52 A4
Thornhaugh St
  WC1 ....93 C1
Thornhill Bridge Wharf
  N1 ....84 C3

Thornhill Cres N1 ....14 B1
Thornhill Gr N1 ....14 C1
Thornhill Ho
  London N1 ....14 C1
  4 W4 ....38 A1
Thornhill Prim Sch
  N1 ....14 C1
Thornhill Rd N1 ....85 B4
Thornhill Sq N1 ....14 B1
Thornicroft Ho
  SW9 ....173 A1
Thornley Pl 2 SE10 ....43 A1
Thornsett Rd SW18 ....71 A3
Thornton Ave
  ....38 A2
  Streatham SW2 ....73 C3
Thornton Ct N7 ....14 A3
Thornton Gdns
  SW12 ....73 C3
Thornton Ho SE17 ....152 A3
Thornton Pl W1 ....103 A4
Thornton Rd
  Mortlake SW14 ....55 C4
  Streatham SW12 ....73 C3
Thornton St SW9 ....173 B2
Thornville St SE8 ....51 C2
Thornycroft Ct TW9 ....44 B1
Thorold Ho SE1 ....136 C4
  6 Streatham SW2 ....74 A4
Thorparch Rd
  SW8 ....161 C1
Thorpebank Rd
  W12 ....29 C1
Thorpe Cl W10 ....31 A3
Thorpedale Rd N4 ....5 B3
Thorpe Ho N1 ....85 A3
Thoverton Rd NW2 ....1 A1
Thoydon Rd E3 ....26 A3
Thrale Rd SW16 ....
Thrale St SE1 ....123 A1
Thrasher Cl 20 E8 ....24 B4
Thrawl St E1 ....111 A3
Thrayle Ho 2 SW9 ....62 B3
Threadgold Ho 8
  N1 ....15 C2
Threadneedle St
  EC2,EC3 ....109 C1
Three Colts La 2
  E1 ....25 A1
Three Colt St E14 ....33 B2
Three Cups Yd
  WC1 ....107 A3
Three Kings Yd
  W1 ....118 A4
Three Mill La E3 ....27 C2
Three Nun Ct EC2 ....109 A2
Three Oak La SE1 ....138 C4
Threshers Pl W11 ....112 A4
Thring Ho SW9 ....172 C2
Throgmorton Ave
  EC2 ....109 C2
Throgmorton St
  EC2 ....109 C2
Thrush St SE17 ....150 C2
Thurland Ho 4
  SE16 ....40 A2
Thurland Rd SE16 ....139 B2
Thurleigh Ave
  SW12 ....60 C1
Thurleigh Ct SW12 ....60 C1
Thurleigh Rd SW12 ....60 C1
Thurloe Cl SW7 ....144 A4
Thurloe Ct SW3 ....144 A3
Thurloe Pl SW7 ....143 C4
Thurloe Place Mews
  SW7 ....143 C4
Thurloe Sq SW7 ....144 A4
Thurloe St SW7 ....143 C4
Thurlow Hill SE21 ....75 B2

Thurlow Ho 17
  SW16 ....74 A1
Thurlow Park Rd
  SE21,SE24 ....75 B2
Thurlow Rd NW3 ....11 C3
Thurlow St SE17 ....152 A1
Thurlow Terr NW5 ....12 C3
Thurlow Twrs SE27 ....74 C1
Thurnscoe NW1 ....82 C3
Thursley Gdns
  SW19 ....69 C2
Thursley Ho 10 SW2 ....74 B4
Thurso Ho NW6 ....78 A1
Thurston Ind Est
  SE13 ....67 A4
Thurston Rd SE8,
  SE13 ....52 A1
Thurtle Rd E2 ....24 B3
Tibbatts Rd E3 ....27 A1
Tibbets Cl SW19 ....69 C3
Tibbet's Corner
  SW19 ....69 C4
Tibbet's Ride SW19 ....69 C4
Tiber Gdns N1 ....84 B3
Tickford Ho NW8 ....90 A3
Tidal Basin Rd E16 ....35 B2
Tidbury Ct SW8 ....160 C1
Tidemill Prim Sch
  SE8 ....51 C3
Tideside Ct 10 NW5 ....13 A4
Tideswell Rd SW15 ....57 B3
Tideway Ct 9 SE16 ....32 C1
Tideway Ho E14 ....41 C4
Tideway Ind Est
  SW8 ....161 A3
Tideway Wharf
  SW13 ....46 A1
Tideway Yd SW13 ....46 A1
Tidey St E3 ....33 C4
Tidworth Ho 13
  SE22 ....64 A4
Tidworth Rd E3 ....26 C1
Tierney Rd SW2 ....74 A3
Tierney Terr SW2 ....74 A3
Tiger Ho WC1 ....93 C4
Tiger Way E5 ....17 A4
Tilbury Cl 16 SE15 ....49 B3
Tilbury Ho 4 SE14 ....50 C4
Tildesley Rd SW15 ....57 B1
Tilehurst NW1 ....92 B3
Tilehurst Rd SW17,
  SW18 ....71 C3
Tile Kiln La N6 ....4 B3
Tileyard Rd N7 ....14 A1
Tilford Gdns SW19 ....69 C3
Tilford Ho 3 SW2 ....74 B4
Tilia Rd E5 ....17 A4
Tilia Wlk 21 SW9 ....63 A3
Tilleard Ho 4 W10 ....23 A2
Tiller Ho 21 N1 ....24 A4
Tiller Rd E14 ....41 C3
Tillet Sq SE16 ....41 A4
Tillet Way 22 E2 ....99 B4
Tilling Ho 8 SE15 ....65 A4
Tilman Ho 2 SE8 ....51 C2
Tilney Ct EC1 ....97 A2
Tilney Gdns 11 N1 ....15 C2
Tilney St W1 ....117 C2
Tilson Cl 2 SE15 ....49 A3
Tilson Gdns SW2,
  SW4 ....74 A4
Tilson Ho SW2 ....74 A4
Tilton St SW6 ....154 B3

Tiltwood The W3 . . . . . .28 B2
Timberland Cl 15
 SE15 . . . . .49 C3
Timberland Rd E1 . .32 A4
Timber Mill Way
 SW4 . . . . .61 C4
Timber Pond Rd
 SE16 . . . . .40 C4
Timber St EC1 . . . . .96 C2
Time Sq E8 . . . . . . .50 C4
Timothy Cl 1 SW4 . .61 B2
Timothy Rd E3 . . . . .33 B4
Timsbury Wlk 6
 SW15 . . . . .68 C3
Tina Ct SW16 . . . . . .74 C1
Tindal St SW9 . . . . .48 A2
Tinniswood Cl N5 . .14 C3
Tinsley Rd E1 . . . . .32 B4
Tintagel Cres SE22 .64 B3
Tintagel Ct EC1 . . . .96 A1
Tintern Cl SW15 . . .58 A2
Tintern Ho NW1 . . .82 B1
 SW1 . . . . .146 A3
Tintern St SW4 . . . .62 A3
Tinworth St SE11 .148 B2
Tipthorpe Rd SW11 .60 C4
Tiptree 7 NW1 . . . . .13 A1
Tisbury Ct W1 . . . .119 B4
Tisdall Pl SE17 . . .151 C3
Tissington Ct 4
 SE16 . . . . .40 C2
Titan Bsns Est 3
 SE8 . . . . .51 C2
Titan Ct TW8 . . . . .36 B1
Titchborne Row
 W2 . . . . .102 B1
Titchfield Rd NW8 . .80 A4
Titchwell Rd SW18 .71 C3
Tite St SW3 . . . . . .158 C4
Titmuss St W12 . . . .39 B4
Tiverton Rd NW6,
 NW10 . . . . .22 C4
Tiverton St SE1 . . .136 C2
Tivoli Ct SE16 . . . .33 B1
Tobago St E14 . . . .41 C4
Tobin Cl NW3 . . . . .12 A1
Toby La E1 . . . . . . .26 A1
Todber Ho W14 . . .126 B2
Todds Wlk N7 . . . . . .5 B2
Tokenhouse Yd
 EC2 . . . . .109 B2
Toland Sq SW15 . . .56 C2
Tolchurch 2 W11 . .31 C3
Tollbridge Cl W10 . .23 A1
Tollet St E1 . . . . . .25 C1
Tollgate Dr SE21 . . .76 A2
Tollgate Ho NW6 . .78 A2
Tollhouse Way N19 . .4 B2
Tollington Ct N4 . . . .5 B2
Tollington Pk N4 . . . .5 B2
Tollington Pl N4 . . . .5 B2
Tollington Rd N7 . .14 B4
Tollington Way N7 . .5 A1
Tolmers Sq NW1 . . .93 A2
Tolpaide Ho SE11 .149 B3
Tolsford Rd E5 . . . .17 A3
Tom Groves Cl E15 .19 C3
Tom Hood Cl E15 . .19 C3
Tom Jenkinson Rd 5
 E16 . . . . .35 C1
Tomkyns Ho SE11 .149 B3
Tomline Ho SE1 . . .122 C1
Tomlin's Gr E3 . . . .26 C2
Tomlinson Cl E2 . . .99 A3
 5 London W4 . . . . .37 A1

Tomlin's Terr E14 . .33 A3
Tomlins Wlk 4 N7 . . .5 B2
Tompion Ho EC1 . . .96 B2
Tompion St EC1 . . . .96 B3
Tom Smith Cl SE10 .53 A4
Tomson Ho SE1 . . .138 C2
Tom Williams Ho
 SW6 . . . . .154 C3
Tonbridge Hos WC1 .94 A3
Tonbridge St WC1 . .94 A3
Toneborough NW8 . .78 B3
Tonsley Hill SW18 . .59 A2
Tonsley Pl SW18 . . .59 A2
Tonsley Rd SW18 . . .59 A2
Tonsley St SW18 . . .59 A2
Took's Ct EC4 . . . .107 B2
Tooley St SE1 . . . .124 A1
Tooting Bec Sta
 SW17 . . . . .72 C1
Topham Ho 8 SE10 .52 B3
Topham St EC1 . . . .95 B2
Topiary Sq TW9 . . .54 B4
Topmast Point E14 . .41 C4
Torbay Ct 18 NW1 . .13 A1
Torbay Mans NW6 . .23 B4
Torbay Rd NW6 . . . .10 B1
Torbay St 15 NW1 . .13 A1
Tor Ct W8 . . . . . . .127 C4
Tor Gdns W8 . . . . .127 B4
Tornay Ho N1 . . . . .84 C2
 London E9 . . . . . . .17 B1
Torquay St W2 . . . .100 A3
Torrens Ct SE5 . . . .63 C4
Torrens Rd SW2 . . .62 B2
Torrens St EC1 . . . .86 A1
Torres Sq E14 . . . .41 C1
Torriano Ave NW5 . .13 C3
Torriano Cotts NW5 .13 B3
Torriano Jun & Inf Schs
 NW5 . . . . .13 C3
Torridge Gdns SE15 .65 B3
Torridon Ho NW6 . .78 A1
Torrington Pl E1 . .125 C2
 WC1 . . . . .105 A4
Torrington Sq WC1 .93 C1
Tortington Ho 11
 SE15 . . . . .50 A3
Torwood Rd SW15 . .56 C2
Tothill Ho SW1 . . .147 C4
Tothill St SW1 . . . .133 C3
Totland Ho SW18 . .59 A1
Tottan Terr E1 . . . .32 C3
Tottenhall 6 NW1 . .12 C1
Tottenham Court Rd
 Sta W1 . . . . . . .105 C2
Tottenham Court Road
 W1 . . . . .105 C1
Tottenham Mews
 W1 . . . . .105 A4
Tottenham Rd N1 . .16 A2
Tottenham St W1 . .105 A4
Totteridge Ho
 SW11 . . . . .167 C2
Touchard Ho N1 . . .97 C3
Toulmin St SE1 . . .136 C3
Toulon St SE5 . . . .48 B3
Toulouse Ct 2
 SE16 . . . . .40 A1
Tournay Rd SW6 . .155 A2
Toussaint Wlk
 SE16 . . . . .139 C2
Tovy Ho SE1 . . . . .153 B1
Towcester Rd E3 . . .27 B1
Tower 42 ★ EC2 . . .110 B1
Tower Bldgs 22 E1 .32 A1

Tower Br App E1,
 EC3 . . . . .124 C3
Tower Bridge★
 E1,EC3,SE1 . . . . .124 C2
Tower Bridge Bsns
 Complex SE16 . . . .40 A3
Tower Bridge Bsns Sq
 SE16 . . . . .138 C4
Tower Bridge Piazza
 SE1 . . . . .124 C1
Tower Bridge Prim Sch
 SE1 . . . . .138 C4
Tower Bridge Rd
 SE1 . . . . .138 C1
Tower Bridge Sq
 SE1 . . . . .138 C4
Tower CI NW3 . . . . .11 C3
Tower Ct WC8 . . . . .80 B2
 WC2 . . . . .106 A1
 London E5 . . . . .7 B4
Towergate SE1 . . .152 A4
Tower Gateway Sta
 EC3 . . . . .124 C4
Tower Hamlets Coll
 E1 . . . . .32 C3
 E14 . . . . .34 A2
 E14 . . . . .34 A3
Tower Hill EC3 . . .124 C4
Tower Hill Sta EC3 124 C4
Tower Hill Terr
 EC3 . . . . .124 B3
Tower Mans SE1 . . .138 C1
Tower Mews E5 . . . .18 A3
Tower Millennium Pier
 EC3 . . . . .124 B2
Tower Mill Rd 1
 SE15 . . . . .49 A3
Tower Rd NW10 . . . .8 C1
Tower Rise TW9 . . .54 A4
Tower Royal EC4 . .123 B4
Towers PI TW10 . . .54 A2
Tower Sq SE2 . . . .106 A1
Towers The
 London TW9 . . . . .54 B3
Tower Terr SE4 . . .66 A3
Tower The ★ EC3 .124 C3
Tower Wharf SE1 .138 C4
Tower Wlk SE1 . . .152 A4
Towncourt Path N4 . .6 B3
Townhall Ave 3
 W4 . . . . .37 C2
Town Hall Rd SW11 .60 B4
Townley Rd SE22 . .64 A2
Townley St SE17 . .151 B2
Townmead Bsns Ctr
 SW6 . . . . .59 B4
Townmead Rd
 London SW6 . . . .166 C1
 Richmond TW9 . . .45 A1
Townsend Ho SE1 153 C3
Townsend Ind Est
 NW10 . . . . .20 B3
Townsend Prim Sch
 SE17 . . . . .152 A3
Townsend St SE1 . .152 A4
Townsend Yd N6 . . .4 A3
Townshend Ct NW8 .80 B2
Townshend Est
 NW8 . . . . .80 A2
Townshend Rd
 NW8 . . . . .80 A3
 Richmond TW9 . . .54 B3
Townshend Terr
 TW9 . . . . .54 B3

Towns Ho 4 SW4 . . .61 C4
Towton Rd SE27 . . .75 B2
Toxteth Ho N4 . . . . .5 B2
Toynbee St E1 . . . .110 C3
Tracey Ave NW2 . . .9 B3
Tracy Ho 2 E3 . . . .26 B2
Tradescant Ho 15
 E9 . . . . .17 B1
Tradescant Rd
 SW8 . . . . .162 B1
Trade Twr 3 SW11 . .59 B4
Trade Winds Ct E1 125 C2
Trading Estate Rd
 NW10 . . . . .20 B1
Trafalgar Ave SE15 .49 B4
Trafalgar Cl 1
 SE16 . . . . .41 A2
Trafalgar Gdns 4 E1 .32 C4
Trafalgar Gr SE10 . .52 C4
Trafalgar Ho SE17 151 A2
Trafalgar Mews 2
 E9 . . . . .18 B2
Trafalgar Rd SE10 . .43 A1
Trafalgar Sq★
 SW1 . . . . .119 C2
Trafalgar St SE17 . .151 C2
Trafalgar Way E14 . .34 B1
Trafford CI E15 . . . .19 A3
Trafford Ho N1 . . . . .87 C2
Tragail SW15 . . . . .58 A2
Traitors Gate ★ EC3 124 C2
Tralee Ct 5 SE16 . .40 A1
Tramway Ave E15 . .19 C1
Trance Way W3 . . .36 C3
Tranmere Ho 7 N7 .14 C3
Tranmere Rd
 SW18 . . . . .71 B2
Tranquil Pass SE3 .53 B1
Tranquil Vale SE3 . .53 A1
Transept St NW1 . .102 B3
Transom CI SE16 . .41 A2
Transom Sq E14 . . .42 A1
Tranton Rd SE16 . .40 A3
Trappes Ho 2 SE16 .40 A2
Travel Clinic, Hospl for
 Tropical Diseases
 WC1 . . . . .93 A1
Travers Ho 6 SE10 .52 C4
Travers Rd N7 . . . . .5 C1
Travis Ho SE10 . . .52 B2
Treadgold Ho 7
 W11 . . . . .30 C2
Treadgold St W11 . .30 C2
Treadway St E2 . . .25 A3
Treasury Buildings
 SW1 . . . . .134 A4
Treaty St N1 . . . . .84 C3
Trebeck St W1 . . . .118 A1
Treborough Ho
 W1 . . . . .103 B4
Trebovir Rd SW5 . .141 C3
Treby St E3 . . . . . .26 B1
Trecastle Way 3
 N7 . . . . .13 C4
Tredegar Rd E3 . . .26 B3
Tredegar Sq E3 . . .26 B2
Tredegar Terr E3 . .26 B2
Trederwen Rd E8 . .24 C4
Treen Ave SW13 . .56 B4
Trees The N16 . . . . .6 C4
Trefil Wlk N7 . . . . .14 A4
Trefoil Rd SW18 . . .59 B2
Tregarvon Rd SW11 .60 C3
Trego Rd E9 . . . . . .18 C1
Tregothnan Rd SW9 62 A4

Tregunter Rd
 SW10 . . . . .142 C1
Treherne Ct SW9 . .48 A2
Trehern Rd 12
 SW14 . . . . .55 C4
Trelawney Est E9 . .17 B2
Trelawney Ho SE1 .136 C4
Trelawn Rd SW2 . . .62 C2
Trellis Sq 1 E3 . . .26 B2
Tremadoc Rd SW4 . .61 C3
Tremaine CI SE4 . . .51 C1
Trematon Ho SE11 149 C2
Tremlett Gr N19 . . .4 B1
Tremlett Mews N19 . .4 B1
Trenchard St SE10 . .42 C1
Trenchold St SW8 .162 A3
Trendell Ho 4 E14 . .33 C3
Trenmar Gdns
 NW10 . . . . .22 A2
Trenmar Lo NW10 . .22 A2
Trentham St SW18 .70 C3
Trent Ho SE15 . . . .65 B3
Trent Rd SW2 . . . . .62 B2
Treport St SW18 . . .71 A4
Tresco Ho SE11 . . .149 B2
Tresco Rd SE15 . . .65 A3
Tresham Cres NW8 .90 A2
Tresham Wlk E9 . . .17 B3
Tressider Ho 10
 SW4 . . . . .73 C4
Tressel Cl 20 N1 . . .15 A1
Tressillian Cres SE4 .66 C4
Tressillian Rd SE4 . .66 C4
Trevanion Rd W14 140 B2
Trevelyan Gdns
 NW10 . . . . .22 B4
Trevelyan Ho 12 E2 .25 C2
 SE5 . . . . .48 A3
Treveris St SE1 . . .122 B1
Treverton St W10 . .22 C1
Treverton Twr W10 .30 C4
Treves Ho 1 E1 . . . .24 C1 99 C1
Treville St SW15 . . .69 A4
Trevithick Ho
 SE16 . . . . .40 A2
 SW8 . . . . .171 B4
 3 London NW5 . . .13 A4
Trevor PI SW7 . . . .130 B3
Trevor Roberts Tutorial
 Coll NW3 . . . . . . .11 C1
Trevor Sq SW7 . . .130 B3
Trevor St SW7 . . . .130 B3
Trevose Ho SE11 . .149 A2
Trewint St SW18 . . .71 B2
Triangle Est The
 SE11 . . . . .149 C1
Triangle Ct SE1 . . .138 C4
Triangle PI SW4 . . .61 C3
Triangle Rd 7 E8 . .25 A4
Triangle The E8 . . .25 A4
 EC1 . . . . .96 B2
 London N19 . . . . . . .4 C1
Trident Ho 9 E14 . .34 B3
Trident St SE16 . . .40 C2
Trieste Ct SW12 . . .72 B3
Trigon Rd SW8 . . .163 A2
Trimdon NW1 . . . . .83 A3
Trimmer Wlk 11
 TW8 . . . . .44 A4
Trim St SE8 . . . . . .51 B4
Trinder Gdns N19 . . .5 A3
Trinder Rd N4,N19 . .5 A3
Trinidad Ho 17 E14 .33 B2
Trinidad St E14 . . .33 B2

Trinity Church Rd SW13 ....47 A4
Trinity Church Sq SE1 ....137 A2
Trinity Cl London SE13 ....67 C3
3 London SW4 ....61 B3
Trinity Cotts TW9 ....54 B4
Trinity Cres SW17 ....72 C2
Trinity Ct 2 N1 ....24 A4
SE16 ....41 A4
WC1 ....94 C2
Trinity Gdns E16 ....35 B2
London SW2,SW9 ....62 B3
Trinity Gn E1 ....32 B4
Trinity Gr 8 SE10 ....52 B2
Trinity Ho SE1 ....137 A2
Trinity Homes 14 SW2 ....62 B3
Trinity Mews SW18 ....70 C3
Trinity Pl EC3 ....124 C3
Trinity Rd Richmond TW9 ....54 B4
Wandsworth SW17, SW18 ....72 A3
Trinity Rise SE24, SW2 ....75 A4
Trinity Sq EC3 ....124 B4
Trinity St 9 E16 ....35 C4
SE1 ....137 B2
Trinity St Mary's CE Prim Sch SW12 ....72 C3
Trinity Way W3 ....29 B2
Trio Pl SE1 ....137 A3
Tristan Ct 41 SE8 ....51 B4
Triton Ct EC2 ....97 C1
Triton Ho 2 E14 ....42 A2
Triton Sq NW1 ....92 C2
Tritton Rd SE21, SE27 ....75 C1
Trocette Mans SE1 ....138 B2
Trojan Ct NW6 ....10 A1
Trojan Ind Est NW10 ....8 B2
Troon Cl 34 SE16 ....40 A1
Troon Ho 11 E14 ....33 A3
Troon St E1 ....33 A3
Tropical Ct 2 W10 ....22 C2
Trossachs Rd SE22 ....64 A2
Trothy Rd SE1 ....153 C3
Trotman Ho SE14 ....50 B2
Trott St SW11 ....168 A3
Trotwood Ho 3 SE16 ....40 A4
Troubridge Ct 12 W4 ....37 B1
Troutbeck NW1 ....92 B3
Troutbeck Rd SE14 ....51 A2
Trouville Rd SW4 ....61 B1
Trowbridge Rd E9 ....18 B2
Trower Ho 5 E9 ....18 A2
Troy Ct W8 ....127 B2
Troyes Ho NW3 ....12 B3
Troy Town SE15 ....64 C4
Troy Town Flats SE15 ....64 C4
Truman's Rd 24 N16 ....16 A3
Trump St EC2 ....109 A1
Trundle St SE1 ....136 C4
Trundleys Rd SE8 ....51 A4
Trundley's Rd SE8 ....40 C1
Trundley's Terr SE8 ....40 C2
Truro Ho 25 W2 ....31 C4
Truro St NW5 ....12 C2
Trussley Rd W6 ....39 B3
Trust Wlk SE21 ....75 A3
Tryon Cres E9 ....25 B4
Tryon St SW3 ....144 C2
Tubbs Rd NW10 ....21 B3
Tudor Cl London N6 ....4 B4
London NW3 ....12 A2
London SW2 ....62 B1
Tudor Ct 5 SE16 ....32 C1
London N1 ....16 A2
London W5 ....36 C4
Tudor Est NW10 ....20 A3
Tudor Gdns SW14 ....56 A4
Tudor Gr E9 ....17 B1
Tudor Ho 34 London E9 ....17 B1
London W14 ....39 C2
Tudor Mews 2 NW10 ....8 C2
Tudor Rd E9 ....25 A4
Tudor St EC4 ....121 C4
Tudor Way W3 ....36 C4
Tufnell Ct 12 E3 ....26 B4
Tufnell Park Mans 2 N7 ....5 A1
Tufnell Park Prim Sch N7 ....13 C4
Tufnell Park Rd N19,N7 ....13 C4
Tufnell Park Sta N19 ....13 B4
Tufton Ct SW1 ....134 A1
Tufton St SW1 ....134 A1
Tuke Sch SE15 ....50 A2
Tullis Ho 12 E9 ....17 B1
Tulse Hill Streatham SW2 ....75 A2
Streatham SW2,SE24 ....74 C4
Tulse Hill Sta SE27 ....75 A2
Tulse Ho SW2 ....62 C1
Tulsemere Rd SE21, SE27 ....75 B2
Tunbridge Ct 1 SE26 ....76 C1
Tunbridge Ho EC1 ....96 A4
Tunis Rd W12 ....30 A1
Tunley Gn 16 E14 ....33 B4
Tunley Rd London NW10 ....21 A4
Upper Tooting SW12, SW17 ....72 C2
Tunnel Avenue Trad Est SE10 ....42 C4
Tunnel Rd SE16 ....40 B4
Tunstall Ct 14 TW9 ....44 B2
Tunstall Rd SW9 ....62 B3
Tunstall Wlk 10 TW8 ....44 A4
Tunworth Cres SW15 ....56 B1
Tupman Ho SE16 ....139 B3
Turberville Ho 1 SW9 ....62 B4
Turene Cl SW18 ....59 B3
Turin St E2 ....24 C2 99 B3
Turk's Head Yd EC1 ....108 A4
Turks Row SW3 ....145 A2
Turle Rd N4 ....5 B2
Turlewray Cl N4 ....5 B3
Turnagain La EC4 ....108 A2
Turnberry Cl 24 SE16 ....40 A1
Turnbull Ho N1 ....86 B4
Turnchapel Mews 1 SW4 ....61 A4
Turner Cl 7 SW9 ....48 A2
Turner Ct 19 SE16 ....40 B4
9 London SE5 ....63 C3
Turner Ho NW8 ....80 A2
SW1 ....147 C3
Turner Ho *continued* WC2 ....120 B3
London N4 ....5 B3
Turner Lo 10 SW19 ....69 C3
Turner Pl SW11 ....60 A2
Turner's Rd E3 ....33 B4
Turner St E1 ....32 A4
E16 ....35 B1
Turneville Rd W14 ....154 C4
Turney Rd SE21 ....75 C4
Turney Sch SE21 ....75 B4
Turnham Green Sta W4 ....38 A2
Turnham Green Terr W4 ....38 A2
Turnham Ho SE4 ....66 A3
Turnham Prim Sch SE4 ....66 A3
Turnham Rd SE4 ....66 A3
Turnmill Ho 8 SW2 ....62 C2
Turnmill St EC1 ....108 A4
Turnour Ho 32 E1 ....32 A3
Turnpike Cl SE8 ....51 B3
Turnpike Ho EC1 ....96 B3
Turnpin La 2 SE10 ....52 B4
Turpentine La SW1 ....146 B1
Turpin Ho SW11 ....170 A4
Turpin Way N19 ....4 C3
Turquand St SE17 ....151 A3
Turret Gr SW4 ....61 B4
Turville Ho NW8 ....90 A2
Turville St E2 ....98 C2
Tuscan Ho 36 E2 ....25 B2
Tuskar St SE10 ....43 A1
Tuttle Ho SW1 ....147 C1
Tweedale Ct E15 ....76 B3
Tweed Ho E14 ....27 B1
Tweezer's Alley WC2 ....121 B4
Twelvetrees Cres E3 ....27 B1
Twig Folly Cl E2 ....25 C3
Twilley St SW18 ....71 A4
Twine Ct E1 ....32 B2
Twisden Rd NW5 ....13 A4
Twyford CE High Sch W3 ....28 A1
Twyford Ho N5 ....6 A1
Twyford Pl WC2 ....106 C2
Twyford St N1 ....84 C4
Twynholm Mans SW6 ....154 A2
Tyburn Tree (site of) W2 ....116 C3
Tyburn Way W1 ....117 A4
Tyer's Est SE1 ....138 A4
Tyers Gate SE1 ....138 A3
Tyers St SE11 ....148 C2
Tyers Terr SE11 ....149 A1
Tyler Cl E2 ....24 B3
Tyler St SE10 ....43 A1
Tylney Ho 19 E1 ....32 A3
Tymperley Ct SW19 ....70 A3
Tyndale La N1 ....15 A1
Tyndale Mans N1 ....15 A1
Tyndale Terr 13 N1 ....15 A1
Tynedale Ct E14 ....42 A1
Tyneham Cl 10 SW11 ....60 C4
Tynemouth St SW6 ....166 C2
Tyne St E1 ....111 A2
Tynsdale Rd NW10 ....8 A2
Tynte Ct E9 ....18 A3
Tynwald Ho 14 SE26 ....76 C1
Type St E2 ....25 C3
Tyrawley Rd SW6 ....166 A4
Tyrrell Ho SW1 ....161 A4
Tyrrell Rd SE22 ....64 C3
Tyrwhitt Rd SE4 ....66 C4
Tysoe St EC1 ....95 C3
Tyssen Rd N16 ....7 B1
Tyssen Sch N16 ....7 C3
Tyssen St N1 ....24 A3
London E8 ....16 B2
Tytherton 30 E2 ....25 B3
Tytherton Rd N19 ....4 C1

U

Uamvar St E14 ....34 A4
Udall St SW1 ....147 A3
Udimore Ho W10 ....30 B4
Uffington Rd NW10 ....22 A4
Ufford St SE1 ....135 C4
Ufton Gr N1 ....15 C1
Ufton Rd N1 ....16 A1
Uhura Sq 19 N16 ....7 A1
Ujima Ct N19 ....5 A3
Ullin St E14 ....34 B4
Ullswater SW15 ....57 C1
Ullswater Ho SE15 ....50 B4
Ullswater Rd Barnes SW13 ....46 C3
West Norwood SE27, SW16 ....75 A2
Ulster Pl NW1 ....92 A1
Ulundi Rd SE3 ....53 A4
Ulva Rd SW15 ....57 C3
Ulverscroft Rd SE22 ....64 C2
Ulverstone Rd SE27 ....75 A2
Ulysses Rd NW6 ....10 B3
Umberston St E1 ....32 A3
Umbria St SW15 ....56 C1
Una Ho 7 NW5 ....13 A2
Under Cliff SE10 ....52 B2
Undercliff Rd SE13 ....67 A4
Underhill Ho 7 E14 ....33 C4
Underhill Pas NW1 ....82 B4
Underhill St NW1 ....82 B3
Undershaft EC3 ....110 A1
Underwood Ho W6 ....39 A3
Underwood Rd E1 ....24 C1 99 C1
Underwood Row N1 ....97 A4
Underwood St N1 ....97 A4
Undine Rd E14 ....42 A2
Unicorn Bldg 14 E1 ....32 C2
Unicorn Sch TW9 ....44 B2
Union Cl E11 ....19 C4
Union Ct London SW4 ....172 A1
45 London W2 ....31 C4
2 Richmond TW10 ....54 A2
Union Dr E1 ....26 A1
Union Gr SW8 ....171 C2
Union Mews SW9 ....172 A1
Union Rd SW8 ....171 C1
Union Sq N1 ....87 A3
Union St E15 ....27 C4
SE1 ....122 C1
Union Wlk E2 ....98 A4
Union Yd W1 ....104 B1
Unity Cl NW10 ....8 C2
Unity Mews NW1 ....83 B2
Univ College Hospl (Annexe) W1 ....103 C4
Univ Coll Jun Sch NW3 ....11 B4
Univ Coll London W1 ....105 A4
WC1 ....93 C1
Univ Coll London *continued* WC1 ....94 B2
University Coll Hospl WC1 ....93 A1
University Coll Sch NW3 ....11 B3
University Mans SW15 ....57 C4
University of North London (Tufnel Park Hall) N7 ....4 B1
University St WC1 ....93 A1
Univ of East London E15 ....27 C4
Univ of Greenwich Rachel Mcmillan Campus SE8 ....51 C4
Univ of Greenwich The SW15 ....68 C4
Univ of London WC1 ....94 A3
Univ of London (King's Coll Hall) SE5 ....63 C4
Univ of London (Queen Mary & Westfield Coll) E1 ....26 A1
Univ of Westminster NW1 ....92 C2
NW8 ....90 A1
W1 ....103 B4
W1 ....104 B2
Unwin Cl SE15 ....49 C4
Unwin Rd SW7 ....129 C2
Upbrook Mews W2 ....101 A1
Upcerne Rd SW10 ....157 A1
Upcott Ho 33 E3 ....27 A2
4 London E9 ....17 B1
Upgrove Manor Way 12 SE24 ....74 C4
Upham Park Rd W4 ....38 A2
Upland Rd SE22 ....64 C1
Uplands Cl SW14 ....55 A2
Upnall Ho 16 SE15 ....50 B4
Upnor Way SE17 ....152 B2
Upper Addison Gdns W14 ....126 A4
Upper Belgrave St SW1 ....131 C2
Upper Berkeley St W1 ....103 A1
Upper Brockley Rd SE4 ....51 B1
Upper Brook St W1 ....117 B4
Upper Caldy Wlk 14 N1 ....15 B2
Upper Cheyne Row SW3 ....158 A4
Upper Clarendon Wlk 13 W11 ....31 A3
Upper Dengie Wlk N1 ....86 C4
Upper Grosvenor St W1 ....117 B3
Upper Ground SE1 ....121 B2
Upper Gulland Wlk 19 N1 ....15 B2
Upper Harley St NW1 ....91 C1
Upper Hawkwell Wlk N1 ....87 A4
Upper Holloway Sta N19 ....4 C2

Upper James St
W1 ....119 A4
Upper John St W1 ....119 A4
Upper Mall W6 ....39 A1
Upper Marsh SE1 ...135 A2
Upper Montague St
W1 ....102 C3
Upper North St E1,
E14 ....33 C4
Upper Park Rd NW3 ..12 B3
Upper Phillimore Gdns
W8 ....127 B3
Upper Rawreth Wlk
N1 ....87 A4
Upper Richmond Rd
SW15 ....57 C3
Upper Richmond Rd W
TW10,SW14,SW15 ..55 B3
Upper St N1 ....86 A3
Upper St Martin's La
WC2 ....120 A4
Upper Tachbrook St
SW1 ....147 A4
Upper Terr NW3 ......2 B1
Upper Thames St
EC4 ....123 A4
Upper Tollington Pk
N4 ....5 C3
Upper Tooting Park
Mans** 1 SW17 ....72 C2
Upper Tooting Pk
SW17 ....72 B2
Upper Tooting Rd
SW17 ....72 B1
Upper Tulse Hill
SW2 ....74 B3
Upper Wimpole St
W1 ....104 A4
Upper Woburn Pl
NW1,WC1 ....93 C2
Upstall St SE5 ....48 A2
Upton Cl NW2 ....1 A1
Urlwin St SE5 ....48 B4
Urlwin Wlk SW9 ......48 A1
Urmston Dr SW19 ....70 A3
Urmston Ho 3 E14 ..42 B2
Ursula Mews N4 ....6 B3
Ursula St SW11 .....168 A3
Urswick Rd E5,E9 ...17 B3
Usborne Mews
SW8 ....163 A2
Usher Rd E3 ....26 B3
Usk Rd SW11 ....59 B3
Usk St E2 ....25 C2
Utopia Village NW1 ..81 B4
Uverdale Rd SW10 ..157 A1
Uxbridge Rd W12 ....30 A1
Uxbridge St
W8 .....31 C1 113 B2

V

Vaine Ho 4 E9 ....18 A2
Vale Cl W9 ....88 C3
Vale Ct W9 ....88 C3
London W3 ....29 B1
Vale End SE22 ....64 B3
Vale Est The W3 .....29 A1
Vale Gr London N4 ....6 B4
London W3 ....28 C1
Vale Row N5 ....6 A1
Valens Ho 1 SW2 ....74 C3
Valentia Pl SW9 ......62 C3
Valentine Ho 11
........................61 B1
Valentine Pl SE1 ....136 A4

Valentine Rd E9 ......17 C2
Valentine Row
SE1 ....136 A3
Vale of Health NW3 ..2 C1
Vale Rd N4 ....6 B4
Vale Rise NW11 ....1 B3
Vale Row N5 ....6 A1
Vale Royal N7 ....14 A1
Vale The SW3 ....157 C4
London NW11 ....1 B3
London W3 ....29 A1
Valette Ho E9 ....17 B2
Valette St E9 ....17 B2
Valetta Rd W3 ....38 B4
Valette St E8 ....17 A2
Valiant Ho 4
SW11 ....167 C3
Vallance Rd
E1 ....24 C1 99 C1
Valliere Rd NW10 ....22 A2
Valmar Rd SE5 ......48 B2
Valmar Trad Est 7
SE5 ....48 B2
Valois Ho SE1 ....138 C2
Valonia Gdns SW18 ..58 B1
Vanbern Ho NW5 .....12 C2
Vanbrugh Ct SE11 ..149 C3
Vanbrugh Fields
SE3 ....53 C3
Vanbrugh Hill SE10,
SE3 ....53 B4
Vanbrugh Ho 8 E9 ...17 B1
Vanbrugh Park Rd
SE3 ....53 B3
Vanbrugh Park Rd W
SE3 ....53 B3
Vanbrugh Pk SE3 .....53 B3
Vanbrugh Rd W4 .....37 C3
Vanbrugh Terr SE3 ...53 B2
Vanburgh Ho 1 E1 ..110 C4
Vancover Ho 3 E1 ...32 A1
Vanderbilt Rd SW18 ..71 B3
Vanderbilt Villas 1
W12 ....39 C4
Vandon Ct SW1 .....133 A2
Vandon Pas SW1 ....133 A2
Vandon St SW1 .....133 A2
Vandyke Cl SW15 ....57 C1
Vandy St EC2 ....98 A1
Vane Cl NW3 ....11 C4
Vane St SW1 ....147 A4
Vange Ho 1 W10 ....30 B4
Van Gogh Ct E14 ....42 C3
Vanguard Bldg 12
E14 ....41 C4
Vanguard St SE8 .....51 C2
Vanguard Trad Ctr

Vanneck Sq SW15 ...56 C2
Vansittart St 7
SE14 ....51 A3
Vantage Mews E14 ...34 B1
Vantrey Ho SE11 ....149 B3
Varcoe Rd SE16 ......40 B1
Vardens Rd SW11 ....59 C3
Varden St E1 ....32 A3
Vardon Cl W3 ....28 C3
Vardon Ho SE10 .....52 B2
Varey Ho E1 ....26 A3
Varley Ho 5 NW6 ....23 C4
Varna Rd SW6 ....154 C1
Varndell St NW1 .....92 C4
Varsity Row SW14 ...45 B1
Vassal Ho E3 ....26 A2
Vassall Rd SW9 .....163 C2
Vat Ho SW8 ....162 B2
Vauban Est SE16 ...139 A1
Vauban St SE16 ....139 A1

Vaudeville Ct N4 .....5 C2
Vaughan Ave W6 ....38 B2
Vaughan Est E2 ......98 C4
Vaughan Ho SE1 ....136 A4
Vaughan Rd SE5 .....63 B4
Vaughan St SE16 ....41 B4
Vaughan Way E1 ....125 C3
Vaughan Williams Cl
........................51 C3
Vauxhall Bridge Rd
SW1 ....147 A3
Vauxhall Cross
SW1 ....148 B1
SW1,SW8 ....148 B1
Vauxhall Gr SW8 ....148 C1
Vauxhall Prim Sch
SE11 ....149 A2
Vauxhall St SE11 ...149 A2
Vauxhall Wlk SE11 ..148 C2
Vawdrey Cl E1 ....25 B1
Vaynor Ho N7 ....14 A4
Vectis Ct SW18 ......59 A1
Veda Rd SE13 ....66 C3
Velde Way 1 SE22 ..64 A2
Vellacott Ho W12 ....30 A3
Velletri Ho 17 E2 ....25 C3
Venables St NW8 ...101 C4
Vencourt Pl W6 ......38 C2
Venetian Rd SE5 .....48 B1
Venice Ct 5 SE5 .....48 B3
Venn Ho N1 ....85 A3
Venn St SW4 ....61 B3
Ventnor Rd SE14 ....50 C3
Venue St E14 ....34 B4
Vera Ct W2 ....100 A2
Vera Rd SW6 ....164 B4
Verbena Gdns W6 ...38 C1
Verdi Ho 2 NW6 ....23 C3
Verdun Rd SW13 ....46 C3
Vere Bank SW19 .....70 B3
Vereker Rd W14 ....140 B1
Vere St W1 ....104 A1
Verity Cl W11 ....31 A3
Verity Ho 19 E3 .....26 B2
Vermeer Ct E14 ......42 C3
Vermont Rd SW18 ...59 A1
Verne Ct 3 W3 ......37 B3
Verney Ho NW8 ......90 A2
Verney Rd SE16 .....40 A1
Verney Way SE16 ....40 A1
Vernon Ct NW2 ......1 B1
Vernon Ho SE11 ....149 A1
Vernon Mews W14 ..140 B3
Vernon Pl WC1 ......106 B3
Vernon Rd E3 ....26 B3
Mortlake SW14 ....55 C4
Vernon Rise WC1 ....95 A4
Vernon Sq WC1 .....95 A4
Vernon St W14 .....140 B3
Vernon Yd
W11 ......31 B2 112 C4
Verona Ct 10 SE14 ..50 C4
London W4 ....46 A4
Veronica Ho SE4 .....66 B4
Veronica Rd SW17 ...73 A2
Verran Rd SW12 ....73 A4
Verulam Ho 5 W6 ...39 B4
Verulam St EC1 ....107 B4
Vervain Ho 2 SE15 ..49 C3
Verwood Ho SW8 ...163 A1
Verwood Lo 6 E14 ..42 C2
Vesage Ct EC1 ......107 C3
Vesey Path 15 E14 ..34 A3
Vespan Rd W12 ......38 C4
Vesta Rd SE4,SE14 ..51 A1
Vestry Mews 12 SE5 .49 A2
Vestry Rd SE5 ....49 A2

Vestry St N1 ....97 B4
Viaduct Pl 28 E2 ....25 A2
Viaduct St E2 ....25 A2
Vian St SE13 ....67 A4
Vibart Gdns SW2 ....74 B4
Vibart Wlk N1 ....84 B4
Vicarage Ave SE3 ....53 C3
Vicarage Cres
SW11 ....167 B3
Vicarage Ct W8 ....128 A4
7 Putney SW15 ......68 C4
Vicarage Dr SW14 ...55 C2
Vicarage Gate W8 ..114 A1
Vicarage Gdns W8 ..113 C1
Mortlake SW14 ....55 C2
Vicarage Gr SE5 .....48 C2
Vicarage Gr SE5 .....48 C2
Vicarage La SE11 ...149 C2
Vicarage Rd SW14 ..55 C2
Vic's
SW1 ....167 C2
Vicarage Cres
SW11 ....167 B3
Vicar's Cl E9 ....25 B4
Vicars Hill SE13 ......67 A3
Vicar's Rd NW5 ......12 C3
Viceroy Cl NW8 ......80 B2
Viceroy Rd SW8 ....172 A4
Vic Johnson Ho 14
E3 ....26 B4
Vickery Ct EC1 ......97 A2
Vickery Ho 3 SW4 ..62 A3
Victor Cazalet Ho
N1 ....86 B4
Victoria & Albert Mus *
SW7 ....129 C1
Victoria Arc SW1 ...132 B1
Victoria Ave EC2 ...110 B3
Victoria Bldgs 8
E8 ....25 A4
Victoria Coach Sta
SW1 ....146 A3
Victoria Emb SW1 ..120 B2
Victoria Gdns
W11 ....31 C1 113 B2
Victoria Gr W8 .....128 C2
Victoria Gr Mews
W2 ....114 A3
Victoria Ho 2
SW8 ....171 B2
1 London SW1 ......146 A2
2 London SW8 ......172 B2
Victoria Ind Est 3
SW9 ....63 A1
Victoria Mans
8 London N7 ....14 C3
London NW10 ....9 A1
Victoria Mews NW6 ..23 C4
Wandsworth SW18 ...71 B3
Victorian Gr N16 .....7 A1
Victorian Rd N16 .....7 B1
Victoria Park Ct 11
E9 ....17 B1
Victoria Park Ind Ctr
........................18 B1
Victoria Park Lofts
........................18 B1
Victoria Park Rd E9 ..17 C1
Victoria Park Sq 8 E2 .25 B2
Victoria Pas NW8 ....89 B2
Victoria Rd NW6 ....23 B4
8 ....128 C2
London N4 ....5 B3
London NW10 ....21 A4
Mortlake SW14 ....55 C4
Victoria Rise SW4 ...61 A4
Victoria Sq SW1 ....132 B2

Victoria St SW1 ....133 A1
Victoria Sta SW1 ...146 B4
Victoria Terr
London N4 ....5 C2
London NW10 ....21 A1
Victoria Villas TW9 ..54 B3
Victoria Yd E1 .....111 B2
Victor Rd NW10 .....22 A2
Victory Day Sch
SW11 ....169 C4
Victory Pl E14 ....33 A2
SE17 ....151 B4
Victory Prim Sch
SE17 ....151 A4
Victory Way SE16 ...41 A4
Victory Wharf E14 ...33 A2
Victory Wlk SE8 .....51 C2
Video Ct N4 ....5 A4
View Cl N6 ....3 B4
Viewfield Rd SW18 ..58 B1
Vigo St W1 ....118 C3
Viking Cl 12 E3 .....26 A3
Viking Ho 3 SE5 ....48 B1
Village Cl NW3 ......11 C3
Village Mount 18
NW3 ....11 B4
Village Sch The
........................12 B2
Village The SW11 ...60 B4
Village Way SE21 ....63 C1
Villa Rd SW9 ....62 C4
Villa St SE17 ....151 C1
Villiers Ct SW11 ....168 B4
Villiers Rd NW2 ......8 C2
Villiers St WC2 .....120 B2
Vince Ct N1 ....97 C3
Vincent Ct SW9 ....173 A3
London N4 ....5 A4
W1 ....102 C2
Vincent Mews 6 E3 ..26 C3
Vincent Rd W3 ......37 B3
Vincents Cl SE16 ....41 A4
Vincent Sq SW1 ....147 B4
Vincent St SW1 .....147 C4
SW1 ....147 C4
Vincent Terr N1 ......86 B2
Vince St EC1 ....97 C3
Vine Ct E1 ....111 C3
Vinegar St E1 ....32 A1
Vinegar Yd SE1 .....138 A4
Vine Hill EC1 ....95 B1
Vine La SE1 ....124 B1
Vine Rd SW13 ......56 B4
Vine Sq W14 ....141 A1
Vines Sch The
SW11 ....60 C3
Vine St EC3 ....110 C1
W1 ....119 A3
Vine St Bridge EC1 ..95 B1
Vineyard Path
TW10 ....54 A2
Vineyard Sch The
TW10 ....54 A1
Vineyard The TW10 ..54 A2
Vineyard Wlk EC1 ...95 B2
Viney Ct 9 SW4 ....61 C1
Vine Yd SE1 ....137 A4
Viney Rd SE13 ......67 A4
Vining St SW2,SW9 ..62 C3
Vinson Ho N1 ....87 C1
Vintners Ct EC4 .....123 A4
Viola Sq W12 ....29 B2
Violet Cl 24 SE8 ....51 B4
Violet Hill NW8 ......78 C1
Violet Hill Ho NW8 ..78 C1
Violet Rd E3 ....27 A1
Violet St E2 ....25 A1
Virgil Pl W1 ....102 C3

Virgil St SE1 . . . . . . .135 A2
Virginia Ct 7 SE16 . .40 C4
Virginia Ho 3 E14 . . . .34 B3
Virginia Prim Sch
 E2 . . . . .98 C3
Virginia Rd E2 . . . . . . .98 C3
Virginia St E1 . . . . . . .125 C3
Virginia Wlk SW2 . . .62 B1
Viscount Ct 11 W11 .31 C3
Viscount St EC1 . . . .108 C4
Vittoria Ho 7 . . . . . . .85 A3
N1
Vittoria Prim Sch
 N1 . . . . .85 A2
Vivian Ho N4 . . . . .6 C4
Vivian Rd E3 . . . . .26 A3
Vivian Sq SE15 . . . . . .65 A4
Vogans Mill SE1 . . . .139 A4
Vollasky Ho 1 E1 . . . .111 B4
Voltaire
 2 London SE5 . . . . .48 C3
 15 Richmond TW9 . .44 B2
Voltaire Ct 5 SW11 .169 C2
Voltaire Rd SW4 . . . . .61 C4
Volt Ave N10 . . . . .21 A2
Vorley Rd N19 . . . . . . .4 B2
Voss St E2 . . . . . . .24 C2 99 C3
Voyager Bsns Est
 SE16 . . . . .139 B2
Vulcan Rd SE4 . . . . . . .51 B1
Vulcan Sq E14 . . . . . . .41 C2
Vulcan Terr SE4 . . . . . .51 B1
Vulcan Way N7 . . . . . . .14 B2
Vyner Ct E5 . . . . .17 A4
Vyner Rd W3 . . . . .28 C2
Vyner St E2 . . . . .25 A4

W

Wadding St SE17 . . . .151 B3
Waddington Rd E15 .19 C2
Waddington St E15 . .19 C2
Wade Ho SE1 . . . . . . .139 A4
Wadeson St E2 . . . . . . .25 A3
Wade's PI E14 . . . . . . .34 A2
Wadham Gdns NW3 . .12 A1
Wadham Rd SW15 . . .58 A3
Wadhurst Rd W4 . . . . .37 C3
Wager St E3 . . . . .26 B1
Waghorn St SE15 . . . .64 C4
Wagner St SE15 . . . . . .50 B3
Wainford Cl SW19 . . .69 C3
Wainwright Ho 3
 E1 . . . . .32 B1
Waite St SE15 . . . . . . .49 B4
Waithman St EC4 . . .108 A1
Wakefield Ho 8
 SE15 . . . . .49 C2
Wakefield Mews
 WC1 . . . . .94 B3
Wakefield St N1 . . . . . .94 B4
Wakeford Cl SW4 . . . .61 B2
Wakeham St 1 N1 . . .15 C2
Wakehurst Rd SW11 .60 B2
Wakeling Ho 8
 SE27 . . . . .75 A1
Wakeling St 1 E14 . .33 A3
Wakelin Ho 10 N1 . . .15 A1
Wakeman Rd NW10 .22 C2
Wakley St EC1 . . . . . . .96 A4
Walberswick St
 SW8 . . . . .162 B1
Walbrook EC4 . . . . . .123 B4
Walbrook Ct 22 N1 . .24 A3
Walburgh St E1 . . . . . .32 A3
Walcorde Ave
 SE17 . . . . .151 A3

Walcot Gdns SE11 . . .149 B4
Walcot Ho 9 SE22 . . .64 A4
Walcot Sq SE11 . . . . .149 C4
Walcott St SW1 . . . . .147 A4
Waldeck Gr SE27 . . . . .75 A1
Waldeck Rd
 Brentford TW8 . . . . .44 C4
 Mortlake SW14 . . . . .55 B4
Waldeck Terr SW14 . .55 B4
Waldegrave Ho 5
 SW15 . . . . .57 B2
Waldemar
 SW6 . . . . .164 B2
Waldemar Avenue Mans
 SW6 . . . . .164 A3
Walden Ct SW8 . . . . .171 C4
Walden St E1 . . . . . . .32 A3
 London SW11 . . . . .169 B2
Waldo Cl SW4 . . . . . . .61 B2
Waldo Rd NW10 . . . . .22 A2
Waldron Ho 7 SW2 . .62 B2
Waldron Mews
 SW3 . . . . .157 C4
Waldron Rd SW18 . . .71 B1
Walerand Rd SE13 . . .52 B1
Waleran Flats SE1 . . .152 A4
Wales Cl SE15 . . . . . . .50 A4
Wales Farm Rd W3 . .28 C4
Waley St 1 E1 . . . . . . .33 A4
Walford Ho 4 E1 . . . .32 A3
Walford Rd N16 . . . . . .16 A4
Walham Ct 15 NW3 . .12 B2
Walham Gr SW6 . . . .155 B2

Walham Green Arc
 SW6 . . . . .155 C2
Walham Yd SW6 . . . .155 B2
Walker Ho NW1 . . . . . .83 B1
Walker Mews 5 SW2 .62 C2
Walkerscroft Mead
 SE21 . . . . .75 B2
Walker's Ct W1 . . . . . .119 B4
Walkers Lo 7 E14 . . .42 B4
Walker's PI SW15 . . . .58 A3
Walkinshaw Ct 14
 N1 . . . . .15 B1
Walkynscroft 1
 SE15 . . . . .50 A1
Wallace Collection*
 W1 . . . . .103 B2
Wallace Ho N7 . . . . . .14 B2
Wallace Rd N1,N5 . . .15 B2
Wallbutton Rd SE4 . . .51 A1
Wall Ct N4 . . . . .5 B3
Waller Rd SE14 . . . . . .50 C1
Wallett Ct 9 NW1 . . .13 B1
Wallflower St W12 . . .29 B2
Wallgrave Rd SW5 . . .142 A3
Wallingford Ave
 W10 . . . . .30 C3
Wallis Alley SE1 . . . . .137 A4
Wallis Cl SW11 . . . . . .59 C4
Wallis Rd E9 . . . . .18 C2
Wallorton Gdns
 SW14 . . . . .55 C3
Wallside EC2 . . . . . . .109 A3
Wall St N1 . . . . .15 C2
Wallwood St E14 . . . .33 C4
Walmer Ho 8 W10 . .30 C3
Walmer Rd
 W11 . . . . .31 A2 112 A3
 London W10 . . . . . . .30 C3
Walmer St 1
 W1 . . . . .102 C4
Walm La NW2 . . . . . . .9 B2
Walnut Cl SE8 . . . . . . .51 B4

Walnut Tree Cl
 SW13 . . . . .46 B2
Walnut Tree Ho
 SW10 . . . . .156 B4
Walnut Tree Rd
 SE10 . . . . .43 A1
 Brentford TW8 . . . . .44 A4
Walnut Tree Walk Prim
 Sch SE11 . . . . .149 B4
Walnut Tree Wlk
 SE11 . . . . .149 B4
Walpole Ave TW9 . . . .44 B1
Walpole Ct
 7 London NW6 . . . .11 B1
 London SE14 . . . . . .39 C3
Walpole Gdns W4 . . . .37 B1
Walpole Mews NW8 . .79 B3
Walpole St SW3 . . . .145 A2
Walsham Cl N16 . . . . .7 C3
Walsham Ho SE14 . . .50 C1
 London SE14 . . . . . .50 C1
Walsham Rd SE14 . . .50 C1
Walsingham
 London SE14 . . . . . .79 C4
Walsingham Lo
 SW13 . . . . .46 C2
Walsingham Mans
 SW6 . . . . .156 B2
Walsingham PI
 SW4,SW11 . . . . .60 C1
Walsingham Rd E5 . . .7 C1
Walter Besant Ho 20
 E1 . . . . .25 C2
Walter Ct 3 W3 . . . . .28 B3
Walter Green Ho
 SE15 . . . . .50 B2
Walter Ho SW10 . . . .157 B2
Walter Northcott Ho 2
 NW6 . . . . .10 C3
Walters Cl SE17 . . . . .151 A3
Walters Ho N1 . . . . . . .86 B4
 10 SE17 . . . . .48 A4
 6 London SE5 . . . . .49 A1
Walter St E2 . . . . .25 C2
Walters Way SE23 . . .65 C1
Walter Terr E1 . . . . . . .32 C3
Walterton Rd W9 . . . .23 C1
Waltham Green Ct
 SW6 . . . . .156 A1
Waltham Ho NW8 . . .78 C4
 London SW9 . . . . . .173 A1
Walton Cl SW8 . . . . . .162 B2
Walton Gdns W3 . . . . .28 A4
Walton Ho E2 . . . . . . .99 A2
 London SW18 . . . . . .58 C1
Walton PI SW3 . . . . . .130 C2
Walton St SW3 . . . . . .130 B1
Walton Way W3 . . . . .28 A4
Walt Whitman Cl 6
 SE24 . . . . .63 A3
Wanborough Dr
 SW15 . . . . .69 A3
Wandle Ct 4 W12 . . .38 A4
Wandle Ho NW8 . . . .102 A4
 Wandsworth SW18 . .71 A4
Wandle Prim Sch
 SW18 . . . . .71 A3
Wandle Rd SW17 . . . .72 A2
Wandle Way SW18 . . .71 A3
Wandon Rd SW6 . . . .156 B1
Wandsworth Bridge Rd
 SW6 . . . . .166 A2

Wandsworth Common
 Sta SW12 . . . . .72 B4
Wandsworth Common
 West Side SW18 . . .59 B2
Wandsworth Gyratory
 SW18 . . . . .59 A2
Wandsworth High St
 SW18 . . . . .59 A2
Wandsworth Plain
 SW18 . . . . .59 A2
Wandsworth Rd
 SW8 . . . . .162 A1
Wandsworth Road Sta
 SW4 . . . . .171 A1
Wandsworth Town Sta
 SW18 . . . . .59 A3
Wangford Ho 13
 SW9 . . . . .63 A3
Wanless Rd SE24 . . . .63 B4
Wanley Rd SE5 . . . . . .63 C3
Wansbeck Rd E3,E9 .18 B1
Wansdown PI SW6 . .156 A2
Wansey St SE17 . . . . .151 A3
Wapping Dock St 11
 E1 . . . . .32 A1
Wapping High St
 E1 . . . . .32 A1
Wapping La E1 . . . . . .32 A1
Wapping Sta E1 . . . . .32 B1
Wapping Wall E1 . . . .32 B1
Warbeck Rd W12 . . . .39 A4
Warburton Cl 8 N1 . .16 A2
Warburton Ct SE15 . .64 C4
Warburton Ho 5
 E8 . . . . .25 A4
Warburton Rd 8
 E8 . . . . .25 A4
Warburton St E8 . . . . .25 A4
Wardalls Ho 13 SE8 . .51 B4
Wardell Ho 12 SE10 .52 B4
Warden Rd NW5 . . . . .12 C2
Wardens Gr SE1 . . . .122 C1
Wardle St E9 . . . . .17 C3
Wardley St SW18 . . . .71 A4
Wardlow 6 NW5 . . . . .13 A4
Wardo Ave SW6 . . . . .164 A4
Wardour Mews
 W1 . . . . .105 A1
Wardour St W1 . . . . . .105 B1
Ward Point SE11 . . . .149 B3
Ward Rd E15 . . . . .27 C4
 London N19 . . . . . . .4 B1
Wardrobe PI EC4 . . . .108 B1
Wardrobe Terr
 EC4 . . . . .122 B4
Wareham Ct 2 N1 . . .16 A1
Wareham Ho SW8 . .162 C2
Warfield Rd NW10 . . .22 C2
Warfield Yd 6
 NW10 . . . . .22 C2
Wargrave Ho 2 . . . . . .98 C3
Warham St SE5 . . . . . .48 A3
Waring Ho E2 . . . . . . .99 C3
Warley Ho N1 . . . . . . .15 C2
Warley St E2 . . . . .25 C2
Warlock Rd W9 . . . . . .23 C1
Warlters Cl N7 . . . . . . .14 A4
Warlters Rd N7 . . . . . .14 A4
Warltersville Mans
 N19 . . . . .5 A4
Warltersville Rd
 N4,N8,N19 . . . . .5 A4
War Memorial Homes
 W4 . . . . .45 C3
Warmington Rd
 SE24 . . . . .63 B1
Warmsworth NW1 . . .82 C4

Warncliffe Ho 3
 SW15 . . . . .57 B2
Warndon St SE16 . . . .40 B2
Warneford St E9 . . . . .25 A4
Warner Ho NW8 . . . . .88 C4
 4 London E9 . . . . . .17 C2
 London SE13 . . . . . .52 A1
Warner PI E2 . . . .24 C2 99 B3
Warner Rd SE5 . . . . . .48 B2
Warner St EC1 . . . . . . .95 B1
Warner Yd EC1 . . . . . .95 B1
Warnford Ho SW15 . .56 A1
Warnham WC1 . . . . . .94 C3
Warnham Ho 6
 SW2 . . . . .74 B4
Warple Mews W3 . . . .38 A4
Warple Way W3,
 W12 . . . . .38 A4
Warren Ave SW14,
 TW10 . . . . .55 A3
Warren Cl SE21 . . . . . .75 B4
Warren Ct N1 . . . . . . .85 B2
Warren Ct N17 . . . . . .13 B4
Warren Gdns E15 . . . .19 C3
Warren Ho 21 E3 . . . .27 A2
Warren Mews W1 . . . .92 C1
Warren St W1 . . . . .92 C1
Warren Street Sta
 NW1 . . . . .93 A2
Warriner Gdns
 SW11 . . . . .169 B3
Warrington Cres
 W9 . . . . .88 C2
Warrington Gdns
 W9 . . . . .88 C1
Warrington PI E14 . . .34 B1
Warspite Ho 5 E14 . .42 A2
Warton Rd E15 . . . . . .27 B4
Warwick A14 . . . . .141 A3
Warwick Ave W9 . . . . .88 C1
Warwick Avenue Sta
 W9 . . . . .88 C1
Warwick Chambers
 W8 . . . . .127 B2
Warwick Cres W2 . . . .100 C4
Warwick Ct WC1 . . . .107 A3
 London NW2 . . . . . .10 A3
Warwick Dr SW15 . . .57 A4
Warwick Ho
 London N4 . . . . .6 B3
 London SW9 . . . . . .173 B1
 6 Putney SW15 . . . .69 B4
Warwick House St
 SW1 . . . . .119 C2
Warwick La EC4 . . . . .108 B1
Warwick Mans
 SW5 . . . . .141 A4
Warwick Park Sch
 SE15 . . . . .49 B2
Warwick Pas EC4 . . .108 B2
Warwick PI W9 . . . . .100 C4
Warwick PI N SW1 . .146 C3
Warwick Rd W14,
 SW5 . . . . .141 A4
Warwick Row SW1 . .132 B2
Warwickshire Path
 SE8 . . . . .51 B3
Warwickshire Rd
 N16 . . . . .16 A4
Warwick Sq EC4 . . . .108 B2
 SW1 . . . . .146 C2
Warwick Sq Mews
 SW1 . . . . .146 C3

Warwick St W1 . . . . . . .119 A4
Warwick Way SW1 .146 B3
Warwick Yd EC1 . . . .97 A1
Wasdale 92 B3
Washbrook Ho W2 . . .100 C4
Washington Cl E6
. . . . .27 A2
Washington Ho
SW1 . . . . .130 C3
Washington Rd
. . . . .46 C3
Watchfield Ct **7**
W4 . . . . .37 B1
Watcombe Cotts
TW9 . . . . .44 C4
Watercress PI N1 . . . .16 A1
Waterden Cres E20 . . .18 C3
Waterden Rd E15 . . . .18 C2
Waterford Rd SW6 . . .156 A1
Watergate EC4 . . . . .122 A4
Watergate Sch
SE13 . . . . .67 A3
Watergate St SE8 . . . .51 C4
Watergate Wlk
WC2 . . . . .120 B2
Water Gdns The
W2 . . . . .102 B2
Waterhead Ho **1** 24 C4
Waterhouse Cl
London NW3 . . . . .11 C3
London W6 . . . . .39 C1
Wateridge Cl E14 . . . .41 C3
Water La SE14 . . . . . . .50 B3
Waterloo Bridge
SE1,WC2 . . . . .121 A3
Waterloo Cl E9 . . . . . . .17 B3
Waterloo East Sta
SE1 . . . . .121 C1
Waterloo Gdns E2 . . . .25 B3
Waterloo Int Sta
SE1 . . . . .135 A4
Waterloo Pier SE1 . . .134 C4
Waterloo Pl SW1 . . . .119 B2
Waterloo Rd SE1 . . . .135 C4
Waterloo Terr N1 . . . .15 A1
Waterloo Ct NW1 . . . . .2 A4
Waterlow Rd N19 . . . . .4 B3
Waterman Bldg **4**
E14 . . . . .41 C4
Waterman St SW15 . . .57 C4
Waterman Way E1 . . . .32 A1
Watermead Ho E9 . . . .18 A3
Watermeadow La
SW6 . . . . .166 C1
Water Mews SE15 . . . .65 B3
Watermint Quay N16 . .7 C4
Water's Edge SW6 . . . .47 B2
Waterside Cl E3 . . . . . .26 B4
SE16 . . . . .139 C3
Waterside Ct SE13 . . . .67 C3
Waterside Pl NW1 . . . .81 C4
Waterside Point
SW11 . . . . .158 B2
Waterson St E2 . . . . . .98 C4
Waters Pl SW15 . . . . . .47 B1
Water St WC2 . . . . . . .121 A4
Water Tower Ho
W8 . . . . .113 B1
Water Tower Pl N1 . . . .86 A3
Waterview Ho E14 . . . .33 A4
Waterworks Rd
SW2 . . . . .62 B1
Watford Cl SW11 . . . .168 B4
Watford Rd E16 . . . . . .35 C4

Watkin Ho N16 . . . . . . .7 B4
Watkinson Rd N7 . . . . .14 B2
Watling Ct EC4 . . . . . .109 A1
Watling Gdns NW2 . . . .10 A2
Watling St EC4 . . . . . .109 A1
4 SE15 . . . . .49 A4
Watney Cotts SW14 . . .55 B4
Watney Mkt **1** 32 A3
Watney Rd SW14 . . . . .55 B4
Watney St E1 . . . . .32 A3
Watson Cl N16 . . . . . . .15 C3
Watson Ho **3** 74 A1
Watson's Mews
W1 . . . . .102 B3
Watson's St SE8 . . . . . .51 C3
Watts Gr E3 . . . . .34 A4
Watts Ho **6** W10 . . . . . .31 A4
Watts St E1 . . . . .32 A1
SE15 . . . . .49 B2
Wat Tyler Rd SE10 . . . .52 C2
Wavel Ct **7** E1 . . . . . . .32 B1
7 Streatham SW16 . .74 A1
Wavel Mews NW6 . . . .11 A1
Wavendon Ave W4 . . . .37 C1
Waveney Ave SE15 . . . .65 A3
Waveney Cl E1 . . . . . .125 C2
Waveney Ho SE15 . . . .65 A3
Waverley Ct W1 . . . . . .103 C4
8 London NW6 . . . . . .10 A1
Waverley Pl NW8 . . . . .79 B2
London N4 . . . . .6 A3
Waverley Rd N8 . . . . . . .5 A4
Waverley Sch (lower)
SE22 . . . . .64 A4
Waverley Sch (Upper)
SE15 . . . . .65 B2
Waverly Ct NW3 . . . . . .12 B3
Waverton Ho **8** E3 . . .26 B4
Waverton Rd SW18 . . .71 C4
Waverton St W1 . . . . .118 A2
Wavertree Ct **9**
SW2 . . . . .74 A3
Wavertree Rd SW2 . . .74 B3
Waxham NW5 . . . . .12 B3
Waxlow Rd NW10 . . . . .20 C3
Wayford St SW11 . . . .168 B1
Wayland Ave E8 . . . . . .16 C3
Wayland Ho SW9 . . . .173 B2
Waylett Ho SE11 . . . . .149 B1
Waylett Pl SE27 . . . . . .75 A1
Wayman Ct E8 . . . . . . .17 A2
Waynflete Sq
16 London W10 . . . . . .30 C2
18 London W10 . . . . . .30 C3
Waynflete St SW18 . . .71 B2
Wayside London NW11 .1 A3
Mortlake SW14 . . . . . .55 B2
Weald Cl SE16 . . . . . . .40 A1
Weardale Ho N4 . . . . . . .6 B4
Weardale Rd SE13 . . . .67 C3
Wearmouth Ho **1**
E3 . . . . .33 B4
Wear Pl **15** E2 . . . . . . .25 A2
Wearside Rd SE13 . . . .67 A3
Weatherbury **6** W2 . . .31 C3
Weatherbury Ho **3**
N19 . . . . .4 C1
Weatherley Cl E3 . . . . .33 B4
Weaver Cl E6 . . . . .25 A1
Weaver Ho **1** 99 B1
Weaver's La SE1 . . . . .124 B1
Weaver St E1 . . .24 C1 99 B1
Weavers Way NW1 . . . .83 B4
6 London NW1 . . . . . .13 A1
Webb Ct W3 . . . . .37 A4
Webber Row SE1 . . . .136 A3
Webber St SE1 . . . . . .136 A3

Webb Est E5 . . . . .7 C4
Webb Ho SW8 . . . . . .161 C1
Webb Pl NW10 . . . . . .21 B2
Webb Rd SE3 . . . . .53 B4
Webb's Rd SW11 . . . . .60 B2
Webb St SE1 . . . . .138 A1
Webheath **5** NW6 . . . .10 B1
Webster Ho **16** N16 . . .16 A3
Webster Rd SE16 . . . .139 C1
Weddell Ho **2** E1 . . . . .25 C1
Wedderburn Rd
NW3 . . . . .11 C3
Wedgewood Ho
SW1 . . . . .146 C1
Wedgewood Mews
W1 . . . . .105 C1
Wedgewood Wlk
NW3 . . . . .11 A3
Wedgwood Ho
17 E2 . . . . .25 C2
SE11 . . . . .135 B1
Wedlake St W10 . . . . . .23 A1
Wedmore Gdns N19 . . .4 C2
Wedmore St N19 . . . . . .4 C1
Weech Rd NW6 . . . . . .10 C4
Weedington Rd
NW5 . . . . .12 C3
Weedon Ho W12 . . . . . .29 C3
Weekley Sq SW11 . . . .59 C4
Weighhouse St
W1 . . . . .103 C1
Weimar St SW15 . . . . .58 A4
Weir Ho **8** SW12 . . . . .73 B4
Weir Rd
Streatham SW12 . . . . .73 B4
Wimbledon SW18,
SW19 . . . . .71 A1
Wirr's Pas NW1 . . . . . .93 C4
Weiss Rd SW15 . . . . . .57 C4
Welbeck Ct W14 . . . . .140 C4
Welbeck Mans **10**
NW6 . . . . .10 C3
Welbeck St W1 . . . . . .104 A2
Welbeck Way W1 . . . .104 A2
Welby Ho N19 . . . . .4 C4
Welby St SE5 . . . . .48 A2
Welford Ct
12 London NW1 . . . .13 A1
London SW8 . . . . .170 C1
Welland Ho SE15 . . . . .65 B3
Welland Mews E1 . . . .125 C2
Wellclose Sq E1 . . . . .125 C4
Wellclose St E1 . . . . . .125 C3
Well Ct EC4 . . . . .109 A1
Wellday Ho **2** E9 . . . . .18 A2
Weller Ho SE16 . . . . . .139 B3
Weller St SE1 . . . . . . .136 C4
Wellesley Ave W6 . . . . .39 A3
Wellesley Ct W9 . . . . . .88 C4
Wellesley Ho NW1 . . . .93 B3
Wellesley Pl NW1 . . . . .93 B3
Wellesley Rd
London NW5 . . . . .12 C3
London W4 . . . . .37 A1
Wellesley St E1 . . . . . .32 C4
Wellesley Terr N1 . . . . .97 A4
Wellfit St **13** SE24 . . . .63 A4
Wellgarth Rd NW11 . . .2 A3
Wellington Arch
SW1 . . . . .131 C4
Wellington Bldgs
14 E3 . . . . .26 C2
SW1 . . . . .145 C1
Wellington Cl
London SE14 . . . . .50 C2
London W11 . . . . .31 C3

Wellington Ct NW8 . . .79 C1
SW1 . . . . .130 C3
SW6 . . . . .166 B3
WC2 . . . . .120 A4
London SW18 . . . . .60 A2
Wellington Gr SE10 . . .52 C3
Wellington Ho N6 . . . . .3 B4
Wellington Hospl
NW3 . . . . .12 B3
Wellington Hospl
(North) NW8 . . . . .79 C1
Wellington Hospl
(South) NW8 . . . . .79 C1
Wellington Mans
N16 . . . . .16 B4
Wellington Mews
London SE22 . . . . .64 C3
London SE7 . . . . .73 L1
Wellington Mus (Apsley
Ho) SW1 . . . . .131 C4
Wellington Pl NW8 . . .89 C4
Wellington Prim Sch
E3 . . . . .26 C2
Wellington Rd NW8 . . .79 C1
London NW10 . . . . .22 C2
Wimbledon SW19 . . . .70 C2
Wellington Row
E2 . . . . .24 C2 99 B4
Wellington Sq
SW3 . . . . .144 C2
Wellington St
WC2 . . . . .120 C4
Wellington Terr **2**
E1 . . . . .32 A1
London SW14 . . . . .55 B2
Wellington Way E3 . . . .26 C2
Well La SW14 . . . . .55 B2
Well Rd NW3 . . . . .2 C1
Wells Ct **1** London SW1 .88 B4
London NW3 . . . . .11 B4
Wells Ho EC1 . . . . .96 A4
9 SE16 . . . . .40 B3
7 W10 . . . . .23 A1
Wells Ho The Mews W3 .11 C4
Wells House Rd
NW10 . . . . .29 A4
Wellside Gdns
SW14 . . . . .55 B2
Wells Mews W1 . . . . . .105 A2
Wells Pl SW18 . . . . . . .71 B4
Wells Rd W12 . . . . .39 B4
Wells Rise NW8 . . . . . .80 C3
Wells Sq WC1 . . . . .95 A3
Wells St W1 . . . . .105 A2
Well St E9 . . . . .17 B1
Wells Terr N4 . . . . .5 C2
Wells Way SW5 . . . . . .49 A4
SW7 . . . . .129 B2
Welly Yd **2** N7 . . . . . . .14 C3
Well Wlk NW3 . . . . .2 C1
Wellwood Ct SW15 . . . .57 B3
Welsford St SE1 . . . . .153 B3
Welsh Ho **10** E1 . . . . . .32 A1
Welshpool Ho **22**
E8 . . . . .24 C4
Welshpool St **1** E8 . . .25 A4
Welstead Ho **1** E1 . . . .32 A3
Welstead Way W4 . . . .38 B2
Weltje Rd W6 . . . . .38 C1
Welton Ho E1 . . . . .32 C4
London SE5 . . . . .49 A2
Welwyn St E2 . . . . .25 B2
Wembury Rd N6 . . . . . . .4 A4
Wemyss Rd SE3 . . . . . .53 B1
Wendell Park Prim Sch
W12 . . . . .38 B4
Wendell Rd W12 . . . . . .38 B4
Wendle Ct SW8 . . . . .162 A3

Wendling NW5 . . . . . . .12 B3
Wendon St E3 . . . . .26 B4
Wendover SE17 . . . . . .152 A2
Wendover Ct **4** NW2 . . .1 C1
W1 . . . . .103 B3
London NW2 . . . . .20 B1
Wendover Ho W1 . . . .103 B3
Wendover Rd NW10 . . .21 B3
Wengham Ho W12 . . . .29 C2
Wenham Ho SW8 . . . .160 C1
Wenlake Ho EC1 . . . . . .96 C2
Wenlock Ct N1 . . . . . . .87 C1
Wenlock Rd N1 . . . . . . .87 A1
Wenlock St N1 . . . . . . .87 B1
Wennington Rd E3 . . . .25 C3
Wensdale Ho E5 . . . . . . .7 C2
wensleydale Ho 8
. . . . .6 B4
Wentworth Cres
SE15 . . . . .49 C3
Wentworth Ct W6 . . . .154 A3
Wandsworth SW18 . . .59 A1
Wentworth Dwellings
E1 . . . . .110 C2
Wentworth Mews
E3 . . . . .26 B2
Wentworth St E1 . . . . .111 A3
Werrington St NW1 . . .83 A1
Werter Rd SW15 . . . . . .58 A3
Wesleyan Pl NW5 . . . . .13 A4
Wesley Ave NW10 . . . .20 C2
Wesley Cl SE17 . . . . . .150 B3
London N7 . . . . .5 B2
Wesley Ho SE24 . . . . . .63 C1
Wesley Rd NW10 . . . . .20 B4
Wesley Sq W11 . . . . . .31 A3
Wessex Ct SW15 . . . . .57 C2
Wessex Gardens Prim
Sch NW11 . . . . .1 A3
Wessex Gdns NW11 . . .1 A3
Wessex Ho **4** London N19 . . . . .4 C1
Wessex St E2 . . . . .25 B2
Wessex Way NW11 . . . .1 A3
Westacott Cl N19 . . . . . .5 A3
West Acton Prim Sch
W3 . . . . .28 A3
West Arbour St **1** 32 C3
West Bank N16 . . . . .7 A4
Westbank Rd NW2 . . . .10 A3
West Block **7** E1 . . . . .32 B2
Westbourne Ave
W3 . . . . .28 C3
Westbourne Cres
W2 . . . . .115 B4
Westbourne Ct
W2 . . . . .100 C2
Westbourne Gdns
W2 . . . . .100 A2
Westbourne Gr
W11 . . . . .100 A1
W2,W11 . . . . . .31 C3 113 A4
Westbourne Gr Mews **7**
W11 . . . . .31 C3
Westbourne Gr Terr
W2 . . . . .100 A1
Westbourne Ho
SW1 . . . . .146 A2
Westbourne Park Rd
W11 . . . . .31 B3
W2 . . . . .31 C3
Westbourne Park Sta
W11 . . . . .31 B4
Westbourne Park Villas
W2 . . . . .31 C3
Westbourne Rd N7 . . . .14 B2

Westbourne St
W2 ....**115** B4

Westbourne Terr
W2 ....**101** A2

Westbourne Terr Mews
W2 ....**100** C2

Westbourne Terr Rd
W2 ....**100** C3

Westbridge Ct W12 .29 C1

Westbridge Prim Sch
SW11 ....**168** A4

Westbridge Rd
SW11 ....**168** A4

West Brompton Sta
SW5 ....**141** C1

Westbook Ho
5 E2 ....25 B2
4 W6 ....39 A3

Westbury Ct SW4 ..61 A1

Westbush Ct **1**
W12 ....39 A4

West Carriage Dr
W2 ....**116** A2

West Central Ave
NW10 ....26 A2

West Central St
WC1 ....**106** A2

Westchester Ho
W2 ....**102** C1

Westcliff Ho **10** N1 .15 C2

Westcombe Ct **1**
SE3 ....53 B3

Westcombe Hill
SE3,SE10 ....53 C4

Westcombe Park Rd
SE3 ....53 B3

Westcombe Park Sta
SE3 ....43 C1

Westcott Ho **11** E14 .34 A2
Westcott Rd SE17 .48 A4
West Cotts NW6 ...10 C3
Westcroft Cl NW2 ..10 A4
Westcroft Ct **3** W6 .38 C2
Westcroft Sq W6 ..38 C2
Westcroft Way NW2 .10 A4

West Cromwell Rd
W14 ....**141** A2

West Cross Route
W10,W11 ....30 C2

Westdean Cl SW18 .59 A1
Westdown Rd E15 ..76 B4

West Dulwich Sta
SE21 ....75 C3

West Eaton Pl
SW1 ....**145** B4

West Eaton Pl Mews
SW1 ....**145** B4

West Ella Rd NW10 .8 A1
West End Ct NW6 ..11 A1
West End La NW6 ..11 C2
Westerdale Ct N5 ..15 A4

Westerdale Rd **2**
SE10 ....43 C1

Westerham NW1 ....**82** C3

Westerham Ho
SE1 ....**137** C2

Western Ave W3 ...28 C3
Western Ave Bsns
Pk W3 ....20 A1

Western Ct
2 London W3 ....28 C3
3 London W9 ....23 B1

Western Eye Hospl The
NW1 ....**102** C4

Western Ho **1** W9 .23 B1
Western La SW12 ..72 C4
Western Mews W9 .23 B1

Western Pl **15** SE16 .40 B4

Western Rd
London NW10 ....20 B1
London SW9 ....62 C4

Western Terr W6 ..38 C1

Western Wharf **4**
SE14 ....51 A4

Westferry Cir E14 .33 C1
Westferry Rd E14 ..41 C3
Westferry Sta E14 .33 C2
Westfield NW3 ......10 C4

Westfield Cl SW10 .**156** C1

Westfield Ct **1**
W10 ....23 C2

Westfield Ho **6**
SE16 ....40 C2

Westfields SW13 ...56 B4
Westfields Ave
SW13 ....56 A4
Westfields Rd W3 ..28 A4
Westfields Sch
SW13 ....56 B4

Westfield Way **11** E1 .26 A1

West Garden Pl
W2 ....**102** B1

Westgate Bsns Ctr
2 W10 ....23 A1
London W10 ....22 C1

Westgate Ct **16**
SW9 ....62 C4

Westgate St **3** E8 .25 A4

Westgate Terr
SW10 ....**156** B4

West Gdns E1 ......32 A2
West Gr SE10 ......52 C2
Westgrove La SE10 .52 B2

West Halkin St
SW1 ....**131** B2

West Hall Rd TW9 ..45 A2
West Hampstead Mews
NW6 ....11 A2

West Hampstead Sta
NW6 ....10 C2

West Hampstead
Thameslink Sta
NW6 ....10 C2

West Harding St
EC4 ....**107** C2

Westhay Gdns
SW14 ....55 A2

West Heath Ave
NW11 ....1 C3
West Heath Cl NW3 .1 C1
West Heath Ct NW11 .1 C3
West Heath Dr NW11 .1 C3

West Heath Gdns
NW3 ....1 C1
West Heath Rd NW3 .2 A1

West Hill N6 ....3 C3
Putney SW15 ....58 A1
West Hill Ct N6 .....3 C1

Westhill Ct W11 ...**113** A4
West Hill Ct N6 .....3 C1

Westhill Pk London N6 .3 B2
London N6 ....3 C2

West Hill Prim Sch
SW18 ....58 C2

West Hill Rd SW18 .58 B1

West Ho **5** SW12 .73 B4
Westhope Ho E2 ...**99** C3

Westhorpe Rd
SW15 ....57 B4

West House Cl
SW19 ....70 A3

West India Ave E14 .33 C1

West India Dock Rd
E14 ....33 C2

West India Quay **1**
E14 ....33 C2

West India Quay Sta
E14 ....33 C2

West Kensington Ct
W14 ....**140** C2

West Kensington Mans
W14 ....**140** C1

West Kensington Sta
W14 ....**140** C2

West La SE16 ......40 A4

Westlake **5** SE16 ..40 B2

Westland Pl N1 ....**97** B4

Westlands Terr **3**
SW12 ....61 B1

Westleigh Ave
SW15 ....57 B2

West London Stad The
W12 ....30 A4

Westly Ct NW2 .....9 C2

Westmacott Ho
NW8 ....**89** C1

West Mall W11 ....**113** C2

Westmark Point **13**
SW15 ....69 A3

Westmead SW15 ...57 A1

West Mews SW1 ..**146** C3

Westmill Ct N4 .....6 B2

Westminster Abbey*
SW1 ....**134** A1

Westminster Abbey
Choir Sch SW1 ...**133** C2

Westminster Boating
Base SW1 ....**161** B4

Westminster Bridge
SE1,SW1 ....**134** B3

Westminster Bridge Rd
SE1 ....**135** A3

Westminster Cath*
SW1 ....**132** C1

Westminster Cath Choir
Sch SW1 ....**147** A4

Westminster Cath RC
Prim Sch SW1 ....**147** C2

Westminster City Hall
SW1 ....**133** A2

Westminster City Sch
SW1 ....**132** C1

Westminster Ct
2 SE16 ....40 C4
3 London SW18 ..58 C2

Westminster Gdns
SW1 ....**148** A4

Westminster Kingsway
Coll
WC1 ....**94** C3
London SW11 .....**169** C4

Westminster Pier
SW1 ....**134** B3

Westminster Sch
SW1 ....**134** A2

Westminster Sta
SW1 ....**134** B3

Westmore Ct SW15 .58 A2

Westmoreland Ho
NW10 ....21 C2

Westmoreland Pl
SW1 ....**146** B1

Westmoreland Rd
SE17 ....48 C4
Barnes SW13 ......46 C2

Westmoreland St
W1 ....**103** C3

Westmoreland Terr
SW1 ....**146** B1

West Norwood Sta
SE27 ....75 A1

Westonbirt Ct **6**
SE15 ....49 B4

Weston Ct N4 ....6 B1

Weston Ed Ctr The
SE5 ....48 B1

West One Ho W1 ..**104** C4
Weston Ho **9** E9 ..25 B4
4 London NW6 ...10 A1
Weston Rise WC1,
N1 ....5 A2
Weston Rise N1,
WC1 ....95 A4

Weston St SE1 ....**137** C4
Weston Wlk **3** E8,
E9 ....17 A1

Westover Hill NW3 .1 C2

Westover Rd SW18 .59 B1

West Park Ave TW9 .45 A2
West Park Rd TW9 .44 C2
West Parkside SE10 .43 B3

West Point SE1 ....**153** B2

Westpoint SW15 ...57 C1

Westpoint Trad Est
W3 ....20 A1

Westport St E1 ....32 C3

West Poultry Ave
EC1 ....**108** A3

West Quarters W12 .29 C3

West Rd SW3 .....**159** A4
SW4 ....61 C2
West Row W10 .....23 A1
Westside SW19 ...72 B3

West Sheen Vale
TW9 ....54 B3

Westside SW1 .....23 C1

West Smithfield
EC1 ....**108** A3

West Sq SE11 ....**136** A1

West St SE **22** E2 ..25 A3
WC2 ....**105** C1

West Temple Sheen
SW14 ....55 A2

West Tenter St E1 .**111** A1

Westvale Mews W3 .38 A4

Westview Cl
London NW10 ......8 B3
London W10 ....30 B3

Westville Rd W12 ..38 C4

West Warwick Pl
SW1 ....**146** C3

Westway W10,W12 .29 C2

Westway (Elevated Rd)
W2 ....**101** B3

Westway Lo **32** W2 .31 C4

Westwell **4** NW5 ..12 C2

Westwick Gdns
W14 ....39 C3

Westwood Gdns
SW13 ....56 B4

Westwood Ho
5 London N4 .....6 C4
London W12 ....30 B1
Westwood Rd SW13 .56 B4

Wetherby Gdns
SW5 ....**142** C3

Wetherby Mans
SW5 ....**142** A2

Wetherby Mews
SW5 ....**142** B2

Wetherby Pl SW7 ..**143** A3

Wetherell Rd E9 ...25 C4

Wetland Centre The
SW13 ....47 A4

Wevco Wharf SE15 .50 A4

Wexford Ho **9** E1 ..32 B4

Wexford Rd SW12 ..72 B4

Weybourne St
SW18 ....71 B2

Weybridge Ct **19**
SE16 ....40 A1

Weybridge Ho N4 ..6 B4

Weybridge Point
SW11 ....**169** A2

Weydown Cl SW19 .70 A3

Weyhill Ho **7** SE5 ..48 B1

Weyhill Rd E1 .....**111** C2

Wey Ho NW8 ......**89** C1

Weymouth Ct **5** E2 .24 B3
15 Streatham SW2 ..74 B4

Weymouth Ho
SW8 ....**162** C1

Weymouth Mews
W1 ....**104** A3
Weymouth St W1 ..**104** A4
Weymouth Terr E2 .24 B3

Whadcoat St N4 ....5 C2

Whaddon Ho
SE5 ....64 A4
London SW1 ......**131** A3

Wharfdale Rd N1 ..**84** B2

Wharfedale St **5**
E5 ....17 C4

Wharfedale St
SW10 ....**142** A1

Wharf Pl E2 ....25 A4
Wharf Rd E15 .....27 C4
N1 ....**86** C1
London NW1 ......**83** C3

Wharfside Rd E16 .35 A4

Wharf St E16 ......35 A4

Wharton Cl NW10 ..8 A2
Wharton Ho SE1 ..**138** C2
Wharton St WC1 ..**95** A3

Whateley Rd SE22 .64 B2

Wheatland Ho **7**
SE22 ....64 A4

Wheatlands Rd
SW17 ....72 C1

Wheatley Ho
London NW5 ....13 A4
3 Putney SW15 ...68 C4

Wheatley St W1 ..**103** C3

Wheat Sheaf Cl E14 .42 A2

Wheatsheaf La
SW8 ....**162** B2
London SW6 ....47 B3

Wheatsheaf Terr
SW6 ....**155** A1

Wheatstone Ho **7**
W10 ....31 A4

Wheatstone Rd
W10 ....31 A4

Wheeler Ct **5**
SW11 ....59 C4

Wheeler Gdns N1 ..**84** B4

Wheelwright St N7 .14 B1

Wheldon Ct SE1 ..**138** C4

Wheler Ho **1**
E1 ....**98** C1

Wheler St E1 .24 B1 **98** C1

Whellock Rd W4 ...38 A3

Whetstone Park
WC2 ....**106** C2

Whewell Rd N19 ...5 A2

Whichcote St SE1 .**121** B1

Whidborne Bldgs
WC1 ....**94** A3

Whidborne Cl SE8 .51 C1

Whidborne St WC1 .**94** A3

Whippingham Ho **17**
E3 ....26 B2

Whiskin St EC1 ...**96** A3

Whistler Mews **2**
SE15 ....49 B3

Whistlers Ave
SW11 . . . .**157** C1
Whistler St N5 . . . . .**15** A3
Whistler Twr
SW10 . . . .**156** C1
Whistler Wlk
SW10 . . . .**157** A2
Whiston Ho **13** **15** A1
Whiston Rd E2 . . . . . .**24** C4
Whitbread Ctr EC1**97** B1
Whitbread Rd SE4 . .**66** B3
Whitburn Rd SE13 . .**67** A3
Whitby Ave NW10 . . .**20** A2
Whitby Ct **1** N7 . . . . .**14** A4
Whitby Ho NW8 . . . . .**78** C1
Whitby St E1 . . . .**98** C2
Whitcher Cl SE14 . . .**51** A4
Whitcher Pl NW1 . . .**13** B2
Whitchurch Ho **10**
W10 . . . .**30** C3
Whitchurch Rd W11 .**30** C2
Whitcomb Ct W1 . . .**119** C3
Whitcombe Mews
TW9 . . . .**45** A2
Whitcomb St W2 . . .**119** C3
Whiteadder Way
E14 . . . .**42** A2
Whitear Wlk E15 . . .**19** C2
Whitebeam Cl
SW9 . . . .**163** A1
Whitebeam Ho **3**
NW3 . . . .**12** B2
White Bear Pl NW3 .**11** C4
White Bear Yd EC1 . .**95** B1
Whitechapel High St
E1 . . . .**111** A2
Whitechapel Rd
E1 . . . .**32** A4 **111** B3
Whitechapel Sta E1 .**32** A4
Whitechurch La
E1 . . . .**111** A2
White City W10 . . . . .**30** B3
White City Cl W12 . .**30** B2
White City Est **21**
W12 . . . .**30** A2
White City Rd W12 . .**30** B2
White City Sta W12 .**30** A2
Whitecliff Ho SW18 .**59** A1
White Conduit St
N1 . . . .**85** C2
Whitecross Pl EC2**109** C4
Whitecross St EC1 . .**97** A1
Whitefield Cl SW15 . .**58** A1
Whitefriars St EC4**107** C1
Whitehall SW1 . . . .**134** A4
Whitehall Ct SW1 . .**120** A1
Whitehall Gdns
SW1 . . . .**120** A1
Chiswick W4 . . . .**45** A4
Whitehall Mans **3**
N19 . . . .**4** C3
Whitehall Park Rd
W4 . . . .**45** A4
Whitehall Pl N19 . . . .**4** B3
Whitehall Pl WC2,
SW1 . . . .**120** A1
White Hart Ct EC2 .**110** A3
White Hart La
London NW10 . . . .**8** B2
Mortlake SW13 . . . . . .**56** A4
White Hart St EC4 .**108** B1
White Hart Yd SE1 .**123** B1
Whitehaven St NW8 .**90** A1
Whitehead Ho SW18 .**71** B4

Whitehead Ho **8**
SW15 . . . .**57** C2
Whitehead's Gr
SW3 . . . .**144** B3
White Ho
London SW11 . . . . . .**167** C2
3 Streatham SW4 . .**73** C4
Whitehorn Ho **6** E1 **32** B1
White Horse La E1 . .**32** C4
Whitehorse Mews
SE1 . . . .**136** A2
White Horse Rd E1 . .**33** A4
White Horse Rd E1 . .**33** A3
White Horse St
W1 . . . .**118** B1
White Horse Yd
EC2 . . . .**109** B2
White Ho The NW1 .**92** C4
White Kennett St
E1 . . . .**110** B2
Whitelands Coll,
Roehampton, Univ of
Surrey SW15 . . . .**70** A4
Whitelands Ho
SW3 . . . .**145** A2
Whiteley Ho **9**
SW4 . . . .**73** C4
Whiteleys Ctr W2 .**100** A2
White Lion Ct EC3 .**110** A1
White Lion Hill
EC4 . . . .**122** B4
White Lion St N1 . . .**85** C1
White Lion Yd W1 .**118** A4
Whitelock Ho **2** E9 .**17** B2
Whiteness Ho SW9 .**173** B4
White Post La E9 . . .**18** C2
White Post St SE14,
SE15 . . . .**50** B3
White's Grounds
SE1 . . . .**138** B4
White's Grounds Est
SE1 . . . .**138** B4
White's Row E1 . . . .**110** C3
White's Sq SW4 . . . .**61** C3
Whitestone La NW3 . .**2** B1
Whitestone Wlk NW3 .**2** B1
Whitethorn St E3 . . .**33** C4
Whitfield Ct SW4 . .**172** A3
Whitfield Gdns
W1 . . . .**105** A4
Whitfield Ho NW8 . .**90** A1
Whitfield Pl W1 . . . .**93** A1
Whitfield Rd SE10,
SE13 . . . .**52** C2
Whitfield St W1 . . . .**105** A4
Whitgift Ho SE11 . .**148** C4
SW11 . . . .**168** A4
Whitgift St SE11 . . .**148** C4
Whitington Ave
EC3 . . . .**110** A1
Whitley Ho SW1 . . .**161** A4
Whitlock Dr SW19 . .**70** A3
Whitman Ho **20** E2 .**25** B2
Whitman Rd E3 . . . . .**26** A1
Whitmore Comm Sch
N1 . . . .**87** B3
Whitmore Gdns
NW10 . . . .**22** B3
Whitmore Ho **20** E1 .**24** A4
Whitmore Rd N1 . . . .**24** A4
Whitnell Ct **7**
SW15 . . . .**57** C2
Whitnell Way SW15 .**57** C2
Whitney Ho **6** SE22 **64** A4
Whitstable Ho **11**

Whittaker Ct SW4 . .**172** B3
Whittaker St SW1 . .**145** B3
Whittaker Way
SE1 . . . .**153** C4
Whittingham Ct W4 .**46** A3
Whittingstall Mans
SW6 . . . .**165** A3
Whittingstall Rd
SW6 . . . .**165** A3
Whittington Hospl The
N19 . . . .**4** B2
Whittlebury Ho N4 . . .**6** B4
Whittlesey St SE1 . .**121** C1
Whitton NW3 . . . .**12** B1
Whitton Wlk E3 . . . . .**26** C2
Whitworth Ho SE1 .**137** A1
Whitworth St SE10 . .**43** A1
Whytlaw Ho **1** E3 . . .**33** B4
Wicker St **3** E1 . . . . .**32** A3
Wickfield Ho SE16 .**139** C3
Wickford Ho **1** E1 . .**25** B1
Wickford St E1 . . . . .**25** B1
Wickham Cl E1 . . . . .**32** B4
Wickham Gdns SE4 .**66** B4
Wickham Mews SE4 .**51** C1
Wickham Mews SE4 .**66** B4
Wickham Rd SE4 . . .**66** B4
Wickham St SE11 . .**148** C2
Wicklow Ho N16 . . . .**7** B3
Wicklow St WC1 . . . .**94** C4
Wick Mews **1** E9 . . .**18** A2
Wick Rd Hackney E9 . .**17** C2
London E9 . . . .**18** B2
Wick Sq E9 . . . .**18** B2
Wickstead Ho TW8 . .**36** B1
Wicksteed Ho SE1 .**137** A1
Wickway Ct **3** SE15 .**49** B4
Wickwood St SE5 . . .**48** A1
Widdenham Rd N7 . .**14** B4
Widecombe Ho **33**
SE5 . . . .**48** B1
Widegate St E1 . . . .**110** B3
Widford **1** NW1 . . . .**13** A2
Widford Ho N1 . . . . .**86** A1
Widley Rd W9 . . . . . .**23** C1
Widnes Ho **6** N7 . . . .**14** C3
Wigmore Hall W1 . .**104** A2
Wigmore Pl W1 . . . .**104** A2
Wigmore St W1 . . . .**103** C2
Wigram Ct SW11 . . .**168** A4
Wigram Ho **6** E14 . .**34** A2
Wigton Pl SE11 . . . .**149** C1
Wilberforce Ho **4**
SW11 . . . .**59** C4
Wilberforce Prim Sch
W10 . . . .**23** A2
Wilberforce Rd
London N4 . . . .**6** A2
London N4,N5 . . . .**6** A2
Wilbraham Ho
SW8 . . . .**162** A1
Wilbraham Pl SW1 .**145** B4
Wilby Mews
W11 . . . .**31** B1 **113** A4
Wilcox Cl SW8 . . . .**162** B2
Wilcox Ho **6** E3 . . . .**33** B4
Wilcox Pl SW1 . . . .**133** A1
Wilcox Rd SW8 . . . .**162** A2
Wildcroft Manor
SW15 . . . .**69** B4
Wildcroft Rd SW15 . .**69** B4
Wild Ct WC2 . . . . . .**106** C2
Wilde Cl E8 . . . .**24** C4
Wilde Pl SW18 . . . . .**71** C4

Wilderness Mews
SW4 . . . .**61** A3
Wilderton Rd N16 . . . .**7** A4
Wild Goose Dr SE14 .**50** B2
Wilding Ho **7** E9 . . .**17** C2
Wild's Rents SE1 . .**138** A2
Wild St WC2 . . . . . .**106** C1
Wildwood Gr NW3 . . .**2** B3
Wildwood Rd NW11 . .**2** A4
Wildwood Rise NW11 .**2** B3
Wildwood Terr NW3 . .**2** A3
Wilfred Fienburgh Ho
N7 . . . .**13** C4
Wilfred St SW1 . . . .**132** C2
Wilfrid Gdns W3 . . . .**28** B4
Wilkes Rd **3** TW8 . . .**44** A4
Wilkes St E1 . . . . . .**111** A4
Wilkie Ho SW1 . . . .**147** C2
Wilkins Ho SW1 . . .**160** C4
Wilkinson Ho N1 . . . .**87** C1
Wilkinson St SW8 . .**162** C1
Wilkinson Way W4 . .**37** C4
Wilkin St NW5 . . . . .**13** A2
Wilks Pl N1 . . . .**24** A3
Willan Wall E16 . . . .**35** B2
Willard St SW8 . . . . .**61** A4
Willbury Ho **7** N7 . . .**13** C3
Willcott Rd W3 . . . . .**28** A1
Willenfield Rd
NW10 . . . .**20** B3
Willesden Community
Hospl The NW10 . . . .**8** C1
Willesden Green Sta
NW2 . . . .**9** B2
Willesden High Sch
NW10 . . . .**22** B4
Willesden Junction Sta
NW10 . . . .**21** B2
Willesden La NW2,
NW6 . . . .**9** C2
Willes Rd NW5 . . . . .**13** A2
Willett Ho **1** SW9 . . .**62** A4
William Banfield Ho
SW6 . . . .**164** C2
William Bonn Meml
Training Coll SE5 . .**48** C1
William Brown Ct
SE27 . . . .**75** A2
William Caslon Ho **26**
E2 . . . .**25** B3
William Channing Ho **6**
E2 . . . .**25** A2
William Cl SE13 . . . .**67** B4
William Davis Prim Sch
E2 . . . .**24** C1 **99** B2
William Dromey Ct
NW6 . . . .**10** B1
William Dunbar Ho
NW6 . . . .**23** B3
William Ellis Sch
NW5 . . . .**3** C1
William Ellis Way
SE16 . . . .**139** C1
William Evans Ho **9**
SE8 . . . .**40** C2
William Gdns SW15 .**57** A2
William Guy Gdns **27**
E3 . . . .**27** A2
William Harvey Ho **1**
SW19 . . . .**70** A3
William Hunt Mans
SW13 . . . .**47** B4
William IV St WC2 .**120** A3
William Margrie Cl **1**
SE15 . . . .**49** C1
William Mews
SW1 . . . .**131** A3

William Morris Acad
W6 . . . .**39** C1
William Morris Ho
W6 . . . .**47** C4
William Morris Way
SW6 . . . .**166** C1
William Patten Prim Sch
N16 . . . .**7** B2
William Rathbone Ho **8**
E2 . . . .**25** A2
William Rd NW1 . . . .**92** C3
William Rushbrooke Ho
SE16 . . . .**153** B4
William Saville Ho **2**
NW6 . . . .**23** B3
Williams Cl SW6 . . .**154** B2
Williams Ho **8** E9 . . .**26** C2
E9 . . . .**25** A4
14 Streatham SW2 . .**74** C3
Williams La SW14 . . .**45** B1
Williamson Cl SE10 . .**43** B1
Williamson Ct
SE17 . . . .**150** C1
Williamson St N7 . . .**14** A4
William Sq SE16 . . . .**33** A2
William St SW1 . . . .**131** A3
William Tyndale Prim
Sch N1 . . . .**15** A1
William Winter Ct **28**
SW2 . . . .**74** C4
Willingham Cl **4**
NW5 . . . .**13** B3
Willingham Terr
NW5 . . . .**13** B3
Willington Rd SW9 . .**62** A4
Willis Ho **7** E14 . . . .**34** A2
Willis St E14 . . . .**34** A3
Willoughby Hall
Dyslexia Ctr NW3 . . . .**11** C4
Willoughby Ho
34 E1 . . . .**32** A1
EC2 . . . .**109** B3
Willoughby Rd NW3 .**11** C4
Willoughby's The
WC1 . . . .**106** A3
Willoughby St
SW14 . . . .**56** A3
Willow Ave SW13 . . .**46** B1
Willowbank SW6 . . . .**58** A4
Willowbank Rd
SE15 . . . .**49** B4
Willow Bridge Rd
N1 . . . .**15** B2
Willow Cotts TW9 . . .**44** C4
Willow Ct EC2 . . . . . .**98** A2
Chiswick W4 . . . .**46** A3
London N7 . . . .**14** B3
London NW6 . . . .**173** B3
40 London W2 . . . . .**31** C4
3 Streatham SW16 . .**74** B1
Willowdene **5** SE15 **50** A3
London N6 . . . .**3** B4
London SE15 . . . .**50** A2
Willow Farm La
SW15 . . . .**57** A4
Willow Hall NW3 . . . .**11** C4
Willow Lo
London NW3 . . . .**12** B2
London W10 . . . .**22** C1
Willow Lo
Fulham SW6 . . . .**47** C2
Putney SW15 . . . .**57** A4
Willow Lodge **10**
SW8 . . . .**61** A4

Willow Pl SW1 .....147 A4
Willow Rd
　London NW3 ......11 C4
　London W5 ....36 A4
Willow St
　EC2 ....24 A1 98 A2
Willows Terr NW10 ...21 C3
Willow Tree Cl E3 ....26 B4
Willow Vale W12 ......29 C2
Willow Way 3 W11 ...30 C2
Willow Wlk SE1 ....152 C4
Willsbridge Ct 1
　SE15 ....49 B4
Willshaw St SE14 ....51 C2
Wilman Gr E8 ....24 C4
Wilmcote Ho W2 ....100 A4
Wilmer Gdns N1 .....24 A4
Wilmer Ho 3 E3 ......26 A3
Wilmer Lea Cl E15 ...19 C1
Wilmer Pl N16 ....7 B2
Wilmers Ct 1
　NW10 ....20 C4
Wilmington Ave W4 45 C3
Wilmington Sq WC1 95 B3
Wilmington St WC1 ...95 B3
Wilmot Cl SE15 ......49 C3
Wilmot Pl NW1 ......13 B1
Wilmot St E2 ....25 A1
Wilna Rd SW18 ....71 B4
Wilsham St
　W11 ....31 A1 112 A2
Wilshaw Ho 8 SE8 51 C3
Wilson Gr SE16 ......40 A4
Wilson Ho
　London NW6 ....9 C1
　London SW8 ....171 B1
Wilson Rd SE5 ....49 A2
Wilson's Pl E14 ......33 B3
Wilson's Rd W6 ....39 C1
Wilson St EC2 ....109 C4
Wiltern Ct NW2 ......10 A2
Wilton Ave W4 ....38 A1
Wilton Cres SW1 ....131 B3
Wilton Ct 11 E1 ......32 A3
　1 Richmond TW10 ...54 A2
Wilton Est E8 ....16 C2
Wilton Ho 8 SE22 ...64 A4
Wilton Mews SW1 ...131 C2
Wilton Pl SW1 ......131 B3
Wilton Rd SW1 .....146 C4
Wilton Row SW1 ....131 B3
Wilton Sq N1 ....87 B4
Wilton St SW1 ......132 A2
Wilton Terr SW1 ....131 B2
Wilton Villas N1 .....87 B3
Wilton Way E8 ....16 C2
Wiltshire Cl SW3 ....144 C3
Wiltshire Ct 2 N4 ....5 B3
Wiltshire Rd SW9 ....62 C4
Wiltshire Row N1 ....87 C3
Wimbart Rd SW2 ......74 B4
Wimbledon Lawn Tennis
　Mus SW19 ....70 A3
Wimbledon Park Ct
　SW19 ....70 B3
Wimbledon Park First
　Sch SW19 ....71 A2
Wimbledon Park Rd
　SW18,SW19 .....70 B3
Wimbledon Park Side
　SW19 ....69 C1
Wimbledon Park Sta
　SW19 ....70 C1
Wimbledon Stadium
　Bsns Ctr SW17 ....71 A1

Wimbledon Windmill
　Mus SW19 ....69 B1
Wimbolt St
　E2 ....24 C2 99 B4
Wimborne Ho E16 ...35 B2
Wimborne Ho 1
　NW1 ....90 B1
　SW8 ....163 A1
　Upper Tooting SW17 73 B1
Wimbourne Ct N1 ....87 B2
Wimbourne St N1 ....87 B2
Wimpole Mews
　W1 ....104 A3
Wimpole St W1 ....104 A2
Winans Wlk SW9 ...173 B1
Winant Ho 7 E14 ....34 A2
Wincanton Rd
　SW18 ....70 B4
Winchelsea Cl
　SW15 ....57 C2
Winchelsea Ho 10
　SE16 ....40 B4
Winchelsea Rd
　NW10 ....20 C4
Winchendon Rd
　SW6 ....165 A4
Winchester Ave
　NW6 ....10 A1
Winchester Cl
　SE17 ....150 B3
Winchester Ct W8 ...128 A4
Winchester Ho
　10 E3 ....26 B2
　SW3 ....157 C3
　W2 ....100 C1
　6 London SE18 ....16 B3
Winchester Pl N6 ....4 A3
　2 London E8 ......16 B3
Winchester Rd N6 ....4 A3
　2 London NW3 ...11 C1
Winchester Sq
　SE1 ....123 B2
Winchester St
　SW1 ....146 B2
　Acton W3 ....37 B4
Winchester Wlk
　SE1 ....123 B2
Winchfield Ho
　SW15 ....56 B1
Winch Ho SW10 ....157 A2
Winchilsea Ho NW8 89 C3
Wincott St SE11 ....149 C3
Windermere 13 NW1 92 B4
Windermere Ave
　NW6 ....23 A4
Windermere Ct
　SW13 ....46 B4
Windermere Ho 2 E3 26 B1
Windermere Point 3
　SE15 ....50 B3
Windermere Rd N19 4 B2
Windham Rd TW9 ....54 B4
Winding La SE8 ......41 A2
Windlass Pl SE8 .....41 A2
Windlesham Gr
　SW19 ....69 C3
Windmill WC1 ......106 C4
Windmill Alley 7
　W4 ....38 A2
Windmill Cl SE1 ....153 C4
　London NW2 ....1 A1
　1 London SE13 ....52 B1
Windmill Dr NW2 ....1 A1
Windmill Dr SW4 ....61 A2
Windmill Hill NW3 ...2 B1
　1 London NW3 ....11 B4
Windmill Ho E14 ...121 C1
Windmill La 11 E15 ..19 C2

Windmill Pas 10
　W4 ....38 A2
Windmill Rd
　London SW18 ....59 C1
　London W4 ....38 A2
　Roehampton SW19 ..69 A1
Windmill Row
　SE11 ....149 B1
Windmill St W1 .....105 B3
Windmill Wlk SE1 ..121 C1
Windrose Cl SE16 ...40 C4
Windrush Cl
　Chiswick W4 ....45 B3
　London SW11 ....59 C3
Windrush Ho NW8 ...101 C4
Windrush Ho NW10 ..20 C4
Windsock Cl 3
　SE16 ....41 B2
Windsor Ct 20 SE16 32 C1
　SW3 ....144 B2
　W2 ....114 A4
　Fulham SW6 ....58 A4
　London W14 ....10 C4
　London SW11 .....167 C2
　2 London SW4 ....61 B3
Windsor Gdns W9 ...23 C1
Windsor Ho 3 E2 ...25 C2
　N1 ....87 A2
　NW1 ....92 B4
　London N4 ....6 B3
　London NW2 ....10 A2
　London W4 ....37 B1
Windsor Pl SW1 ....147 A4
Windsor Rd
　London N7 ....5 A1
　London N19 ....4 C2
　Richmond TW9 ......44 B1
Windsor St N1 ....86 B4
Windsor Terr N1 .....97 A4
Windsor Way W14 ..140 A4
Windsor Wharf E9 ...18 B3
Windsor Wlk SE5 ....48 C1
Windspoint Dr SE15 50 A4
Windus Rd N16 ....7 B3
Windus Wlk N16 ......7 B3
Wine Cl E1 ....32 B2
Wine Office Ct
　EC4 ....107 C2
Winford Ct 18 SE15 ..49 C2
Winford Ho E3 ......18 B1
Winforton St SE10 ...52 B2
Winfrith Rd SW18 ...71 B3
Wingate Ho 28 E3 ...27 A2
　8 London N16 .....15 C4
Wingate Rd W6 ......39 A3
Wingfield Ct 10 E14 34 C2
Wingfield Ho 2
　NW6 ....78 A2
Wingfield Mews
　SE15 ....64 C4
Wingfield St SE15 ...64 C4
Wingford Rd SW2 ...62 A1
Wingham 2 NW5 ....12 C2
Wingmore Rd SE24 ..63 B4
Wingrad Ho 19 E1 ...32 B4
Wingrave SE17 ......151 B3
Wingrave Rd W6 .....47 B4
Wingreen NW8 ....78 B4
Winicotte Ho W2 ....101 C4
Winifrede Paul Ho 7
　NW5 ....13 A4
Winkley St 3 E2 ....25 A3
Winkworth Cotts 13
　E1 ....25 B1
Winnett St W1 ......119 B4

Winnington Ho
　5 SE5 ....48 B3
　19 W10 ....23 A2
Winscombe St N19 ...4 A2
Winsham Gr SW11 ..60 C2
Winsham Ho NW1 ...93 C4
Winslade Rd SW2 ....62 A2
Winsland Mews
　W2 ....101 B2
Winsland St W2 ....101 B2
Winsley St W1 .....105 A2
Winslow SE17 ......152 A1
Winslow Rd W6 ......47 B4
Winstanley Rd
　SW11 ....59 C4
Winston Ho WC1 ....93 C1
Winston Rd N16 .....15 C4
Winston Wlk 4
　W4 ....37 C2
Winterbourne Ho 10
　W11 ....112 A3
Winter Box Wlk
　TW10 ....54 B2
Winterbrook Rd
　SE24 ....63 B1
Winterfold Cl SW19 70 A2
Winterleys 7 NW6 ...23 B3
Winterton Ho 18 E1 32 B3
Winterton Pl
　SW10 ....157 A4
Winterwell Rd SW2 ..62 A2
Winthorpe Rd SW15 58 A3
Winthrop Ho 10
　W12 ....30 A2
Winthrop St E1 ......32 A4
Winton Prim Sch
　N1 ....84 C1
Wirral Ho 16 SE26 ..76 C1
Wisden Ho SW8 ....163 A3
Wise Rd E15 ....27 C4
Wiseton Rd SW17 ...72 B3
Wisley Ho SW1 ....147 B2
Wisley Rd SW11 .....60 C2
Wisteria Rd SE13 ....67 C3
Wistow Ho 12 E2 ....24 C4
Witanhurst La N6 ....3 C3
Witan St E2 ....25 A2
Witchwood Ho 11
　SW9 ....62 C4
Witcombe Point 13
　SE15 ....49 C2
Witham Ct SW17 ....72 B1
Witham Ho 33 SE5 ...48 B1
Witherington Rd
　N5 ....14 C3
Withers Pl EC1 ......97 A2
Withycombe Rd
　SW19 ....69 C4
Withy Ho 4 E1 ....25 C1
Witley Ho 2 SW2 ....74 B4
Witley Point 8
　SW15 ....69 A3
Witley Rd N19 ....4 B2
Wittering Ho
　SW11 ....169 A2
Wivenhoe Cl SE15 ...65 A4
Wix Prim Sch SW4 ..61 A3
Wix's La SW4 ....61 A3
Woburn Ct 18 SE16 ..40 A1
　2 London SE6 .....54 B4
Woburn Pl WC1 .....94 A1
Woburn Sq WC1 ....93 C1
Woburn Wlk WC1 ....94 A1
Wodehouse Ave
　SE5 ....49 B2

Wodehouse Ct 10
　W3 ....37 B3
Woking Cl SW15 ....56 B3
Wolcot Ho NW1 .....83 A1
Wolfe Cres 34 SE16 40 C4
Wolfe Ho 13 W12 ....30 A2
Wolfson Ct SE1 .....139 A4
　London NW11 ....1 A4
Wollaston Cl SE1 ...150 C4
Wolseley Ave SW18,
　SW19 ....70 C2
Wolseley Gdns W4 ..45 A4
Wolseley Rd W4 .....37 B2
Wolseley St SE1 ....139 A3
Wolsey Ho NW6 .....11 B1
Wolsey Mews NW5 ..13 B2
Wolsey Rd N1 ....15 C3
Wolsey St E1 ....32 B4
Wolverley St 2 E2 ..25 A2
Wolverton SE17 ....152 A2
Wolverton Gdns
　W6 ....39 C2
Wontner Cl 5 N1 ...15 B1
Wontner Rd
　SW17 ....72 B2
Woodall Cl 2 E14 ...34 A2
Woodberry Down N4 ..6 B4
Woodberry Down Com
　Prim Sch N4 ....6 B4
Woodberry Gr N4 ....6 B4
Woodbine Terr E9 ...17 B2
Woodborough Rd
　SW15 ....57 A3
Woodbourne Ave
　SW16 ....73 C1
Woodbourne Cl
　SW16 ....74 A1
Woodbridge Cl 10 N7 ..5 B2
Woodbridge Ct N16 ..6 C1
Woodbridge St EC1 96 A2
Woodchester Sq
　W2 ....100 A3
Woodchurch Ho
　SW9 ....173 B4
Woodchurch Rd
　NW6 ....11 A1
Wood Cl E2 ..24 C1 99 B2
Woodcock Ho 2
　E14 ....33 C4
Woodcote Ho 4
　SE8 ....51 B4
Woodcroft Mews
　SE8 ....41 A2
Wood Dene 6 SE15 ..50 A2
Woodfall Rd N4 ......5 C2
Woodfall St SW3 ...144 C1
Woodfarrs SE5 ....63 C3
Wood Field NW3 ....12 B3
Woodfield Ave
　SW16 ....73 C1
Woodfield Cl SE19 ..75 B1
Woodfield Ctr The
　N4 ....5 C4
Woodfield Gr SW16 73 C1
Woodfield Pl W9 ....23 B1
Woodfield Rd W9 ....23 B1
Woodger Rd W12 ....39 B4
Woodhall 8 NW1 ....92 C3
Woodhall Ave SE21 ..76 B1
Woodhall Dr SE21 ...76 B1
Woodhall Ho SW18 59 C1

Woodheyes Rd NW10 8 A3
Wood Ho 6 NW6 ...23 B3
London SW4 ...171 C2
Woodhurst Rd W3 28 B2
Woodison St E3 ...26 A1
Wood La W12 ...30 B2
Woodland Cres
SE10 ...52 B4
SE16 ...40 C4
Woodland Gr SE10 ...43 A1
Woodlands SW4 ...61 A3
Woodlands Ave W3 ...28 A1
Woodlands Ct
NW10 ...22 C4
Woodlands Gt SW15 58 B2
Woodlands Park Rd
SE10 ...53 A4
Woodlands St
SW13 ...56 B4
Woodlands St 2 E8 ...16 B2
Woodlands The N6 ...15 A4
Woodlands Way
SW15 ...58 B2
Woodland Wlk
8 SE10 ...43 A1
London NW3 ...12 A3
Woodlane High Sch
W12 ...30 A3
Woodlawn Cl SW15 58 B2
Woodlawn Rd SW6 47 C2
Woodlea Rd N16 ...7 A1
Woodleigh Gdns
SW16 ...74 A1
Woodmans Gr NW10 .8 B3
Woodmans Mews
W12 ...30 A4
Woodmere Cl 10
SW11 ...60 C4
Woodpecker Mews
SE13 ...67 C3
Woodpecker Rd 6
SE14 ...51 A4
Wood Point 6 E16 .35 C4
Woodquest Ave
SE24 ...63 B2
Woodruff Ho SW2 .62 C1
Woodrush Cl 4
SE14 ...51 A3
Woodseer St E1 111 B4
Woodsford SE17 151 B1
Woodsford Sq
W14 ...126 B4
Woods Ho SW8 ...170 C4
Wood's Mews W1 ...117 B4
Woodsome Rd NW5 ..4 A1
Wood's Pl SE1 ...138 B1
Woodspring Rd
SW19 ...70 A2
Wood St EC15 ...109 A2
Wood St W4 ...38 A1
Woodstar Ho 8
SE15 ...49 C3
Woodstock Ave
NW11 ...1 A4
Woodstock Ct
SE11 ...149 A2
SE12 ...72 A2
Woodstock Gr W12 .39 C4
Woodstock Ho 2
N5 ...15 B4
Woodstock Mews
W1 ...103 C3
Woodstock Rd
London N4 ...5 C3
London NW11 ...1 A4

Woodstock Rd continued
London W4 ...38 A3
Woodstock St W1 104 A1
Woodstock Terr
E14 ...34 A2
Woodthorpe Rd
SW15 ...57 A3
Woodview Cl N4 ...6 A4
Woodville Ct 3
SE10 ...52 B4
Woodville Ho SE1 138 C2
Woodville Rd NW6 ..23 B3
London N16 ...16 A3
London NW11 ...1 A4
Woodwarde Rd
SE22 ...64 A1
Woodwell St SW18 .59 B2
Wood Wharf SE10 ..52 B4
Woodyard Cl NW5 ...12 C3
Woodyard La SE21 ..76 A4
Woolcombes Ct 4
SE16 ...32 C1
Wooler St SE17 ...151 C2
Woolf Ct 7 W3 ...37 B3
Woolf Mews WC1 ...94 A3
Woolley Ho SW9 ...63 A4
Woollon Ho 1 E1 ...32 B3
Woolmore Prim Sch
E14 ...34 B2
Woolmore St E14 ...34 B2
Woolneigh St SW6 166 A1
Woolpack Ho 1 E9 .17 B3
Woolridge Way E9 ..17 B1
Woolstaplers Way
SE16 ...153 B4
Woolstone Ho 7
E2 ...24 C4
Woolven Ho SE3 ...53 B4
Wooster Gdns E14 .34 C3
Wootton St SE1 ...121 C1
Worcester Ct
W2 ...31 C4
Worcester Dr W4 ...38 A4
Worcester Gdns
SW11 ...60 B2
Worcester Ho
SE11 ...135 B1
2 Putney SW15 ...69 B4
Worcester Mews 2
NW6 ...11 A2
Wordsworth Ho
NW6 ...23 C2
Wordsworth Pl 1
NW5 ...12 B3
Wordsworth Rd
SE1 ...153 A3
London N16 ...16 A4
Worfield St SW11 ..158 B1
Worgan St SE11 ...149 A2
SE16 ...40 C4
Working Men's Coll The
NW1 ...82 C2
World's End Pas
SW10 ...157 B2
World's End Pl
SW10 ...157 B2
Worlidge St W6 ...39 B1
Worlingham Rd
SE22 ...64 B3
Wormholt Park Prim
Sch W12 ...29 C2
Wormholt Rd W12 ..29 C2
Wormwood St EC2 110 A2
Wornington Rd
W10 ...31 A4

Wornum Ho 3
NW6 ...23 A3
Woronzow Rd NW8 .80 A3
Worple St SW14 ...55 C4
Worple Way TW10 ..54 A3
Worship St
EC2 ...24 A1 98 A1
Worsley Gr E5 ...16 C4
Worsopp Dr SW4 ...61 B2
Worth Gr SE17 ...151 B1
Worthington Ho
EC1 ...95 C4
18 Streatham SW2 .74 C4
Wotton Ct 8 E14 ...34 C2
Wotton Rd 18 SE8 ..51 B4
Wouldham Rd E16 ..35 B3
Wrayburn Ho SE16 139 C3
Wray Cres N4 ...5 B2
Wray Ct N4 ...5 B2
Wrayburn Ho 1 SW2 74 A3
Wren Ave NW2 ...9 B4
Wren Cl E16 ...35 B1
Wren Ho 27 E3 ...26 B3
SW1 ...147 B1
Wren Landing E14 .33 C1
Wrenn Ho SW13 ...47 B4
Wren Rd SE5 ...48 C2
Wren St WC1 ...95 A2
Wrentham Ave
NW10 ...22 C3
Wren View N6 ...4 B3
Wrestlers Ct EC3 ...110 A2
Wrexham Rd E3 ...26 C3
Wrigglesworth St
SE14 ...50 C3
Wright Cl SE13 ...67 C3
Wright Rd SW15 ...57 A2
Wright's Gn SW4 ...61 C3
Wright's La W8 ...128 A2
Wrights Rd E3 ...26 B3
Wrights Wlk SW14 ..55 C4
Wrotham Ho SE1 ...137 C2
Wrotham Rd 11
NW1 ...13 B1
Wrottesley Rd
NW10 ...21 C3
Wroughton Rd
SW11 ...60 B1
Wroxton Rd SE15 ...50 B1
Wulfstan St W12 ...29 C3
Wyatt Cl SE3 ...41 B4
Wyatt Dr SW13 ...47 A3
Wyatt Ho NW8 ...89 C1
London SE3 ...53 A1
Wyatt Park Mans 1
SW2 ...74 A2
Wyatt Park Rd SW2 74 A2
Wyatt Rd N5 ...6 B1
Wybert St NW1 ...92 C2
Wycherley Cl SE3 ...53 B3
Wychwood End N6 ..4 B4
Wychwood Ho N4 ...6 B4
Wyclif Ct EC1 ...96 A3
Wycliffe Ho 13 N16 .16 A4
Wyclif St EC1 ...96 A3
Wycombe Ct SE3 ...53 C3
Wycombe Gdns
NW11 ...1 C2
Wycombe Ho NW8 .90 A2
Wycombe Pl SW18 .59 B1
Wyersdale Ho N4 ...6 B4
Wye St SW11 ...167 C1
Wyfold Rd SW6 ...154 A1
Wyke Rd E3 ...18 C1
Wyldes Cl NW11 ...2 B3
Wyllen Cl E1 ...25 B1

Wymering Mans 6
W9 ...23 C2
Wymering Rd W9 ...23 C2
Wymondham Ct
NW8 ...79 C4
Wymond St SW15 ...57 B4
Wynan Rd E14 ...42 A1
Wynard Terr SE11 149 A2
Wyndham Cres N19 ..4 B1
Wyndham Deedes Ho 2
E2 ...24 C3
Wyndham Ho SW1 145 B3
Wyndham Mews
W1 ...102 C3
Wyndham Pl W1 ...102 C3
Wyndham Rd SE5 ..48 B3
Wyndham St W1 ...102 C4
Wyndham Yd W1 ...102 C3
Wyndhams Ct 8
Dalston E8 ...16 B1
Wynford Rd N1 ...85 A2
Wynne Ho SE14 ...50 C2
Wynne Rd SW9 ...173 B1
Wynnstay Gdns
W8 ...127 C2
Wynter Ho SW9 ...173 A1
Wynter St SW11 ...59 B3
Wynton Pl W3 ...28 A3
Wynyard Ho SE11 149 A2
Wynyatt St EC1 ...96 A4
Wytham Ho NW8 ...89 C1
Wythburn Ct W1 ...102 C2
Wythburn Pl W1 ...102 C2
Wyvil Prim Sch
SW8 ...162 B2
Wyvil Rd SW8 ...162 A2
Wyvis St E14 ...34 A4

Y

Yabsley St E14 ...34 B1
Yaldam Ho SE1 ...152 A3
Yalding Ho 20 E5 ...17 A3
Yalding Rd SE16 ...153 B4
Yale Ct NW6 ...11 A3
Yardley St WC1 ...95 B3
Yarmouth Pl W1 ...118 A1
Yarnfield Sq 14
SE15 ...49 C2
Yarrow Ho 10 E14 ..42 B3
London W10 ...30 B4
Yatesbury Ct E5 ...18 A3
Yates Ct NW2 ...9 C2
Yates Ho 2 ...99 C4
Yatton Ho W10 ...30 B4
Yeadon Ho W10 ...30 B4
Yearby Ho W10 ...22 B1
Yeate St N1 ...15 C1
Yeats Cl NW10 ...8 A2
Yeldham Ho W6 ...39 C1
Yeldham Rd W6 ...39 C1
Yelverton Rd
SW11 ...167 C1
Yeoman St SE25 ...77 A1
Yeoman Ho SE1 ...153 A2
Yeoman's Row
SW3 ...130 B1
Yeoman St SE8 ...41 A2
Yeoman's Yd E1 ...125 A4
Yeo St E3 ...34 A4
Yeovil Ho London N7 .5 B2
W10 ...22 B1
Yerbury Prim Sch
N19 ...4 C1
Yerbury Rd N19 ...4 C1
Yesodey Hatorah Sch
N16 ...7 B4
Yewfield Rd NW10 ..8 B2

Yew Gr NW2 ...9 C4
Yew Ho SE14 ...51 B1
Yew Tree Rd W12 ...29 B2
Yoakley Rd N16 ...7 A2
Yoke Cl N7 ...14 A2
Yonge Pk N4,N7 ...5 C1
York Ave SE17 ...151 A2
Mortlake SW14 ...55 B2
York Bldgs WC2 ...120 B3
York Bridge NW1 ...91 B2
York Cl 17 SE5 ...48 B1
York Gate NW1 ...91 C1
York Gr SE15 ...50 B2
York Hill SE27,SW16 .75 A1
York Ho N1 ...84 C1
SE1 ...135 A1
SW3 ...145 A2
W1 ...102 C4
W8 ...128 A4
London N5 ...6 A1
3 London N7 ...13 C2
London W3 ...28 B2
Richmond TW10 ...54 C2
Richmond TW9 ...44 C2
York House Pl W8 128 A4
Yorkley Ho 10 ...22 B1
York Mans SW5 ...169 C4
W1 ...103 B4
York Mews NW5 ...13 A3
York Pl WC2 ...120 B3
London SW11 ...59 C4
York Place Mans
NW1 ...103 A4
York Rd SE1 ...135 A4
London SW11,SW18 ..59 C4
London W3 ...28 C3
4 Richmond TW10 ..54 B2
York Rise NW5 ...4 A1
York Road Bsns Ctr
SW11 ...167 C1
Yorkshire Cl N16 ...7 A1
Yorkshire Grey Yd
WC1 ...106 C3
Yorkshire Rd E14 ...33 A3
York Sq 14 E14 ...33 A3
York St Chambers
W1 ...102 C4
York Terr E NW1 ...91 C1
York Terr W NW1 ...91 B1
Yorkton St E2 ...24 C3
York Way N1 ...84 B3
London N1,N7,NW1 ..14 A1
York Way Ct N1 ...84 B3
Young's Bldgs EC1 ..97 A2
Youngs Ct SW11 ...169 C3
Young St W8 ...128 A3
Yoxall Ho W10 ...22 B1
Yukon Rd SW12 ...73 A4
Yuletide Cl NW10 ...8 A2

Z

Zampa Rd SE16 ...40 B1
Zander Ct E2 ...24 C2 99 C4
Zangwill Ho NW6 ...23 B3
Zealand Ho 11 SE5 .48 B1
Zealand Rd E3 ...26 A3
Zennor Rd SW12 ...73 B3
Zenoria St SE22 ...64 B3
Zetland Ho W8 ...128 A2
Zetland St E14 ...34 B4
Zion Ho 6 E1 ...32 B3
Zoar St SE1 ...122 C2
Zodiac Ho 3 E3 ...26 C1
Zoffany St N19 ...4 C2

List of numbered locations

This atlas shows thousands more place names than any other London street atlas. In some busy areas it is impossible to fit the name of every place.

Where not all names will fit, some smaller places are shown by a number. If you wish to find out the name associated with a number, use this listing.

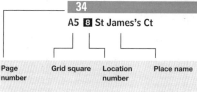

34			
A5 **8** St James's Ct			
Page number	Grid square	Location number	Place name

1
B1 1 Mortimer Cl
2 Sunnyside Ho
3 Sunnyside
4 Prospect Pl
B4 1 Berkeley Ct
2 Exchange Mans
3 Beechcroft Ct
4 Nedahall Ct
C1 1 Portman Hts
2 Hermitage Ct
3 Moreland Ct
4 Wendover Ct

2
B1 2 Stamford Cl

4
1 Hunter Ho
2 Fisher Ho
3 Lang Ho
4 Temple Ho
5 Palmer Ho
B2 1 Flowers Mews
2 Sandridge St
3 Bovingdon Cl
4 Laurel Cl
5 Forest Way
6 Larch Cl
7 Pine Cl
8 Alder Mews
9 Aspen Cl
B3 1 Calvert Ct
2 Academy The
3 Whitehall Mans
4 Pauntley St
5 Archway Hts
6 Pauntley Ho
C1 1 Melchester Ho
2 Norcombe Ho
3 Weatherbury Ho
4 Wessex Ho
5 Archway Bsns Ctr
C2 1 Bowerman Ct
2 Hargrave Mans
3 Church Garth
4 John King Ct
C3 1 Louise White Ho
2 Levison Way
3 Sanders Way

C4 1 Eleanor Rathbone Ho
2 Christopher Lo
3 Monkridge
4 Marbleford Ct
5 High London
6 Garton Ho
7 Hilltop Ho
8 Caroline Martyn Ho
9 Arthur Henderson Ho
10 Margaret Mcmillan Ho
11 Enid Stacy Ho
12 Mary McArthur Ho
13 Bruce Glasier Ho
14 John Wheatley Ho
15 Keir Hardie Ho
16 Monroe Ho
17 Iberia Ho
18 Lygoe Ho
19 Lambert Ho
20 Shelbourne Ho
21 Arkansas Ho
22 Lafitte Ho
23 Shreveport Ho
24 Packenham Ho
25 Orpheus Ho
26 Fayetville Ho
27 Bayon Ho

5
A1 1 Northview
2 Tufnell Park Mans
A2 1 Christie Ct
2 Ringmer Gdns
3 Kingsdown Rd
4 Cottenham Ho
5 St Paul's Ct
6 Rickthorne Rd
7 Stanley Terr
A3 1 Beeches The
2 Lambton Ct
A4 1 Marie Lloyd Gdns
2 Jessie Blythe La
3 Leyden Mans
4 Brambledown
5 Lochbie
6 Edith Cavell Cl
B2 1 Berkeley Wlk
2 Lazar Wlk

3 Thistlewood Cl
4 Tomlins Wlk
5 Andover Ho
6 Barmouth Ho
7 Chard Ho
8 Methley Ho
9 Rainford Ho
10 Woodbridge Cl
11 Allerton Wlk
12 Falconer Wlk
B3 1 Lawson Ct
2 Wiltshire Ct
3 Hutton Ct
C2 1 Brookfield
2 Churnfield

6
B4 1 Finmere Ho
2 Keynsham Ho
3 Kilpeck Ho
4 Knaresborough Ho
5 Leighfield Ho
6 Lonsdale Ho
7 Groveley Ho
8 Wensleydale Ho
9 Badminton Ct
C2 1 Chestnut Cl
2 Sycamore Ho
3 Lordship Ho
4 Clissold Ho
5 Beech Ho
6 Laburnum Ho
7 Ormond Ho
C4 1 Selwood Ho
2 Mendip Ho
3 Ennerdale Ho
4 Delamere Ho
5 Westwood Ho
6 Bernwood Ho
7 Allerdale Ho
8 Chattenden Ho
9 Farningham Ho
10 Oakend Ho

7
A1 1 Gujarat Ho
2 Marton Rd
3 Painsthorpe Rd
4 Selkirk Ho
5 Defoe Ho

6 Edward Friend Ho
7 Sheridan Ho
8 Barrie Ho
9 Arnold Ho
10 Macaulay Ho
11 Stowe Ho
12 Carlyle Ho
13 Shaftesbury Ho
14 Lillian Cl
15 Swift Ho
16 Dryden Ho
17 Scott Ct
18 Kingsfield Ho
19 Uhura Sq
A3 1 Godstone Ct
2 Farnham Ct
3 Milford Ct
4 Cranleigh Ct
5 Haslemere Ct
6 Belmont Ct
7 Hockworth Ho
8 Garratt Ho
9 Fairburn Ho
B1 1 Lawrence's Bldgs
2 Cottage Wlk
3 Batley Pl
B2 1 Garnham St
2 Garnham Ct
3 Sanford La
4 Sandford Wlk
5 Abney Gdns
6 Fleet Wood
B3 1 Stamford Hill Mans
2 Montefiore Ct
3 Berwyn Ho
4 Clent Ho
5 Chiltern Ho
6 Laindon Ho
7 Pentland Ho
B4 1 Regent Ct
2 Stamford Lo
C1 1 Ravenscourt
2 Mellington Ct
3 Rendlesham Ho
4 Florence Ct
5 Burnaston Ho
C2 1 Cazenove Mans
2 Chedworth Ho
3 Aldergrove Ho
4 Abbotstone Ho

5 Briggeford Cl
6 Inglethorpe Ho
7 Ashdown Ho
C3 1 Stamford Grove E
2 Stamford Mans
3 Grove Mans
4 Stamford Grove W

8
A1 1 Beveridge Rd
C2 1 Regency Mews
2 Tudor Mews

10
A1 1 Fountain Ho
2 Kingston Ho
3 Waverley Ct
4 Weston Ho
5 Mapes Ho
6 Athelstan Gdns
7 Leff Ho
B1 1 Alma Birk Ho
2 Brooklands Ct
3 Brooklands Court Apartments
4 Cleveland Mans
5 Buckley Ct
6 Webheath
C1 1 Linstead St
2 Embassy Ho
3 Acol Ct
4 Kings Wood Ct
5 Douglas Ct
6 King's Gdns
7 Carlton Mans
8 Smyrna Mans
9 New Priory Ct
10 Queensgate Pl
11 Brondesbury Mews
C2 1 Dene Mans
2 Sandwell Cres
3 Sandwell Mans
4 Hampstead West
5 Redcroft
C3 1 Orestes Mews
2 Walter Northcott Ho
3 Polperro Mans
4 Lyncroft Mans
5 Marlborough Mans
6 Alexandra Mans

7 Cumberland Mans
8 Cavendish Mans
9 Ambassador Ct
10 Welbeck Mans
11 Inglewood Mans

11

A2 **1** Beswick Mews
2 Worcester Mews
3 Minton Mews
4 Doulton Mews
5 Laurel Ho
6 Sandalwood Ho
7 Iroko Ho
8 Banyan Ho
9 Ebony Ho
10 Rosemont Mans
B1 **1** Harrold Ho
2 Glover Ho
3 Byron Ct
4 Nalton Ho
B2 **1** Petros Gdns
2 Heath Ct
3 Imperial Twrs
4 Fairhurst
5 St John's Ct
6 New College Ct
7 Chalford
8 Sutherland Ho
B4 **1** Windmill Hill
2 Highgrove Point
3 Gainsborough Ho
4 Heath Mans
5 Pavilion Ct
6 Holly Berry La
7 New Campden Ct
8 Holly Bush Vale
9 Gardnor Mans
10 Mansfield Pl
11 Streatley Pl
12 New Ct
13 Bird In Hand Yd
14 Spencer Wlk
15 Wells Ct
16 Perrin's Ct
17 Village Mount
18 Benham's Pl
19 Prince Arthur Ct
20 Prince Arthur Mews
21 Monro Ho
22 Ellerdale Cl
23 Holly Bush Hill
24 Prospect Pl
C1 **1** New College Par
2 Northways Par
3 Noel Ho
4 Campden Ho
5 Centre Hts
6 Hickes Ho
7 Swiss Terr
8 Leitch Ho
9 Jevons Ho
10 Langhorne Ct
11 Park Lo
12 Avenue Lo
C2 **1** Belsize Park Mews
2 Baynes Mews
3 McCrone Mews
C3 **1** Belsize Court Garages
2 Roscommon Ho
3 Akenside Ct

12

A2 **1** Banff Ho
2 Glenloch Ct
3 Havercourt
4 Holmfield Ct
5 Gilling Ct
6 Howitt Cl
7 Manor Mans
8 Straffan Lo
9 Romney Ct
10 Lancaster Stables
11 Eton Garages
B1 **1** Hancock Nunn Ho
2 Higginson Ho
3 Duncan Ho
4 Mary Wharrie Ho
5 Rockstraw Ho
6 Cleaver Ho
7 Chamberlain St
8 Sharples Hall St
9 Primrose Mews
10 Rothwell St
11 St Georges Mews
B2 **1** Alder Ho
2 Hornbeam Ho
3 Whitebeam Ho
4 Aspen Ho
5 Rowan Ho
6 Beech Ho
7 Chestnut Ho
8 Oak Ho
9 Willow Ho
10 Sycamore Ho
11 Maple Ho
12 Hazel Ho
13 Elaine Ct
14 Faircourt
15 Stanbury Ct
16 Priory Mans
17 Grange The
B3 **1** Cayford Ho
2 Du Maurier Ho
3 Isokon Flats
4 Palgrave Ho
5 Garnett Ho
6 Stephenson Ho
7 Park Dwellings
8 Siddons Ho
9 Mall Studios
10 Park Hill Wlk
11 Wordsworth Pl
12 Fraser Regnart Ct
13 St Pancras Almshouses
14 Walham Ct
15 Wellington Ho
C1 **1** Bridge Ho
2 Hardington
3 Mead Cl
4 Rugmere
5 Tottenhall
6 Beauvale
7 Broomfield
C2 **1** Silverbirch Wlk
2 Penshurst
3 Wingham
4 Westwell
5 Chislet
6 Burmarsh
7 Shipton Ho
8 Stone Gate
9 Leysdown
10 Headcorn
11 Lenham
12 Halstow

13 Fordcombe
14 Cannington
15 Langridge
16 Athlone Ho
17 Pentland Ho
18 Beckington
19 Hawkridge
20 Edington

13

A1 **1** Ferdinand Ho
2 Harmood Ho
3 Hawley Rd
4 Hawley Mews
5 Leybourne St
6 Barling
7 Tiptree
8 Havering
9 Candida Ct
10 Lorraine Ct
11 Donnington Ct
12 Welford Ct
13 Torbay Ct
14 Bradfield Ct
15 Torbay St
16 Leybourne Rd
17 Haven St
18 Stucley Pl
A2 **1** Ashington
2 Priestley Ho
3 Leonard Day Ho
4 Old Dairy Mews
5 Monmouth Ho
6 Alpha Ct
7 Una Ho
8 Widford
9 Hey Bridge
10 Roxwell
A4 **1** Denyer Ho
2 Stephenson Ho
3 Trevithick Ho
4 Brunel Ho
5 Newcomen Ho
6 Faraday Ho
7 Winifrede Paul Ho
8 Wardlow
9 Fletcher Ct
10 Tideswell
11 Grangemill
12 Hambrook Ct
13 Calver
B1 **1** Durdans Ho
2 Philia Ho
3 Bernard Shaw Ct
4 Foster Ct
5 Bessemer Ct
6 Hogarth Ct
7 Rochester Ct
8 Soane Ct
9 Wallett Ct
10 Inwood Ct
11 Wrotham Rd
12 Caulfield Ct
13 Bruges Pl
14 Reachview Cl
15 Lawfords Wharf
B3 **1** Eleanor Ho
2 Falkland Ho
3 Kensington Ho
4 Willingham Cl
5 Kenbrook Ho
6 Aborfield
7 Great Field
8 Appleford
9 Forties The
B4 **1** Benson Ct

2 Tait Ho
3 Manorfield Cl
4 Greatfield Cl
5 Longley Ho
6 Lampson Ho
7 Davidson Ho
8 Palmer Ho
9 Lambourn Cl
10 Morris Ho
11 Owen Ho
C1 **1** Hillier Ho
2 Gairloch Ho
3 Cobham Mews
4 Bergholt Mews
5 Blakeney Cl
6 Weavers Way
7 Allensbury Pl
C2 **1** Rowstock
2 Carters Cl
3 York Ho
4 Hungerford Rd
5 Cliff Ct
6 Camelot Ho
C3 **1** Blake Ho
2 Quelch Ho
3 Lee Ho
4 Willbury Ho
5 Howell Ho
6 Holmsbury Ho
7 Leith Ho
8 Betchworth Ho
9 Rushmore Ho
10 Dugdale Ho
11 Horsendon Ho
12 Colley Ho
13 Coombe Ho
14 Ivinghoe Ho
15 Buckhurst Ho
16 Saxonbury Ct
17 Charlton Ct
18 Apollo Studios
19 Barn Cl
20 Long Meadow
21 Landleys Field
22 Margaret Bondfield Ho
23 Haywood Lo
C4 **1** Fairlie Ct
2 London Metropolitan Univ (Carleton Grange Hall)
3 Trecastle Way
4 Hilldrop Est
5 Hyndman Ho
6 Carpenter Ho
7 Graham Ho

14

A3 **1** Kimble Ho
2 Saxonbury Ct
3 Poynder Ct
4 Pangbourne Ho
5 Moulsford Ho
A4 **1** Arcade The
2 Macready Pl
B1 **1** Kerwick Cl
2 Rydston Cl
3 Skegness Ho
4 Frederica St
5 Ponder St
6 Kings Ct
7 Freeling St
B4 **1** Buckmaster Ho
2 Loreburn Ho
3 Cairns Ho
4 Halsbury St

5 Chelmsford Ho
6 Cranworth Ho
C1 **1** Mountfort Terr
2 Davey Lo
3 Carfree Cl
4 New College Mews
C3 **1** Slaney Pl
2 Wells Yd
3 Milton Pl
4 Hartnoll Ho
5 St James School Flats
6 Widnes Ho
7 Tranmere Ho
8 Victoria Mans
9 Formby Ct
10 Mersey Ho
11 Birkenhead Ho

15

A1 **1** Islington Park Mews
2 Evelyn Denington Ct
3 Bassingbourn Ho
4 Cadmore Ho
5 Adstock Ho
6 Garston Ho
7 Flitton Ho
8 Datchworth Ho
9 Battishill St
10 Almeida St
11 Edward's Cotts
12 Hyde's Pl
13 Tyndale Terr
14 Spriggs Ho
15 Barratt Ho
16 Spencer Pl
17 Chadston Ho
18 Whiston Ho
19 Wakelin Ho
20 Tressel Cl
21 Canonbury Ct
22 Shillingford St
23 Halton Ho
A4 **1** Chestnuts The
2 Bowen Ct
3 Peckett Sq
B1 **1** Haslam Ho
2 Horsfield Ho
3 Astey's Row
4 Melville Pl
5 Wontner Cl
6 Hedingham Cl
7 Eric Fletcher Ct
8 Ashby Ho
9 Annette Cres
10 Bentham Ct
11 New Bentham Ct
12 Cardigan Wlk
13 Lindsey Mews
14 Walkinshaw Ct
15 Laundry La
B2 **1** Crowline Wlk
2 Bardsey Wlk
3 Handa Wlk
4 Lismore Wlk
5 Sark Ho
6 Clephane Rd
7 Sybil Thorndike Ho
8 Guernsey Rd
9 Guernsey Ho
10 Herm Ho
11 Florence Nightingale Ho
12 Jersey Ho

13 Jethou Ho
14 Upper Caldy Wlk
15 Caldy Ho
16 Alderney Ho
17 Marquess Rd S
18 Oronsay Rd
19 Upper Gulland Wlk
20 Gulland Wlk
21 Church Rd
B3 1 Pearfield Ho
2 Larchfield Ho
3 Beresford Terr
4 Pondfield Ho
5 Ashfield Ho
6 Elmfield Ho
B4 1 Fountain Mews
2 Woodstock Sq
3 Henson Ct
4 Taverner Sq
C2 1 John Kennedy Ct
2 John Kennedy Lo
3 Ball's Pond Pl
4 Haliday Wlk
5 Rona Wlk
6 Threadgold Ho
7 Wakeham St
8 Saffron Ct
9 Callaby Terr
10 Tilney Gdns
11 Westcliff Ho
12 Ilford Ho
13 Ongar Ho
14 Greenhills Terr
15 Romford Ho
C4 1 Ledo Ho
2 Salween Ho
3 Prome Ho
4 Arakan Ho
5 Rangoon Ho
6 Mandalay Ho
7 Karen Ho
8 Wingate Ho
9 Jubet Ho
10 Orde Ho
11 Chindit Ho
12 Mabel Thornton Ho
13 Crawshay Ho
14 Avon Ho
15 Connaught Mans
16 Jonson Ho
17 Herrick Ho
18 Donne Ho
19 Grasmere Ho
20 Thirlmere Ho

16
A1 1 Dorchester Ct
2 Wareham Ho
3 Dorset Ct
4 Stratton Ct
5 Swanage Ct
6 Blandford Ct
7 Portland Ct
8 Oscar Faber Pl
9 Lancaster Cl
A2 1 Kingsland Gn
2 Kingsland Pas
3 Metropolitan Benefit Societies Almshouses
4 Nimrod Pas
5 De Beauvoir Pl
6 Warburton Cl
7 Buckingham Mews
A3 1 Hewling Ho
2 Matthias Ho

3 Port Royal Pl
4 Cressington Cl
5 King Henry's Yd
6 Bronte Ho
7 Sewell Ho
8 Lydgate Ho
9 Patmore Ho
10 Congreve Ho
11 Elton St
12 Conrad Ho
13 Southwell Ho
14 Neptune Ho
15 Campion Ho
16 Webster Ho
17 Meredith Ho
18 Beckford Ho
19 Ashley Ct
20 Hayling Cl
21 Millard Cl
22 Salcombe Rd
23 Truman's Rd
24 Templeton Cl
25 John Campbell Rd
26 Gillett St
27 Bradbury St
A4 1 Londesborough Ho
2 Knebworth Ho
3 Knebworth Ho
4 Bransby Ct
5 Imperial Ave
6 Leonard Pl
7 Shakspeare Mews
8 Binyon Ho
9 Shelley Ho
10 Browning Ho
11 Burns Ho
12 Andrew Marvell Ho
13 Wycliffe Ho
14 Blake Ho
15 Marlowe Ho
16 Fletcher Ho
17 Chaucer Ct
B1 1 Hilborough Rd
2 Shoreditch Ct
3 Evergreen Sq
B2 1 Prospect Ho
2 Woodland St
3 Crosby Wlk
4 Kirkland Wlk
5 Bowness Cl
6 Carlisle Wlk
7 Skelton Cl
8 Camerton Cl
9 Buttermere Wlk
10 Houghton Cl
11 Hayton Cl
B3 1 Miller's Terr
2 Chow Sq
3 Drysdale Flats
4 Gateway Mews
5 Birkbeck Mews
6 Winchester Pl
B4 1 Coronation Ave
2 Morris Blitz Ct
3 Shacklewell Ho
4 Alexandra Ct
C1 1 Aldington Ct
2 Bayton Ct
3 Rochford Wlk
C3 1 Kingsdown Ho
2 Glendown Ho
3 Moredown Ho
4 Blakeney Cl
5 Beeston Cl
6 Benabo Ct

7 David Devine Ho
8 Kreedman Wlk
9 Hermitage Row
10 Grafton Ct
11 Lushington Terr

17
A1 1 Fortescue Ave
2 Pemberton St
3 Weston Wlk
4 Bayford St Ind Ctr
5 Bayford St
6 Sidworth St
7 Helmsley St
A2 1 Bohemia Pl
2 Graham Mans
3 Marvin St
4 Boscobel Ho
5 Royal Oak Rd
6 Colonnades The
7 Sylvester Ho
8 Sylvester Path
9 Doctor Spurstowe Almshos
10 Great Eastern Bldgs
11 Sojourner-Truth Cl
A3 1 Birchington Ho
2 Bicknor Ho
3 Boxley Ho
4 Adisham Ho
5 Cranbrook Ho
6 Marden Ho
7 Broome Ho
8 Crandale Ho
9 Cheriton Ho
10 Ditton Ho
11 Langley Ho
12 Dymchurch Ho
13 Elham Ho
14 Bodney Mans
15 Pembury Pl
16 Downs Ct
17 Perrywood Ho
18 Stapelhurst Ho
19 Pegwell Ho
20 Yalding Ho
21 Northbourne Ho
22 Monkton Ho
23 Milsted Ho
24 Athlone Cl
25 Clarence Pl
26 Gould Terr
27 Quested Ct
28 Brett Pas
29 Marcon Ct
A4 1 Sutherland Point
2 Embley Point
3 Downs La
4 Gaviller Pl
5 Robert Owen Lo
6 Apprentice Way
7 Arrowe Ct
8 Gilwell Ct
9 Sutton Ct
10 Kinnoull Mans
11 Rowhill Mans
12 Sladen Pl
13 Mothers Sq The
14 Richborough Ho
15 Sandgate Ho
16 Sheppey Ho
B1 1 Pitcairn Ho
2 Lyme Grove Ho
3 Shakespeare Ho
4 Upcott Ho

5 Loddiges Ho
6 Parkinson Ho
7 Sloane Ho
8 Vanbrugh Ho
9 Cambridge Pas
10 Lyttleton Ho
11 Victoria Park Ct
12 Tullis Ho
13 Fairchild Ho
14 Forsyth Ho
15 Tradescant Ho
16 Mason Ho
17 Capel Ho
18 Cordwainers Ct
19 Bridgeman Ho
20 St Thomas's Pl
21 Barclay Ho
22 Clayton Ho
23 Danby Ho
24 Sherard Ho
25 Catesby Ho
26 Petiver Ct
27 Leander Ct
28 Philip Turner Est
29 Grendon Ho
30 Shore Mews
31 Shore Bsns Ctr
32 Kendal Ho
33 Classic Mans
34 Tudor Ho
35 Park Ho
36 Alpine Gr
37 Clarendon Ct
B2 1 Woolpack Ho
2 Elvin Ho
3 Thomas Ho
4 Hockley Ho
5 Retreat Ho
6 Butfield Ho
7 Brooksbank Ho
8 Cresset Ho
9 Brooksbank St
10 Lennox Ho
11 Milborne Ho
12 Collent Ho
13 Middlesex Pl
14 Devonshire Hall
15 Brent Ho
C1 1 Stuart Ho
2 Gascoyne Ho
3 Chelsfield Point
4 Sundridge Ho
5 Banbury Ho
C2 1 Musgrove Ho
2 Cheyney Ho
3 Haynes Ho
4 Warner Ho
5 Gilby Ho
6 Gadsden Ho
7 Risley Ho
8 Baycliffe Ho
9 Sheldon Ho
10 Offley Ho
11 Latimer Ho
12 Ribstone Ho
13 Salem Ho
14 Fieldwick Ho
15 Lever Ct
16 Matson Ho
17 Wilding Ho
18 Rennell Ho
19 Dycer Ho
20 Granard Ho
21 Whitelock Ho
22 Harrowgate Ho
23 Cass Ho

24 Lofts on the Park
C4 1 Cromford Path
2 Longford Ct
3 Overbury Ho
4 Heanor Ct
5 Wharfedale Ct
6 Ladybower Ct
7 Ilkeston Ct
8 Derby Ct
9 Rushmore Cres
10 Blackwell Cl

18
A2 1 Wick Mews
2 Wellday Ho
3 Selman Ho
4 Vaine Ho
5 Trower Ho
B2 1 Merriam Ave

19
C4 1 Mulberry Ct
2 Rosewood Ct
3 Gean Ct
4 Blackthorn Ct
5 Cypress Ct

20
1 Fitzsimmons Ct
2 Bernard Shaw Ho
3 Longlents Ho
4 Mordaunt Ho
5 Wilmers Ct
6 Stonebridge Sh Ctr

21
B3 1 New Crescent Yd
2 Harlesden Plaza
3 St Josephs Ct

22
C2 1 Westfield Ct
2 Tropical Ct
3 Chamberlayne Mans
4 Quadrant The
5 Queens Park Ct
6 Warfield Yd
7 Cherrytree Ho

23
A1 1 Sycamore Wlk
2 Westgate Bsns Ctr
3 Buspace Studios
4 Bosworth Ho
5 Golborne Gdns
6 Appleford Ho
7 Adair Twr
8 Gadsden Ho
9 Southam Ho
10 Norman Butler Ho
11 Thompson Ho
12 Wells Ho
13 Paul Ho
14 Olive Blythe Ho
15 Katherine Ho
16 Breakwell Ct
17 Pepler Ho
18 Edward Kennedy Ho
19 Winnington Ho
A2 1 Slomon Ho
3 Stansbury Ho

4 Tilleard Ho
5 Selby Ho
8 Mundy Ho
9 Macfarren Ho
10 Mounsey Ho
11 Courtville Ho
12 Croft Ho
13 Batten Ho
14 Bantock Ho
15 Banister Ho
16 Symphony Mews
17 Bliss Mews

A3 1 Lancefield Ct
2 Verdi Ho
3 Wornum Ho

B1 1 Western Ho
2 Russell's Wharf

B2 1 Boyce Ho
2 Farnaby Ho
3 Danby Ho
4 Purday Ho
5 Naylor Ho
6 St Judes Ho
7 Leeve Ho
8 Longhurst Ho
9 Harrington Ct
10 Mulberry Ct
11 Quilter Ho
12 Romer Ho
13 Kilburn Ho

B3 1 Claremont Ct
2 William Saville Ho
3 Western Ct
4 Bond Ho
5 Crone Ct
6 Wood Ho
7 Winterleys
8 Carlton Ho
9 Fiona Ct

C1 1 Westside Ho
2 Sutherland Ct
3 Fleming Ct
4 Hermes Cl

C2 1 Masefield Ho
2 Austen Ho
3 Fielding Ho
4 Park Bsns Ctr
5 John Ratcliffe Ho
6 Wymering Mans
7 Pavilion Ct
8 Nelson Cl

C3 1 Wells Ct
2 Cambridge Ct
3 Durham Ct

C4 1 Ryde Ho
2 Glengall Pass
3 Leith Yd
4 Daynor Ho
5 Varley Ho
6 Sandhy Ho
7 Colas Mews
8 Bishopsdale Ho
9 Lorton Ho
10 Marshwood Ho
11 Ribblesdale Ho
12 Holmesdale Ho
13 Kilburn Vale Est
14 Kilburn Bridge

24

A3 1 Bracer Ho
2 Scorton Ho
3 Fern Cl

4 Macbeth Ho
5 Oberon Ho
6 Buckland Ct
7 Crondall Ct
8 Osric Path
9 Caliban Twr
10 Celia Ho
11 Juliet Ho
12 Bacchus Wlk
13 Malcolm Ho
14 Homefield St
15 Crondall Pl
16 Blanca Ho
17 Miranda Ho
18 Falstaff Ho
19 Charmian Ho
20 Myrtle Wlk
21 Arden Ho
22 Sebastian Ho
23 Stanway Ct
24 Jerrold St
25 Rosalind Ho
26 Cordelia Ho
27 Monteagle Ct
28 John Parry Ct
29 James Anderson Ct
30 Ben Jonson Ct
31 Sara Lane Ct
32 Walbrook Ct

A4 1 Portelet Ct
2 Trinity Ct
3 Rozel Ct
4 St Helier Ct
5 Corbiere Ho
6 Kenning Ho
7 Higgins Ho
8 Cavell Ho
9 Girling Ho
10 Fulcher Ho
11 Francis Ho
12 Norris Ho
13 Kempton Ho
14 Nesham Ho
15 Crossbow Ho
16 Catherine Ho
17 Strale Ho
18 Horner Hos
19 Stringer Hos
20 Whitmore Ho
21 Nightingale Ho
22 Fletcher Ho
23 Arrow Ho
24 Archer Ho
25 Meriden Ho
26 Rover Ho
27 Bowyer Ho
28 Longbow Ho
29 Tiller Ho
30 Canalside Studios
31 Bishopgate
32 Holburn
33 Fenchurch

B3 1 Queensbridge Ct
2 Godwin Ho
3 Kent Ct
4 Brunswick Ho
5 Weymouth Ct
6 Sovereign Mews
7 Dunloe Ct
8 Cremer Bsns Ctr
9 Allgood St
10 Horatio St
11 Cadell Ho
12 Horatio Ho
13 Shipton Ho

B4 1 Hilborough Ct
2 Scriven Ct
3 Livermere Ct
4 Angrave Ct
5 Angrave Pas
6 Benfleet Ct
7 Belford Ho
8 Orme Ho
9 Clemson Ho
10 Longman Ho
11 Lowther Ho
12 Lovelace Ho
13 Harlowe Ho
14 Pamela Ho
15 Samuel Ho
16 Acton Ho
17 Loanda Cl
18 Phoenix Cl
19 Richardson Ct
20 Thrasher Cl
21 Mary Secole Cl
22 Canal Path
23 Pear Tree Cl
24 Hebden Ct
25 Charlton Ct
26 Laburnum Ct
27 Mansfield Ct
28 Garden Pl

C2 1 Lorden Wlk

C3 1 London Terr
2 Sturdee Ho
3 Maude Ho
4 Haig Ho
5 Jellicoe Ho
6 Ropley St
7 Guinness Trust Bldgs
8 Ion Ct
9 Moye Cl
10 Morrel Ct
11 Courtauld Ho
12 Drummond Ho
13 Atkinson Ho
14 Gurney Ho
15 Halley Ho
16 Goldsmith's Sq
17 Ken Wilson Ho
18 Shahjalal Ho
19 Crofts Ho
20 April Ct
21 Sebright Ho
22 Beechwood Ho
23 Gillman Ho
24 Cheverell Ho
25 Besford Ho
26 Dinmont Ho
27 Wyndham Deedes Ho
28 Sheppard Ho
29 Mary James Ho
30 Hadrian Est
31 Blythendale Ho
32 George Vale Ho
33 Lion Mills
34 Pritchard Ho

C4 1 Broke Wlk
2 Rochemont Wlk
3 Marlborough Ave
4 Rivington Wlk
5 Magnin Cl
6 Gloucester Sq
7 Woolstone Ho
8 Marsworth Ho
9 Cheddington Ho
10 Linslade Ho

11 Cosgrove Ho
12 Blisworth Ho
13 Eleanor Ct
14 Wistow Ho
15 Muscott Ho
16 Boxmoor Ho
17 Linford Ho
18 Pendley Ho
19 North Church Ho
20 Debdale Ho
21 Broadway Market Mews
22 Welshpool Ho
23 Ada Ho

25

A1 1 Rochester Ct
2 Weaver Ct
3 Greenheath Bsns Ctr
4 Glass St
5 Herald St
6 Northesk Ho
7 Codrington Ho
8 Heathpool Ct
9 Mocatta Ho
10 Harvey Ho
11 Blackwood Ho
12 Rutherford Ho
13 Bullen Ho
14 Fremantle Ho
15 Pellew Ho
16 Ashington Ho
17 Dinnington Ho
18 Bartholomew Sq
19 Steeple Ct
20 Orion Ho
21 Fellbrigg St
22 Eagle Ho
23 Sovereign Ho
24 Redmill Ho
25 Berry Ho
26 Grindall Ho
27 Collingwood Ho

A2 1 Charles Dickens Ho
2 Adrian Bolt Ho
3 William Rathbone Ho
4 Southwood Smith Ho
5 Rushmead
6 William Channing Ho
7 John Cartwright Ho
8 Charles Darwin Ho
9 Thomas Burt Ho
10 John Fielden Ho
11 Gwilym Maries Ho
12 Joseph Priestley Ho
13 Wear Pl
14 John Nettleford Ho
15 Thornaby Ho
16 Stockton Ho
17 Barnard Ho
18 Gainford Ho
19 Stapleton Ho
20 James Middleton Ho
21 Kedleston Wlk
22 Queen Margaret Flats
23 Hollybush Ho
24 Horwood Ho
25 Norden Ho
26 Newcourt Ho

27 Seabright St
28 Viaduct Pl
29 Sunlight Sq

A3 1 Dinmont St
2 Marian St
3 Claredale Ho
4 Bradley Ho
5 Connett Ho
6 Winkley St
7 Temple Dwellings
8 Argos Ho
9 Helen Ho
10 Lysander Ho
11 Antenor Ho
12 Paris Ho
13 Nestor Ho
14 Hector Ho
15 Ajax Ho
16 Achilles Ho
17 Priam Ho
18 Peabody Est
19 Felix St
20 Cambridge Cres
21 Peterley Bsns Ctr
22 Beckwith Ho
23 Parminter Ind Est
24 Ted Roberts Ho
25 Cambridge Ct
26 West St
27 Millennium Pl
28 William Caslon Ho
29 Hugh Platt Ho
30 Mayfield Ho
31 Apollo Ho
32 Tanners Yd
33 Teesdale Yd

A4 1 Welshpool St
2 Broadway Ho
3 Regents Wharf
4 London Wharf
5 Warburton Ho
6 Warburton St
7 Triangle Rd
8 Warburton Rd
9 Williams Ho
10 Booth Cl
11 Albert Ct
12 King Edward Mans
13 Victoria Bldgs

B1 1 William's Bldgs
2 Donegal Ho
3 Frederick Charrington Ho
4 Wickford Ho
5 Braintree Ho
6 Doveton Ho
7 Doveton St
8 Cephas Ho
9 Sceptre Ho
10 Bancroft Ho
11 Stothard St
12 Redclyf Ho
13 Winkworth Cotts
14 Ryder Ho
15 Hadleigh Ho
16 Hadleigh Cl
17 Amiel St
18 Stathard Ho
19 Barbanel Ho
20 Colebert Ho
21 Kenton Ho
22 Ibbott St
23 Stannard Cotts
24 Rennie Cotts
25 Rickman St
26 Rickman Ho

27 Pemell Cl
28 Pemell Ho
29 Leatherdale St
30 Gouldman Ho
31 Lamplighter Cl
32 Hamilton Lo
33 Cleveland Gr
34 Montgomery Lo
35 Bardsey Pl
36 Cromwell Lo
37 Colin Winter Ho
38 Allport Mews
B2 1 Mulberry Ho
2 Gretton Ho
3 Merceron Ho
4 Montfort Ho
5 Westbrook Ho
6 Sugar Loaf Wlk
7 Museum Ho
8 Burnham Est
9 Globe Terr
10 Moravian St
11 Shepton Hos
12 Mendip Hos
13 Academy Ct
14 Pepys Ho
15 Swinburne Ho
16 Moore Ho
17 Morris Ho
18 Burns Ho
19 Milton Ho
20 Whitman Ho
21 Shelley Ho
22 Keats Ho
23 Dawson Ho
24 Bradbeer Ho
25 Forber Ho
26 Hughes Ho
27 Silvester Ho
28 Rogers Est
29 Pavan Ct
30 Stafford Cripps Ho
31 Sidney Godley (VC) Ct
32 Butler Ho
33 Butler St
34 Thorne Ho
35 Bevin Ho
36 Tuscan Ho
B3 1 Evesham Ho
2 James Campbell Ho
3 Thomas Hollywood Ho
4 James Docherty Ho
5 Ebenezer Mussel Ho
6 Jameson Ct
7 Edinburgh Ct
8 Roger Dowley Ct
9 Sherbrooke Ho
10 Calcraft Ho
11 Burrard Ho
12 Dundas Ho
13 Ponsonby Ho
14 Barnes Ho
15 Paget Ho
16 Maitland Ho
17 Chesil Ct
18 Reynolds Ho
19 Cleland Ho
20 Goodrich Ho
21 Rosebery Ho
22 Sankey Ho
23 Cyprus Pl
24 Royston St

26 Stainsbury St
27 Hunslett St
28 Baildon
29 Brockweir
30 Tytherton
31 Malmesbury
32 Kingswood
33 Colville Ho
B4 1 Hallett Ho
4 Christ Church Sq
5 Swingfield Ho
6 Greenham Ho
7 Dinmore Ho
8 Anstey Ho
9 Weston Ho
10 Carbroke Ho
11 Bluebell Cl
12 Cherry Tree Cl
13 Georgian Ct
14 Park Cl
15 Regency Ct
16 Norris Ho
C1 1 Raynham Ho
2 Pat Shaw Ho
3 Colmar Cl
4 Withy Ho
5 Stocks Ct
6 Downey Ho
7 Bay Ct
8 Sligo Ho
9 Pegasus Ho
10 Barents Ho
11 Biscay Ho
12 Solway Ho
13 Bantry Ho
14 Aral Ho
15 Pacific Ho
16 Magellan Ho
17 Levant Ho
18 Adriatic Ho
19 Genoa Ho
20 Hawke Ho
21 Palliser Ho
22 Ionian Ho
23 Weddell Ho
C2 1 Stubbs Ho
2 Holman Ho
3 Clynes Ho
4 Windsor Ho
5 Gilbert Ho
6 Chater Ho
7 Ellen Wilkinson Ho
8 George Belt Ho
9 Ayrton Gould Ho
10 O'Brian Ho
11 Sulkin Ho
12 Jenkinson Ho
13 Bullards Ho
14 Sylvia Pankhurst Ho
15 Mary Macarthur Ho
16 Trevelyan Ho
17 Wedgwood Ho
18 Pemberton Ct
19 Walter Besant Ho
20 Barber Beaumont Ho
21 Brancaster Ho
22 Litcham Ho
C3 1 Kemp Ho
2 Piggott Ho
3 Mark Ho
4 Sidney Ho
5 Pomeroy Ho
6 Puteaux Ho
7 Doric Ho

8 Modling Ho
9 Longman Ho
10 Ames Ho
11 Alzette Ho
12 Offenbach Ho
13 Tate Ho
14 Norton Ho
15 St Gilles Ho
16 Harold Ho
17 Velletri Ho
18 Bridge Wharf
19 Gathorne St
20 Bow Brook The
21 Palmerston St
22 Peach Walk Mews
23 Lakeview
24 Caesar Ct

26
A1 1 Formosa Ho
2 Galveston Ho
3 Arabian Ho
4 Greenland Ho
5 Coral Ho
6 Anson Ho
7 Lindop Ho
8 Moray Ho
9 Azov Ho
10 Sandalwood Cl
11 Broadford Ho
A3 1 Bunsen Ho
2 Bunsen St
3 Beatrice Webb Ho
4 Margaret Bondfield Ho
5 Wilmer Ho
6 Sandall Ho
7 Butley Ct
8 Josseline Ct
9 Dalton Ho
10 Brine Ho
11 Ford Cl
12 Viking Ho
13 Stanfield Rd
14 Ruth Ct
15 School Bell Cloisters
16 Schoolbell Mews
17 Medhurst Cl
18 Olga St
19 Conyer St
20 Diamond Ho
21 Daring Ho
22 Crane Ho
23 Exmoor Ho
24 Grenville Ho
25 Hyperion Ho
26 Sturdy Ho
27 Wren Ho
28 Ardent Ho
29 Senators Lo
30 Hooke Ho
31 Mohawk Ho
32 Ivanhoe Ho
33 Medway Mews
B2 1 Trellis Sq
2 Sheffield Sq
3 Howcroft Ho
4 Astra Ho
5 Byas Ho
6 George Lansbury Ho
7 Regal Pl
9 Coborn Mews
10 Cavendish Terr
11 Buttermere Ho

12 Tracy Ho
13 Hanover Pl
14 Coniston Ho
15 St Clair Ho
16 Verity Ho
17 Icarus Ho
18 Whippingham Ho
19 Winchester Ho
20 Hamilton Ho
21 Longthorne Ho
B3 1 Roman Square Mkt
2 John Bond Ho
3 McKenna Ho
4 Dennis Ho
5 McBride Ho
6 Libra Rd
7 Dave Adams Ho
8 Sleat Ho
9 Ewart Pl
10 Brodick Ho
11 Lunan Ho
12 Mull Ho
13 Sinclairs Ho
14 Driftway Ho
15 Clayhall Ct
16 Berebinder Ho
17 Stavers Ho
18 Barford Ho
19 Partridge Ho
20 Gosford Ho
21 Gullane Ho
22 Cruden Ho
23 Anglo Rd
24 Dornoch Ho
25 Dunnet Ho
26 Enard Ho
27 Fraserburgh Ho
28 Forth Ho
29 Ordell Ct
30 William Pl
B4 1 Hampstead Wlk
2 Waverton Ho
3 Elton Ho
4 Locton Gn
5 Birtwhistle Ho
6 Clare Ho
7 Magpie Ho
8 Atkins Ct
9 Tait Ct
10 Ranwell Ho
11 Ranwell Cl
12 Tufnell Ct
13 Pulteney Cl
14 Vic Johnson Ho
C1 1 Fairmont Ho
2 Healy Ho
3 Zodiac Ho
4 Buick Ho
5 Consul Ho
6 Bentley Ho
7 Cresta Ho
8 Daimler Ho
9 Riley Ho
10 Jensen Ho
11 Lagonda Ho
12 Ireton St
13 Navenby Wlk
14 Burwell Wlk
15 Leadenham Ct
16 Sleaford Ho
C2 1 Jarret Ho
2 Marsalis Ho
3 Lovette Ho
4 Drapers Almshouses
5 Mallard Point

6 Creswick Wlk
7 Bevin Ho
8 Huggins Ho
9 Williams Ho
10 Harris Ho
11 Marina Ct
12 Electric Ho
13 Matching Ct
14 Wellington Bldgs
15 Grafton Ho
16 Columbia Ho
17 Berkeley Ho

27
A1 1 Broxbourne Ho
2 Roxford Ho
3 Biscott Ho
4 Stanborough Ho
5 Hillstone Ct
A2 1 Bradley Ho
2 Prioress Ho
3 Alton Ho
4 Foxley Ho
5 Munden Ho
6 Canterbury Ho
7 Corbin Ho
8 Barton Ho
9 Jolles Ho
10 Rudstone Ho
11 Baxter Ho
12 Baker Ho
13 Insley Ho
14 Hardwicke Ho
15 Glebe Terr
16 Priory St
17 Sadler Ho
18 Ballinger Point
19 Henshall Point
20 Dorrington Point
21 Warren Ho
22 Fairlie Ct
23 Regent Sq
24 Hackworth Point
25 Priestman Point
26 Wingate Ho
27 Nethercott Ho
28 Thelbridge Ho
29 Bowden Ho
30 Kerscott Ho
31 Southcott Ho
32 Birchdown Ho
33 Upcott Ho
34 Langmead Ho
35 Limscott Ho
36 Northleigh Ho
37 Huntshaw Ho
38 Chagford Ho
39 Ashcombe Ho
40 Shillingford Ho
41 Patrick Connolly Gdns
42 Lester Ct
43 Franklin St
44 Taft Way
45 Washington Cl
46 Elizabeth Ho
47 William Guy Gdns
48 Denbury Ho
49 Holsworthy Ho

28
A1 1 Lantry Ct
2 Rosemount

21 Jean Pardies Ho
22 Clichy Ho
23 Le Moal Ho
24 Odette Duval Ho
25 Dagobert Ho
26 Charles Auffray Ho
27 Boisseau Ho
28 Paymal Ho
C1 1 Clarence Mews
2 Raleigh Ct
3 Katherine Cl
4 Woolcombes Ct
5 Tudor Ct
6 Quayside Ct
7 Princes Riverside Rd
8 Surrey Ho
9 Tideway Ct
10 Edinburgh Ct
11 Falkirk Ct
12 Byelands Cl
13 Gwent Ct
14 Lavender Ho
15 Abbotshade Rd
16 Bellamy's Ct
17 Blenheim Ct
18 Sandringham Ct
19 Hampton Ct
20 Windsor Ct
21 Balmoral Ct
22 Westminster Ct
C2 1 Barnardo Gdns
2 Roslin Ho
3 Glamis Est
4 Peabody Est
5 East Block
6 Highway Trad Ctr The
7 Highway Bsns Pk The
8 Cranford Cotts
9 Ratcliffe Orch
10 Scotia Bldg
11 Mauretania Bldg
12 Compania Bldg
13 Sirius Bldg
14 Unicorn Bldg
15 Keepier Wharf
C3 1 Pattison Ho
2 St Thomas Ho
3 Arbour Ho
4 Bladen Ho
5 Antill Terr
6 Billing Ho
7 Dowson Ho
8 Lipton Rd
9 Chalkwell Ho
10 Corringham Ho
11 Ogilvie Ho
12 Edward Mann Cl
13 Lightermans Mews
C4 1 Roland Mews
2 Morecambe Cl
3 Stepney Green Cl
4 Milrood Ho
5 Panama Ho
6 Galway Ho
7 Caspian Ho
8 Darien Ho
9 Rigo Ho
10 Flores Ho
11 Taranto Ho
12 Aden Ho
13 Frances Grey Ho
14 Master's St
15 Diggon St

33
A2 1 St Georges Sq
2 Drake Ho
3 Osprey Ho
4 Fleet Ho
5 Gainsborough Ho
6 Victory Pl
7 Challenger Ho
8 Conrad Ho
9 Lock View Ct
10 Shoulder of Mutton Alley
11 Frederick Sq
12 Helena Sq
13 Elizabeth Sq
14 Sophia Sq
15 William Sq
16 Lamb Ct
17 Lockside
18 Ionian Bldg
19 Regents Gate Ho
A3 1 Coltman Ho
2 Repton Ho
3 Causton Cotts
4 Darnley Ho
5 Mercer's Cotts
6 Troon Ho
7 Ratcliffe Ho
8 Wakeling St
9 York Sq
10 Anglia Ho
11 Cambria Ho
12 Caledonia Ho
13 Ratcliffe La
14 Bekesbourne St
15 John Scurr Ho
16 Regents Canal Ho
17 Basin App
18 Powlesland Ct
A4 1 Waley St
2 Edith Ramsay Ho
3 Andaman Ho
4 Atlantic Ho
5 Pevensey Ho
6 Solent Ho
7 Lorne Ho
8 Cromarty Ho
9 Greaves Cotts
10 Donaghue Cotts
11 Ames Cotts
B2 1 Hamilton Ho
2 Imperial Ho
3 Oriana Ho
4 Queens Ct
5 Brightlingsea Pl
6 Faraday Ho
7 Ropemaker's Fields
8 Oast Ct
9 Mitre The
10 Bate St
11 Joseph Irwin Ho
12 Padstow Ho
13 Bethlehem Ho
14 Saunders Cl
15 Roche Ho
16 Stocks Pl
17 Trinidad Ho
18 Grenada Ho
19 Kings Ho
20 Dunbar Wharf
21 Limekiln Wharf
B3 1 Dora Ho
2 Flansham Ho
3 Gatwick Ho
4 Ashpark Ho

5 Newdigate Ho
6 Salmon St
7 Midhurst Ho
8 Redbourne Ho
9 Southwater Cl
10 Aithan Ho
11 Britley Ho
12 Cheadle Ho
13 Elland Ho
14 Butler Ho
15 Fitzroy Ho
16 Leybourne Ho
B4 1 Wearmouth Ho
2 Elmslie Point
3 Grindley Ho
4 Stileman Ho
5 Baythorne St
6 Wilcox Ho
7 Robeson St
8 Couzens Ho
9 Perley Ho
10 Whytlaw Ho
11 Printon Ho
12 Perkins Ho
13 Bowry Ho
14 Booker Cl
15 Tunley Gn
16 Callingham Cl
17 Tasker Ho
C2 1 West India Ho
2 Birchfield Ho
3 Elderfield Ho
4 Thornfield Ho
5 Gorsefield Ho
6 Arborfield Ho
7 Colborne Ho
8 East India Bldgs
9 Compass Point
10 Salter St
11 Kelly Ct
12 Flynn Ct
13 Mary Jones Ho
14 Horizon Bldg
15 Berber Pl
C3 1 Landin Ho
2 Charlesworth Ho
3 Gurdon Ho
4 Trendell Ho
5 Menteath Ho
6 Minchin Ho
7 Donne Ho
8 Denison Ho
9 Anglesey Ho
10 Gough Wlk
11 Baring Ho
12 Hopkins Ho
13 Granville Ho
14 Gladstone Ho
15 Russell Ho
16 Pusey Ho
17 Overstone Ho
18 Stanley Ho
19 Old School Sq
C4 1 Bredel Ho
2 Linton Ho
3 Matthews Ho
4 Woodcock Ho
5 Limborough Ho
6 Maydwell Ho
7 Underhill Ho
8 Meyrick Ho
9 Ambrose Ho
10 Carpenter Ho
11 Robinson Ho
12 Bramble Ho
13 Bilberry Ho

14 Bracken Ho
15 Berberis Ho
16 Busbridge Ho
17 Metropolitan Cl
18 Invicta Cl
19 Bellmaker Ct
34
A2 1 Westcott Ho
2 Corry Ho
3 Malam Gdns
4 Devitt Ho
5 Leyland Ho
6 Wigram Ho
7 Willis Ho
8 Balsam Ho
9 Finch's Ct
10 Poplar Bath St
11 Lawless St
12 Storey Ho
13 Abbot Ho
14 Landon Wlk
15 Goodhope Ho
16 Goodfaith Ho
17 Winant Ho
18 Lubbock Ho
19 Goodwill Ho
20 Martindale Ho
21 Holmsdale Ho
22 Norwood Ho
23 Constant Ho
24 Woodall Cl
A3 1 Colebrook Ho
2 Essex Ho
3 Salisbury Ho
4 Maidstone Ho
5 Osterley Ho
6 Norwich Ho
7 Clarissa Ho
8 Elgin Ho
9 Shaftesbury Lo
10 Shepherd Ho
11 Jeremiah St
12 Elizabeth Cl
13 Chilcot Cl
14 Fitzgerald Ho
15 Vesey Path
16 Ennis Ho
17 Kilmore Ho
A4 1 Sumner Ho
2 Irvine Ho
3 David Ho
4 Brushwood Ho
5 Limehouse Cut
6 Colmans Wharf
7 Foundary Ho
8 Radford Ho
B2 1 Discovery Ho
2 Mountague Pl
3 Virginia Ho
4 Collins Ho
5 Lawless Ho
6 Carmichael Ho
7 Commodore Ho
8 Mermaid Ho
9 Bullivant St
10 Anderson Ho
11 Mackrow Wlk
12 Robin Hood Gdns
B3 1 Langdon Ho
2 Balfron Twr
3 Tabard Ct
4 Delta Bldg
5 Kilbrennan Ho
6 Thistle Ho
7 Heather Ho

8 Tartan Ho
9 Trident Ho
B4 1 Mills Gr
2 Duncan Ct
C2 1 Settlers Ct
2 Susan Constant Ct
3 Adventurers Ct
4 Bartholomew Ct
5 Atlantic Ct
6 Cape Henry Ct
7 Wotton Ct
8 Studley Ct
9 Wingfield Ct
C3 1 Lansbury Gdns
2 Thesus Ho
3 Theseus Ho
4 Adams Ho
5 Sam March Ho
6 Arapiles Ho
7 Athenia Ho
8 Jervis Bay Ho
9 Helen Mackay Ho
10 Gaze Ho
11 Ritchie Ho
12 Circle Ho
13 Dunkeld Ho
14 Braithwaite Ho
15 Rosemary Dr
16 Sorrel La
17 East India Dock Road Tunnel

35
B1 1 Newton Point
2 Sparke Terr
3 Montesquieu Terr
4 Crawford Point
5 Rathbone Ho
6 George St
7 Emily St
8 Fendt Cl
9 Sabbarton St
B2 1 Radley Terr
2 Rathbone Mkt
3 Thomas North Terr
4 Bernard Cassidy St
5 Mary St
6 Hughes Terr
7 Swanscombe Point
8 Rawlinson Point
9 Kennedy Cox Ho
10 Cooper St
C1 1 Capulet Mews
2 Pepys Cres
3 De Quincey Mews
4 Hardy Ave
5 Tom Jenkinson Rd
6 Hanameel St
7 Kennacraig Cl
8 Gatcombe Rd
9 Badminton Mews
10 Holyrood Mews
11 Britannia Gate
12 Dalemain Mews
C2 1 Clements Ave
2 Martindale Ave
C4 1 Odeon Ct
2 Edward Ct
3 Newhaven La
4 Ravenscroft Cl
5 Douglas Rd
6 Ferrier Point

7 Harvey Point
8 Wood Point
9 Trinity St
10 Pattinson Point
11 Clinch Ct
12 Mint Bsns Pk

36

A1 **1** Burford Ho
2 Hope Ct
3 Centaur Ct
4 Phoenix Ct
C1 **1** Surrey Cres
2 Forbes Ho
3 Haining Cl
4 Melville Ct
5 London Stile
6 Stile Hall Par
7 Priory Lo
8 Kew Bridge Ct
9 Meadowcroft
10 St James Ct
11 Rivers Ho

37

A1 **1** Churchdale Ct
2 Cromwell Cl
3 Cambridge Rd S
4 Oxbridge Ct
5 Tomlinson Cl
6 Gunnersbury Mews
7 Grange The
8 Gunnersbury Ct
A4 **1** Cheltenham Pl
2 Beaumaris Twr
3 Arundel Ho
4 Pevensey Ct
5 Jerome Twr
6 Anstey Ct
7 Bennett Ct
8 Gunnersbury Ct
B1 **1** Arlington Park Mans
2 Sandown Ho
3 Goodwood Ho
4 Windsor Ho
5 Lingfield Ho
6 Ascot Ho
7 Watchfield Ct
8 Belgrave Ct
9 Beverley Ct
10 Beaumont Ct
11 Harvard Rd
12 Troubridge Ct
B2 **1** Chiswick Green Studios
2 Bell Ind Est
3 Fairlawn Ct
4 Dukes Gate
5 Dewsbury Ct
6 Chiswick Terr
B3 **1** Blackmore Twr
2 Bollo Ct
3 Kipling Twr
4 Lawrence Ct
5 Maugham Ct
6 Reade Ct
7 Woolf Ct
8 Shaw Ct
9 Verne Ct
10 Wodehouse Ct
11 Greenock Rd
12 Garden Ct

13 Barons Gate
14 Cleveland Rd
15 Chapter Cl
16 Carver Cl
17 Beauchamp Cl
18 Holmes Ct
B4 **1** Belgrave Ct
2 Buckland Wlk
3 Frampton Ct
4 Telfer Cl
5 Harlech Twr
6 Corfe Twr
7 Barwick Ho
8 Charles Hocking Ho
9 Sunninghill Ct
10 Salisbury St
11 Jameson Pl
C1 **1** Chatsworth Lo
2 Prospect Pl
3 Townhall Ave
4 Devonhurst Pl
5 Heathfield Ct
6 Horticultural Pl
7 Merlin Ho
8 Garth Rd

38

A1 **1** Glebe Cl
2 Devonshire Mews
3 Binns Terr
4 Ingress St
5 Swanscombe Rd
6 Brackley Terr
7 Stephen Fox Ho
8 Manor Gdns
9 Coram Ho
10 Flaxman Ho
11 Thorneycroft Ho
12 Thornhill Ho
13 Kent Ho
14 Oldfield Ho
A2 **1** Chestnut Ho
2 Bedford Ho
3 Bedford Cnr
4 Sydney Ho
5 Bedford Park Cnr
6 Priory Gdns
7 Windmill Alley
8 Castle Pl
9 Jonathan Ct
10 Windmill Pas
11 Chardin Ho
12 Gable Ho
A3 **1** Fleet Ct
2 Ember Ct
3 Emlyn Gdns
4 Clone Ct
5 Brent Ct
6 Abbey Ct
7 Ormsby Lo
8 St Catherine's Ct
A4 **1** Longford Ct
2 Mole Ct
3 Lea Ct
4 Wandle Ct
5 Beverley Ct
6 Roding Ct
7 Crane Ct
B1 **1** Miller's Ct
2 British Grove Pas
3 British Grove S
4 Berestede Rd
5 North Eyot Gdns
B2 **1** Flanders Mans

2 Stamford Brook Mans
3 Linkenholt Mans
4 Prebend Mans
5 Middlesex Ct
B3 **1** Stamford Brook Gdns
2 Hauteville Court Gdns
3 Ranelagh Gdns
C2 **1** Hamlet Ct
2 Derwent St
3 Westcroft Ct
4 Black Lion Mews
5 St Peter's Villas
6 Standish Ho
7 Chambon Pl
8 Court Mans
C4 **2** Victoria Ho
3 Lycett Pl
4 Kylemore Ct
5 Alexandra Ct
6 Lytten Ct
7 Becklow Mews
8 Northcroft Ct
9 Bailey Ct
10 Spring Cott
11 Landor Wlk
12 Laurence Mews
13 Hadyn Park Ct
14 Askew Mans

39

A2 **1** Albion Gdns
2 Flora Gdns
3 Lamington St
4 Felgate Mews
5 Galena Ho
6 Albion Mews
7 Albion Ct
8 King Street Cloisters
9 Dimes Pl
10 Clarence Ct
11 Hampshire Hog La
12 Marryat Ct
A4 **1** Westbush Ct
2 Goldhawk Mews
3 Sycamore Ho
4 Shackleton Ct
5 Drake Ct
6 Scotts Ct
B2 **1** Bridge Avenue Mans
2 Bridgeview
3 College Ct
4 Beatrice Ho
5 Amelia Ho
6 Edith Ho
7 Joanna Ho
8 Mary Ho
9 Adela Ho
10 Sophia Ho
11 Henrietta Ho
12 Charlotte Ho
13 Alexandra Ho
14 Bath Pl
15 Elizabeth Ho
16 Margaret Ho
17 Peabody Est
18 Eleanor Ho
19 Isabella Ho
20 Caroline Ho
21 Chancellors Wharf
22 Sussex Pl

B2 **1** Phoenix Lodge Mans
2 Samuel's Cl
3 Broadway Arc
4 Brook Ho
5 Hammersmith Broadway
B4 **1** Verulam Ho
2 Grove Mans
3 Frobisher Ct
4 Library Mans
5 Pennard Mans
6 Lanark Mans
7 Kerrington Ct
8 Granville Mans
9 Romney Ct
10 Rayner Ct
11 Sulgrave Gdns
12 Bamborough Gdns
C3 **1** Grosvenor Residences
2 Blythe Mews
3 Burnand Ho
4 Bradford Ho
5 Springvale Terr
6 Ceylon Rd
7 Walpole Ct
8 Bronte Ct
9 Boswell Ct
10 Souldern Rd
11 Brook Green Flats
12 Haarlem Rd
13 Stafford Mans
14 Lionel Mans
C4 **2** Vanderbilt Villas
3 Bodington Ct
4 Kingham Cl
5 Clearwater Terr
6 Lorne Gdns
7 Cameret Ct
8 Bush Ct
9 Shepherds La
10 Rockley Ct
11 Grampians The
12 Charcroft Ct
13 Addison Park Mans
14 Sinclair Mans

40

A1 **1** Hockney Ct
2 Toulouse Ct
3 Lowry Ct
4 Barry Ho
5 Lewis Ct
6 Gainsborough Ct
7 Renoir Ct
8 Blake Ct
9 Raphael Ct
10 Rembrandt Ct
11 Constable Ct
12 Da Vinci Ct
13 Gaugin Ct
14 Michelangelo Ct
15 Monet Ct
16 Weald Cl
17 Jasmin Lo
18 Birchmere Lo
19 Weybridge Ct
20 Florence Ho
21 Gleneagles Cl
22 Sunningdale Cl
23 Muirfield Cl
24 Turnberry Cl
25 St Andrews Cl
26 Kingsdown Cl
27 St Davids Cl

28 Galway Cl
29 Edenbridge Cl
30 Birkdale Cl
31 Tralee Ct
32 Woburn Ct
33 Belfry Cl
34 Troon Cl
35 Holywell Cl
A2 **1** Market Pl
2 Trappes Ho
3 Thurland Ho
4 Ramsfort Ho
5 Hambley Ho
6 Holford Ho
7 Pope Ho
8 Southwell Ho
9 Mortain Ho
10 Radcliffe Ho
11 Southwark Park Est
12 Galleywall Road Trad Est
13 Trevithick Ho
14 Barlow Ho
15 Donkin Ho
16 Landmann Ho
17 Fitzmaurice Ho
18 Dodd Ho
A3 **1** Perryn Rd
2 Chalfont Ho
3 Prestwood Ho
4 Farmer Ho
5 Gataker Ho
6 Gataker St
7 Cornick Ho
8 Glebe Ho
9 Matson Ho
10 Hickling Ho
11 St Andrews Ho
A4 **1** Butterfield Cl
2 Janeway Pl
3 Trotwood Ho
4 Cranbourn Ho
5 Cherry Garden Ho
6 Burton Ho
7 Morriss Ho
8 King Edward The Third Mews
9 Cathay St
10 Rotherhithe St
B2 **1** Damory Ho
2 Antony Ho
3 Roderick Ho
4 Pedworth Gdns
5 Beamish Ho
6 Gillam Ho
7 George Walter Ho
8 Richard Ho
9 Adron Ho
10 Westlake
11 McIntosh Ho
B3 **1** Blick Ho
2 Neptune Ho
3 Scotia Ct
4 Murdoch Ho
5 Edmonton Ct
6 Niagara Ct
7 Columbia Point
8 Ritchie Ho
9 Wells Ho
10 Helen Peele Cotts
11 Orchard Ho
12 Dock Offices
13 Landale Ho
14 Courthope Ho
B4 **1** Mayflower St
2 St Mary's Est

3 Rupack St
4 Frank Whymark Ho
5 Adams Gardens Est
6 Hatteraick St
7 Hythe Ho
8 Seaford Ho
9 Sandwich Ho
11 Winchelsea Ho
12 Kenning St
13 Western Pl
14 Ainsty St
15 Pine Ho
16 Beech Ho
17 Larch Ho
18 Seth St
19 Turner Ct
20 Risdon Ho
21 Risdon St
22 Aylton Est
23 Manitoba Ct
24 Calgary Ct
25 Irwell Est
26 City Bsns Ctr
27 St Olav's Sq
C2 1 John Kennedy Ho
2 Brydale Ho
3 Balman Ho
4 Tissington Ct
5 Harbord Ho
6 Westfield Ho
7 Albert Starr Ho
8 John Brent Ho
9 William Evans Ho
10 Raven Ho
11 Egret Ho
12 Fulmar Ho
13 Dunlin Ho
14 Siskin Ho
15 Sheldrake Ho
16 Buchanan Ct
17 Burrage Ct
18 Biddenham Ho
19 Ayston Ho
20 Empingham Ho
21 Deanshanger Ho
22 Codicote Ho
C4 1 Schooner Cl
2 Dolphin Cl
3 Clipper Cl
4 Deauville Ct
5 Colette Ct
6 Coniston Ct
7 Virginia Ct
8 Derwent Ct
9 Grantham Ct
10 Serpentine Ct
11 Career Ct
12 Lacine Ct
13 Fairway Ct
14 Harold Ct
15 Spruce Ho
16 Cedar Ho
17 Sycamore Ho
18 Woodland Cres
19 Poplar Ho
20 Adelphi Ct
21 Basque Ct
22 Aberdale Ct
23 Quilting Ct
24 Chargrove Ct
25 Radley Ct
26 Greenacre Sq
27 Maple Leaf Sq
28 Stanhope Ct
29 Hawke Pl
30 Drake Cl

31 Brass Talley Alley
32 Monkton St
33 James Ho
34 Wolfe Cres

41
A2 1 Trafalgar Ct
2 Hornblower Cl
3 Cunard Wlk
4 Caronia Ct
5 Carinthia Ct
6 Freswick Ho
7 Graveley Ho
8 Husbourne Ho
9 Crofters Ct
10 Pomona Ho
11 Hazelwood Ho
12 Cannon Wharf Bsns Ctr
13 Bence Ho
14 Clement Ho
15 Pendennis Ho
16 Lighter Cl
17 Mast Ct
18 Rushcutters Ct
19 Boat Lifter Way
B1 1 Gransden Ho
2 Daubeney Twr
3 North Ho
4 Rochfort Ho
5 Keppel Ho
6 Camden Ho
7 Sanderson Ho
8 Berkeley Ho
9 Strafford Ho
10 Richman Ho
11 Hurleston Ho
12 Grafton Ho
13 Fulcher Ho
14 Citrus Ho
B2 1 Windsock Cl
2 Linberry Wlk
3 Lanyard Ho
4 Golden Hind Pl
5 James Lind Ho
6 Harmon Ho
7 Pelican Ho
8 Bembridge Ho
9 Terrace The
10 George Beard Rd
11 Colonnade The
12 Pepys Ent Ctr
C1 1 Hudson Ct
2 Shackleton Ct
3 Perry Ct
4 Maritime Quay
C2 1 Olympian Ct
2 Aphrodite Ct
3 Mercury Ct
4 Poseidon Ct
5 Neptune Ct
6 Artemis Ct
7 Hera Ct
8 Ares Ct
9 Cyclops Mews
10 Magellan Pl
11 Britannia Rd
12 Deptford Ferry Rd
13 Ironmonger's Pl
14 Radnor Wlk
15 Ashdown Wlk
16 Rothsay Wlk
17 Dartmoor Wlk
18 Ringwood Gdns
19 Dockers Tanner Rd
20 Apollo Bldg

21 Nova Bldg
C3 1 St Hubert's Ho
2 John Tucker Ho
3 Clare Grant Ho
4 Gilbertson Ho
5 Bowsprit Point
6 Scoulding Ho
7 Cord Way
8 Cressall Ho
9 Alexander Ho
10 Kedge Ho
C4 1 Jefferson Bldg
2 Waterman Bldg
3 Pierpoint Bldg
4 Franklin Bldg
5 Bellamy Cl
6 Bosun Ct
7 Edison Bldg
8 Vanguard Bldg

42
A2 1 Brassey Ho
2 Triton Ho
3 Warspite Ho
4 Rodney Ho
5 Conway Ho
6 Exmouth Ho
7 Akbar Ho
8 Arethusa Ho
9 Tasman Ct
B2 1 Betty May Gray Ho
2 Castleton Ho
3 Urmston Ho
4 Salford Ho
5 Capstan Ho
6 Frigate Ho
7 Galleon Ho
8 Barons Lo
B3 1 Cardale St
2 Hickin St
3 John McDonald Ho
4 Thorne Ho
5 Skeggs Ho
6 St Bernard Ho
7 Kimberley Ho
8 Kingdon Ho
9 Lingard Ho
10 Yarrow Ho
11 Sandpiper Ct
12 Nightingale Ct
13 Robin Ct
14 Heron Ct
B4 1 Llandovery Ho
2 Rugless Ho
3 Ash Ho
4 Elm Ho
5 Cedar Ho
6 Castalia Sq
7 Walkers Lo
8 Antilles Bay
9 Alice Shepherd Ho
10 Oak Ho
11 Ballin Ct
12 Martin Ct
13 Grebe Ct
14 Kingfisher Ct
C2 1 Verwood Lo
2 Fawley Lo
3 Lyndhurst Lo
4 Blyth Cl
5 Farnworth Ho
6 Francis Cl

43
A1 1 Bellot Gdns
2 Thornley Pl
3 King William La
4 Bolton Ho
5 Miles Ho
6 Mell St
7 Sam Manners Ho
8 Hatcliffe Almshouses
9 Woodland Wlk
10 Earlswood Cl
B1 1 Baldrey Ho
2 Christie Ho
3 Dyson Ho
4 Cliffe Ho
5 Moore Ho
6 Collins Ho
7 Lockyer Ho
8 Halley Ho
9 Kepler Ho
C1 1 Layfield Ho
2 Westerdale Rd
3 Mayston Mews

44
A4 1 Ferry Sq
2 Wilkes Rd
3 Albany Par
4 Charlton Ho
5 Albany Ho
6 Alma Ho
7 Griffin Ct
8 Cressage Ho
9 Tunstall Wlk
10 Trimmer Wlk
11 Running Horse Yd
12 Mission Sq
13 Distillery Wlk
14 Primrose Ho
B2 1 Lawman Ct
2 Royston Ct
3 Garden Ct
4 Capel Lo
5 Devonshire Ct
6 Celia Ct
7 Rosslyn Ho
8 Branstone Ct
9 Lamerton Lo
10 Kew Lo
11 Dunraven Ho
12 Stoneleigh Lo
13 Tunstall St
14 Voltaire
C2 1 Clarendon Ct
2 Quintock Ho
3 Broome Ct
4 Lonsdale Mews
5 Elizabeth Cotts
6 Sandways
7 Victoria Cotts
8 North Ave
9 Grovewood
10 Hamilton Ho
11 Melvin Ct
12 Power Ho
13 Station Ave
14 Blake Mews

46
B1 1 Melrose Rd
2 Seaforth Lo
3 St John's Gr
4 Sussex Ct
5 Carmichael Ct
6 Hampshire Ct
7 Thorne Pas
8 Beverley Path

47
C4 1 Cobb's Hall
2 Dorset Mans
3 St Clements Mans
4 Bothwell St
5 Hawksmoor St

48
A1 1 Langport Ho
2 Iveagh Ho
3 Newark Ho
4 Edgehill Ho
5 Hopton Ho
6 Ashby Ho
7 Nevil Ho
A2 1 Fairbairn Gn
2 Hammelton Gn
3 Foxley Sq
4 Silverburn Ho
5 Butler Ho
6 Dalkeith Ho
7 Turner Ct
8 Bathgate Ho
9 Black Roof Ho
A4 1 Faunce Ho
2 Garbett Ho
3 Harvard Ho
4 Doddington Pl
5 Kean Ho
6 Jephson Ho
7 Cornish Ho
8 Bateman Ho
9 Molesworth Ho
10 Walters Ho
11 Cruden Ho
12 Brawne Ho
13 Prescott Ho
14 Chalmer's Wlk
15 Copley Cl
B1 1 Bergen Ho
2 Oslo Ho
3 Viking Ho
4 Jutland Ho
5 Norvic Ho
6 Odin Ho
7 Baltic Ho
8 Nobel Ho
9 Mercia Ho
10 Kenbury Gdns
11 Zealand Ho
12 Elsinore Ho
13 Norse Ho
14 Denmark Mans
15 Dane Ho
16 Canterbury Cl
17 York Cl
18 Kenbury Mans
19 Parade Mews
20 Winterslow Ho
21 Lilford Ho
22 Cutcombe Mans
23 Bartholomew Ho
24 Guildford Ho
25 Boston Ho
26 Hereford Ho
27 Weyhill Ho
28 Lichfield Ho
29 Lansdown Ho
30 Honiton Ho
31 Pinner Ho
32 Baldock Ho
33 Widecombe Ho

48 B1

34 Nottingham Ho
35 Witham Ho
36 Barnet Ho
37 Empress Mews
B2 1 Bertha Neubergh Ho
2 Mornington Mews
3 Badsworth Ho
4 Sycamore Ct
5 Elm Tree Ct
6 Samuel Lewis Trust Dwellings
7 Valmar Trad Est
8 Keswick Ho
9 Mitcham Ho
B3 1 Boundary Ho
2 Day Ho
3 Burgess Ho
4 Carlyle Ho
5 Myers Ho
6 Thompson's Ave
7 Palgrave Ho
8 Winnington Ho
9 Brantwood Ho
10 Lowell Ho
11 Jessie Duffett Ho
12 Otterburn Ho
13 Crossmount Ho
14 Venice Ct
15 Bowyer St
16 Livingstone Ho
17 Gothic Ct
18 Coniston Ho
19 Harlynwood
20 Carey Ct
21 Finley Ct
22 Grainger Ct
23 Hayes Ct
24 Moffat Ho
25 Marinel Ho
26 Hodister Cl
27 Arnot Ho
28 Lamb Ho
29 Kipling Ho
30 Keats Ho
31 Kenyon Ho
32 New Church Rd
33 Sir John Kirk Cl
C1 1 Selborne Rd
2 Hascombe Terr
C2 1 Joiners Arms Yd
2 Butterfly Wlk
3 Cuthill Wlk
4 Colonades The
5 Artichoke Mews
6 Peabody Bldgs
7 Brighton Ho
8 Park Ho
9 Peabody Ct
10 Lomond Ho
11 Lamb Ho
12 Kimpton Ct
13 Belham Wlk
14 Datchelor Pl
15 Harvey Rd
C3 1 Masterman Ho
2 Milton Ho
3 Pope Ho
4 Chester Ct
5 Marvel Ho
6 Flecker Ho
7 Landor Ho
8 Evelina Mans
9 Habington Ho
10 Langland Ho
11 Drinkwater Ho
12 Procter Ho
13 Shirley Ho
14 Drayton Ho
15 Bridges Ho
16 Cunningham Ho
17 Hood Ho
18 Herrick Ho
19 Dekker Ho
20 Sansom St
21 Houseman Way
22 Coleby Path
23 Jago Wlk
C4 1 Queens Ho
2 Arnside Ho
3 Horsley St
4 St Peter's Ho
5 St Johns Ho
6 St Marks Ho
7 St Stephens Ho
8 St Matthew's Ho
9 Red Lion Cl
10 Boyson Rd
11 Bradenham

49
A1 1 Springfield Ho
2 Craston Ho
3 Walters Ho
4 Edgecombe Ho
5 Fowler Ho
6 Rignold Ho
7 Chatham Ho
A2 1 Barnwell Ho
2 Brunswick Villas
3 St Giles Twr
4 Bentley Ho
5 Dawson Ho
6 Dryden Ho
7 Mayward Ho
8 Longleigh Ho
9 Fairwall Ho
10 Bodeney Ho
11 Sandby Ho
12 Vestry Mews
13 Netley
14 Lakanal
15 Racine
A3 1 Tower Mill Rd
2 Tilson Cl
3 Dorton Cl
4 Granville Sq
5 Farnborough Way
6 Hordle Prom W
7 Samuel Jones Ind Est
8 Dibden Ho
9 Marchwood Cl
10 Pilgrims Cloisters
11 Beacon Ho
12 Teather St
13 Stacy Path
14 Rumball Ho
15 Ballow Cl
16 Rill Ho
A4 1 Pearse St
2 Watling St
3 Gandolfi st
4 Andoversford Ct
5 Downend Ct
B2 1 Colbert
2 Voltaire
3 Finch Mews
4 Charles Coveney Rd
5 Crane St
6 Curlew Ho
7 Mallard Ho
8 Tern Ho
9 Crane Ho
10 Falcon Ho
11 Bryanston Ho
12 Basing Ct
13 Marcus Ho
14 Sheffield Ho
B3 2 Whistler Mews
1 Painswick Ct
2 Sharpness Ct
3 Hordle Prom N
4 Mattingly Way
5 Calypso Cres
6 Samuel St
7 Hordle Prom S
8 Cinnamon Cl
9 Savannah Ct
10 Thames Ct
11 Amstel Ct
12 Danube Ct
13 Tilbury Ct
14 Hordle Prom E
15 Oakcourt
16 Palm Ct
17 Rowan Ct
18 Blackthorn Ct
19 Pear Ct
21 Lidgate Rd
B4 1 Wallsbridge Ct
2 Cam Ct
3 Quedgeley Ct
4 Saul Ct
5 Quenington Ct
6 Westonbirt Ct
7 Wickway Ct
C1 1 William Margrie Cl
2 Choumert Sq
3 Parkstone Rd
4 Atwell Rd
C2 1 Angelina Ho
2 Jarvis Ho
3 Richland Ho
4 Honeywood Ho
5 Wakefield Ho
6 Primrose Ho
7 Hardcastle Ho
8 Dunstall Ho
9 Purdon Ho
10 Flamborough Ho
11 Lambrook Ho
12 Witcombe Point
13 Yarnfield Sq
14 Winford Ct
15 Portbury Cl
16 Robert Keen Cl
C3 1 Thornbill Ho
2 Vervain Ho
3 Woodstar Ho
4 Tamarind Ho
5 Hereford Retreat
6 Haymerle Ho
7 Furley Ho
8 Applegarth Ho
9 Freda Corbett Cl
10 Rudbeck Ho
11 Henslow Ho
12 Lindley Ho
13 Collinson Ho
14 Sister Mabel's Way
15 Timberland Cl
16 Hastings Cl
17 Neville Cl
18 Sidmouth Ho
19 Budleigh Ho
20 Stanesgate Ho
21 Braemore Ho
22 Ely Ho
C4 1 Bowles Rd
2 Western Wharf
3 Northfield Ho
4 Millbrook Ho
5 Denstone Ho
6 Deerhurst Ho
7 Caversham Ho
8 Battle Ho
9 Cardiff Ho
10 Bridgnorth Ho
11 Exeter Ho
12 Grantham Ho
13 Aylesbury Ho
14 Royston Ho

50
A1 1 Walkynscroft
2 Ryegates
3 Hathorne Cl
4 Pilkington Rd
5 Russell Ct
6 Heaton Ho
7 Magdalene Cl
A2 1 Willowdene
2 Pinedene
3 Oakdene
4 Beechdene
5 Hollydene
6 Wood Dene
7 Staveley Cl
8 Carnicot Ho
9 Martock Ct
10 Kendrick Ct
A3 1 Tortington Ho
2 Credenhill Ho
3 Bromyard Ho
4 Hoyland Ct
5 Willowdene
6 Ashdene
7 Acorn Par
8 Carlton Gr
9 Springall St
10 Harry Lambourn Ho
B1 1 Honiton Gdns
2 Selden Ho
3 Hathway Ho
4 Hathway St
5 Station Ct
B3 1 Ambleside Point
2 Grasmere Point
3 Windermere Point
4 Laburnham Ct
5 Romney Cl
6 Hammersley Ho
7 Hutchinson Ho
8 Hammond Ho
9 Fir Tree Ho
10 Glastonbury Ct
11 Highbridge Ct
12 Filton Ct
13 Chiltern Ct
14 Cheviot Ct
B4 1 Penshurst Ho
2 Reculver Ho
3 Mereworth Ho
4 Camber Ho
5 Chilam Ho
6 Otford Ho
7 Olive Tree Ho
8 Aspen Ho
9 Lewis Silkin Ho
10 Richborough Ho
11 Dover Ho
12 Eynsford Ho
13 Horton Ho
14 Lamberhurst Ho
15 Canterbury Ind Pk
16 Upnall Ho
17 Sissinghurst Ho
18 Rochester Ho
19 Leybourne Ho
20 Lullingstone Ho
C3 1 Richard Anderson Ct
2 Palm Tree Ho
3 Edward Robinson Ho
4 Antony Ho
5 Gerrard Ho
6 Palmer Ho
7 Pankhurst Cl
C4 1 Harrisons Ct
2 Grantley Ho
3 Sunbury Ct
4 Tilbury Ho
5 Graham Ct
6 Connell Ct
7 St Clements Ct
8 Henderson Ct
9 Jemotts Ct
10 Verona Ct
11 Heywood Ho
12 Francis Ct
13 Hind Ho
14 Donne Ho
15 Carew Ct
16 Burbage Ho
17 Newland Ho
18 Dobson Ho
19 Dalton Ho
20 Greene Ct
21 Redrup Ho
22 Tarplett Ho
23 Stunnell Ho
24 Gasson Ho
25 Bryce Ho
26 Barnes Ho
27 Bartwith Ho
28 Bannister Ho
29 Apollo Ind Bsns Ctr

51
A3 1 Batavia Ho
2 Marlowe Bsns Ctr
3 Batavia Mews
4 Woodrush Cl
5 Alexandra St
6 Primrose Wlk
7 Vansittart St
8 Granville Ct
9 Cottesbrook St
A4 1 Portland Ct
2 Phoenix Ct
3 Rainbow Ct
4 Hawke Twr
5 Woodpecker Rd
B3 1 Austen Ho
2 Exeter Way
3 Crossleigh Ct
4 Mornington Pl
5 Maple Ho
B4 1 Chester Ho
2 Lynch Wlk
3 Arlington Ho
4 Woodcote Ho
5 Cornbury Ho

6 Prospect Pl
7 Akintaro Ho
8 Mulberry Ho
9 Laurel Ho
10 Linden Ho
11 Ashford Ho
12 Wardalls Ho
13 Magnolia Ho
14 Howard Ho
15 Larch Cl
16 Ibis Ct
17 Merganser Ct
18 Wotton Rd
19 Kingfisher Sq
20 Sanderling Ct
21 Dolphin Twr
22 Mermaid Twr
23 Scoter Ct
24 Shearwater Ct
25 Brambling Ct
26 Kittiwake Ct
27 Guillemot Ct
28 Marine Twr
29 Teal Ct
30 Lapwing Twr
31 Cormorant Ct
32 Shelduck Ct
33 Eider Ct
34 Pintail Ct
35 Tristan Ct
36 Skua Ct
37 Rosemary Ct
38 Violet Ct
39 Diana Cl
C2 1 Admiralty Cl
2 Barton Lo
3 Sylvia Cotts
4 Pitman Ho
5 Heston Ho
C3 1 Sandpiper Cl
2 Flamingo Ct
3 Titan Bsns Est
4 Rochdale Way
5 Speedwell St
6 Reginald Pl
7 Fletcher Path
8 Frankham Ho
9 Cremer Ho
10 Wilshaw Ho
11 Castell Ho
12 Holden Ho
13 Browne Ho
14 Lady Florence Ctyd
15 Covell Ct
C4 1 Dryfield Wlk
2 Blake Ho
3 Hawkins Ho
4 Grenville Ho
5 Langford Ho
6 Mandarin Ct
7 Bittern Ct
8 Lamerton St
9 Armada St
10 Armada Ct
11 Benbow Ho
12 Oxenham Ho
13 Caravel Mews
14 Hughes Ho
15 Stretton Mans

52

A3 1 Finch Ho
2 Jubilee The
3 Gordon Ho
4 Haddington Ct
5 Maitland Cl

6 Ashburnham Retreat
B1 1 Ellison Ho
2 Pitmaston Ho
3 Windmill Cl
4 Hermitage The
5 Burnett Ho
6 Lacey Ho
B2 1 Penn Almshouse
2 Jarvis Ct
3 Woodville Ct
4 Darnell Ho
5 Renbold Ho
6 Lindsell St
7 Plumbridge St
8 Trinity Gr
9 Hollymount Cl
10 Cade Tyler Ho
11 Robertson Ho
B3 1 Temair Ho
2 Glaisher St
3 Prince of Orange La
4 Lombard Ho
5 St Marks Cl
6 Ada Kennedy Ct
7 Arlington Pl
8 Topham Ho
9 Darnell Ho
10 Hawks Mews
11 Royal Pl
12 Swanne Ho
13 Maribor
14 Serica Ct
15 Queen Elizabeth College
B4 1 Greenwich Mkt
2 Turnpin La
3 Durnford St
4 Sexton's Ho
5 Bardsley Ho
6 Wardell Ho
7 Clavell St
8 Stanton Ho
9 Macey Ho
10 Boreman Ho
C4 1 Frobisher Ct
2 Hardy Cotts
3 Palliser Ho
4 Bernard Angell Ho
5 Corvette Sq
6 Travers Ho
7 Reade Ho
8 Maze Hill Lo

53

B3 1 Westcombe Ct
2 Klefiens Ct
3 Ferndale Ct
4 Combe Mews
5 Mandeville Ct
6 Heathway
7 Pinelands Cl
C3 1 Mary Lawrenson Pl
2 Bradbury Ct
3 Dunstable Ct
C4 1 Nethercombe Ct
2 Holywell Cl

54

A1 1 Lancaster Cotts
2 Lancaster Mews
3 Bromwich Ho
4 Priors Lo
5 Richmond Hill Ct
6 Glenmore Ho

7 Hillbrow
8 Heathshot
9 Friars Stile Pl
10 Spire Ct
11 Ridgeway
12 Matthias Ct
A2 1 Litchfield Terr
2 Union Ct
3 Carrington Lo
4 Wilton Ct
5 Egerton Ct
6 Beverley Lo
7 Bishop Duppa's Almshouses
8 Regency Wlk
9 Clearwater Ho
10 Onslow Avenue Mans
11 Michels Almshouses
12 Albany Pas
13 Salcombe Villas
A3 1 St John's Gr
2 Michel's Row
3 Michelsdale Dr
4 Blue Anchor Alley
5 Clarence St
6 Sun Alley
7 Thames Link Ho
8 Benns Wlk
B1 1 Chester Ct
2 Evesham Ct
3 Queen's Ct
4 Russell Wlk
5 Charlotte Sq
6 Jones Wlk
7 Hildtch Ho
8 Isabella Ct
9 Damer Ho
10 Eliot Ho
11 Fitzherbert Ho
12 Reynolds Pl
13 Chisholm Rd
B2 1 Alberta Ct
2 Beatrice Rd
3 Lorne Rd
4 York Rd
5 Connaught Rd
6 Albany Terr
7 Kingswood Ct
8 Selwyn Ct
9 Broadhurst Cl
B3 1 Towers The
2 Longs St
3 Sovereign Ct
4 Robinson Ct
5 Calvert Ct
6 Bedford Ct
7 Hickey's Almshouses
8 Church Estate Almshouses
9 Richmond International Bsns Ctr
10 Abercorn Mews

55

A3 1 Hershell Ct
2 Deanhill Ct
3 Park Sheen
4 Furness Lo
5 Merricks Ct
C4 1 Rann Ho
2 Craven Ho
3 John Dee Ho
4 Kindell Ho

5 Montgomery Ho
6 Avondale Ho
7 Addington Ct
8 Dovecote Gdns
9 Firmston Ho
10 Glendower Gdns
11 Chestnut Ave
12 Trehern Rd
13 Rock Ave

56

B1 1 Allenford Ho
2 Swaythling Ho
3 Tatchbury Ho
4 Penwood Ho
5 Bramley Ho
6 Shalden Ho
7 Dunbridge Ho
8 Denmead Ho
9 Charcot Ho
10 Portswood Pl
11 Brockbridge Ho
12 Hurstbourne Ho
C2 1 Theodore Ho
2 Nicholas Ho
3 Bonner Ho
4 Downing Ho
5 Johsen Ho
6 Fairfax Ho
7 Devereux Ho
8 David Ho
9 Leigh Ho
10 Clipstone Ho
11 Mallet Ho
12 Arton Wilson Ho

57

B2 1 Inglis Ho
2 Ducie Ho
3 Warncliffe Ho
4 Stanhope Ho
5 Waldegrave Ho
6 Mildmay Ho
7 Mullens Ho
C1 1 Balmoral Ho
2 Glenalmond Ho
3 Selwyn Ho
4 Keble Ho
5 Bede Ho
6 Gonville Ho
7 Magdalene Ho
8 Armstrong Ho
9 Newnham Ho
10 Somerville Ho
11 Balliol Ho
12 Windermere Ho
13 Little Combe Cl
14 Classinghall Ho
15 Chalford Ct
16 Garden Royal
17 South Ct
18 Anne Kerr Ct
19 Ewhurst
C2 1 Geneva Ct
2 Laurel Ct
3 Cambalt Ho
4 Langham Ct
5 Lower Pk
6 King's Keep
7 Whitnell Ct
8 Whitehead Ho
9 Halford Ho
10 Humphry Ho
11 Jellicoe Ho
C3 1 Olivette St
2 Mascotte Rd

3 Glegg Pl
4 Crown Ct
5 Charlwood Terr

58

A2 1 Claremont
2 Downside
3 Cavendish Cl
4 Ashcombe Cl
5 Carltons The
6 Draldo Ho
7 Millbrooke Ct
8 Coysh Ct
9 Keswick Hts
10 Lincoln Ho
11 Avon Ct
B2 1 Burlington Mews
2 Cumbria Ho
3 St Stephen's Gdns
4 Atlantic Ho
5 Burton Lo
6 Manfred Ct
7 Meadow Bank
8 Hooper Ho
C2 1 Pembridge Pl
2 Adelaide Rd
3 London Ct
4 Windsor Ct
5 Westminster Ct
6 Fullers Ho
7 Bridge Pk
8 Lambeth Ct
9 Milton Ct
10 Norfolk Mans
11 Francis Snary Lo
12 Bush Cotts
13 Downbury Mews
14 Newton's Yd

59

A2 1 Fairfield Ct
2 Blackmore Ho
3 Lancaster Mews
4 Cricketers Mews
B4 1 Molasses Ho
2 Molasses Row
3 Cinnamon Row
4 Calico Ho
5 Calico Row
6 Port Ho
7 Square Rigger Row
8 Trade Twr
9 Ivory Ho
10 Spice Ct
11 Sherwood Ct
12 Mendip Ct
13 Chalmers Ho
14 Coral Row
C3 1 Burke Ho
2 Fox Ho
3 Buxton Ho
4 Pitt Ho
5 Romsey Ho
6 Beverley Ho
7 Florence Ho
8 Linden Ct
9 Dorcas Ct
10 Johnson Ct
11 Agnes Ct
12 Hilltop Ct
13 Courtyard The
14 Old Laundry The
15 Oberstein Rd

278 | **59 C3**

16 Fineran Ct
16 Sangora Rd
16 Harvard Mans
C4 1 Benham Ct
2 Milner Ho
3 McManus Ho
4 Wilberforce Ho
5 Wheeler Ct
6 Sporle Ct
7 Holliday Sq
8 John Parker Sq
9 Carmichael Cl
10 Fenner Sq
11 Clark Lawrence Ct
12 Shaw Ct
13 Livingstone Rd
14 Farrant Ho
15 Jackson Ho
16 Darien Ho
17 Sheppard Ho
18 Ganley Ct
19 Arthur Newton Ho
20 Chesterton Ho
21 John Kirk Ho
22 Mantua St
23 Heaver Rd

60
A4 1 Kiloh Ct
2 Lanner Ho
3 Grifton Ho
4 Kestrel Ho
5 Kite Ho
6 Peregrine Ho
7 Hawk Ho
8 Inkster Ho
9 Harrier Ho
10 Eagle Hts
11 Kingfisher Ct
12 Lavender Terr
13 Temple Ho
14 Ridley Ho
15 Eden Ho
16 Hertford Ct
17 Nepaul Rd
C1 1 Rayne Ho
2 St Anthony's Ct
3 Earlsthorpe Mews
C4 1 Shaftesbury Park Chambers
2 Selborne
3 Rush Hill Mews
4 Marmion Mews
5 Crosland Pl
6 Craven Mews
7 Basnett Rd
8 Woodmere Cl
9 Tyneham Cl

61
A4 1 Turnchapel Mews
2 Redwood Mews
3 Phil Brown Pl
4 Bev Callender Cl
5 Keith Connor Cl
6 Tessa Sanderson Pl
7 Daley Thompson Way
8 Rashleigh Ct
9 Abberley Mews
10 Willow Lodge
11 Beaufoy Rd

B1 1 Joseph Powell Cl
2 Cavendish Mans
3 Westlands Terr
4 Cubitt Ho
5 Hawkesworth Ho
6 Normanton Ho
7 Eastman Ho
8 Coelhy Ho
9 Poynders Ct
10 Selby Ho
11 Valentine Ho
12 Gorham Ho
13 Deauville Mans
14 Deauville Ct
B2 1 Timothy Cl
2 Shaftesbury Mews
3 Brook Ho
4 Grover Ho
5 Westbrook Ho
6 Hewer Ho
7 Batten Ho
8 Mandeville Ho
9 George Beare Lo
B3 1 Polygon The
2 Windsor Ct
3 Trinity Cl
4 Hanscomb Mews
5 Studios The
6 Bourne Ho
B4 1 Clapham Manor Ct
2 Clarke Ho
3 Gables The
4 Sycamore Mews
5 Maritime Ho
6 Floris Pl
C1 1 Parrington Ho
2 Savill Ho
3 Blackwell Ho
4 Bruce Ho
5 Victoria Ho
6 Belvedere Ct
7 Ingram Lo
8 Viney Ct
9 Bloomsbury Ho
10 Belgravia Ho
11 Barnsbury Ho
C3 1 Kendoa Rd
2 Felmersham Cl
3 Abbeville Mews
4 Saxon Ho
5 Gifford Ho
6 Teignmouth Cl
7 Holwood Pl
8 Oaklands Pl
C4 1 Chelsham Ho
2 Lynde Ho
3 Greener Ho
4 Towns Ho
5 Hugh Morgan Ho
6 Roy Ridley Ho
7 Lendal Terr
8 Slievemore Cl
9 Cadmus Cl

62
A2 1 King's Mews
2 Clapham Court Terr
3 Clapham Ct
4 Clapham Park Terr
5 Queenswood Ct
6 Oak Tree Ct
7 Park Lofts
A3 1 Morris Ho
2 Gye Ho
3 Clowes Ho

4 Thomas Ho
5 Stuart Ho
6 Storace Ho
7 Bedford Ho
8 Ascot Ct
9 Ascot Par
10 Ashmere Ho
11 Ashmere Gr
12 Vickery Ho
13 Stafford Mans
14 Beresford Ho
A4 1 Callingham Ho
2 Russell Pickering Ho
3 Lopez Ho
4 Coachmaker Mews
B2 1 Beatrice Ho
2 Florence Ho
3 Evelyn Ho
4 Diana Ho
5 Brixton Hill Ct
6 Austin Ho
7 Manor Ct
8 Camsey Ho
9 Romer Ho
10 Gale Ho
11 Byrne Ho
12 Farnfield Ho
13 Marchant Ho
14 Rainsford Ho
15 Springett Ho
16 Mannering Ho
B3 1 Freemens Hos
2 Roger's Almshouses
3 Gresham Almshouses
4 Exbury Ho
5 Glasbury Ho
6 Dalbury Ho
7 Fosbury Ho
8 Chalbury Ho
9 Neilson-Terry Ct
10 Pavilion Mans
11 Daisy Dormer Ct
12 George Lashwood Ct
13 Marie Lloyd Ct
14 Trinity Homes
15 Lethaby Ho
16 Edmundsbury Ct Est
17 Regis Pl
18 Belvedere Pl
19 Alpha Ho
20 Beta Pl
21 Cedars Ho
B4 1 Turberville Ho
2 Thrayle Ho
3 Percheron Ct
4 Draymans Ct
C1 1 Eccleston Ho
2 Scarsbrook Ho
3 Purser Ho
4 Rudhall Ho
5 Hardham Ho
6 Heywood Ho
7 Haworth Ho
8 Birch Ho
9 Lonsdell Ho
10 Lomley Ho
11 Laughton Ho
12 Bascome St
13 Dudley Mews
14 Herbert Mews

16 Blades Lo
17 Dick Shepherd Ct
18 Charman Ho
19 Morden Ho
20 Bishop Ct
21 Blackburn Ct
22 Leigh Ct
23 John Conwey Ho
C2 1 Crownstone Ct
2 Brockwell Ct
3 Nevena Ct
4 St George's Residences
5 Hanover Mans
6 Fleet Ho
7 Langbourne Ho
8 Turnmill Ho
9 Cossar Mews
10 Carter Ho
C3 1 Electric Mans
2 Electric La
3 Connaught Mans
4 Clifton Mans
5 Hereford Ho
6 Chaplin Ho
7 Brixton Oval
8 Lord David Pitt Ho
9 Marcus Garvey Way
10 Montgo Ct
11 Bob Marley Way
12 Leeson Rd
C4 1 Buckmaster Cl
2 Albermarle Ho
3 Goodwood Mans
4 Angell Park Gdns
5 Fyfield Rd
6 Howard Ho
7 Harris Ho
8 Broadoak Ct
9 Burgate Ct
10 Witchwood Ho
11 Blacktree Mews
12 Chartham Ct
13 Chilham Ct
14 Northgate Ct
15 Westgate Ct
16 Dover Mans

63
A3 1 Mahatma Ganhi Ind Est
2 Dylan Rd
3 Bessemer Park Ind Est
4 Pablo Neruda Cl
5 Langston Hughes Cl
6 Walt Whitman Cl
7 James Joyes Wlk
8 Alice Walker Cl
9 Louise Bennett Cl
10 Chadacre Ho
11 Burwood Ho
12 Pyrford Ho
13 Wangford Ho
14 Ashford Ho
15 Kenwood Ho
16 Moyne Ho
17 Elveden Ho
18 Carrara Wlk
19 Broughton Dr
20 Tilia Wlk
21 Angela Davis Ind Est
A4 1 Mallams Mews
2 Amberley Ct

3 Harper Ho
4 Leicester Ho
5 Station Ave
6 Wellfit St
7 Loughborough Ct
8 Belinda Rd
9 Higgs Ind Est
C3 1 Shaftesbury Ct
2 Mayhew Ct
3 Morris Ct
4 Swinburne Ct
5 Perth Ct
6 Tayside Ct
7 Matlock Ct
8 Hunter Ct
9 Turner Ct

64
A2 1 Velde Way
2 Delft Way
3 Arnhem Way
4 Isel Way
5 Kempis Way
6 Terborah Way
7 Steen Way
8 Deventer Cres
9 Nimegen Way
10 Hilversum Cres
11 St Barnabas Cl
A4 1 Harfield Gdns
2 Karen Ct
3 Seavington Ho
4 Appleshaw Ho
5 Birdsall Ho
6 Whitney Ho
7 Wheatland Ho
8 Wilton Ho
9 Walcot Ho
10 Whaddon Ho
11 Melbrook Ho
12 Ledbury Ho
13 Tidworth Ho
14 Riseholme Ho
15 Ringmer Ho
16 Petworth Ho
17 Stagshaw Ho
18 Ivybridge Ho
19 Inwood Ho
20 Gatcombe Ho
21 Gatebeck Ho
22 Felbridge Ho
23 Cowdray Ho
B3 1 Dulwich Mews
2 St James's Cloisters
C2 1 Dorothy Charrington Ho
2 Keswick Ct
3 Kendall Ct
4 Halliwell Ct

65
A4 1 Tilling Ho
2 Goodwin Ho
3 Citron Terr
4 Cheam St
C3 1 Laxton Path
2 Barlings Ho
3 Bayfield Ho
4 Coston Wlk
5 Coverham Ho
6 Gateley Ho
7 Dereham Ho
8 Greenwood Ho
9 Hilton Ho
10 Goodall Ho

11 Horsley Ho
12 Jordan Ho

68

1 Farnborough Ho
2 Rushmere Ho
3 Horndean Cl
4 Highcross Way
5 Timsbury Wlk
6 Foxcombe Rd
7 Ryefield Path
8 Greatham Wlk
9 Gosport Ho
10 Stoatley Ho
11 Milland Ho
12 Clanfield Ho
13 Fareham Ho
C4 1 Woodcott Ho
2 Lyndhurst Ho
3 Wheatley Ho
4 Allbrook Ho
5 Bordon Wlk
6 Chilcombe Ho
7 Vicarage Ct
8 Shawford Ct
9 Eastleigh Wlk
10 Kings Ct

69

A3 1 Ramsdean Ho
2 Purbrook Ho
3 Portsea Ho
4 Blendworth Point
5 Eashing Point
6 Hindhead Point
7 Hilsea Point
8 Witley Point
9 Buriton Ho
10 Grately Ho
11 Hascombe Ho
12 Dunhill Point
13 Westmark Point
14 Longmoor Point
15 Cadnam Point
D4 1 Cumberland Ho
2 Devonshire Ho
3 Cornwall Ho
4 Norfolk Ho
5 Leicester Ho
6 Warwick Ho
7 Sutherland Ho
8 Carmarthen Ho
9 Worcester Ho
10 Rutland Ho
C3 1 Sandringham Cl
2 Eastwick Ct
3 Oatlands Ct
4 Banning Ho
5 Grantley Ho
6 Caryl Ho
7 Duncombe Ho
8 Chilworth Ct
9 Kent Lo
10 Turner Lo
11 Marlborough
12 Parkland Gdns
13 Lewesdon Cl
14 Pines Ct
15 Ashtead Ct
16 Mynterne Ct
17 Arden
18 Stephen Ct
19 Marsham Ct
20 Doradus Ct
21 Acorns The

22 Heritage Ho
23 Conifer Ct
24 Spencer Ho
25 Chartwell
26 Blenheim
27 Chivelston
28 Greenfield Ho
29 Oakman Ho
30 Radley Lo
31 Simon Lo
32 Admirals Ct
C4 1 Brett Ho
2 Brett House Cl
3 Sylva Ct
4 Ross Ct
5 Potterne Cl
6 Stourhead Cl
7 Fleur Gates
8 Greenwood

70

A3 1 William Harvey Ho
2 Highview Ct
3 Cameron Ct
4 Galgate Cl
5 Green Ho The
6 King Charles Wlk
7 Florys Ct
8 Augustus Ct
9 Albert Ct
10 Hertford Lo
11 Mortimer Lo
12 Allenswood
13 Ambleside

72

C2 1 Upper Tooting Park Mans
2 Cecil Mans
3 Marius Mans
4 Boulevard The
5 Elmfield Mans
6 Holdernesse Rd
C3 1 Heslop Ct
2 St James's Terr
3 Boundaries Mans
4 Station Par
5 Old Dairy Mews
C4 1 Hollies Way
2 Endlesham Ct

73

A3 1 Holbeach Mews
2 Hildreth Street Mews
3 Coalbrook Mans
4 Hub Buildings The
A4 1 Meyer Ho
2 Faraday Ho
3 Hales Ho
4 Frankland Ho
5 Graham Ho
6 Gibbs Ho
7 Anslie Wlk
8 Rokeby Ho
9 Caister Ho
10 Ivanhoe Ho
11 Catherine Baird Ct
12 Marmion Ho
13 Devonshire Ho
B4 1 Limerick Ct
2 Homewoods
3 Jewell Ho
4 Glanville Ho
5 Dan Bryant Ho
6 Olding Ho

7 Quennel Ho
8 Weir Ho
9 West Ho
10 Neville Ct
C3 1 Sinclair Ho
2 MacGregor Ho
3 Ingle Ho
4 St Andrews Mews
C4 1 Riley Ho
2 Bennett Ho
3 White Ho
4 Rodgers Ho
5 Dumphreys Ho
6 Homan Ho
7 Prendergast Ho
8 Hutchins Ho
9 Whiteley Ho
10 Tressider Ho
11 Primrose Ct
12 Angus Ho
13 Currie Ho

74

A1 1 De Montfort Par
2 Leigham Hall Par
3 Leigham Hall
4 Endsleigh Mans
5 John Kirk Ho
6 Raeburn Ct
7 Wavel Ct
8 Homeleigh Ct
9 Howland Ho
10 Beauclerk Ho
11 Bertrand Ho
12 Drew Ho
13 Dowes Ho
14 Dunton Ho
15 Raynald Ho
16 Sackville Ho
17 Thurlow Ho
18 Astoria Mans
A2 1 Wyatt Park Mans
2 Broadlands Mans
3 Stonehill's Mans
4 Streatleigh Par
5 Dorchester Ct
A3 1 Beaumont Ho
2 Christchurch Ho
3 Stapleford Cl
4 Chipstead Ho
5 Coulsdon Ho
6 Conway Ho
7 Telford Avenue Mans
8 Telford Parade Mans
9 Wavertree Ct
10 Hartswood Ho
11 Wray Ho
A4 1 Picton Ho
2 Rigg Ho
3 Watson Ho
4 MacArthur Ho
5 Sandon Ho
6 Thorold Ho
7 Pearce Ho
8 Mudie Ho
9 Miller Ho
10 Lycett Ho
11 Lafone Ho
12 Lucraft Ho
13 Freeman Ho
14 New Park Par
15 Argyll Ho
16 Dumbarton Ct
17 Kintyre Ho

18 Cotton Ho
19 Crossman Hos
20 Cameford Ct
21 Parsons Ho
22 Brindley Ho
23 Arkwright Ho
24 Perry Ho
25 Brunel Ho
26 New Park Ct
27 Tanhurst Ho
B1 1 Carisbrook Ct
2 Pembroke Ct
3 Willow Ct
4 Poplar Ct
5 Spa View
6 Mountview
B3 1 Charlwood Ho
2 Earlswood Ho
3 Balcombe Ho
4 Claremont Ct
5 Holbrook Ho
6 Gwynne Ho
7 Kynaston Ho
8 Tillman Ho
9 Regent Lo
10 Hazelmere Ct
11 Dykes Ct
B4 1 Archbishop's Pl
2 Witley Ho
3 Outwood Ho
4 Dunsfold Ho
5 Deepdene Ct
6 Warnham Ho
7 Albury Lo
8 Tilford Ho
9 Elstead Ho
10 Thursley Ho
11 Brockham Ho
12 Capel Lo
13 Leith Ho
14 Fairview Ho
15 Weymouth Ct
16 Ascalon Ct
17 China Mews
18 Rush Common Mews
C3 1 Valens Ho
2 Loveday Ho
3 Strode Ho
4 Ethelworth Ct
5 Harbin Ho
6 Brooks Ho
7 Godolphin Ho
8 Sheppard Ho
9 McCormick Ho
10 Taylor Ho
11 Saunders Ho
12 Talcott Path
13 Derrick Ho
14 Williams Ho
15 Baldwin Ho
16 Berkeley Ct
17 Churston Cl
18 Neil Wates Cres
19 Burnell Ho
20 Raymond Ho
C4 1 Ellacombe Ho
2 Booth Ho
3 Hathersley Ho
4 Brereton Ho
5 Holdsworth Ho
6 Dearmer Ho
7 Cherry Cl
8 Greenleaf Cl
9 Longford Wlk

10 Scarlette Manor Wlk
11 Chandlers Way
12 Upgrove Manor Way
13 Ropers Wlk
14 Tebbs Ho
15 Bell Ho
16 Worthington Ho
17 Courier Ho
18 Mackie Rd
19 Hamers Ho
20 Kelyway Ho
21 Harriet Tubman Cl
22 Estoria Cl
23 Leckhampton Pl
24 Scotia Rd
25 Charles Haller St
26 Sidmouth Ho
27 Hunter Ct
28 Onslow Lo
29 William Winter Ct
30 Langthorne Lo

75

A1 1 Thanet Ho
2 Chapman Ho
3 Beaufoy Ho
4 Easton Ho
5 Roberts Ho
6 Lloyd Ct
7 Kershaw Ho
8 Wakeling Ho
9 Edridge Ho
10 Jeston Ho
11 Lansdowne Wood Cl
C2 1 Coppedhall
2 Shackleton Ct
3 Bullfinch Ct
4 Gannet Ct
5 Fulmar Ct
6 Heron Ct
7 Petrel Ct
8 Falcon Ct
9 Eagle Ct
10 Dunnock Ct
11 Dunlin Ct
12 Cormorant Ct

76

C1 1 Tunbridge Ct
2 Harrogate Ct
3 Bath Ct
4 Leamington Ct
5 Porlock Ho
6 Cissbury Ho
7 Eddisbury Ho
8 Dundry Ho
9 Silbury Ho
10 Homildon Ho
11 Highgate Ho
12 Richmond Ho
13 Pendle Ho
14 Tynwald Ho
15 Wirrall Ho
16 Greyfriars

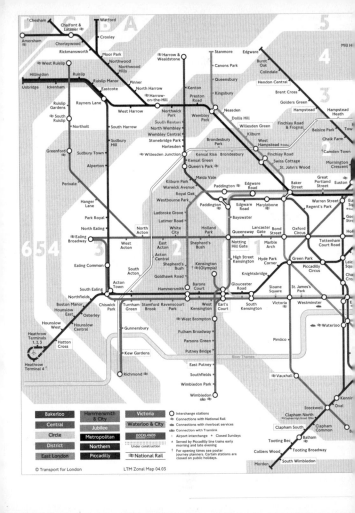

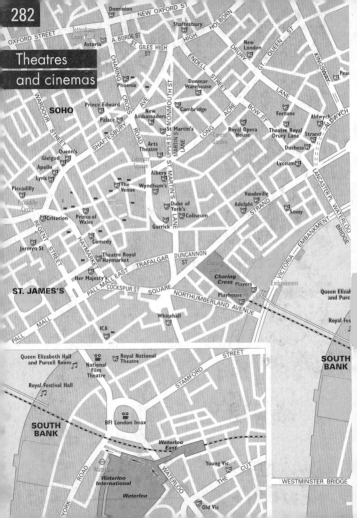

Theatres
and cinemas

OXFORD STREET
Tottenham Court Road
A. BORDE ST.
Astoria
CHARING CROSS ROAD
Dominion
NEW OXFORD ST
ST. GILES HIGH ST
Shaftesbury
HIGH
HOLBORN
DRURY
New
London
GT. QUEEN ST
KINGSWAY
Peac

Phoenix

WARDOUR STREET

SOHO

Prince Edward
Palace

Gielgud
Queen's
Apollo
Lyric

Piccadilly
Piccadilly
Circus

REGENT STREET

Criterion
Prince of
Wales

Comedy

Jermyn St Street

HAYMARKET

Theatre Royal
Haymarket

Her Majesty's

ST. JAMES'S

PALL MALL EAST
COCKSPUR ST

PALL MALL

ICA

New
Ambassadors

SHAFTESBURY AVENUE

Arts
Theatre

Leicester
Square

The
Venue

Albery
Wyndham's

Donmar
Warehouse

ENDELL STREET

Cambridge

UPPER ST MARTIN'S ST MONMOUTH ST

LONG ACRE

BOW ST

Fortune

Aldwych
ALDWYCH
Strand

Royal Opera
House

Covent
Garden

Theatre Royal
Drury Lane

Duchess

Lyceum

LANCASTER PL

WATERLOO

BRIDGE

Duke of
York's

ST MARTIN'S LANE

Coliseum

Garrick

Vaudeville
Adelphi

STRAND

Savoy

Charing
Cross

Players

Playhouse

VICTORIA EMBANKMENT

Embankment

Queen Elizabeth
and Purc

Royal Fes

DUNCANNON ST

TRAFALGAR
SQUARE

NORTHUMBERLAND AVENUE

Whitehall

Charing
Cross

SOUTH
BANK

Queen Elizabeth Hall
and Purcell Room

Royal Festival Hall

National
Film
Theatre

Royal National
Theatre

STREET

STAMFORD

SOUTH
BANK

BFI London Imax

Waterloo
East

YORK ROAD

Waterloo

Waterloo
International

Waterloo

WATERLOO

THE CUT

Young Vic

Old Vic

WESTMINSTER BRIDGE

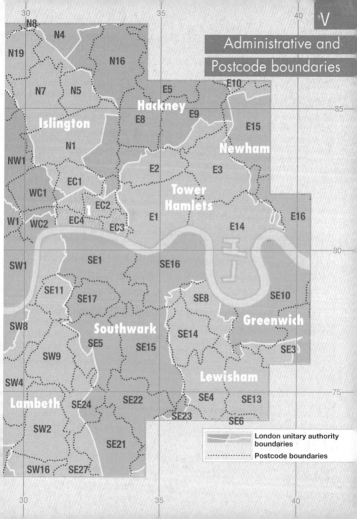

V

Administrative and
Postcode boundaries

London unitary authority
boundaries
.... Postcode boundaries

VI

Key to map symbols

(22a) Motorway with junction number	Railway with station
Primary route – single, dual carriageway	London Underground station
A road – single, dual carriageway	Docklands Light Railway station
B road – single, dual carriageway	Bus or coach station
Through-route – single, dual carriageway	Ambulance, police, fire station
Minor road – single, dual carriageway	Hospital, accident and emergency entrance
Road under construction	
Rural track, private road or narrow road in urban area	Market, public amenity site
Path, bridleway, byway open to all traffic, road used as public path	Information centre, post office
Tunnel, covered road	VILLA House Roman, non-Roman antiquity
Gate or barrier, car pound	100 304 House number, spot height – in metres
P P&R Parking, park and ride	Christian place of worship
Three Legged Cross Junction name	Mosque, synagogue
Pedestrianised area	Other place of worship
Restricted access area	65 Adjoining page number
Congestion Charge Zone boundary Roads within the zone are outlined in red	NW6 Postcode boundary
Houses, important buildings	City of Westminster Unitary authority boundary
Woods, parkland/common	Water, tidal water
	River or canal – minor, major
	Stream

Scale

3½ inches to 1 mile : 1:18103

0	220yds	440yds	660yds	½ mile

0	250m	500m	750m	1km

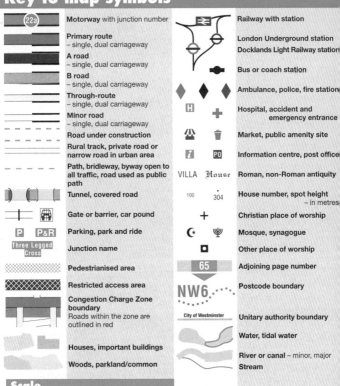

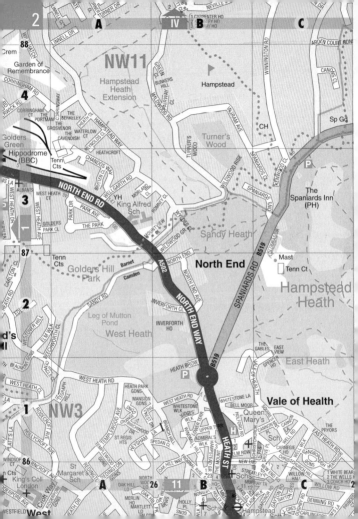

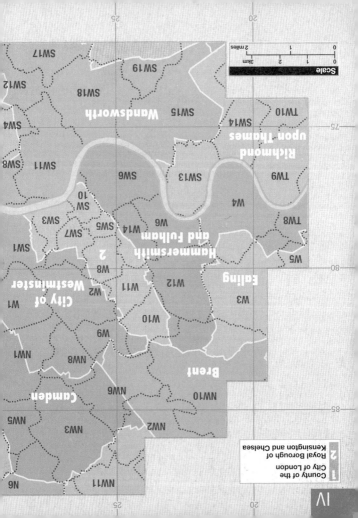

IV

1	County of the City of London
2	Royal Borough of Kensington and Chelsea

Scale

0   1   2   3km
0   1   2 miles

City of Westminster

Camden

Brent

Ealing

Hammersmith and Fulham

Wandsworth

Richmond upon Thames

N6
NW11
NW5
NW3
NW2
NW1
NW8
NW6
NW10
N1
W1
W2
W11
W10
W9
W12
W3
W8
SW1
SW7
SW3
SW10
SW5
W14
W6
W4
W5
TW8
TW9
TW10
SW4
SW8
SW11
SW6
SW13
SW14
SW15
SW18
SW12
SW17
SW19
SW16

25
20
75
80
85

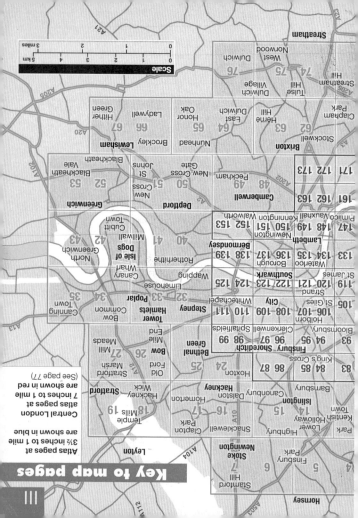